A History of Financial Crises

"Once-in-a-lifetime" financial crises have been a recurrent part of life in the last three decades. It is no longer possible to dismiss or ignore them as aberrations in an otherwise well-functioning system. Nor are they peculiar to recent times. Going back in history, asset-price bubbles and bank runs have been an endemic feature of the capitalist system over the last four centuries. The historical record offers a treasure trove of experience that may shed light on how and why financial crises happen and what can be done to avoid them – provided we are willing to learn from history.

This book interweaves historical accounts with competing economic crisis theories and reveals why commentaries are often contradictory. First, it presents a series of episodes from tulip mania in the seventeenth century to the subprime-mortgage meltdown. In order to tease out their commonalities and differences it describes political, economic, and social backgrounds, identifies the primary actors and institutions, and explores the mechanisms behind the asset-price bubbles, crashes, and bank runs. Second, it starts with basic economic concepts and builds five competing theoretical approaches to understanding financial crises. Competing theoretical standpoints offer different interpretations of the same event, and draw dissimilar policy implications.

This book analyses divergent interpretations of the historical record in relation to how markets function, the significance of market imperfections, economic decision-making processes, the role of the government, and evolutionary dynamics of the capitalist system. It is written for university students and demonstrates that the discipline of economics is far more diverse than standard textbooks may convey. The theoretical and historical content complements economics, finance, history, and political science curricula.

Cihan Bilginsoy is Professor of Economics, University of Utah, USA.

D0162476

Economics as Social Theory
Series edited by Tony Lawson
University of Cambridge

Social Theory is experiencing something of a revival within economics. Critical analyses of the particular nature of the subject matter of social studies and of the types of method, categories and modes of explanation that can legitimately be endorsed for the scientific study of social objects are re-emerging. Economists are again addressing such issues as the relationship between agency and structure, between economy and the rest of society, and between the enquirer and the object of enquiry. There is a renewed interest in elaborating basic categories such as causation, competition, culture, discrimination, evolution, money, need, order, organization, power probability, process, rationality, technology, time, truth, uncertainty, value etc.

The objective for this series is to facilitate this revival further. In contemporary economics the label "theory" has been appropriated by a group that confines itself to largely asocial, ahistorical, mathematical "modelling". Economics as Social Theory thus reclaims the "theory" label, offering a platform for alternative rigorous, but broader and more critical, conceptions of theorizing.

Other titles in this series include:

A History of Financial Crises

Dreams and follies of expectations

Cihan Bilginsoy

LONDON AND NEW YORK

First published 2015
by Routledge
2 Park Square, Milton Park, Abingdon, Oxon OX14 4RN

and by Routledge
711 Third Avenue, New York, NY 10017

Routledge is an imprint of the Taylor & Francis Group, an informa business

British Library Cataloguing in Publication Data
A catalogue record for this book is available from the British
Library

Library of Congress Cataloging in Publication Data
Bilginsoy, Cihan.
  A history of financial crises : dreams and follies of
  expectations / Cihan Bilginsoy. – First Edition.
    pages cm – (Economics as social theory)
  1. Financial crises–History. 2. Banks and banking–History.
  3. Corporations–Finance–History. I. Title.
  HB3722.B565 2014
  338.5′42–dc23   2014022357

ISBN: 978-0-415-68724-9 (hbk)
ISBN: 978-1-315-78087-0 (ebk)
ISBN: 978-0-415-68725-6 (pbk)

Typeset in Palatino
by Sunrise Setting Ltd, Paignton, UK

To the memory of Sadi Bilginsoy and Raika Bilginsoy

Contents

Illustrations

Figures

Table

Preface

Dozens of books have been published since 2008 on the topic of the subprime-mortgage crisis by academics, journalists, and finance and policy experts for the general public and professional economists. They examine what happened, how, and why from various distinct perspectives. While there are substantial differences in interpretations, these books are informative and insightful, and often fascinating and entertaining. Scholarly works on the roots of the crisis, appropriate remedies, and prescriptions on how to avoid another crisis in the future filled library shelves faster than the reading capacity of most people. In this embarrassment of riches how does one justify yet another book on the subject?

This book has several features that distinguish it from the currently available books. First, it is written for college students, to be used either as a source in a free-standing course on financial crises or as a supplement in related courses. The idea for this book was conceived during the days after the fall of Lehman Brothers in September 2008. There was immense interest among students from all majors in the topic, as demonstrated by the large audiences in lectures, seminars, round-table discussions, and the growing number of videos on the internet. Demand for knowledge created its supply, and new courses were offered in many institutions on the causes and outcomes of the crisis of 2007–8. The University of Utah followed this trend and created a course that introduced students from a cross-section of disciplines to the subject of financial crises by interweaving historical experience, economic theory, and intellectual history. This book is an outcome of that effort.

Second, unlike other books published in the past few years, this is not a book on the crisis of 2007–8, although it dwells on the topic at some length. Instead, it draws from the experience of the last 400 years to underscore that, claims of a "once in a lifetime event" notwithstanding, financial crises have occurred with astonishing frequency throughout the history of capitalism. I start from the premise that the knowledge of history and identification of similarities and differences between these crisis episodes are essential ingredients in understanding how and why financial crises occur, and cover a wide range of historical experience by presenting selected episodes of asset-price bubbles and bank runs, from the Dutch tulip fever of the seventeenth century to the subprime-mortgage crisis of this century.

Third, the narrative of the book integrates historical accounts with alternative economic theories that explore why financial crises happen. Currently, there is no consensus among economists regarding the sources of financial crises. Thus, this book helps students to develop their critical-thinking skills by presenting points of agreement and contention among the competing economic theories that attempt to explain boom-bust cycles in financial markets. The interweaving of historical records and theoretical positions permits a systematic illustration and comparison of the alternative hypotheses in historical contexts.

Fourth, there is an ulterior motive to the project. The topic of financial crises is a lure to attract students to learn and appreciate how economists make sense of the world, and why they may disagree about the sources of and cures for economic problems. I trace divergent opinions on the subject of financial crises to deeper disagreements concerning economic behavior, market structures, and the roles of institutions and government. The theoretical core of this book is organized around the larger questions of economists' views on how people make economic decisions, how their environment shapes the outcomes of these decisions, and how the evolution of institutions affects economic outcomes. Organizing the theoretical discussion explicitly around these basic points of contention will, hopefully, offer students reference points for economists' visions and ways of thinking, which may be put to use to understand other controversial topics. After all, perspectives on current public-policy debates, e.g. on provisioning health and education, controlling climate change, the minimum wage, or regulating financial markets, reflect participants' theoretical orientations. Familiarity with the intellectual foundations of these competing perspectives will facilitate better-informed evaluations of the debates.

While the book is written for the express purpose of classroom use, it is not a traditional textbook. Textbooks typically present the accepted wisdom in a field. If authors touch upon anomalies or pathologies that are not explained well by the standard theory they usually address them in the closing chapters, which are the ones most likely to be omitted as the semester rapidly winds down. However, in the case of financial crises there is currently no accepted wisdom. In fact, the collective failure to foresee the oncoming catastrophe of 2007–8 compelled many prominent economists to question whether there is an inherent flaw in the conduct of economic research. Recent debates among even some of the most prominent mainstream economists on the state of the discipline amply demonstrate that there exist strong differences of opinion on this subject. It is misleading and unfair to pretend otherwise in the classroom. While there may be students who simply ask for the "right answer," I believe most of them appreciate learning about the limits of economic knowledge, the sources of disagreements, and how these seemingly arcane debates inform public-policy deliberations that affect their daily lives. Thus, this book is designed to present a plurality of theoretical positions, or as an "anti-textbook."

In terms of the subject matter the most closely related book is Charles P. Kindleberger's *Manias, Panics and Crashes: A History of Financial Crises*. First published in 1978, this classic went through six editions, with the later editions expanded and updated by Robert Z. Aliber. In terms of content and organization there are several differences between the two books. Kindleberger organizes his book around the stages of a stylized financial crisis based on the Minsky credit-cycle model and illustrates each phase of the cycle in historical detail. His book presents historical episodes as well as competing mainstream theoretical positions as warranted by the course of its core theoretical narrative.

I follow a different organization, by which I develop the historical and theoretical strands in dedicated sections independently and integrate them. The first reason for my choice is that the audience I am targeting has little, if any, prior knowledge of the historical episodes and will benefit from more fully developed accounts of what happened and how. Thus, I select a limited number of crises and describe these episodes in some detail. The second reason is that my intended audience is likely to have limited knowledge about economic theory, too. I develop basic economic ideas, such as utility maximization, price determination, and expectations formation, from the bottom up, and build upon this foundation five parallel, competing theoretical approaches that offer alternative explanations of financial crises.

These competing theoretical standpoints offer different interpretations of the same event, often with different policy implications. The value of my approach is that it explains the contradictory commentaries on financial crises by linking them to their underlying theories of how markets function, the significance of market imperfections, the economic decision-making process, the role of government, and the evolutionary dynamics of the capitalist system.

Another closely related book is Edward Chancellor's *Devil Take the Hindmost: A History of Speculation*. My selection of historical episodes is similar to Chancellor's and, like him, I take the time to give details about each episode. However, our two books are written for different (albeit overlapping) audiences. Chancellor writes for the educated general public, and my intention was to write a more academic work for college students. While Chancellor occasionally takes economic theorists to task, the present work offers a more systematic and complete treatment of the differences and similarities between competing schools of thought. Further, in my historical narrative I spend more time on the mechanics of asset-price bubbles and banking crises and less time on historical anecdotes. One consequence of this trade-off is that Chancellor's account of what happened is more entertaining than mine.

There is also some overlap with Carmen M. Reinhart and Kenneth Rogoff's *This Time is Different: Eight Centuries of Financial Folly*, which offers a long, historical perspective on financial crises. Rather than examining specific booms and busts (with the notable exception of the subprime crisis), their book provides detailed data from dozens of countries to detect common experiences across time and space. It focuses primarily on sovereign-debt defaults, hyperinflations, and currency crises that I leave outside the scope of this study. The present emphasis is on asset-price bubbles and banking failures that largely take place in the private sector.

Some notes on the pedagogy

Because this book is intended for college students three points are worth mentioning regarding its pedagogical approach. First, this is a self-contained book that does not require prior knowledge of economics or statistics. All the relevant concepts are developed in the text, though in brief compared with typical textbooks. Second, the presentation moves quite fast and, at times, covers somewhat abstract, sophisticated material that is usually presented in advanced economics courses. Thus, certain sections may be challenging, even for students with some economics background. I assume that students, particularly the novices, will have the guidance and assistance of an instructor. Depending on the level of the course, the instructor may cover lightly or skip some of the material without harming the narrative's continuity. Third, I attempt to keep the exposition non-technical, exclude mathematical and graphical exposition, and, instead, rely on numerical examples and answers that can be intuited. I broke this rule in only one instance: the standard asset-valuation equation. After some trial and error I discovered that some students found the visual summary of the argument in the form of a mathematical expression economical and convenient.

Perhaps the most important pedagogical point relates to the ordering, content, and continuity of the chapters. These decisions were driven, first, by the objective of combining economic and intellectual history and theory, and, second, by the rhythm of the semester. One way of organizing the material is to follow a block-recursive model, presenting the theory first and then applying it to individual historical episodes. I do not believe that a heavy initial dose of abstract theory is student-friendly. Students retain abstract ideas better when they are immediately associated with concrete illustrations. Therefore, I decided to mix things up and create a five-stage narrative.

In the first stage (Chapters 2 to 4) I present the three "classical" asset bubbles from the seventeenth and eighteenth centuries, somewhat lighter reading than pure theory. The second part (Chapters 5 to 6) is theoretical. It introduces basic economic concepts, describes the five alternative approaches to explain bubbles, and uses historical information on the classical bubbles to illustrate these theories. The thrust of this section is the discussion of how asset prices are determined and why they may differ from their "intrinsic" values and become bubbles. The application of competing theories in the context of the classic bubbles demonstrates how scholars often offer contradictory interpretations of the same event.

In the third stage (Chapters 7 to 10), I return to history, covering the British and the American experience from the beginning of the nineteenth century to the crash of 1929. The presentation of the historical record and its interpretations from different perspectives are combined in these chapters. The fourth part (Chapters 11 to 12) contains the second theoretical section. This time the discussion focuses on why the fundamental price matters and what to do if markets fail to get prices right. Related debates over the efficiency of markets and the role of regulation also set the stage for what happened next. The final stage (Chapters 13 to 17) covers the story of the financialization of the economy through the 1980s, 1990s, and 2000s, ending with the subprime-mortgage boom and bust.

Two more features of the narrative are worth mentioning. First, throughout the book the historical chapters also serve to present institutional features. In the context of the Mississippi and the South Sea companies, for instance, I discuss the essentials of money and credit, securities markets, commercial paper, balance sheets, and leveraging, while the British experiences of 1829, 1837, and 1846 are ideally suited to introduce the dilemmas of the lender of last resort. Second, though the book is self-contained, the chapters are not necessarily so. There are, at times, loose ends in individual chapters that are tied up after developing theoretical tools in later chapters. Later chapters also rely on the institutional detail introduced in previous chapters. Thus, the narrative is cumulative.

Finally, to help students keep track of the story, at the end of the chapters I have added historical timelines as well as a list of new key terms and concepts. There is also a glossary at the end of the text for the reader's convenience.

Acknowledgments

Many students at the University of Utah endured the class notes that eventually became this book. I do not think they really know how valuable their questions and comments were in selecting and organizing the content and shaping the presentation. Günseli Berik shared enthusiasm, industry, and a few bouts of misery, but she did not share my doubts about the viability of the project. She also was the best sounding board to discuss many early ideas. Mehmet Bilginsoy, a sophomore in college, read the entire manuscript, marked many passages "does not make sense," and gave me the target audience's perspective on the narrative. All the remaining confusing passages and flaws are my responsibility. Alev Bilginsoy's attempt to rewrite the first paragraph she read was a constant reminder of how much I need to improve my expository skills. Professor Norman Waitzman's comments were critical in identifying the institutional information that needed to be presented in the early chapters. I benefitted greatly from Professor Robert J. Shiller's online database and he gave me permission to reproduce much of it in charts. Sharon Lynn Bear edited the manuscript under a tight time constraint. Tara Minshull gave permission to use her artwork on the cover. Amy Kimball prepared Figure 12.3. Ayşe and Kemal Bilginsoy offered summer quarters that were ideal for work and for much appreciated distraction.

In the early stages of this project I worked with Senior Publisher Robert Langham and Editorial Assistant Simon Holt at Routledge. But I missed the deadlines and both Rob and Simon moved on. So I ended up testing interminably the patience of Economics Editor Andy Humphries and Editorial Assistant Lisa Thomson. Lisa tolerated my many requests for extensions. Tim Hyde copy-edited and put the finishing touches on the final manuscript.

I am grateful to all.

Credits

Cover art: *Let Nature Catch You* by Tara Minshull. Photograph from her *Cinematic Worlds* collection.

Figure 2.3 is reproduced from Earl A. Thompson, "The Tulipmania: Fact or Artifact," *Public Choice*, 130(1) (2007), p. 101, Figure 1. Copyright© 2007 Springer. Reprinted by permission of Springer Science and Business Media.

Figure 3.2 is based on data from Antoin E. Murphy, *John Law: Economic Theorist and Policy-Maker*. Clarendon Press (1997). Copyright© Antoin E. Murphy. Reprinted by permission of Oxford University Press.

Figures 7.1 and 7.3 are based on data from Arthur G. Gayer, W.W. Rostow and Anna Jacobson Schwartz, *The Growth and Fluctuations of the British Economy 1790–1850: An Historical, Statistical, and Theoretical Study of Britain's Economic Development*. Oxford University Press (1953). Reprinted by permission of Oxford University Press.

Figure 7.2, fixed investment data are from B.R. Mitchell, "The Coming of Railway and United Kingdom Economic Growth," *The Journal of Economic History*, 24(3) (1964). Copyright©1964 The Economic History Association. Reprinted by permission of Cambridge University Press.

Figure 8.1 is based on data from Benjamin Horace Hibbard, *A History of the Public Land Policies*. University of Wisconsin Press (1965). Copyright© Regents of the University of Wisconsin. Reprinted by permission of the University of Wisconsin Press.

Figures 8.2 and 9.1 are based on data from Susan B. Carter, Scott Sigmund Gartner, Michael R. Haines, Alan L. Olmstead, Alan L. Richard Sutch and Gavin Wright (eds) *The Historical Statistics of the United States, Millenial Edition* (2006). Copyright©2006 Cambridge University Press. Reprinted by permission of Cambridge University Press.

Figure 8.3 is from Walter Buckingham Smith and Arthur Harrison Cole, *Fluctuations in American Business 1790–1860*, pp. 184–5, Harvard University Press (1935). Copyright©1935 by the President and Fellows of Harvard College. Reprinted by permission of the publisher.

Figures 9.2 and 9.3 are based on data from *NBER Macrohistory Database Online*. Reprinted by permission.

Figures 9.4, 10.3, 12.6, 13.2, and 14.3 (in part) are based on data from S&P Dow Jones. The S&P 500® index and the Dow Jones Industrial Average are proprietary to and are calculated, distributed, and marketed by S&P Opco, LLC (a subsidiary of S&P Dow Jones Indices LLC), its affiliates and/or its licensors and has been licensed for use. S&P® and S&P 500® are registered trademarks of Standard & Poor's Financial Services LLC, and DJIA®, Dow Jones Industrial Average®, and Dow Jones® are registered trademarks of Dow Jones Trademark Holdings LLC. ©2014 S&P Dow Jones Indices LLC, its affiliates and/or licensors. All rights reserved. Reprinted by permission.

Figures 10.2, 12.4, 12.5, 12.7, 13.1, 13.3, 14.1, 14.2, and 15.1 are based on Robert J. Shiller's online data. Reprinted by permission.

Figure 14.3 (in part) is based on data from NASDAQ Indices. Reprinted by permission.

Figures 15.4, 15.5, 15.6, 15.7, and 15.8 are based on data from Inside Mortgage Finance, *The 2012 Mortgage Market Statistical Annual*, *Volumes I and II* (2012). Copyright©2012 Inside Mortgage Finance Publications. www.insidemortgagefinance.com. Reprinted by permission.

Figures 10.1, 15.1 (in part) and 16.2 are based on data from FRED, Federal Reserve Bank of St. Louis. LIBOR data are used by permission of ICE Benchmark Administration.

Abbreviations

AIG:	American International Group
AIGFP:	AIG Financial Products
ARM:	Adjustable-rate mortgage
BMK:	Bagehot–Minsky–Kindleberger (model)
BSM:	Black–Scholes–Merton (model)
CAPE:	Cyclically adjusted P/E ratio
CDO:	Collateralized debt obligation
CDS:	Credit default swap
CERN:	European Organization for Nuclear Research
CFTC:	Commodity Futures Trading Commission
CME:	Chicago Mercantile Exchange
CMO:	Collateralized mortgage obligation
DJIA:	Dow Jones Industrial Average
EMH:	Efficient-market hypothesis
Fannie Mae:	Federal National Mortgage Association
FDIC:	Federal Deposit Insurance Corporation
Fed:	Federal Reserve System
FHA:	Federal Housing Administration
FRB:	Federal Reserve Board (pre-1935)
FRBNY:	Federal Reserve Bank of New York
Freddie Mac:	Federal Home Loan Mortgage Corporation
FSLIC:	Federal Savings and Loan Insurance Corporation
JCHS:	Joint Center for Housing Studies (of Harvard University)
GDP:	Gross domestic product
Ginnie Mae:	Government National Mortgage Association
GSE:	Government-sponsored enterprise
IIA:	Independence of irrelevant alternatives (axiom)
IMF:	International Monetary Fund
IO:	Interest-only (mortgage-backed security)
ISDA:	International Swaps and Derivatives Association
LBO:	Leveraged buyout
LIBOR:	London interbank offered rate
LTCM:	Long-Term Capital Management

LTV:	Loan-to-value ratio
MBS:	Mortgage-backed security
MC:	Mississippi Company
MP:	Member of Parliament
NYC:	New York City
OCC:	Office of the Comptroller of Currency
OTC:	Over-the-counter
PDCF:	Primary Dealer Credit Facility
P/E ratio:	Price-earnings ratio
PO:	Principal-only (mortgage-backed security)
QE:	Quantitative easing
Repo:	Repurchase agreement
S&L:	Savings and loan association
S&P:	Standard and Poor's
S&P 500:	S&P 500 Index
SPV:	Special purpose vehicle
SEC:	Securities and Exchange Commission
SIV:	Structured investment vehicle
TAF:	Term Auction Facility
TARP:	Troubled Asset Relief Program
TBTF:	Too big to fail
TSTF:	Too systemic to fail
VaR:	Value-at-risk
WaMu:	Washington Mutual

"m," "b," and "t" denote million, billion, and trillion respectively

1   Introduction

Consider a household which plans to buy a home, a firm that plans to build a new plant, or a government that plans to improve highways. If their income is insufficient to finance the projects these households, firms, and governments are called *deficit units*. On the other side of the ledger there are *surplus units*, households, firms and governments with incomes greater than their expenditures and which want to increase their income further by investing their savings. The role of the *financial system* is to facilitate transactions between these two types of units. In financial markets the deficit units bid for the excess funds of the surplus units by selling instruments of debt (e.g. short-term commercial paper, IOUs, bonds) or ownership (shares) to raise funds to carry out planned expenditures (Figure 1.1). These instruments entitle the surplus units to returns or income streams in the form of interest payments or dividends to be received at future dates. But financing is not always direct; the surplus units do not always meet the deficits units "face to face" as direct buyers of financial instruments. The financial system also includes intermediary institutions such as banks, credit unions, pension funds, insurance companies, hedge funds, and mutual funds, which facilitate financial transactions. As shown in Figure 1.2, these *financial intermediaries* stand between the surplus and deficit units and serve as hubs that gather savings of the surplus units and market them to the deficit units. They also collect the returns and distribute them among the surplus units after deducting the fees for their services.

If everything goes well and mutually beneficial exchanges take place, both sides of the trade improve their well-being. On the deficit-unit side households enjoy their new homes, firms expand their capacity and raise profits, and the governments provide new highways that save time and reduce traffic hazards. The surplus units receive returns and add to their wealth.

There is, of course, always the possibility that the actual outcomes may be different from the plans. There are always risks associated with forward-looking actions. The homebuyer may be unable to make mortgage payments and face foreclosure. A recession may force a firm to abandon

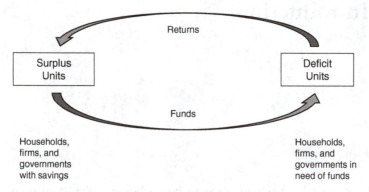

Figure 1.1 Direct financing.

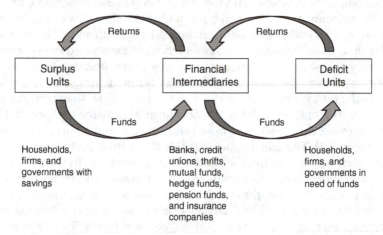

Figure 1.2 Financial intermediation.

its new plant and face bankruptcy. The surplus units may not be able to collect the expected payments. The fact that the future is unknown is what really makes financial markets shine. They price the risk and match borrowers who pursue high-risk projects with portfolio holders who can tolerate more risk in return for higher interest or dividends. They offer means to manage risk in forms of portfolio diversification and trading instruments of insurance. Finally, they make risk more affordable by distributing it among many wealth holders. Thus, *financial markets* are markets in which economic agents raise funds, invest in assets, and manage risk by trading instruments such as short- and long-term loans, stocks, and derivative contracts.

From a social perspective, finance lubricates the channels of commerce and production. Merchants need lines of credit because buying and selling are usually temporally separated. Producers rely on credit to pay their daily production costs. Allocation of surplus funds among the deficit units creates new industries, products, and neighborhoods. The construction of merchant fleets and the emergence of long-distance trading companies that globalized the economy in the seventeenth and the eighteenth centuries required large numbers of investors both to amass sufficient funds and to distribute risk among many stakeholders. At the dawn of the industrial revolution large-scale projects such as canals and railways required the mobilization of savings across the economy through loans and common stocks. Not surprisingly, many economists today fervently advocate the development and growth of financial markets across the globe with the expectation that they will be the handmaidens of economic growth.

However, the enthusiasm about the beneficence of the financial system is hardly universal. Skeptics point out that the laudatory accounts of textbook descriptions of the financial system overlook its unappealing features. Certain financial innovations are merely bets against future market movements, and, as such, move money around without creating much social value. Financial markets may not function efficiently due to various kinds of frictions and imperfections, such as differential access to information, perverse incentives, and price manipulation. The troubles of a few institutions may spread to the rest of the system quickly due to financial institutions' interdependence, especially during periods of heightened risk and excessive debt creation. The outcomes of this contagion are often a generalized run on banks, pervasive defaults, and stock-market crashes. Even worse, these crashes may spill over to the *real sector* (industry, commerce, agriculture, services) and trigger a generalized economic contraction. Boom-and-bust cycles throughout financial history are the primary evidence offered in support of this view. These observations are usually coupled with the recommendation that it is necessary to impose rules and regulations on financial institutions by public authorities to alleviate excessive speculative activity and reduce the likelihood of crises.

The "vision" thing

Financial crises have been a recurrent feature of the capitalist economy. The earlier classic episodes are the Dutch tulip mania, the Mississippi Bubble, and the South Sea Bubble that took place in the seventeenth and eighteenth centuries. Throughout the nineteenth century speculation in land and railways, stock-market booms and busts, and subsequent periods of stagnation were rampant in Britain and the US. The crash of 1929 is still recognized as the ultimate financial meltdown, and the launching pad of the Great Depression. After a lull that lasted until the 1980s financial crises came back with a vengeance. In the US savings and loan institutions failed in the 1980s at the cost of hundreds of billions of dollars to the taxpayers. 1987 witnessed the biggest one-day Wall Street crash. The hedge fund Long-Term Capital Management was saved by a consortium of investment banks and the Federal Reserve System in 1998. The dot-com bubble burst in 2000. Finally, the subprime-mortgage crisis of 2007–8 triggered fears of another Great Depression. However, there is still no consensus among economists on whether these events were ordinary responses of the markets to exogenous shocks or symptoms of endemic market failures.

One might think that experts, with the benefit of historical hindsight, must have by now determined the sources of financial instability, learned to anticipate the tell-tale signs of looming problems, and designed measures to avert a crisis. This is not the case. A common response among the commentators in the face of widespread defaults, bank failures, and asset-price crashes is surprise. After the near meltdown of the financial system in 2008 US Vice-President Cheney, in an Associated Press interview in January 2009, stated, "I wouldn't have predicted that. . . I don't think anybody saw it coming." President George W. Bush wrote in his memoirs that he was "blindsided" by the crisis. The president and the vice-president may be excused for their inadequate forecasting abilities due to the numerous issues that demanded their attention daily, from wars in Iraq and Afghanistan to security leaks in the administration—and they were not specialists in financial turmoil. It is the job of experts in academia, business, and government to take note of the potholes and hazardous conditions in the economy, inform the public and the policymakers, issue warnings, and make recommendations.

But they also failed—collectively. Throughout the decades preceding the crisis most of the experts hailed the incessant rise in home prices, securitization of debt instruments, and the proliferation of opaque financial derivatives as beneficial forces that created an age of unprecedented prosperity and demonstrated the omnipotence of the "free market system" (a euphemism for capitalism unfettered by government regulations). They ignored or downplayed how these new markets and instruments increased the fragility of the financial system and elevated the risk exposure of the entire financial system and the economy. The dominant conceptual framework propounded by economists and promoted, among others, by Alan Greenspan and Ben Bernanke (successive chairs of the Federal Reserve System), bank executives, and real-estate-industry insiders was that innovations in financial markets stimulated the flow of savings to securities and reduced risk across the system. These savings ostensibly enabled technological revolutions, enhanced productivity, and improved the global standard of living. Potential problems, such as the subprime-mortgage defaults, were thought to be isolated in remote corners of the financial world, unlikely to spill over to the rest of the system.

The media held the party line by constantly talking up the riches to be attained in the financial markets.

What these economists, policymakers, business people, regulators, and much of the public shared was a particular "vision" or frame of mind that shaped how they observed and conceptualized the developments in the economy. Economist Joseph Schumpeter drew attention to the role of this frame of reference in economic analysis:

> [I]n order to be able to posit ourselves any problems at all, we should first have to visualize a distinct set of coherent phenomena as a worthwhile object of our analytical efforts. In other words, analytical effort is of necessity preceded by a preanalytic cognitive act that supplies the raw material for the analytic effort. In this book this preanalytic cognitive act will be called Vision.
>
> (1954: 41)

Schumpeter's *preanalytic vision* is the researcher's perception of the "world in which we live" that selects certain facts as important or relevant and ignores others. It precedes the analytical work of constructing theoretical models to conceptualize the vision. The preanalytic vision is obviously closely related with ideology.

> In fact, [ideology] enters on the very ground floor, into the preanalytic cognitive act of which we have been speaking. Analytic work begins with material provided by our vision of things, and this vision is ideological almost by definition. It embodies the picture of things as we see them, and wherever there is any possible motive for wishing to see them in a given rather than another light, the way in which we see things can hardly be distinguished from the way in which we wish to see them.
>
> (Schumpeter 1954: 42)

The important point here is that ideology is an essential ingredient of the preanalytic vision and an indispensable component of the endeavor to make sense of the world.[1] As such, it may restrict the researcher to thinking in limited structures, and fail to discern contrarian trends and to ask appropriate questions. In light of Schumpeter's comments, ideological proclivities explain the failure of a large majority of the experts to see the oncoming subprime meltdown. The dominant vision in the post-1980 period precluded systemic financial fragility and crisis. Most experts, despite the benefit of historical hindsight, failed to anticipate the telltale signs of looming problems because, within their frame of reference, unfettered markets were inherently stable, and innovations only further improved the resilience and stability of the financial system.

Alan Greenspan made the same point at a post-2008 congressional hearing: "An ideology is, is a conceptual framework with the way people deal with reality. Everyone has one. You have to—to exist, you need an ideology."[2] He further announced that the subprime crisis revealed an error in his ideology: "I found a flaw in the model that I perceived as the critical functioning structure that defines how the world works." During the same hearing, he explained:

> I made a mistake in presuming that the self-interests of organizations, specifically banks and others were such that they were best capable of protecting their own shareholders and equity in firms . . . So the problem here is something which looked to be a very solid edifice and, indeed, a critical pillar to market competition and free markets, did break down. . . . [T]hat shocked me. I still do not understand why it happened and, obviously, to the extent that I figure out what happened and why, I will change my views.

What happens when events that are deemed anomalous from the perspective of the dominant "vision" occur? Various outcomes are possible, depending on the frequency, significance, and severity of such occurrences. Sometimes the anomalies are ignored or dismissed by the public, investors, and experts. Believers in the magic of the markets adhere to the "once in a lifetime" cliché and relegate crashes to mere aberrations. After passing through stages of blame and atonement investors pick up the pieces and proceed to the next speculative boom, sharing the sentiment expressed by the "four most dangerous words" in investing attributed to Sir John Templeton: "This time it's different." Academics who side with the dominant orthodoxy of the supremacy of unfettered markets offer versions or interpretations of events to align them with their framework.

However, conceptual complacency is not universal. Crises, especially when they are severe and long-lasting, may lead to alternative visions of how the economy works and theoretical fault lines. Market turbulences, in fact, motivated many economists to design models to explain the conditions under which financial markets fail to function efficiently and apply these theories to episodes of boom and crash. While these economists imply that financial markets do not guarantee socially optimal outcomes, there is substantial variation among the visions of these alternative models. One set of models focuses on consequences of the imperfectly competitive market structures. Another set emphasizes the decision-making process of investors. Others go further by positing a vision of capitalist dynamics as inherently unstable and fragile rather than harmonious, balanced, and steady.

As for this book, it acknowledges a plurality of explanations (although it does not subscribe to the relativist view that all theories are valid on their own terms and that there is no discoverable, objective truth). Its objective is to lay out the preanalytics and analytics of competing explanations of financial crises, illustrate them in historical perspective, and present the current state of the debate in the economics discipline. It is important to appreciate the differences between alternative approaches and their implications because, as current discussions over the regulation of financial markets attest, theories inform the public policies that influence people's everyday lives.

Types of financial crises and the scope of the book

A financial crisis occurs when a large number of wealth holders attempt to liquidate their assets simultaneously due to the fear that the value of their holdings will depreciate. Three types of asset may underlie three types of crisis: bank deposits (or other short-term loans to banks), securities (government debt, private bonds, and stocks), and currencies. When banknote holders, depositors, and other short-term lenders grow uneasy about a bank's solvency they rush to redeem their loans to banks. Concerns about depreciation of the value of securities force their owners to sell their portfolios. The expectation that a national currency will lose value vis-à-vis other currencies leads to a run from the currency.

Once agents' apprehension is kindled and spreads, the crisis can easily become a self-fulfilling prophecy and turn into a bank run, bond- or stock-market crash, or a currency collapse. In each of these instances owners of these assets try to convert their wealth to safe alternatives, which may take the form of gold, cash, Treasury bills, and so forth, depending on time and geography. What is common to all financial crises is that, when many wealth holders try to dump these assets simultaneously, buyers disappear and liquidity evaporates. The positive-feedback mechanism between expectations of declining values and excess supply of assets in the market exacerbates the price collapse. Increasing risks of default and bankruptcy of the deficit units make lenders less willing to make loans and a credit freeze sets in, with potentially disastrous consequences for the entire economy.

The scope of the book is limited to banking and private security-market crises. The reason for the narrow boundaries is pragmatic. The primary question is how well financial markets function in allocating of savings and disseminating information. Crises that emerge in the private sector of the economy offer a more appropriate focus to address these questions. Government-debt crises open up the stage for an entirely different set of questions related to fiscal policy and deficits, which lie outside the scope of this work. Consideration of currency crises, such as the 1994 Mexican peso and 1997 Thai baht crises, in turn, requires development of ideas about balance of payments and exchange rates. An adequate treatment of these additional topics is unfeasible in a one-semester course model, for which this book is designed. Therefore, the subject of currency crises is left outside the scope of the book.

Plan of the book

This book presents, in chronological order, a series of financial booms and busts, their primary actors, relevant institutions, mechanics of expansion and crash, and consequences. Chapters 2, 3, and 4 present accounts of the three classic financial crises: the Dutch tulip mania of 1636–7, the Mississippi Bubble of 1719–20, and the South Sea Bubble of 1720. Tulip mania has always captured the imagination of the commentators: imagine paying several years' income for a single tulip bulb. Rare tulip bulbs were traded among aficionados for very large sums throughout the 1620s and 1630s in the United Provinces. However, the emphasis here is not the incredulous stories about the purchase of luxury items by the collectors; the more interesting part of the story for the present purpose relates to the transferable forward contracts that were traded among a relatively new class of traders for speculative purposes. Tulip mania refers to the twentyfold increase in and sudden crash of the average price of bulb forward contracts between November 1636 and February 1637.

The Mississippi and South Sea bubbles took place almost simultaneously in Paris and London respectively. Both were initiated by private companies to restructure government debt held by the public. The strategy in both cases was to create a publicly held commercial company and swap shares of the company with the outstanding government debt. To motivate bondholders to swap the debt they held for company shares the Mississippi and South Sea companies promised potential shareholders high profits from the commercial activities of the companies and devised means to raise expectations of share-price appreciation. Rapidly rising share prices attracted more investors in anticipation of capital gains. The value of the Mississippi shares increased from 500 to close to 10,000 livres between May and December 1719, and toppled in May 1720. The share price of the South Sea Company rose from £100 to £900 in the first six months of 1720 but collapsed back to its original level in September of the same year. Chapters 3 and 4 detail the mechanics of the creation of the two companies, their internal contradictions, and their eventual collapses.

In addition to chronicling these events, in Chapters 2, 3, and 4, I introduce several economic concepts and institutions that are pivotal to understanding financial markets. In the context of tulip mania, for instance, I present spot and forward markets, hedging, and short selling. Chapter 3 starts by presenting a discussion of money and credit, how the banking system creates money through credit extension, and insolvency and illiquidity crises.

In these three chapters I describe what happened and how, but do not probe the question of why prices behaved the way they did or explain the willingness of the investors to pay astounding prices for the assets. Simply saying that they were seeking capital gains is not an explanation because it begs the question of why investors did not anticipate that prices were apt to collapse and ignored the heightened risk of loss of wealth. What is missing in these chapters is the theory. Asset-price bubbles are defined as persistent and cumulative deviations of the market price from the fundamental or intrinsic price. To make sense of this definition it is necessary to lay out the meaning of the fundamental price. Chapter 5 presents the standard theory of price determination that links prices to "fundamental" factors via the "rational" decision-making of economic agents. The first part of Chapter 5 reviews the standard-fare economic analysis that covers utility and profit maximization, supply, demand, and price determination in the commodities markets. Next, it shows how bond and stock prices are related to fundamentals that are summarized by the discounted expected income streams of these securities.

The second part of Chapter 5 delves into the six issues that are central to the theories of asset-price bubbles and banking crises. As all investment decisions are future-oriented and no one has perfect foresight, the first issue concerns how to operationalize uncertainty in modeling forward-looking decision-making. The second is the discussion of the rational-expectations hypothesis that has become the workhorse of modern mainstream economic models. Third, I introduce the idea of the "rational bubble" or the theoretical possibility of an asset-price bubble when agents form expectations "rationally." The fourth topic is the meaning of "rational" behavior in the context of standard economic analysis. While the rest of the world uses the word "rational" synonymously with "reasonable," economists define the term narrowly as optimizing behavior. Fifth, I present challenges to the idea of rationality-as-optimization from within the economics discipline. The final issue is the debate over whether speculation stabilizes or destabilizes asset prices. These discussions lay the groundwork to appreciate competing crisis theories, which are presented in Chapter 6.

In Chapter 6 I identify five competing approaches to explain financial booms and busts and illustrate these competing hypotheses in the context of the three classical bubbles. These approaches are distinguished in terms of their takes on how economics agents make financial decisions and the economic environment in which they are located. According to the first approach, which also serves as the reference category, asset prices are outcomes of optimizing decisions of economic agents in perfectly competitive markets. This position implies that asset prices fully reflect the available information on market fundamentals, and theoretically rules out the possibility of bubbles. The second approach contends that asset-price bubbles may occur and attributes them to distortions created by government interference in markets. The third approach retains the optimization assumption, but argues that markets are not perfectly competitive. Endemic imperfections and frictions make financial markets prone to crises. The fourth approach follows the work of the behavioralist economists, who object to the optimizing decision-making assumption. They trace the sources of financial crises to investors' reliance on rules of thumb and the interdependence of investment decisions. The fifth approach follows the work of three economists, Bagehot, Minsky, and Kindleberger, who view financial booms and busts as consequences of the internal dynamics of the credit cycle of the capitalist system.

Chapter 7 returns to the historical record. This chapter considers the banking and stock-market crisis in Britain during the first half of the nineteenth century. There are three important themes in this chapter. The first is the consequences of a technological revolution, i.e. railways, on the development of financial markets, speculation, stock-price appreciation, and collapse. The second theme is the banking system's connection with this process, or, specifically, the relationship between bank credit extension and stock-price movements. The third theme is the conflicting private and public roles of the Bank of England and the need for a lender of last resort to save the banking system from collapsing when credit channels are blocked.

The subjects of Chapters 8 and 9 are the arc of the US banking system, from its first experiment with central banking in 1791 to the establishment of the Federal Reserve System in 1913, and the recurrent boom-and-bust cycles in land and railroads. The widely varied US banking experience, including free banking, state monopolies, outright prohibition, and the hierarchical national banking system, offers a wealth of information on how policymakers and banks, in the absence of a central overseer of the system, searched for ways to stabilize the banking system, and the successes and failures of this endeavor. The fortunes of asset markets were closely intertwined with the banking system. The first half of the nineteenth century witnessed bouts of land speculation fed by bank credit; in the second half of the century railroads were the leading sector of the economy, as well as the primary source of growth and hazard in the financial markets. It was a very turbulent century, with financial crises in almost every decade. In Chapters 8 and 9 I select six of these episodes to tell the story of the American experience: the land panics of 1819 and 1837, the land and railroad securities panic of 1857, the railroad securities panics of 1873, the currency and industrial panic of 1893, and, jumping into the new century, the run on New York City financial-trust companies in 1907.

Chapter 10 is devoted to the Wall Street Crash of 1929, which illustrates various themes that run through the book, including the mechanisms behind the boom and fragility in securities markets, the dilemmas of Federal Reserve policymakers regarding stock-price overvaluation, and the enthusiasm of academics and stakeholders in cheering on and talking up the bubble economy. This chapter summarizes the debate over the sources of stock-market growth in the 1920s and the subsequent crash, which remain contentious to the present day. In addition it discusses in more detail the relationship between the financial crash and the depression in the real economy.

Chapters 11 and 12 dig deeper into the theoretical issues raised in Chapters 5 and 6 and explore the question of the significance of the equality of the market price and the fundamental price. Why does it matter? The answer is related to the welfare implications of deviations of price from its intrinsic value. Some light on this question is already shed in the historical chapters, where sustained deviations from the fundamental price were shown to have resulted in undesirable resource allocation.

Chapter 11 tackles the question of how resources are allocated via market prices and the efficiency properties of market outcomes. The chapter starts with a detour into the intellectual history of moral philosophers, Adam Smith's "invisible hand," and reinterpretation of this concept by current standard-fare economics. It then presents two defenses of unfettered markets: the allocative- and informational-efficiency defenses. The chapter concludes with a discussion of why the price system may fail to bring about efficient outcomes due to imperfections and frictions endemic to markets, or interdependent actions of economic agents.

In Chapter 12 I discuss the allocative- and informational-efficiency arguments with reference to financial markets. It will be noted immediately that the debates over market efficiencies are already familiar from the theoretical taxonomy of Chapter 6. The fundamentals-based and policy-based distortions approaches uphold the view that, left to their own devices, markets attain efficient outcomes. The other three approaches are skeptical that this is always the case. Chapter 12 summarizes the theoretical arguments of the two opposing sides on the social-welfare implications of financial markets. It also presents the efficient-market hypothesis and the arguments of its critics. These debates are important from the public-policy perspective because the failure of allocative or informational efficiency inevitably leads to the question of the need for market regulation. The discussion of these questions also sets the stage in Chapter 12 for post-1980 debates.

Chapters 13, 14, 15, and 16 recount three acts of a play. The banking regime put into place in the 1930s produced an extended phase of boring but stable financial relations that lasted until the 1970s. In the 1980s and 1990s, however, many of the financial regulations of the 1930s were dismantled or unenforced for being out of date, unnecessary, and harmful. Deregulation widened the realms of financial institutions' operations. The immense growth of derivatives trading (securitized debt instruments, options, and swaps) was perceived as a force that deepened and stabilized markets. The financial sector more than doubled its share in the economy. However, these decades also brought back market turbulence.

Chapter 13 focuses on the developments in financial markets in the 1980s, i.e. leveraged buyouts, junk bonds, the savings and loan crisis, and the stock-market crash of 1987. Chapter 14 discusses the growth of securitization of mortgage debt and swap derivatives and also describes two financial calamities of the decade: the implosion of the hedge fund Long-Term Capital Management and the dot-com boom and bust. Chapters 15 and 16 cover the latest installment in the narrative, the subprime-mortgage crisis of 2007–8. The narrative of these four chapters underscores that the last and the most momentous act since 1929 was not happenstance or a freak accident but the outcome of forces that had been building in the economy since the 1980s.

One side effect of the subprime-mortgage crisis has been soul searching within the economics profession. The fact that economists largely failed to anticipate the financial meltdown led many leading economists to question whether the way they learn, teach, and practice economics is also in crisis. Criticisms of the dominant theoretical paradigm included its excessive reliance on an axiomatic approach based on optimizing economic agents, on building models that are formally pleasing and elegant but have little relevance to the "real world," on an intentional dismissal of history, and on wearing the ideological blinds of free-market efficiency. In the public-policy sphere the ongoing parallel discussion is whether the sweeping deregulation of the previous decades should be reversed and private financial institutions' wings clipped to avoid excessive risk-taking in the future. The concluding chapter takes stock of the legacy of the 2007–8 crisis for the economics discipline and the restructuring of financial architecture.

Key terms and concepts

Deficit unit
Financial intermediaries
Financial market
Financial system
Preanalytic vision
Real sector
Surplus unit

Endnotes

1 Schumpeter (1954) recognized the dangers of ideological bias and wrote at length on how scientific procedural rules would alleviate ideological errors if not eradicate them totally.
2 Greenspan quotations are from Cassidy (2009: 205–6).

References

Cassidy, John. 2009. *How Markets Fail: The Logic of Economic Calamities*. New York: Farrar, Straus and Giroux.

Schumpeter, Joseph A. 1954. *History of Economic Analysis*. New York: Oxford University Press.

2   Tulip mania

The tulip is arguably the most elegant and exotic object of speculation in the colorful history of financial crises. Real estate, securities, even gold can hardly match the charm of delicate colors and sensuously flared petals. In the early seventeenth century Dutch botanists and wealthy merchants were passionate admirers of tulips, and bulb prices were on the rise throughout the 1620s and early 1630s. As the country became more prosperous, demand for tulips grew in excess of supply until a single bulb of a rare species could command the price of a house on the main canal, and perhaps even more. Today hardly a news item on financial crises fails to mention the inordinate sums of money the Dutch were willing to pay for a single tulip bulb. However, what has come to be known as tulip mania was not simply rising demand for a luxury product. Rather, it refers to the twentyfold increase in the average price of tulip-bulb forward contracts, including for the more common bulbs, in just three months, and its subsequent abrupt collapse. Some details of the story are contentious, and disputes continue over the magnitude of price changes, backgrounds of market participants, and outcomes of the crash, but all commentators agree that something extraordinary happened in the United Provinces in the winter of 1636–7.[1]

Background

The tulip, a wildflower native to the Central Asian steppes, was cultivated by the Ottoman Turks during the sixteenth century. In addition to its sturdiness the tulip is a very versatile plant that can yield many new varieties through cross-breeding. The Ottoman cultivators cross-bred hundreds of varieties of colors and shapes, and the flower quickly became an icon of beauty and the favorite adornment in the palace gardens. Stylized tulip motifs were ubiquitous on tiles, vases, marbled paper, prayer rugs, and the outfits that sultans donned both in the palace and on the battlefield.

When the tulip was introduced to the West during the second half of the sixteenth century Europeans were initially interested more in the plant's medicinal and culinary properties. However, it gradually gained favor among botanists and connoisseurs who bred the flower, as well as the wealthier burghers who made it the showpiece of their gardens. While devotees spread throughout France and central Europe, the center of tulip passion, both in terms of cultivation and adornment, was the Dutch United Provinces (today's Netherlands). Exchanges of bulbs among aficionados and purchases of bulbs at high prices were frequent during the first decades of the seventeenth century.

The willingness to pay large amounts for these collector's items is probably not astonishing, given the United Provinces' vast accumulation of wealth. At the turn of the seventeenth century the United Provinces was a highly urbanized cosmopolitan republic in the European sea of peasantry and monarchy. This confederation of cities, organized around a central parliament in Amsterdam, had become the most prominent center of commerce, finance, manufacture, and art in Europe. The nation's rise to economic prominence occurred in a particular political and military context. Until the mid sixteenth century the Netherlands was part of the Spanish Empire. The Dutch revolted in 1568 and the war against Spanish rule lasted until 1648. An early outcome of the war was the secession and rise of the northern United Provinces as an economic and commercial powerhouse. When the Spanish occupied Antwerp and the southern provinces (today's Belgium) in 1585 many skilled craftsmen and merchants migrated to the new Dutch republic and contributed to the concentration of skills, capital, and wealth. The Spanish blockade of the Scheldt estuary, the maritime access to Antwerp, in the same year made Amsterdam the gateway to central Europe and, eventually, the hub of European trade with the Americas, southern Asia, and the Far East. During most of the first two decades of the seventeenth century the war with Spain was in a lull—and because the Netherlands did not take part in the Thirty Years' War (between Spain, France, and the German and Scandinavian states), which lasted from 1618 to 1648 and wreaked havoc across central Europe, they were able to divert resources from military outlays and quickly became leaders in commerce, finance, manufacturing, shipbuilding, and channel construction. The Dutch Golden Age spanned the entire seventeenth century.

The economic fortunes of the Netherlands rose with trade. The Dutch established colonies in the Caribbean, South and North America, and, most importantly, in the Far East. The Dutch East India Company, the crown jewel of Dutch commerce, was chartered in 1602 and granted the monopoly on trade with Asia by the government. With the decline of Spanish naval dominance the company's activities grew significantly. The company contested with and prevailed over the British and Portuguese in the islands of Java and Borneo, established trade posts and colonies across the Far East, and became the largest trading company in Europe. As the primary supplier of luxury goods such as spices and porcelain, which were cheap at source but in high demand in Europe, the Dutch East India Company yielded enormous profits to its shareholders.

As a result of wars and concomitant defaults of states on their loans, many European financial centers, such as Paris, Bruges, Antwerp, and Liege, declined in the second half of the sixteenth century. Against this background, the Bank of Amsterdam and the Amsterdam bourse emerged as the leading financial institutions in Europe. The Bank of Amsterdam, established in 1609, was the largest European bank for most of the century. Amid the chaos of multitudes of coins of dubious value arriving from all corners of Europe it launched the widely adopted "bank money," or credit against deposits of coin and bullion, which standardized currency and facilitated commercial transactions. This orderly monetary system attracted merchants from across Europe to Amsterdam. Financial instruments sold on the Amsterdam exchange included stocks, bonds, and insurance contracts; but the Dutch East India Company was the star of the Amsterdam stock market. While *joint-stock companies*, i.e. businesses owned by shareholders, had been around in various forms since the thirteenth century, the Dutch East India Company was the first to issue common stock that was tradable on a stock exchange. The ease of convertibility to cash made Dutch East India Company shares more attractive to investors and enhanced the company's ability to finance long-distance trade. The exchange also boasted a very active futures market in commodities (e.g. timber, spices, and hemp) and securities.

In the first three decades of the seventeenth century wealth was rapidly accumulated by the large merchant class and, to a lesser extent, smaller merchants, professionals, and skilled master craftsmen. The Dutch Golden Age of painting, led by masters such as Rembrandt and Frans Hals, was in full bloom. The Dutch did not have the reputation of being ostentatious consumers, though the wealthy built large homes and gardens, and patronized the arts. Rare tulips decorated the gardens and were reproduced in paintings.

A digression on forward and futures contracts, hedging, and short selling

Many financial practices that were commonplace on the seventeenth-century Amsterdam exchange changed little over the centuries, and they will be encountered frequently in this historical account. Thus, it is worthwhile describing a few of these at this stage.

A *forward* or *futures market* permits two parties to trade a commodity or an asset for future delivery at a price agreed today.[2] It is different from a *spot market*, where the commodity or asset is traded for immediate delivery. Merchants and portfolio holders can hedge their exposure to price fluctuations through forward transactions, or transfer the risk of unfavorable price changes to other parties. *Hedging* avoids the risks of a position in one market by taking the offsetting position in another market. Consider a spice merchant whose goods are still in transit from the Far East. Ownership of the spices means that the merchant is *long* in spices or is in a *long position*. A long position exposes the merchant to risk. If the price of spices happens to fall by the time ships drop anchor in Amsterdam harbor the merchant would suffer losses. The solution is to offset the long position by selling the incoming spices for future delivery at a price set today. This hedge locks in a cash value for the spices and insulates the merchant from future price fluctuations. By selling the spices forward the merchant takes a *short position* in the forward market. The merchant's long and short positions are offsetting. Similarly, a stockholder could avoid the losses from a possible decline in the value of his portfolio by selling stocks in the futures market.

The merchant may engage in a forward transaction with one of two types of counterparties. The first type is another merchant, such as a spice wholesaler, who wishes to hedge against the risk of an increase in price. Such a transaction requires a coincidence of needs between two hedgers. The second type of counterparty is the speculator. *Speculation* is conventionally defined as trading assets or commodities with the intention of profiting from short- or medium-term movements in their prices. The simple rule of speculation is to "sell if the price is expected to fall and buy if the price is expected to rise." In the spice-market example the speculator would purchase spices forward if she anticipates that the future spot price will be higher than the contracted forward price. Thus, the speculator assumes the risk the hedger wants to avoid; she sells peace of mind to the merchant, similar to "insurance."

A closely related practice is *short selling* or *shorting*. Suppose that a speculator expects the price of a stock to decline in the future and that this expectation is not commonly held by others in the market. The speculator can profit from her hunch by making a bet against the market. This takes the form of short selling, which consists of borrowing a security from a lender today and selling it to another party for future delivery.

Figure 2.1 illustrates how short selling works (the dark arrows denote the movement of shares and forward contracts; the dashed lines are cash payments). Suppose on May 1 the one-month forward price of a share is $10, and a speculator believes the stock is overpriced; she expects the spot price a month from now would be $8. On May 1 she borrows ten shares, say, of the stock from a lender, usually a broker, and simultaneously signs a one-month forward contract to deliver ten shares to a buyer at $100. On June 1 the contract is settled; the shorter delivers the shares to the buyer and receives $100 in return. Next, the shorter has to return the borrowed shares to the broker. She buys ten shares on the spot market on June 1 and returns them to the broker. If the price indeed turns out to be $8 she pays only $80 for the shares, and her profit is $20. However, if the price has increased to $13, then she has lost $30.[3] The Dutch public authorities were deeply distrustful of forward trading of securities on the grounds that

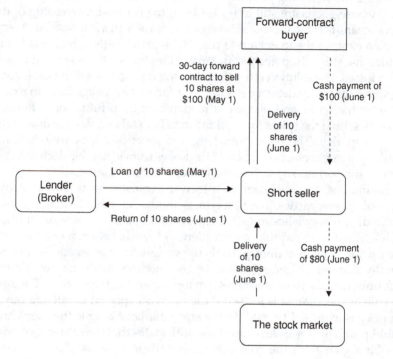

Figure 2.1 Short selling.

widespread or coordinated shorting of a stock could be sufficient to depress its price. To avoid destabilization of markets by self-fulfilling actions and manipulations of speculators they prohibited *naked shorting*, or selling a stock in the forward market without borrowing the security. Courts implemented the edict by refusing to enforce such contracts (Garber 2000).

Early Dutch tulip market: collectors and growers

Dutch horticulturalists cross-bred hundreds of varieties of tulip bulbs. There were two basic categories of bulb: breeders and varietals. Breeders were common, plain, single-colored bulbs that were abundant and cheap. Varietals, also known as broken tulips, were multicolored specimens and the real objects of passion. Varietals were often named after their cultivators or towns, coupled flamboyantly with military titles, such as Admiral, General, and Viceroy—or, when these ranks did not sate the hunger for hyperbole, Admiral of Admirals and General of Generals. The inimitable Semper Augustus with vivid red flares against a pure white background was the uncontested emperor of tulips, so exquisite and rare that it was seldom ever traded.

Tulips were grown either from seeds or by cultivating the offsets that the mother bulb created by cloning itself. Growing a tulip from seed took a long period of time (seven to ten years), and rare varieties could not be grown in this way. In fact, the varietals were "biological accidents." The source of delicate colors and patterns of the broken tulips, unbeknownst to the cultivators, was the mosaic virus spread by aphids that infected the bulbs. The virus did not infect the seeds, so rare bulbs could be acquired only from the offsets of the mother bulb. A mother bulb yielded perhaps two or three clones per year, and it took two to three years for offsets to become mature bulbs. Even then it was not certain that the clones would be reproductions of the rare species because colors and patterns depended on variations in the degree of infection. Further, while the more heavily infected bulbs yielded more beautiful and desirable flowers, they were also weaker and destined for a shorter lifespan. They also produced fewer offsets, which added to their rarity.

Due to the variability of these growing methods, one characteristic of the tulip-bulb market was the high level of uncertainty surrounding the transactions because it was difficult to discern the characteristics and quality of specific bulbs, let alone differences between bulbs. For example, if a seller switched the promised bulb with an inferior one, the fraud could not be discovered before the bulb bloomed the following year. Further, buyers could never be sure what they had bought because even the same bulb did not necessarily yield an identical flower every year, and there was no guarantee that offsets were exact clones of the mother bulb.

The initial participants in the tulip market were the connoisseurs: botanists, amateur cultivators, and collectors. Exchanges and gifts of seeds, bulbs, and botanical information took place in a closely knit network of aficionados across Europe, who bred and collected new varieties. The node of the network was Carolus Clusius, the foremost botanist of the late sixteenth century, who in 1594 founded the botanical garden of the University of Leiden. He planted tulips and other flowers for their aesthetic rather than utilitarian value, a botanical novelty at the time.

Rising wealth and changing tastes were the primary movers of demand for luxury products. Tulips were increasingly used to adorn the gardens of German and Austrian princes and became a fashion statement in women's décolletage or coiffure in Paris ballrooms. However, their popularity was unmatched among people of prominence in the Netherlands—important merchants, professionals, regents—whose wealth was growing at a rapid pace. The growth of a wealthy merchant class and the concomitant refinement of tastes, spread of fashion, and perhaps a bit of vanity raised the demand for rare bulbs. The supply of bulbs, however, did not grow commensurately because cultivation was primarily in the hands of a small number of connoisseurs, and because of the aforementioned technical hurdles to growing varietals in large numbers.

During the first two decades of the seventeenth century the tulip market expanded as supply moved from the hands of connoisseurs to professional growers, who started to offer breeder bulbs and varietals in larger numbers. The bulb market was easy for suppliers to enter because, in contrast with the structure of most other trades that were organized under the guild system, there were no restrictions on who could engage in tulip cultivation, and the capital requirements were modest (a small piece of land and some bulbs and seeds). On the demand side, the Dutch middle class increasingly entered the market as buyers, and more people with means established gardens in their backyards or outside the city walls. The market also extended internationally as growers started selling bulbs in bulk across Europe and even to the Ottoman Empire. With the increase in the number of professional cultivators, some varietals became more available, and their price increases were restrained. However, the taste for novelty products induced growers to introduce new varietals to the market, and rare bulbs continued to command very high prices. Exorbitant bids on the rarest tulip bulbs by Dutch collectors were recorded in the 1620s. By one account, f12,000 (the "f" stands for Dutch guilder), the equivalent of an average artisan's income over 40 years, was offered for ten Semper Augustus bulbs. The owner reportedly turned down the offer (Dash 1999: 81). Into the 1630s demand for varietals continued to increase in excess of supply, and their prices were on the rise.

In the Netherlands tulips flowered for only about two weeks from May to June; traditionally, tulip bulbs were traded in early summer. As patterns and colors cannot be inferred from the bulb, the trade was not a simple transaction. Once flowers bloomed prospective buyers inspected the flowers and negotiated a price with the seller for the bulbs of specific flowers and made a purchase contract. The transaction between the buyer and the seller was completed only after the flowers withered and their bulbs were lifted from the soil in the presence of witnesses. The buyer wrapped the bulbs in paper and kept them dry indoors. They were replanted in September and remained in the ground throughout the winter and the spring. There was also an active auction market during the remainder of the year, while bulbs were still in the ground and not in bloom. Since owners kept detailed records of their holdings, bulbs belonging to merchants in default or to the deceased were often auctioned by creditors or heirs to be delivered after blooming.

As professional cultivation spread and the market expanded, growers published "tulip books," catalogues of the watercolors, or gouaches, of the flowers with descriptions and sometimes prices to disseminate information on the multitude of varieties available. Because the slightest variation in color or pattern was sufficient to christen a new varietal these books fell short of capturing all that was offered in the market. Nonetheless, tulip books signaled a more mature and expansive market.

Enter the florists

After 1630 the complexion of the tulip-bulb market started changing. Steady increases in bulb prices attracted a different type of actor, the florist, to the market, whose primary motivation was to take advantage of rising prices by selling bulbs at a higher price than she had paid to realize *capital gains*. For this group the bulb was not simply a commodity that was purchased and admired for its colors and patterns, it was an *asset*, an object in which wealth could be held and expected to grow.

According to Scottish journalist Charles Mackay (2009 [1852]), people across all levels of society, including nobles, farmers, and even chimney sweeps, speculated in bulbs in anticipation of quick and easy profits. However, the social class encountered most frequently in the accounts of speculative activity is the artisan, e.g. weavers, brewers, and carpenters (Posthumus 1929). In these accounts florists were often characterized as people who knew or cared little about the bulbs or the aesthetic qualities of the flowers. They are said to have used their savings and mortgaged their homes, looms, and livestock to purchase bulbs and bulb contracts, with dreams of quick riches.

Anne Goldgar (2007: 137) disputes these descriptions of florists. On the basis of archival research she argues that speculative activity was not spread across different classes but limited to small groups of easily identifiable middle-level to well-off merchants, professionals, and master craftsmen—in short, citizens of some import who were closely connected by familial, religious, neighborhood, and professional networks. These networks facilitated communication and information flows. Their exclusivity implies that the overall florist market was, in fact, composed of many localized markets of interconnected individuals. The florists' demand for bulbs derived as much from an attempt to emulate a higher class of consumer as from a search for a lucrative place to put their savings. Hence, their motives were not entirely speculative. Bulb trading was a side activity for florists because they maintained their usual occupations and did not forego the tools of their trade. Thus, Goldgar warns that descriptions of wild frenzy and collective madness were "contemporary propaganda" that cautioned people against losing their heads. She maintains that, while florists may not have been experts, it is an exaggeration to say that they were totally uninformed about the sources of supply and demand or the quality of bulbs.

With the expansion of the florist trade, the tulip market was transformed. The first important innovation in the new bulb market was that the object of trade was no longer the bulb but the forward bulb-purchase contract. Forward trades in commodities and assets were already common on the Amsterdam exchange, and the practice was swiftly put into use in the bulb market by speculators. Bulb trading transformed from a summer spot exchange into a year-round activity. At any time prior to blooming the owner and buyer could sign a forward contract for bulbs (or clones) that were still in the ground. The contract required the exchange of cash for the bulb at the predetermined price once it was dug up from the ground, with the proviso that the buyer may verify the flower before-hand. The sales agreement permitted the buyer to renege on the contract in the event that the bulb was found to be a different variety upon inspection of the flower. The contract could also require the buyer to pledge his property to protect the seller from non-payment (van der Veen 2009). Moreover, the contractual purchase obligation was transferable, i.e. the buyer could sell the forward contract to a third party.

Second, also around 1634, the unit of bulb trading was standardized. Previously bulbs had been priced individually; after 1634 they were priced by weight. Variants of rare bulbs were priced by individual weight measured in aces (equal to 1/20 of a gram), and the more common bulbs were sold in batches (pound goods). The price of a bulb to be lifted from ground the following June became a function of its expected weight at that time. Standardization of the unit of trading signaled the growth of the bulb market and the increasing number of participants.

The third important innovation in the florist segment of the bulb market was the credit system. Entry into the trade required access to funds to finance bulb purchases. Florists who were short of funds had to start by dealing with cheaper bulbs. Those with some starting capital were able to purchase more valuable bulbs, the prices of which were rising at a faster rate and which promised higher capital gains. A continuous increase in prices, however, required greater access to funds to match competing bids. The typical recourse for raising more funds was to borrow from a financial institution, such as a bank.[4] The common practice among florists, however, was for the seller to extend personal credit to the buyer by agreeing to deliver bulbs in return for a *promissory note* (IOU) from the buyer.

Because forward contracts were transferable transaction chains soon emerged, through which the same bulb contract was traded several times over against IOUs. Figure 2.2 depicts such a chain. Florist A purchases bulbs from a bulb owner (who could be a grower) to be delivered the following spring in return for promissory note IOU_A worth $f100$. Commonly, the buyer did not make a down payment in this exchange. Florist A then sells the forward contract to Florist B in return for IOU_B of $f120$. Note that Florist A, without putting any money down, makes a return of $f20$ (provided that the transactions eventually clear). In the next step Florist B sells the contract to Florist C in return for IOU_C of $f140$. The chain can continue as long as the holder of the contract finds a party willing to purchase the contract. The Dutch called the process the wind trade: exchanging unseen bulbs in the ground for pieces of paper. As long as the florist has sold the contract at a price higher than she paid for it she makes capital gains, at least on paper. All transactions in the chain are to be cleared simultaneously on the bulb-delivery date (after the blooming season). All IOUs are

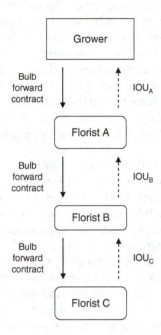

Figure 2.2 Bulb forward-contract transaction chain.

cashed: Florist C pays B f140, B pays A f120, and A pays the grower f100. Florist C also submits the forward contract to the grower and receives the bulb. In the end both A and B make capital gains of f20, the grower receives f100 for the bulb, and C is the owner of the bulb in return for f140. If Florist C wants to own the bulb this chain of transactions is mutually beneficial. The hazard for the speculative buyer, of course, is the failure to sell the contract to another party at a favorable price.

In finance purchasing an asset on borrowed funds multiplies the gains (or losses) of the buyer and is known as *leverage*. Access to credit in bulb-contract purchases had two important implications. First, a rising number of participants entered the market by leveraging whatever little capital they owned. Second, they were able to bid up the price of bulb contracts and add momentum to the escalation of prices.

Posthumus (1929) dates the emergence of the speculative tulip market at 1633 or early 1634. The Dutch were already familiar with speculative activity, and speculation on Dutch East India Company shares and commodities was common, although limited to wealthy merchants. Tulip-bulb contracts allowed other social classes to engage in speculative activity, and speculation took place in the midst of heightened uncertainty in the bulb trade. In addition to the unknowns related to the botanical properties of the bulb, such as its ability to reproduce the same flower the next season, questions about the future expected spot price, the weight of the bulb when it is pulled from the ground, the number and size of prospective clones, and whether the purchased bulb even existed became pertinent to traders' decision-making. Some authors have pointed to the Dutch people's proclivity for gambling as an explanation for their attraction to the bulb trade in the face of these unknowns (Kindleberger and Aliber 2011: 59). Others have attributed the attraction to the Dutch's fatalistic attitudes in the midst of the bubonic plague that ravaged the United Provinces between 1635 and 1637, decimating a fifth of the population (Garber 2000).

Florists often traded bulb contracts at so-called "colleges," or inns and taverns, which were common locations for many types of transactions. Bulb-contract trades were carried out through bilateral negotiations or auctions, and they were highly ritualized. In bilateral negotiations traders sat around tables in inns or taverns and made offers by marking wooden plates. Upon agreement on a price the buyer purchased the contract on credit but paid, in cash, what was known as "wine money" to seal the contract—an amount for food, wine, tobacco, tips, and even alms. In the event a party stepped back from negotiations he was required to compensate the counterparty through payment of a penalty called "grief money." Wine and grief money were the only instances in which cash was used. The practice of no-cash-down payment implied potentially infinite leverage or unlimited issuance of promissory notes by buyers as long as sellers were willing to accept paper. Growth in personal credit permitted spiraling prices. Only the reluctance of the seller to accept debt in return for the contract could have restrained the explosion of borrowing, but the confidence in rising prices probably allayed any fears that sellers might have had about the ability of the borrowers to pay in the future. The readiness to extend and accept personal credit, in turn, permitted a cycle that pushed prices higher and further reinforced the confidence of all parties.

While these transformations were taking place in the markets the original tulipophiles—aficionados, wealthy collectors, and big merchants who purchased rare bulbs for their own pleasure, using their own funds—refrained from participating in the speculative florist segment of the market.

The boom

With the increasing number of traders, particularly those who traded on personal credit, bids kept climbing. In February 1637 one rare Admirael van Enkhuizen bulb with an offset was sold for ƒ5,200 in an auction (Goldgar 2007: 203). By way of comparison, the annual income of an artisan at the time was around ƒ300. The price is astronomical even in comparison with "luxury" products: in 1640, for instance, the premier artist of the day, Rembrandt, was commissioned to paint what has come to be known as *The Night Watch*, a painting that measured 13 by 16 feet, for ƒ1,650, about a third of the price of the Admirael. The Admirael sale took place at the end of the period of tulip mania, the brief episode between November 1636 and February 1637, when there was a massive increase in the price of both the rare and relatively common bulbs.

The price data are limited, however, and it is difficult to generate a consistent bulb-price index. The available information from the anonymous pamphlets of *Dialogues between Waermont and Gaergoedt* (meaning Truemouth and Greedy-goods respectively) that was first published in 1637, as well as from tulip books, notary records on disputed contracts, and auction records, is scattered and incomplete. There were also substantial variations in price from one city to another. The price series compiled by Earl Thompson, which is frequently cited in the literature, shows the average price of tulip bulbs from November 1636 to February 1637 (Figure 2.3). This index is the average price of several varieties of bulbs and has the obvious shortcoming of erratic frequency of observations; and the basket of bulbs that underlie each observation and the weights used in calculating averages are not necessarily the same from one observation to the next. Nonetheless, Thompson's index is consistent with the sharp increase in prices in December 1636 and January 1637 and the collapse in February 1637 recorded in various accounts and, therefore, appears to provide an adequate approximation of the overall price pattern. The index increased from 10 on November 10, 1636 to 178 by December 12, 1636. The average price peaked on February 3, 1637, at 203.

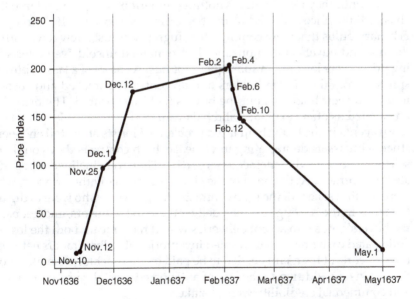

Figure 2.3 Bulb forward-contract-price index, November 1636–May 1637.
Source: Thompson (2007).

The spiraling prices were not limited to varietals. By January 1637 demand had outstripped supply by so much that even the more common bulbs, such as Switsers and Croonen, which were sold by the pound, were added to the speculative market. Switsers were sold for *f*60 in the fall of 1636 but were increased in price to *f*125 on December 31, 1636. Within two months, by February 3, 1637, the price was *f*1,500 (Goldgar 2007: 202). The willingness of buyers to bid up prices was probably a sign of the widespread optimism about prospective capital gains. It was also an indication of the precariousness of the situation. If price increases slowed and capital gains were diminished speculative traders would revise their expectations of price appreciation downward. From that point on speculators would have an incentive to sell contracts. As the number of sellers multiplied and buyers vanished excess supply would push prices down. Lower prices, in turn, would create a positive feedback loop of expectations of further price decreases and the dumping of more contracts on the market.

The crash

The internal contradiction of a bubble is that it will survive only if holders and buyers of an asset believe that the bubble will sustain itself. As long as there are new rounds of buyers who are willing to make higher bids the bubble will survive. However, when prospective buyers vanish bubble-asset holders experience a Wile E. Coyote moment: they stay suspended in mid-air until they realize there's nothing underfoot and plummet into the chasm. Bulb prices crashed at the beginning of February 1637. In early February bulbs that were commanding high prices just a few days earlier did not find buyers at auction, and they remained unsold even after asking prices were lowered in subsequent rounds. As news of a lack of buyers spread across the market holders of bulb contracts panicked and rushed to unload their holdings; but the buyers had disappeared. The price fall accelerated as offers exploded and bids vanished.

All agents in the bulb chain faced problems. Florists at the tail end were stuck with assets depreciating in value, i.e. bulb contracts they could not sell, and debts owed to their counterparties. They were inclined to repudiate the contracts. At the head of the chain were usually the growers, who were the first sellers of the bulb contracts. For growers, who were to dig up the bulbs in the coming summer, deliver them to the buyers, and get paid, the buyers' refusal to accept deliveries would have meant both the loss of anticipated cash flow and unwanted inventories of bulbs. Traders between the two ends of the chain needed to be paid by their debtors to make good their loans. In addition to the loss of anticipated capital gains their honor and commercial credibility were at stake.

Once they realized that buyers were unlikely to honor their contracts growers from different cities met in Amsterdam and announced on

February 23, 1637, that they would accept 10 percent of the original contract price to settle debts on all contracts signed after November 30, 1636 (the Amsterdam growers rejected the proposal). However, the proposal was not legally binding. Buyers balked; they wanted liquidation at 0 percent of the original price, or permanent settlement of all contracts without any compensation to the growers. Lacking the force of law, the growers' offer was not accepted. What followed was a state of confusion and disorder about what to do with thousands of outstanding forward contracts. The central government remained impartial and left it to local authorities to sort out the disputed contracts.

In April 1637 the Court of Holland decided to suspend all bulb contracts temporarily and asked city magistrates to collect information about the bulb trade and resolve disputes locally once determinations were made regarding who owed what to whom. The central parliament made this decision binding on all cities, but cities did not take action and left the resolution of disputes to buyers and sellers, who dealt with the contracts via bilateral negotiations. Suspension of contracts was to the advantage of the buyers because the blooming season was arriving. Growers needed to remove bulbs from the ground shortly and deliver them to buyers in exchange for payment, which was difficult when buyers were not present for the transaction. Thus, growers were forced to settle at a fraction of what they had hoped for. After a year, in May 1638, the Haarlem city council ruled that all contracts be cancelled at 3.5 percent of the original sale price, and other cities adopted this decision.

The aftermath

According to Posthumus (1929) and Kindleberger and Aliber (2011: 111), the tulip crisis of 1637 had an adverse effect on the Dutch economy as wealth declined, but there is little evidence to support this claim. There are two reasons why the impact of the crisis was negligible on the economy. First, the bulb trade was marginal to the economy. Most florists were dealing in bulbs as a side activity, and the collapse of bulb prices did not necessarily mean widespread bankruptcies and suspension of their usual economic activities. Florists earned their livelihood through other means, and, after the collapse of the tulip-bulb market, they were able to continue with their established trades. For speculators, expected capital gains evaporated because promissory notes that circulated among traders were practically worthless. However, the debts owned and owed were largely personal and, in the aggregate, offset each other. Moreover, large merchants had not participated in the florist market and were insulated from the crash. There were, however, certain sections of the society who suffered. Growers who ended up with large quantities of unwanted inventories faced losses. Florists who had mortgaged their real assets, such as homes and livestock, to purchase bulbs faced financial difficulties and perhaps bankruptcy. Nevertheless, these problems did not spill over to the rest of the economy; the entire episode was brief and localized.

The second reason that the effect of the tulip crisis was negligible to the overall economy was that that credit used in the bulb market originated from sellers within the market, not from financial institutions. After the crash credit losses were isolated in the bulb market. As we shall see in future chapters, financial crashes are detrimental to the rest of the economy when they cause the payment and credit systems to come to a halt due to widespread defaults and repudiation of contracts. Once financial institutions restrict lending to reduce their risk exposure and the credit flow becomes glacial there is collateral damage to the other sectors of the economy. Manufacturing, agriculture, and commerce need a constant flow of credit to carry out their day-to-day operations. Credit freezes starve these sectors of funds and engender lower levels of activity, slower circulation of commodities, and overall stagnation. However, the likelihood of such a credit freeze in the 1630s in the Netherlands, where the banking sector was insulated from the tulip trade, was remote.

This is not to say that there were no adverse societal consequences. Goldgar (2007) emphasizes the profound negative effect of tulip mania on the social and commercial sectors of the Dutch public due to the deterioration of mutual trust among individuals. Widespread refusal to honor contracts harmed the reputation of merchants and master craftsmen, who were otherwise held in high esteem. There were many instances of drawn-out litigation. Once one's word was no longer one's honor trust in counterparties broke down, and disputes became more difficult to mediate. In the Netherlands the severe social dislocation diminished restraint and civility as the public searched for scapegoats or conspirators, and blamed what had happened on the more secluded Jewish and Mennonite communities.

Sadly, the exquisite varietals of tulips for which the wealthy were willing to pay a king's ransom before and after the boom are extinct today. Botanical advances eradicated the mosaic virus along with the colors and patterns it created. Multitudes of Admirals and Generals, as well as the unique Semper Augustus, survive today only in the gouaches of growers' catalogues.

Timeline

1600–30	Tulip market expands with exchanges between connoisseurs, as well as sales to wealthy merchants; gradually, professional horticulturalists emerge and gardening becomes fashionable among middle and upper-middle classes.
1630	Florists enter market.

1631	Dutch economy booms as the recession of 1620s, caused by reignition of Spanish War, subsides.
1633–early 1634	Speculative tulip market emerges.
December 1634	First recording of sale of bulbs by weight.
1635	Bubonic plague starts in United Provinces and kills 20 percent of population over next two years.
Fall 1636	Growth of forward market in bulbs and spread of payments by promissory notes.
November 1636	Tulip-bulb forward-contract prices start rising sharply—start of the bubble. Average price rises twentyfold over next three months.
February 3, 1637	Bulb prices reach peak and collapse.
February 23, 1637	Growers offer to settle contracts signed after November 30, 1636, at 10 percent of price. Florists reject offer.
April 25, 1637	Court of Holland decides all contracts will be temporarily suspended while city magistrates collect information about bulb trade and then resolve disputes locally.
April 27, 1637	Central parliament makes Court of Holland decision binding on all cities. Contracts suspended, but cities don't take action.
May 1636	Bulb prices at pre-bubble levels.
May 1638	Haarlem city council rules all contracts can be canceled at 3.5 percent of original sale price.

Key terms and concepts

Capital gain/loss
Forward contract
Forward market
Futures contract
Futures market
Hedging
Joint-stock company
Leverage
Long position
Naked shorting
Promissory note
Short position
Short selling (shorting)
Speculation
Spot market

Endnotes

1 The historical narrative, descriptions of the bulb market, and the social environment in this chapter draw heavily on Posthumus (1929), Dash (1999), Goldgar (2007), and Garber (2000).
2 While *futures* and *forward contracts* perform the same functions, they are not identical. Futures contracts are standard contracts that are traded on exchanges, whereas forward contracts are bilateral agreements designed to the specifications of the counterparties. However, the distinction is not important in the present context, and, therefore, I use these terms interchangeably.
3 The actual transactions would be more involved due to factors such as borrowing costs, margin payments to the lender, and commissions.
4 Chapter 3 discusses the banking system.

References

Dash, Mike. 1999. *Tulipmania: The Story of the World's Most Coveted Flower and the Extraordinary Passions It Aroused.* New York: Three Rivers Press.

Garber, Peter M. 2000. *Famous First Bubbles: The Fundamentals of Early Manias.* Cambridge, MA: MIT Press.

Goldgar, Anne. 2007. *Tulipmania: Money, Honor, and Knowledge in the Dutch Golden Age.* Chicago: University of Chicago Press.

Kindleberger, Charles P. and Robert Z. Aliber. 2011. *Manias, Panics, and Crashes: A History of Financial Crises.* 6th ed. New York: Palgrave Macmillan.

Mackay, Charles. 2009 [1852]. *Memoirs of Extraordinary Popular Delusions and the Madness of Crowds.* Mansfield Centre, CT: Martino.

Posthumus, N. W. 1929. "The Tulip Mania in Holland in the Years 1636 and 1637." *Journal of Economic and Business History* 1 (3): 434–66.

Thompson, Earl A. 2007. "The Tulipmania: Fact or Artifact?" *Public Choice* 130 (1/2): 99–114.

van der Veen, A. Maurits. 2009. *The Dutch Tulip Mania: The Social Foundations of a Financial Bubble.* Athens, GA: Department of International Affairs, University of Georgia.

3   The Mississippi Bubble

Episodes of financial euphoria and despair feature fascinating characters who are revered one moment and reviled the next. They inspire fictional heroes and villains, from Anthony Trollope's Augustus Malmotte to Oliver Stone's Gordon Gekko. However, fiction is often a pale imitation of real life. The Medicis, the Rothchilds, J. P. Morgan, and their ilk easily surpass fictional financiers in power, glamour, and intrigue. The archetype of larger-than-life financial wizards was John Law, a Scotsman, whose audacity and ambition are unmatched in the history of finance. As a young man he was a dandy, a womanizer, and a gambler, but, at around 30 years of age, he turned to economics; at 45 he started implementing his grand financial design.

Within four years Law was in charge of France's banking, its treasury, mint, overseas trade, and colonial development. In the same year that he became the de facto prime minister of France the edifice he created collapsed, and Law had to flee the country. However, his economic theory left its mark in the intellectual realm, even though economists' assessments tend to be ambivalent in the face of Law's monumental failure. According to Karl Marx, he had "the pleasant character mixture of swindler and prophet." Alfred Marshall referred to him as "that reckless, and unbalanced, but most fascinating genius." The foremost historian of economics in the twentieth century, Joseph Schumpeter, recognized him as a revolutionary economist of his time: "[Law] is a class by himself. He worked out the economics of his projects with a brilliance and, yes, profundity, which places him in the front ranks of monetary theorists of all time."[1]

John Law was born in 1671 in Edinburgh, Scotland, into a family of finance. His father, who died when Law was 12 years old, was a goldsmith. At the time goldsmiths, in addition to buying and selling gold, accepted deposits and made loans. Bankrolled by the mortgaged family estate, John Law lived lavishly in London until, at the age of 23, he killed a man in a duel over what appeared to be a web of amorous liaisons. He was imprisoned for murder and sentenced to death. In 1695, having appealed the verdict, Law escaped, apparently with the assistance of the authorities. He traveled to France and Italy, where he built sizeable wealth at the gambling tables, thanks to his exceptional prowess in calculating odds.

In Amsterdam he observed the operations of the Bank of Amsterdam and the Dutch East India Company, Europe's largest bank and joint-stock company respectively. These observations formed the foundations of his economic thinking and his financial designs to raise vast quantities of funds through a combination of paper-money creation and common-stock sales. Law developed his economic ideas in two books, *Essay on a Land Bank*, published in 1704, and *Money and Trade*, published in 1705. He needed the support of political authorities to put his ideas into practice, but convincing them was not easy. He proposed the idea of a national land bank, which would issue notes to the borrowers against the security of the land of the country (instead of precious metals), in London, Edinburgh, Paris, and Turin between 1704 and 1712 but was unsuccessful. In 1716 the French government, in the midst of a severe fiscal crisis and in desperate need of funds, warmed to the idea of a bank that would ease its debt problems.

Money, credit, banking, and government debt in the early eighteenth century

To understand Law's rise and fall it is essential to describe the financial environment of his time. The nature of money and credit, the banking system, and government debt are the essential elements of this backdrop.

Money

Money is a means of exchange, a store of value, and a unit of account. The first function refers to money being used as payment, or currency, to purchase commodities and assets. The second function refers to money as a form in which wealth can be kept. The third function refers to its use as a metric, e.g. to express prices, income, and wealth.[2] In principle, anything a society agrees to accept as money can be money. In the past individual commodities, such as shells, salt cubes, wampum, and cigarettes performed this function. However, the most familiar form of *commodity money* is gold or silver coins, or *specie money*. The relative scarcity of gold and silver, their universal recognition as valuable metals, and the ease by which they can be minted in coins of different metal content and denominations made them obvious candidates to perform the functions of money. Commodity money has intrinsic use value of its own. Gold, for instance, is sought after in jewelry for its malleability and shine, and in electronics for its conductivity.[3]

The value of a gold or silver coin, in terms of the number of bushels of wheat it can purchase, say, would vary with the relative supply of precious metals. The pillaging of the Americas and the inflow of gold and silver increased the European specie supply in the sixteenth century. As the quantity of goods and services produced for exchange did not increase proportionately with the quantity of the specie the outcome was too much money chasing too few commodities. Depreciation of the value of specie money—inflation—ensued. The value of a coin also depends on its quality. Worn, filed, chipped, or debased coins, which have lower precious-metal content, are worth less.

In a specie-money economy without *depository institutions*, such as banks, the money stock consists of the coins in circulation. However, coins are heavy and bulky and can be cumbersome in making large payments. Their safekeeping is also expensive and risky. Considering these draw-backs, it was a common practice to hold the specie at a goldsmith in return for a receipt, or scrip, written to the bearer. The scrip holder used it as the means of payment in purchases. Once the seller who received the receipt as payment submitted it to the goldsmith the buyer's specie account was debited and the seller's account credited by the amount of the transaction. The emergence of the goldsmith as a depository institution changed the composition of the money stock of the economy. It was now equal to the sum of the total deposits, which, in turn, was equal to the value of receipts in the hands of the public and the circulating specie, that is, specie outside of goldsmiths' vaults. The goldsmith as a deposit-taking, scrip-issuing institution was the precursor of the modern banking system.

Credit

Exchange of commodities through the intermediation of money is more efficient than barter exchange because the latter requires the transacting parties' needs to coincide. The most important instrument that facilitates exchanges, however, is not money; it is credit. *Credit* is a contract or an agreement whereby one party—the lender—agrees to provide a good, service, or money to the second party—the borrower—in return for a payment to be received sometime in the future. To secure the loan the borrower usually posts *collateral* in the form of a property or financial asset that he agrees to forfeit to the lender in the event he defaults on the loan. Credit is as old and as common as money. Use of promissory notes, orders, and checks in transactions has been common since 2000 BCE in the Middle East, Hellenic Greece, Egypt, and China (Braudel 1981: 472). In Europe, after the fifteenth century most exchanges among merchants and manufacturers involved commercial credit or *commercial paper* (promissory notes or bills of exchange) that permitted deferment of payment, lubricated channels of transaction, and allowed faster circulation of commodities. Consider the transactions among three parties: a wholesaler, a retailer, and the final customer. Suppose that the retailer does not have surplus funds and would not be able to pay the wholesaler until after the sale to the final customer. It is likely that the two transactions do not take place simultaneously. One way to solve the problem to the benefit of all three parties is for the retailer to get credit or a loan from the wholesaler. The credit may take the form of a *bill of exchange*, in which case the retailer (drawer of the bill) receives the goods by signing an order to pay a specified amount to the wholesaler (bearer of the bill) at a future date. It is likely that the exchange would cost more for the retailer in comparison with handling the transaction with a cash payment because the wholesaler would seek to be compensated for the postponement of the payment and the risk of not getting paid. Essentially, the wholesaler extends credit to the retailer, and the difference between the amounts of the credit and the cash payment is the interest on the loan.

The contract is settled when the retailer pays the debt to the wholesaler on the specified date. However, the wholesaler does not need to hold on to the bill of exchange until this date. It is possible, and common, for the bill to traverse the market when the wholesaler endorses it to another party, likely at a discount, for another exchange, provided the other party is willing to accept it as payment. Through a chain of endorsements a single bill could be used in a multitude of transactions, but there would be a single final payment from the initial drawer (the retailer) to the final bearer of the bill at the due date.

Banking

A preponderance of bills of exchange helped banks find a new source of profit: bank credit. Idle coins in a vault could be extended as loans to customers at interest. Bank credit often took the form of *discounting*, which meant that the bank purchased bills of exchange from the bearer of commercial paper at a discount. Discounting effectively made it possible for the bank to extend credit to the initial drawer of commercial paper. With the emergence of banks as specialized lending institutions, sellers were more disposed to accept buyers' commercial paper, knowing that it could be cashed in before the due date. They were less concerned with whether another trading partner would accept it as payment. Put differently, the commercial paper was now more *liquid*, or more easily converted into money. In addition to being a source of profit for banks, discounting benefited the real sector of the economy by further lubricating the channels of circulation of commodities.

Discounting of commercial paper had a profound effect on the monetary sphere. If the wholesaler who sold the bill to the bank redeposited the specie in the banking system, where it would be safe in the vault, and carried out his own transactions using receipts, then the outcome would be an increase in total deposits and the money stock without any increase in specie. That is, lending and redepositing augmented the money supply by creating more deposit money.

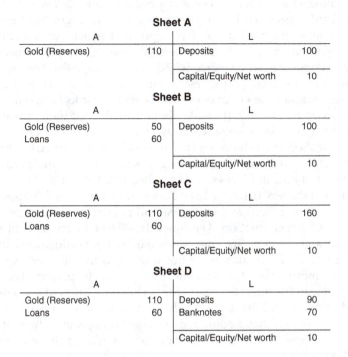

Sheet A

A		L	
Gold (Reserves)	110	Deposits	100
		Capital/Equity/Net worth	10

Sheet B

A		L	
Gold (Reserves)	50	Deposits	100
Loans	60		
		Capital/Equity/Net worth	10

Sheet C

A		L	
Gold (Reserves)	110	Deposits	160
Loans	60		
		Capital/Equity/Net worth	10

Sheet D

A		L	
Gold (Reserves)	110	Deposits	90
Loans	60	Banknotes	70
		Capital/Equity/Net worth	10

Figure 3.1 Banking-sector balance sheets.

The evolution of the banking system can be summarized by the balance sheet (Figure 3.1). The balance sheet reports the total assets and liabilities of a company. Suppose that the total value of gold coins or money in circulation is worth $110, and initially there is no bank. Then a farsighted individual establishes a bank with $10 of capital, collected by selling shares to the public. Next, make two simplifying assumptions: the public keeps all the gold coins in the bank due to the safety and convenience it offers, and there is only one bank in the economy (or, equivalently, the balance sheet represents the banking system of the whole economy). The assets of the bank, or what it owns, are the $110 worth of gold recorded on the left side of balance sheet A of Figure 3.1. Liabilities of the bank, or what it owes, are reported on the right side of the balance sheet as deposits of $100. The difference between the assets and liabilities of the bank is its capital of $10, which is also referred to as *equity* or *net worth*. It also is recorded on the right side so that the assets and liabilities are balanced.

In the next step suppose the bank, in search of revenue opportunities, makes loans of $60 from its gold holdings. The impact on the balance sheet is illustrated on Sheet B. On the asset side gold reserves drop to $50, and loans become $60. However, because the public is assumed not to hold any cash but to use bank receipts in exchange, all of these gold loans would be redeposited into the borrowers' deposit accounts. Balance Sheet C records the bank's assets and liabilities: assets are $110 in gold and $60 in loans. Liabilities of the bank are $160 of deposits. The net worth is still $10. The total specie held by the bank is the total reserves at hand to meet the demands of depositors who wish to withdraw their deposits. The ratio of reserves to deposits is called the *reserve ratio*. The banking system in which the reserve ratio is less than one—that is, where banks back only a fraction of deposits by reserves (to make them available for withdrawal) and loan out the remainder—is known as the *fractional-reserve system*.

The next innovation in the banking system was bank money. After the sixteenth century banks started extending credit not only in specie-backed deposits but also in pieces of paper called *banknotes*. The Bank of England perfected the practice after 1694. This innovation turned "deposits" into "notes in circulation" and further simplified the transaction process and enhanced the circulation of commodities. The balance sheet of a bank that both accepts deposits and issues banknotes is illustrated in Sheet D of Figure 3.1. Banknotes were not written to the "bearer" and were, therefore, more easily transferable from person to person. They were also divisible in the sense that they were printed in different denominations and, thus, could be used easily in transactions of variable amounts. Holders of banknotes could redeem them for specie at the issuing bank. The reserve ratio is now the ratio of reserves to the sum of deposits and banknotes.

The advantage of a lower reserve ratio for banks is higher profitability, though this comes at a cost. The disadvantage is that banks become vulnerable as the reserve ratio declines. Balance Sheets C and D show that the bank faces two kinds of risk. The first is the *illiquidity risk*. *Liquidity* refers to the ease with which an asset can be converted into money. The lending-redepositing scheme implies that the bank keeps a fraction of the total deposits as specie reserves (or the reserve ratio is below unity). Deposits and banknotes are redeemable for specie at any time, whereas the bank makes longer-term loans that are to be collected at a future date. Deposits and banknotes are more liquid than bank loans. The *maturity mismatch* between its assets and liabilities exposes the bank to potential trouble. Even if the loans are sound and certain to be paid back, the inability to convert long-term loans to cash at short notice exposes the bank to illiquidity risk if depositors at any time wanted to withdraw their deposits en masse[4] (as faced by Jimmy Stewart's George Bailey in *It's a Wonderful Life*). A bank that faces a heightened illiquidity risk would try to strengthen its cash reserves through borrowing from other parties or partially liquidating its loan portfolio (that is, selling its loans to other parties or not renewing existing loans).

The second type of risk is *insolvency risk*, which concerns the quality of bank assets and refers to the possibility of the bank's net worth becoming negative. A bank is *solvent* if it can meet its long-term financial obligations, which requires timely collection of the loans it has extended. Suppose that a bank suffers from poor management and has a large inventory of non-performing loans, and its borrowers are defaulting in rising numbers. The value of its loans, a significant component of the bank's assets, would decline. Once the value of assets falls below the value of liabilities and its net worth becomes negative, the bank is insolvent. As it owes more than it owns, the bank cannot meet its obligations and faces bankruptcy. Even prudent banks may not be free from insolvency risk. During periods of economic contraction, rising defaults and distress sales of assets by over-indebted businesses reduce collateral values across the board and thereby adversely affect the value of bank assets and net worth. A bank that faces insolvency may temporarily attempt to fend off the problem by borrowing, although it may be difficult to find lenders under such conditions. Alternatively, it may attempt to increase its capital base through new injections, which may take the form of issuing new stock or even selling the company partially or fully to another party.

Banking crises occur when a large number of banks are exposed to illiquidity or insolvency risks simultaneously. Illiquidity and insolvency crises may, of course, be linked. A *bank run* occurs when there is a generalized loss of confidence in the banking system that compels large numbers of depositors and note holders to redeem their deposits and banknotes to hard cash. When a bank run forces otherwise solvent banks to raise liquidity by selling their assets at a loss the banks' net worth declines, and insolvency risk increases. Conversely, in the presence of a generalized insolvency crisis banks often limit lending either due to concerns about other banks' default risk, or to protect their own reserves in the event of a contagion. A liquidity freeze ensues when banks refuse to extend credit by purchasing other banks' assets.

The correct diagnosis of whether the source of a banking crisis is illiquidity or insolvency is important from a policy perspective. Lending to liquidity-constrained banks resolves the problem by buying them time to call back loans and strengthen their reserves. Clearing houses established by banks in the US performed this function locally with mixed success in the nineteenth century, before the establishment of the Federal Reserve System. There are also instances of banks pooling resources to provide liquidity to their troubled brethren to contain the problem and prevent it from spilling over to other institutions. However, a coordinated effort is not always forthcoming (individually, each bank has an incentive to withdraw from the process) or may be inadequate. Then, a publicly supported institution, a central bank, is necessary to serve as the *lender of last resort* and offer loans to illiquid banks. Another means to allay public anxiety and bank runs that cause illiquidity problems is insuring bank deposits. The insolvency crisis is a more difficult problem to deal with because it is a structural issue that cannot be averted by opening credit lines. Many economists favor adopting regulatory measures to prevent imprudent bank behavior that may create insolvency risk. Such measures may include imposing capital requirements (a minimum ratio of equity to loans) and monitoring banks' loan performance by regulators to assure judicious lending behavior.

Historically, various types of banks with different objectives and practices have coexisted. Two examples from the seventeenth century are noteworthy: the Bank of Amsterdam and the Bank of England.

We first encountered the Bank of Amsterdam in Chapter 1. Although it was primarily the Spanish who brought gold and silver into Europe during the sixteenth and seventeenth centuries, these metals found their way to northern Europe through three channels: first, bullion was smuggled and pirated; second, the Spanish specie payments to northern countries' manufacturers rose with inflation; and, third, the military occupation of the southern Dutch provinces and ongoing wars increased Spanish expenditures. Much of the specie ended up in Amsterdam, the financial capital of Europe. These coins were of very mixed quality. The Dutch chartered the Bank of Amsterdam in 1609 with the express purpose of creating a standard monetary unit by collecting coins of various sources and qualities at their intrinsic value and issuing banknotes against them. Standardization of the value of currency facilitated exchanges and attracted more resources to Amsterdam, contributing to it becoming Europe's foremost financial center. The Bank of Amsterdam was an example of a pure deposit bank: it did not extend credit. It only issued transferable paper money to depositors and kept the number of banknotes it issued to 100 percent of its gold reserves. These banknotes, however, were so trustworthy and popular that merchants were willing to pay a premium for them. This state of affairs lasted for more than a century (although the bank did provide occasional, short-term lending to the Dutch East India Company). The credibility of the bank eroded as economic circumstances deteriorated during the Fourth Anglo-Dutch War in 1780, and the City of Amsterdam began to ask for loans. The bank closed down in 1812.

The Bank of England was chartered in 1694 to establish a system of money and credit in England and to facilitate a resolution to the government's troubled finances. It was the only bank the government permitted to be established as a joint-stock company. Its primary functions were to make loans to the government and to manage government debt. It also took deposits from the public, discounted commercial paper, and issued banknotes. It became a central player in the resolution of financial crises in England in the eighteenth and nineteenth centuries, and was a precursor to modern central banks.

Discussions of money and credit are at times confusing because the line of delineation between the two can very quickly become ambiguous. For instance, a bill of exchange is credit, but once it is endorsed and is accepted as means of payment it is a very close substitute for currency and effectively functions as money. Banknotes are even more likely to be accepted because they do not need endorsement. Thus, these instruments of credit, these pieces of paper, were as good as specie, at least insofar as the holders had confidence that the issuer would honor them.

Government debt

The final component of the financial environment is *government debt*. European states and the papacy had a constant need to feed and equip armies to fight the perpetual wars among themselves. These expenses were in part funded by taxes, fees, and creative means, such as lotteries and the selling of government offices. When these methods did not suffice states borrowed by selling to the public various types of government paper, such as bonds and annuity contracts. Holders of sovereign debt were entitled to interest payments or annuities. Liquidity of these *debt instruments* varied due to an assortment of restrictions on their transferability. They were often traded in financial markets at a discount because the state was usually in arrears in their payments, and there was a risk that the state would refuse to pay. Monarchs at times indeed repudiated their loans when they were unable to service them. France, in the early seventeenth century faced chronic difficulties in paying its debt and defaulted on some of its loans.

John Law in France

King Louis XIV died in 1715 after reigning for 72 years. Before he died the Sun King left the monarchy to his five-year-old great-grandson and appointed his nephew Philippe II, the Duke of Orleans, as regent. France was in a dire financial situation following wars that had lasted decades. The tax system was inefficient, and corruption was pervasive. Total public revenues covered only two thirds of state outlays and forced the state to borrow even more to cover the budget deficit. Debt payments were in arrears. In the financial markets government debt was traded at a discount of more than 50 percent, which signaled prevalent public skepticism regarding the government's ability to pay its debts.

The French tax-collection system was privatized. The government auctioned tax-farming leases for the collection of indirect taxes. Leaseholders collected taxes for a six-year term in return for fixed annual payments to the government. Direct taxes, e.g. on income and wealth, were collected by the sale of public offices to buyers that entitled them to a certain percentage of the taxes they collected. Additional funds were raised by the sale of government monopolies, e.g. tobacco and mint, to the highest bidder.

The government borrowed either in the form of long-term, lifetime, or perpetual annuities, or short-term (floating) debt. Interest on long-term debt was to be paid from specific tax revenues, but the revenue source of short-term debt was not earmarked. *Financiers* served as intermediaries in the financing of government expenditures by borrowing from the public and lending to the government.[5] They were held in low public esteem because they were often considered profiteers who exploited the financial distress of the state. Behind the scenes, however, the state's principal creditor was the rich aristocracy (Murphy 1997). They lent to the state through the intermediation of the financiers and, therefore, were not subject to public scrutiny. It was nonetheless common for the government to default on portions of the debt when it had sufficient political power vis-à-vis the financiers.

In comparison with the contemporary Dutch and British systems the French banking system was primitive, and the state could not resort to bank borrowing. There was a generalized shortage of specie money, and the credit system was broken. Agriculture, manufacturing, and commerce had stagnated, and the economy overall was in distress.

John Law was already known by the French authorities from his earlier visits to Paris, when he had promoted his land bank scheme. Upon his return in 1716 the regent selected him as the point man to alleviate the fiscal troubles of France. His task was to set in motion France's economy and to solve its public-finance problem. Law's diagnosis for the first part of the job was that the shortage of money and credit hindered the flow of commodities and, thus, production. Law had theoretically solved the problem in his published work: revive an economy that faced unemployment and idle resources by increasing credit and paper money (and replacing the limited specie money with paper money). He expected an abundance of credit to stimulate manufacturing, agriculture, and commerce, and to utilize unemployed resources. This task required the establishment of a note-issuing bank.

The second part of the task was more urgent: pulling the French state back from default and putting its fiscal house in order. Authorities who had already repudiated a portion of the debt were in search of a permanent solution to the persistent fiscal imbalance. Law devised and implemented a remedy in due course: restructure the French public debt by creating a joint-stock company and swapping government debt held by the public for equity of the company. The swap was to make the company the state's sole creditor and lower the state's fiscal burden by charging a lower interest rate. The plan's success, of course, required the public's willingness to exchange government bonds for company equity, or company shares to be more attractive than government bonds in terms of returns and risk.

After their establishment the bank and the company acted in unison, and, for a while, the system appeared to be successful. In a letter written in 1722, after the downfall of his system, Law reminisced:

> The Prince headed a rich nation and increased his revenues while reducing the burden on his people. There was no unutilized land or unemployed workers. Manufactures, navigation, and trade increased.

The peasants were fed and clothed and owed nothing to the king or to their master. Credit together with specie had made money so abundant that one could ordinarily borrow at the notaries at 1/2 percent and only repay the principal at will . . . when [paper money] was preferred and commanded a premium over specie.

(Murphy 1997: 319)

Step 1: The General Bank

Law's plan to alleviate France's fiscal troubles was implemented in three steps. The first was to establish a bank that would unlock and lubricate channels of commerce by credit extension. He received permission from the regent to establish the General Bank, a private bank with a 20-year charter and a modest capital base of 6mL (the "L" stands for livre, which was the monetary unit of account) in May 1716. Capital was raised by selling shares to the public. In the *initial public offering* (IPO) 1,200 shares were sold at 5,000L per share. Buyers were asked for only a quarter of the purchase price up front and the rest in the future. Law, the regent, and the regent's inner circle were among the largest shareholders. Shareholders paid for about a quarter of the shares in specie and the rest in floating government paper. This was the starting point of the collection of government debt in the hands of the businesses that Law managed.

The General Bank was authorized to accept deposits, discount bills of exchange, and issue banknotes backed by specie. After a shaky start, by January 1717 it was a well established and very profitable bank. In April 1717 it became the bank of the government and its notes were made *legal tender*, accepted for both tax payments and government disbursements. Law had guaranteed the notes against debasement of metal currency: they would be redeemed in the weight of the metal coins at the time the paper was issued. Soon General Bank notes were being used in many types of transactions, and the public preferred to hold Law's notes above others because the alternatives did not carry a comparable metallic-content guarantee. The specie reserve of the bank was a respectable 50 percent of the banknotes (Velde 2004).

At Law's insistence the General Bank was nationalized in December 1718 by the regent, who bought its shares and renamed it the Royal Bank. The new bank had a wider sphere of influence, as it had permission to open branches and faced fewer constraints in issuing banknotes. Most notably, the metallic-content guarantee did not apply to the Royal Bank notes.

Step 2: The Mississippi Company

The second stage in Law's scheme was to create a publicly owned commercial company. In August 1717 he purchased the defunct Mississippi

Company, which had owned trading rights with the French colony of Louisiana. The company had the monopoly right to establish a trade post and colonize a wide swath of land (comprised of roughly the middle third of the US, the Mississippi River watershed from today's Louisiana to Minnesota, and the West Indies) and trade beaver pelts with Canada (then in high demand among the Parisian hat makers). Under the new name of the Company of the West, Law relaunched it as a joint-stock corporation.[6] The company issued 200,000 shares in August 1717 at the face value of 500L per share (dividends were calculated as a percentage of the face value). The actual market price, however, was much lower, 146L to 160L, indicating an initial lackluster demand for shares. Buyers of shares, as in the case of the General Bank, paid again primarily in floating government paper, which itself was being traded at a 60–70 percent discount. Thus, the establishment of the company was the second round of the conversion of debt to equity. The regent, in the name of the king, was among the largest shareholders.

Shares of the Mississippi Company initially generated limited enthusiasm. By the beginning of 1719 their open-market price had crept up to 450L, still below the face value. Even this price overstated the true market value because large purchases by Law and the regent kept the price high. However, this state of affairs was to change shortly. In the spring of 1719 Law began a series of mergers and acquisitions that ultimately created a conglomerate around the Mississippi Company. The first acquisition, paid for with government paper, was the tobacco monopoly in August 1718 from the government in lieu of the interest payments that the state failed to meet. Law bought the Senegal Trading Company for cash in December 1718 and acquired the East Indies and China trade companies in May 1719 (and renamed the new business Company of the Indies). In June the North Africa Trading Company joined the fold. Purchase of the Royal Mint, the lease for collection of all indirect taxes, and the authority to collect direct taxes followed in the summer of 1719. The outcome was the largest conglomerate of its time. It promised its shareholders profits from more streamlined and efficient operations of overseas trade, colonial development, domestic-tax collections, domestic monopolies, and interest payments on government debt owned by the company.

Financing these mergers, as well as paying for the expenses of building and equipping a new fleet for colonial development and overseas trade, and the administration of the company, required substantial sums of money. Law raised funds by selling two more issues of Mississippi Company stocks in June and July 1719 (50,000 each with face values of 500L and 1,000L respectively), bringing the total number of shares to 300,000. The appeal of stocks to wealth holders lies in the dividends and capital gains they are expected to generate. Law resorted to various methods to stimulate public interest in the stock and boost the share price.

First, he and friends personally underwrote the shares issued in June at 550L, 10 percent higher than the face value. Law also permitted buyers to make payments in installments, paying only 50L up front and spreading the rest over 20 months. Under the installment plan the buyers of the IPO were said to *subscribe* to the shares. In return they were handed a certificate (scrip), and the shares would be issued only after full payments were made. The scrip was traded in the stock market alongside the shares. The installment plan not only made shares more attractive, it permitted buyers to leverage their purchases, which raised the demand for shares. Under the latter plan 500L would purchase not one but ten shares at face value, with the balance of 4,500L to be paid in the future. The company also stipulated that only the current owners of previous issues could purchase the new issue.

These measures had three outcomes. First, they kept the IPO market thin and allowed price manipulation by Law. Second, they created demand for older issues and raised their prices. Third, the measures created, in effect, an options market. A call option is a contract whereby a party purchases the right to purchase an asset at (by) a specific date at a specific price. The buyer has the right not to exercise the option, in which case his sole expense is the payment made to purchase the option. By making a down payment subscribers to the Mississippi shares were effectively purchasing the right to buy the share, with the full price to be paid over a period of time. They would be able to decide not to buy the share in the event its price fell, at the cost of losing their initial payment.

Law's efforts paid off, and the share price started rising sharply. In late May the share price was 490L. New shares were oversubscribed in June, and the share price climbed again. Figure 3.2 shows the share price's increase from August 1719 to November 1720. By August 9, 1719, it had risen to 2,830L, and by August 26 to 3,600L, a sevenfold rise in three months.

Step 3: Conversion of the long-term national debt

Law's boldest move came at the end of August 1720. As mentioned, the public bought shares of the General Bank and the first issues of the Mississippi Company in part by short-term government paper. Law had started converting publicly held state debt to private equity. On August 27, 1719, when he purchased the right to collect taxes, Law also reached an agreement with the government to take over the entire long-term national debt of France, which amounted to 1,600mL, and to become the state's sole creditor.

The plan again consisted of swapping government bonds for company equity. However, the logistics of this swap were a bit more complicated. First, the state issued vouchers to government-bond holders, and debt

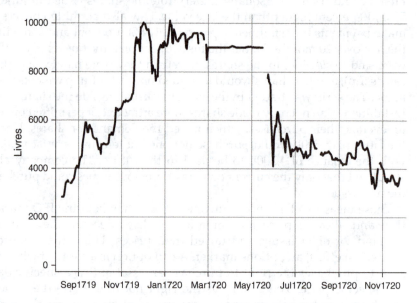

Figure 3.2 Mississippi Company stock price, 1719–20 (daily).

Source: Murphy (1997: 208).

Note: In mid May 1719 the price was 450L.

holders were required to redeem vouchers against specie, the Royal Bank notes, or the newly issued Mississippi Company shares. By mid September 1719, when the market price of shares was close to 6,000L, the company issued 300,000 more shares at a par value of 5,000L.

Why would debt holders and the government take part in this scheme? From the perspective of the debt-holding public the swap meant conversion of fixed-income annuities to flexible-income equities. Such a conversion would have been attractive provided the expected dividend income plus the expected capital gains on the stock were higher than the 4.5 percent interest the crown paid on the long-term national debt. Thus, success of the swap required the promise of high profits from commercial ventures of the Mississippi Company and the continued rise of the share price. From the perspective of the government the conversion was gainful because the agreement between Law and the government lowered the annual interest it paid on debt from 4.5 percent to 3 percent.

The national-debt-private-equity swap transformed the government's borrowing mechanism and inserted the Royal Bank and the Mississippi Company in the middle of France's public finances. Prior to Law's plan taxes were collected by tax farmers and delivered to the state (after

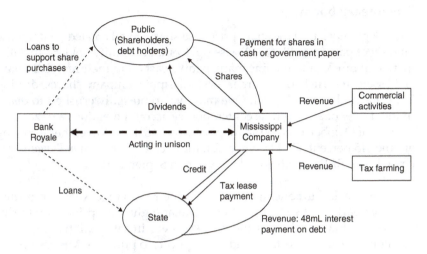

Figure 3.3 Mississippi Company debt-conversion scheme.

deducting administrative costs and lease profits), and the government made interest/annuity payments to bondholders from these revenues. Figure 3.3 (adopted from Velde 2004) illustrates how, in the new system, the bank and the company became France's financial hub. The company sold shares to the public in return for cash and government debt. After the full transfer of government paper the company held the entire national debt. There were three potential sources of revenue for the company. The first source was the 48mL annual interest on national debt,[7] the second source was tax farming, and the third source was the commercial activities, including international trade, colonization, mint operations, and so forth. Profits generated from these operations were to be paid to the shareholders as dividends.

The dashed lines on the left side of Figure 3.3 show how the Royal Bank supported the operations of the company. The two institutions acted in unison. First, the bank issued banknotes to extend loans to the public so that the demand for shares remained buoyant. Second, it routinely met the company's need for cash. Third, its power to issue banknotes enabled Law to extend share-price guarantees to the public. Finally, the bank issued banknotes to meet the state's demands for additional funds. The Mississippi Company and the Royal Bank effectively acted as a single entity. Their headquarters were in the same building, and Law was both the chief executive of the company and the director of the bank. Gradually, the Mississippi Company transformed into a financial enterprise, and its commercial operations were virtually discontinued.

The uneasy boom

After September 1719 the share price rose sharply and created an immense amount of paper wealth for Mississippi Company equity holders. In anticipation of quick capital gains many people cashed in their real and financial assets and rushed to purchase Mississippi Company shares, driving the price higher and higher. One man was reportedly crushed to death in the frenzy of buying (one contemporary account mentions a dozen). By the end of October 1719 the share price was 6,463L; in November it rose by another 45 percent. On December 2 it hit 10,025L. The term *millionaire* was coined. The British-embassy clerk wrote in September:

> The Rue de Quinquempoix, which is their Exchange Alley, is crowded from early in the morning to the late at night with princes and princesses, dukes and peers and duchesses etc. in a way all that is great in France. They sell estates and pawn jewels to purchase Mississippi.
> (Murphy 1997: 205)

Demand for shares also came from abroad: the Dutch and the English were prominent buyers. The British ambassador in Paris received letters from friends and relatives requesting that he buy stocks in the company and the bank.

Law devised several methods to sustain the demand for shares and thereby keep the share price high and rising. First, as early as July 1719 he announced that the company would pay a 12 percent dividend (of par value), far in excess of the return on government annuities (the market value at the time was approximately the same as par value). Second, the installment-based share sales continued, allowing buyers to leverage their resources. Third, Law engaged in frequent, aggressive price "management." When new issues doubled the number of shares and lowered the price in the second half of September 1719 the company stopped the decline by announcing that it would be buying its shares back at 4,500L, and the price resumed its upward trend. In early December 1719 the price declined by 22 percent but recovered as the Royal Bank made loans to prospective buyers at convenient terms against the collateral of shares so that they could buy more shares.

The apparent success of the conglomerate advanced Law's fortunes, and on January 5, 1720, he was appointed France's Controller General and Superintendent General of Finance. Just a few days later, on January 8, the peak share price of 10,100L was reached, a twentyfold increase from its original issue price in just eight months. Law, however, had started growing apprehensive because the system's internal contradictions were becoming sharper.

The first problem was maintaining debt holders' interest in shares. Conversion of debt was compulsory, but the bondholders could choose between cash and company shares. Law's plan required persuading debt holders to convert government bonds to Mississippi Company equity instead of cash. The objective was achieved by keeping expectations of capital gains elevated. It was a delicate task because, given the option feature of money subscriptions, there was always the risk of subscribers backing off from the equity and sending the share price tumbling. Moreover, as installment payments started coming due in late 1719, subscribers sold some of their certificates to raise funds to meet their payments, which put downward pressure on the share price and forced Law to announce price guarantees to stop the decline.

The second problem involved the unstable increase in paper money. As shown in Figure 3.3, there were several sources of banknote growth. First, the bank was expanding loans to support share purchases. Second, it issued banknotes to assist the company in meeting its own operational expenses. The company was in constant need of these funds because only a fraction of the share price was being paid in cash at the time of subscription and there was insufficient inflow of revenue from its commercial operations. Third, the regent put pressure on the bank for more loans to fund state expenditures, and Law acquiesced. Royal Bank notes rose in volume by 92 percent, from 400mL to 769mL, in four months, between the end of August and the end of December 1719. The specie reserve had become precariously low, and the bank could not have survived a rush to convert banknotes to gold.

To ensure that the public would be willing to hold paper money and not demand specie the government took measures in December 1719 to promote the use of banknotes and penalize the use of specie. Royal Bank notes were made legal tender. The use and hoarding of coins, bullion, and objects made of precious metal by the public, with a few exceptions, such as the Church, was prohibited. Specie holdings were limited to 500L by individuals, any excess was confiscated upon discovery, and hoarders were fined. Simultaneously, the government further promoted the use of banknotes by raising the value of banknotes vis-à-vis specie, despite the fact that the quantity of specie was not on the rise. This measure, of course, contradicted the excessive growth in the quantity of paper money. The system was balanced precariously on the edge, sustainable only as long as the public had confidence in the bank and was willing to hold banknotes instead of gold.

Modern commentators on Law are reasonably charitable, e.g. Murphy (1997), Velde (2004). They do not question his intelligence or personal integrity, or accuse him of engaging in fraudulent activities. The objective of Law's price "management" (not many commentators call it manipulation) was not to benefit personally at the expense of naïve shareholders (although he speculated and gambled extensively at the international level, he did not take advantage of the Mississippi shareholders) but to complete the conversion of government debt to private equity and put government finances on a solid basis. He did not want share prices to go much higher than 10,000L, and he intended to deflate the share price once the goal of fiscal stabilization was attained. He also realized the unsustainability of the paper-money expansion and planned to absorb notes from the market gradually. However, once the foundations of the system started shaking Law's options were limited, and his efforts to manage the share price consisted of a series of improvisations that met severe popular and political opposition at every turn.

In February 1720, when the share price was hovering above 9,500L and the volume of banknotes in circulation was above 1,000mL, the company stopped supporting the share price. The outcome was a sharp decline in the price of stock; from February 22 to 29 the share price fell by 26 percent, from 9,545L to 7,825L. As shareholders who faced capital losses grumbled and protested, the company retreated and guaranteed a minimum price of 9,000L in March and started trading shares at this fixed price (Figure 3.2). The price guarantee implied that the bank was to act according to the dictates of the company and supply as many banknotes as needed to purchase shares at the announced support price. At the same time the company abandoned the debt-equity swap and started using banknotes to purchase government bonds from the public. The money supply went out of control, reaching 1,262mL by the end of March and 2,000mL by the end of April 1720.

The bust

Toward the end of May 1720 the company officially took over the Royal Bank. At that point the banknote stock was 2,100mL. The fact that shares were guaranteed to be purchased at the support price implied that the total liquidity was even higher, by as much as another 1,800mL. The increase in the supply of notes raised doubts about the ability of the bank to convert them to specie and threatened its credibility. Law returned to the idea of bringing paper and specie into balance by deflating the share price and withdrawing banknotes from circulation. On May 21 he declared gradual reductions in both the share price (from 9,000L to 5,000L) and the quantity of banknotes over the next seven months. The response was a sell-off that lowered the price sharply, by 17 percent, in the following six days, before the declaration was revoked by the regent (Figure 3.2). Law's star was descending.

According to Murphy (1997), the concentration of power in the hands of Law had created substantial resentment among the prominent people of the old order, especially the nobility and financiers who had previously controlled the financial system, as well as their allies in the parliament. Their economic and political power had diminished under Law, but they were forced to keep their opposition in check while Law had the solid support of the regent. However, as the system disintegrated and popular dissatisfaction spread, they grew louder and held Law accountable for tearing down the kingdom. The regent promptly dismissed Law from the office of Controller General and put him under house arrest on May 29. The share price then dropped even faster, down to 4,116mL on May 31, a 46 percent decline since the May 21 declaration. Public hostility rose to dangerous levels as the bank appeared to have difficulty converting banknotes to specie (even at a discount). Shareholders who faced huge capital losses participated in street protests, and British investors decided to sell their Mississippi Company stock at a loss (which, in turn, created an immediate increase in British stock prices). Within a week the regent brought Law back, albeit with diminished powers, to arrest the panic. Law's return indeed created a temporary bump in the stock price.

What followed in the next few months was a tug of war between Law and the parliament, with the regent trying to hold on to his own political power, against the background of rising social unrest. The government used the cavalry to control street demonstrations and took extra measures to ensure the provisioning of staples, such as bread. However, the tide had turned against Law, and his system was systematically dismantled. Between the beginning of June and the end of October 1720 a series of policy measures were implemented to reduce the quantity of banknotes and reintroduce specie money into the economy. In July 1720 there was a run on the bank, and convertibility of paper to specie was suspended. The parliament approved the return to issuing annuities as the primary instrument of government debt. In September 1720 the value of Royal Bank accounts was reduced to a quarter by decree and the support price of the shares was reduced to 2000L, which meant huge losses for both the banknote holders and the shareholders who had purchased shares at the peak of the boom. The bubonic plague that started in Marseilles in August and spread throughout southern France further increased the economic uncertainty and added to the public's flight from banknotes to the safety of specie. In November all existing banknotes were converted to annuities, and the Royal Bank closed down on November 27. Law fled France in December 1720, leaving his family and brother, who had served as a deputy, behind.

The company was put into receivership in March 1721. It is interesting to note that there was still demand for shares before its ultimate demise. New issues in July 1720, for instance, were marketed at 9,000L (1,000L on first installment), when the current market price was around 5,000L. The public demand for these shares was sustained in part by the need for an outlet to dump the devalued banknotes.

The aftermath

The long-lasting effects of the Mississippi Bubble were a lack of confidence of the French in banks, paper money, and the credit system, and a professed preference for specie. The scarcity of credit and paper money stifled commerce for years to come. The immediate beneficiary of the scheme was the state, due to the huge reduction in its debt. Holders of banknotes and company shares were the losers, and many went bankrupt. However, the experiment was closely followed in other European countries and, ironically, inspired the British to create their own debt-equity swap. The collapse of the Mississippi Company and the growing affluence of the South Sea Company were linked intimately: as confidence declined in Law's design, international investors shifted from Paris to London, deflating one share price and inflating another.

Law became the object of condemnation in France and was vilified. In his remaining years he traveled to the Netherlands and England and attempted to get an official pardon for the capital offense of his youth. He had accumulated massive wealth during his years in France, but most of it was in real estate and he left it behind when he fled. He lived the rest of his life in relatively modest circumstances. When he died in Venice, in 1726, his wealth consisted of an extensive collection of Old Masters paintings and little else. His long-lasting economic-policy legacy was the idea of stimulating a stagnant economy through the extension of liquidity and removing the strictures on money supply that stifled the full employment of resources.

Timeline

May 1716	John Law sets up General Bank in Paris.
August 1717	Law buys Mississippi Company (MC) and sets it up as Company of the West.
September 1717	First issue of MC shares (200,000).
December 4, 1718	General Bank nationalized and renamed Royal Bank.
March 1719	Restrictions on use of silver coins in large transactions.
May 1719	MC absorbs East Indies and China trade companies.
June 17, 1719	MC takes over North Africa Trading Company and makes second issue of shares (50,000) at nominal price of 500L; old shares trading at 650L; Royal Bank notes stock at 160mL.
July 1719	Third issue of shares (50,000); share price over 1,000L; MC takes over mint; Royal Bank note stock reaches 400mL.
August 1719	MC buys national debt and swaps it with shares; buys lease on tax farms for nine years; share price reaches 5,000L.

September 1719	Fourth and fifth issues of shares.
October 2, 1719	Sixth issue of shares.
November 1719	Share price around 6500L; banknote stock around 640mL.
December 1719	Royal Bank notes legal tender; government imposes restrictions on use and hoarding of specie, bullion, and jewelry.
January 5, 1720	Law appointed Controller General of Finances.
January 9, 1720	Share price peaks at 10,100L.
February 22, 1720	Law declares discontinuation of share-price support; share price declines 26% in one week. Regent withdraws declaration.
March 5, 1720	MC guarantees support price at 9,000L.
May 21, 1720	Law declares reduction in share price (from 9,000L to 5,000L over next seven months) and quantity of banknotes; share price falls 17 percent in following six days before declaration revoked by regent.
May 22, 1720	MC takes over Royal Bank.
May 29, 1720	Law dismissed from office of Controller General; share price at 4,116L on May 31, a 46 percent decline since May 21 declaration.
June 1, 1720	Prohibition of specie hoarding repealed.
June 2, 1720	Law brought back to power as Superintendent of Commerce; share price rises to 6,350L by June 6.
June 1720	Return to annuities in government borrowing; Royal Bank creates deposit accounts to absorb banknotes and facilitate transfers between accounts.
Mid July 1720	Street demonstrations by people who want to convert banknotes to specie; parliamentary unrest.
October 10, 1720	Royal Bank notes no longer legal tender for taxes nor (after November 1) for all other transactions.
November 27, 1720	Royal Bank closes down.
December 1720	Law leaves France.
March 1721	MC put into receivership.

Key terms and concepts

Bank run
Banknote
Bill of exchange
Collateral

Commercial paper
Commodity money
Credit
Debt instrument
Depository institution
Discounting of commercial paper
Equity
Fiat money
Financiers
Fractional-reserve system
Government/sovereign debt
Illiquidity risk
Initial public offering (IPO)
Insolvency risk
Legal tender
Lender of last resort
Liquidity
Maturity mismatch
Money
Net worth
Reserve ratio
Solvency
Specie money
Subscription

Endnotes

1 All quotes are from Murphy (1997). Murphy offers a detailed account of John Law's life, economic thinking, and the rise and fall of the Mississippi Company against the social and political background of seventeenth-century France. This chapter's historical narrative also draws from Garber (2000) and Velde (2004, 2009).

2 Income and wealth are commonly measured in monetary units (e.g. "Jane's annual income is $20,000," "Joe's portfolio is worth $1,000,000"), and, therefore, money is often used interchangeably with income and wealth in daily language (e.g. "Jane does not make a lot of money," "Joe has lots of money"). However, money is not synonymous with either income or wealth, and the reader should be aware of this semantic trap. First, an individual receives income in return for a service provided, or as an entitlement. In principle, income can be measured and paid in any form, including coconuts or toilet paper, neither of which is money. Second, the wealth of an individual may certainly include money in the form of cash and deposits, but it also includes stocks and bonds, which are measured in dollars but certainly are not money. It is certainly more convenient to state both income and wealth in monetary units, which is a universal metric to measure value.

3 By contrast, *fiat money*, or paper currency, that is common today is a relatively recent invention. Fiat money has no intrinsic use; it is merely a piece of paper with some ink and artwork on it. It derives its value from government fiat (it is the legal tender) and social convention.

4 A note-issuing bank is also exposed to illiquidity risk when it does not have sufficient specie reserves to back its notes.
5 There was a close link between the government debt and the tax-farming system because the right to collect taxes was purchased by financiers.
6 While the company name changed at each incarnation, it is commonly referred to by its original name, the Mississippi Company, in the literature. From this point onward I continue with this practice.
7 The company simply deducted this amount from the annual fixed payments it had to make to the state for the tax-farming lease.

References

Braudel, Fernand. 1981. *Civilization and Capitalism, 15th–18th Century, vol. 1: The Structures of Everyday Life*. New York: Harper and Row.

Garber, Peter M. 2000. *Famous First Bubbles: The Fundamentals of Early Manias*. Cambridge, MA: The MIT Press.

Murphy, Antoin E. 1997. *John Law: Economic Theorist and Policy-maker*. Oxford, UK: Clarendon Press.

Velde, Francois. 2004. *Government Equity and Money: John Law's System in 1720 France*. Working Paper No. WP-03-31. Chicago: Federal Reserve Bank of Chicago.

Velde, Francois. 2009. "Was John Law's System a Bubble? The Mississippi Bubble Revisited." Pp. 99–120 in *The Origins and Development of Financial Markets and Institutions: From the Seventeenth Century to the Present*, edited by Jeremy Atack and Larry Neal. Cambridge, New York: Cambridge University Press.

4   The South Sea Bubble

While the Mississippi Company was struggling in Paris during the spring of 1720, the fortunes of another firm were rising across the channel in London. In fact, investors who liquidated their Mississippi Company shares and transferred funds to London contributed directly to the initiation of the South Sea Bubble. A modest government-debt-private-equity swap had already been executed in England by the South Sea Company a few years before Law carried out his plan in France. However, Law's boldness was an inspiration to the managers of the South Sea Company to expand the scale of their enterprise and take over the English government debt in its entirety in 1720.[1]

Background

At the turn of the eighteenth century England was predominantly an agricultural country, characterized by small-scale cottage industries. The technological and industrial revolution and the emergence of the urban industrial proletariat and capitalist class were yet to come. The political system was dominated by the Tories, associated broadly with the landed aristocracy. The other major political faction, and the main rival of the Tories, was the Whigs, who were allied with the country's commercial and financial interests. International trade and colonization were expanding under mercantilist policies that targeted export surpluses and domestic accumulation of specie reserves. The state granted selected trade companies monopoly rights in the domestic market and provided them with protection from foreign competitors through trade barriers, subsidies, and regulations, as well as the artillery power of the Royal Navy on the high seas. The expansion of international trade and colonization led to a rapid accumulation of wealth and brought the country to the threshold of a financial revolution. Commodities, bills of exchange, and other debt instruments were traded on the Royal Exchange in the City of London, the commercial and financial center of London since the sixteenth century. The number of joint-stock companies, whose shares were traded on the stock market, multiplied after the Glorious

Revolution of 1688, which established the constitutional monarchy and increased the security of private-property rights. By the end of the seventeenth century wealth holders were increasingly diversifying their portfolios by buying paper assets, such as government bonds, private bonds, and stocks.

The stock market emerged in London after 1690, and shares of approximately 150 joint-stock companies were being traded at the end of 1695 (Neal 1990: 46). However, having garnered a reputation of being noisy, vulgar, rude, and unscrupulous, stockbrokers were removed from the Royal Exchange in 1698. They then set up shop in the coffee houses along Exchange Alley—winding, narrow streets across from the Royal Exchange. The coffee houses, most famously Jonathan's and Garraway's, functioned as hubs of information, post offices, business offices, and trading floors. Although trading was decentralized and spread across establishments in the alley, widespread use of the forward, option, and repurchase contracts in addition to spot transactions signaled a sophisticated stock market. Although new joint-stock companies needed a royal charter to issue and sell stock, this rule was seldom observed.

Shareholders traded stocks through the intermediation of stockbrokers and stockjobbers. The *stockbroker* was merely a conduit who matched the seller and buyer in return for a commission. The *stockjobber* was a *market maker*, who traded for his own account, held stocks in his own inventory, and profited from the spread between the ask and bid prices. In practice, the same individual often acted as both a broker and a jobber. Protecting investors from fraudulent practices of intermediaries and ensuring the solvency of intermediaries were sources of concern for public officials. Regulations were introduced from time to time to license brokers, limit their number, control commissions, and ban jobbing and forward contracts. These regulations, however, were ineffectual because they were loosely worded and scarcely enforced (Dale 2004: 35).

The principal economic problem that faced the state at the beginning of the eighteenth century was the national debt, an outcome of spending incurred during the War of the Spanish Succession. At the end of the war in 1713 the British national debt amounted to £53.3m. Because taxes fell far short of meeting expenditure the state had issued a variety of debt instruments to raise funds, including short-term (floating) debt, *redeemable and irredeemable long-term annuities,* and lottery loans. These debt instruments were traded in the financial market but were not very liquid due to various restrictions on their trade and transfer. In addition, borrowing costs varied by type of loan: interest rates were lower on annuities and higher on short-term and lottery loans. The state had the option of calling redeemable annuities, which made it possible to convert them to lower-interest debt when interest rates declined, but this could not be done in the case of irredeemable debt. As the heterogeneous nature of debt instruments added to the burden of debt servicing, consolidation of the national debt was an attractive option from the government's perspective. Joint-stock companies were to play an important role in this enterprise, purchasing and restructuring the national debt.

The South Sea Company: early years

Robert Harley, chief minister to Queen Anne, chartered the South Sea Company in 1711. The company was the brainchild of John Blunt and other partners of the Sword Blade Company, which, at the time, was engaged in banking and land speculation. Political support for the South Sea charter came from the Tory party, who viewed the charter as a counterbalance to the Bank of England and the financial interests of the City of London, both of which were represented in Parliament by the Whigs. The objective of the company was to ease the debt problem of the British government by purchasing short-term national debt from the public and consolidating it at terms that were advantageous to the government. It was already common for joint-stock companies to act as financiers of the state. When the Bank of England was chartered in 1694, for instance, it loaned the entire proceeds of its initial stock sale to the government to relieve the crown's fiscal burden. In the following years it acted as the primary account keeper and debt manager of the state.

Blunt and his partners could not establish a bank as a lending vehicle because, by law, the Bank of England was the only bank that could be chartered as a joint-stock company. Instead, they chose to launch a joint-stock trade company, whose shares were to be exchanged for £9.47m of short-term government debt (debt not secured by a specific tax), held by the public. Members of the court of directors of the new South Sea Company included partners of the Sword Blade Company as well as many political Tory appointees. Blunt, however, with the support of his inner circle, exercised absolute authority in the establishment and day-to-day operations of the company as well as in the planning and implementation of debt conversions in the later years (Dale 2004: 96–7).

The terms of the debt conversion were simple: £100 worth of stock was to be exchanged for £100 worth of government debt, both at par value. The company restructured the debt by converting it to a long-term perpetual annuity (which implies that the principal would not be repaid) at a 6 percent interest rate, substantially lower than the 9 percent that the government was paying on the short-term debt. For the privilege of the debt-equity conversion the company also made a lump-sum payment to the government. In return, Parliament granted the South Sea Company a monopoly to trade with Spanish colonies in the South Seas—almost the entire Central and South American coast. Figure 4.1 presents the swap arrangement. Debt holders and the company swapped the state's short-term debt for private company equity; consequently, the debt holders

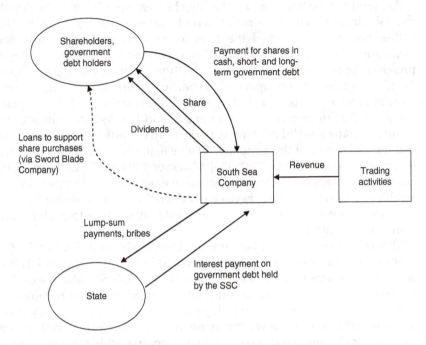

Figure 4.1 South Sea Company debt-conversion scheme.

became shareholders, and the company held the restructured debt. The company paid dividends to shareholders from its revenues, which consisted of the government's payments of interest on the debt and the proceeds of its commercial ventures.

The arrangement benefited the government because it eased its debt-servicing problem: its interest burden was relieved by three percentage points, and payments on the principal were canceled. For the debt-holding public the advantages were threefold. First, as the market value of government debt was discounted by as much as 40 percent at the time, the conversion of debt to equity at par meant capital gains for the public, provided the share price held up. Second, although shareholders received a lower return on government debt held by the South Sea Company relative to what they would have received had they held on to government paper themselves, they would potentially profit from the company's commercial activities. Third, it was difficult to convert short-term government debt to money or other assets. By contrast, private shares were far more liquid and easily transferable. Short-term-paper holders were willing to exchange high-interest, illiquid public debt for highly tradable stock, and 97 percent of the targeted debt was converted to shares.

At the end of the Spanish War the Utrecht Treaty of 1713 gave the British the Asiento, the exclusive contract to trade slaves across the Atlantic. The British government granted the right to trade slaves to the South Sea Company. The slave trade presumably expanded the commercial profit prospects of the company. The dominant view among researchers, however, is that the company operated primarily as a financial and not a commercial enterprise; its first trading ship did not sail until 1714. Skeptics point out that there were severe limitations in the Asiento contract, the company managers did not have experience in long-distance trading, and commercial profits of the company, relative to its size, were not significant (Chancellor 2000: 60; Dale 2004: 45, 49; Dickson 1993: 66–7). Dickson (1993) attributes the approximately 6 percent average annual increase in the stock price of the company between 1713 and 1718 to declining interest rates following the end of the Spanish War rather than to profits from commercial activities.

This traditional position has recently been challenged. Paul (2011: 63) reports that the South Sea Company traded between 10,000 and 11,000 slaves with Spanish America between 1714 and 1718. She also states that the South Sea Company was an efficient and profitable slaver because the slave-mortality rate on company ships was lower than the industry average (Paul 2011: 65). Whatever the merits of these competing positions on the company's commercial prospects, it is incontrovertible that in 1719 the company's trading activities were held back by rising hostilities between the Spanish and the British, and there was no slave trade in 1720, the year of the bubble.

In 1719 the company's financial activities grew more aggressive. First, another type of government obligation, annuities paid on the 1710 Lottery Loan, was converted to £1.1m worth of South Sea stock. Annuitants were happy to convert debt to stock, given that government payments were in arrears, shares were more liquid than annuities, capital gains were expected on the stock, and shares promised permanent dividends, while annuities were scheduled to expire. Almost 70 percent of the loan was converted. The government was again pleased because it paid a lower interest rate after the conversion, and it had the option of retiring debt by buying it from the company. In addition, the company extended the government a loan of £544,142, which enhanced the deal. This loan was to be funded by the issue of new equity, to be sold at market price (rather than at par). As the market value was higher than the par value by 14 percent, the sale of new equity created an immediate surplus cash inflow for the company.

By the end of 1719 the total national debt of the British government was approximately £50m, about £12m of which was held by the South Sea Company, and £6.6m by the Bank of England and the British East India Company. The bulk of the debt was still in the hands of the public, a potential source of revenue that was waiting to be tapped.

The second round of debt conversion

In late 1719 Blunt and his partners proposed to Parliament that the South Sea Company swap the remaining £31.5m worth of government paper held by the public for new South Sea shares and convert it to a lower-interest debt of 5 percent (4 percent after 1727). The company also promised the government a lump-sum payment of £1.5m for the privilege of the debt-equity swap, and yet another payment of £1.6m if all annuities were exchanged for shares. South Sea Company managers made the initial proposal to the government on January 22, 1720. The Bank of England made a similar proposal five days later and started a bidding war. On February 1 the South Sea Company raised its offer to £7.5m and bribed government officials, politicians, and the king's friends and mistress with another £1.3m by distributing stock options free of charge.[2] The company's bid prevailed, and Parliament enacted the South Sea Bill into law on April 7, 1720.

The law authorized the company to issue a total of 315,000 shares at £100 par value, totaling £31.5m, which was equal to the volume of debt to be purchased. The scheme's profitability revolved around the conversion rate between equity and debt, and setting the latter was left to the company. If the debt was converted to shares at par—that is, if each share was exchanged for an annuity valued at £100—the company would suffer losses because it still had to pay the government £7.5m for the privilege of purchasing the debt. If each share was to be exchanged for an annuity valued at, say, £200, however, half of the shares would be sufficient to pay the debt, and proceeds from the sale of the remaining shares in the stock market would constitute a net cash flow into the coffers of the company. While the number of shares was limited by law, the upper bound of the cash flow that originated from the sale of shares was limited only by the market price at which the shares were sold.[3]

There were limitations, however, to how high a price could be charged per share. Slightly less than half of the debt was held in irredeemable annuities, which meant that the government could not force the holders to sell them or exchange them for another asset. Although the higher liquidity of stocks made them more attractive to debt holders, too high a share price would have meant a lower value of government paper and a disincentive to exchange debt for equity. From the perspective of the company, the means to persuade the public to switch to equity was to keep the market price of shares rising. As long as the share price was expected to increase, anticipated capital gains would give debt holders a reason to exchange government paper for shares, even at an initially unfavorable rate of exchange. The company started running up the share price even before the passing of the South Sea Bill by spreading rumors in coffee houses and the press and exaggerating the prospects of its trade in the Americas. As a result, the share price rose from £130 to £173 in February 1720 (Figure 4.2). The sharp spike in March, which raised the

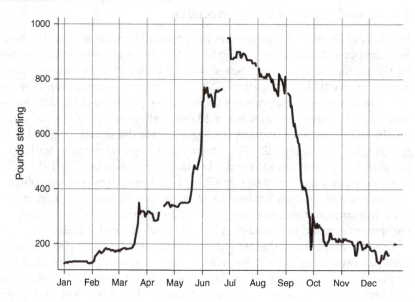

Figure 4.2 South Sea Company stock price, 1720 (daily).
Source: Neal (1996).

price to £310 by the end of the month, was attributable to the inflow of funds from Paris to London by speculators who were growing jittery about the future of the Mississippi Company.

April 1720 was an extremely active month for the South Sea Company. Initially, the company sold new shares for cash to make the contractual lump-sum payment to the government and pay the promised bribes, and to buy redeemable annuities (the last in accordance with the government's requirements). The total size of the first money subscription on April 14 was £2.25m at par value. However, shares were sold to an enthusiastic public at £300, 200 percent premium over par, and generated a £6.75m potential cash flow for the company. The total cash influx, however, was much smaller due to the various tactics that company managers implemented to keep the share price rising. The price was boosted in part by the ability of buyers to leverage their purchases by buying in installments. The company accepted a 20 percent down payment, with the balance to be paid over the following 16 months. Buyers of the new shares were handed transferable subscription receipts, and these receipts were traded in a parallel market alongside the existing shares of the company. Unlike the Mississippi Company installment sales, these were not options, as the contracts did not permit the buyers to renege on their purchase.

The company also announced on the day of the first money subscription that it would be raising dividends (to be paid in stock) in midsummer from 3 percent to 10 percent, which further attracted investor interest. In addition, the company used cash inflows to extend loans to share buyers via its sister enterprise, the Sword Blade Company (shown by the dashed line in Figure 4.1). Investors borrowed against the collateral of shares they owned to purchase additional shares. A sum of £250 was lent against £100 of stock, up to £3,000 maximum, at 5 percent interest. Carswell (1993: 125) describes the operation as one of flooding the market with cash through loans, watching the share price soar, and then cleaning it up by selling subscriptions in return for cash. The Sword Blade Company also issued paper, which the South Sea Company accepted as payment for shares (although these notes were not accepted as money elsewhere). Moreover, South Sea managers reportedly purchased their own stock to keep the demand high.

In the second money subscription of April 29, 1720 (15,000 shares at £100 par value), there was enough demand to drive the price to £400, £60 over the current spot price. The terms of this second subscription were more generous than the first, asking for only 10 percent down. Money subscriptions were very successful in raising the share price but not in generating a commensurately large cash flow. The first two money subscriptions would have yielded close to a £13m cash flow to the company, but, as shares were only partially paid upfront, the inflow of cash totaled £2m (Dale 2004: 204). This was still a substantial sum but hardly sufficient in the view of the South Sea Company's outlay, which included promised payments to the government, bribes, operating costs of the company, and loans to the public. The company suffered from a shortage of cash.

The debt-equity swap began on April 28, 1720. The company registered annuitants, who wished to convert irredeemable debt to shares, before it set the terms at which the exchange would take place. Only on May 19 did the directors announce the conversion rate: £375 of debt per share. At that time the spot market price of each share was £340, so the conversion rate was not too far off the spot rate. Of all the irredeemable annuities, 63 percent (£9.4m) was subscribed. The large size of the swap was deemed a success by investors and made the stock more attractive. It also meant, however, that the substantial growth in the number of shares in the market could depress the share price if annuitants who converted to equity were to cash in by selling their stocks. In recognition of this danger the directors delayed issuance of shares to the annuitants by eight months, until December 1720.

The boom

The South Sea stock-price upsurge took place between mid May and the end of June 1720 (Figure 4.2). In a five-week period, between May 16 and June 22, it rose by 117 percent, from £352 to £765. The most conspicuous action of the company during this period was the third money subscription, on June 17, when £5m worth of new stock (at £100 par value) was sold at a 1,000 percent premium, which implied a potential cash flow of £50m. The demand for shares continued to be fed by the company's sale methods. Installment sales required only a 10 percent down payment. Loans became more generous: £400 for every £100 of collateral stock deposited in the Sword Blade Company. Lending against share deposits raised the share price in two ways: it raised the demand for and restricted the supply of stocks in the market. The total amount of loans made by the Sword Blade Company was £11.2m by the end of August (Neal 1990: 105). Despite the monumental volumes of money subscriptions, cash inflow continued to be restricted due to the installment payment scheme. Meanwhile, the slave trade had halted, and commercial success from Spanish American trading was elusive. The primary source of profit was the 5 percent interest revenue from government debt.

South Sea shareholders included public figures, from the king down to members of the government, members of Parliament (MPs), and aristocrats. Listing prominent people among the shareholders helped the company to maintain a rising share price by raising the company's profile and lending it credibility. Shareholders also included rich farmers, bankers, and military officers. Domestic and international bankers, financiers, and speculators were attracted first by expected dividends and later by the prospect of capital gains. In May 1720 there was a large influx of capital from Dutch speculators, who further fueled the boom. One special group of shareholders were women of means, for whom stocks were attractive because ownership of shares had fewer gender-specific legal strings attached in comparison with more traditional assets, such as land or rental property.

The boom period of the South Sea Company featured the new phenomenon of "bubble companies." These new joint-stock companies, in the fields of technology, finance, insurance, mining, and trade, promised high-profit opportunities to prospective stock buyers who crowded Exchange Alley. In popular accounts, these companies were usually mocked as fanciful, improbable, or outright fraudulent enterprises that promoted projects such as importing jackasses from Spain, developing the wheel of perpetual motion, curing venereal disease, trading in human hair, extracting gold from lead, and even a scheme that was too secret to be made public. English inventor James Puckle promoted a machine gun designed to shoot round and square bullets, one for Christian foes and the other for Moslems. In all likelihood, there was an element of exaggeration in these popular accounts; and some of the emerging companies were legitimate enterprises. The new joint-stock companies benefitted from the atmosphere that the South Sea Company created. They sold stock in installments to a public eager for quick capital gains. Proliferation of new stocks contributed to the speculative environment. Banks made loans to investors and speculators against the collateral of shares. Investors and speculators channeled borrowed funds into common stocks and boosted shares prices to new heights.

New joint-stock companies and the growing volume of common stocks also meant an intensification of the competition that the South Sea Company faced in Exchange Alley. One route the South Sea managers took to overpower their competition was to challenge the legitimacy of the bubble companies directly. It was common for British joint-stock companies to engage in activities outside their original charter. Even the South Sea Company's sister enterprise, the Sword Blade Company, was originally chartered to manufacture hollow sword blades, but it had been operating as a financial company for two decades. To undermine their competitors the South Sea directors pressured Parliament to pass an act that prohibited joint-stock companies from pursuing businesses outside their charter. Thus, what came to be known as the Bubble Act passed on June 11, 1720.

In the summer of 1720 the share price of the South Sea Company peaked, although the exact level and timing are subjects of dispute. Neal (1990: 111) states that from June 22 to August 22 the company had closed its stock-transfer books to prepare for the £10 per share midsummer stock dividend. He notes that reported prices between these dates were forward prices and not comparable with the spot stock prices for the periods before and after.[4] Spot prices at the close and the opening of the books were in the mid £700s, which might have meant that the share price remained roughly unchanged over the summer. Dale (2004: 118) contests this argument by pointing out that subscription receipts were transferable during summer, and their prices indicate that the price boom continued until mid July.

Interpretations of the data notwithstanding, the company shares clearly commanded higher prices throughout the summer in comparison with the previous spring. The company took advantage of this by registering the remaining annuities against shares on July 14 and August 6. Overall, the debt-equity exchange was a success. At the end of these conversions, 84 percent of the £31.5m government debt was swapped for equity. The fourth money subscription of 12,500 shares followed on August 14 at a 1,000 percent premium over the par value of £100, with only 20 percent down and the remainder to be paid over two years. Throughout this process, however, liquidity pressures on the company continued to mount. Although money subscriptions nominally amounted to large volumes of cash, the actual cash inflow continued to be restricted due to installment sales and did not cover the expenses and the loans that the company extended. More ominously, liquidity pressures in the general market were emerging.

The panic

When the South Sea Company books were reopened on August 23, the share price stood at £740. The market experienced one final surge on

August 31 at £810 and then rapidly unraveled, the share price dropping to £565 on September 15 and then to £310 on September 30. Economic and financial historians draw attention to several precipitating factors, although they do not necessarily agree on the relative significance of each.

The first factor was the general liquidity shortage in the market. Neal (1990) points out that there was a credit shortage in the overall economy due to the heightened demand for the South Sea and other bubble-company shares, installment payments due in the summer, and the flow of credit toward other projects in Europe. In the face of the drain of their reserves, the Bank of England and other financial institutions reduced the loans they made on stocks. The outcome was a shortage of liquidity in the marketplace.

According to Dale (2004: 134), the story is more nuanced. He argues that the problem was not an externally created shortage of liquidity in the economy but the changing behavior of lenders. Softening of the stock market after midsummer raised concerns among bankers about their net worth because they held stock both as direct investment and as collateral for the loans they extended. A rising default risk and uncertainty regarding the financial health of borrowers forced bankers to reassess lending policies and ration credit; that is, they extended credit only to favored customers or customers who could provide high-quality collateral. Thus, the economy faced not only a shortage of liquidity but an internally generated credit squeeze in view of the banks' perception of borrowers' impending insolvency and their own deteriorating balance sheets.

Whether the source of stress was exogenous or endogenous to the banking system, both interpretations imply that credit dried up. The dearth of funds meant investors' and speculators' ability to bid for shares diminished, and a gradual weakening of share prices. In addition, payments on South Sea shares sold on an installment basis were due in August. In the midst of the scramble for credit it became more difficult for shareholders who did not have the cash to finance installment payments by borrowing. When buyers on installment plans unloaded some of their stock portfolio to raise cash for the upcoming payments the decline in price spilled over to the general market.[5]

The second factor that contributed to the price decline was the enforcement of the Bubble Act on August 17 and 18, when four joint-stock companies were served legal notices for violating the act. The unintended consequence of this action was panic in the market.[6] These firms' share prices dropped and reduced the net value of shareholders, who included both individuals and banks. The problem spilled over to other stocks rapidly as lower collateral values and net worth induced banks to restrict credit, and shareholders started selling their portfolios in order to meet cash needs.

News of the burst of the Mississippi Bubble in May 1720 might also have raised doubts among investors. Similarities between the Mississippi and

South Sea companies were evident, and the French crash may very well have induced some investors and speculators to start selling shares and cashing in capital gains. Dutch investors, for instance, left the market in early summer. Such an action can escalate when the leveling of the share price causes other speculators to offload their holdings in view of evaporating capital gains and start a mass sell-off.

The actions of the South Sea directors also did not help matters. In August and September of 1720 they attempted to support the price by buying their own shares, which not only failed to alter the unfavorable trend but added to the company's liquidity problem. In September, in response to the collapsing price, the directors promised a 30 percent Christmas cash dividend, as well as a 50 percent annual cash dividend for the next 12 years. Investors did not believe that the company could pay enhanced dividends, and their short-term credit problems were, in any event, more pressing. Lacking credibility, the dividend announcements backfired. They lowered the confidence in the company's prospects and, consequently, hastened the price collapse.

The outcome was a generalized collapse in Exchange Alley. By the end of September the South Sea share price had dropped 62 percent from the opening of the transfer books on August 23 (Figure 4.2).

The resolution

To raise much-needed cash and to stop the stock-price slide, the company directors approached their arch rival, the Bank of England. On September 19 the bank initially agreed, under some government pressure, to underwrite South Sea bonds to ease the liquidity problem of the company and to convert its own holdings of government debt into South Sea stock to support the stock price. However, it ultimately did not abide by this "bank contract" and officially reneged on November 9. One probable motivation for the Bank of England's decision was self-preservation. Declining depositor and banknote-holder confidence in the solvency of banks could have created a panic and a generalized run on banks.

In fact, the banking system was becoming unstable in the fall of 1720. The Sword Blade Company had failed to redeem its notes on September 24 and then closed its doors for good. The Bank of England was already facing deposit withdrawals and diminishing reserves in September 1720 and had stopped discounting bills of exchange to replenish its reserves. A deal with the now discredited South Sea Company could have dealt a blow to public trust in the bank. According to one story, to ward off the crisis the Bank of England slowed down the specie-payment process in late September through payment in small change and repetitive counting; the bank managers even placed their associates at the head of depositor queues, only to have the gold coins brought back surreptitiously through the back door to be used in the next round of payments (Kindleberger and

Aliber 2011: 200). The parade of satisfied ersatz depositors, the bank holiday, and the passage of time had the desired calming effect on the public. The arrival of 100,000 gold guineas from the Netherlands finally replenished the reserves and averted the bank run (Carswell 1993: 168). It is also possible that the Bank of England decided not to honor the bank contract because it was seeking a better deal. In fact, a new and more advantageous arrangement was struck between the bank and the South Sea Company in February 1722 (Dickson 1993: 167).

People who purchased shares in the spring and unloaded them before the burst of the bubble enjoyed huge capital gains. The government also benefited from the debt-equity swap due to the consolidation of the debt at lower interest rates. However, vanishing fortunes over the course of a month created widespread public indignation. Government debt holders who had converted debt to company shares (who numbered about 30,000, according to Dale (2004: 142)) at seemingly advantageous terms were now left with shares that were deflated in value. They asked for restitution. People who had purchased stocks a few months earlier also suffered large losses. Subscribers to new shares wanted their money back or the subscription terms altered, and they went as far as invading the House of Commons to demand compensation. Prominent South Sea Company investors who suffered losses included the poet John Gay, essayist Jonathan Swift, and composer Georg Handel. Sir Isaac Newton had sold his stock in April 1720 at a capital gain of 100 percent, but could not resist re-entering the market as the price continued escalating (Carswell 1993: 108, 165). In the end, according to his niece, he lost £20,000. He is alleged to have said, "I can calculate the movement of the stars, but not the madness of men."[7] The poet Alexander Pope's letters indicate that he was torn between holding on to and selling his stock (Chancellor 2000), but he managed to unload his shares before the collapse. However, Pope recommended on August 22 that Lady Montague, the first lady of letters, buy South Sea shares, and she took her friend's advice. Not only did she lose money, she was exposed to blackmail by her paramour, whose money she had also invested.

The government preferred that the South Sea Company and its counterparties sort out their own affairs. However, in the face of deep public resentment and the unwillingness of the prominent private institutions (the Bank of England and the British East India Company) to assist the South Sea Company, the government did not have any choice but to get involved to resolve the chaos. According to the government, the situation "had a most fatal and general influence on all publick and private credit" (Carswell 1993: 230). The first task was to respond to the demands of the multitude of losers by settling loans, subscriptions, and future payments. With the Restore the Public Credit Act of August 1721, the government announced its reluctant intervention into the market. With this act, the government provided some relief to the company by forfeiting the £7m it was owed, an early example of a bailout. The loans that the company extended were reduced to 10 percent of their value to help investors who had borrowed against the collateral of the company stock (and the collateral stock was transferred to the company).[8] Prices charged on money subscriptions were reduced. Debt holders who converted government debt to company stock were credited with additional stock. All remaining unsold stock was distributed proportionately among the shareholders.

The government's other task was to address the ire of the public, who demanded retribution for the fraudulent activities of the company directors and corrupt politicians. The company had bribed members of the government and Parliament. The purchase of political favor through bribery was not an uncommon activity, and it might have been considered a regular cost of doing business. However, there were also widespread allegations that Blunt, his inner circle, and politicians with insider contacts avoided losses and, in fact, profited by selling their shares before the burst of the bubble. The government also had received its share of criticism for abdicating its responsibility to protect shareholders. The House of Commons initiated an investigation into the company's activities and insider deals in January 1721. The company directors who were MPs were expelled from Parliament or lost any political positions they might have held. Several prominent politicians and well connected individuals were found guilty of corruption, and a few were imprisoned. The revenue from the confiscation of the property of convicted directors and politicians and the fines levied amounted to £2.3m; this was used to compensate investors.

At the end of 1720 the share price was £200 and, by the middle of 1721, had reverted to its pre-January 1720 value. The company itself was not insolvent because it still owned the huge government debt, which provided annual interest payments. In addition, it held the trade monopoly in the South Seas and even engaged in Arctic whaling after 1725. In 1752 it ceased as a trading company and functioned as a manager of government debt until its dissolution in the nineteenth century. The South Sea daily share-price series from 1711 to 1736 shows that April–September 1720 was truly an extraordinary period. With the exception of these six months the share price fluctuated around £100.

There were multitudes of people who suffered loss of wealth, but the impact of the crash on the general economy was not deep, perhaps owing to the government's efforts to settle contracts in the aftermath of the crisis and avoid large-scale banking failures. Manufacturing, trade, and agriculture were not influenced adversely. One lasting impact may have been the loss of business confidence. In response to the speculative excesses of the period the government passed acts that prohibited unincorporated joint-stock companies, short sales, and futures and options trades. These measures could have arrested the development of finance in England, but they were loosely worded and enforced, and apparently proved immaterial to the evolution of the market (Dale 2004; Paul 2011).

The Mississippi and South Sea bubbles: a comparison

The core of both the Mississippi Company's and the South Sea Company's operations was the debt-equity swap. For the schemes to work it was critical for the debt holders to exchange the government bonds they held for company stock. One factor that would have attracted debt holders to shares was the expected profitability of the companies. Risk and liquidity advantages would also have encouraged the equity swap. The French might have viewed private equity as less risky in the aftermath of previous government defaults, and the South Sea shares were more easily transferable than British government debt. In addition to these factors, in both episodes voluntary conversion was achieved by creating an environment of high and rising price expectations so that debt holders switched from bonds to equity in anticipation of capital gains.

There were, however, significant differences between the two enterprises. Unlike the South Sea Company, the Mississippi Company occupied a central place in the economy, and its commercial operations covered a far greater diversity of activities. In addition, the Mississippi Company was a monopoly and had no competitors in the domestic stock market. In contrast, the South Sea Company was not only in continuous strife with the Bank of England for the privilege of the conversion of government debt, it competed with other joint-stock companies for customers in Exchange Alley. The latter problem became more severe after 1719, when the South Sea Company was extending the scale of its operations in the midst of a proliferation of joint-stock companies in London. Finally, the Mississippi Company was in control of the banking system and was able to create, in principle, unlimited quantities of money through banknote issues to support its share price and pay its operating expenses. This unlimited access to the Royal Bank notes eventually created high inflation and undermined confidence in the bank's ability to convert notes to specie. The South Sea Company's financing sources were limited to its own cash inflow, loans from the Sword Blade Company, and whatever it could borrow in the rest of the financial market. Thus, unlike the Mississippi Company, the South Sea Company persistently faced cash shortages.

The long-term outcomes of the two crashes were dissimilar. While the British economy did not experience long-term distress, the French economy suffered from a distrust of paper money and banking for many decades, which adversely affected the secular growth and development of manufacturing and commerce. Historian Fernand Braudel (1979: 136) attributes the difference in impact of the crises on the two countries, in part, to the state of the development of capitalism in those countries. Compared to France, Britain was economically, politically, and socially more advanced, and modern financial markets had already established deep roots. The Mississippi scandal drove the French, encumbered with feeble economic and financial institutions and the deep-seated financial interests of the ruling aristocratic class, to retreat to the *ancien regime*.

It is nevertheless true that the outcome could have been far worse for the British economy because the crash had the potential to spill over to the rest of the banking system and the economy. The Bank of England was threatened by the bank run and, if not for its tactics of delay and diversion, as well as emergency loans from abroad, it might have faced very serious problems. Public trust in the financial and the political systems was sufficiently shaken for the state to be forced to enact a partial bailout for the shareholders to stabilize confidence. Without these measures the burst of the South Sea Bubble might have had a longer-lasting adverse effect on the British economy.

On the three classic bubbles

Figures 2.3, 3.2, and 4.2 depict ten to twentyfold increases in the price of an asset in a matter of a few months, followed by sharp collapses. These were extraordinary events. The asset-price inflations and consequent crashes, however, did not create major, immediate dislocations in the general economy, such as those seen in the Wall Street crashes of 1929 and 2007–8. Thus, they may be seen as odd, dramatic, but ultimately inconsequential incidents that do not deserve more than the attention of a trivia buff. However, from an economist's perspective, they are much more than curiosities; they are fascinating puzzles that challenge the way economists think about how individuals make decisions and how markets function.

The central issue is how to explain the significant increase in share prices. Why were people willing to pay such seemingly excessive prices? Did they expect the offspring of the tulip bulbs to generate returns to cover the price they paid? Did investors really believe that the future profitability of the commercial ventures of the Mississippi and South Sea companies would be high enough to justify astronomical stock prices? Were the risk and liquidity advantages of equities over government paper large enough to warrant such a high demand for private equities? Is it possible that investors believed that share prices would rise indefinitely, so that there would always be capital gains? Were there "smart money" investors who took advantage of unsophisticated investors and added fuel to the speculative fire by first buying into the bubble and then selling their stocks to unsuspecting, naïve buyers, who did not understand that the price increase was unsustainable? Did people, facing uncertainty about the future and imperfect information, make financial decisions based on extraneous factors unrelated to expected profitability ("Well, the king is buying!")? Did investors adopt a herd mentality and imitate other market participants instead of basing their decisions on the best information about expected returns on assets? These questions indicate only some of the hypotheses that economists pose to make sense of these asset-price bubbles. To assess these competing hypotheses it is necessary first to delve into theories of asset price determination.

Timeline

September 1711	South Sea Company (SSC) chartered to convert £9.47m short-term government debt to company stock in return for annual interest payments from government.
1713	War of Spanish Succession ends; Asiento right is granted to SSC.
1718	Hostilities with Spain renewed.
December 1718	SSC share price £118.
1719	Parliament passes bill to convert £1.5m 1710 Lottery Loan annuities to SSC shares; SSC proposes conversion of £31.5m long-term annuity to company shares.
January 1, 1720	SSC share price £128.
February 7, 1720	South Sea Bill to convert £31.5m public debt to SSC equity enacted; company permitted to issue 315,000 shares at £100 par value.
April 1, 1720	SSC share price £310.
April 14, 1720	First money subscription at £400 per share.
April 28, 1720	First registration of irredeemable annuities for conversion (2/3 registered).
April 29, 1720	Second money subscription at £400 per share.
May 2, 1720	SSC share price £339.
May 19, 1720	Announcement of terms of conversion for first registration of irredeemable annuities; SSC stock priced at £375.
June 1, 1720	SSC share price £720.
June 11, 1720	Bubble Act passes.
June 17, 1720	Third money subscription at £1,000.
June 22, 1720	Books closed for two months to pay dividends; SSC share price £765.
June 29, 1720	SSC share price peaks at £950.
July 14, 1720	Registration of redeemable annuities for second conversion.
August 6, 1720	Registration of remaining annuities for second conversion.

August 12, 1720	Announcement of terms of conversion for first registration of irredeemable annuities; SSC stock priced at £800.
August 14, 1720	Fourth money subscription at £1,000.
August 17, 1720	Bubble Act enforced; legal notices for violating act served on four companies.
August 23, 1720	Company books open; share price £740.
September 1720	South Sea share price starts collapsing.
September 19, 1720	Bank of England (BoE) agrees to help SSC (bank contract).
September 24, 1720	Sword Blade Company fails.
October 1, 1720	SSC share price £290.
November 9, 1720	BoE reneges on bank contract.
December 1720	SSC share price £200.
January 1721	Secret committee to investigate SSC operations.
August 1721	Parliament passes Act to Restore Public Credit.

Key terms and concepts

Irredeemable government debt
Market maker
Redeemable government debt
Stockbroker
Stockjobber

Endnotes

1 This historical account of the South Sea bubble is drawn from Carswell (1993), Chancellor (2000), Dale (2004), Neal (1990), and Paul (2011).
2 For an appreciation of the order of magnitude of these sums, in the early 1700s a middle-level artisan's annual income was around £200.
3 Unlike modern accounting standards, the practice at the time was to take the surplus cash inflow from the sale of shares at a premium and tally it as profit distributable to shareholders (Chancellor 2000: 62; Dale 2004: 80).
4 While the shares of the Mississippi Company were easily traded in the market, trading of South Sea shares required registration in the company's books.
5 Paul (2011: 85) contests the view that the need for cash for upcoming installment payments would have forced investors to raise cash. She argues that investors could have cut their losses by dumping scrip or refusing to continue payments.
6 Harris (1994) doubts that the enforcement of the Bubble Act could have triggered a panic because it had passed two months earlier and was not news to the public.
7 This oft repeated quote is attributed to Newton in *The Church of England Quarterly Review* (1850: 142).
8 This provision conveniently helped the 138 MPs who were borrowers themselves.

References

Braudel, Fernand. 1979. *Civilization and Capitalism, 15th–18th Century, vol. 2: The Wheels of Commerce*. New York: Harper and Row.

Carswell, John. 1993. *The South Sea Bubble*, rev. ed. Dover, NH: Alan Sutton.

Chancellor, Edward. 2000. *Devil Take the Hindmost: A History of Financial Speculation*. New York: Plume.

The Church of England Quarterly Review. 1850. "Review of *Chronicles and Characters of the Stock Exchange* by John Francis." XXVII: 128–54.

Dale, Richard. 2004. *The First Crash: Lessons from the South Sea Bubble*. Princeton, NJ: Princeton University Press.

Dickson, P. G. M. 1993. *The Financial Revolution in England: A Study in the Development of Public Credit, 1688–1756*. Aldershot, Hampshire, England: Gregg Revivals.

Harris, Ron. 1994. "The Bubble Act: Its Passage and its Effects on Business Organization." *The Journal of Economic History* 54 (3): 610–27.

Kindleberger, Charles P. and Aliber, Robert Z. 2011. *Manias, Panics, and Crashes: A History of Financial Crises*, 6th ed. New York: Palgrave Macmillan.

Neal, Larry. 1990. *The Rise of Financial Capitalism: International Capital Markets in the Age of Reason*. Cambridge, New York: Cambridge University Press.

Neal, Larry. 1996. *Course of the Exchange, London, 1698–1823 and Amsterdamsche Beurs, Amsterdam, 1723–1794*. Ann Arbor, MI: Inter-university Consortium for Political and Social Research. doi:10.3886/ICPSR01008.v1.

Paul, Helen J. 2011. *The South Sea Bubble: An Economic History of its Origins and Consequences*. New York: Routledge.

5 Rationality, fundamentals, and prices

First principles

In commentaries on changing asset prices the term "fundamentals" comes up frequently. While it is not always defined precisely, fundamentals denotes a variety of economic, political, and institutional factors that are expected to influence, in a predictable fashion, company profits and risks and, therefore, security prices. They may include consumer preferences, technological innovations, the state of the world economy, political stability, and government policies. Occasionally, however, experts admit that they are baffled when security prices appear to change in the absence of any perceptible change in the observed fundamentals. When that occurs analysts either attribute the price change to some unknown fundamental factor and embark on research to discover it, or inquire whether there are extraneous, non-fundamental factors that cause a systematic deviation of the market price from its intrinsic value that is warranted by the fundamentals.

Economists define the asset-price bubble as a cumulative or sustained deviation of the market price from its intrinsic or fundamental value. The critical element of the bubble, as Stiglitz (1990) states, is that investors believe the deviation will persist and that they will realize capital gains in the future. Sir Thomas Browne's adage regarding diuturnity applies to bubbles as well: a bubble "is a dream and folly of expectation." Such a deviation cannot sustain itself indefinitely and eventually collapses to bring the market price back in line with its fundamental value.

This definition presents an obvious point of contention. Only the market price is observable; the fundamental price is unobservable. As only one price is observed, how does one distinguish between the market price and the fundamental price, or pass judgment on whether the observed actual price is a deviation from the intrinsic value of an asset? In fact, many economists vehemently dispute the idea that a bubble can exist and believe that the observed market price is the same as the fundamental price. If this theory is true then the bubble is a just legend, a figment of the imagination and an example of careless economic reasoning. Other economists, who accept that bubbles are possible, offer a variety of competing explanations of their causes and dynamics, although a consensus or a dominant view has yet to emerge. At the root of the debate among the competing explanations lie differences in economists' conceptions of economic behavior, the nature of uncertainty, market structure, and the dynamics of the credit system.

This chapter examines how economists make sense of financial bubbles and illustrates the competing ideas in the context of the three classic bubbles described in the previous chapters. This task requires an initial discussion of the foundational concepts of rationality, uncertainty, and expectations that are embedded in the theory of price determination. Standard introductory economics textbooks introduce these concepts in the context of commodities markets. Because readers are likely to be more familiar with commodities markets than financial markets the former is a convenient entry point for current purposes as well. I start with the determination of the fundamental price of a commodity and move on to the fundamentals of asset prices. The chapter concludes with discussions on six topics that play central roles in interpretations of financial crises: operationalizing uncertainty, hypothesis of rational expectations, possibility of rational bubbles, plausibility of the notion of rationality as optimization, alternative notions of rationality, and whether speculation is stabilizing or destabilizing.

Fundamentals of commodity prices

The previous chapters chronicled three bubble events but did not offer explanations for why prices behaved the way they did. To explain these episodes it is necessary to develop a theory that identifies the factors and mechanisms that set in motion and sustained the price increase, and later instigated the collapse. Only through the lens of a theory can one organize, understand, and explain the historical "facts." However, this enterprise is a contested terrain. There are always competing theories that offer alternative interpretations of a specific event. The battle between the theories is a matter of interest to the general public because theories have public-policy implications concerning how financial markets should be organized and regulated, which, in turn, affect the daily lives of everyone.

Theories that attempt to explain economic processes and predict outcomes are stated in the form of models. *Economic models* are artificial constructs that depict relationships and chains of causation between variables. The world is an extremely complex place, and it would be impossible to emulate it in all its details. In addition, such an effort would not be desirable or productive because not all of the features are likely to be pertinent to the question at hand. Thus, models are necessarily stripped-down, simplified representations of reality that disregard "irrelevant" factors and focus on the "important" factors. There is, of course, usually more than one theory or model to explain an observed phenomenon. These competing models are distinguished in terms of their assumptions concerning the behavior of economic agents and their environment, relative importance assigned to various factors, and the cause and effect relations between variables.

The central variable of interest is price, and this chapter presents standard *perfect-competition* models of commodity and security pricing. I start with the commodity-price-determination model. Consider a stylized tulip bulb market in Haarlem, United Provinces, circa 1620. In this market buyers (consumers) purchase bulbs to enjoy the beauty of the flowers, and growers (producers) cultivate bulbs for profit. All exchanges are spot transactions: bulbs are exchanged for cash between the buyer and the seller. A *perfectly competitive market* is one in which the following assumptions hold: first, there are no variations in tulip bulbs, i.e. a homogeneous bulb is traded; second, each buyer and seller is small relative to the size of the market, and the actions of an individual agent do not have a perceptible effect on market supply or demand; third, there is free entry into and exit from the market by producers so that profit opportunities are fully exploited; finally, no agent holds an informational advantage over others. The available information about the state of the demand for and supply of bulbs is evenly distributed across all buyers and sellers.[1] The latter assumption implies that all agents trade on equally advantageous terms, and there is a single price for bulbs in the market. If identical bulbs are sold at different prices in two locations then economic agents can engage in *arbitrage*, i.e. they can make no-risk profits by simultaneously buying bulbs at the lower price and selling them at the higher price. The outcome is a convergence of prices, called the *law of one price* or *no-arbitrage condition*.

Figure 5.1 illustrates the standard price-determination model in a competitive economy. The objective is to explain how Box D, the bulb price, is reached. To answer this question one has to move backwards from Box D.

Market demand and supply (Box C)

The bulb price in the spot market is determined by the interaction of market demand for and market supply of bulbs. The *market demand* for bulbs is the sum of individual demands of buyers and shows the total number of bulbs consumers would be willing to purchase at each price. It describes buyers' intended purchases at different prices and does not, by itself, show the actual number of bulbs purchased or the price at which they are traded. Thus, it is a relationship between bulb price and quantity of bulbs demanded, not a specific combination of price and quantity. Similarly, the *market supply* of bulbs is the sum of quantities offered by individual growers at each price. It is also a relationship between price and quantity that describes producers' and sellers' intentions and does not by itself show how much is actually sold in the market.

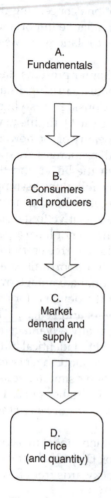

Figure 5.1 Determination of the commodity spot price.

To understand how market demand and supply jointly determine the price suppose that bulbs are traded initially at *f*10 each. Then suppose that the economy experiences a shock that causes market demand to grow, e.g. Far East trade expands and generates more wealth. Provided there are no other changes in market demand or supply, the shock would create an excess demand for bulbs at the initial price, and competing buyers would bid up the price. The displacement could also originate on the supply side. An expansion in supply due to favorable weather conditions, for instance, would create a surplus of bulbs in the marketplace, and competition among sellers would push the price below the initial price of *f*10.

Thus, behind the price change are factors that shift either the market demand or supply. To understand fully how market demand or supply change, however, one needs to look closer at where market demand and supply originate, or how individual buyers and sellers make their bid and offer decisions.

Optimizing economic agents: consumers and producers (Box B)

The standard economic theory models an individual consumer's demand for and a producer's supply of bulbs as outcomes of benefit-cost calculations. On the demand side the objective of the consumer is to maximize the benefit derived from the consumption of tulip bulbs, given tastes and preferences, income (endowments), and prices of other commodities. As more bulbs are consumed the total utility increases (albeit at a diminishing rate); the more, the better. The opportunity cost of each bulb purchased is the unit price, or the amount of money that could have been used in the purchase of some other good. The consumer's objective is to buy a combination of quantities of goods that maximize her utility. Intuitively, utility maximization may be visualized as the consumer rank ordering all feasible baskets of goods—that is, combinations of quantities of bulbs, beer, bread, boots, and so forth that can be acquired within a budget—and choosing the basket that yields the highest level of satisfaction. The highest utility for the total amount spent is achieved when the composition of the consumption basket is such that the last dollar spent on each commodity yields the same amount of additional utility.[2]

Readers who are mathematically inclined will recognize that this setup is a constrained *optimization* problem: maximize an objective utility function subject to a budget constraint. The constraint is determined by the given income and prices of commodities. Economics majors routinely learn to express this decision problem mathematically, solve it using linear algebra or calculus, illustrate the solution with graphs, and carry out exercises that describe how the optimal basket changes in response to exogenous shocks, such as a change in income. This formal solution is interpreted as the replication of the choice that the economic agent makes in real life. Note that the consumer's allocation decision is pertinent only if the consumer's endowment is finite. If unlimited resources are available then the consumer can afford unlimited quantities of everything to attain infinite utility and does not face any restrictions or trade-offs in making choices.

On the supply side economics posits that bulb growers are optimizing decision makers as well. Their objective is to maximize profits, i.e. the difference between total revenue and total cost, given the bulb price, input costs, and technology. Production requires a firm to combine inputs in specific quantities, similar to a cook who prepares a dish. Often several available techniques of production are available, each using inputs in different intensities. For example, pesto can be prepared either by grinding basil leaves, garlic, and pine nuts in a mortar (labor intensive) or blending them in a food processor (capital intensive). The available techniques of production constitute the state of the technology. Given input prices, the price of the product, and the state of the technology, the producer determines the quantities of primary *factors of production* (land, labor, machinery, and equipment) and intermediate inputs and produces the quantity of output that maximizes total profit. The producer will be willing to supply a higher quantity as long as the price, or the revenue from the additional unit sold, is higher than its cost of production. Parallel to the consumer's decision-making problem, the producer's task may be viewed as rank ordering all of the alternative input combinations in accordance with the profit pay-off and selecting the one that is most profitable.

Factors that influence the consumer's demand for and the producer's supply of bulbs (remember, these are respectively what the consumer is willing to purchase and what the producer is willing to offer at each price) follow directly from this setup. On the demand side individual demand reflects first the tastes and preferences of the individual. The more the consumer enjoys watching tulips bloom in her yard, the more she will be willing to spend on bulbs. Changing fashions, acquisition of new tastes, and higher levels of utility associated with the consumption of tulips induce consumers to allocate more of their income to bulbs (and less to other goods). Second, an increase in consumer income, or more generally, endowment, will lead to an increase in the number of bulbs demanded because consumers can now afford more of them.[3] Third, changes in the prices of other goods and services will also alter the demand for bulbs. A higher price of hyacinths, for instance, will lead to the substitution of relatively cheaper tulips for hyacinths and a higher demand for tulip bulbs. The change in individual demand then reflects the consumer's response to the changing environment by reweighing the benefits of an additional bulb against the cost and revising her purchase decision accordingly.

On the supply side fluctuations in an individual firm's supply originate from changes in the unit cost of production. A technological innovation that raises input productivity or a reduction in input prices both lower the unit cost of production. More favorable weather conditions, particularly in the case of agricultural products, will also lead to a lower unit cost of production. At the initial price the lower unit cost of production implies a higher profit and induces the producer to raise the quantity she is willing to supply.

In economics utility maximization and profit maximization are referred to as the "rationality postulates." Rationality in this context means that both the consumers and the producers rank the outcomes of their actions respectively in terms of the utility and profits they yield, and choose the outcome that maximizes the value of the objective function. This preference ordering must satisfy three conditions. First, the agent must have well defined preferences so that she can rank all possible outcomes: for the two outcomes A and B, she prefers A to B, or B to A, or is indifferent between A and B. This is known as the *completeness* axiom. Second, if she prefers A to B and B to C, then the consistency of preferences requires her to prefer A to C. This is the *transitivity* axiom. Third, if the agent prefers A to B when given a choice only between A and B then adding C to the choice set should not change preference ordering between A and B; A should still be preferred to B. This is *the independence of irrelevant alternatives* (IIA) axiom.

The rationality postulate, in the sense of the independent individual optimizing behavior describe above, is the foundation of mainstream economics. Economics as a discipline promotes the application of rational-choice methodology by extending the choice universe of the rational agent beyond the commodity market to almost everything under the sun. It explains the number of hours an individual works in terms of allocation of the fixed number of hours in a day between work and leisure so that the total utility from the combination of leisure and purchase of goods is maximized. Saving is modeled as the outcome of allocation of expected lifetime income across annual consumption spending, such that the utility derived from lifetime consumption is maximized. Parents' decisions regarding the number of their progeny is reduced to a maximization of returns to having children, e.g. assistance in old age, subject to the available family resources and the cost of raising children. Standard economics formulates practically all economic and social outcomes as benefit-maximizing and cost-minimizing solutions to allocation problems.

Fundamentals of the commodity spot price (Box A)

The previous section already partially identified the fundamental factors that determine the agents' optimizing consumption and production decisions. In the case of the tulip bulbs the fundamentals that determine demand are tastes and preferences, endowments (including biological, natural, intellectual, and geographical attributes that determine income), and the prices of other commodities. On the supply side fundamentals are prices of inputs and technology. (Moving from individual to market supplies and demands, one can add to these fundamentals the numbers of consumers and producers, or the market size, as well.) Combining the demand and supply side, the fundamentals that determine the intrinsic price of tulip bulbs are, then, tastes and preferences, endowments, technology, and prices of other commodities and inputs.

Further reflection would suggest that the fundamentals set should be expanded a bit further. A Dutch merchant's current demand for bulbs may depend on his expectations regarding the likelihood of the safe passage of spice ships that cross the Indian Ocean, or his expected future income. If the war is over and the odds of his incoming ships being attacked by the enemy are less the merchant is more likely to indulge in several new bulbs today. Thus, the list of fundamentals should include, in addition to the current states, the anticipated future states of tastes and preferences, endowments, technology, and other prices.[4]

Many economists add institutions as another category of the fundamentals. Institutional factors comprise what can be best described as "rules of the game." The legal system, recognition and enforcement of property rights, political structure, regulatory environment, and import-export regimes are some examples of institutional factors that would influence supply and demand decisions, and, therefore, the price.

Finally, identification of the fundamentals is also contingent on the scope of the analysis. When one adopts a narrow perspective and looks, for example, only at the tulip market, competing goods and input prices are among the fundamentals that affect the bulb price. However, these other prices, just like bulb prices, are determined in their respective markets through interaction of pertinent market supplies and demands. When a wider multi-market perspective is adopted to understand how bulb prices are determined simultaneously with all of the other prices one observes that the prices of other commodities and inputs are themselves market outcomes, not fundamentals.

The objective of the price theory sketched above is to predict how the price and quantity of tulip bulbs traded change as the economic environment is altered. In economic models there are two types of variables. The first type is the *endogenous variable*. Endogenous variables' values are determined within the model itself. In the standard competitive pricing model the price of the commodity and the quantity traded are examples of endogenous variables. By contrast, *exogenous variables* are external to the model. Their values are determined independently of the internal workings of the model and are taken as data by the economist. In the price model tastes and preferences, endowments, technology and institutions (and, depending on the scope of analysis, prices of other goods and inputs) are taken as exogenous variables. These exogenous factors are obviously in constant flux, but, from the perspective of the model, how and why they change are of little or no interest. The objective of the pricing model is to determine how the endogenous variables, i.e. the price and the quantity traded, respond to the changes in exogenous factors.

Equipped with this model, one can now attempt to explain the rising value of variegated tulip bulbs in Haarlem during the 1620s (before tulip mania). Tulips became increasingly fashionable in Europe, and more and more people of means wished to acquire the flowers for their beauty.

Thanks to the expansion of the Far East trade, Amsterdam becoming the hub of global trade, and the growth of manufacturing that generated more wealth, large Dutch merchants could afford more luxury items, such as tulips. Growing incomes of professionals and master craftsmen created a middle class that imitated the lifestyle of the wealthy. Changes in tastes and endowments caused the demand for tulips to expand and put upward pressure on the price. On the supply side the entry of specialized professional cultivators into the market expanded the number of bulbs offered in the market. Given their low reproduction rates and technical constraints on the growers' ability to mass cultivate them, however, the supply of rare bulbs could be increased only very slowly, and it was impossible for the supply to rise as much as the demand. Consequently, excess demand for rare bulbs boosted the price. The story is somewhat different in the case of bulbs that are more common. There was an increase in demand for them from lower- and middle-class buyers. The supply of more common bulbs, however, increased at a faster pace with the rise in the number of professional growers and the less-challenging conditions of cultivation. Consequently, prices of common bulbs were more stable—at least until the speculative boom of the mid 1630s.

Fundamentals of security prices

Now consider a portfolio holder, a Parisian or a Londoner in 1719, say, who allocates her wealth among money, government bonds, and joint-stock-company shares. The portfolio holder may also choose to allocate some of her total savings to non-financial assets, e.g. jewelry, real estate, paintings, rare wines, but, for the sake of simplicity, these alternatives may be ignored. The bond is a contract between the issuer—usually government or corporations—and the investor. The issuer promises to make periodic fixed payments over the lifetime of the bond and then one lump-sum payment upon its expiration to the investor. Periodic payments are called *coupons*, and the lump-sum payment upon maturity is the *principal*, *face*, or *par* value of the bond (which is not the same as the market price of the bond).[5] The buyer of the contract, in effect, lends the market value of the bond to the issuer. In contrast, equity, or the common stock, is a certificate of partial ownership of a publicly owned company. The shareowner virtually owns a piece of the tangible and intangible assets, e.g. buildings, machines, software, and intellectual property, and is entitled to receive a proportionate share of the distributed profits or dividends. In contrast to coupon payments, dividends are variable because their size depends on the profitability of the company. Finally, money, unlike bonds or stocks, does not yield any return to the holder. However, the portfolio holder may wish to keep some of her wealth in the form of money because it has the advantage of higher liquidity, or ease of convertibility into other assets or commodities.

Securities are traded in the *primary* and *secondary* markets. The initial public offering (IPO) of common shares (called money subscriptions in Paris and London during the eighteenth century) and bonds take place in the primary market, usually with the assistance of an *underwriting* firm that has expertise in valuing and marketing initial offerings of securities. After investors purchase securities in the primary market they may trade them in the secondary market. London's Royal Exchange or Exchange Alley, and the New York Stock Exchange are examples of organized physical secondary markets. They also come in many other forms, such as curb markets, dealer networks, and virtual electronic exchanges. The market price of a financial asset is determined by its supply and demand in the secondary market. Although large quantities of stocks and bonds are traded in the secondary markets on any given day, typically, this volume constitutes only a small fraction of the total stock of securities. One implication of this observation is that asset prices can become very volatile if many portfolio holders suddenly decide to sell large portions of their holdings.

The rationality postulate applies to behavior in the asset markets as well. Suppose that the portfolio holder is risk averse, which means that, all else being equal, she prefers less risk to more (a plausible assumption). An optimizing investor's objective is to maximize the total expected return of her portfolio, given tastes and preferences (risk tolerance, time preference), and the financial technology (types of available financial instruments). Note that the portfolio holder maximizes the expected return because securities are claims on future income flows. Future dividend payments, interest rates, and default risks that affect returns are not known with certainty and investors' decisions are based on their best forecasts of these variables.

The larger portfolio-decision problem, the allocation of the total wealth among competing assets in accordance with the individual's goals, risk tolerance, and time horizon, lies outside the scope of our current interest. The simpler and more relevant question here concerns determination of the price at which the portfolio holder would buy or sell a specific security.

The present value of future income

One critical concept that needs to be explained first is *present value*. Preference ranking between two assets requires a comparison of the income flows they would generate. The comparison of two income flows is not as straightforward as adding the annual returns because the value of $1 changes over time, even with zero rate of inflation. The calculation of the income flow requires *discounting the future.* For the sake of simplicity, suppose that the inflation rate is zero, so that the purchasing power of money does not change over time. Now, $980 today is not worth $980 next year because if today's $980 were kept in a bank account with 2 percent interest, then its one-year *future value* would be approximately $1,000 [= $980· (1 + 0.02)]. Reading this relationship in reverse, the *present value* of $1,000 that one would collect a year from now is $980 [= $1,000/ (1 + 0.02)]. By the same token, the present value of $1,000 to be collected two years from now would be even lower, approximately $961 [$1,000/ (1 + 0.02)²] because it collects compound interest (or interest received in the second year on the first year's interest earning). In these examples the future is discounted at 2 percent. A comparison of income streams of alternative assets with different maturities, as well as risks, requires the conversion of the income streams to their present values, using the appropriate discount rates.[6]

Bond price

A bond is a contract between the borrower and lender that obliges the borrower to make periodic payments to the lender over the lifetime of the bond and the principal payment upon maturity. It is a piece of paper (real or virtual) that is composed of two parts. The top part states the maturity (in years, say) and the par value, which is the principal to be paid to the bondholder upon maturity. The bottom part consists of coupons with a fixed value assigned by the issuer. In number these coupons are equal to the number of years in which the bond matures. Each year the issuer makes the bondholder a fixed coupon payment. The ratio of coupon payment to the face value is called the *coupon rate*. Suppose that the face value of a bond is $1,000, its maturity is two years, and the coupon is $50: the coupon rate is 5 percent (= $50/$1,000). The bondholder receives $50 coupon payments in two consecutive years, and collects $1,000 in the second year. Because coupon payment is fixed the bond is known as a *fixed-income security*.

Consider a bond with a face value of F, a coupon of C, and a maturity of n periods. An investor who considers buying this bond in period 0 would receive C in every period until n and C + F in period n when the bond matures. Letting d stand for the discount rate, the present value of the income stream V_0^B is then:

$$V_0^B = \frac{C}{1+d} + \frac{C}{(1+d)^2} + \ldots + \frac{C}{(1+d)^{n-1}} + \frac{C+F}{(1+d)^n}. \tag{5.1}$$

The successive terms on the right-hand side of Equation 5.1 are the present values of the amounts the bondholder would collect from period 1 to n. As the coupon payments and the face value are fixed, the discount rate is the critical variable in determining the present value.[7] Present value is inversely related to the discount rate.

The discount rate depends on three factors. The first is the *safe interest rate*—the interest rate on the safe alternative because the bond must yield at least as much as the safe instrument. Two reasonably safe instruments today are savings accounts, insured by the Federal Deposit Insurance Corporation, and Treasury bills (the US government is unlikely to default). If the safe interest rate is higher then the discounted future income stream, or present value of the asset, will be lower. Second, the discount rate should also include the *risk premium* to compensate the bondholder for the risk of default by the issuer. If the likelihood of not being paid back is higher the value of the asset for the buyer will be lower. The third factor is the *liquidity premium.* Under conditions where the liquidity is valued highly, as in the case of restrictions on the transfer of the bond, the liquidity premium is higher and the present value is lower.

At what price would an investor be willing to purchase a bond? The benefit of the bond to the buyer is the income stream it generates. If the income stream is higher than the price then the buyer has the incentive to purchase. If the price is higher than the value of the income stream an optimizing investor would not purchase the bond because she would suffer losses. The critical variable in the purchase decision, then, is the present value of the income stream.

Continuing with the numerical example above, suppose that the safe interest rate is 2 percent, and risk and liquidity premiums amount to 6 percent: the present value of the bond is approximately \$946 $\left[= \dfrac{\$50}{1 + 0.08} + \dfrac{\$50 + \$1{,}000}{(1 + 0.08)^2} \right]$. If the bond is offered at \$950 there would be no buyers because the offer price exceeds what the bond pays by \$4, a net loss to the buyer. Given the lack of demand, competition would drive the bond price down. Conversely, if the bond is offered at \$940, there is a net gain of \$6 to the buyer, which would create excess demand and a rise in price. Thus, competitive forces push the price of the bond at time 0 (P_0^B) to the present value of the income stream of the bond: $P_0^B = V_0^B$. In a competitive market in which buyers and sellers take advantage of all profit opportunities the price of the bond should be equal to the present value of the income stream that the bond generates.

As in the case of the competitive commodity market, arbitrage will ensure that the law of one price will hold in the bond market. If two assets that are identical in terms of their discounted income flows are traded at different prices arbitrageurs can ensure profits by simultaneously selling the overvalued asset and buying the undervalued asset. The rising supply of the overvalued asset and the rising demand for the undervalued asset will bring the prices in line. When asset prices are such that there is no likelihood of realizing a gain without taking on more risk then the *no-arbitrage condition* is satisfied.

Alternatively, when the price is equal to the present value of the income stream one may read Equation 5.1 in reverse to determine the yield on the bond given the price, maturity, and coupon and the face value. According to the numerical example above, an investor who purchases this bond for

$946 and holds it until maturity would earn an 8 percent yield per year. A lower market price, $900, say, implies a higher annual yield (10.8 percent)[8]; because the yield is higher than the discount rate the bond is underpriced. This would create excess demand for the bond, thereby raising its price and lowering its yield. The important point to keep in mind is that the bond price and yield are inversely related.

Hence, the fundamental behind the bond price is the discount rate, which, in turn, is determined by the safe interest rate, the risk premium, and the liquidity premium. These factors are manifestations of the preferences of investors, financial technology, and institutions. Risk premium reflects the risk tolerance of investors, or their preferences regarding risk. Liquidity premium is related to the state of financial technology. Bonds are more easily convertible to cash in mature financial markets with organized exchanges. Both the financial technology and the monetary and fiscal institutions, e.g. the conduct of central-bank policy and government budgets, influence the interest rate on savings accounts or Treasury bonds.

Note that throughout this discussion it is assumed that the investor holds the bond until maturity. Hence, the yield calculated above is called the *yield to maturity*. This is not, however, necessarily the *rate of return* on the bond. If the bondholder sells the bond at the end of the first year and realizes a capital gain the rate of return should reflect this gain as well. The issue of capital gains is considered below in the context of the stock price.

Stock price

Equity or common-stock investors are part owners of a publicly traded company. If an investor owns 100 shares of a company that has issued a total of 10,000 shares then she owns 1 percent of the company's assets and is entitled to receive 1 percent of the company's distributed profits. If the share price is $10 then the investor's total shares are worth $1,000, and the company's market valuation or *capitalization* is $100,000. Similar to bonds, the price of a share reflects expected present value of its future income stream. However, while the coupon payments are known with certainty, this is not true for future profits. Dividend distributions vary with the profitability of the company. Hence, common stocks are known as *flexible income securities*. Dividends are likely to be high during periods of high profitability and as small as zero when the company's fortunes decline. Therefore, shareowners face greater variability in earnings, or greater risk. One implication of this is that the risk premium is typically higher for equities than it is for bonds.[9] Further, unlike bonds, equities do not mature at a specific date; they pay dividends as long as the company distributes profits.

The price of a stock is also based on the discounted income flow it is expected to generate. Suppose that an investor plans to buy a share in year 0 and plans to hold it indefinitely. The expected present value of the income stream formed in year 0 (V_0^S) would depend on the annual expected dividends (*ED*) and the discount rate (*d*).

$$V_0^S = \frac{E_0 D_1}{1+d} + \frac{E_0 D_2}{(1+d)^2} + \frac{E_0 D_3}{(1+d)^3} + \dots \tag{5.2}$$

E denotes the expected value of the variable. The subscript 0 next to *E* denotes that the expectation of the respective variable is formed in period 0, or based on the information that is available to the investor at time 0. *D* is dividend and its subscript denotes the time period. For instance, $E_0 D_1$ is the investor's expectation of the value of the dividend of period 1 based on the information available in period 0.

As in the case of bonds, the discount rate is determined by the safe interest rate, risk, and liquidity premiums. Markets forces, i.e. demand for and supply of the stock, will equate the price of the stock with the present value of the income flow. Arbitrage will ensure that the stock price will be equal to the expected present value of the dividend flow: $P_0^S = V_0^S$. Then:

$$P_0^S = \frac{E_0 D_1}{1+d} + \frac{E_0 D_2}{(1+d)^2} + \frac{E_0 D_3}{(1+d)^3} + \dots \tag{5.2'}$$

Thus, the fundamentals of the current stock price are expected dividends and the discount rate, conditional on the currently available information. The higher the expected profitability, or the lower the discount rate, the higher the expected present value of the dividend stream and the stock price.[10] Hence, any new information that raises profit expectations, mitigates risk, or improves the ease of transferability of shares will make the stock more attractive and raise demand and, consequently, the price.

However, this example of stock-price determination is oversimplified. People do not necessarily hold a share indefinitely, and, when they sell the share, they may experience capital gains or losses if the sale price is different from the initial purchase price. How does the stock-price-determination story change in the presence of prospective capital gains? For illustrative purposes, consider that each investor holds the stock for only one year and then sells it. Figure 5.2 may help to visualize the stock's price in this scenario. The discounted income flow and, therefore, the price at time 0 (P_0^S) is determined by discounted values of the expected dividend and the expected stock price at the end of period 1, conditional on the available information in period 0 [$E_0 D_1$, $E_0 P_1^S$]. How is $E_0 P_1^S$ determined? If investors form price expectations in line with the standard asset-pricing theory presented here then $E_0 P_1^S$, in turn, will be determined by the expected dividend and the expected resale price in

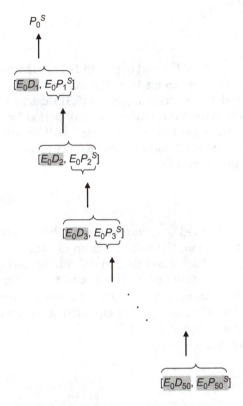

Figure 5.2 Determination of the stock price.

Notes: It is assumed that the share is held for only one period. ED and EP^S refer to the discounted expected values of the dividends and stock price respectively. Subscripts denote time. All expectations are based on information available in time 0.

period 2 $[E_0D_2, E_0P_2^S]$. Putting these pieces together, the value of the stock today is determined by discounted expected dividends of the first and second periods and the expected price at the end of the second period. By the same logic, the expected price at the end of period 2 is determined by the expected dividend and the expected resale price in period 3. If we follow this chain for 50 periods, as in Figure 5.2, we see that the current price is determined by the shaded variables: expected dividends from period 1 to 50 and the expected price in period 50, all discounted to period 0.

I next illustrate this result mathematically. In the first step note that the price is equal to the sum of the discounted expected values of the dividend (E_0D_1) and resale price $(E_0P_1^S)$ of period 1, conditional on the information that the investor has at her disposal in year 0, when she is deciding whether to purchase the security:

$$P_0^S = V_0^S = \frac{E_0 D_1}{1+d} + \frac{E_0 P_1^S}{1+d}. \tag{5.3}$$

What is $E_0 P_1^S$, or the expected price, at the end of period 1? The standard economic model posits that optimizing agents form their expectations by making use of the asset-price-determination equation (5.3). Just as the share price in period 0 depends on the expected dividend of period 1 and the expected price in period 1, the expected price in year 1 will be determined by the expected dividend in year 2 and the expected price in year 2, given the information in the current period:

$$E_0 P_1^S = \frac{E_0 D_2}{1+d} + \frac{E_0 P_2^S}{1+d}. \tag{5.4}$$

Note that price expectations are formed in accordance with the underlying economic model of price formation. Equation 5.4 is an illustration of the *rational expectations hypothesis,* which states that an optimizing agent's expectation of the future stock price will be consistent with the relevant theory. See Equation 5.3: the optimizing agent will gather information on variables on the right-hand side of the asset-pricing equation and process this information in accordance with this equation.

Substituting $E_0 P_1$ from Equation 5.4 into 5.3:

$$P_0^S = \frac{E_0 D_1}{1+d} + \frac{E_0 D_2}{(1+d)^2} + \frac{E_0 P_2^S}{(1+d)^2}. \tag{5.5}$$

The spot price in year 0 is determined by the present values of expected dividends of periods 1 and 2 and the expected price in period 2, again all expectations being conditional on the information available in year 0. Applying the rational expectations hypothesis to $E_0 P_2^S$:

$$E_0 P_2^S = \frac{E_0 D_3}{1+d} + \frac{E_0 P_3^S}{1+d} \tag{5.6}$$

and substituting back into (5.5):

$$P_0^S = \frac{E_0 D_1}{1+d} + \frac{E_0 D_2}{(1+d)^2} + \frac{E_0 D_3}{(1+d)^3} + \frac{E_0 P_3^S}{(1+d)^3}. \tag{5.7}$$

Repeating these recursive substitutions, for, say, 50 years, we obtain:

$$P_0^S = \frac{E_0 D_1}{1+d} + \frac{E_0 D_2}{(1+d)^2} + \frac{E_0 D_3}{(1+d)^3} + \ldots + \frac{E_0 D_{50}}{(1+d)^{50}} + \frac{E_0 P_{50}^S}{(1+d)^{50}}. \tag{5.8}$$

This is the same result obtained in Figure 5.2.

Mathematically, it can be observed that the denominators on the right-hand side of Equation 5.8 grow exponentially as time passes. Provided the numerator does not grow as fast as the denominator, the last term will approach zero with the passage of time. In other words, if the discounted expected future price approaches zero in the limit as time goes to infinity (infinite future is infinitely discounted), then price is the same as that obtained in Equation 5.2. Again the current price of the share is determined exclusively by the fundamentals, i.e. the stream of discounted expected dividends from now to infinity and beyond, conditional on the current information. Whether the investor holds a share indefinitely or only for a short period of time does not affect the security's price determination.

The information set, used to assist the investor in making a decision on whether to acquire shares in a company, is likely to include factors such as the performance of the company, the degree of competition it faces, new technologies it is implementing, new products it is introducing into the market, and government regulations. It is to the advantage of the investor to form as accurate a prediction of discounted dividend flow as possible. The gist of the rational expectations hypothesis is that optimization in the realm of expectation formation requires the agent to utilize all of the information at her disposal as best she can. An important corollary of this argument is that everything that is currently known about the fundamentals, including expected changes in their values, is incorporated in the price of the asset.

If the researcher accepts the standard asset-pricing theory summarized by Equations 5.2 or 5.8 as the true model then the asset-price booms and busts discussed in the previous chapters are attributable only to changes in the fundamentals on the right-hand side of the asset-pricing equation, i.e. expected dividends and the discount rate. If this is true then, against all appearances, the observed bubble patterns do not represent anomalous market behavior but are somehow outcomes of agents' optimizing responses to changes in the fundamentals. Descriptions of financial-market oscillations driven by bouts of "euphoria" and "despair" are inconsistent with classical asset-price-determination theory because psychological factors do not have a place among the fundamentals.

Unknown future: risk vs. uncertainty

Before moving on to interpretations of financial crises it is necessary to address several interrelated methodological issues. The first methodological issue concerns decision-making under conditions of uncertainty. As portfolio decisions are forward looking and no one has perfect foresight, investors and speculators need to ascertain the possible future states of the economy. There are two alternative approaches to modeling decision-making in the face of the unknown future. The first assumes that economic actors know the possible future outcomes and the probability of each outcome. In the language of statistics the outcome is a *random variable*, the value of which is drawn from a known *probability distribution*. The simplest illustration of the probabilistic approach comes from games of chance. In roulette the design of the wheel and betting options are well defined and common knowledge. The player can calculate the expected earnings mathematically based on odds of and pay-offs for each possible outcome. The probability of the ball's falling into pocket 3, for instance, is 1/38, and the pay-off for this outcome is 1 to 35. Thus, if the player bets $1 on pocket 3, the expected gain is −$0.0526 [= (−$1)(37/38) + ($35)(1/38)]. The player is expected to lose, on average, 5.26 percent on his bet.

The expected return on a stock can be calculated similarly if possible pay-offs and their probabilities are known. Suppose that the shareholder expects the possible returns from holding a share over a certain period to be $0, $20, $40, $60, or $80 per share with the respective probabilities of 10, 25, 40, 20, and 5 percent. These data are summarized in Figure 5.3 by a histogram that illustrates the probability distribution of the returns per share. The pay-off is measured on the horizontal axis. The height of each bar measures the probability of the respective pay-off. The sum of the probabilities measured by the bars is equal to 100 percent because the five outcomes exhaust all of the possibilities. The actual value of the returns will be drawn from this distribution. The expected return (or mathematical expectation of the return) is the mean value of the distribution, which is calculated as the weighted average pay-off: $(0.10)(\$0) + (0.25)(\$20) + (0.40)(\$40) + (0.20)(\$60) + (0.05)(80) = \$37$. The spread of the probability distribution, commonly measured by its standard deviation, is a measure of the volatility of returns (interpreted as the riskiness of the asset). As the probability distribution widens, the likelihood of observing outcomes farther

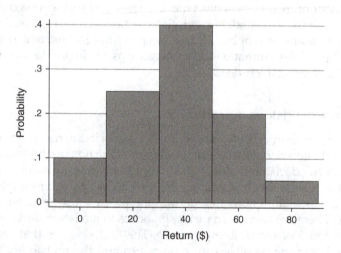

Figure 5.3 Probability distribution of returns per share.

away from the mean increases. This approach to modeling decision-making reduces the investor's uncertainty about the future to probabilistically calculable *risk.*

Not all economists subscribe to the idea of reducing uncertainty to risk and probability distributions. Frank Knight (1984 [1921]) and John Maynard Keynes (1936) draw a distinction between risk and uncertainty and emphasize that probability calculus is an adequate procedure to calculate the expected returns of an asset only when the probability distribution of possible outcomes is well defined and known, as they are in a casino game. In the economic and financial world, however, probability distributions of outcomes are often unknown and/or ambiguous, and, therefore, probabilistic decision-making is unfeasible or unreliable. Such a state of lack of knowledge about the future is called *intrinsic uncertainty.*

The distinction between risk and intrinsic uncertainty has profound consequences for the methodology of economics. In the absence of a probability distribution optimization-based economic analysis faces a colossal problem: if the probabilistic calculation of assets' expected returns and riskiness is not possible how can agents rank outcomes and choose the highest return, or determine the value of an asset? Under conditions of rapid transformative change the situation may become even more complicated as it may be difficult even to ascertain possible outcomes, let alone assign odds, with any degree of confidence. We are then in a world of, in the words of former US Secretary of Defense Donald Rumsfeld, "unknown unknowns." Keynes argues that under conditions of intrinsic uncertainty agents use alternative decision-making rules or rely on convention or rules of thumb as opposed to optimization.

Unfortunately, the standard economics texts often ignore intrinsic uncertainty altogether and use the terms *risk* and *uncertainty* interchangeably. The reader is warned that, this common practice notwithstanding, the distinction between these two terms merits constant attention in the discussion of financial crises.

The rational expectations hypothesis

The rational expectations hypothesis was mentioned above in the context of stock-price determination. In the late 1950s Carnegie Mellon University was the home institution of economists John Muth and Herbert Simon, who were developing the diametrically opposing behavioral hypotheses of rational expectations and bounded rationality (to be introduced later) respectively. According to the rational expectations hypothesis, an individual's subjective expectation of the value of an outcome should be consistent with the objective mathematical expectation that follows from the related theoretical/statistical model. The idea can again be illustrated by the game of roulette. In roulette there exists an objective probability distribution of expected pay-offs that is determined by the design of the wheel (numbers of black, red, green, odd, and even pockets) and the betting rules of the game. The objective mathematical expectation of bet's earnings can be calculated by using the information on the possible outcomes and pay-offs, as illustrated in the previous section. The player, on the other hand, has in mind a subjective probability distribution of the pay-offs based on her knowledge of the game. Provided the player has complete information on the design of the wheel and the rules of the game, and converts this information into knowledge by calculating the odds (as any optimizing player should do), then her subjective probability distribution of earnings should coincide with the objective distribution. The objective mean rate of return to the bet is −5.26 percent, as calculated earlier—and a smart player should know the objective odds.

Turning to economics, the objective probability distribution of returns from an asset will be determined by the probabilities of possible outcomes of the fundamentals and the theoretical model of price determination, which explains the relationship between the fundamentals and returns. The omniscient economist, equipped with theoretical knowledge, data, and computing power, utilizes the appropriate model (i.e. the standard asset-pricing equation) to process the available information on the fundamentals (i.e. the expected dividends and discount rate), to assess the objective probability distribution of the returns, and calculate the expected return, or the mean of the distribution (just as the house does on roulette).

Now consider the decision-making process of the investor. Is there a correspondence between her subjective distribution of the investment's pay-off and the objective distribution of the return as determined by the model, similar to the correspondence observed at the casino? Provided the decision problem is well defined, as in roulette, the answer to this question should be yes. Just as it is nonsensical for the gambler to ignore the fundamentals of roulette in making bets, it is suboptimal for an optimizing economic agent not to take into consideration the fundamentals of asset-price determination in assessing the present value of the dividend flow. From the perspective of the agent the optimal method of forming expectations is, first, to utilize all of the available information on the fundamentals, because anything that is pertinent but ignored will impair the forecast; and, second, to process this information in accordance with the relevant economic theory of asset-price determination, as that is the most efficient way to utilize the information. Thus, the individual investor calculates the expected outcomes and makes choices as though she knows the relevant economic model, and possesses the power of calculation to make efficient use of all available information. Consistency of the subjective and objective probability distributions is the foundation of the rational expectations hypothesis.[11]

Suppose that economic agents have access to reliable probability distributions of possible outcomes, know the rules of the game or the model, and form rational expectations of future returns. Under these conditions how would the expected and the actual observed values of the return compare? Because the world is full of unpredictable events (e.g. surprise weather conditions, Federal Reserve announcements, political strife in the Middle East) the actual observed value, in all likelihood, will turn out to be different from the expected value. However, the difference between the observed and expected values, or the *expectational error*, will be non-systematic over time, or, on average, will be equal to zero. By way of explanation, note that the random events that affect discounted returns are, by definition, unpredictable. Had they been anticipated they would have been a part of the investor's information set and embodied in the expected price. As they are unpredictable their expected value is zero. Put differently, systematic errors imply that the economic agent is systematically under- or overestimating returns; she is either repeatedly overlooking a relevant piece of information or is not processing the available information as well as she should, both of which lead to suboptimal outcomes and contradict optimizing behavior. Therefore, only unanticipated, irreducible, and expectational errors are in accordance with the rational expectations hypothesis.[12]

While the rational expectations hypothesis may appear to belong to economic arcana, it plays a prominent role in asset-price-bubble theories. As demonstrated above, in the context of the standard asset-pricing model the market price cannot systematically deviate from the intrinsic price so long as investors base their decisions on the fundamentals and expectations are formed rationally. However, the rational expectations hypothesis by itself does not imply that there cannot be bubbles. Once the link between the price and the fundamentals is severed bubbles are theoretically possible even when expectations are formed rationally. Consider an alternative asset-pricing model according to which the current asset price is determined by the fundamentals summarized in Equation 5.2 plus some extraneous factor (such as herding behavior, which is ruled out by the fundamentals-based analysis). The rational expectations hypothesis would then suggest that the investor would be willing to pay a price that would exceed the fundamental value. I consider this possibility in the next section.

Rational bubbles?

In her book on tulip mania Anne Goldgar (2007: 227) objects to the commentators who claimed that the florists' willingness to pay huge sums for bulbs was "irrational." What is irrational, she protests, about buyers paying large sums if they anticipated selling the bulbs at even higher prices in the future? She, of course, has a point. Her objection is consistent with the rational expectations hypothesis, which implies that there is nothing irrational or suboptimal about paying an "excessive" price if the buyer believes the asset will continue to gain value over and above its fundamental worth. The possibility of such a systematic deviation has come to be known as the *rational bubble hypothesis.* I will discuss bubble theories fully in the next chapter. However, the rational bubble hypothesis relates directly to the standard asset-pricing model as well as the notions of optimization and rational expectations presented in this chapter. A discussion of the hypothesis is appropriate because it facilitates a deeper understanding of optimizing behavior and its relationship with the fundamentals. This section first explains the nature of the rational bubble, and then discusses its relationship to optimizing behavior.

Recall that Equation 5.3 expresses the price of a stock in period 0 in terms of the expected dividend and expected price in period 1. If expectations are formed rationally, and the discounted value of the expected price goes to zero as time goes to infinity, the solution to Equation 5.3 is as given by Equation 5.2′. That is, the current price is determined exclusively by the fundamentals. But mathematicians inform us that 5.2′ is only one of the possible solutions to the so-called difference equation, i.e. 5.3. Another equally legitimate solution to Equation 5.3 is:

$$P_0^S = \frac{E_0 D_1}{1+d} + \frac{E_0 D_2}{(1+d)^2} + \frac{E_0 D_3}{(1+d)^3} + \frac{E_0 D_4}{(1+d)^4} + \dots + B_0. \tag{5.9}$$

The mathematical derivation of Equation 5.9 is not of interest for the present purposes. What is important is that, in plain language, Equation 5.9 states that the investor expects the price to exceed the discounted expected dividend stream by B_0, and, therefore, at time 0 she is willing pay a higher price, as much as B_0, than is justified by the fundamentals. This extra amount B_0 is called the bubble component of the price (Blanchard and Watson 1982).

The possible values of B_0 make the bubble behavior in Equation 5.9 interesting. One possible time path for the bubble component is that it may increase exponentially. To simplify the exposition assume that the risk and liquidity premiums are zero, so that the discount rate is equal to the safe interest rate, and let the latter be 2 percent. What should the value of B_0 be for the investor to pay, say, $100 extra over the intrinsic value of this security? With a one-year time horizon the value of B_0 should be at least $102 [= $100(1 + 0.02)] because otherwise it makes more sense to invest $100 in the safe asset. Next consider a time horizon of two years. If the investor is planning to hold the asset for two years then the opportunity cost of investing $100 in period 0 would be even higher at $104.04 [= 100(1 + 0.02)^2]. In the event she plans to sell the asset at the end of period 1 the result does not change. She knows that the prospective buyer will be willing to pay the additional $102 in period 1 only if he knows that the value will be higher, at $104.04, in period 2 to cover the opportunity cost of investing in the safe asset. Looking farther into the future, B_0 should rise at the compound rate $100(1 + 0.02)^3$, $100(1 + 0.02)^4$, and so forth, or the price in period 0 must rise exponentially. As long as the opportunity cost of investing the additional \$100 is covered by the exponential growth of the bubble component then the purchase decision is perfectly consistent with the pricing model illustrated by Equation 5.9 and with the rational expectations hypothesis.[13]

The rational bubble theory highlights that agents' belief in the role of non-fundamentals in determining the asset price is self-reinforcing. If agents believe that the price will rise for extraneous reasons and act accordingly the price will rise. This idea gave rise to a rich theoretical literature, much of which is devoted to the question of whether rational bubbles are logically admissible in a world of optimizing agents; and economic theorists point out various conditions under which optimizing behavior precludes a rational bubble (e.g. Tirole 1982). A few examples of the contradiction between optimizing behavior and the existence of the rational bubble will give a flavor of these discussions.

First, an exponentially growing bubble is nonsensical because it leads to the absurd proposition that, eventually, all the wealth in the economy will be insufficient to buy a single share unless wealth itself grows at an even faster rate than the price. Second, a bubble will not even begin if substitute assets are widely available because investors will switch to alternative, cheaper assets and slow down the expansion in demand. Third, if an asset is easily reproducible (consider a corporation that can flood the market with new issues of stocks or a living painter's artwork) bubbles cannot be sustained. Fourth, there cannot be bubbles in securities with a finite lifespan, such as non-perpetuity bonds, because investors know that their value cannot grow exponentially; optimizing agents know that the price could not rise forever and, therefore, will not buy into the bubble in the first place. Fifth, investors buy into a bubble plan to sell at a future date to realize capital gains; if there are a finite number of investors there will be a finite number of transactions, and no one will want to keep the security beyond a certain future date (because there will be no one left to sell to). In this case no one has an incentive to purchase the asset in the last period. By the same token, there is no incentive to buy the asset in the next to the last period. By backward induction, the deviation from the intrinsic price will never start.

The rational expectations hypothesis does not inquire why economic agents would pay attention to extraneous or non-fundamental factors in decision making. Not surprisingly, the staunch proponents of the standard fundamentals-based model dismiss the rational bubble idea, e.g. Meltzer (2002). Even Blanchard and Watson (1982), who originated the theory, suggest that rational bubbles may emerge under restrictive conditions when the fundamentals are difficult to assess, such as in the gold or art markets. As discussed in the next chapter, however, the hypothesis may be relevant when financial markets are not perfectly competitive.

The rationality postulate

The foundational assumption of rationality (as optimization) can be questioned on several grounds. First, is the assumption realistic? Second, what are the consequences of optimization if individual choice sets are determined by non-fundamental factors? Third, even if the fundamentals exclusively determine the choice set does individual optimization imply social-welfare maximization as well?

Is rationality (as optimization) a realistic assumption?

The assumption of optimizing behavior focuses exclusively on the objective of the economic agent and the particular decision that achieves the objective. Cognitive processes through which the consumer, producer, or investor perceives the available choices, deliberates, gathers and processes information, learns from mistakes, reasons about the pros and cons of alternatives, and chooses a course of action are deemed unimportant and irrelevant and are left outside the scope of the analysis. Simon (1976), a critic of this approach, calls rationality as optimization, or focusing on goals rather than the process of decision-making, *substantive rationality*.

One nagging question about the premise of substantive rationality is whether modeling of the economic agent as an optimizer is realistic. There are decision-making problems in which the optimization postulate is clearly plausible. In the classic example of the problem of the traveling salesman, for instance, the task of the salesman is to minimize the distance of the route (or gas cost) in visiting a given number of addresses in a day to market Tupperware. Given the geographic distribution of homes and the cost of gas, the salesman faces a "well defined" problem in the sense that the length or cost of each alternative route can clearly be calculated and ranked. The route the time- or cost-saving salesman chooses would likely coincide with the economist's formal solution to the optimization problem obtained by mathematical methods.

Another example is the problem of the casino, where betting options, outcome probabilities, and pay-offs are common knowledge. Armed with this information, the player can calculate the expected winnings and choose the game that maximizes expected earnings or minimizes expected losses. Again, as possible courses of action and outcomes, in the probabilistic sense, are clearly delineated, the agent can rank them according to her objective function and pick the option that maximizes expected earnings. This latter approach has come to be known as *expected utility maximization*, following the work of the mathematician John von Neumann and economist Oskar Morgenstern in the 1940s.

Dissenting economists point out that these examples are not representative of the decision problems that economic agents commonly encounter. Real-life problems are often not well defined in the above sense due to the dearth of information or limited access to it, or an incomplete under-standing of how to utilize available information. A casino game is not an adequate metaphor for expected returns on an investment, the outcomes of which may extend to a distant unknown future; the investor may not have reliable information on the probabilities of the outcomes or even what the possible outcomes may be. If these claims are true then the assumption that economic agents continuously optimize is implausible.

These procedural questions on the realism of optimizing behavior are dismissed in standard textbook economics on several grounds. The defense's first argument is that rationality (in the optimization sense) is a fundamental generalization that is an obvious and self-evident fact of daily experiences (e.g. Robbins 1935). It is considered an indisputable postulate out of which flow a series of deductions concerning economic or allocative human activity. Second, Milton Friedman (1953b) argues that, from a methodological perspective, the realism of assumptions does not matter, and, therefore, questioning the realism of the optimization assumption is a pointless exercise. According to this view, the ultimate test of a theory is not the realism of its assumptions but, rather, whether its theoretical predictions are supported by empirical evidence. In this context standard economic models posit that agents make consumption, production, and portfolio decisions *as if* they optimize, and make predic-tions about responses of individuals to exogenous shocks, e.g. higher income levels, higher tulip prices. Provided the predictions of the theo-retical model are supported by empirical evidence, the theory passes the test of acceptance, and questioning the realism of assumptions is meth-odologically inappropriate. Friedman's position is widely adopted in mainstream economics textbooks.

The third justification, usually attributed to Alchian (1950), is "economic Darwinism": competition weeds out economic agents who do not comply with the dictates of the market. An auto producer who does not adopt the best technology to minimize costs will be driven out of the market by com-petitors; thus, the market imposes rationality. In the context of financial markets this argument is made forcefully by Eugene Fama (1965). Naïve investors who overpay for a share will face losses because the *smart money*, or optimizers, will exploit the price difference and benefit at their expense. The smart money will dump the overpriced stock on the hapless investors or short the stock by selling borrowed stocks in the forward market. This will bring price back to its intrinsic level and in the process wipe out the naïve investors. Thus, *market rationality* is sufficient to keep prices in line with the fundamentals even if not every investor makes optimal decisions.

Non-fundamentals and the information cascade

Suppose there are two neighboring Middle Eastern restaurants, Cedars and Olives, that are very similar in terms of apparent quality, menu, prices, decoration, and so forth, so that customers who crave a plate of stuffed grape leaves on a Saturday night are indifferent to choosing one restaurant over the other. Given these fundamentals, each customer on a given night is likely to choose a restaurant randomly, and diners are expected to be distributed evenly between the two restaurants. However, consider the following possible outcome. The first couple to arrive may choose Cedars by flipping a coin. However, what if the second couple is influenced by the first couple, who they see dining through the restaurant window ("Do they know something we do not? Could it be that Cedars is a better restaurant?"), and chooses Cedars? If newcomers also pay attention to the extraneous information of the observed choices of other diners then the outcome is a disproportionately larger demand for Cedars that cannot be explained by the fundamentals. Moreover, Olives, which is as good a restaurant, may realize losses and even go out of business.

This is an example of an *information cascade*, in which individual optimizing responses create a herd-like, group behavior that is, in the aggregate, suboptimal. All diners are making the best use of the information that is available, but the information fails to disseminate the fundamentals or the true value of the dining experience (Shiller 2005: 160). Extraneous factors such as information cascades may create unwarranted price hikes in the absence of changes in the fundamentals.

The fallacy of composition

Now assume that all consumers and firms are rational in an economist's narrow sense of optimization and that they do not pay attention to extraneous factors. There still remains the question of whether optimization at the individual level is compatible with optimization at the social level. If each individual maximizes utility is aggregate social welfare maximized as well?

When, in 2004, Oprah Winfrey gave everyone in her live audience (as many as 276 people) a brand new car, she must have improved the utilities of them all. After all, no one refused the gift. However, did the additional cars improve their social welfare as well? The question may be made transparent if one considers a hypothetical scenario where Oprah gives everyone in the nation a brand new car. Again, probably no one will refuse, but it is highly doubtful that the level of social welfare will rise. The outcome is likely to be endless traffic jams, parking-lot shortages, and worsening air pollution, all of which reduce the quality of life. This is an example of the *fallacy of composition*: what is true for individuals is not necessarily true for the community. Thus, it is necessary to recognize the possibility that, even if all individuals make optimizing decisions, the aggregate outcome may be suboptimal.

Another example of the fallacy of composition is bank runs. Bank runs are instances of depositors redeeming deposits due to concerns about the solvency of banks. From his or her own perspective each depositor is smart to minimize exposure to risk by getting in line to redeem deposits. However, the outcome is detrimental for the system as a whole because, due to maturity mismatch and the fractional-reserve system, not even solvent banks can withstand the demand for cash. As a result, individually optimal decisions can create a system-wide hazard and social-welfare deterioration.

Alternatives to rationality as optimization

Economists' conception of rational decision-making has come to be known as *rational choice theory* and has gained adherents in other social sciences, particularly in political science. It will be noted that the concept of rationality as optimization is quite different from what is meant by rationality in daily life. For economists rationality is a purely subjective choice that obeys the axioms of completeness, transitivity, and the IIA. For the public, however, rationality is synonymous with being reasonable, deliberative, thoughtful, or sensible, and using common sense, judgment, and wisdom. The two definitions may overlap but also include types of behavior that are excluded from the other. For instance, many people are likely to agree that smoking is an unwise decision, given its health hazards, and may consider it an "irrational" choice. From the economist's perspective, however, smoking is a perfectly rational choice if an individual prefers immediate satisfaction to long-term health, and his preference ordering is consistent in the sense that it obeys the transitivity and IIA axioms. Conversely, rationality as thoughtful deliberation may not imply optimization because, often, the three axioms may not be practicable in the face of intrinsic uncertainty about the future and cognitive limitations.

Unfortunately, distinctions between different notions of rationality are often lost in discussions among people who overlook these nuances, and the discourse deteriorates into the false dichotomy of "rational" vs. "irrational." This is a false dichotomy because the alternative to optimization is not necessarily "irrationality." It could simply be a different type of rationality. An increasing number of economists, psychologists, and decision theorists are indeed skeptical of the adequacy of the optimization postulate on the grounds that it is based on extreme and unrealistic assumptions.

There are two interrelated strands of inquiries in the search for alternatives to optimization. The first strand, mentioned above, argues that, given the limitations on cognitive abilities of human beings to gather and process information, and the intrinsic uncertainty of the future, forward-looking decisions are not always reducible to probability-based expected utility maximization. Decision problems are not always as well defined as the problems that face the traveling salesman or the casino player. However, skepticism of optimization does not mean that individuals are erratic, impulsive, unpredictable, inconsistent, or unreasonable, as the terms irrationality or non-rationality imply. According to Keynes (1936), as probability calculus is of little help in forward-looking investment decisions, investors follow conventions and rules of thumb in making decisions. Simon (1976) proposed to construct economic theory based on *bounded* or *procedural rationality* that focuses not on the goals but on the cognitive processes by which agents make their decisions.

Rather than identifying rationality with the optimal solution to an allocation problem, Simon defines rationality in terms of how agents who face a decision problem collect and process information, and reason and deliberate to arrive at a course of action. Substantive rationality answers the question of *what* the agent chooses on the assumption of optimizing behavior; procedural rationality answers the descriptive question of *how* the agent makes a choice and demonstrates that the very process of decision-making may lead the agent to a suboptimal but reasonable choice. Simon's (1976) alternative to optimizing behavior is *satisficing* behavior, or choosing the basket that meets the conditions of satisfying and sufficing. Much of this approach has its roots in psychological research, which has traditionally been kept out of economics, but which has been making inroads over the last three decades.

The second strand of inquiry challenges empirically the idea that individual preferences are always consistent. Behavioral economist Thaler's dinner party is an example (Thaler and Sunstein 2009). Thaler's guests were stuffing themselves with cashews before dinner. When Professor Thaler removed the nuts the guests thanked him for doing so because they were spoiling their appetites. It appeared that the guests, including economists committed to the optimization postulate, had inconsistent preferences. If they were optimizers either they should not be gorging themselves on the nuts or they should not be grateful for their confiscation.

Behavioral economists view optimizing behavior not as the untouchable core of the discipline but as a testable hypothesis, something that may be supported or refuted by experience. They design experiments to test whether people's choices violate the optimization hypothesis. One famous experiment is the *certainty effect* or the Allais paradox, named after the French economist Maurice Allais, who conducted it among academic economists in 1952.

Psychologist Daniel Kahneman (2011: 313) offers a simplified version of Allais' paradox. Consider the following two options. Option A: a 61 percent chance of winning $520,000; option B: a 63 percent chance of winning $500,000. Which one would you choose? In experiments people were more likely to choose option A, which offers a substantially larger prize at the cost of a small decline in the probability of winning. Next consider a second set of options. Option C: a 98 percent chance of winning $520,000; and option D: a 100 percent chance of winning $500,000. In this case subjects were more likely to choose option D over C. However, the choices of A and D constitute an inconsistent preference ordering. If the $20,000 prize differential dominates the two-percentage-point-lower chance of winning in deciding between A and B then, similarly, C should trump D. Moreover, the odds of winning $520,000 are even higher in the second set of options. Kahneman points out that, while this result is a paradox for economists committed to the notion that consistent preferences are the bedrock of decision-making, non-economists more easily recognize that people do not assign weights to outcomes strictly in terms of probabilities. When an outcome with certainty is available they are more likely to choose it, even if it is probabilistically less rewarding than the alternative option.

Allais' fellow economists ignored him in 1952, but contradictory preference orderings continued reappearing. Two more examples may illustrate the point. For the first example of a psychological bias that runs against the grain of consistent preference ranking consider the *framing effect*, i.e. that people's responses are sensitive to whether the same choice set is presented as a gain or loss—and people are more inclined to avoid losses than acquire gains. For instance, patients who are told that the probability of death in an elective surgery is 20 percent are less likely to choose the operation in comparison with patients who are told that the probability of survival is 80 percent (Tversky and Kahneman 1986). Under the optimization postulate there should not, on average, be a difference because patients are given identical information. The second example is the voting paradox, which refers to the question of why people vote in large numbers when they know that the impact of an individual vote is practically nil. The answer may lie in the impact of social norms, magical thinking (if I vote others will as well), or the categorical imperative (we would be worse off if *everyone* abstained from voting), all of which appear to lie outside the realm of economists' cost-benefit framework.

Jon Elster (2007: 215–30) offers a lengthy list of other examples of inconsistent preference ordering and reasons why they exist. Tversky and Kahneman summarized this line of research:

> How do people assess the probability of an uncertain event or the value of an uncertain quantity? . . . [P]eople rely on a limited number of heuristic principles which reduce the complex tasks of assigning probabilities and predicting values to simple judgmental operations. *In general, these heuristics are quite useful, but sometimes they lead to severe and systematic errors* [italics added].
>
> (1974: 1124)

The last sentence in this quote is highlighted because it suggests an environment that is quite different from the previously described world of optimizing agents who make only non-systematic errors.

The evolving field of experimental economics conducts laboratory experiments (often using undergraduate students as subjects) to test whether human subjects make choices in accordance with consistent preference orderings. Behavioral economics explains the findings that contradict optimization postulate on psychological, behavioral, or evolutionary foundations. In response, adherents to the principle of optimizing decision-making either seek ways to explain the seemingly anomalous results within the confines of utility maximization or discount them as trivial. Many mainstream economists dismiss the validity of these experiments by questioning the relevance of the artificial laboratory environment to real-world decision-making. Moreover, there is always the question of whether experiments can definitively invalidate the optimization postulate because the alleged inconsistency of preferences may be explained by agents' preferences changing or agents becoming better processors of information during the experiment.

Stabilizing and destabilizing speculation

The objective of the speculator is to make capital gains by making bets on the future direction of asset prices. If the speculator expects that the price of an asset will increase in the future, and this belief is not shared by the market (so that the asset is currently undervalued according to the speculator), then she would purchase the asset with her own or borrowed funds in anticipation of selling later at a higher price. Conversely, if the speculator believes that the price will fall then she can make a bet against the market by shorting the asset. If she is right she can turn a profit. This is, of course, a risky activity. If the price turns out to be different from the speculator's expectation losses may occur.

Speculators have been a much maligned group throughout history, stereotyped as greedy subjects of Mammon, manipulators and schemers who prey on hard-working, honest people. US presidents since Thomas Jefferson have warned against them and blamed them for various economic calamities. Franklin Roosevelt denounced in his 1934 State of the Union Address "those reckless speculators with their own or other people's money whose operations have injured the values of the farmers' crops and the savings of the poor."

In economics the debate over the merits or evils of speculation is not as rancorous. It revolves around the issues of whether speculation is *stabilizing* or *destabilizing*, and whether speculators perform an economically and socially useful function. The theoretical orientation of orthodox theory is to view market processes as solutions that mitigate allocation problems. Thus, it is not surprising that many orthodox economists believe that speculators play a beneficial role in markets.

Perhaps the most prominent of the alleged useful functions of speculation is the prevention of deviations of market price from the intrinsic price. The case for stabilizing speculation is related to the concepts of market rationality (Friedman 1953a; Fama 1965). Again suppose that there are two types of trader: sophisticated investors, or the smart money, who make full use of information; and naïve, non-optimizing investors who do not use information efficiently. Is it possible that the latter group's actions can create a sustained, positive deviation from the fundamental price leading to a bubble? Thanks to the sophisticated investors, this possibility can be disregarded. The sophisticated investors have a better idea of where the fundamental price lies, and when they observe that the asset is overpriced they exploit the profit opportunity by dumping their holdings of the stock on the naïve traders at the currently excessive price, or borrowing the security to sell in the forward market. The rising supply of the security brings the price back down to the fundamental level. Thus, speculation by smart money is stabilizing, and speculators perform the beneficial function of keeping the market price at the level warranted by the fundamentals. Speculation is, of course, a risky activity. If the price of the shorted asset did not decline as anticipated speculators would suffer losses. Thus, according to Friedman, their profit is a well deserved compensation for the risk they undertake.

Friedman (1953a) makes his case for stabilizing speculation on a priori grounds. It is based on deductive reasoning that flows from optimizing behavior. Destabilizing speculation that aggravates a divergence from the fundamental price is illogical or inconceivable because anyone who buys when a security is overpriced and sells when underpriced would be wiped out by the actions of smart money. Only the smart money can survive, and their survival attests to the fact that speculation cannot be destabilizing.

However, economic historians, on a posteriori grounds, are skeptical about the idea of stabilizing speculation, and many tend to dismiss it (e.g. Kindleberger 1993: 267). Based on historical experience and empirical evidence, historians contend that speculative behavior has been an integral component of deviations from the fundamental price and subsequent financial crises since the time of the three classic bubbles. There are multiple obstacles that stand in the way of sophisticated investors that may prevent them from carrying out stabilizing speculation. Institutional constraints on borrowing the asset may limit shorting. It is possible that there may be a relatively small number of smart-money investors; they may face financial limitations on their ability to hold on to their positions; and the costs and risks of shorting may be inordinately high. Lack of confidence in their assessment of the true fundamentals may hold sophisticated investors back from performing the stabilizing function. Under these conditions the convergence to the fundamental price through speculators' actions is not guaranteed. In fact, speculators may choose to buy into overvalued assets in anticipation of selling before the collapse of the bubble and thereby exacerbate the deviation from the fundamental price.

Key terms and concepts

Arbitrage
Bounded rationality
Certainty effect
Completeness axiom
Coupon
Coupon rate
Destabilizing speculation
Discount rate
Economic model
Endogenous variable
Exogenous variable
Expectational error
Expected utility maximization
Face value
Factors of production
Fallacy of composition
Fixed-income security
Flexible income security
Framing effect
Heuristic
Independence of irrelevant alternatives axiom (IIA)
Information cascade
Intrinsic uncertainty
Law of one price
Liquidity premium
Market capitalization
Market demand
Market rationality
Market supply
No-arbitrage condition
Optimization
Par value
Perfect competition
Present value
Primary market
Principal value
Probability distribution
Procedural rationality
Random variable
Rate of return
Rational bubble hypothesis
Rational choice theory
Rational expectations hypothesis

Risk
Risk premium
Safe interest rate
Satisficing
Secondary market
Smart money
Stabilizing speculation
Substantive rationality
Transitivity axiom
Underwriting
Yield to maturity

Endnotes

1 This condition would be satisfied if all agents had perfect information and perfect foresight. While this extreme condition is sufficient for the symmetric distribution of information, it is not necessary.
2 Consider the situation in which the last dollars spent on beer and bulbs yield 20 and 10 "utils" (fictional units of utility) respectively. Then the optimizing consumer would improve total utility by purchasing more beer and fewer bulbs. Given diminishing marginal utility, this action would reduce the gap between marginal utilities per dollar between the two goods and raise total utility. Suppose that the dollar transferred to an additional pint of beer adds 18 utils. Because the reduction in bulb purchases costs 10 utils the reallocation would raise total utility by 8. Assuming that goods are divisible, the transfer of spending from bulbs to beer should continue until the last dollars spent on the two goods produce the same amount of utility.
3 There are exceptions to this statement. In the case of inferior goods, as income increases the customer may switch from, say, hamburger to steak.
4 Expectations presumably are based on the current information set about the possible future states of the economy. The assumption of *no informational advantage* implies that there are no systematic differences between agents' information sets and expectation-formation procedures.
5 There are many different kinds of bonds, and this description does not strictly hold for all of them. For instance, issuers of no-coupon bonds do not make periodic payments but make a single payment of the par value upon maturity. Issuers of perpetuity bonds make coupon payments indefinitely, and the bonds have no maturity date.
6 If the inflation rate was non-zero then the appropriate discount rate would be the interest rate *minus* the inflation rate, or the *real* interest rate.
7 For the sake of simplicity, we assume that the discount rate does not change over time.
8 The arithmetic is more complicated with longer maturity bonds, but financial calculators simplify the computation.
9 Another factor that raises the risk of equity ownership is that, if the company goes bankrupt, bondholders, typically, are paid first from the sale of the company's assets. There are also tax considerations that may affect the choice between bonds and common stock.
10 Note that the present value of the income stream and, therefore, the price will be a finite figure only if the discounted expected dividends decline to zero as time goes to infinity.

11 I will consider the issue of "realism" of assumptions later in this chapter.
12 In this discussion we assumed that the correct economic model is the standard asset-pricing model. As is indicated repeatedly throughout the text, economists frequently disagree on what the correct model is. The rational expectations hypothesis is silent on the subject of the correct economic model. It is theory-neutral. It posits that the formation of expectations should be consistent with the predictions of the "relevant" theory without identifying the latter.
13 More sophisticated rational bubble patterns are conceivable. Blanchard and Watson (1982), for instance, suggest a more complex rational bubble and crash model. Suppose agents expect the bubble component to burst in the next period with some probability, and, in each successive period, this probability grows. The expected pay-off for holding the asset is then the average of the expected gain and loss of the next period weighted by the probabilities of inflation and implosion of the bubble respectively. Over time the probability of the bubble bursting rises (and that of inflation declines). At some point the pay-off turns negative and the bubble collapses.

References

Alchian, Armen. 1950. "Uncertainty, Evolution and Economic Theory." *Journal of Political Economy* 58: 211–21.

Blanchard, Olivier J. and Mark W. Watson. 1982. "Bubbles, Rational Expectations and Financial Markets." Pp. 295–315 in *Crises in the Economic and Financial Structure*, edited by Paul Wachtel. Lexington, MA: Lexington Books.

Browne, Thomas. 1658. *Hydriotaphia Urn Burial; Or, A Discourse of the Sepulchral Urns Lately Found in Norfolk.* eBooks@Adelaide. The University of Adelaide Library. https://ebooks.adelaide.edu.au/b/browne/thomas/hydriotaphia/

Elster, Jon. 2007. *Explaining Social Behavior: More Nuts and Bolts of Social Sciences.* Cambridge, NY: Cambridge University Press.

Fama, Eugene F. 1965. "The Behavior of Stock-market Prices." *The Journal of Business* 38 (1): 34–105.

Friedman, Milton. 1953a. "The Case for Flexible Exchange Rates." Pp. 157–203 in his *Essays in Positive Economics.* Chicago: University of Chicago Press.

Friedman, Milton. 1953b. "Methodology of Positive Economics." Pp. 3–43 in his *Essays in Positive Economics.* Chicago: University of Chicago Press.

Goldgar, Anne. 2007. *Tulipmania: Money, Honor, and Knowledge in the Dutch Golden Age.* Chicago: University of Chicago Press.

Kahneman, Daniel. 2011. *Thinking, Fast and Slow.* New York: Farrar, Straus, and Giroux.

Keynes, John Maynard. 1936. *The General Theory of Employment, Interest, and Money.* London: Macmillan.

Kindleberger, Charles P. 1993. *A Financial History of Western Europe, 2nd ed.* New York, Oxford: Oxford University Press.

Knight, Frank. 1984 [1921]. *Risk, Uncertainty and Profit.* Chicago: University of Chicago Press.

Meltzer, Allan H. 2002. *Rational and Irrational Bubbles.* Keynote Address for the Federal Reserve Bank of Chicago–World Bank Conference on Asset Price Bubbles, Chicago.

Robbins, Lionel. 1935. *An Essay on the Nature and Significance of Economic Science,* 2nd ed. London: Macmillan.

Shiller, Robert J. 2005. *Irrational Exuberance*, 2nd ed. New York: Currency Doubleday.

Simon, Herbert A. 1976. "From Substantive to Procedural Rationality." Pp. 139–48 in *Method and Appraisal in Economics*, edited by Spiro Latsis. New York: Cambridge University Press.

Stiglitz, Joseph E. 1990. "Symposium on Bubbles." *Journal of Economic Perspectives* 4 (2): 13–18.

Thaler, Richard H. and Cass R. Sunstein. 2009. *Nudge: Improving Decisions on Health, Wealth, and Happiness*. New York: Penguin Books.

Tirole, Jean. 1982. "On the Possibility of Speculation under Rational Expectations." *Econometrica* 50 (5): 1163–82.

Tversky, Amos and Daniel Kahneman. 1974. "Judgment under Uncertainty: Heuristics and Biases." *Science, New Series* 185 (4157): 1124–31.

Tversky, Amos and Daniel Kahneman. 1986. "Rational Choice and the Framing of Decisions." *The Journal of Business* 59 (4, Pt. 2): S251–S278.

6 Explaining asset-price bubbles and banking crises

In his *Memoirs of Extraordinary Popular Delusions and the Madness of Crowds* Scottish journalist Charles Mackay (2009 [1852]) describes tulip mania, the Mississippi Bubble, and the South Sea Bubble as collective delusions spread across all ranks of society. The same state of mind and herd mentality that tempted people to participate in witch hunts and apocalyptic fantasies, which are among the vignettes that Mackay portrays, was evident in the rush to buy assets with dreams of getting rich(er) overnight. Popular songs, allegorical prints, and sarcastic poems that proliferated at the peak and during the aftermath of these episodes also painted pictures of out-of-control greed and a populace devoid of common sense. While these descriptions are amusing and commonplace, they fall short of explaining why bubbles emerge. Their frequent embellishments also provide an easy foil for commentators who dispute the verisimilitude of the historical accounts. Between the two perceptions of the human condition, i.e. individual optimization under competitive conditions that rules out bubbles, and the collective frenzy that makes them ubiquitous, there is a diverse set of theories that acknowledge the existence of bubbles. These theories attempt either to reconcile bubbles with the canons of the standard economic theory or search for explanations based on alternative behavioral foundations or evolutionary capitalist market dynamics.

This chapter is an introduction to the theories of financial crises. It will focus mainly on asset-price bubbles and, to a lesser extent, on banking crises. I classify the competing hypotheses into five categories. First, the orthodox, fundamentals-based approach is characterized by optimizing agents who operate in perfectly competitive markets. Each economic agent is an independent decision maker, guided by the available information on the fundamentals. Consequently, the fundamental and market prices are identical, and the bubble is just an economic myth. The second category accepts the primacy of the fundamentals but recognizes the possibility of asset-price bubbles. Its explanation for bubbles is that government-policy interventions in the economy distort relative prices and create deviations from the fundamentals. The third category tweaks the orthodoxy. It retains the optimization postulate but recognizes bubbles and banking crises as possible outcomes of pervasive imperfections and frictions in the market. The fourth category replaces the optimization postulate with behavioral foundations of decision-making. Bubbles are outcomes of the interaction of non-optimizing decision-making with social and psychological dynamics. The fifth category focuses on institutional characteristics of capitalist economies and concludes that financial crises that feature manias and panics are endemic to the evolution of competition and the credit cycle in a loosely regulated financial sector. This chapter presents each approach and illustrates it in the context of the classical bubble episodes.

The criteria for this five-way classification draw from methodological questions on economic behavior, and market structures and dynamics. I chose these criteria because they permit relating the discussion of financial crises to larger debates in economic analysis.[1] The reader should be forewarned that, like a roadmap, a taxonomy offers a simplified way to traverse a complex landscape of competing theories. This comes at a cost. There are, at times, ambiguities or overlaps that blur the lines of delineation between the categories, as well as substantial differences of opinion within each category. I will make note of these secondary problems as they appear.

The fundamentals-based orthodoxy: bubble? What bubble?

The foundation of the fundamentals-based position on bubbles is that, when all or a sufficient number of agents make independent optimizing decisions in a perfectly competitive environment, price movements reflect only the changes in the fundamentals, and there is no distinction between the intrinsic price and the market price; they are identical. Therefore, a bubble cannot happen. Once the economic model rules out bubbles on a priori grounds the task for fundamentals-based analysis is to provide an explanation for the price phenomena that may look to others like a bubble. Economists take several routes in their search for this explanation: (a) trivialize the incident, (b) question the data, and (c) appeal to the fundamentals.

Trivialize the incident

In his interpretation of tulip mania Garber (1989, 1990, 2000) disregards historical accounts. First, he declares that tulip mania is a much embellished legend, initially propagated by moralistic pamphlets and then accepted as the truth after centuries of repetition in popular accounts and "around the campfires [of] . . . fledgling economists" (Garber 1989: 535). Morality tales were spread by what Garber (1989) calls the Dutch ruling "elite" or "oligarchy and its magistrates," who attempted to dissuade people from what they considered to be "unsafe" speculative areas of economic activity, and promote "safe" activities, i.e. those regulated by public authorities. Goldgar's (2007) archival study of tulip mania also observes that exaggeration was commonplace in the popular accounts of tulip mania. However, a preponderance of historical evidence indicates that something did happen, and especially perplexing is the rise and fall of the common-bulb forward prices.

Second, Garber (1989) dismisses tulip mania as a trifling incident because he considers that the speculative bulb market was driven by inebriated, fatalistic traders who bought and sold contracts in taverns while bubonic plague ravaged the population. The historical accuracy of Garber's characterization of florists as amateur traders is disputable. It is true that large merchants did not trade in the speculative bulb market, but florists were not necessarily amateurs whose faculties were impeded by wine and beer; many were middle-class professionals and artisans with strong informational networks (Goldgar 2007). Further, during the seventeenth and eighteenth centuries it was common practice for taverns and inns to function as locations of business, and the bulb trade was a formalized activity with well defined rules (Dash 1999; Goldgar 2007).

Third, Garber (1989) downplays the significance of tulip mania because it did not create major economic disruption, and, therefore, is of little consequence. It is indeed true that asset-price boom-bust cycles sometimes leave the economy at large intact. At other times the impact can be catastrophic. Regardless of the scope of the subsequent economic troubles, however, most economists are unlikely to ignore these episodes because they are invaluable "natural" experiments and offer opportunities to learn about the economy, which a researcher can hardly afford to overlook.

Question the data

The second route that economists take to shed doubt on the bubble interpretation is to question the accuracy or interpretation of the price record. Garber (1989) provides price series on various bulbs in an attempt to demonstrate that there were, in fact, no significant changes in the bulb prices (with the exception of the astonishing increase in ordinary-bulb prices in December 1636–January 1637). Cochrane (2001) states that installment-based sales of Mississippi Company shares in the primary market make interpretation of share prices problematic. Subscribers made a non-refundable down payment and then paid the remainder in installments. Thus, what they were buying were not shares but options on shares; they had the choice of not exercising their option if the market soured.

Yet another version of the argument disputes whether the observed prices were really the market prices. Velde (2009) agrees that the Mississippi shares were overvalued but that this was not a bubble because observed prices were artificial prices created via various measures, including lending against the security of shares, support pricing, and price-fixing.

Ultimately, prices reflected Law's manipulations, not the market forces. Similarly, Neal (1990) discounts the substantial increase in the South Sea stock price during the summer of 1720 because the company's books were closed during the summer, and the recorded prices were forward prices that were not comparable to spot prices recorded before and after the summer. (However, he does not dispute that the rest of the episode was a bubble; see below.)

Appeal to the fundamentals

According to fundamentals-based analyses, bubble-shaped price behavior is ultimately explainable by changes in the fundamentals. Again there are several distinct lines of arguments. Garber (1989) draws attention to the fact that it takes time for farm products such as tulip bulbs to reproduce, and the rising price is simply an outcome of lagging supply. Over time relative scarcity and price of the new varietal bulbs are expected to decline due either to the rising rate of reproduction or availability of substitutes. In support of this hypothesis Garber gives examples of temporary hikes in the prices of flowers such as hyacinths and tulips, observed in later periods in the European markets, which were eventually mitigated as cultivators expanded their supply or the fashion changed.

The more common line of argument with regard to price behavior starts with the standard asset-valuation formula. The variable that has attracted the most attention is the expected cash flow. Garber (1990, 2000) challenges the view that the Mississippi and the South Sea stocks were overpriced. He argues that the increase in the Mississippi share price is not surprising in view of investors observing John Law's early successes in founding the General Bank, revitalizing the French economy, carrying out fiscal reform and financial restoration, creating the largest holding company through mergers, and retaining the support of the politically powerful. Investors were confident, based on available information, that the company's commercial ventures would be successful and yield high returns. In anticipation of rising profits they rushed to purchase shares.

In the case of the South Sea Company the successful initial conversion of public debt to equity and parliamentary support for the company improved its prospects and increased the demand for shares. The fact that the performance of neither company was successful does not mean that shareholder actions were disconnected from the fundamentals, as investors were basing their decisions on the best information that was available when decisions were being made: the price was right, *given the available information at the time.*[2] Ultimately, the Mississippi and South Sea companies were ventures that went awry, but these are ordinary occurrences in a market economy, and one should not assign a bubble interpretation to an enterprise merely because it initially looked highly promising but eventually folded. Asserting that this was a bubble, according to this view, is simply second-guessing and passing judgment on investor decisions with the luxury of hindsight.

Several other researchers move beyond asserting the plausibility of expected high profitability and search for evidence that supports the thesis that investor optimism was, indeed, justified. Frehen, Goetzmann, and Rouwenhorst (2013) discuss three financial innovations (government debt-equity swap, risk-sharing via joint-stock companies, and joint-stock companies operating outside their charters) and the growth of the Atlantic trade as developments that raised profit prospects and fueled investor optimism. Comparison of the South Sea, (British) Royal African, the Dutch West Indies, (British) Old East Indies, and the Dutch East Indies companies' share prices indicate that the first three, which engaged in occidental trade, also experienced stock-price booms in the summer of 1720. The share prices of the two oriental trade companies, however, were basically flat. The authors interpret this finding as a sign of the prospect of high profits related to the Atlantic triangular trade. Paul (2011) argues that the hopes of the South Sea Company shareholders were hardly misplaced because the company actually had very good profit prospects from trading goods and slaves and establishing a colony. She further states that the company was financially viable and that it actively engaged in the profitable transatlantic slave trade from 1713 to 1739. However, Paul's data do not explain why, in the entire history of the company, the singular share-price boom and bust happened in 1720, when the slave trade had halted due to rising hostilities with the Spanish.

The argument that share prices accurately reflected the available information on the profit prospects of the Mississippi and South Sea companies remains contentious. Historical accounts of bubbles have usually maintained that the commercial activities of these companies were not profitable and that their only steady source of income, i.e. interest payments on government debt, did not justify the escalation of their share prices (Kindleberger and Aliber 2011). According to Chancellor (2000: 94), prior to the peak of the South Sea share price it was common knowledge that shares were overpriced. Therefore, continued purchases of the share contradict economists' notion of fundamentals-driven behavior. Dale *et al.* (2005) observe that South Sea Company subscription receipts and shares were very close substitutes, and, therefore, movements of their prices must have been parallel. Statistical analysis of the price data shows, however, that prices paid for the later subscriptions of South Sea stock were far in excess of the value of the underlying stock and that this differential widened over time. The widening gap, again, contradicts the predictions of fundamentals-based analysis.

Other fundamentals of the share price are in the denominator terms on the right-hand side of the standard share price-equation (5.8). Neal

(1990: 111) attributes the initial surge in the South Sea share price, in part, to bondholders' desire to exchange cumbersome, illiquid government debt for private shares that could be cashed easily. It is also possible that share-holders may have reasoned they had a better chance to protect their wealth against a unilateral government default if the debt were consolidated into a single entity as opposed to being distributed among thousands. Thus, claims on bonds via ownership of company stock may have been viewed as less risky and increased the demand for shares. However, the role of the liquidity and risk premiums was limited to triggering the early interest in the stock. It cannot account for the subsequent price boom.

The theory should explain the collapse of the price as well as its rise. The fundamentals-based position again searches for reasons for the crash in the asset-pricing equation. One obvious candidate is "bad news," or the arrival of unfavorable new information on expected profits. The news of John Law's fall from power, for instance, could have been one example of bad news that deflated the optimism of investors in the Mississippi Company and consequently drove the stock price down (Garber 2000). In the case of the South Sea Bubble, according to Neal (1990), the bad news was the liquidity shortage, precipitated exogenously by foreign investors who were channeling their funds from London to elsewhere in Europe. As liquidity disappeared and banks reduced the extension of credit to replenish their reserves, demand for shares financed by bank loans could not be maintained.

The most frequently mentioned source of bad news, however, is the onset of a recession. A recession may influence stock prices through two channels. First, contraction of economic activity lowers profitability of companies and, thus, the dividend-income flow. The second channel operates through liquidity and risk premiums. When economic activity contracts, and the likelihood of defaults and bankruptcies rises, lending institutions, such as banks, limit credit extension to protect themselves. Liquidity and risk premiums rise, and security prices drop. If investors have financed security purchases by borrowing they may be forced to sell their assets to meet their debt obligations and thereby exacerbate the price decline.

All economists agree that scarcity of liquidity and credit, difficulty in repaying loans drawn to purchase assets, and the consequent pressure to sell assets are common features of the crash stage of bubbles. What distin-guish different schools are their views on the source of the liquidity short-age. Fundamentals-based approaches argue that forces initiated by exogenous factors, such as a recession or capital outflow, explain the liquidity shortage and the subsequent security-price decline. Others are more likely to argue that the liquidity shortage is the outcome of internal tensions of a bubble that force lenders, at some stage, to become more risk averse and to restrict credit. This distinction will be drawn more sharply later in this chapter.

Broadening the fundamentals, or an "intrinsic bubble"

Occasionally, the economist may be at a loss to identify the fundamentals of bubble-like behavior. Meltzer (2002), a prominent proponent of the fundamentals-based approach, counsels that the seemingly anomalous price movements merely signal economists' failure to notice the subtle fundamental factors. If the fundamentals are not immediately identifiable then the economist's task is to search for and uncover them rather than to resort to explanations that lie outside "legitimate" orthodox analysis. Once the hidden fundamentals are uncovered they will provide a full explanation of price formation, and economics will be free of the bubble nonsense. The *intrinsic bubble theory* is a step in this research direction.

Intrinsic-bubble theorists focus specifically on overreactions of investors to changes in the fundamentals. According to Froot and Obstfeld's (1991) version of the theory, investors overreact to dividend news, which causes demand and the price to increase more than is warranted by the new information. The overreaction, in turn, is the source of the deviation from the fundamental price. A negative bubble is equally possible when investors overreact to adverse news. Froot and Obstfeld offer some evidence from the twentieth-century US stock market to support the hypothesis that prices respond in a non-linear way to dividends, but they do not discuss why investors would behave in this fashion.

Zeira (1999) explains the overreaction in terms of informational dynamics. Consider an economy that undergoes a massive transformation, such as the introduction of a new technology. Examples may include the proliferation of the financial joint-stock companies in Britain in 1720, debt-equity swap on an unprecedented scale, the introduction of the railroads during the 1830s, and the launch of the internet in the 1990s. During such periods of rapid technological change investors may not have adequate knowledge of the limits of the market or profitability. Expectations of market expansion and profit growth are updated steadily as the most recent favorable information flows in. Although it is commonly known that markets cannot expand indefinitely and that growth eventually slows down, investors cannot ascertain the timing of the slowdown due to the lack of adequate knowledge on the limits of the market. As investors can recognize the slowdown only with a delay, the momentum of their expectations leads to prices overshooting the fundamentals during the slowdown. Only when the correct information on market capacity and declining dividend growth reaches investors do they realize that they had overestimated the price of the stock and readjust expectations downward. Once the dust settles and they dump the overvalued stock the price returns to its fundamental value. In this case we observe a correction of the market price. Zeira (1999) characterizes his approach as one that expands the scope of the fundamentals, and, therefore, the intrinsic-bubble explanation of a deviation from the fundamental value is perfectly consistent with the orthodoxy. Neal (1990) attaches the intrinsic-bubble interpretation to the early (February to mid May 1720) climb of the South Sea share price, when investors could not assess the fundamentals correctly in the midst of the massive privatization of government debt.

Assessing overvaluation

If the fundamental price is not directly observable how can one know whether the market price has deviated from the fundamental price? This question compelled economists to devise empirical measures of over- and undervaluation of asset prices. The conventional *price-earnings (P/E) ratio*, which is the market value of the share divided by earnings per share, is one possible metric. When the P/E ratio hovers substantially above its "historical norms," the share is often considered overvalued. The short-coming of this interpretation is that it is based on past values of earnings, and past performance may not be a good indicator of future profitability. Past earnings may become outdated very quickly, especially during periods when a "new economy" emerges, characterized by the rapid transformation of technology, organization of production, and growing profit opportunities. If past values fail to predict future prices then the P/E ratio relative to historical norms will fall short of settling the dispute over the possibility of overvaluation.

The alternative way to use this metric is to ask whether the current P/E ratio is "reasonable" under "plausible" projections regarding the expected profitability and discount rates over a "reasonable" time horizon. In one application of this approach to the value of Mississippi Company shares Velde (2009) noted that John Law promised in December 1719 a dividend of 200L per share when the market price was approximately 9,000L, which meant an implied P/E ratio of 45. Velde notes that the 200L dividend did not justify the observed share price. Based on his estimates of the expected revenue stream of the company, Velde projects that the share price should have been around 1,650L to 2,130L, or about 20 percent of its peak value. Thus, the Mississippi Company share price was overvalued by a factor of about five (again, Velde viewed the discrepancy as an outcome of Law's market "management" rather than as a bubble).

The government did it: policy-induced distortions

The Austrian school of economics, led in the twentieth century by Ludwig von Mises and Friedrich Hayek, also trusts the power of the market to set prices correctly, but does not rule out asset-price bubbles. It views bubbles as outcomes of distortions created by the extraneous interference of political power and monetary authority in the market system. This perspective is the foundation of libertarian economic thought that advocates leaving markets to their own devices to ensure that prices are determined by the fundamentals, and banishing government interventions in the economy to prevent distortions of market outcomes.

The core of the Austrian objections to government interference in the economy is that it distorts relative prices. The most important relative price in this context is the interest rate. The interest rate is the price at which surplus units loan funds to deficit units, and fluctuations in the interest rate are the mechanism that ensures the quantities of loanable funds supplied and demanded are matched. If, for some reason, savers decide to postpone consumption and create an excess of savings then competition among the savers who seek borrowers lowers the interest rate. At lower interest rates firms become willing to borrow to invest in fixed capital and expand their capacity, and homebuyers become more willing to sign mortgage contracts. Fluctuations in the interest rate keep the supply of demand for funds in balance.

The Austrian economic model posits that there are two types of goods produced in the economy: final-consumption goods, e.g. shoes, autos, dental services purchased by consumers, and capital goods, e.g. machinery, equipment, buildings purchased by firms. The latter are used in the production of consumption goods. In response to the lower interest rate described above fewer consumption goods and more capital goods will be produced—an outcome that is perfectly consistent with households' changing preferences. With growth in the capital-goods sector production becomes more future-oriented, productivity increases, and genuine economic growth follows.

However, when the cost of borrowing declines artificially for reasons unrelated to the fundamentals problems emerge. The source of the artificial decline in the rate of interest is related to the expansion of money and credit, either directly by the central bank or by commercial banks under the fractional-reserve system. Credit expansion creates the illusion of greater availability of savings or loanable funds, lowers the interest rate, and produces an unnatural, unwarranted boom in the capital-goods-producing sector. The lower interest rate translates to higher production of capital goods—machines and equipment, as well as residential and non-residential buildings.

Because consumer preferences are unchanged and production of capital goods expands without a corresponding reduction in consumer goods temporary overemployment occurs. The Austrian school calls the expansion in the capital-goods industries *malinvestment* because it is wasteful spending, resulting from distorted interest rates that are not warranted by households' saving behavior. The rapid growth in the number of housing subdivisions in the 1990s and early 2000s that were eventually abandoned, uncompleted, or torn down is, according to this approach, an example of malinvestment caused by the Federal Reserve keeping interest rates very low.

The false boom in the capital-goods sector is unsustainable because households' preferences between consumption and saving have not changed. Too many capital goods are produced. The artificial boom eventually comes crashing down as the newly produced buildings, machinery, and equipment remain unsold or idle, waiting to be liquidated. Firms with stocks of wasteful capital goods may go bankrupt, and a recession ensues. The Austrian school's advice to policymakers at this stage is to refrain from intervening in the economy to alleviate the downturn because the recession, bankruptcies, and foreclosures are socially desirable processes that will cleanse the system of past errors, distortions, and unprofitable ventures.

According to the Austrian-school economists, the increase in stock prices and bubbles are by-products of artificially low interest rates and credit abundance. The stock market becomes buoyant because the artificial boom is driven by the expansion of capital-goods industries. Shares are certificates of ownership of capital-goods industries, and their prices increase with the rise in demand for capital goods. Extension of credit for the purchase of securities drives security prices higher. However, investors and speculators are not to blame for the bubble; they are merely economic agents who respond to the perverse incentives created elsewhere. Government institutions should be held responsible for the reckless creation of more credit and money.

French (2009) applies this argument to the classic bubbles. He reasons that in the case of tulip mania the inflow of specie to the United Provinces from the rest of Europe had expanded sharply through both trade and piracy. The Bank of Amsterdam issued paper money against deposits of coins and bullion, and the money supply expanded in excess of what was needed to perform transactions—by 42 percent in 1636 alone. The surplus of money stimulated speculative activity in the bulb trade, which eventually created the bubble. But the postulated link between monetary expansion and the bulb price in this case is precarious, as there was no commensurate increase in the prices of other assets. Moreover, the Bank of Amsterdam was solely a deposit bank, with a reserve ratio of 100 percent. Credit in the bulb market was extended personally by the sellers, not by the banks. The relationship between money and credit expansion and equity prices is more readily evident in the Mississippi and South Sea episodes. French interprets each episode as a causal chain connecting an excessive quantity of money and credit to speculation and bubbles. The issue of virtually unlimited banknotes by the Royal Bank contributed to the Mississippi Bubble, and the emergence of modern fractional-reserve banking and the expansion of bank loans at the turn of the eighteenth century in London facilitated the South Sea Bubble.

The close link between money and credit expansion and speculative booms is acknowledged by many economists. After all, buyers' ability to leverage their purchases and bid up prices depends on their access to funds. What is controversial is the direction of the causal link between the two variables. Not all economists subscribe to the Austrian view that expansion of money and credit causes speculation. While all bubbles are associated with the expansion of money and credit, the reverse is not true; the 39 percent increase in the money stock in the Dutch provinces in 1639, for instance, did not create a repetition of the mania. The alternative interpretation (to be discussed later) of the correlation between credit and asset prices reverses the direction of causality and views the growth in money and credit supply as a passive factor that responds to speculative demand. Investors and speculators demand more credit to purchase securities and banks merely increase loans to accommodate the rising demand for credit.

Finally, it is worthwhile drawing attention to the similarities between the fundamentals-based approach and the views of the Austrian school. Both are cynical about government-policy interventions and confident about markets' ability to "get the price right," or set the price at a level that fully reflects the intrinsic value of the asset. The fundamentals-based approach generally does not concur with the Austrian theory of the business cycle or the latter's views on the appropriate conduct of monetary policy in the face of a recession. It accepts that excessive money and credit expansion as well as other policy interventions influence the decisions of economic agents and affect prices and market outcomes adversely, but discounts the bubble rhetoric. These factors are incorporated into the right-hand side of the asset-price-determination equation as determinants of the present value of income streams, and the intrinsic value of the security.

Market frictions and imperfections

Within mainstream economic theory there is a considerable breadth of theoretical diversity including deviations from the fundamentals-based approach. Nonetheless, economists are very reluctant to surrender the principle of optimization as it is too central an organizing framework of model building. Most would probably agree with Ben Bernanke's (1983: 258) sentiment that, "I do not deny the possible importance of irrationality [viz. non-optimizing behavior] in economic life; however, it seems that the best research strategy is to push the rationality postulate as far as it will go." Economists find it more tolerable to jettison the postulate of the perfectly competitive market. The consequences of markets with imperfections or frictions, e.g. the failure of perfect-competition assumptions or the presence of spillover effects, have featured in economic analysis since the 1930s.

The rational bubble, presented in the last chapter, offers a convenient organizing framework to illustrate how bubbles may arise in the presence of optimizing behavior and market imperfections. The rational bubble formalizes the possibility of a bubble under rational expectations, but the source of the bubble component of the price in Equation 5.9 is hardly explicable in the context of optimizing behavior in perfectly competitive markets. The market-imperfections argument offers a way to explain the bubble component by appealing to endemic frictions in the market that may cause even sophisticated investors to base their decisions on extraneous factors. Individual optimizing actions may then initiate deviations from the fundamental price, add momentum to a deviation and transform it to a bubble, or prevent corrective forces from mitigating deviations from the fundamental price. Below I give several examples of market imperfections and their contributions to bubble formation. Subsequent chapters will provide more examples.

Extrinsic bubble

One source of uncertainty about the price is the future state of the fundamentals. However, the market is a social system, and if extrinsic factors, such as the behavior of rivals and their optimism or fear, are commonly believed to influence prices then prices may change for reasons that are unrelated to the fundamentals. Such extrinsic beliefs are called *sunspots*. These extraneous factors are an additional source of uncertainty and price volatility. For instance, if an optimizing investor believes that her competitors' level of optimism is relevant to the future price movements her forecast of the future will rely, in part, on variables that are unrelated to the fundamentals but seemingly informative about her competitors' sentiments.

These beliefs, when widely shared, are self-fulfilling and, therefore, may create a cumulative rise (or fall) from the intrinsic price. Such a deviation, known as an *extrinsic bubble*, may underlie the bubble component in the rational-bubble model given by Equation 5.9. An example of the extrinsic-bubble model would be the attribution of stock-price increases to investors' belief that high prices would prevail because political power in London and Paris in 1719 and 1720 was invested in markets. The literature on the extrinsic-bubble model is theoretical, and it is suggested that it may have some explanatory power for the classical bubbles (Azariadis 1981; Dale *et al.* 2005).

Heterogeneous investors and short-sale constraints

There is a wide class of bubble models based on heterogeneous investors operating in an environment in which market frictions impose constraints on arbitrage or short selling. These models contest Fama's (1965) argument that the existence of smart-money investors ensures the correction of deviations and reversion to the intrinsic price. Not only may the smart money fail to correct deviations it may contribute to the growth of the bubble. Consider a situation in which two types of investors hold different beliefs about asset prices. The first group is the smart money, composed of sophisticated traders who have better access to information (perhaps they are insiders) and superior means of processing this information. They make investment decisions optimally in accordance with the classic asset pricing formula. In the second group are the unsophisticated *noise traders*, who do not use all of the available information, do not have the means to process information optimally, or rely on extraneous factors, such as rumor, instinct, or arbitrary signals; they are not optimizers. Is it possible that the noise investors' excessive optimism or pessimism can push the security price persistently away from what is justified by the fundamentals?

As mentioned in the previous chapter, the standard theory predicts that, when investors are heterogeneous in the sense described above, market rationality will prevail in the wake of stabilizing speculation. An upward deviation from the fundamental price would be corrected by the smart money via short selling. Short sellers borrow the overpriced security and sell it in the futures market to the naïve investors, who are willing to overpay. The difference between the forward price and the spot price at the time the forward contact is settled, net of borrowing costs, is the gain (or loss) of the short seller. Provided there are plenty of short sellers who have access to funds so that they can hold on to short positions as long as is necessary, the excess supply of the security will bring the price back down to its intrinsic value.

However, market imperfections that limit short selling may prevent price corrections. Schleifer and Summers (1990) list several types of risk that can curb the enthusiasm of the smart money. The first is the *fundamental risk*. If the market rises and the fundamental value of the stock turns out to be higher than the short seller's expected future spot price then the shorter will suffer losses. The presence of the fundamental risk may keep short sellers' bets against the naïve investors in check. The second type of risk the shorter faces is the *noise trader risk*, which refers to the possibility of the persistence of large numbers of aggressive noise traders who prevent the spot price from declining on the date the short contract clears. The third type of risk is the *synchronization risk* (Abreau and Brunnermeier 2002). In the absence of a synchronized effort the corrective action of a single shorter may be insufficient to reverse the price deviation. Not knowing with certainty when other sophisticated investors will attack the bubble, the individual short seller may refrain from betting against overvaluation. In response to the noise trader and synchronization-risk concerns it may be argued that a deviation cannot persist forever, and convergence to the fundamental value will ultimately be attained. In the event that convergence takes longer than anticipated a smart-money investor will hold on to her position by renewing her bet and eventually collect the reward. Her ability to take that route, however, may be circumscribed by the rising cost of borrowing as she renews her loans. If the capital market is imperfect the shorter may incur restrictions on borrowing or higher periodic borrowing fees during the contract period, which can increase substantially if the price correction is delayed.

Moreover, in view of these obstacles, the smart money may opt to *ride the bubble* rather than to attack it. The motivation to take advantage of naïve investors is another explanation of the bubble component of the rational-bubble model. Sophisticated investors may know that the asset is overvalued, but, in weighing the costs and risks of short selling against the capital gains that can be earned by participating in the bubble, they may choose to buy into the market, with plans to unload their holdings and get out before the bubble bursts. Consequently, they push the price even higher. If their timing is right and they can bail out before the crash they make profits at the expense of the naïve traders, or the "greater fools," who are caught with depreciated assets in their portfolio when the price plummets. An example of bubble riding took place during what Neal (1990) describes as the second phase of the South Sea Bubble. Dutch investors recognized that price manipulations by Blunt and his partners would keep the price rising. They contributed to the price growth by buying South Sea shares in mid May. Shortly after, in June 1720, they sold the shares at a considerable capital gain.

Temin and Voth (2004) also offer evidence for bubble riding from the trading record of Hoare's Bank, a financial institution that invested in South Sea shares on its own account while making loans to its customers against the collateral of the South Sea stock. The authors maintain that Hoare's did not have access to privileged information through its customers or any other means. However, the bank discontinued extending credit to customers against the stock's collateral before the peak of the boom, which suggests that Hoare's Bank recognized that shares were overvalued and expected the value of the collateral to decline. Further, despite the acknowledged overvaluation, Hoare's continued to purchase South Sea shares until the peak of the boom, only to liquidate its positions at a substantial profit shortly after the price started to decline. Temin and Voth attribute Hoare's decision to ride the bubble through the peak either to the naïveté of unsophisticated investors or the low likelihood of massive sales by sophisticated investors.

Another example of a departure from perfectly competitive market assumptions is the behavior of misinformed outsiders whose beliefs differed from those of insiders during tulip mania. According to Thompson (2007), several prominent Dutch bulb traders, who had contacts in parliament, had signed forward contracts with the growers for bulbs to be delivered in the spring of 1637. They had planned to sell the bulbs to German princes who were building new castles. When these prospective sales fell through due to the unexpected defeat of the German allies in the Thirty Years' War and the German peasant revolts the traders pressured the

Dutch parliament to convert the original purchase contracts signed after October 30, 1636, to call options at 0 percent of the contracted price so that they could be freed from their obligations to the growers. Unsurprisingly, the growers objected.

The conflict between the traders and growers, as well as the traders' strong alliance with parliamentarians, was public knowledge by late November 1636. Throughout December 1636 and January 1637 florists, believing that the traders would win in the end and potential losses would be limited to the cost of options that were priced as low as 0 percent, jumped into the market. Bulb forward contracts signed after the October 30 cut-off date continued to be traded in the market, with prices rising at every sale. The astronomical prices that buyers paid were in line with optimizing behavior because there was no downside to the trade. Buyers experienced little risk because they did not make any down payments and stood to profit if they could sell contracts to other parties at higher prices. They could ignore the possibility of a lack of buyers because they believed the contracts were call options priced at 0 percent of the value of the contract.

According to Thompson (2007), the growers announced on February 24, 1637, that they would settle forward contracts at 0–10 percent of their price as a compromise to traders and their political allies, the exact value to be determined later by the legislature and courts. Unfortunately for the final holders of purchase contracts, the cut-off date was set as November 30 instead of October 30. Thompson suggests that the final cut-off date was known by privileged traders who had access to insider information, but not by outsiders. Thus, the insiders were able to sell the contracts they signed in November to the unsuspecting, misinformed outsiders, who believed that they were effectively purchasing zero-cost call-option contracts. The misinformed outsiders' purchases, which were perfectly consistent optimal responses to the perceived fundamentals, created the alleged tulip mania.

The validity of Thompson's (2007) historical account is a matter of debate for historians to sort out. For the present purposes the argument is interesting because it offers an illustration of economists' reasoning related to how deficient information among optimizing buyers may create and sustain a price deviation. It also calls attention to the possibility that economic and political insiders may shift their losses to outsiders, and perhaps even make profits at the expense of the latter.

Asymmetric information and bank runs

Bank runs were mentioned in Chapter 5 as an example of the fallacy of composition. Even when banks are solvent a generalized loss of confidence in the banking system generates a run on banks by depositors, banknote holders, and other short-term lenders to banks. Due to the fractional-reserve system and the maturity mismatch of assets and lia-bilities even solvent banks will not have sufficient liquidity to meet the demand to redeem deposits, banknotes, and short-term debt. The options of borrowing funds from other institutions or liquidating assets are also limited in a generalized banking panic. From the perspective of an econ-omist it is paradoxical that while a bank run is an optimal response indi-vidually for those who made loans to the bank it is impossible for all of them to withdraw their money, and their collective action produces the suboptimal outcome of threatening the entire banking system.

J. P. Morgan said in the midst of the banking panic of 1907, "If people will keep their money in the banks, everything will be all right" (Bruner and Carr 2007: 100–1). George Bailey made the same appeal to little avail in *It's a Wonderful Life*. The theoretically interesting question is, "Why would people who are supposedly fundamentals-driven optimizers not follow Morgan's advice but, instead, panic and hurt themselves as well as the banking system?" One line of reasoning underscores how market imperfections disconnect individual agents' optimizing actions from the fundamentals and create socially suboptimal outcomes. Two of the best known explanations of this type are by Diamond and Dybvig (1983) and Calomiris and Gorton (1991).

According to Diamond and Dybvig's (1983) *random-withdrawal hypoth-esis*, banks offer their depositors an insurance against the risk of unex-pected expenditures in the future. Deposits can be liquidated at any time at par value, although this is not true for less liquid bank assets. Second, and here is a market imperfection, markets are incomplete in the sense that there is no market in which holders of bank debt[3] can sell these obligations and insure themselves against the likelihood of a bank failure. The third point of the model is that deposit withdrawals cannot be made simultaneously by all customers. They must get in line and redeem on a first-come-first-served basis rather than through a pro-rata distribution. Under these circumstances the concerns of bank-debt holders about others redeeming their debt, and the incentive to avoid being the last one in the line, create a mass attack on the bank. The con-sequent panic is a self-fulfilling outcome, as debt holders' misgivings are sufficient to start a bank run. To explain how such beliefs emerge economists have examined the institutional structure of the banking system. I will illustrate this point in Chapter 8 in the context of the US experience.

Calomiris and Gorton (1991) offer an alternative liquidity-crisis model that emphasizes *asymmetric information* between bankers and bank-debt holders regarding the performance of the bank's asset portfolio. According to this argument, banks produce business and household loans. Provided that the bank originates and holds loans, the bank's product is non-marketable; there is no "price" for the bank's loan portfolio that signals information to the general public about the quality and performance of the bank's assets. Only the bank managers, by virtue of their position, can follow the portfolio closely over time. Thus, one of the standard assumptions of perfect competition, that information is distributed symmetrically among agents, is violated. Managers have better information on the returns and risks of bank loans than do bank-debt holders, and the latter are fully aware of this fact. In this context problems arise when bank-debt holders receive unfavorable news, such as the onset of a recession or rising defaults, and reassess the risks faced by the banks. Given their incomplete information set, they are not able to judge which banks have precarious portfolios and whether risks faced by their own bank have also risen. To minimize their own risk exposure bank-debt holders' optimal action is to cash in their deposits and banknotes or not to roll over their short-term debt. Consequently, what was probably a small tremor, such as a normal recession, may turn into a shockwave as bank-debt holders simultaneously attempt to redeem their holdings.

The random-withdrawal and asymmetric-information hypotheses have different policy implications. On the one hand, if liquidity crises result from random withdrawal then, in the absence of private bank-debt insurance markets, government-sponsored deposit insurance, such as the Federal Deposit Insurance Corporation, may be a solution to the banking crisis. Another solution would be to create a semi-public lender of last resort, such as the central bank, to which banks can turn to borrow reserves. Pro-rata redemption of the deposits and notes would also alleviate the bank run.

The asymmetric-information explanation of bank runs casts doubt on the appropriateness of government-sponsored deposit insurance and a semi-public lender of last resort as solutions to bank runs. The potential of a banking panic acts as a monitoring device over bankers. Bank managers who are cognizant of the possibility of panics have the incentive to make prudent loan decisions, better manage risk, and create private institutions to monitor each other and facilitate interbank reserve loans during difficult times. Deposit insurance and the lender of last resort could be harmful because they remove market discipline for bankers and create *moral hazard* by incentivizing banks to engage in high-risk, high-return lending practices as the cost of failure is now passed on to another party. Moreover, banks may not use the lender-of-last-resort facility in times of need. If extension of these loans is public information then recourse to them would signal to the depositors and note holders that the bank is in trouble and, perhaps, intensify the run. The appropriate solution, according to the asymmetric-information diagnosis, is to create market institutions to disseminate information, share the bank risk, and insure bank debt. One example of such institutions is the clearing houses, commonplace after the 1850s in the US (discussed in Chapter 8). Most economists are skeptical, however, about the effectiveness of such private institutions in the midst of a major crisis.

The behavioralist approach

According to the standard asset-pricing theory, the smart money prevents the occurrence of bubbles. Various market-imperfection models propose that the smart money may not be sufficient for the prevalence of market rationality or the correction of deviations from the market price. Both the standard asset-pricing and market-imperfection accounts recognize noise investors and non-optimizing behavior, but neither delves into the question of why they exist in the first place. The label noise trader hardly suggests a deep interest in what motivates this group of people.

In contrast, behavioral economics situates non-optimizing behavior at the center of the asset-bubble discussion and attempts to explain the prevalence of deviations from the fundamental price as a possible outcome of the cognitive, informational, and computational limitations faced by investors. This approach emphasizes that non-optimizing behavior is not a phenomenon that is observed solely among less informed and unsophisticated investors, but that it is common, in varying degrees, to all investors, including the smart money. Non-optimizing behavior is not an individual flaw but, rather, the result of objective conditions in an intrinsically uncertain and ambiguous environment within which people operate. It is not that people are unintelligent, capricious, arbitrary, or emotional when making financial decisions. Rather, under conditions in which the decision problem is not clearly delineated and optimization is not feasible, they rely on alternative decision rules. Moreover, investors are social beings. They do not make decisions independently and in isolation from other market participants, i.e. solely on the basis of individually perceived fundamentals. They interact with and influence each other, and the dynamics of social interaction create the possibility that extraneous factors will affect market outcomes.

John Maynard Keynes (1936), the most influential economist of the twentieth century, stated that in the presence of intrinsic uncertainty, or the absence of reliable probability distributions of future states of the economy, investors cannot act as cost-benefit calculators. Given their inability to compute discounted expected profits with a high degree of confidence, Keynes argued, investors do not and cannot make their decisions in accordance with the standard asset-pricing theory based on probabilistically calculated expected returns and risks.

Another influence on the behavioralist approach was Herbert Simon (1956), who contributed to economics, management, psychology, computer science, and political science. He argued that optimization is not a realistic behavioral assumption in view of imperfect information, as well as the cognitive and computational limitations of the human mind. The costs of collecting information and deliberating impose limits on the optimizing abilities of individuals and compel them to use, again, heuristics or experience-based practical guidelines, e.g. rules of thumb, common sense, educated guesses, or intuition in decision-making. He proposed that bounded rationality or the search for satisficing choices, i.e. choices that meet certain criteria that both satisfy and suffice, among a limited number of alternatives is a better description of human behavior than is optimization (Simon 1956). A satisficing basket may not be optimal but it meets the criterion of being "good enough."

Optimizing vs. non-optimizing decision rules may appear to be a distinction without a difference, as, in both cases, agents appear to be doing the best for themselves given the constraints. However, as the work of the behavioralist economists, who extend Keynes' and Simon's insights, demonstrates, there is an important difference between the two. Optimization or substantive rationality is related to the goal of decision-making, or the analytical determination of a basket that solves the decision problem; the process of selecting the basket is not of interest. The behavioralist approach shifts attention to how people collect information, deliberate, and reason, or the decision-making process, which is a question of procedural rationality. Understanding the decision-making process is the key to the behavioralist explanation of why market prices may deviate from intrinsic prices and cause asset-price bubbles.

In his behavioralist account of financial crises Robert Shiller (2005) describes how investors' environments shape the decision-making process. According to Shiller, a bubble is an outcome of individual, social, and cultural dynamics, which amplify and transform an initial deviation from the intrinsic price. Sustained over- or undervaluation of an asset is the consequence of the combination of the shortcomings of human psychology and market dynamics that make non-fundamental factors relevant to decision-making.

The precipitating factors that cause deviations from the intrinsic price are historically contingent and geographically specific market trends that have been in place for some time prior to triggering the bubble. For the crises of the 1980s and the 1990s, for instance, Shiller (2005) identifies a host of variables at work, including, but not limited to, advances in information technology, demographics of the baby-boom generation, ownership-society ideology, rising cultural and social glorification of business success and wealth, lower long-term interest rates, greater tolerance for gambling and risk-taking, and highly optimistic media coverage of securities markets. The higher interest in the market triggers higher security prices.

These precipitating factors are a necessary but insufficient condition for the emergence of a bubble. A bubble also requires amplification of the initial price increases through feedback mechanisms, which operate at individual and cultural levels. At the individual level, first, higher prices boost individual investors' confidence about the overall market's prospects as well as their confidence about their own stock-selecting abilities. The outcomes are more trading and even higher prices. Second, higher asset prices raise the value of portfolios. Greater wealth pushes spending on goods and services, increases profits, and feeds back to the asset price. Third, the booming economy creates expectations of even higher profits, which, in turn, fuel investor enthusiasm, and more people enter the market. Investors' expectations of higher returns create self-fulfilling asset-price increases. At the cultural level news media add fuel to the fire with favorable news about price movements and capital gains, and draw attention to the riches to be reaped in financial markets. The "new era" of economic and social thinking that predicts and promises a bright and more certain future dominates public discourse.

The most important component of Shiller's account, however, is the decision-making process at the individual level. The human behavior posited here is not based on pop-psychology notions of "craziness of crowds," "collective mania," or some vague notion of "emotions-driven" investing; instead, the behavior is explained in the tradition of Keynes, Simon, and behavioral scientists, who draw attention to the limitations that decision makers face. Given the ambiguity of the future, Shiller states, investors often rely on arbitrary *quantitative and qualitative moral anchors*, or beliefs, in their buy and sell decisions. The notion of anchoring is rooted in psychology and suggests that people tend to use arbitrary pieces of information in their subsequent judgments and decisions (Kahneman 2011: 119). A typical example is the final price paid for a car: it is influenced by the initial price, which is only the starting point of the negotiation. Examples of quantitative anchors used by investors are past price changes, the most recently remembered price, or milestone stock values. A qualitative or moral anchor is the narrative that allegedly describes and justifies movements of an individual stock or the market. According to Shiller, the inordinate influence of stories and anecdotes over statistics and charts in human decision-making is, at least in part, a product of evolutionary biology. Neither quantitative nor moral anchors necessarily mirror or even relate to the fundamentals.

Psychological research points out that heuristics, in terms of which these anchors are selected, are subject to systematic biases that are inherent in human behavior. Psychologists offer a long list of such biases. A few examples will suffice here to illustrate their nature and significance. *Cognitive dissonance* refers to the resistance to accepting new evidence when it contradicts pre-existing beliefs. The *representativeness heuristic* describes the tendency to overgeneralize and jump to conclusions based on limited evidence. Decision-making is also subject to the *availability heuristic*, or placing too much weight on and generalizing from the agent's own or more readily available experiences. People's selection and interpretation of data tend to confirm their prior beliefs and thought systems. This *confirmation bias* implies that events that do not confirm prior opinions tend to be ignored. In addition, people tend to have *hindsight bias*, or view events as more predictable once outcomes are known and, thus, overestimate their own ability to forecast the future; they are inclined to contend that they "knew it all along." Finally, *conservation bias* suggests that people tend to adhere persistently to previous forecasts, even in the face of newly available, contradictory information.

Thus, anchors are not only arbitrary, they also reflect very human biases. Three somewhat paradoxical implications follow from this observation. The first is the overconfidence in one's own stock picking abilities and the subsequent high volume of trading. An investor's high returns may be due merely to the overall buoyancy of the market, but the investor is more likely to attribute it to her ability to select a lucrative portfolio. The high level of comfort with perceived skills is likely, in turn, to direct her to expand her volume of trading. Second, anchors reduce the day-to-day volatility of prices and produce market inertia due to people's resistance to altering their decisions. Third, given their arbitrary nature, anchors also are very fragile. When news stories about dramatic changes can no longer be ignored investors are susceptible to breaking their anchors. Violent reactions are possible in periods when agents' conventional rules of thumb no longer appear to be relevant. Euphoria can suddenly turn into despair. Sudden implosions and crashes that follow relatively steady courses of price paths may be attributable to such instances of rupture.

Finally, anchors would not be of much significance if they varied among investors. If quantitative benchmarks and market narratives are distributed randomly across market participants it is probable that they will somehow even out and not have a notable aggregate effect on the market. Their use will matter more, however, if the same or similar anchors are used by large groups of people. The latter is more likely because people share similar experiences and thought processes. As mentioned, investors do not make decisions independently from each other; rather, they are likely to interact and influence each other. An individual investor may be "pressured" by neighbors to conform to their behavior. Perhaps more important is the possibility that the investor may reconsider any contrarian thoughts she harbors when she is in the minority, especially when others are benefitting from running with the market. Because they either use common anchors or they are influenced by their community at large investors are interdependent, and their actions easily create positive-feedback mechanisms, such as *herd behavior*.

If these claims have any validity then investors adopt non-optimizing decision rules based on factors disconnected from the fundamentals. Their interdependent actions may create sustained, cumulative deviations from intrinsic prices and explain why asset buyers are prone to what Fed Chairman Alan Greenspan once called "irrational exuberance," or speculative fever that raises asset prices to unsustainable levels.

In support of his model Shiller (2005) first presents statistical evidence on security prices that is inconsistent with predictions of the fundamentals-based approach (more on this in Chapter 12). Second, he provides historical evidence from twentieth-century US financial crises that illustrates the operation of the precipitating factors and feedback mechanisms and contradicts fundamentals-based explanations. Third, he surveys financial markets participants. In his survey of financial traders in the aftermath of the 1987 Wall Street crash, for instance, Shiller questions subjects about their modes of thinking and what they were paying attention to prior to the crisis, and concludes that the fundamentals were hardly a prominent factor in explaining the motivations for their actions.

Turning back to the classical bubbles, collecting direct evidence for the behavioralist explanation after the passage of centuries is a formidable task. Contemporary accounts, however, give clues about whether some of the forces Shiller emphasizes were at work. While historical clues are often anecdotal and exaggerations are ubiquitous, some researchers note that the three classic episodes and Shiller's descriptions of twentieth-century events have common features. For instance, the ideological setting of 1710s Britain, as expressed by Mandeville's *The Fable of the Bees* glorification of self-interest, individual enrichment, and luxury (Chancellor 2000) is similar to Shiller's description of the conditions in the US that precipitated the crises in the 1980s. Shiller sees evidence for the amplification mechanisms that fed tulip mania in the *Dialogues of Waermont and Gaergoedt* pamphlet and Mackay's (2009 [1852]) descriptions of how the stories of success and the promise of quick capital gains tempted people to enter the bubble in increasing numbers.

Shiller (2005: 248) also surmises that the well developed print media in the United Provinces would have disseminated news and served as a feedback mechanism that fueled speculative activity. Although some economists, such as Garber, distrust the historical verisimilitude of the stories, and the "madness" recounted in these historical accounts is likely to be exaggerated, the possible role of feedback mechanisms cannot be ruled out cavalierly. Van der Veen (2009) identifies a positive-feedback mechanism in the florists' social connectedness (through trade, religion, or marriage), a point upon which Goldgar (2007) also comments at length. Van der Veen argues that these interlinkages within small, localized markets created an information cascade, whereby participants ignored any private information they might have had about asset prices and relied increasingly on their observations of other people's behavior when making buy and sell decisions. Consequently, prices were increasingly disconnected from the fundamentals.

Bagehot–Minsky–Kindleberger: the financial delicacy/instability hypothesis

The fifth and final approach to understanding bubbles and banking crises follows the work of nineteenth-century English political and economic essayist Walter Bagehot and twentieth-century US economists Hyman Minsky and Charles Kindleberger (who I will refer to collectively as BMK). What distinguishes the BMK theory from the previous classes of theories is its methodological approach to understanding financial crises. The critical unit of analysis in all of the models discussed thus far is the individual decision maker.[4] While the behavioral approach permits inter-dependent actions, the individual is still the central analytical unit, and economic outcomes are explained in terms of her decision-making. In contrast, the individual recedes to the background in the BMK approach, and the institutional and structural features of the capitalist system come to the fore.

The deductive reasoning that flows from individual behavioral axioms, which is the hallmark of optimizing models, is now left aside. The focus is now on the examination of credit cycles in an institutional and historical context, and the construction of hypotheses that will explain these cycles. The BMK approach does not treat the financial crisis merely as an outcome of departures from the ideal of perfectly competitive markets or the peculiarities of human and market psychology, although both are likely to be relevant and important factors. Rather, financial turmoil is an innate feature of the dynamics of the capitalist economy and symptomatic of its inherent structural instability (Minsky 1975). In this account the banking system plays a central role in initiating and propagating credit cycles. Bank runs and asset-price bubbles are products of these credit cycles.

Bagehot served as the editor-in-chief of the newspaper *The Economist*. His classic book (1999 [1873]) *Lombard Street* is a treatise on the structure of financial markets in nineteenth-century Britain. In it he discusses the role of banks in the initiation and propagation of turbulences, the impact of financial breakdown on the real economy, and the necessity of a lender of last resort to alleviate banking crises. Minsky (1975) drew attention to the innate fragility of the capitalist financial system throughout his career and asked whether a calamity comparable to the Great Depression could happen again. He found a following among unorthodox economists known as post-Keynesians but was dismissed or ignored by mainstream economists. Kindleberger, an economic historian at Massachusetts Institute of Technology, interpreted Western financial history and crises through the theoretical lens of Minsky's hypothesis of financial instability (Kindleberger 1993; Kindleberger and Aliber 2011).

The theoretical core of the BMK approach is Minsky's hypothesis of financial instability or fragility. The starting point of the Minsky model is the observation that the banking system's willingness to extend credit depends on the expected profitability of the borrowers' projects and their ability to pay back loans. When prospects are brighter and expected future profits are higher businesses plan more fixed-investment projects and demand more credit, and banks become more willing to extend credit in view of lower default risk and in anticipation of higher earnings. Three interrelated points follow from these observations. First, in this narrative the banking system's credit extension is endogenous: it responds to the demand for credit. Second, credit expansion is pro-cyclical: during periods of economic upswing, when markets expand and profits increase, credit rises. Third, credit extension creates a positive-feedback mechanism: more credit amplifies the economic expansion and subsequently raises profit expectations; in anticipation of higher profits businesses demand more credit to expand their scale of production; banks respond to rising demand by offering more credit and feed further economic growth.

Yet this period of prosperity carries the seed of its own undoing. The nature of debt transforms over the expansion, and the stable financial system changes into an unstable set of financial relations that ultimately brings down the entire structure. In his chapter titled "Why [Money Market] is Often Dull, and Sometimes Excited" Bagehot (1999 [1873]) impressed on the reader that internal dynamics make the credit system "delicate." Minsky (1994) named his thesis the *financial instability hypothesis*:

> The first theorem of the financial instability hypothesis is that the economy has financing regimes under which it is stable and financing regimes in which it is unstable. The second theorem of the financial instability hypothesis is that over periods of prolonged prosperity, the economy moves from financial relations that make for a stable system to those that make for an unstable system.
>
> (157)

In his discussion of the transformation of the debt structure and destabilization of the financial system Minsky (1994) identifies three types of financing regimes. The first is *hedge financing*, under which the expected cash flow of the firm (or, generically, the borrower) is sufficient to pay both the interest and the principal on its debt. Hedge financing implies stable and sustainable financial relations, whereby all contractual obligations are fulfilled. The second regime is *speculative financing*, in which the cash flow of the firm is sufficient to meet interest payments on loans but not the principal. Under speculative financing the firm is required to sell its assets or assume more debt to finance the payments on the principal of the debt (or to roll over the existing loans). Finally, *Ponzi financing* is the regime under which the firm's income flow is insufficient to cover the interest or the principal payments on outstanding debt. To continue making these payments it has to raise new loans. Unless the cash-flow position improves the situation is unsustainable, and the firm eventually defaults. The central thesis of the financial instability hypothesis is that the nature of finance changes from a stable to an unstable regime over the course of the cycle.[5]

Kindleberger's stylized model describes transformation of the nature of credit and its implications by dividing the financial boom-and-bust cycle into five phases: displacement, expansion, euphoria, distress, and panic-crash (Kindleberger and Aliber 2011). While Minsky (1975) originally offered his hypothesis of endogenously unfolding crises to explain the turbulences in the mature twentieth-century capitalist economy, Kindleberger applies the model to interpret financial crises throughout history and believes that it is pertinent to earlier bubbles, as "details proliferate; structure abides" (Kindleberger and Aliber 2011: 34).

The first two stages of the credit cycle are *displacement* and *expansion*. A displacement is a large, exogenous event that positively affects perceptions of profit opportunities. It may initially be confined to a particular sector of the economy, but it must be substantial enough to influence the economic outlook and behavior and change planning horizons. Typical examples of a displacement are a new technology (railways, the internet), financial innovations (derivatives), institutional transformation (deregulation), new commodities (cars, computers), and wars. These events trigger a substantial spurt in economic growth that eventually spills over to the rest of the economy and initiates a generalized expansion, the second stage of the credit cycle. The volume of credit increases with the level of economic activity as banks extend credit to firms that need financing for fixed-capital projects and portfolio investors who invest in securities. Pro-cyclical credit, in turn, feeds back into further growth of production and trade, amplifies the expansion, and heightens profit prospects as well as security prices. Kindleberger and Aliber (2011: 53) identify the political and financial revolution of late seventeenth-century England as a displacement that initiated the expansion that preceded the South Sea Bubble. During the 1690s joint-stock companies proliferated. They dispersed risk across shareholders, limited individual liability, and enhanced capital accumulation.

During phases of prosperity, when profit expectations are realized, hedge financing is dominant in the financial markets, and security prices are expected to move concurrently with optimistic profit expectations. In Kindleberger's account, however, instability encroaches into the system as expansion transforms into *euphoria*. In this stage optimistic expectations become self-fulfilling through feedback loops. Rising real-estate and security prices increase wealth, consumption spending, and, therefore, production and profits. Higher stock prices and lower costs of raising cash also stimulate investment spending in physical capital. On the credit-supply side competition among banks to maintain their market shares leads to relaxation of lending standards, such as lowering margin requirements and down payments. As the quality of loans decline, the share of the speculative and Ponzi financing units in the financial system rises.

During euphoria, as asset prices appreciate, the objective of asset purchases changes from seeking earnings from enterprises' long-term ventures to seeking capital gains. Buyers leverage their capital gains by taking short-term loans against the collateral of their assets. As higher asset values increase the value of the collateral that borrowers post, borrowers' capacity to take on additional loans increases. This positive-leverage-feedback mechanism adds momentum to the asset-price inflation. Leveraging also raises the risk exposure of borrowers and lenders, and interconnections between actors in financial markets transform individual risk to *systemic risk*. In their euphoric state many borrowers and lenders may fail to recognize systemic risk. The smart money's actions at this stage may be destabilizing if these investors, either because of intrinsic uncertainty or arbitrage cost and risk constraints, do not bet against the market and choose to ride the bubble. Policymakers and monetary authorities may grow uneasy about the credit expansion and seek to purge the speculative excesses and inflationary pressures. Such endeavors usually meet with stiff resistance from banking interests that wish to protect their profits. In addition to flexing its political muscle the banking system has proven to be immensely creative in devising vehicles to circumvent limits on leverage and systemic risk (such as off-balance-sheet shadow banking vehicles, discussed in Chapters 15 and 16) imposed by authorities.

The euphoria stage in the classic bubbles was observed in the London and Paris exchanges when domestic and international speculators purchased shares at ever rising prices on borrowed money, despite common knowledge (according to most historians) that the revenues from commercial activities were practically nil, and interest revenues on government debt were far from justifying the prices that buyers paid for shares. Credit expansion played a critical role in buyers' ability to bid up prices. The rise in the South Sea Company's share price could not have been achieved if the demand were not fueled by loans from the Sword Blade Company and other London banks. Similarly, John Law could not have maintained high and rising share prices without the banknote issue against the collateral of the Mississippi Company shares. Bank credit did not play a role in tulip mania, but personal credit with no down payment or margin requirements facilitated rising bulb-contract prices, seemingly without bounds.

The next stage of the credit cycle is *distress*, which indicates degradation of confidence in the system, mounting doubts about the sustainability of higher asset prices, and the implicit (and gradually overt) acknowledgement of an increasingly hazardous financial environment. Signs of distress include banks becoming more cautious about their ability to collect the loans they have extended. They begin raising interest rates and limiting credit. Changes in policy regimes may also play a role in creating distress. Concerned with the economic boom and inflation, the monetary authority may take measures to raise interest rates and slow economic growth, which will diminish profits and capital gains. Declining credit growth and slowing economic growth reduces revenues, and individual firms encounter difficulties in servicing their debt. As the ability of the borrowers to continue servicing debt becomes dubious, banks become even more conservative and further limit credit to reduce their exposure to the higher likelihood of defaults and bankruptcies. Emerging distress in the economy in combination with slowing credit growth also decreases portfolio holders' demand for assets, decelerating and flattening asset-price changes. Once speculators realize that capital-gain opportunities are on the verge of disappearing they start selling off their assets. Lenders, concerned with declining collateral values, begin calling in loans and building up their cash reserves in preparation for the oncoming turbulence. The credit squeeze forces businesses in the real sector of the economy to cut back production. Conservative hedge-finance firms may suddenly find themselves transformed into specula-tive-finance units when the slowdown in the economy dries up their cash flow.

In London the signs of distress during the South Sea Bubble were an increasing shortage of liquidity due to the flow of funds out of the country (which may have been exacerbated by the exogenous profit opportunities elsewhere in Europe) and banks' unwillingness to extend loans in view of flattening stock prices and concerns about the potential decline of the value of their own assets. The signs of distress appeared as early as December 1719 in Paris in the form of shareholders selling holdings in response to dilution of shares, sending the price tumbling down. Law's implementation of price-support measures merely extended the distress period and postponed the inevitable collapse.

The final stage of the cycle, *panic-crash*, is the implosion of the bubble and the collapse of asset prices. The outstanding feature of this phase of the credit cycle is *debt deflation*, which refers to the fact that as the value of borrowers' assets relative to their debt shrinks, the relative burden of debt rises and exacerbates their financial distress. Investors and speculators rush to sell assets that have depreciated in value and convert them to the safety of cash before prices decline further. The positive feedback loops of deleveraging fuels despair. In the face of declining asset and collateral prices, as well as the rising likelihood of defaults, banks also participate in the rush to liquidity by calling loans and refusing rollover of mature debt. Banks that have made high-risk loans against the security of overvalued collaterals during the euphoria stage become more vulnerable to adverse shocks and face insolvency. The dreaded *Minsky moment* is reached when indebted agents are forced to sell their good assets to meet their financial obligations, resulting in a general price collapse.

The collateral damage of the financial meltdown on the real sector can be disastrous. The liquidity freeze causes the crisis to spill over to agriculture, industry, and commerce and creates general stagnation. The outcome is a vicious cycle of bankruptcies, defaults, declining collat-eral values, and insolvencies. The collapse is sometimes a sudden and dramatic crash, often accompanied by a panic asset sale. It may also occur in a more orderly fashion if leading private financial institutions or government authorities can exercise some control over events by providing liquidity or bailouts to faltering institutions, and calming the panicking public.

How and when the financial system shifts from a state of distress to one of free fall is difficult to determine. The distress may last a few days, several months, or even longer. Then any incident, such as the default or bankruptcy of a firm or a bank, a news item about a seller failing to find buyers, or a policy change announced by a monetary authority, can trigger a cascade of asset sales. In the case of tulip mania the incident was as simple as the sellers of bulbs not being able to find buyers. As the word of the lack of buyers spread, the panic was ignited by speculators trying to unload their contracts at any price. The specific trigger, in any case, is less important than the fact that the market was operating at unsustainable levels and that the implosion was inevitable.

While the credit cycle narrative of the BMK approach incorporates elements of market imperfection and behavioral approaches, it places these elements in the larger context of institutions and structures of the capitalist finance system. Market-imperfection arguments focus on the microstructures of the market. In the behavioral approach human and market psychology is at the forefront. In BMK the emphasis is on the internal dynamics of the macro system. Especially pertinent to this point is the comparison of explanations of banking failures. Market-imperfection theories attribute banking crises to liquidity problems that may emerge when individual depositors make optimizing decisions under conditions of incomplete markets or asymmetric information. According to the BMK approach, bank panics are outcomes of the declining quality of debt and emerging borrowing constraints (Kindleberger and Aliber 2011: 63; Minsky 1975). Thus, at the heart of the problem is the insolvency of at least some of banks, and illiquidity is primarily the consequence of the response of economic agents to the rising risk of default.

The BMK approach is in agreement with the Austrian approach regarding the centrality of credit in a financial crisis. However, the two schools differ in terms of the role they assign to credit. The Austrian school identifies credit expansion as the penultimate cause of the crisis. While BMK accepts that the explosive growth of asset prices is impossible without credit expansion, it treats credit expansion as the endogenous or accommodating factor. Rising credit is a symptom of borrowers' attempts to take advantage of rising profit and capital-gain opportunities, and of the readiness of both lenders and borrowers to take on more risk in expectation of higher returns.

Accordingly, the policy prescriptions of the two schools are widely dissimilar. The remedy to bubbles and banking crises, according to the Austrian economists, is to remove controls on the banking system altogether, including the abolishment of the modern central bank that holds the monopoly to issue money, to let banks create banknotes backed by gold or some other scarce commodity, and to adopt a 100 percent reserve requirement. The quantity of money in the economy would be controlled by supply and demand, similar to that of any other commodity. Market discipline would ensure that imprudent banks that fall short of supporting their obligations with gold would not survive, and, thus, the quantity of money and credit in the economy would be under control and free from artificial expansion. Only "good" money survives.

The policy recommendations of the BMK approach focus on measures to prevent the excessive credit expansion generated by market incentives and systemic risk. The imposition and adjustment of minimum reserve and equity-loan ratios on banks, and margin payments, such as borrowers making a down payment when purchasing a home, are examples of such regulations. Longer-term structural means to eradicate the credit cycle include reducing the dependence of households on debt by pursuing full-employment policies to ensure steady and high incomes, and disconnecting fixed-investment spending from credit conditions through greater social control over capital accumulation.

Concluding comments

The divergence of the observed market price of an asset from its fundamental value is understandably of great interest to economists, but it is hardly a purely academic matter. The economic, political, and ideological implications of bubbles have a bearing on the daily lives of everyone, as the following three points demonstrate.

The first relates to the allocative function of the market. In November 2009 Lloyd Blankfein, chief executive officer of the investment bank Goldman Sachs, defended the bonuses of bank executives by explaining that the executives were "doing God's work."[6] He was not referring to the establishment of a new church on Wall Street but suggesting that financial markets and their executives produce social goods and make the world better for everyone. Properly functioning financial markets match borrowers and lenders in terms of their risk and return profiles by setting security prices commensurate with their risks and expected returns. To the extent that institutions perform the intermediation function effectively and security prices reflect the fundamentals, financial markets create value, improve the social good, and "do God's work." Without intermediation firms would find it more difficult to grow, innovate, create wealth, and hire workers; households would face obstacles in purchasing homes and durables.

The possibility of bubbles, however, sheds doubt on how well financial markets fulfill this "matching" task. Persistent overvaluation of a security, i.e. demand being higher than the discounted expected earnings flow, implies that the related fixed-capital projects are absorbing excessive amounts of funds, e.g. the excessive construction of railways in 1840s England, fiber-optic networks in the US during the 1990s, homes in the US in the 2000s, that could have been put to better use elsewhere. Worse, mispricing and related speculative activity may create instability, to the detriment of the society.

The second point relates to the cost of a crash. As discussed in previous chapters, the implosions of the three early bubbles had adverse consequences for the economy, ranging from the weakening of the social compact in the Netherlands, through the loss of trust in joint-stock companies in England, to the launching of an era of financial stagnation in France. A crash can create a large disruption or exacerbate a downturn in economic activity, as exemplified in 1929 and 2008, through the suspension of credit and the adverse effect of shrinking wealth on the demand for goods and services. Bagehot (1999 [1873]) observed more than a century ago:

> The problem of managing a panic must not be thought of as mainly a "banking" problem. It is primarily a mercantile one. All merchants are under liabilities; they have bills to meet soon, and they can only pay those bills by discounting bills on other merchants. In other words, all merchants are dependent on borrowing money, and large merchants are dependent on borrowing much money. At the slightest symptom of panic many merchants want to borrow more than usual; they think they will supply themselves with the means of meeting their bills while those means are still forthcoming. If the bankers gratify the merchants, they must lend largely just when they like it the least; if they do not gratify them, there is a panic.
>
> (52)

Clearly, society has an interest in avoiding costly crashes.

The third point relates to current debates over public policy. From a fundamentals-based perspective markets work efficiently as long as they are free from government interference. If policymakers, under the guidance of a "gullible" economist from one of the other camps, intervene in the economy to fix the ostensible market deficiencies so that misallocation of funds or a prophesied crash can be avoided then the market will be prevented from doing what it does best. Distorted incentives and real misallocations will ensue, and economic welfare will suffer. Worse, such interventions may constitute a threat to political freedom. Other economists' confidence in the market's omnipotence is more nuanced, although their levels of skepticism vary. In view of the likelihood of the emergence of bubbles and their enduring negative consequences, these other economists are more likely to advocate the implementation of preventative regulatory measures. These contending positions are debated not only in the economic but also in the political arena. Informed political choices require understanding of the intellectual foundations of competing views on economic policymaking and the economic role of the state.

Key terms and concepts

Asymmetric information
Asymmetric-information hypothesis (of bank runs)
Debt deflation
Displacement (Kindleberger)
Distress (Kindleberger)
Euphoria (Kindleberger)
Expansion (Kindleberger)
Extrinsic bubble
Financial instability hypothesis
Fundamental risk
Hedge financing (Minsky)
Herd behavior
Intrinsic bubble
Malinvestment
Methodological individualism
Minsky moment
Moral hazard
Noise trader
Noise trader risk
Panic-crash (Kindleberger)
Ponzi financing (Minsky)
Price-earnings (P/E) ratio
Qualitative anchor
Quantitative anchor
Random-withdrawal hypothesis (of bank runs)
Riding the bubble
Speculative financing (Minsky)
Sunspots
Synchronization risk
Systemic risk

Endnotes

1 Alternative categorizations emphasize other aspects of bubble theories. Camerer (1989) distinguishes between rational bubbles, fads, and information bubbles. Brunnermeier (2008) identifies four types: rational expectations with symmetrical information, rational expectations with asymmetric information, limited arbitrage, and heterogeneous belief bubbles.
2 Garber (1990, 2000) notes that information may not have been distributed symmetrically across agents and that some investors may have based their decisions

on misleading information. As a result, they may have been overly optimistic. Nonetheless, he maintains that agents were acting in accordance with their perception of the fundamentals, and, therefore, the outcome of this over-optimism, in retrospect, cannot be interpreted as a bubble.

3 "Bank-debt holder" refers to those who made loans to the banks, namely depositors, banknote holders, and other short-term lenders to banks.

4 Knowledge about social phenomena acquired through the study of actions and motivations of individuals is called *methodological individualism*. This approach is the hallmark of neoclassical economics.

5 The terms *hedge*, *speculative*, and *Ponzi* financing are introduced in Minsky (1975). It should be pointed out that these labels are used to mean different things in standard economics, and, in fact, several economists take exception to Minsky's definitions (see the comments on Minsky's article in Kindleberger and Laffargue 1982).

6 Blankfein was not the first banker to invoke God's name in congressional hearings. During the 1932 Senate hearings that investigated stock-exchange practices after the crash of 1929 Albert H. Wiggin, President of Chase National Bank, stated, "I think the market was a God-given market" (Wigmore 1985: 27).

References

Abreau, Dilip and Markus K. Brunnermeier. 2002. "Synchronization Risk and Delayed Arbitrage." *Journal of Financial Economics* 66: 341–60.

Azariadis, Costas. 1981. "Self-fulfilling Prophecies." *Journal of Economic Theory* 25: 380–96.

Bagehot, Walter. 1999 [1873]. *Lombard Street: A Description of the Money Market.* New York: John Wiley and Sons.

Bernanke, Ben S. 1983. "Nonmonetary Effects of the Financial Crisis in the Propagation of Inflation." *American Economic Review* 73 (3): 257–76.

Bruner, Robert F. and Sean D. Carr. 2007. *The Panic of 1907: Lessons Learned from the Market's Perfect Storm.* Hoboken, NJ: John Wiley and Sons.

Brunnermeier, Markus K. 2008. "Bubbles." In *The New Palgrave Dictionary of Economics*, 2nd ed., edited by Steven N. Durlauf and Lawrence E. Blume. Palgrave Macmillan. Online: www.dictionaryofeconomics.com/article?id= pde2008_S000278.

Calomiris, Charles W. and Gary Gorton. 1991. "The Origins of Banking Panics: Models, Facts, and Bank Regulation." Pp. 109–73 in *Financial Markets and Financial Crises*, edited by R. G. Hubbard. Chicago: University of Chicago Press.

Camerer, Colin. 1989. "Bubbles and Fads in Asset Prices." *Journal of Economic Surveys* 3 (1): 3–41.

Chancellor, Edward. 2000. *Devil Take the Hindmost: A History of Financial Speculation.* New York: Plume.

Cochrane, John H. 2001. [Review of "Famous First Bubbles: The Fundamentals of Early Manias," by Peter M. Garber.] *Journal of Political Economy* 109 (5): 1150–4.

Dale, Richard, Johnnie E. V. Johnson, and Leilei Tang. 2005. "Financial Markets Can Go Mad: Evidence of Irrational Behavior during the South Sea Bubble." *Economic History Review* 58 (2): 233–71.

Dash, Mike. 1999. *Tulipmania: The Story of the World's Most Coveted Flower and the Extraordinary Passions it Aroused.* New York: Three Rivers Press.

Diamond, Douglas W. and Philip H. Dybvig. 1983. "Bank Runs, Deposit Insurance, and Liquidity." *Journal of Political Economy* 91 (3): 401–19.

Fama, Eugene F. 1965. "The Behavior of Stock-market Prices." *The Journal of Business* 38 (1): 34–105.

Frehen, Rik G. P., William N. Goetzmann, and K. Geert Rouwenhorst. 2013. "New Evidence on the First Financial Bubble." *Journal of Financial Economics* 108 (3): 585–607.

French, Douglas E. 2009. *Early Speculative Bubbles and Increases in the Supply of Money*, 2nd ed. Auburn, AL: Ludwig von Mises Institute.

Froot, Kenneth A. and Maurice Obstfeld. 1991. "Intrinsic Bubbles: The Case of Stock Prices." *American Economic Review* 81 (5): 1189–214.

Garber, Peter M. 1989. "Tulipmania." *Journal of Political Economy* 97 (3): 535–60.

Garber, Peter M. 1990. "Famous First Bubbles." *Journal of Economic Perspective* 4 (2): 35–54.

Garber, Peter M. 2000. *Famous First Bubbles: The Fundamentals of Early Manias*. Cambridge, MA: The MIT Press.

Goldgar, Anne. 2007. *Tulipmania: Money, Honor, and Knowledge in the Dutch Golden Age*. Chicago: University of Chicago Press.

Kahneman, Daniel. 2011. *Thinking, Fast and Slow*. New York: Farrar, Straus, Giroux.

Keynes, John Maynard. 1936. *The General Theory of Employment, Interest, and Money*. London: Macmillan.

Kindleberger, Charles P. 1993. *A Financial History of Western Europe*, 2nd ed. New York: Oxford University Press.

Kindleberger, Charles P. and Robert Z. Aliber. 2011. *Manias, Panics, and Crashes: A History of Financial Crises*, 6th ed. New York: Palgrave Macmillan.

Kindleberger, Charles P. and Jean Pierre Laffargue. 1982. *Financial Crises: Theory, History, and Policy*. New York: Cambridge University Press.

Mackay, Charles. 2009 [1852]. *Memoirs of Extraordinary Popular Delusions and the Madness of Crowds*. Mansfield Centre, CT: Martino.

Meltzer, Allan H. 2002. *Rational and Irrational Bubbles*. Keynote Address for the Federal Reserve Bank of Chicago-World Bank Conference on Asset Price Bubbles, Chicago.

Minsky, Hyman P. 1975. *John Maynard Keynes*. New York: Columbia University Press.

Minsky, Hyman P. 1994. "The Financial Instability Hypothesis." Pp. 153–7 in *The Elgar Companion to Radical Political Economy*, edited by Philip Arestis and Malcolm C. Sawyer. Aldershot, UK: Edward Elgar.

Neal, Larry. 1990. *The Rise of Financial Capitalism: International Capital Markets in the Age of Reason*. Cambridge, New York: Cambridge University Press.

Paul, Helen J. 2011. *The South Sea Bubble: An Economic History of its Origins and Consequences*. New York: Routledge.

Schleifer, Andrei and Lawrence H. Summers. 1990. "The Noise Trader Approach to Finance." *Journal of Economic Perspectives* 4 (2): 19–33.

Shiller, Robert J. 2005. *Irrational Exuberance*, 2nd ed. New York: Currency Doubleday.

Simon, Herbert A. 1956. "Rational Choice and the Structure of the Environment." *Psychological Review* 63 (2): 129–38.

Temin, Peter and Voth, Hans-Joachim. 2004. "Riding the South Sea Bubble." *American Economic Review* 94 (5): 1654–68.

Thompson, Earl A. 2007. "The Tulipmania: Fact or Artifact?" *Public Choice* 130 (1/2): 99–114.

van der Veen, A. Maurits. 2009. *The Dutch Tulip Mania: The Social Foundations of a Financial Bubble*. Athens, GA: Department of International Affairs, University of Georgia.

Velde, Francois. 2009. "Was John Law's System a Bubble? The Mississippi Bubble Revisited." Pp. 99–120 in *The Origins and Development of Financial Markets and Institutions: From the Seventeenth Century to the Present*, edited by Jeremy Atack and Larry Neal. Cambridge and New York: Cambridge University Press.

Wigmore, Barrie A. 1985. *The Crash and its Aftermath: A History of Securities Markets in the United States, 1929–1933*. Westport, CT: Greenwood Press.

Zeira, Joseph. 1999. "Informational Overshooting, Booms, and Crashes." *Journal of Monetary Economics* 43: 237–57.

7 Technological revolutions and speculation

Nineteenth-century British railways and banks

Speculative bubbles often accompany emerging revolutionary technologies. The industrial revolution in Britain offers two classic examples of innovation: canals and railways. During the 1700s the development of large-scale industrial production in Britain required the mass transportation of raw materials and manufactured goods, and horse-drawn carriages on dirt roads were proving inadequate to transport merchandise in large volumes. With the creation of the canal and the railway networks, however, the growing needs of manufacturers and mine owners began to be met, and the success of these innovations in carrying freight cheaply provided impetus to the growth of industrial production. Canal construction started in the 1750s and boomed during the last decade of the century. With the advent of the non-stationary steam engine in the 1820s, however, the era of canals came to an end. Railroad transportation was the undisputed technological marvel of the nineteenth century.

Both canals and railways were large capital investments that required vast sums of financing, for which private funding was insufficient. Consequently, canal and railroad companies were established as joint-stock companies, and funds were raised by selling shares to the public. These stocks periodically became objects of speculation, and their prices experienced extraordinary peaks followed by drastic collapses.

Commentators often draw parallels between the boom and bust of nineteenth-century railways and those of twentieth-century telecommunications companies, in which the British experience is a cautionary tale that modern investors should have heeded more than 150 years later; but there are other aspects of the railway manias that offer learning opportunities for the present, and a number of nineteenth-century debates continue to be the subjects of current discussions. These include the need for the regulation of industries, the possibility that markets misallocate resources, the interface of political and economic power, the role of the government in avoiding speculation and responding to crashes, the control of credit to prevent speculation, and the advantages and disadvantages of the banks' access to a lender of last resort.

Canals

At the dawn of the industrial revolution canals were the principal innovation in transportation infrastructure. Throughout history rivers have
been used for the transit of goods and passengers, but transportation by
natural waterways is constrained by geography. With the advent of artificial canals, however, transporters could negotiate natural obstacles with
the help of locks, tunnels, and aqueducts. Canals expanded the scope of
inland navigation and delivered raw materials and merchandise across a
much wider area in accordance with the needs of trade. The first canals
to serve the growing industrial production were completed in the 1750s
in northern England. The power was simply supplied by animals pulling
boats, but a single horse was able to pull a much heavier load along a
canal than many horses on dirt roads. During the subsequent 20 years
more than a thousand miles of canals were built in the English midlands
and the north. They facilitated capital and wealth accumulation by providing cheap transportation of items such as coal, iron, and agricultural
and manufactured goods. According to one report in the 1830s, transporting a ton of bales of grain from Manchester to London cost £20
by road and £4 by inland waterway (Gayer *et al.* 1953).[1] By 1830, the end
of the inland navigation era, the total canal stock of Britain measured
4,000 miles.

Due to the large capital requirements of construction canal companies
were organized as joint-stock enterprises. Promoters of a new canal
announced the project through newspapers and pamphlets and invited
investors to subscribe to its shares. Subscribers initially paid a fraction of
the share price and pledged to pay the remainder once construction
started and the managers made calls for payment. In line with the dictates
of the Bubble Act of 1720 promoters petitioned Parliament for the privilege
of establishing a joint-stock company. Once parliamentary authorization
was obtained the company was incorporated and could proceed with the
compulsory land purchases and construction.

From 1750 to 1789 Parliament granted authorization for 48 canals (Ward
1974). The financing of these projects was largely a provincial activity
(Ward 1974). Shareholders were primarily local landowners, merchants,
tradesmen, and manufacturers. These investors were familiar with the
location and the expected volume of traffic and anticipated benefitting
from the long-term profitability of the company. The sole source of their
profit was the tolls paid by the barge operators, as canal owners were not
allowed to operate boats. These tolls were sufficient to make early canal
ownership a profitable business. Many of these early canals indeed yielded
high returns and stimulated both promoter and investor interest in additional projects (Hadfield 1984: 108).

The canal boom started in 1790 with an unprecedented rise in the number of promotions for canal-share subscriptions, and previously local

capital markets expanded on a national scale. Individuals of various occupations, such as company clerks, attorneys, and innkeepers, became self-styled local share brokers and attracted investors from across the country by advertising forthcoming canal-share subscriptions in distant towns' newspapers, spreading the news of profit opportunities. Indeed, between 1790 and 1794 Parliament authorized 51 new projects (Ward 1974: 164), which, had they all been built, would have more than doubled the number of existing canals and increased their total length several times over. At its peak canal construction was so extensive that its absorption of resources from other economic activities became a source of concern for policymakers. In 1793 Parliament even considered, but dismissed, the idea of stopping canal building during harvest time to ensure a sufficient number of hands in the fields (Burton 2004: 14).

In addition to investors, many small speculators motivated by quick capital gains rather than longer-term profitability responded to the share promotions (Simmons and Biddle 1997: 68). As soon as they were entitled to shares by subscription speculators could start trading these scrip, even before the canal project received parliamentary authorization. The demand for shares was high enough that subscriber meetings overflowed from inns and churches to fields. However, for the most part, the share market was thin: the turnover was low in the secondary market for stock and scrip of the old canals, and promoters of new canals frequently prevented outsiders from entering the market by keeping subscription meetings secret and restricting sales to locals (Hadfield 1984: 111; Ward 1974: 86–7). The thin market contributed to the frenzy of purchasing new share issues. Promoters of several highly speculative projects took advantage of the situation by appealing directly to outside money. Shares of projects such as the building of the Ellesmere and Crinan canals, which were marketed to outsiders, were oversubscribed.

While some of them proved to be highly profitable in later years, new canals generally did not match the financial success of the earlier generation. Many were not viable and were often abandoned before completion (Hadfield 1984: 112). Moreover, the cost of construction frequently exceeded the initial estimates, and managers made calls on subscribers to raise additional funds. These calls disproportionately affected those speculators who did not have additional cash and had intended to hold shares for a short period before selling at a higher price (Gayer *et al.* 1953: 418). The speculative fever peaked in the winter of 1792–3 and ended with the economic crisis of 1793. Dividends of canal shares declined alongside the volume of commerce, and share prices plummeted (Hadfield 1984: 109–10). In 1793, as banks discontinued lending and liquidity became scarce, the government issued Exchequer bills (short-term Treasury paper) to the public that could be used as a means of exchange.

Early years of the railways and the 1825 boom and panic

In the early nineteenth century industrialization in Britain was progressing at full force. The last vestiges of mercantilism and restrictions on competition in commerce and industry were removed in the 1820s. When Parliament repealed the nearly defunct Bubble Act of 1720 in 1825 and granted limited liability privileges to businesses in increasing numbers, savings were increasingly channeled to incorporated businesses. The number of limited-liability joint-stock companies multiplied.

Railways emerged as a groundbreaking innovation only after companies were organized as joint-stock enterprises because their construction and management required extraordinary amounts of fixed capital. The first wave of railway promotion in the form of public companies came in the early 1820s. By 1825 promoters had announced 70 railway projects, 40 of which reached Parliament for authorization, with very few actually realized. The most notable achievement of the sector in this period was the establishment of Stockton and Darlington Railway Company as the first publicly owned, non-stationary steam-powered passenger-railway company in England. The company was authorized in 1821 and started operating in 1825. It carried both cargo and passengers on a 26-mile-long track.

These developments were taking place against the background of easy credit, a booming stock market, and a prospering economy. Between 1821 and 1824 trade and manufacturing, particularly the iron industry, were operating at close to full-capacity levels (Gayer *et al.* 1953: 194). The abundance of credit was a result of two factors. First, in prior years, the Bank of England had increased (albeit reluctantly) the issue of notes to assist the Treasury's efforts to retire the war debt of the Napoleonic Wars and to meet pension obligations (Neal 1998). The bank had also lowered its discount rate in 1822. Nevertheless, its contribution to the expansion of money and credit was modest; it had ample specie reserves, as much as a third of its liabilities, in October 1824. The second and more important factor was the country banks' expansion of their small-denomination-note issues, with the consent of the Treasury, to finance the expansion of heavy manufacturing and public-works projects.

The interest rate on government debt was very low, and British investors were searching for investments with higher rates of return. The most exciting of these investments were the mining shares and government bonds of the newly independent Central and South American countries (including the fictitious South American Republic of Poyais) that were freed from Spanish rule and recognized by the British government in 1824. These securities were marketed aggressively by British agents. Investors, joined soon by speculators, eagerly subscribed to these securities that promised high returns (Chancellor 2000: 98; Neal 1998). They invested both their own money and funds borrowed from banks in bonds and stocks. The British stock market, fed by cheap credit and subscription-based sales, boomed after 1823 and peaked in April 1825. The boom in railway stocks was a marginal component of this general euphoria.

The boom faded when the British economy was caught in the financial crisis of 1825. The crisis hit in April as misgivings about the returns and riskiness of the distant Latin American securities surfaced and confidence deteriorated. Both domestic and foreign security prices declined in mid 1825. As subscription payments on securities came due, investors and speculators were forced to sell some of their holdings to raise funds. Unfortunately, however, buyers had disappeared in the wake of declining prices and expectations of further downside (Gayer *et al.* 1953: 190).

Rising default risk on their loans and the declining value of collateral they held put banks in a precarious position. Country banks that had played an important role in the expansion of credit rushed to the London banks to withdraw deposits and discount paper to replenish their reserves. London banks, in turn, approached the Bank of England with the same purpose. The Bank of England, however, was alarmed by declining security prices and its own depleting specie reserves, and, rather than lending, it contracted notes in mid 1825 and raised its discount rate. Monetary tightening led to failures among the rural and London banks. A liquidity shortage immediately spilled over to industry and commerce as merchants, manufacturers, and farmers found it increasingly difficult to roll over their loans, sell commercial paper, and, in short, continue their commercial activities. They cut expenditures to build up cash reserves. Banks were pressured from all sides by the withdrawal of deposits, declining collateral values, and the impending insolvency of parties whose commercial paper they had discounted. A contemporary observer reported:

> A panic had seized the public. Men would not part with their money on any terms, nor for any security. Persons of undoubted wealth and real capital were seen walking about the streets of London not knowing whether they should be able to meet their engagements for the next day.
>
> (Joplin 1832: 11)

The government had arrested the canal panic of 1793 by issuing liquidity in the form of Exchequer bills. However, they did not wish to repeat this action to resolve the current crisis. The land-owning aristocracy that dominated Parliament had little sympathy for the financial interests who were believed to have created the problem through their greed and excess. Prime Minister Lord Liverpool viewed speculation as the root of evil and blamed country banks for facilitating speculation by overextending banknotes. He went on record in the spring of 1825 that the government would not bail out the banks in the event of a financial emergency (Kindleberger 1993: 93). In December 1825, when the market was collapsing, Lord Liverpool and the chancellor of the exchequer were in agreement that "the evil would work its own cure" (Joplin 1832: 10). However, while Lord Liverpool considered a governmental rescue to be politically unacceptable, he was not opposed to a rescue by private interests. After all, the liquidity freeze also hurt manufacturers, merchants, and farmers who were innocent of speculation. He pressured the Bank of England to end the panic by activating its discount facility. On December 14 the bank abruptly changed its tight money stance, started discounting the more creditworthy banks' bills, and aggressively issued new notes. Infusion of a large loan of bullion from the Bank of France brought the financial panic to a halt. Bagehot (1999 [1873]) quotes Mr. Harman, a director of the Bank of England:

> We lent it by every possible means and in modes we have never adopted before: we took in stock on security, we purchased Exchequer bills, we made advances in Exchequer bills, we not only discounted outright, but we made advances on the deposits of bills of exchange to an immense amount, in short, by every possible means consistent with the safety of the bank, and we were not on some occasions over-nice. Seeing the dreadful state in which the public were, we rendered every assistance in our power.
>
> (51–2)

It is interesting to observe in this context the multiple, and at times conflicting, roles that the Bank of England played during this time of crisis. First, it was a private bank with obligations to its owners and was expected to oversee the financial interests of its shareholders by generating profits. This task required the expansion of banknotes and loans relative to the specie reserves as much as was possible, albeit within the bounds of prudent banking. Second, it served as the bank of the government and was required to be responsive to its needs. Third, the bank enjoyed special status and privileges: it was the only bank permitted to be a joint-stock company; it was the central depository institution in which other banks kept their reserves; and it was the only institution that discounted bills on demand (other banks performed the service only for their customers). Further, its designation as "government bank" was an implicit assurance to the public that it would never be permitted to fail. In return for these privileges and the power they represented the bank was also expected to serve the public interest. Specifically, the bank was expected to use its unique status to watch over the stability of the British monetary and banking system.

These three roles were not necessarily compatible, as its experiences during the 1820s illustrate. First, the bank's purchase of low-interest government annuities in 1824 (which the public had ignored due to their low rate of return) to fulfill its responsibilities with respect to the government was hardly in line with the private interests of shareholders. Second, before 1825, unlike other banks, the Bank of England could not expand credit liberally in pursuit of profit. As the central depository institution, it was compelled to keep high levels of specie reserves to sustain the lending institutions in the event of a confidence crisis and bank run. Indeed, the bank came in for sharp criticism for engaging in inflationary finance even when it made only a modest contribution to the pre-1825 monetary ease. Third, in mid 1825 the decision to contract credit and minimize the bank's insolvency risk was reasonable from the shareholders' perspective. However, from a public-interest perspective it was seen as a detrimental move that limited liquidity and fanned the flames of financial collapse. The bank's belated action to assume the responsibility of providing liquidity by discounting other banks' commercial paper prevented the financial crisis and depression from intensifying, but it was a risky move from the perspective of its shareholders.

The financial panic peaked in December 1825, but the British economy bore the injuries throughout the following years. From September to December 1825 bankruptcies throughout the economy increased steadily, totaling 514. During the following four months there were 1,145 additional bankruptcies (Gayer *et al.* 1953: 205). Of the British banks, 73, or close to 10 percent, declared bankruptcy (Neal 1998). Until 1832 the British economy experienced chronic unemployment and excess capacity, as well as declining commodity and security prices. With the exception of a mild recovery in 1827–8 the economy was in a depression.

The railway panic of 1836–7

The 1820s were the formative years of the railways. It took some time for society to come to terms with the revolutionary technology, and various interests voiced their opposition to railway construction as late as the 1840s. Various landowners were concerned about the tracks that partitioned their land and farms, the levels of compensation for compulsory acquisition of their land, the possibility of adverse consequences of machines spewing fire and ash on land and livestock, and the impact of competition on their returns from canal investments. Canal owners were destined to lose the most from expansion of this new powerful competitor, although railways initially served primarily as extensions of canals and did not directly compete with them. The opposition of aristocratic landowners and canal interests to railways was effective in slowing down the passage of railroad acts in Parliament and limiting the expansion of new railways in the late 1820s (Burton 2004).

The first railroad designed to compete directly with the canals was the Liverpool and Manchester Railway Company (L&MR), authorized in 1826 and opened in 1830. The length of its track was 35 miles. L&MR was revolutionary in several ways. Civil engineers demonstrated their ability to lay tracks between Liverpool and Manchester through hills and swamps. In October 1829 Robert Stephenson's *Rocket* locomotive won the prize for best engine in L&MR's Rainhill Trials competition, demonstrating that the non-stationary steam engine was unquestionably the future power source of rail transportation. Rail transit that reached incomparable speeds of 30 miles per hour through tunnels and over bridges and viaducts spelled the ultimate demise of canals as the leading means of moving merchandise. By 1830 total railway-route length reached 98 miles. Threats by land, canal, and turnpike owners to obstruct the passage of parliamentary acts of authorization lingered only a short while longer. The economic interests of landowners soon lined up with the fortunes of railways, as many landowners required efficient transportation of minerals and metals mined on their land. Canal-company opposition faded away as railway companies first compensated and then took over the canal companies.

By the mid 1830s businesses, investors, and the public accepted the technological superiority of railways and preferred it to alternative means of transportation. The first railway boom was well under way. However, enthusiasm was blended with a dose of skepticism, the primary sources of which were uncertainty over the costs of railway construction and the growth of passenger demand, or, in short, the profitability of the railway enterprises (Bryer 1991; Odlyzko 2010b). The costs of building new railways were difficult to predict, and construction expenses often turned out to be twice the initial budget. Future passenger demand for services was uncertain because steam-engine speeds frightened many people.

Promoters of the early railroad projects were primarily local merchants, manufacturers, and tradespeople. On the technical side, promoters hired surveyors and engineers to conduct initial land surveys on selected routes and to evaluate the physical feasibility of projects. On the financial and management side, they recruited men of prominence, such as landowners and industrialists, to enhance the credibility of the project. They formed committees, who put together a prospectus that detailed the route, expected traffic, revenues, and costs of the project, and invited investors to subscribe to the company's shares through public meetings and trade papers.

With the prospectus and the subscription list in hand, the committees hired an agent to draw up a bill and apply to Parliament for authorization (by the annual November 30 deadline). The bill was considered successively by two parliamentary committees to ensure that all affected parties, i.e. owners and leaseholders of the property on which tracks would be built, residents on the neighboring lands, and competitors, were informed about the project, their objections and reservations were heard and recorded, and promoters demonstrated that at least half of the capital of the project was subscribed. Only after the bill was approved by the parliamentary committees, had passed the House of Commons and the House of Lords, and received royal assent did it become a private act of Parliament that authorized the promoters to acquire land and proceed with construction (Simmons and Biddle 1997: 400–1). If the bill was rejected at any stage promoters could reintroduce it only in the following annual parliamentary session.

Beyond authorization, legislators and the government did not interfere with the railways. Even in the early 1830s, when promoters started petitioning for longer-distance lines and paved the road for a national rail system, Parliament and the government did not entertain the idea of participating in planning or designing a network.

Investors in railway companies included large merchants and industrialists, as well as middle-class professionals and small provincial merchants and manufacturers. The practice of selling transferable scrip for a fraction of the par value of the share price, usually 5 percent to 10 percent, continued. Scrip buyers were to pay the remainder when managers of the company called for it. Thus, trading of scrip before authorization took place in the midst of uncertainties related to technical feasibility, cost, demand, and whether the proposal would obtain parliamentary approval. Nonetheless, scrip sales widened the investor base and enabled the middle classes and people of modest means to enter the market. However, many came to regret the obligation of making good on calls for capital once the construction started because actual costs typically exceeded projections (Bryer 1991; Mitchell 1964).

From 1832 to 1835 Britain experienced a boom similar to the 1820s cycle, albeit of a much larger magnitude. Industry operated at full employment, and commodity and security prices climbed steadily. Railways had become an integral component of the economy. In fact, rising railway construction was the most important source of the boom in coal and iron production. In the financial area credit conditions eased as new legislation after 1826 permitted the establishment of joint-stock banks with the privilege of issuing notes, provided they operated outside a 65-mile radius of London. By 1836 a considerable number of these banks were in operation. At the same time the Bank of England was allowed to establish branches outside London. It did so promptly and started competing with country banks by offering lower discount rates (Conant 1969 [1927]: 117). Lower interest rates fueled investor interest in common stocks, particularly railway, bank, and insurance shares.

Railway traffic, especially that of passengers, grew beyond the most optimistic expectations. Encouraged by the growing acceptance of railways, promoters initiated new schemes. Between 1832 and 1835 petitions for 55 new railways reached Parliament, and projects with an expected capital of £13.2m were authorized (Figure 7.1). By 1837 these figures jumped to 110 new projects and £36.4m of approved capital. Parliament authorized 1,000 miles of new railways in 1836, a 500 percent increase from 1835, and another 600 miles in 1837.

Fixed-capital investment in planned railways and new routes followed new authorizations with a lag of approximately one year. Fixed-capital-investment expenditure in railways doubled annually between 1835 and

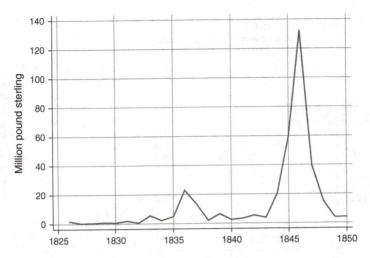

Figure 7.1 Railway capital authorized in Britain, 1825–50 (annual).
Source: Gayer *et al.* (1953: 437).

1837, from £1.6m to £3.3m to £6.0m (Figure 7.2). Between 1835 and 1837 the route length increased by 242 miles and almost doubled the total length of railways constructed during the previous two decades.

The surge in railway-stock prices coincided with the increase in promotions and authorizations. The rush to buy railway stocks started in mid 1835, and the railway-share-price index rose by 117 percent between May 1835 and May 1836 (Figure 7.3). It is interesting to compare the stock-price movements with the rate of return. Based on semi-annual company reports, Arnold and McCartney (2004b) estimate that only from 1831 to 1834 did the average annual rate of return on railway equity exceed 4 percent, which was the minimal interest rate on long-term debt. From 1834 to 1839 the average rate of return was a mere 1.8 percent, and during the mania years of 1835 and 1836 returns were 2.6 percent and 1.2 percent respectively. Thus, railways, overall, do not give the impression of being a highly profitable venture in the 1830s, especially when compared with the cost of borrowing. In other words, railway-stock-price growth does not appear to be commensurate with observed profitability.

These figures are calculated using imperfect data that come from a period when accounting was in its formative years. Therefore, statistics on rates of return are not always systematic or reliable, especially before 1840. Two additional points need to be borne in mind when interpreting these figures. First, the low rates of return may be attributed to the fact that railways have a long development stage, and many were still under construction or were expanding. Thus, they may not have reached their full profit

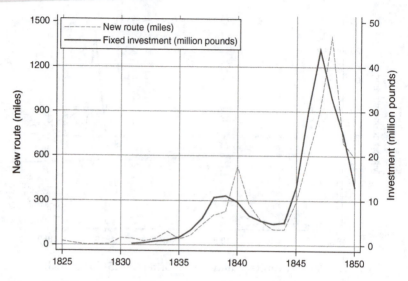

Figure 7.2 New routes and fixed investment in British railways, 1825–50 (annual).

Source: New-route data from Mitchell (1988: 541); fixed-investment data from Mitchell (1964: 335).

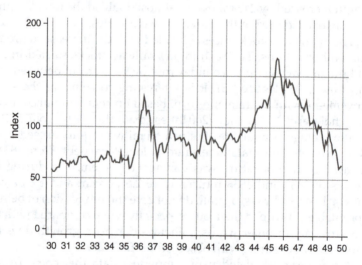

Figure 7.3 British railroad-share-price index, 1830–50 (monthly).

Source: Gayer *et al.* (1953: 375).

potential, and the long-term expectations of profitability were probably more promising. Second, while the average return was unimpressive, there was substantial variation across the firms, which suggests that there were some highly profitable businesses. The high variation of profitability may be attributed to some companies' ability to charge higher prices due to limited competition and by catering to high-value passenger and freight traffic (Simmons and Biddle 1997: 399). These caveats may explain the optimism of investors with regard to the fundamentals, despite the observed low-profit rates. However, what is puzzling, then, is why the railway-stock index dropped by 41 percent within 12 months, from 1836 to 1837.

One factor that may have contributed to the share-price drop is the change in the monetary conditions in 1836. Credit conditions were becoming tighter as tensions were building in the British banking system due to specie outflow abroad and declining reserves. Due to monetary stringency in the US Americans were cashing in the British securities they held and reducing British imports. As a consequence, British banks' reserves were drained as cash was remitted to the US (Gayer *et al.* 1953: 272). Banks that were confronted with diminishing reserves limited credit expansion and started calling in their loans; in addition, they asked for assistance from the Bank of England. In response to its own diminishing reserves, the Bank of England raised its discount rate twice during the summer of 1836. Unlike the experience of 1825, however, the Bank of England continued to extend credit to banks hurt by the American trade and, to some extent, alleviated the liquidity shortage. Accordingly, relatively few banks failed.

The credit shortage, nevertheless, damaged the railway sector. Many companies were experiencing chronic cost overruns in constructing railways. Their regular means of financing construction expenses were drawing bank credit, making calls on subscribers, and issuing new shares. Bank loans, which financed about 30 percent of the total construction cost, were exhausted when banks cut credit extension. Credit contraction in combination with the difficulty of posting collateral when prices of assets were declining, meant many subscribers who did not have ready cash could no longer take loans to meet their payment obligations. To raise funds these subscribers sold shares. Speculators also dumped their shares in view of the vanishing capital gains and mounting financing constraints, which added to the momentum of the stock-price decline. Lower stock prices also prevented railway companies from raising significant funds by issuing new shares.

The immediate impact of the financial crisis was on parliamentary authorizations. Authorized capitalization, that had peaked in 1936 at £22.8m, dropped sharply with the crisis, reflecting perhaps both the lack of new applications and the unwillingness of Parliament to pass additional acts (Figure 7.1). Annual authorization figures remained below £10m until 1844. Many projects authorized before and during the boom were not realized, and some partially built projects were abandoned, while others never started. Railway construction, however, did not come to a complete halt, as work on some projects that had started before the crisis continued. As shown in Figure 7.2 fixed-capital investment in railway construction increased steadily even after the crisis and peaked in 1838–9 at £22m. As observed in Figures 7.1 and 7.2, however, between 1840 and 1844 the railroad industry was in a lull in terms of all three measures, i.e. the value of capital authorized by Parliament, fixed-capital investment in railways, and new routes completed.

By 1843 the railway stock of Britain had reached 2,000 route miles. According to Arnold and McCartney (2004b), the average rate of return had recovered somewhat and rose from 3.0 percent to 4.4 percent between 1840 and 1843, still barely above the cost of borrowing. The average railway-share price fluctuated at levels far below the 1836 peak (Figure 7.3), often selling at a discount. Lackluster investor demand recovered only after 1843. Odlyzko (2010b), however, argues that the demand for services on rail lines constructed in the 1830s turned out to be very high in the 1840s, enough to make large profits despite overruns in the costs of construction and operation. Those who invested in the previous decade and were able to hold on to their stocks realized high dividends in the mid 1840s.

The railway fever of 1845

The depressed state of the British economy lasted until 1842. Declining demand from rail iron was a contributing factor to the stagnant industrial output (Gayer *et al.* 1953: 292). Bullion outflow due to purchases of US securities and rising grain imports (following bad weather and disastrous harvests) drained reserves, and banks tightened credit. After 1842 the economy started improving, with bountiful harvests and easing monetary conditions (Gayer *et al.* 1953: 330). Economic growth was at a healthy 5 percent per annum in the middle of the decade (Campbell and Turner 2010). In the meantime, following the sharp expansion of routes in the late 1830s, railways entered the stage of maturity. Not only were new lines opening up, but existing lines were being used more intensively.

Enthusiasm for railways was fueled by expanding passenger traffic, thanks to overall prosperity, the convenience of trains, and lower fares. The London–Bristol trip by coach, for instance, took 12 to 15 hours; by train it was 4.5 hours and cheaper (Simmons and Biddle 1997: 328). On June 13, 1842, Queen Victoria and Prince Albert were the first reigning British monarchs to make a train journey. In spite of her apprehensions about the speed (the engineer was advised to go slow), on June 14, 1842, the Queen wrote to her uncle that she found the half-hour experience "free from dust and crowd and heat, and I am quite charmed with it" (Queen Victoria 1908: 404).

Between 1843 and 1846 overall revenues from passenger and merchandise traffic rose by more than 40 percent (Campbell 2010). Opposition from landowners disappeared as land values around rail tracks increased.

The new technology was not just a more comfortable, faster, and economical mode of transportation, it was anticipated to be a life-changing transformation that would disseminate information faster, bring people closer together, and make the world smaller (Chancellor 2000: 125–6). In addition, it created challenges for policymakers.

The government, railways, and the banking system

The mercantilist era of government-sanctioned monopolies had long passed and been replaced by the economic doctrine of laissez-faire that promoted unregulated competition and free exchange. The role of government in the new economic order was limited to providing a legal framework for the exercise of individual rights, maintaining public order, and enforcing laws to defend private property. Unregulated markets were expected to promote social welfare by providing goods in accordance with consumer demand at the lowest cost, utilizing the most effective and least costly methods of production. Free competition was deemed superior to regimes that assigned regulatory or interventionist economic roles to the government. While the British government and Parliament explicitly subscribed to free-market doctrine, they were, nevertheless, forced to address two issues in the 1840s.

The first issue concerned the viability and desirability of competition in railways. New promotions of railways were decentralized ventures, and routes were built in a piecemeal manner, without any coordination. However, the hands-off stance of the government and market forces did little to rein in the monopolistic power of the railway companies. Other means of transportation could not compete with railways due to their technological inferiority. In the previous era competition in canal transport had been achieved by separating ownership of canals from barge operation, and by permitting multiple barge navigators to use the same canal. Within the railway industry, however, the high costs of locomotive ownership as well as access to stations and water tanks made the competitive canal model unviable. Tracks and trains were owned and managed by the same company. Where multiple companies operated between two locations the more direct line enjoyed an advantage. Thus, some companies were able to engage in monopolistic practices, such as charging exorbitant prices or refusing to provide certain services, e.g. third-class passenger wagons, which raised the ire of some members of Parliament (MPs).

The promotion of competition by building new lines would not solve the problem, either, because railways were *natural monopolies*. Multiple lines between two locations were wasteful when a single track was sufficient to meet total passenger and freight demand. The standard solution to the problem of balancing abusive monopolistic practices and wasteful competition is to have a single provider who offers a service between two points, and to regulate the provider to ensure proper price and quality. The relevant regulatory authority in Britain was the Board of Trade. In response to parliamentary inquiries its president, William Gladstone, proposed regulations in February 1844 to reduce fares and provide an improved third-class service. In return, the government would give existing railways protection from new competition. However, companies enjoying wide profit margins were unwilling to give them up. Railway directors fiercely opposed the regulation act, which they presented as government intrusion into private enterprise and a power grab, and they successfully lobbied Parliament. Of course, the fact that many railway directors and committee members were sitting in the House of Commons helped their cause. In the end railway interests prevailed, and the Board of Trade's recommendations were heavily diluted when the final act passed.

According to Arnold and McCartney (2004a: 129), while they viewed protection from competition as a desirable objective, railway owners and managers were unwilling to cooperate with the regulators because they did not believe in the credibility of government guarantees. Instead, in the following years, they tried to stifle competition by merging established lines. Nevertheless, intense competition persisted among new promotions. Companies competed by building alternative routes between two terminal towns and, once the trunk lines were in place, fought over branch- and connection-line construction (Simmons and Biddle 1997: 101).

The second issue government addressed concerned the regulation of banks and credit extension. The overextended credit and speculative fever of 1835–6 were still fresh in the minds of politicians in the early 1840s. Increasing exports of gold bullion to America between 1840 and 1844 also raised questions about the sustainability of bank reserves and the stability of the British financial system. To keep credit extension in check and to ensure the stability of the banking system Robert Peel's government passed the Bank Charter Act of 1844 (also known as the Peel Act). The act gave the Bank of England exclusive rights to issue banknotes in England and Wales, and required other banks to withdraw their banknotes gradually from circulation. It also limited the banknote-creating capacity of the Bank of England by imposing the requirement that new banknote issues should be backed fully by gold or up to £14m of government bonds. Restrictions on banknote issues were expected to restrain inflationary and speculative pressures. The flaw in the design was that, even without banknote issuance, banks could create money by making loans through deposits accounts. Not surprisingly, the Peel Act did not prevent banks from extending loans freely and was ineffective in suppressing speculation. However, it turned out to be very effective in exacerbating the liquidity freeze and worsening the crisis when financial markets collapsed in 1846.

The boom

The biggest railway boom started in 1844. By 1845 there were 761 petitions awaiting parliamentary approval (Campbell and Turner 2010). In 1844 Parliament approved railway petitions with a projected total market capitalization of £20m (Figure 7.1). Concurrently, railroad-share prices started their sustained climb. Between 1842 and 1845 railway profitability exceeded 4 percent. It was not exceptional but a high point by historical standards (with substantial variability among the individual lines). More importantly, the largest railway companies were paying dividends as high as 10 percent of their par value, four times higher than the short-term interest rate (Chancellor 2000: 130). The investors were local merchants and industrialists, mostly from outside London, and the "middle class," which included professionals (e.g. lawyers, physicians, officers, clergy), "white-collar" groups (e.g. teachers, engineers, servants), farmers, and women (Bryer 1991). The larger and wealthier middle class, a product of the industrial revolution, played an important role in encouraging interest in railway stocks. Government debt that paid interest as low as 3 percent in 1844 was not an attractive option, and the middle class increasingly channeled their savings to railway stocks. However, the London capital market, the core of British financial wealth, stayed out of the growth of the railway-stock market.

George Hudson, the railway baron, epitomized the boom. Hudson, a draper by trade, came into a large inheritance in 1827 at the age of 27 and afterwards became active in local Tory politics, banking, and railways. In 1835 he was a member of York City Council and a promoter of the York and North Midland Railway. A year later he became director of the railway and in 1837 was elected Lord Mayor of York. An ambitious, brash, and arrogant man, his business and political fortunes flourished for the next two decades as he accumulated immense wealth. He played a leading role in the merging of railway companies, and, by 1844, he was in charge of operations of more than 1,000 miles of track, almost half of all the route miles in Britain. After Hudson spearheaded the industry's successful opposition to Gladstone's regulatory measures trade journals and the industry-friendly press celebrated his leadership, awarding him the moniker "Railway King" (until then Hudson had been mockingly known as the "Yorkshire Balloon" (Arnold and McCartney 2004a: 133)). Later, as a Tory MP, Hudson was the strongest defender of railway interests in Parliament, as well as a ubiquitous, if disdained, presence among London's upper crust.

Hudson was matchless in promoting railways. He had an active interest in several newspapers, which served as vehicles to promote the expansion schemes of the companies he managed (Arnold and McCartney 2004a: 148). The openings of his new railway lines were always ostentatious affairs, designed to publicize both the enterprise and the man. He was avaricious in his business dealings and unscrupulous in management practices. He was a ruthless cost-cutter, willing to hire inexperienced or incompetent staff and drivers as long as wages were kept low and hours long. These hiring practices risked the lives of passengers and staff and several times led to fatal accidents (Arnold and McCartney 2004a: 84).

Railway promoters continually brought new railway-line projects to the attention of prospective investors and spread the news of high dividends in railway journals. It was common practice to pay dividends out of capital and to exaggerate profitability. The press was instrumental in fueling investor enthusiasm, and the number of railway journals multiplied. The rail press, whose lifeline was advertisements, and some non-rail press supported and praised the promotions unconditionally and contributed to the inflation of share prices. Many promotions were used by company directors as a means to enrich themselves at the expense of investors. Directors of the Liverpool, Manchester, and Newcastle Junction Railway, for instance, secretly kept most of the shares for themselves and issued only a fraction to the public. They then hyped the company to attract investors. They recruited George Hudson to the committee to elevate the credibility of the company; he agreed to join in return for free shares (worth £25,000 at par). Once the share price started rising the directors, including Hudson, sold their shares at a premium (Arnold and McCartney 2004a: 147). Price manipulation was not unusual. Hudson made similar capital gains in 1844 on the Manchester and Birmingham line. Profiteering by the inner circle of directors and committee members was prevalent, and the practice earned its own nickname: *stagging*.

Insiders with privileged information were not the only actors who were after quick capital gains. Speculation was widespread across the society. At the bottom rung were those scrip holders who lacked the means to make payments once construction started and managers made calls on subscribers. Their only hope was to sell the scrip at a premium (Chancellor 2000: 135).

Much of the speculation involved the rural branch and connection lines, and, consequently, many scrip and share buyers were from the countryside. Multiple railway proposals often competed for authorization to build a line along a certain route. At times competing projects sold scrip at a premium simultaneously, despite the fact that only one company could have operated at a profit due to the natural monopoly of the line. Country banks were established to provide credit against the collateral of shares and expansion of credit fueled a speculative frenzy. New provincial exchanges emerged to accommodate trading in shares and scrip. The interest on railway-share-collateralized loans reached as high as 80 percent. However, as long as share prices increased—and capital gains as high as 500 percent were reported—speculation leveraged by bank loans continued. By July 1845 the railroad-share-price index reached 168, an 80 percent increase since early 1843.

As the number of promotions escalated in 1844 and the workload exceeded the capabilities of parliamentary committees, Parliament considered altering the petition procedure. It proposed that all petitions be examined by a committee of railway experts from the Board of Trade before being sent to individual parliamentary committees. Many parliamentary-committee members also served on railway-company committees and had personal interests in ensuring that the planned projects had their stamp of approval. They strongly opposed this proposal, which they claimed to be a breach of their authority and a potential assault on their financial interests. Again the railway interest prevailed, and the committee of Board of Trade experts disbanded in 1845. Parliamentary committees could not cope with the large number of proposals and performed only perfunctory evaluations. In effect Parliament was complicit in the overexpansion of railways and railway-stock speculation.

As mentioned, parliamentary authorizations responded to promotions with about a one-year lag. In 1845 and 1846 the projected capitalization of authorized railways surged to £60m and £133m respectively (Figure 7.1). Fixed-capital investment jumped to £13m in 1845, £30m in 1846, and £44m in 1847. Route mileage increased by 293 in 1845, 595 in 1846, 909 in 1847, and 1,400 miles in 1848 (Figure 7.2).

The bust

By the summer of 1845 a crisis of confidence was brewing in certain quarters. Several newspapers, particularly *The Times* and *The Economist*, raised questions about the sustainability of railway promotion and construction, as well as the long-term destructive effects of railway speculation. Projected fixed-capital investment in authorized railways was large enough to absorb all of the capital funds in the country and starve other industries. Even in 1847, after the railway mania had imploded, new authorizations had collapsed, and many projects had been abandoned, fixed investment in ongoing railway construction exceeded £40m. This sum, equivalent to 7 percent of British gross domestic product (GDP), prompted *The Economist* (2008) to call the 1840s railway mania "arguably the greatest bubble in history."[2] Throughout the boom, however, the railway-friendly press dismissed concerns about the unsupportable growth of railways as "erroneous" and "alarmist" (Arnold and McCartney 2004a: 158; Campbell and Turner 2010; Chancellor 2000: 136–7).

The government and Parliament also observed the growing mania with unease and considered curbing speculation, but they were unable to decide on a course of action or even agree on whether any measures were necessary. Prime Minister Peel believed that the Bank Charter Act of 1844 would eventually keep the credit expansion in check, despite the fact that there were no signs of dissipating enthusiasm in 1845. In August 1845 the idea of raising the discount rate of the Bank of England, which was around

2.5 percent, was floated but eventually discarded due to doubts about its effectiveness in arresting the mania, as well as the worry that a rate increase might trigger a panic.

A credit shortage started in 1845. First, a disastrous harvest, the Irish potato blight, and concern about famine slowed economic growth. Higher grain imports lowered gold reserves and compelled the Bank of England to restrict credit. Subsequently, the discount rate was raised in October and November 1845. Second, as construction on the newly authorized railways got underway, companies started calling in capital. Average monthly calls for capital from the period of January 1843–September 1845 to the period of October–December 1845 increased by an order of 15. In the meantime a record number of promotions continued to sell new subscriptions to meet the November 30 petition deadline (Campbell and Turner 2010). Sales of scrip by subscribers to meet the capital calls and the abundance of new scrip caused railway-share prices to fall. Vanishing capital gains forced speculators to dispose of their shares, which added to the downward price pressure. Investors' scramble to banks to raise funds was futile as banks limited credit in response to the declining value of stock posted as collateral and depleting reserves. In the vicious cycle of credit stringency and a declining stock market despair replaced euphoria. In December the railway-share-price index was 20 percent below its July peak.

This was only the beginning of the long-term decline in railway shares. In response to the sharpening conflict between railway-company directors, who were making calls on capital, and scrip holders, who were trying to avert their obligations, Parliament passed the Dissolution Act in 1846 to facilitate the termination of railway companies. Many projects folded, while others were acquired by larger companies. Nevertheless, construction on existing projects continued, and their calls to pay for inputs and labor put pressure on scrip- and shareholders. The outcome was devastating for speculators as well as middle-class, long-term investors, who were facing diminishing incomes and tighter borrowing constraints.

In the midst of declining railway prices and the credit shortage the Bank Charter Act of 1844 had severely limited the Bank of England's activities. The act had been ineffectual in limiting credit because banks were able to extend loans by creating deposit accounts during the boom. In the presence of a liquidity freeze, however, the act prevented the Bank of England from strengthening the reserves of country banks and providing the liquidity that commerce and industry needed to operate. In fact, its depleting reserves forced the bank to limit discounting commercial paper. Over a two-year period the bank raised the discount rate and imposed limitations on advances on bills it would accept, but the drain on its reserves continued. The pressure on the Bank of England, in combination with commercial failures, led to loss of confidence in the banks and aggravated the liquidity crisis.

Finally, on October 25, 1847, the British government permitted the Bank of England to disregard the 1844 Bank Charter Act. The bank started a massive discounting operation, and the financial crisis ended as the bank expanded credit. The bank's actions not only saved the banking system but also warded off a further deepening of the crisis in the real sector of the economy. While the actions of the Bank of England eased the liquidity crisis and averted a total collapse of economic activity, the fortunes of the railway industry did not recover for quite some time. The average-railway-share index dropped until 1850 due to the continuing burden on scrip- and shareholders to meet calls for capital and chronic cost overruns. In December 1849 the index was 63 percent lower than its July 1845 peak. The rates of return on equity of the surviving railroads were below 3 percent until 1860, well below short-term interest rates (Arnold and McCartney 2004b).

George Hudson's fortunes did not fare any better. During the post-mania mergers he was initially able to expand his empire by acquiring more railways. However, in 1848 he was accused of corrupt and fraudulent business practices. Committees of inquiry established by railway companies concluded that Hudson had inflated revenues, paid dividends out of capital, and appropriated large sums of company funds for personal use. His business and personal reputation, already questionable due to charges of insider trading and stagging, was further damaged. He was forced to step down from railway directorships and York politics in 1849.

The former railway king spent the rest of his years clearing his name and battling with creditors and company directors who sought the return of misappropriated funds. Hudson paid many of his obligations but was nevertheless incarcerated in debtors' prison several times after losing his seat in the Commons. Only the generosity of his remaining few friends afforded him a bit of comfort before he died in 1871. Some of his harshest critics, however, viewed Hudson, his many flaws notwithstanding, as a product of a corrupt system. The *Illustrated London News*, in 1849, condemned the *zeitgeist* of the 1840s mania:

> [Hudson was] neither better nor worse than the morality of 1845. He rose to wealth and importance in an immoral period; he was a creature of an immoral system and . . . it is rather too much to expect of him that he should be purer than his time or his associates.
>
> (quoted in Arnold and McCartney 2004a: 239)

The aftermath

Between 1845 and 1850 total railway routes in Britain more than doubled, reaching 6,600 miles. Fixed-capital investment in railways, however, peaked in 1847 and then declined precipitously. The peak year in new routes was 1848, when 1,400 miles of railways were put into operation. Although the total route length fell far short of that authorized before

1847, which was estimated to reach 20,000 miles, it was still the most extensive transportation network in the world. Thus, despite all the problems it caused, railway mania provided the country with a vast transportation infrastructure. However, the network was hardly optimal. As it was developed without coordination between the various railway companies there were duplicate lines between terminal locations with relatively minor differences in routes and many unviable branch lines, which ultimately closed down. Suboptimal lines and over-construction may account for the low returns on railway investments; the average rate of return on equity between 1847 and 1855 was merely 3 percent. By January 1850 average share prices were 56 percent lower than their 1845 peak. Thus, railways transformed the economic structure but proved, on average, to be a poor financial investment.

Inefficiencies in the British system led many to question the virtues of a laissez-faire approach to building railways. Would the public interest have been better served by planning and coordination? European countries that industrialized later than Britain thought so. In Belgium, France, and Germany states were involved to various extents in the design and construction of the railway network and the management of the train service.

Understanding British railway manias

The economic-history literature on the British experience in the first half of the nineteenth and late eighteenth centuries is rich, but there have been few interpretations of the stock-price movements in light of the modern debates in finance. Most historical accounts traditionally attribute the price boom and collapse to speculative excesses. In recent years, however, in line with developments in finance literature, dedicated analyses of the behavior of British railway shares have been conducted.

As mentioned, the average profitability of railways was never outstanding, but this does not necessarily mean that investors who were observing current and past performance were unrealistic about returns on their investments. It can always be argued that high share prices were simply reflections of expected future profitability in a transformational industry. Given this caveat, it is still a reasonable exercise to question how reasonable prices were in view of revenue projections. Odlyzko (2010a) argues, for instance, that in the 1840s prices were totally disconnected from any plausible profit expectations. His rough calculations show that the 10 percent dividend figure, often mentioned in the press, would have required revenues to increase five- to tenfold in five years. He views such growth of revenues as improbable and concludes that investors' willingness to pay high prices against virtually impossible odds shows they were "deluded by the collective psychology of the Mania" (Odlyzko 2010a: 172).

Campbell (2010) notes that the question of how well prices reflect the fundamentals can be answered by studying whether changes in the current stock price are consistent with changes in future dividends. A positive response of price to dividend growth may be taken to confirm that the fundamentals explain the share price. Statistical tests indicate that the pricing of railway shares was consistent with short-term changes in dividends, but not so with long-term changes. Put differently, investors did a good job in predicting near term (two-year) changes in dividends; however, they lacked longer-term foresight on changing fundamentals and ended up overpricing the shares. Campbell also finds that, controlling for their discounted dividends, railway stocks were overvalued relative to non-railway stocks in the long run but not in the short run. The analysis does not, however, explain why prices deviated from the fundamentals in the long run. The deviation could have been the outcome of investors failing to see that far ahead or focusing on the short term due to the misinformation disseminated by railway companies.

Finally, Bagehot's (1999 [1873]) deliberations on the "delicate" nature of the credit market are a precursor to the credit-cycle model of Minsky. Bagehot draws attention to the fact that, due to the high degree of division of labor and specialization, a high degree of interdependence existed between banks and producers (e.g. manufacturers, merchants, farmers). Therefore, any shock to the system was easily transmitted across the economy. Within- and cross-sector interconnections caused bank loans, the credibility of borrowers, and profitability to move in tandem and reinforce each other. A positive shock that raised profitability, first, in a large sector and, subsequently, in the broader economy (such as the development of canals and railways with their powerful backward and forward linkages) initiated a spiral of higher profitability, firms' credit worthiness, and bank loans (Bagehot 1999 [1873]: 149). With prosperity prices increased and warranted even further extension of bank funds for firms to meet their operating expenses and carry out production and trade (Bagehot 1999 [1873]: 155). The rising demand for credit in due course put upward pressure on interest rates. The expansion in demand for credit was also fed by both the optimism of producers with regard to their future sales and rising speculation in financial assets. Fraud and deceptive practices generated by the upward movement of the cycle fostered speculator enthusiasm.

Overextension of credit also caused borrowers and lenders to overreact to any adverse event that injured economic fortunes, such as the draining of specie abroad or a bad harvest. Under unfavorable conditions the economy unwound quickly because the credit system was "delicate":

> The peculiar essence of our banking system is an unprecedented trust between man and man: and when that trust is much weakened by hidden causes, a small accident may greatly hurt it, and a great accident for a moment may almost destroy it.
>
> (Bagehot 1999 [1873]: 158–9)

The liquidity shortage was the symptom of a deeper problem. Once banks observed a sector-specific or economy-wide distress, not knowing what was on the balance sheets of individual borrowers, they limited credit across the board to ensure solvency. Firms hurried to discount their bills to build cash reserves in the event they were pressured by the demands of their creditors. Speculators sold assets to cash in capital gains or, if they were leveraged, to meet margin calls, and pushed asset prices down. The generalized rush to liquidity, not to purchase assets and goods but to hoard in anticipation of hard times, caused financial markets to collapse with (as in 1825 and 1846) or without (as in 1836) a panic. The orderliness of financial markets' recovery depended on the willingness of the Bank of England to discount various financial instruments and to allay the fear that the channels of commerce would remain blocked.

Bagehot advocated that the Bank of England's reserves should be made available liberally and widely to banks in times of severe liquidity shortage to prevent the aggravation of the crisis and the panic. This does not imply, however, indiscriminate lending by the lender of last resort. The Bagehot doctrine states that the lender of last resort should lend freely but at penalty rates in accordance with the public's demand for money and against good collateral, not to shore up any specific banking institution but to support the entire banking system against the threat of panic:

> The end is to stay the panic; and the advances should, if possible, stay the panic. And for this purpose there are two rules:—First. That these loans should only be made at a very high rate of interest. This will operate as a heavy fine on unreasonable timidity, and will prevent the greatest number of applications by persons who do not require it. . .Secondly. That at this rate these advances should be made on all good banking securities, and as largely as the public ask for them. The reason is plain. The object is to stay alarm, and nothing therefore should be done to cause alarm. But the way to cause alarm is to refuse some one who has good security to offer. The news of this will spread in an instant through all the money market at a moment of terror; no one can say exactly who carries it, but in half an hour it will be carried on all sides, and will intensify the terror everywhere. . .The amount of bad business in commercial countries is an infinitesimally small fraction of the whole business. That in a panic the bank, or banks, holding the ultimate reserve should refuse bad bills or bad securities will not make the panic really worse; the 'unsound' people are a feeble minority, and they are afraid even to look frightened for fear their unsoundness may be detected. . . If it is known that the Bank of England is freely advancing on what in ordinary times is reckoned a good security—on what is then commonly pledged and easily convertible—the alarm of the solvent merchants and bankers will be stayed.
>
> (Bagehot 1999 [1873]: 197–8)

However, in the dust and smoke of a financial crisis it may not be easy to identify high-quality collateral; the quality of the collateral itself may decline the longer the panic lasts; and the lender of last resort may be subject to political pressures or show favoritism. Thus, implementation of the Bagehot doctrine raises challenges; but the majority of the economics profession today is in favor of its implementation, subject to various stipulations to address the challenges encountered in practice.

Timeline

1750s	First industrial-era canals completed.
1750–89	Parliament authorizes 48 canals.
1790–4	Parliament authorizes 51 canals.
1792–3	British canal-promotion and construction boom.
1793	Canal boom ends and depression starts.
1821	Parliament authorizes S&D, first joint-stock railway company.
1821–4	British economy booms in midst of abundant credit.
1824	Market in Latin American securities expands.
1825	S&D Railway Company starts operating; Parliament repeals Bubble Act and limited-liability privilege expands; security prices peak; Latin American securities market collapses; security prices decline in general; Bank of England (BoE) raises discount rate and limits credit; in December starts pumping liquidity by discount paper.
1825–7	British economy in recession
1826	New banking legislation allows joint-stock banks outside London.
1828–32	British economy in depression.
1830	L&MR (authorized in 1826) starts operation.
1832–4	British economy booms.
1832–5	Parliament authorizes railways with projected capital of £13m.
1835	Bank reserves decline due to specie flow abroad.
1836	Reserve depletion continues; BoE raises discount rate twice; railway-company share prices collapse after summer; Parliament authorizes railways with projected capital of £23m.
1837	New railway authorizations start declining; economic contraction starts.
1842	British economy recovers.
1844	Railway regulations proposed by the Board of Trade but rejected by Parliament; Bank Charter Act passes Parliament; Parliament authorizes new railways with projected capital of £20m.

1845	Railroad-share-price index rises 80 percent on 1843; capital calls by railway companies rise; some newspapers warn of speculative bubble but ignored; measures to pinch bubble considered but discarded; share prices start declining after August 1845.
1846	Parliament authorizes new railways with projected capital of £60m; Parliament passes Dissolution Act to terminate railway companies.
1847	Parliament authorizes new railways with projected capital of £133m; government permits BoE to ignore Bank Charter Act of 1844.
1848	Committees formed to investigate fraudulent business practices of railway companies.

Key terms and concepts

Laissez faire
Natural monopoly
Stagging

Endnotes

1 Railroads, in turn, were to reduce the cost further by one-third to one-half.
2 By way of comparison, fixed investment in communications infrastructure during the dot-com bubble of the 1990s (a technological revolution often compared to the nineteenth-century railway revolution) totaled 1 to 1.5 percent of US GDP.

References

Arnold, A. J. and S. McCartney. 2004a. *George Hudson: The Rise and Fall of the Railway King.* New York: Hambledon and London.

Arnold, A. J. and S. McCartney. 2004b. "Were They Ever 'Productive to the Capitalist?' Rates of Return on Britain's Railways, 1830–55." *Journal of European Economic History* 33 (2): 373–410.

Bagehot, Walter. 1999 [1873]. *Lombard Street: A Description of the Money Market.* New York: John Wiley and Sons.

Burton, Anthony. 2004. *On the Rails: Two Centuries of Railways.* London: Aurum Press.

Bryer, R. A. 1991. "Accounting for the 'Railway Mania' of 1845—A Great Railway Swindle?" *Accounting, Organizations and Society* 16 (5/6): 439–86.

Campbell, Gareth. 2010. *Bubbling Dividends.* (MPRA Paper No. 29840). Online: http://mpra.ub.uni-muenchen.de/29840/.

Campbell, Gareth and John Turner. 2010. *"The Greatest Bubble in History": Stock Prices during the British Railway Mania.* (MPRA Paper No. 21820). Online: http://mpra.ub.uni-muenchen.de/21820.

Chancellor, Edward. 2000. *Devil Take the Hindmost: A History of Financial Speculation*. New York: Plume.

Conant, Charles A. 1969 [1927]. *A History of Modern Banks of Issue*. New York: Augustus M. Kelley.

The Economist. 2008. "The Beauty of Bubbles." December 18. Online: www.economist.com/node/12792903.

Gayer, Arthur G., W. W. Rostow and Anna Jacobson Schwartz. 1953. *The Growth and Fluctuations of the British Economy 1790–1850: An Historical, Statistical, and Theoretical Study of Britain's Economic Development*. London: Oxford University Press.

Hadfield, Charles. 1984. *British Canals: An Illustrated History*, 7th ed. North Pomfret, VT: David and Charles.

Joplin, T. 1832. *Case for Parliamentary Inquiry into the Circumstances of the Panic: In a Letter to Thomas Gisborne, Esq., M.P.* London: J. Ridgway and Sons, Piccadilly.

Kindleberger, Charles P. 1993. *A Financial History of Western Europe*, 2nd ed. New York: Oxford University Press.

Mitchell, B. R. 1964. "The Coming of Railway and United Kingdom Economic Growth." *The Journal of Economic History* 24 (3): 315–36.

Mitchell, B. R. 1988. *British Historical Statistics*. Cambridge, New York: Cambridge University Press.

Neal, Larry. 1998. "The Financial Crisis of 1825 and the Restructuring of the British Financial System." *Federal Reserve Bank of St. Louis* 80 (3): 53–76.

Odlyzko, Andrew. 2010a. *Collective Hallucinations and Inefficient Markets: The British Railway Mania of the 1840s*. Minneapolis: University of Minnesota. Online: www.dtc.umn.edu/~odlyzko/doc/hallucinations.pdf.

Odlyzko, Andrew. 2010b. This Time is Different: An Example of a Giant, Wildly Speculative, and Successful Investment Mania. *The B.E. Journal of Economic Analysis and Policy (Topics)* 10 (1): Article 60. Online: www.bepress.com/bejeap/vol10/iss1/art60.

Queen Victoria. 1908. *The Letters of Queen Victoria*, vol. 1. London: John Murray.

Simmons, Jack and Gordon Biddle, Eds. 1997. *The Oxford Companion to British Railway History*. New York: Oxford University Press.

Ward, J. R. 1974. *The Finance of Canal Building in Eighteenth-century England*. London: Oxford University Press.

8 The American experience I
The antebellum era

During the nineteenth century the US evolved from a newly independent backwater to an industrial powerhouse. At the beginning of the century the country was an agrarian economy in which cotton was the critical commercial crop and the primary source of export earnings. Foodstuff production and small-scale manufacturing catered to the domestic market. As geographic frontiers expanded mid century, grains also became an important export item, and agriculture remained the dominant economic activity for a while longer. From mid century onward, however, railroads were the foundation of economic growth. The growing rail network stimulated manufacturing via backward and forward linkages.

The US financial system from the end of the eighteenth to the beginning of the twentieth century was in a continuous state of flux, with periodic crises followed by deep recessions and even depressions. It lacked a central banking institution to oversee the banks and act as a lender of last resort in times of need. First, the federal government started and ended two early experiments with a national bank fashioned after the Bank of England. Subsequently, a range of banking practices were introduced, including state-chartered banks, "free" banking, state monopoly banks, coordinated self-regulation, outright prohibition of banks, and a hierarchical national banking system. However, chronic banking crises continued with astonishing frequency. In the absence of a lender of last resort banks and the federal government tried various measures to alleviate banking crises, with mixed success. Finally, the Federal Reserve System was created in 1913 as the lender of last resort.

Contributing to the turbulence in US financial markets were waves of land speculation fed by domestic bank credit, a high dependence on foreign funds to build transportation infrastructure, heavily indebted Western railroads operating with excess capacity, the pro-cyclical volatility of bank credit, the interconnection of banks and securities markets, and the impact of agricultural cycles on monetary conditions. This environment also contained economic and political debates and strife, some of which endure to the present day. Disputes over hard vs. soft money (i.e. specie vs. paper money), and skepticism and distrust of the large banking institutions by popular groups (including small businesses, farmers, and small banks) surfaced during banking crises and asset-price crashes. There were runs on banks by depositors and note holders, as well as the eventual suspension of convertibility of paper into specie, in 1819, 1837, 1857, 1873, 1884, 1890, 1893, and 1896. The six most important crises were related to land speculation in 1819 and 1837, the land- and railroad-securities panic of 1857, the railroad-securities panic of 1873, the currency and industrial panic of 1893, and, in the new century, the run on New York City (NYC) financial trust companies in 1907. This chapter examines the antebellum period (1781–1860).[1]

The US financial system: the early years and the 1819 crisis

The post-Revolutionary War US financial system was primitive and fragmented. The federal government was burdened with large debts from the war, and there was no functional taxation system, which made debt service virtually impossible. In addition to banknotes, federal and state paper and dozens of foreign coins were circulating as money, which created multiple exchange rates and a cumbersome monetary system. The new republic needed a financial system, but the structure of the prospective system was a contentious matter in the innermost political circles. Alexander Hamilton's and Thomas Jefferson's opposing economic and political visions on whether the US needed a European-style national financial institution that would also serve as the government's bank influenced not only the post-Revolutionary War arrangements but also, according to Johnson and Kwak (2010), the evolution of the US financial system over the next century.

In 1789 Hamilton became Secretary of the Treasury and laid the foundations for a fiscally powerful, solvent federal government. Hamilton was in favor of building strong, centralized political and economic institutions to put the country on a resilient fiscal and financial footing. Under his watch, the existing federal and state debts were combined and restructured into bonds that paid interest in hard money. These new securities were sold to both domestic and foreign investors. In addition, new taxes on imports and whiskey secured a steady flow of federal revenues. Hamilton also envisioned a publicly chartered, private bank modeled after the Bank of England to bring order to the US monetary system, manage the government's revenues and payments, provide credit to both the government and the private sector, and oversee banks to prevent overextension of credit.

However, the new republic was a heterogeneous collection of former colonies, and, after years of fighting the British crown, citizens had a profound distrust of concentrated power. Further, Secretary of State Thomas Jefferson was deeply suspicious of large banks and bankers, as such institutions would centralize economic as well as political power and undermine democracy. Jefferson and the Southern members of Congress also viewed a strong, central financial institution as a vehicle that would serve the commercial interests of the Northern states and threaten Southern agricultural interests, whose credit needs could be met by local institutions. They questioned the constitutionality of a central bank that would be a tool to extend federal authority over the states.

The first Bank of the United States

Hamilton's economic vision prevailed, securing him the first round of the Jefferson–Hamilton debate. Against Jefferson's objections the first Bank of the US was chartered as a national bank in 1791 for a period of 20 years. The bank had its home office in Philadelphia and branch offices in eight cities. One fifth of its $10m equity, larger than the combined capital of the banks in existence, was funded by the federal government, the remainder by domestic and foreign investors. The foreigners, predominantly British, were heavily represented among the shareholders, but they had no voting rights. The public paid for its shares of the bank in specie and government bonds.

Although it was the largest shareholder, the government was not permitted to participate in the management of the bank. The bank performed the regular banking functions of accepting deposits and discounting promissory notes and bills of exchange; in addition, it was authorized to issue convertible notes that were accepted as legal tender in payment of taxes. Hamilton adopted the *bimetallic standard*, which meant that the value of the convertible paper money was set in both gold and silver. The quantity of notes issued was a multiple of the specie reserves; thus, the bank was able to augment the nation's money supply. While it made loans to the private sector, the bank's largest customer was the federal government. It provided short-term loans to the government, managed its fiscal affairs (including Jefferson's 1803 Louisiana Purchase), collected revenues, and functioned as a clearing house for government debt. Overall, the bank proved to be a profitable enterprise, yielding average annual dividends of 8 percent over its lifetime (Stedman 1905: 53). In addition, the bank performed the central-bank duty of regulating state-chartered banks to prevent over-issuance of banknotes. Owing to its size, prestige, and geographic spread of branch offices, the first Bank of the US was the repository of many of the notes of state-chartered banks. The bank was able to restrain the state banks from over-expanding credit by redeeming these notes for conversion to specie.

A dynamic, competitive financial system soon developed. Within a decade more than a hundred banks were chartered by the states. These banks were able to attract large amounts of capital because they were established as limited-liability corporations.[2] The anarchy of the monetary system ended as convertible notes and deposits of the Bank of the US and state-chartered banks replaced the multitude of coins and paper monies. In addition, the securities markets expanded; the primary items traded were government debt, and bank and transportation (turnpike, canal, bridge) stocks and bonds. According to Rousseau and Sylla (2005), the US market was similar to the British market in terms of the numbers of securities traded and, by 1825, matched it in terms of capitalization. The depth of the market meant US securities were highly liquid. European investors participated heavily in the US stock market and, in fact, held most of the securities.

Despite its success the Bank of the US faced hostility. The coalition of its opponents included citizens in the Southern and Western states, who resisted the discipline that the bank attempted to impose on state banks that did not pay specie on demand, and Jeffersonian Republicans, who continued to question the bank's constitutionality. Some even expressed concerns about the bank becoming a British instrument that meddled in the affairs of the US economy (even though foreigners were non-voting shareholders). In 1811 Congress did not renew the charter of the bank, by a margin of one vote.

The second Bank of the United States and the crisis of 1819

The need for a national bank re-emerged during the Anglo-American War of 1812–15. During the war the money stock expanded at a very rapid pace. Among other instruments, the federal government raised funds for war expenses by selling short-term, "small Treasury notes," which served as money, as they were used for payment of taxes, duties, and federal debt. In the absence of any external supervision state banks freely expanded banknote issue, which led to runaway inflation and the eventual suspension of convertibility of notes to specie in 1814 and 1815 with the consent of the government. To restore fiscal and monetary order Congress chartered the second Bank of the US in 1816 for a 20-year period, with a mission statement similar to that of the first Bank of the US. The bank opened for business in 1817, with headquarters in Philadelphia and 18 branches across the country.

The establishment of the second Bank of the US coincided with an economic boom and the expansion of the Western and Southern frontiers. The high global price of cotton, the backbone of the US economy at the time, and expanding international trade were the main forces behind the boom (North 1966a: 179). Southern cotton was the primary commercial crop exported to Europe. The Northeast supplied manufactured goods, either domestically produced or imported, as well as banking, transportation, and insurance services. Manufacturing was not yet capable of competing internationally in terms of cost or quality. The geographic division of labor had the South generating export earnings, which permitted import expansion and production in the North to feed and equip the domestic market.

During the 1810s the geographic boundaries of the US economy expanded as settlers moved to Alabama, Mississippi, Ohio, Indiana, and Missouri in increasing numbers to purchase and cultivate public lands. Many settlers could not afford to purchase land outright, but the federal government permitted buying land on credit. Both the second Bank of the US and state banks extended credit to the settlers against the collateral of land. Land purchases accelerated in the second half of the 1810s and peaked in 1818 at 3.5m acres, but they dropped precipitously when the US was faced with its first big depression and financial panic in 1818–19 (Figure 8.1). Overextension of credit had made the balance sheets of state-chartered banks unstable. In 1818, facing depleting specie reserves, the second Bank of the US and state-chartered banks started recalling loans and demanding immediate payment, but many debtors did not have the money to pay off their loans. As banks contracted credit, panic ensued, foreclosures and bankruptcies swelled, and overextended banks closed their doors. The South was hit worse than the North, and the ensuing depression lasted until 1824. The second Bank of the US, the only national and the largest bank, became a special object of ire when it redeemed for specie the checks and notes of the state-chartered banks that it had accumulated as deposits. The Western and Southern states blamed the bank for causing the crisis (Stedman 1905: 78).

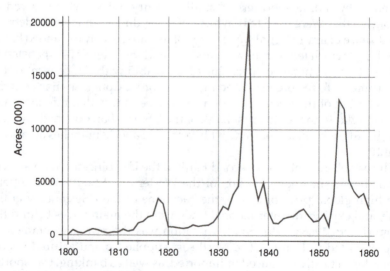

Figure 8.1 Public land purchases in the US, 1800–60 (annual).

Source: Hibbard (1965: 100, 103, 106).

Interpretation

There are three competing explanations of the land boom and bust of 1818–19. The first two interpretations are distinguished in terms of the relative weight they place on rising agricultural prices (a fundamental of the land price) and speculation. In explaining the fundamental forces behind the Southern and Western expansion and the land boom, North (1966a) focuses on the higher export demand for US cotton and grain in the aftermath of the Napoleonic Wars that ravaged western Europe. Export demand raised agricultural prices and thus the demand for land. In addition, the opening up of the former Native American lands, construction of new roads, and improvement in river transportation facilitated people's movement to the West. Migration from Europe had also risen after the brief pause during the war years and augmented the westward movement. According to this interpretation, credit expansion played an accommodating role to these real forces by facilitating land purchases.

In contrast, Smith and Cole (1969: 53–4) note that the correlation between land sales and immigration (even allowing for time lags) is not close and that the irregularity of land purchases over time does not align with the continuity of improvement of transportation facilities. Smith and Cole, along with several other historians, conclude that the fundamentals alone cannot explain the 1818 spike in land sales. Instead, they highlight capital-gain expectations as the primary motive in the surge of land acquisitions. Land speculation was a familiar business in the US and featured many founding fathers among its practitioners (Sakolski 1932). The expansion of the country's geographic boundaries provided more opportunities to speculators to acquire land on borrowed funds. During the nineteenth century the term "land speculator" encompassed a wide range of people. At one end of the spectrum were prominent speculators with the means to acquire land before the settlers and pioneers. These speculators parceled out large tracks of the best land and sold it to the new arrivals at a premium. At the other end were small farmers who purchased more land than they could cultivate in anticipation of selling the spare acreage at a higher price (North 1966b: 125).

North (1966a: 182–3) accepts that the initial agricultural-price surge might have created over-optimism among farmers and land speculators, fed their expectations of further appreciation, and compelled them to invest in land, but considers it of secondary importance. In contrast with historians (e.g. Gates 1942) who argue that speculation caused massive harm to individual settlers as well as the overall economy, however, North (1966b: 132) claims that speculators performed beneficial services by developing and improving the land, thereby adding to its value.

Competing explanations of the crash follow directly from these two lines of reasoning. According to North (1966a: 182), declining cotton prices, as a consequence of expanding production, were the primary source of the depression. The inflow of resources into cultivation, in the form of developed land, population movements, and credit availability, over time increased the cotton supply and pushed the price down. Economic contraction in Europe also lowered demand for US farm products. When plans based on high cotton prices collapsed land buyers with mortgages were ruined.

Accounts that rely more heavily on the behavior of speculators do not deny the role of changes in the fundamentals but underscore that the latter was only the proximate cause that triggered the crisis. The real problem with the system was the unsustainably high debt burden of farmers and speculators and the overall escalation of risk. The first drop in agricultural prices burst the speculative bubble and created a vicious cycle of credit restraint. According to this latter interpretation, the lax monetary stance of the second Bank of the US and the state banks, and the abundance of credit extended primarily for land acquisition and development, played a critical role in the land boom and the crash. The argument, in line with the Bagehot–Minsky–Kindleberger approach, explained in Chapter 6, is that the bank credit extension was responding to mounting speculative forces. As the boom progressed, banks expanded more credit. The credit growth, in turn, made banks' situations unstable due to the dubious quality of many of the loans, which made the system more vulnerable to an adverse shock. Indeed, as soon as the shock of declining cotton prices hit the economy and the specter of defaults and foreclosures rose banks abruptly limited credit and recalled loans.

The third explanation of the cause of the boom and crisis also focuses on the role of money and credit but reverses the causal relationship. Economists and historians of the Austrian school lay the blame for the country's financial troubles on the second Bank of the US and, indirectly, the federal government. Rothbard (2002) argues that it was the unsustainable banknote expansion by the bank and the government's unwillingness to enforce specie conversion by state banks in 1814 that created the artificial boom and malinvestment in land in the first place. The boom was unsustainable because paper money had grown out of proportion with specie. In the end the bank was forced to curtail credit severely to replenish specie reserves and protect itself. On a deeper level, however, the fault lay with the federal government, which committed a violation of property rights by allowing banks to suspend payments in 1814 rather than forcing them to accept the consequences of their irresponsible actions. Thus, the solution to the monetary chaos is strict adherence to hard money that requires the backing of all banknotes by specie (Rothbard 2002: 83).

According to this view, market discipline ensures the health and stability of the system by eliminating the weak spots or liquidating any bank that cannot convert notes or deposits to specie on demand. Banks, like any other company, are rewarded in accordance with the degree of satisfaction their product generates. Money is no different from any other commodity. Individuals decide whether to deposit money in a bank or accept or refuse its banknotes based on their confidence in the bank.

Whether money really is like any other commodity is a critical point of contention between the Austrian laissez-faire approach and its critics. For instance, the bankruptcy of a cotton farmer or a textile manufacturer is unlikely to create significant ripple effects across the economy, which demonstrates, the critics contend, that money is very different from cotton or textiles. Money and credit perform unique functions as the lubricators of channels of commerce. Money has the peculiar characteristic of being the asset of choice in the face of an oncoming liquidity crisis. Moreover, a shock to the system in the form of bankruptcy of a bank can easily be transmitted across the economy due to interconnections among banking institutions. These features of the financial system underscore its exposure to systemic risk, or the relative ease of the transformation of a local turbulence into a threat to the entire financial system and, indeed, the whole economy.

The land panic of 1837

Langton Cheves became the president of the second Bank of the US in 1819 and restored the bank's reputation, which had been severely tarnished by misconduct in previous years. In 1822 he was succeeded by Nicholas Biddle, who, according to most modern commentators, proved to be an accomplished central banker with evenly matched skills and arrogance. The bank expanded its network by opening more branch offices. While the mismanagement of its initial years was behind it, the bank still faced a formidable alliance of opponents. It was unpopular among the Western and Southern state-chartered banks for keeping their credit expansion in check, as well as among small businesses and trades people who needed access to more credit. Banks located in the emerging financial centers, such as NYC, resented the privileged relationship of the second Bank of the US with the government. The constitutionality of a national bank continued to be questioned. Finally, President Jackson was a Jeffersonite who was skeptical of paper money and big centralized financial institutions, which he believed favored economic and political elites at the expense of the public.

Bank president Biddle's overconfidence and association with Jackson's political opponents did not help the bank either. The financial support that the bank offered to Jackson's political opponents escalated the conflict. The second Bank of the US applied for re-charter in 1832, four years before it was set to expire, and Congress renewed the charter. President Jackson, whose re-election platform was built on ending the political and economic concentration of power, promptly vetoed the bill and ended the US's second national-bank experiment and the second round of the

Jefferson–Hamilton debate. The federal government withdrew its deposits from the second Bank of the US and distributed them to the state-chartered banks that proliferated in the 1830s.

The 1830s boom

After the mid 1820s the US resumed its fast pace of growth. Improved transportation facilities opened access to land resources and expanded the internal market. The Erie Canal opened in 1825, and, in the following year, the first railroad was completed in Massachusetts, with a total track of four miles. The length of tracks in operation expanded from 23 to 1,437 miles between 1830 and 1837 (Figure 8.2), and the railroad network started to advance inland from the Eastern seaboard. Railroad stocks were listed on the New York Stock and Exchange Board after 1830. In addition, the number of steamboats that operated on the Mississippi River quadrupled between 1825 and 1835.

Europe was a rich source of funds for US infrastructure investment. The federal government had paid the national debt in full by 1835 and acquired the reputation of a credible borrower in international financial markets, which attracted even more funds from European lenders. Much of this foreign capital was channeled to canal, railroad, and bank securities. Municipalities and states, led by Ohio, Indiana, Illinois, and Michigan, incurred a substantial portion of the total foreign indebtedness to finance infrastructure construction that targeted lowering the transportation costs of agricultural commodities. Between 1831 and 1837 the

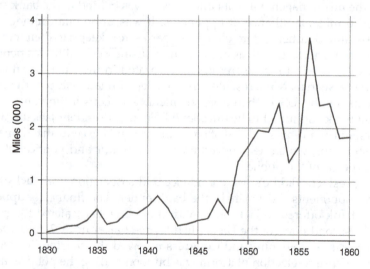

Figure 8.2 New railroads in operation in the US, 1830–60 (annual).
Source: Carter *et al.* (2006: Series Df884).

aggregate foreign debt of the US increased almost threefold. While the US trade balance was in chronic deficit, which would normally have depleted specie, the country net accumulated gold and silver due to capital inflow from abroad. Political opinion regarding European enthusiasm for US securities was divided. The Whigs, who opposed President Jackson and his Democratic party, viewed foreign capital as a vehicle for economic development and welcomed it, but among the Jacksonians, who were concerned about the impact of growing foreign influence on US securities markets and financial stability, it was a subject of consternation.

During the 1830s the US experienced another speculative episode, the object of which was again land. As shown in Figure 8.1, land purchases in the 1830s dwarfed the 1814–19 land rush. The sale of federal public lands increased fivefold between 1834 and 1836 and reached a peak of 20m acres in 1836. Similar to the previous episode, the fundamentals for the expansion of land purchases were in place (Ratner *et al.* 1979: 179). Improvement in transportation facilities (canals, railroads, steamships), an increase in the number of immigrants from Europe, and favorable agricultural prices all played a role, especially in the fertile Mississippi and Ohio River valleys. The federal government promoted Western settlement by reducing the minimum plot size over time (from 320 acres in 1800 to 40 in 1832) and keeping the public land price low.

While it required payments for land to be made in specie, the federal government also accepted convertible banknotes as payment. Government land offices across the South and the West administered the sale of public lands. Long lines of buyers in front of these offices gave rise to the idiom "land office business," which refers to a thriving volume of trade. North (1966a) again emphasizes the role of higher cotton prices in inducing Southern farmers to purchase land for clearing and cultivation. As with the case of 1818, however, many authors do not consider these fundamentals sufficient to explain the spike of 1836, and point to the expansion of speculative activity fueled by the abundance of money as the reason (Hammond 1957; Smith and Cole 1969; Stedman 1905). According to Hammond, the low price that the government charged for land to make it available to settlers attracted speculators, who were organized professionals with bank connections, in prodigious numbers. In addition, the rising demand for land was not limited to agricultural plots in rural areas. Land was purchased with an eye on future urban development in the new territories. Moreover, real-estate prices in established metropolitan areas like NYC and Chicago were on the rise.

Sources of monetary growth

The quantity of money in the economy sharply increased during the 1830s. There are two competing explanations of the source of monetary growth.

The traditional view traces the expansion to President Jackson's veto of the second Bank of the US, which removed whatever discipline there was on the state-chartered banks. Within the three years following 1833 the number of state-chartered banks increased by 50 percent, to about 600 (Hammond 1957: 453). Bank capital increased by 164 percent, and loans increased by 383 percent. In 1837 the total stock of banknotes was four times the specie reserves (Stedman 1905: 95), and was growing fastest in the South and the West.

President Jackson's decision to transfer Treasury deposits to the so-called "pet" banks (banks that were supposedly loyal to the administration numbered as many as 91 in 1836) is also viewed as a factor that added to credit expansion. These Treasury funds were substantial. Between 1828 and 1836 government revenues exceeded expenditures by a factor of 1.6. The primary source of revenue was customs, but public land sales were also important. In 1836 revenues from land sales constituted half of government revenues (Hammond 1957: 451). As this revenue flow was deposited in the state banks their capacity to make loans increased.

The changing agrarian structure transformed the debt pattern of Western farmers. Farmers were increasingly producing for the market rather than for self-consumption and, therefore, borrowed in large volumes not only for land acquisition and development but also to finance purchases of farm equipment, raise livestock, and transport their products to market. The bulk of bank lending, however, was made to small businesses and merchants, many of whom were engaged in land speculation. Banks loaned to speculators by issuing more banknotes, and, as these banknotes were re-deposited in the banking system, creating the illusion of higher resources, banks could expand loans even further to meet the demands of land speculators. The rising ratios of loans to bank equity and banknotes/deposits to specie reserves were the warning signs of undercapitalized banks and liquidity risks. Nevertheless, as capital-gain expectations whetted the appetites of speculators and raised demand for land, credit continued to expand.

The alternative view of the source of monetary growth is that it was not due to President Jackson's policies or excessive banknote expansion. Rather, the money stock increased because banks were accumulating specie, thanks to silver inflows from Mexico and security purchases by the Europeans. Temin (1969: 90) offers evidence that, in fact, reserve ratios did not increase while the money supply was rising. As incoming silver strengthened reserves, banks created more paper money. The higher money stock was channeled to purchases of land, which the government was offering at a constant price. Temin also maintains that, in contrast to the traditional view, land sales did not feed back to credit expansion because the government withdrew the money it accumulated from land sales from circulation.

Austrian-school economists adhere to Temin's argument and clear the state-chartered banks of having instigated reckless credit expansion and encouraged land speculation. In their view, closing the second Bank of the US did not cause imprudent lending by state banks, as the reserve ratios of banks were no higher after the bank closed (Rothbard 2002). The trouble was that the banks were not required to keep specie to back all of the notes they issued and were permitted to hold only a portion of deposits as reserves; therefore, the inflow of specie and rising deposits led to a disproportionate increase in the money supply. The culprit in monetary expansion, then, was banking regulation or the fractional-reserve system sanctioned by the government. The Jackson administration, admirably according to this view, had intended to fix this problem by imposing a 100 percent reserve requirement but, unfortunately, did not accomplish this task.

The crash

Two policy shocks from the Jackson administration and the reversal of inflow of British capital triggered an implosion of speculative activity and the collapse of the economy in 1837. The relative importance of these shocks is again a subject of debate.

The first policy shock was the Specie Circular of 1836. The Jackson administration had been observing with apprehension the sale of public land for banknotes. Ever distrustful of paper money, the White House was alarmed by the quality of these notes, against which the government was dispensing public land, and decided to put a stop to the paper money-land exchange. In July 1836 President Jackson issued the Specie Circular, which required payment for government land purchased after August 15, with few exceptions, to be in gold or silver. The circular expressed concern about the excessive growth of paper money as well as the monopolization of public lands in the hands of speculators at the expense of settlers and immigrants. The measure effectively lowered the demand for paper money and induced a rush to specie.

The second shock was the Deposit Act, which was passed in the same summer and required distribution of the federal budget surplus held in pet banks to the states. On January 1, 1837, the first round of transfers allocated 25 percent of government deposits from pet banks to the states, which implied a flow of specie from Western to Eastern banks. The rush to specie and withdrawal of federal deposits jointly lowered reserves of Western banks and created liquidity pressure on them. The second round of the federal deposit redistribution was announced for the end of March 1837, spreading more fear among Western banks. Martin Van Buren, who took the office of the presidency in March 1837, promised to continue Jackson's policies, to the disappointment of banks and borrowers who had been hurt by the monetary developments. A precipitous run from paper money ensued as pet banks rushed to gold and silver to meet federal government redemptions and note-holder demands to convert paper to specie.

Temin (1969: 147), however, argues that the more important adverse shock originated from the financial crisis in Britain and declining cotton export prices. British banks were losing reserves in 1836 and called in their loans and restricted their US operations. The Bank of England raised its discount rate in July and August 1836 and early 1837 to stop the reserve drain. As the British economy contracted, real wages and demand for textiles declined. The subsequent decline in the cotton price added extra pressure on US farmers and exporters as well as on the banks that had extended credit to them. The credit structure was built upon the security of cotton, and the lower price of cotton meant higher risks for US cotton farmers, brokers, merchants, and their banks. The combination of the end of foreign lending and depressed export demand for cotton led to the loss of specie reserves in NYC banks (Temin 1969: 136).

As a result of monetary contraction in the US the volume of land speculation collapsed as fast as it had risen. Public land sales declined from 20,000 acres in 1836 to 5,600 acres in 1837. The consequent economic crisis spread quickly across the economy. The South was hit first—and worst. In April 1837 there was a generalized collapse in New Orleans, where banks, mercantile houses, and brokers became insolvent. Business failures were also common in the North throughout the spring. As NYC banks contracted credit by discontinuing to discount bills, merchants, many from the West and the South, were unable to make payments, and failures grew cumulatively. There was no institution in the US comparable to the Bank of England that could have rescued banks by acting as the lender of last resort. On May 10, after several bank runs, NYC banks stopped payment on gold and silver and the specie suspension lasted for about a year.

The aftermath

Under the fractional-reserve system, the higher demand for specie (lower demand for notes) reduces the volume of bank loans and causes the economy to contract. The initial contraction in 1837 was relatively short and mild and primarily affected a few urban areas. It was followed by a short respite in 1838, thanks to rising cotton prices and lower British interest rates. Banks resumed specie payment. However, price, wage, and monetary deflation returned in 1839 and lasted for another four years. This depression hit the West and the South the hardest as domestic and international trade shrank, and many Northern states were forced to abandon their large-scale infrastructure projects.

Economists disagree about the depth of the post-1838 depression. Hammond (1957) and Friedman and Schwartz (1963) compare it to the

Great Depression of the 1930s. According to North (1966a: 202) employment indeed declined, but the magnitude of job losses was kept in check by the fact that wages declined even faster than prices. Lower real wages and cheaper labor acted as a buffer that prevented the recession from worsening. Temin (1969: 160) notes that adverse economic conditions were unevenly distributed across sectors; consumption, agricultural production, and textile production, in fact, did not fall. Infrastructure projects, such as canals and railways, were hit harder. Rothbard (2002), taking his cue from Temin's study, hails this recession as a prime example of the power of markets to liquidate waste and overproduction, i.e. the malinvestment in infrastructure and land created by excessive credit and artificially low interest rates.

One interesting postscript to this story is that the government acquiesced to NYC banks' suspension of specie conversion in May 1837, which lasted a year. Was suspension, or, as the Austrian economists describe it, the "usurpation of private property," a mistake? Temin (1969: 115) draws attention to the fact that the suspension did not mean banks ceased operation altogether. In fact, the coordinated suspension of convertibility provided breathing room for the suffocating financial system; banks did not meet the redemption demands of their customers but neither did they attempt to redeem the notes they held from other banks. Once they were freed from the need to hold specie reserves banks could continue to make loans and partially release the credit bottleneck. To the extent that most people were both borrowers and lenders in a given locality, they were willing to use these loans, made in the form of banknotes or deposits, in making payments.

Further, in Boston, banks agreed not to engage in excessive credit extension during suspension. They enforced the agreement by mutual inspection of each other's books and imposing sanctions on any bank that did not abide by the agreement. Thus, during the suspension period banks continued many of their regular operations, with the exception of redemption of notes for specie. This experience is an early example of local banks warding off a liquidity crisis by coordinating their actions. Banks suspending convertibility was a recurrent occurrence throughout the nineteenth century and, according to Calomiris and Gorton (1991), prevented bank failures from spreading further. As long as coordination, mutual trust, and verification could be maintained among banks, the lack of bullion to back paper did not hinder payments, finance, or commerce.

There was much finger pointing in the aftermath of the crisis. The Whigs blamed Jackson's financial policies for creating the liquidity crisis, and Van Buren defended the Democratic administration by holding the Whigs culpable for the promotion of paper money and the excessive expansion of credit. The federal government provided a measure of comfort to the financial system by providing liquidity in the form of Treasury-note issuance eight times between 1837 and 1843. The Specie Circular was repealed in 1848, but land sales remained dormant despite the policy shift. The widespread sentiment among borrowers was indignation; anger was directed especially at foreign banks, which asked for payment on loans. Several states, including Pennsylvania, Michigan, Indiana, and Maryland, defaulted or threatened to repudiate their international debt, which brought the inflow of foreign capital to a temporary halt. Consequently, European investors shunned the US securities markets until the mid 1840s.

The banking panic of 1857

After the mid 1840s the US economy experienced another period of growth and transformation. The country's borders expanded in the 1840s when Texas was annexed, Utah and Arizona (the entire Southwest region) became territories, and settlements on the Pacific coast were developed. Migration from Germany and Ireland and the 1848 California gold rush added to the population move to the West. The tide of migration continued until 1854 and contributed to the third peak of public land sales (Figure 8.1).

Cotton, while still important, was no longer the singular dominant commercial product in the US economy. Grains became a major export item, especially during times of war between the European powers. The Northeast and the Northwest were now more closely integrated economies, trading manufactured goods and foodstuffs. The manufacturing base had expanded to textiles, leather goods, clothing, and machinery for farms, steamboats, and railways. Samuel Morse's invention of the telegraph facilitated commerce and finance by shrinking distances and speeding the flow of information. Telegraph wires connected all major cities by 1850. The momentous change, however, was the emergence of railroads as the principal industry to shape the future of the US. Underneath the prosperous surface, though, problems festered. The banking system and railroads were systematically overextended and undercapitalized, the securities market was vulnerable to external shocks, and, in the twilight of the Civil War, the country was sitting on a keg of political gunpowder.

The banking system

The specie stock of the country crested after the California gold rush. Shipment of gold from California to NYC increased fivefold between 1849 and 1853. Higher specie reserves, in turn, permitted banks to expand their operations and extend credit on a much larger scale. After the closing of the second Bank of the US the idea of a national bank had faded, and the only banks in operation were those that were chartered by state legislatures. Banking practices varied substantially. Some states in which suspicion of banks was prevalent prohibited banks outright, e.g. Texas, Iowa, Arkansas, or established state-level monopoly banks, e.g. Indiana and Missouri. In the former, banking activities were carried out by such institutions as insurance companies or branches of banks from other states.

The most distinctive variety of banking until 1863, however, was *free banking*. Michigan in 1837 and New York and Georgia in 1838 were the first states to pass new laws on bank regulation that began the era of free banking. Many other states followed suit after 1849. Under this system legislative acts by states were no longer required to establish a new bank; all that was necessary was the payment for a fraction of the bank's capital, a promise to come up with the rest, and a pledge to comply with a set of conditions. These banks were permitted to issue banknotes, which were convertible to gold or silver coins on demand, provided they posted the equivalent value in state or federal bonds with state banking supervisors. To limit leverage state legislatures imposed requirements to hold hard-coin reserves against outstanding banknotes. The outcome of the new banking regulation was a significant increase in the number of banks and the volume of credit. Politically, free banking was hailed as a win for the Jefferson–Jackson camp and a blow to the ostensibly corrupt, monopolistic, centralized banking system favored by Hamilton and the federalists (Hammond 1957).

Free banks' trustworthiness and performance varied. New York free banks, for instance, operated smoothly after a rocky initial period (Dwyer 1996). In contrast, fraud and corruption were said to be frequent, especially early on, in Michigan and later in Indiana, Illinois, and Wisconsin. In Michigan specie reserves were on one occasion discovered to consist of glass and nails covered by a layer of coins (Hammond 1957: 601). In addition, a group of Michigan bankers were reported to have pooled and transferred their reserves from one bank to another in advance of the bank examiner making his rounds (Galbraith 1975: 107). In the Western states *wildcat banking* operations were carried out with little supervision. Hammond (1957: 618–9) describes the system of wildcat bankers in Indiana and Wisconsin as follows: anyone with a few thousand dollars purchases discounted Southern state bonds from a broker, deposits these with the state Treasurer for notes to be printed, uses these notes to pay the debt to the broker and to purchase more bonds for a second round of note issuance, sets up the bank office hidden in a "deep forest" or in an "Indian reservation" to avoid note holders who may want to redeem banknotes for specie, and enjoys the interest payments on the state bonds for the few years that the bank remains in operation. In the West free banks frequently suspended payments.

More recent research suggests that the many accounts of instability, mismanagement, undercapitalization, and fraud in the free-banking era are exaggerated and that a reputation for rampant insolvency and reckless behavior among free banks was not entirely deserved, despite the high frequency of closures. Dwyer (1996) concludes that the performance of these banks improved over time, most likely due to legal responses to the problems encountered; the failures were more likely to be attributable to external factors that reduced demand for their banknotes than to their imprudent behavior.

During this period NYC emerged as the undisputed financial center of the US. Notes of the Western banks found their way to the East Coast, where they circulated at discount rates that varied with their issuers' reputations and their distance from NYC. Many Western banks kept reserves in NYC banks to facilitate circulation and acceptance of their notes in the East, which turned large NYC banks into ad hoc reserve banks. NYC was also the gateway for capital inflow from abroad.

One important innovation during this era was the expansion of demand deposits and checking accounts (Gorton 1984). Checks were used primarily in the cities as a means of making payments, but they did not circulate like banknotes. They were accepted at par; their acceptance below par or refusal signaled to the account holder that there may be doubt about the reliability of the bank, which could facilitate a bank run.

Checking accounts also led large banks to establish *clearing houses*, which eventually served as a source of liquidity in times of need.[3] The first clearing house was established in 1853 in NYC as a central location to settle interbank claims at the end of the day and avoid the highly inefficient system of porters carting checks between multiple banks to be converted to specie. The clearing house also issued gold certificates in large denominations in return for a specie deposit from a member bank of the clearing house. Accounts were increasingly settled by these certificates, which, in turn, reduced the use of coins.

Clearing houses soon functioned as more than simple hubs of settlement: they made loans to member banks that were short on reserves by issuing loan certificates against the collateral of paper assets. These loan certificates were accepted by other banks in the settlement of interbank claims (at a discount) and freed the borrowing bank's precious-metal reserves to meet depositors' demands. Thus, clearing houses performed a stabilizing function by distributing the risk of a bank failure across their member banks. Clearing houses were soon established in Boston, Baltimore, Philadelphia, and Chicago. By the 1870s they were operating in all of the metropolitan centers. According to Kindleberger and Aliber (2011: 6), clearing-house certificates and deposit accounts were a factor in expanding the country's credit capacity.

The dominant position of NYC banking and the proliferation of smaller banks in the expanding agricultural West created seasonal, geographical shifts of money. During the late summer and fall Western and Southern farmers withdrew their deposits from local banks. The local banks drew upon their reserves from NYC banks. Money flowed from the East to the West and the South, and reserves in the East diminished. By winter, however, following the sale of crops, deposits of the proceeds, and payment of loans, money flowed back to the East. This cycle could, of course, be disrupted easily by a bad harvest or declining crop prices, both of which would result in farmers' failure to pay back their loans. These seasonal factors were a source of vulnerability for both the country and smaller NYC banks.

Securities markets

Infrastructure projects, such as railway construction, required large-scale, long-term lending, for which domestic savings were insufficient. Many of the long-term loans for fixed-capital investments originated in Europe, primarily in London, and, to a lesser extent, Paris, Brussels, and other financial centers. Foreign investments, which were interrupted after the 1837 crisis, resumed in the 1850s and were made primarily in railroad and banking securities. There were firms that specialized in procuring long-term financing for large capital projects by marketing bonds and stocks to foreign and domestic investors. After 1850 these unincorporated partnerships came to be known as *investment banks*. They underwrote bonds to finance private investment projects, mainly railways, and government debt during the Mexican War and the Civil War. These firms established close ties with European financial centers, especially London, and were proficient in marketing US securities abroad.

Domestic savings were primarily used to finance short-term loans. The majority of banks offered short-term lending to merchants, farmers, and businesses in the form of banknotes and deposits that met the economy's need for a medium of exchange and turned the wheels of commerce (Hammond 1957: 671). The working capital of the railroads soaked up the bulk of this lending. NYC banks also made loans to stockbrokers against the collateral of securities. Trading on NYC security exchanges expanded with the growing volumes of private securities, primarily railway bonds and stocks, in addition to federal and state bonds.

The growth of railways boosted the stock market. As illustrated by the bellwether railroad-share-price index in Figure 8.3, the stock market was turbulent, due in part to pressures from abroad. The 1853 market drop was attributed to a sudden calling of bank loans and the British cashing in US securities (Conant 1969 [1927]: 638). Scandals also frequently shook the market (Sobel 1988: 90–1). In 1854 Robert Shuyler, President of the New Haven and Harlem railroad companies, printed and sold fraudulent stocks and escaped to Canada with proceeds totaling $2.6m. Erie Railroad diluted its stock by raising its capital twelvefold. The forging and dilution of shares by managers and the transferring of takings into their private accounts were not isolated incidents.

Figure 8.3 US railroad-share-price index, 1850–60 (monthly).
Source: Smith and Cole (1969: 184).

Railroads

Railroads were on their way to becoming the leading industry in the US. Between 1848 and 1856 the total railroad tracks in operation increased from 4,600 to 22,000 miles (Figure 8.2). By the 1850s the Eastern rail network was well established. New railroad tracks to the West continued to be laid at a swift pace for frontier settlement, the delivery of grains to Eastern ports for export, and the growth of domestic commerce. The government actively promoted construction of new railroads by granting public lands to railroad companies. Mobile and Ohio railroad companies, for instance, received 1m acres of land; Illinois Central was granted 2.6m acres (Stedman 1905). A new wave of public land purchases accompanied the expansion of the railroads. In 1854 and 1855 settlers and speculators bought approximately 25m acres of public land along the projected railroad routes.

Competition intensified with the construction of new railroads, causing profit margins to decline and the debt burden to keep rising (Fishlow 1965). Western railroads suffered from chronic overcapacity and undercapitalization. Nonetheless, the British continued investing in railroads, and even sat on the boards of some railroad companies. Optimism abounded, and tracks were built into the wilderness with the confidence that they would create their own communities and markets (Conant 1969 [1927]), and, for a while, the traffic appeared relentless. According to Calomiris and Schweikert (1991), as late as the spring of 1857 1,000 settlers arrived in Kansas daily, many of whom were willing to borrow at high interest rates to purchase farms. Given uncertainties about the growth of the Western frontier and the amount of passenger and freight traffic, however, there was a strong speculative component to the Western railroad construction.

The future of railroad and land values was also tied to politics. The most significant political problem in the West was the conflict between abolitionists and slave owners. As the frontier expanded into the West, the debate on the extension of slavery to the Western territories came to the fore of political debate. Various compromises were attempted by Congress, such as the Kansas–Nebraska Act of 1854, which established the Nebraska and Kansas territories and left the decision on slavery in these territories to the settlers. The Supreme Court's 1857 Dred Scott decision ended all compromise efforts by ruling that Congress did not have the power to legislate slavery in the new territories. The conflict escalated between the pro-slavery and abolitionist forces who competed for the fertile lands of the new territories, leading to bloody confrontations and a growing source of political uncertainty.

The crash

1856 was a year of relative economic stability, but this was soon to change, as declining land values in the summer of 1857 brought about foreclosures on mortgaged property. From March to July, the monthly stock index declined by 18 percent. However, the early decline in the stock market was received merely as a correction amid the "madness of railroad building" (Hammond 1957: 709). NYC financial circles for the most part maintained their confidence and optimism for the future even after banks started reducing credit in early August and the stock-market decline continued. The collapse occurred in August as bankruptcies of mercantile firms increased.

On August 11, 1857, the bankruptcy of H. H. Wolfe and Company, a reputable and conservative flour and grain company, shook Wall Street. However, what transformed the aforementioned economic slide into a disaster was the failure of the Ohio Life Insurance and Trust Company, which had extensive ties with the troubled Western railroads. Charles Stetson, President of Ohio Life Insurance, announced on August 24 that, as the company had invested excessively in railroads and these loans were not performing, it would suspend payments at its NYC branch. Together with rumors of embezzlement in the NYC offices the announcement started a bankers' panic. To build reserves some NYC banks that had extended credit to Ohio Life Insurance started calling in loans they had extended to other smaller banks and enterprises. Hammond (1957: 711) reports that initially it was the newer, inexperienced banks that led the panic, while calm ruled in the large banks.

Banking difficulties increased in September as deposits and banknotes were converted to specie and the gold reserves of NYC banks declined. Moreover, as many of these banks were agents for country banks and converted the latters' notes to gold at a discount, country-bank notes flooded the NYC market, adding to the depletion of specie. To replenish reserves NYC banks restricted credit. This contraction of loans to brokers led to the collapse of stock prices and set off a cycle of declining collateral values and rising solvency risk. Several railroad companies that were unable to meet loan obligations went into receivership. The panic then spread to the rest of the country, and Western banks continued to withdraw their reserves from NYC. The sinking of the *S.S. Central America*, which was carrying 10 tons of California gold valued at almost $2m to NYC, in a hurricane across Cape Hatteras on September 11, 1857, shook people's confidence in the banking system and added to the panic.

The stock market took a very large hit. The railroad-share-price index dropped 36 percent between August and October 1857 (Figure 8.3). A decline in land values created defaults on mortgages and foreclosures. The Bank of Pennsylvania failed on September 25, and the state's banks suspended conversion. In the following days several brokerage and securities houses folded. The New York Clearing House made promises to supply sufficient credit to the city banks as late as October 12, but these were futile in the face of the magnitude of the specie outflow. On October 13 the banking panic hit full force, and the city banks finally suspended payment of specie. New England banks suspended convertibility on October 15, and the rest of the country followed suit. Only the Mississippi Valley banks were able to avert the panic due to their conservative lending practices, ability to cooperate locally, and wide geographical dispersion of depositors (Hammond 1957: 712).[4]

As in the case of the 1837 crisis, the suspension of specie payment broke the downward spiral of the stock market because it halted the calling in of loans and prevented borrowers from selling their securities or goods at bare-minimum prices and declaring bankruptcy (Calomiris and Schweikert 1991). The recovery of the banking sector was swift. Banks resumed operations shortly after December 11, and there were relatively few bank failures. The stock market recovered initially and rose to its August 1857 level by March 1858, though it subsequently slid back down (Figure 8.3). Only in 1862 did the railroad-share-price index reach its 1857 levels.

In the rest of the economy, however, the ensuing recession was deep. According to the National Bureau of Economic Research, official chronicler of US business cycles, economic activity contracted from June 1857 to December 1858. Many railroad companies, including Illinois Central, New York and Erie, and Central Michigan, failed. The North was hit hard because the export market for grain had shrunk, and heavily indebted farmers could not buy the products of Northeastern manufacturers.

The South was not affected as much. Cotton exports increased throughout the late 1850s, keeping the Southern agrarian economy sound. This made Southern leaders confident; they thought that the foundations of the Northern economy, i.e. industry and finance, were feeble, whereas the prosperity of the South, which was based on agriculture, was enduring.

The stance of the federal government, as in the previous crises, was that of a semi-detached observer who provided occasional assistance. The Treasury briefly purchased state bonds with gold to alleviate the liquidity crisis, but it was insufficient to meet the public's demand for specie. President Buchanan blamed the crisis on paper money and encouraged a stricter adherence to specie money by holding a gold dollar for every three paper dollars issued and revoking the charter of any bank that suspended convertibility. The Northern economy finally recovered in the summer of 1860, when Europe increased its wheat imports from the US sevenfold.

Interpretation

Most explanations of what has come to be known as the Western Blizzard of 1857 emphasize either the fundamentals or the unsustainable speculative forces as the source of the crisis. Calomiris and Schweikert (1991) attribute the decrease in value of Western land and railroad securities to the rising political uncertainty of the status of territories. The declining political power of the North and rising conflict between the abolitionists and pro-slavery forces in the Western territories reduced frontier settlement and diminished railway-passenger traffic. Subsequently, the Western railroads' combination of lower profitability and higher default risk reduced the value of their securities. The opposing viewpoint is that lower profitability and higher default risks were not just outcomes of 1850s politics. Rather, they were symptomatic of a structural problem created by the overextension of loans that led to the overbuilding of railroads and their consequent undercapitalization and underutilization (Hammond 1957; Sobel 1988; Stedman 1905).

Pastor and Veronesi (2009) offer a very different type of explanation for the changes in railroad-stock prices that relies on the fundamentals. Their hypothesis is that railroads were a technological revolution—and over the life cycle of a technological revolution the risk characteristics of stocks change. The changing nature of risk causes stock prices to rise and fall. To understand their hypothesis one must be able to distinguish between *idiosyncratic* and *systematic* risk.[5]

Idiosyncratic risk is specific to an individual corporation (related to its management, profitability, and costs) or industry. A specific event, such as the explosion of a deep sea well that interrupts production and creates an environmental catastrophe, would lower the profitability of the involved oil company and reduce its share price. The emergence of a viable energy resource to compete with oil would also lower the company's share price, as well as the share prices of all oil companies. These firm- and industry-specific risks are idiosyncratic risks. Investors can protect themselves against this risk by *diversification*; they can purchase shares of other oil companies or of corporations across many industries. Provided the returns are not positively correlated, the losses in one portion of the portfolio will be compensated by wins elsewhere.

Systematic risk, or market-wide risk, is a vulnerability to events that produce uncertainty for the entire economy. For example, a recession or economy-wide decline in profits is likely to have a generalized adverse effect on share prices across the board. Unlike idiosyncratic risk, systematic risk cannot be avoided through diversification, as almost all share prices are affected simultaneously and in the same direction.

According to Pastor and Veronesi (2009), during the early stage of a technological revolution little is known about the productivity of a new innovation, or even whether it will be successful. The new technology is initially implemented on a small scale and, therefore, is marginal to the economy at large as well as to investment portfolios. Its risk is idiosyncratic: that is, the variability of expected returns on the investment reflects exclusively the risks associated with the new innovation. Because its shares are of marginal importance in portfolios and are not strongly correlated with the movement of the overall stock market idiosyncratic risk can be mitigated by portfolio diversification. A low risk premium, in turn, implies a low discount rate. In combination with high expected returns the low discount rate implies a high discounted expected profit flow and a high share price.

The wider adoption of a successful innovation and its implementation on a large scale, however, changes the nature of the risk. As the new technology becomes a major industry and integrates with the "old" economy, e.g. microprocessors, originally designed for computers, have become a component in a wide range of products, from automobiles to cameras, variations in its stock price are more closely correlated with overall market variations. This risk becomes systematic and cannot be mitigated through diversification. Further, the variability of the returns increasingly reflects fluctuations in the broader market. Thus, the risk premium and the discount rate increase in the mature stages of the technology and, in turn, lower the discounted expected returns.

Combining these two stages of the life cycle of a technological revolution, Pastor and Veronesi (2009) hypothesize that the stock price associated with a new innovation initially rises and subsequently falls, similar to the bubble shape observed in many instances. In the early stages of a technological revolution the share price of the technology firm rises due to expected dividends associated with productivity gains and the low risk factor. As the technology is adopted on a larger scale and integrates with and transforms the old economy, the risk of investing in the technology firm increasingly becomes systematic and non-diversifiable. The rising risk premium dominates the positive productivity/earnings effect and lowers the stock price.[6]

Applying their hypothesis to the nineteenth-century US, Pastor and Veronesi (2009) contend that, until the 1840s, the railroad was a new industry, and its potential to compete with canals and rivers in transporting passengers and freight was highly dubious. Only during the 1850s did the railroad become the dominant form of transportation, eventually being adopted on a large scale by the old economy around 1857. Thus, the railroad-stock crash of 1857 was due to the rising discount rates that reflected the transformation of low idiosyncratic risk to high systematic risk.

Timeline

1791	Congress charters first Bank of the US.
1811	Congress does not renew charter of first Bank of the US.
1812–15	Anglo-American War.
1814–15	Suspension of convertibility of banknotes to specie.
1815	Last round of Napoleonic Wars in Europe.
1816	Second Bank of the US established.
1818	Peak of first land boom; start of financial panic and depression.
1819	Financial panic and depression; Cheves becomes president of second Bank of the US and rebuilds its reputation.
1822	Biddle becomes president of second Bank of the US.
1832	Congress renews charter of second Bank of the US, but President Jackson vetoes bill.
1833	President Jackson removes federal deposits from second Bank of the US and distributes them to state-chartered banks.
1833–66	Number of state-chartered banks rises by 50 percent.
1834	Start of second land boom.
1835	National debt of US paid off in its entirety.
1836	Peak of second land boom; Jackson administration issues Specie Circular; Congress passes Deposit Act; Bank of England raises discount rate twice.
1837	First round of transfer of Treasury surplus funds to states under Deposit Act; low cotton prices in Britain; collapse of public land sales.
April 1837	New Orleans banks fail.
May 1837	NYC banks stop convertibility of banknotes to specie.
1838	Rising cotton prices; NYC banks resume specie payment; slight improvement in economic conditions.
1839–43	Return of depression and deflation.

1848	California gold rush.
1853	Establishment of NYC Clearing House.
1854–5	Start of third land boom.
1857	Supreme Court issues Dred Scott decision; bank failures; stock-price collapse; NYC banks suspend convertibility.
1860	Economy recovers from recession with rising grain exports.

Key terms and concepts

Bimetallism
Clearing house
Diversification
Free banking
Idiosyncratic risk
Investment bank
Systematic risk
Wildcat banking

Endnotes

1 Much of the historical narrative of this chapter comes from Chancellor (2000), Geisst (1997), Hammond (1957), North (1966b), Smith and Cole (1969), Sobel (1988), and Stedman (1905).
2 In the British banking system limited-liability privilege was enjoyed only by the Bank of England.
3 For the evolution of clearing houses in the US see Gorton (1984).
4 The crisis of 1857 was distinguished by its global character. The US's ordeals soon spilled over to the British economy through the failure of both the financial and mercantile houses, and from there to other European centers.
5 The reader should note also that systematic risk and systemic risk are distinct concepts and should not be confused.
6 Frehen *et al.* (2013) claim that the Pastor–Veronesi argument is also valid in the context of the South Sea Bubble.

References

Calomiris, Charles W. and Gary Gorton. 1991. "The Origins of Banking Panics: Models, Facts, and Bank Regulation." Pp. 109–73 in *Financial Markets and Financial Crises*, edited by R. Glenn Hubbard. Chicago: University Of Chicago Press.

Calomiris, Charles W. and Larry Schweikert. 1991. "Panic of 1857: Origins, Transmission, Containment." *Journal of Economic History* 51 (4): 807–34.

Carter, Susan B., Scott Sigmund Gartner, Michael R. Haines, Alan L. Olmstead, Richard Sutch and Gavin Wright, Eds. 2006. *The Historical Statistics of the United States* (Millennial Ed., Series Df884). Cambridge, NY: Cambridge University Press. Online: hsus.cambridge.org/HSUSweb/HSUSEntryServlet.

Chancellor, Edward. 2000. *Devil Take the Hindmost: A History of Financial Speculation*. New York: Plume.

Conant, Charles A. 1969 [1927]. *A History of Modern Banks of Issue*. New York: Augustus M. Kelley.

Dwyer, Gerald P. 1996. "Wildcat Banking, Banking Panics, and Free Banking in the United States." *Federal Reserve Bank of Atlanta Economic Review*, December, 1–20.

Fishlow, Albert. 1965. *American Railroads and the Transformation of the Antebellum Economy*. Cambridge, MA: Harvard University Press.

Frehen, Rik G. P., William N. Goetzmann and K. Geert Rouwenhorst. 2013. "New Evidence on the First Financial Bubble." *Journal of Financial Economics* 108 (3): 585–607.

Friedman, Milton and Anna J. Schwartz. 1963. *A Monetary History of the United States, 1867–1960*. Princeton, NJ: Princeton University Press.

Galbraith, John Kenneth. 1975. *Money: Whence it Came, Where it Went*. New York: Bantam Books.

Gates, Paul Wallace. 1942. "The Role of the Land Speculator in Western Development." *Pennsylvania Magazine of History and Biography* 66 (3): 314–33.

Geisst, Charles R. 1997. *Wall Street: A History from its Beginnings to the Fall of Enron*. Oxford, UK: Oxford University Press.

Gorton, Gary. 1984. "Private Clearinghouses and the Origins of Central Banking." *Business Review, Federal Reserve Bank of Philadelphia*, January–February, 3–12.

Hammond, Bray. 1957. *Banks and Politics in America from the Revolution to the Civil War*. Princeton, NJ: Princeton University Press.

Hibbard, Benjamin Horace. 1965. *A History of Public Land Policies*. Madison, WI: University Of Wisconsin Press. (Original Work Published 1924)

Johnson, Simon, and James Kwak. 2010. *13 Bankers: The Wall Street Takeover and the Next Financial Meltdown*. New York: Pantheon Books.

Kindleberger, Charles P. and Robert Z. Aliber. 2011. *Manias, Panics, and Crashes: A History of Financial Crises*, 6th ed. New York: Palgrave Macmillan.

North, Douglass C. 1966a. *Growth and Welfare in the American Past: A New Economic History*. Englewood Cliffs, NJ: Prentice-Hall.

North, Douglass C. 1966b. *The Economic Growth of the United States, 1790–1860*. New York: W. W. Norton and Company.

Pastor, Lubos, and Pietro Veronesi. 2009. "Technological Revolutions and Stock Prices." *American Economic Review* 99 (4): 1451–83.

Ratner, Sidney, James H. Soltow and Richard Sylla. (1979). *The Evolution of the American Economy*. New York: Basic Books.

Rothbard, Murray N. 2002. *A History of Money and Banking in the United States: The Colonial Era to World War II*. Auburn, AL: Ludwig von Mises Institute.

Rousseau, Peter L. and Richard Sylla. 2005. "Emerging Financial Markets and Early US Growth." *Explorations in Economic History* 42: 1–26.

Sakolski, A. M. 1932. *The Great American Land Bubble: The Amazing Story of Land Grabbing, Speculations, and Booms from Colonial Days to the Present Time*. New York: Harper and Brothers.

Smith, Walter Buckingham, and Arthur Harrison Cole. 1969. *Fluctuations in American Business, 1790–1860*. New York: Russell and Russell.

Sobel, Robert. 1988. *Panic on Wall Street: Classic History of America's Financial Disasters with a New Exploration of the Crash of 1987*. New York: Truman Talley Books/Dutton.

Stedman, Edmund Clarence. 1905. *The New York Stock Exchange: Its History, its Contribution to National Prosperity, and its Relation to American Finance at the Outset of the Twentieth Century*, vol. I. New York: Stock Exchange Historical Company.

Temin, Peter. 1969. *The Jacksonian Economy*. New York: W. W. Norton and Company.

9 The American experience II
The gilded age

The second part of the narrative of the American experience starts with the establishment of the *national banking system* in the 1860s. This pyramid system, with nationally chartered, central-reserve city banks on top and country banks on the bottom, failed to bring an end to the recurrent bank panics, liquidity freezes, or the economic stagnation that followed them. The idea of the lender of last resort surfaced only after the formidable powers of J. P. Morgan, the leading banker of the time, with the support of the US Treasury, very narrowly avoided another financial meltdown during the "Bankers' Panic" of 1907. The narrative arc of the nineteenth-century American experience came to a close when financial and political powers agreed to set up a semi-public national-reserve system that would act as the lender of last resort, oversee bank operations, and keep financial crises at bay. The objective of this chapter is to trace the evolution of banks and securities markets and their interactions with the railroads, i.e. the growth sector of the economy, in the course of three major crises that took place between the Civil War and the establishment of the *Federal Reserve System* (Fed), i.e. the panics of 1873, 1893, and 1907.

During the post-Civil War decades, railroads were still the leading industry and absorbed most of the domestic and foreign capital available to the country. However, they continued to suffer from chronic under-capitalization, debt, and overcapacity, and much of the rail system yielded low returns. The fastest growing segment of the economy was manufacturing. The US was no longer a predominantly agricultural country. Competition was as intense in manufacturing as in railroads. But by the last decade of the century behemoth trusts had merged smaller manufacturers to limit the "ruinous" rivalry among the manufacturers and railroads, and to maintain profitability.

In the financial markets, large New York City (NYC) banks grew in power and influence and functioned as ad hoc reserve banks for the nation, although they were not always successful in averting crises. These banks often clashed with the agrarian and small businesses that favored easier access to loans. Securities markets grew in importance alongside expanding railroads and manufacturing. There was little self-discipline in the securities markets, and company executives commonly engaged in price manipulation, stock dilution, and insider trading, and enriched themselves at the expense of shareholders. By the end of the century large banks that underwrote corporate securities demanded assurances from corporations that executives would not engage in dishonest practices, and bankers sat on the boards of corporations as self-appointed protectors of shareholders' and lenders' interests. The same bankers, however, were not willing to make their own operations transparent. All investors and depositors needed to know, bankers declared, was that J. P. Morgan was in charge and looking after their interests.[1]

The railroad panic of 1873

To finance Civil War expenditures the Lincoln administration issued paper currency called *greenbacks*, which were legal tender (except in payment for import duties and interest on the national debt) but not backed by specie. During the Greenback Period (1862–79) specie payments were suspended, and the use of gold was limited to payments for international transactions. An abundant supply of greenbacks, in combination with rising demand for agricultural and manufactured goods and public construction stimulated the economy. The leading industry was still the railroads. From 1865 to 1873 total railroad length doubled to 70,000 miles (Figure 9.1). Congress continued to provide impetus to the growth of railroads with land grants and bond subsidies. New railroads were expected

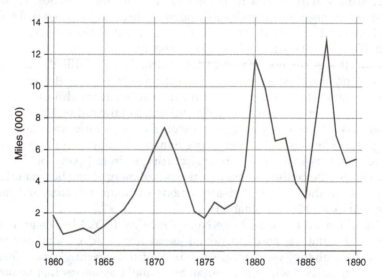

Figure 9.1 New railroads in operation in the US, 1860–90 (annual).

Source: Carter *et al.* (2006: Series Df884).

to open up new markets, boost settlement in the West, and raise the value of railroad lands. Yet while the inflow of foreign and domestic funds continued and the railway network kept growing, all was not well in the industry. Intense competition for traffic and fares lowered profitability. As Western railroads carried grain to the Eastern seaboard for export to Europe, fluctuations in the shipment of agricultural products added to the volatility of profits. In 1873 railroads were earning close to 5 percent of their market capitalization, but the more profitable lines were in the East. According to Stedman (1905: 219), Western states and territory lines earned an average of 2 percent, and Southern lines earned less than 1 percent. Moreover, the costs of borrowing were high, and railroads bore a heavy debt burden.

The national banking system

One of the key transformations that took place in the financial market after 1863 was the ending of the free-banking era. A series of banking acts that passed between 1863 and 1865 created a system of national banks, with the Office of the Comptroller of Currency (OCC) as the central supervisor. The OCC was given the authority to grant federal charters to the national banks. The national banks were required to keep Treasury securities to back their notes (creating a ready market for government bonds and helping to finance the Civil War) and to accept each other's notes at par value. To prevent counterfeiting the OCC printed all banknotes.

Under the National Banking Act the reserve system had three distinct tiers. At the top were the banks located in central-reserve cities (NYC and, after 1887, Chicago and St. Louis). The middle tier consisted of reserve city banks (18 originally, later expanding to 47 cities), and the bottom tier included the remaining banks in the periphery, or "country" banks. All national banks were subject to capital controls and reserve requirements. For instance, central-reserve city banks and reserve city banks were required to hold 25 percent reserves against notes and deposits, and reserve city banks could hold half of their reserves as deposits in a central-reserve city bank. Reserve requirements for country banks were 15 percent of notes and deposits, and they could hold three fifths of their reserves as deposits in reserve or central-reserve city banks.

The banking acts also dispensed with notes of the state-chartered banks. The federal government had imposed a 10 percent tax on state banks' notes, and, consequently, these banks stopped issuing banknotes and transformed themselves into demand-deposit institutions. Thus, the emergence of the US's current dual national-state banking system can be traced back to the 1860s.

One outcome of the national banking system was that the geographically thinly distributed and relatively immobile reserves did not readily respond to fluctuations in money demand through transfers across banks.

The hierarchical structure empowered the banks on top to decide the fate of those at the bottom. In times of crisis the reserve banks could decide which country banks would survive and which would fail by accepting or refusing loan extensions. The hierarchical banking structure became a source of conflict, whereby smaller banks often railed against larger banks for restricting liquidity. Finally, the new system brought to an end the circulation of the multitude of banknotes that were exchanged at various discounts. National bank notes backed by US Treasury notes and traded at par proved to be a more efficient means of exchange and paved the road toward a national currency.

Securities markets and the robber barons

Alongside the growth in railroads, manufacturing, and mining securities markets expanded, and new exchanges opened. The New York Stock Exchange (NYSE) could no longer accommodate either the rising trade volume or the number of brokers and traders. Many of these brokers and traders did not have a chance to become members of the NYSE and, as a result, started the Public Stock Board in a basement in 1862. The Open Board of Stock Brokers followed in 1864, and trading on the curb market extended trading hours until 6pm. Gallagher's Evening Trading sessions were held from 5pm until midnight. In 1862 the Gold Room was founded, wherein gold and gold contracts (which had become a relatively scarce commodity due to the flooding of the paper money market with greenbacks) were traded. In response to the rising volume of trade in 1864 some traders left the Gold Room and founded the New York Gold Exchange. The multiplicity of exchanges, in which many of the same assets were traded, provided more opportunities for speculation and market manipulation. Objects of speculation included mining and petroleum stocks and gold, but the main attraction was railroad securities.

Stock dilution, outright embezzlement, and other unsavory practices were prevalent throughout the 1860s. None of these were new, but they grew in both variety and scale during this time—and their stage was crowded with larger-than-life characters. The quartet of Daniel Drew, Cornelius Vanderbilt, Jay Gould, and James Fisk, Jr. epitomized the era of robber barons. All four came from modest backgrounds to become railroad owners and executives, as well as movers and shakers of Wall Street. With the exception of Vanderbilt they viewed railroads primarily as a vehicle for speculative gains rather than an enterprise to be built and maintained. The barons amassed and lost vast fortunes in epic battles to control railroads and manipulate railroad stocks, sometimes as comrades in arms and sometimes as foes in trenches.

Drew was among the first to recognize that ownership of a business expanded the scope of stock manipulation. Early in his career he had worked as a cattle driver, allegedly "fattening" the stock with the help of salt and water prior to their sale. In the 1830s he ran a steamship company on the Hudson River and became a rival to Vanderbilt. After the demise of the steamship business, due to the spread of the railways, Drew started to speculate in railroad stocks and discovered that direct involvement in the management of the enterprise offered more opportunities to realize financial gains. Influence over the board of directors of a company could be exercised to dilute the stock by issuing more shares and achieving gains at the expense of other shareholders. In 1857 he had complete control of the Erie Railroad, whose stock he watered down to expand his own wealth. Drew was a pioneer and the prototype of many directors who issued unauthorized shares, paid dividends out of capital, and shorted their own stock—and then pushed the stock price down to cover the shorts.

One widespread practice of the time was to form *corners*. The objective of a corner was to collect a sufficient number of shares to drive the price of a stock higher and to catch the bears who had sold the stock short in anticipation of buying it back low. A corner could be formed either by an individual or an informal set of partners who pooled their resources. When the stock was effectively cornered the operator could demand a high price from short sellers who were legally required to cover their positions. Jacob Little, the "Great Bear of Wall Street," was an early master. When he cornered Morris Canal and Banking he pushed the stock price from $10 to $185 between January 1834 and December 1835 and made a fortune (losing everything, however, in 1857 and dying destitute). By the 1860s the magnitude of corners, particularly in railroad stocks, had amplified. Vanderbilt, who had made his fortune in shipping (earning him the moniker "Commodore"), was over 60 years old when he became involved in the railroads. In 1865 he and John Tobin cornered Harlem Railroad stock when members of the city government sold the stock short, knowing that the railroad's contract would be revoked. Vanderbilt and Tobin were able to drive the price from $80 to $285, and the short sellers had no choice but to buy the stock from the two partners to cover their sales. Vanderbilt and Tobin netted a profit of $3m from the Harlem corner (Sobel 1988: 120).

The practice of *pools* facilitated corners by combining the resources of several speculators who shared the profits proportionately. Henry "the Silent" Keep put his own twist on the practice by creating *blind pools*, wherein participants were kept in the dark about the investments. Keep, as the pool manager, kept the information private to prevent an investor from cheating. He had a solid enough reputation to attract plentiful funds, and he earned millions of dollars for himself and his associates.

The most infamous corner episode was Jay Gould's attempt to manipulate the gold market in 1869. Gould had worked as a surveyor and tannery owner before he became a Wall Street speculator. He entered the railroad business after 1860 and by the time of his death had accumulated wealth of more than $70m. Gould was universally despised and vilified as the most ruthless and unscrupulous of the tycoons. In August 1869 he started to purchase gold and gold contracts to corner the market. The ostensible objective was to raise the price of gold vis-à-vis the greenback and, therefore, the British pound (the pound price of gold was very stable). The depreciated paper dollar would have made surplus US grain cheaper internationally and helped farmers. Gould stood to benefit from the increased foreign demand for Western grain because his own Erie and Wabash railroads were the primary lines used to transport it to the East. A successful corner would, of course, also yield ample profit at the expense of the gold short sellers.

Gould used personal connections to drive the price of gold higher. He asked an acquaintance in the first family to dissuade President Grant from selling government gold in the open market. By mid September 1869, however, the price of gold was stagnant, and the corner was facing a collapse. Gould convinced his one-time partner, James Fisk, Jr., to enter the market and drive up the price. Fisk was a boisterous extrovert and the most flamboyant of the tycoons. He had worked as a peddler, salesman, and, during the Civil War, cotton smuggler. He became a stockbroker in 1864, and by 1869, at the age of 33, he was such a prominent player on Wall Street that he entertained President Grant on his yacht.

Fisk started buying gold contracts with fervor, primarily via the railroad companies and banks he controlled. By September 23 he had $40m in gold contracts, twice the gold supply in NYC, and, on that date, panicking bears, fearful of further appreciation, started buying gold to cover their shorts. They sold securities to raise funds for gold purchases, which eventually caused the stock market to collapse. Unbeknownst to all, including Fisk, they were buying the gold from Gould, who had received news a day earlier that President Grant would not cooperate and that the Treasury was getting ready to sell gold. In anticipation of the price fall Gould had already decided that it was time to sell.

On September 24, 1869, the panic of Black Friday struck when rumors of European intentions to funnel gold to the US started circulating, along with the news of the Treasury selling gold against government bonds. Gold prices collapsed as market participants rushed to unload gold contracts. Gould, however, had been able to sell most of his gold holdings surreptitiously in the previous two days at the top of the market. Fisk, who had purchased gold contracts in the name of other parties, simply repudiated all obligations. Any discontent he might have had toward Gould must have been temporary because Gould paid him his share of the profits. The gold corner, however, reinforced Gould's reputation as a master manipulator who could bend the market to his will.

Economists have two conflicting interpretations of Black Friday. According to Wimmer (1975), it was a demonstration of the corrective powers of stabilizing speculation. From September 22 to 24, he argues, the actions of Gould and Fisk were only temporarily destabilizing because the government did not declare its neutrality and gave the impression of being complicit in the corner. The bump in the price was due to the government's lack of transparency. Moreover, even if the government had sided with Gould, Wimmer maintains, corrective speculative gold flows from Europe would have stabilized the US market. The alternative view is that the gold corner was an example of destabilizing speculation under conditions where some agents enjoy informational advantages over others (Kindleberger and Aliber 2011: 46). Gould's actions not only drove the gold price higher but also influenced the expectations of outsiders who jumped on the bandwagon and accentuated the price hike for a brief period of time.

Expansion of the existing exchanges and the opening up of new ones coincided with the growing interdependence of the banking system and the securities markets. Although bank lending against the security of stock had been practiced since the 1700s, it became more widespread over time. NYC bankers supplied *call loans* to brokers to finance *margin accounts*. A margin account is a leveraging instrument for the securities buyer. It enables investors and speculators to purchase securities from the broker against the collateral of the security and a margin payment in cash. The margin payment is calculated as a fraction of the loan. The broker effectively extends a loan to the customer to be used to buy the security.

The combined value of the cash and the security collateral is higher than the value of the loan, which gives the broker a margin of safety to cover the credit risk.[2] If the value of the security held as collateral declines the broker makes a *margin call* to the borrower to make up the difference by posting more cash. If the customer cannot pay the broker sells shares to raise the cash.

The broker, in turn, finances the loan by borrowing from a bank against the collateral of the securities. These are highly liquid loans that can be called by the bank at any time. They earn daily interest, known as the *call rate*. The growth of call loans facilitated the participation of small-time buyers in the stock market, stimulated turnover of shares, and boosted speculative trades. It also benefited brokerage services by generating more fees. Call loans were widely used by speculators to leverage capital gains.

The interlinking of banking and the stock market had important consequences. First, manufacturers, merchants and farmers complained that speculative call loans crowded out or created a shortage of commercial loans, which they considered the more "legitimate" economic activity. Second, the stock market became more sensitive to monetary conditions, particularly to the flow of money across the nation during agricultural cycles. When money flowed to the West during late summer and fall NYC banks lost reserves and called their loans. As borrowers sold securities to meet their obligations the stock market dropped. The flow of money to the

East in January eased credit conditions and rekindled the stock market. Third, stock-market volatility created turbulence in the banking system as fluctuations in collateral values forced banks to expand or limit credit to stock investors and speculators.

Another class of financiers made their fortunes by underwriting long-term government and corporate loans to domestic and foreign investors. In contrast to the likes of Gould, Drew, and Fisk, these financiers, exemplified by investment bankers Jay Cooke and John Pierpont Morgan, often came from established families and were tutored in investment banking and business in their youth. They exercised wide influence in the securities markets because investors often sought their assurance before purchasing bonds. However, they were not infallible. In fact, the panic of 1873 was not triggered by the antics of Gould and Fisk but by the failure of Jay Cooke and Company, the largest investment banking house, to dispose of the railroad bonds it had underwritten.

The panic

As mentioned earlier, the Western railroads' undercapitalization, excess capacity, and low profitability were chronic problems. Because the price that Western railroads charged for freight fluctuated with grain prices the declining price after 1865 hurt the railroads directly (Sobel 1988: 157). Moreover, from 1865 to 1871 the wholesale-price index declined by 30 percent and remained low. Deflation raised the debt burden and transferred wealth from debtors to creditors. Farmers and railroads, the largest debtors, were hit worst. Railroads tried to make up for the losses by laying new tracks and expanding their operations, funded primarily by floating securities in London. The inflow of capital from abroad allowed the railroads to grow but also made the US financial markets more vulnerable to economic and political developments in Europe.

In the meantime the federal and state governments were encouraging railroad construction through land grants. One of the companies that benefitted from government largesse was the Northern Pacific Railroad, chartered in 1864 to lay 2,000 miles of track from Lake Superior to Puget Sound. The construction of the Northern Pacific was financed by Jay Cooke and Company. Jay Cooke had built his reputation as a prominent financier and innovative banker when he formed a syndicate of Wall Street bankers during the Civil War to sell Union government loans across the nation to small investors through a network of brokerage houses and agents. After the war Cooke continued as the primary underwriter of US government debt and marketed both government debt and private securities in the US and Europe.

Cooke and Company had underwritten $100m worth of Northern Pacific bonds in 1869. Politicians were bribed, newspapers were bought, and the bonds were initially widely promoted both domestically and internationally through promises of new lands and riches. However, the laying of the tracks was fraught with technical difficulties, and construction had become a huge vacuum, sucking up cash. By August 1873 the total track mileage in operation had reached only 455 miles. Plans to sell bonds to a European syndicate to meet financing needs fell through in 1872 as a result of the outbreak of the Franco-Prussian War and British discontent over the Alabama arbitration. The domestic market's response to the bond offer was lackluster because it was already saturated with railroad securities. Cooke and Company used its own funds to make up the difference.

Outside factors aggravated Cooke's problems. In February 1873 President Grant signed the Coinage Act, which embraced the gold standard and demonetized silver. The outcome was a limited money supply and higher interest rates. Credit contraction added to mounting fears of an imminent financial crisis. By the spring of 1873 recollections of 1837 and 1857 were common in the NYC press, and writers questioned whether the country was on the edge of another collapse. The initial impact on the stock market was small, and the railroad-stock-price index declined by only 3 percent between January and August 1873. On August 28, however, newspapers reported that two other railroad lines were experiencing financial troubles, and in September the system started to give way (Figure 9.2).

The slide toward panic started on September 8 and gained momentum on September 15 when some railroad companies went under, and several

Figure 9.2 US railroad-share-price index, 1869–79 (monthly).

Source: National Bureau of Economic Research (NBER) (2014).

banking houses, including Daniel Drew's firm, and insurance companies suspended operations as their non-performing loans to railroad companies pushed them into insolvency. The first signs of panic in the stock market were observed on Wednesday, September 17, but there were still rumors and hope that Cornelius Vanderbilt was organizing support to lift stock prices. However, on September 18, known as Black Thursday, the NYC office of Cooke and Company failed to raise funds through borrowing or selling stocks and was forced to close its doors. Within hours the panic hit full force, and the Philadelphia and Washington branches of the leading financial house in the country were shut down.

The question in everyone's mind was: who could be trusted if Cooke and Company was insolvent? On Friday, September 19, the panic spread to banks, trust companies, which operated like banks but were less regulated, and brokerage houses. Depositors en masse tried to withdraw their funds, but banks were unable to meet their demands and tried to build up reserves by discontinuing credit extension and calling in loans. Stockholders who faced margin calls attempted to meet their obligations by selling shares, but there were no buyers. Stock prices plummeted. On Saturday, September 20, the Board of Exchange temporarily closed the NYSE, and the effects of the panic spread to Philadelphia and Chicago. The railroad-stock-price index declined 8.2 percent in September and 9.1 percent in October (Figure 9.2). The total decline in the index was 26 percent between January and November 1873. Various stopgap measures by bankers helped slow the drain of cash from banks. With considerable reluctance the Grant administration yielded, albeit only partially, to the pleas of the bankers and pumped $17m into the market by purchasing government bonds. Stock exchanges opened on September 30 with some semblance of normality.

Jay Gould profited from the crash because he had shorted stocks. Daniel Drew went bankrupt and never recovered. Vanderbilt's purchases of the shares in his enterprises were insufficient to keep the stock price high, but he suffered only paper losses because he owned his stocks outright. Vanderbilt nevertheless lamented, "There are many worthless railroads in this country without any means to carry them through . . . Building railroads from nowhere to nowhere at public expense is not a legitimate undertaking" (Sobel 1988: 180). He blamed "respectable" NYC banks for underwriting these unsound railroad bonds and "giv[ing] a moral guarantee to their secureness." Investors and speculators who purchased stocks with loans and did not sell before the collapse lost the most.

The banking panic had stopped by the end of September 1873, but bankruptcies in the financial sector continued, and money was scarce. The adverse effects of the liquidity freeze spread to the real sector as commerce and industry failed to raise funds for their working-capital needs. New railroads declined sharply, to a fraction of their 1870–2 levels, and did not pick up until 1879 (Figure 9.1). The US economy underwent what has come to be known as the Long Depression, which lasted until 1879. Approximately 18,000 businesses failed between 1873 and 1875, including a quarter of the country's railroad firms. The average price level of commodities declined by one third during the depression, and the rising debt burden bankrupted many farmers and businesses. Factories laid off workers, and unemployment reached 14 percent in 1876. The Long Depression also gave rise to sharpening labor–capital conflict. Railway workers went on strike in West Virginia, protesting poor working conditions and two wage cuts in the same year. The strikes quickly spread to Maryland, Pennsylvania, Illinois, and Missouri. The Great Railroad Strike of 1877 brought railway transportation to a standstill for 45 days. Strife between striking workers and the local militia, federal troops, and the National Guard left more than 100 dead. The longest period of economic contraction in US history lasted for 65 months, from October 1873 to March 1879.

Jay Cooke's life as the foremost investment banker was over. J. P. Morgan succeeded Cooke as the supreme custodian of the investment-banking business and much more.

The panic of 1893[3]

The distinguishing feature of the two decades after 1870 was the sharpening conflict between the proponents of hard and soft money. Hard money refers to currency backed strictly by gold and implies a more restrictive credit regime. Soft money refers to paper currency that is not tied to precious metals and implies easier access to credit. (Given the abundance of silver in the US in the late nineteenth century, silver-backed currency was also considered soft money.)

Hard vs. soft money was an ongoing debate in the US, as observed in President Jackson's opposition to the second Bank of the US and the paper currency. After the Civil War proponents of hard money first passed the Coinage Act of 1873 that demonetized silver and terminated the bimetallic system. Then hard-money backers in Congress limited the volume of greenbacks in circulation in 1874 and passed the 1875 Resumption Act, which made paper fully convertible to gold on January 1, 1879. In the coming decades gold became relatively scarce as mining slowed down, while gold demand increased due to more countries adopting the gold standard. Moreover, the federal government was running chronic surpluses, which it used to buy back national debt. As banks held government bonds as reserves (in addition to gold), the declining volume of government debt reduced reserves and worsened monetary stringency.

The support for hard money in the last two decades of the nineteenth century also reflected big-business interests. By this time the US had become an industrial power. Manufacturing had become the prominent economic activity, and mill towns and factories proliferated across the country. The emerging industries included steel and petroleum, the large-scale, low-cost production methods of which provided the economy with new intermediate commodities, such as steel rails and kerosene. In manufacturing and railways, however, intense competition over market share and overproduction kept profit margins low. Ways to raise profit margins included consolidating businesses to curb competition, capturing foreign markets, maintaining low production costs, and keeping the labor-union movement in check. Big business was in favor of tight money to keep input (grain, labor, and raw materials) prices low and to expand export markets with the help of low-price final goods. The role of the gold standard in this context was to keep the money supply and credit tight.

Tight money had adverse consequences for small businesses, merchants, and farmers who relied on loans to operate their businesses. The hard-money regime reduced their access to credit. The shortage of money relative to the growth of output also added a deflationary bias to the economy. Farmers and workers were especially hurt by agricultural prices and wages that dropped faster than the overall price level. In addition, deflation increased the debt burden on borrowers. Discontent among these groups led to the emergence of populist and progressive political movements. They demanded access to cheap money by the repeal of the act that demonetized silver (known as the "Crime of '73") so that they could pay their debts in weaker dollars and stop the transfer of wealth from borrowers to banks.[4]

In the realm of politics the first step to resolve the conflict between the proponents of hard and soft money was the 1890 Sherman Silver Purchase Act, by which the Treasury purchased 4.5m ounces of silver per month to be paid in Treasury notes, redeemable in gold or silver. The soft-money regime was now in place. As compensation big business had the McKinley Tariff Act of 1890, which raised tariffs an average of 48 percent to protect domestic manufacturing from foreign competition. By 1892 the US was de facto back on the bimetallic standard, whereby paper was convertible to both gold and silver.

Although the bimetallic money regime of 1892 had initially created an upswing in economic activity, it soon became a source of instability in the monetary sphere. Silver quickly supplanted gold in circulation and for payment of debts. *Gresham's Law*, according to which "bad money drives out good money," was in evidence with a vengeance as undervalued gold disappeared from circulation. Europeans converted their US securities to gold and shipped it to London and Paris, and they accepted only gold as payment in international transactions. In anticipation of higher premiums US banks converted greenbacks and other government obligations to gold and hoarded the coins and bullion. This contracted credit, and gold conversions depleted government gold reserves sharply.

There were two other noteworthy factors related to the panic of 1893. First, while railroad construction had spearheaded growth for decades, it was still the soft underbelly of the economy. New railroads rose sharply in the late 1880s, their tracks reaching a total of almost 28,000 miles (Figure 9.1). However, the industry was still undercapitalized, and the average rate of return was low. In 1892 only 44 percent of the shares yielded dividends to their owners (Steeples and Whitten 1998: 22). In the meantime railway companies needed to meet interest payments on the large volume of debt they had floated to finance construction. Second, the near bankruptcy in 1890 of London investment bank Baring Brothers and the rescue effort led by the Bank of England slowed the inflow of gold from Europe. The subsequent European depression reduced foreign demand for US products. Capital inflow from Britain to the US declined by 65 percent between 1890 and 1893 and limited the funding for investment in fixed capital (Steeples and Whitten 1998: 28).

The panic of 1893 took place against the backdrop of a run on gold, overextended railways, and contracting foreign-capital inflow and external markets. The financial reverberations started in early 1893, with the stockprice index falling by 10 percent in the first two months (Figure 9.3). The first big shock to the system was the bankruptcy of the Philadelphia and Reading Railroad Company in February, with a debt of $125m. Although there was a temporary respite and some degree of optimism in the stock market in March, gold outflow persisted. When Grover Cleveland became president in March the Treasury's gold was barely above the legal minimum-reserve limit. By the end of April gold reserves had fallen even further. The ability of the Treasury to convert its obligations to gold was in doubt, and the US government was facing default. The administration sought to replenish its reserves by selling more bonds.

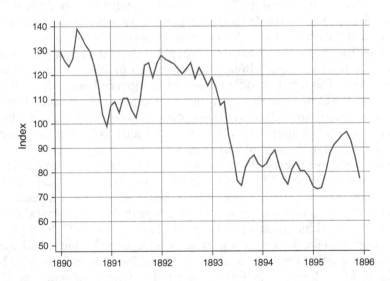

Figure 9.3 Average price of 40 common stocks in the US, 1890–6 (monthly).
Source: NBER (2014).

Severe credit limitations impeded the operations of enterprises, many of which were already overburdened with debt. The failure of the National Cordage Company, due to a lack of credit and declining orders, on May 4 was the beginning of the collapse of the economy. Cordage was overextended, and banks had started calling in their loans. When it failed to raise additional funds from banks Cordage declared insolvency and went into receivership. The demise of this behemoth sent shock waves across financial markets. Within the national banking system banks higher up in the pyramid were facing rising demands for reserves from the banks below. By mid May NYC banks were refusing to accept silver dollars or notes of the Western and Southern banks, which initiated a surge of bank runs and closures in the West. The run from silver to gold accelerated at the end of June when India discontinued silver purchases. Contraction in credit and a loss of confidence in the solvency of companies lowered stock and bond prices. Throughout July bank and business failures continued. News and rumors of business failures across the spectrum—railroads, banks, mining, iron and steel, textiles—caused the stock-market index to fall by 46 percent between April and August of 1893.

In August 1893 Congress repealed the Sherman Silver Purchase Act, and the Treasury stopped buying silver. The abandonment of bimetallism was expected to halt the depletion of gold, stabilize prices, and renew confidence in financial markets, but business failures continued throughout that year and the next. In 1893 5 percent (642) of all banks failed. In industry railroads were hit the hardest: by the end of the year 119 companies, accounting for 28,000 miles of lines (15 percent of the total mileage) had been placed in receivership. The Cleveland administration limited its response to salvaging the Treasury's gold reserves and rescuing the gold standard and then waited for the crisis to run its course.

Worsening economic conditions brought a period of intense social unrest. Coal-miner and Pullman-worker strikes in 1894 led to violence across cities. The urban middle classes were squeezed not only by dire economic conditions but also by the loss of their savings in failed banks and were forced to walk away from their mortgages. The depression, which started in January 1893, continued until June 1897, with the exception of a respite in the second half of 1894.

In the 1896 presidential elections Democrats nominated, with the support of the populists, William Jennings Bryan over Grover Cleveland. Bryan ran on the populist platform of bringing back silver coinage, denouncing the gold standard, and proclaiming that "[big business] shall not crucify mankind upon a cross of gold." However, in 1897 the depression eased with the discovery of gold in the Klondike and South Africa as well as new gold-extraction technology that raised the gold supply. In addition, failed harvests in Europe and rising foreign demand for US grain increased the inflow of gold. Expansion of the money supply mollified populist demands, and Bryan lost to the Republican William

McKinley, who was supported by Eastern big business. As gold reserves grew and confidence returned to financial markets US industry recovered as well.

The financial leader who emerged unrivaled through the panic was J. P. Morgan. Politicians, financiers, and foreign investors saw him as a stabilizing figure who could bring some sense of order to financial markets. His name lent credibility to even the US government in the eyes of the foreign lenders. When the Cleveland administration attempted to alleviate the Treasury's gold shortages in 1893 it was able to sell bonds to foreign as well as domestic buyers through bank syndicates organized by Morgan, which, incidentally, earned roughly 10 percent fees for the banks.

The last decade of the century witnessed a transformative change: a tidal wave of consolidation of small companies into large conglomerates. By 1890 Morgan had already concluded that competition among the railroad companies over traffic and fares had led to deteriorating profits. He initiated a campaign to rehabilitate and consolidate multiple companies into a smaller number that would share the market, end cut-throat competition, and exploit economies of scale. Between 1897 and 1904 4,277 companies were merged into 257 giant enterprises, including Rockefeller's Standard Oil, Harriman's Union Pacific Railroad, Morgan's International Harvester, and AT&T.

The largest consolidation was US Steel. In 1901 Morgan brought together Carnegie Steel and seven other steel-related companies—including iron mines, smelters, plants, and shipping lines—to create a company whose capitalization in stocks and bonds amounted to $1.4b, or 7 percent of the US GDP. The investment banks that financed these mergers made huge sums in commissions and profits. For instance, the syndicate that Morgan put together to underwrite $225m of US Steel securities earned $50m in commissions and fees (Smith and Sylla 1993). J. P. Morgan and Co.; Kidder, Peabody and Co.; Brown Brothers; and Kuhn, Loeb and Co. were the luminaries of Wall Street, and Goldman Sachs and Lehman Brothers were rising stars. Bankers became prominent in the boardrooms of manufacturing, transportation, railway, and mining companies and were directly involved in their management. In the political arena, however, populists and progressives were alarmed by the centralization of financial and industrial power in a few hands. One by-product of the industrial mergers was the anti-trust movement.

Bank runs revisited

The frequency of banking panics during the national-banking period has attracted a great deal of attention in the bank-run literature. An interesting question that springs from the US experience is why banking panics, i.e. sudden and generalized demands to convert deposits and banknotes into hard currency, occurred with such high frequency. One line of reasoning introduced in Chapter 6 underscored that market imperfections may cause optimizing actions to become disconnected from the fundamentals and lead to socially suboptimal outcomes. To reiterate, there are two prominent arguments that attribute banking panics and bank runs to such imperfections. Diamond and Dybvig (1983) emphasize that, in the absence of markets to insure deposits, and under first-come-first-served redemption rules, depositors are prone to rush to banks when there are any doubts about their soundness. Calomiris and Gorton (1991) focus on bank-debt holders' response to negative news under conditions of asymmetric information. While they trace the imperfections in different sources, both explanations see banking crises as an illiquidity problem.

An issue that Diamond and Dybvig (1983) have not addressed is the initial source of the demand to redeem deposits or banknotes, or why otherwise optimizing agents would panic. According to several commentators, in the second half of the nineteenth century in the US the initial source was the seasonal demand for currency for agricultural payments. Farmers demanded more money during planting and harvesting seasons, and country banks needed to satisfy this redemption demand. If the seasonal shock was strong enough bank reserves were depleted, and country banks were required to draw funds from reserve banks that were higher up in the national banking hierarchy. The reason that this may generate a panic lies in the spatial separation of country banks and the structure of the national banking system. First, each country bank knew that it had to hasten to the reserve city bank, knowing that other country banks would be doing the same thing and that latecomers may come back empty-handed. In this way the system created incentives for country banks to rush to withdraw deposits from reserve city banks. Second, because they were spatially separated the country banks could not coordinate among themselves to avert this obviously suboptimal action. The panic then moved up the banking pyramid. Calomiris and Gorton (1991) note that, according to this explanation, the institutional structure of the three-tiered national banking system imposed by the government was culpable for making US banks vulnerable to bank runs.

According to Calomiris and Gorton (1991), however, the source of US bank runs was exogenous negative events, including the onset of recession, the rising number of defaults in railroads and mercantile companies, and the bursting of land bubbles. Deposit and banknote holders revised their assessment of the health of their own banks on hearing this news. Lacking information on their own bank's loan-portfolio performance and the likelihood of its failure, holders took defensive action by asking to redeem their deposits and notes. Gorton (2012: 12) emphasizes that, in this account, expansion of credit is a significant risk factor that increases the fragility of the system. The larger the volume of bank credit, i.e. the larger the number of borrowers and size of loans, the larger the default risk.

The emphasis on fragility, of course, overlaps with views put forth by the Bagehot-Minsky-Kindleberger (BMK) approach. The primary difference between the BMK approach and those presented above is that BMK views the banks' problem as one of solvency, not liquidity. As noted in Chapter 6, BMK argues that credit expansion is endogenous to the system, and rising default risk is the outcome of the changing quality of loans over the credit cycle. The real weakness of the banking system is not the government-imposed institutional structure or information sets of the stakeholders but the fact that banks engage in increasingly risky behavior to meet the demands of borrowers who take high risks—and higher leveraging raises the vulnerability of the banking system. Bank runs and liquidity risks are the outcomes of default risk, or rising fears of counter-party insolvency.

The Bankers' Panic of 1907

Background

At the beginning of the twentieth century the US was the world's leading industrialized country. Its economy grew with few interruptions from 1897 to 1907. "Destructive competition" was replaced by *industrial trusts*. These trusts were financed by issuing hundreds of millions of dollars' worth of stocks and bonds, which were a boon to the securities exchanges and the underwriters. The Dow Jones Industrial Average (DJIA) reached a historical peak of 103 on January 26, 1906.

However, chronic stresses and recurrent shocks created a shortage of money and spelled trouble for financial markets in 1906. The availability of credit became more restricted as the growth of gold reserves fell short of industrial growth. Eastern bank reserves continued to fluctuate with seasonal variation in money demand in the West. The first big shock in 1906 was the flow of money to the West in the aftermath of the San Francisco earthquake and fire in April. The depletion of reserves caused Eastern banks to call in loans from stockbrokers and lowered stock prices. Then Congress authorized the Interstate Commerce Commission to set maximum railroad rates in July, which reduced railroad-stock prices. Finally, the Bank of England raised its discount rate twice in the fall to slow the outflow of capital from London and protect its reserves. The adverse effects of these developments were temporary, and the US stock market remained high for the rest of the year. However, the dangers of depleting reserves and the possibility of bank failures were on the minds of the financiers.

The impact of tight money and credit was felt harshly in 1907. Early in the year one long-term railroad-bond sale failed. Stocks began to decline steadily, despite the fact that corporations were reporting higher earnings (Figure 9.4). During the "silent" or "mysterious" panic between March 1

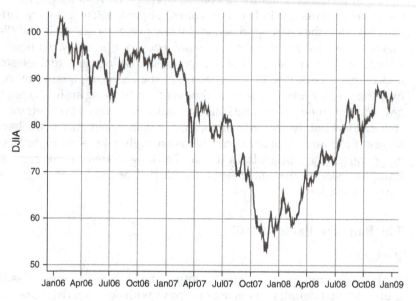

Figure 9.4 Dow Jones Industrial Average, 1906–8 (daily).

Source: S&P Dow Jones Indices.

and 25 the DJIA declined by 16 percent. Railroad and copper stocks were hit hardest. Margin calls became more common, call rates rose as high as 25 percent, and several brokerage firms declared bankruptcy (Bruner and Carr, 2007: 23). A series of external shocks further tightened liquidity. The Bank of England faced depleted reserves after it saved the Alexandria (Egypt) Stock Exchange by shipping gold from London. London discontinued refinancing and new loans to the US, and gold started flowing from the US to Britain. Next there was a wave of banks failures in Japan. The French then started to convert US securities to gold and ship it to Paris, which further drained US reserves.

Securities markets were unstable during the summer of 1907. Westinghouse found buyers for only a third of its new stock issue. Then in June a $29m municipal-bond offer of NYC failed to find buyers; the city tried again in August and was successful, but only because J. P. Morgan agreed to underwrite the issue. The copper market collapsed in July. Shocks originated from politics as well, and President Theodore Roosevelt, who had promised an anti-trust crusade, blamed industrial trusts and Wall Street for the country's financial instability. On August 3 the courts fined Standard Oil $29.25m for anti-trust violation, and the business press accused the president of destabilizing the market. Stock prices had been declining since late spring, and the DJIA index had fallen by 35 percent in the first eight months of 1907 (Figure 9.4). Finally, with the arrival of fall, the seasonal migration of money to the West put more pressure on Wall Street.

The weakest link in the banking system was the *trust companies* (different from the industrial trusts mentioned above). These firms were originally established to handle the financial affairs of private estates, but they performed bank functions, such as collecting deposits and making loans. Unlike banks, however, they were not subject to OCC supervision or reserve and capital requirements, nor did they benefit from clearing-house protection, with the exception of a few large ones, including the Knickerbocker Trust Company. Trusts were profitable, but they were also more vulnerable to a run by the depositors.

The failed corner

The Bankers, Panic of 1907 was triggered by Otto Heinze, who attempted to corner shares of the United Copper Company, whose value had been declining since the collapse of the copper market.[5] United Copper Company was the core of the Heinze enterprises. Once a Montana copper magnate, Augustus Heinze had become an important player on Wall Street in 1906. With the financial assistance of Charles T. Barney, President of the Knickerbocker Trust Company, Augustus and his partner, Charles Morse, gained control of or influence in many financial institutions, including state and national banks and trust and insurance companies. Augustus became President of the Mercantile National Bank, owned a seat on the NYSE, and established a brokerage house (run by Otto and another brother). Although Augustus, Morse, and Barney opposed the idea of a corner and declined to lend funds, Otto Heinze went ahead on his own on Monday, October 14, and purchased copper share contracts on borrowed money to raise the share price. He was unsuccessful. On Tuesday the share price of the United Copper Company began to collapse, and by Wednesday Otto was ruined.

The ripple effects of the failed corner spread quickly. Otto Heinze was unable to pay the loans he took to corner the market. On Thursday, October 17, the Heinze brokerage house was bankrupt, and Otto was suspended from the stock exchange. Depositors started a run on the Mercantile and Charles Morse's two other banks. By Sunday, October 20, the boards forced Augustus Heinze and Charles Morse to resign from all of their banking interests.

The next domino to topple was the Knickerbocker Trust Company, one of the largest NYC trusts, when Barney's association with Heinze and Morse proved to be a liability. On October 18 depositors were withdrawing their money from the company, and the board of the trust asked Barney to resign as president on Monday, October 21. On the same day Knickerbocker was dropped by its clearing house, signaling the loss of confidence in the trust in financial circles. On October 22 a massive bank run started, and Knickerbocker was forced to suspend operations. Most of the withdrawal demands came not from retail customers but from other banks that had made loans to Knickerbocker. Thus, the 1907 incident came to be known as the Bankers' Panic. The panic spread when financial institutions raised interest rates on loans and started a credit squeeze.

Panic management

Wall Street's hopes of ending the panic rested on J. P. Morgan, the most powerful banker in terms of wealth, experience, and connections. On Sunday, October 20, Morgan, with the assistance of two lieutenant bank presidents, reviewed the financial statements of Knickerbocker and concluded that the company was unsalvageable; they then decided to focus their efforts on containing the panic and ensuring the survival of other shaky trusts. On October 23, when a bank run started on the Trust Company of America, Morgan led presidents of trust companies to put together an $8.25m loan package to avert the crisis. Treasury Secretary George B. Cortelyou, in consultation with Morgan, announced a $25m government deposit to banks the next day. John D. Rockefeller of Standard Oil added another deposit of $10m to strengthen reserves. After liquidating some of its own assets the Trust Company of America was on a firm footing for the moment. However, volatility did not subside. On that same day the Westinghouse Manufacturing Company was placed in receivership, the Pittsburg Stock Exchange suspended trading, and the Lincoln Trust in NYC was struggling. A number of smaller banks and trusts could not meet the withdrawal demands of depositors and were forced to shut down by October 24.

Banks were unwilling to continue extending the call loans that lubricated daily exchanges on the stock market. As loans to brokers shrank so did the demand for stocks. Lower stock prices forced margin buyers to sell their stocks to meet margin requirements. Stock prices plummeted. The president of the NYSE asked for Morgan's help at 1:30 pm on October 24 to prevent early closure of the stock market and a possible meltdown of public confidence in stocks. Within half an hour Morgan contacted 14 bank presidents, and by 2:16 pm, he had arranged a $23.6m loan to the stock exchange that again saved the day. The next morning, Friday, October 25, the panic continued at the NYSE, and more funds were needed. Morgan was able to organize help, but the bankers, who were concerned for their own survival, were more reluctant and this time pledged only $9.6m. This amount turned out to be sufficient to keep the market open until the regular closing hour.

Morgan and his associates spent the weekend trying to devise a means to strengthen public confidence in banks and the stock market. They asked newspaper publishers and clergy to spread the word that financial markets rested on a solid foundation and that they would withstand the recent shocks. Sunday editorials and sermons temporarily allayed fears and calmed the public. Further, the New York Clearing House issued and distributed to banks, under Morgan's directives, certificates amounting to $100m to be used to settle interbank exchanges so that banks could keep their reserves intact. Again Morgan's authority was critical in persuading bankers to accept these certificates.

However, the prospect of relief was quashed by yet more bad news when the mayor of NYC informed Morgan on Sunday that the city had failed to float new bonds, and, unless $20m was found by Thursday, November 1, the city would be bankrupt. After he met with the mayor on Monday and Tuesday Morgan arranged for the New York Clearing House to underwrite $30m worth of city bonds by scrip that would be accepted by the banks. The mayor suffered the indignity of turning over the city's books to Morgan's men, who would be the monitors of the city's finances.

Morgan's powers were twice more put to the test on Friday, November 2. First, the brokerage firm of Moore and Schley had borrowed extensively against the collateral of Tennessee Coal, Iron and Railroad Company (TC&I) stock. The stock was not performing well. If lenders had called in loans and forced Moore and Schley to liquidate its holdings of TC&I stock, the share price would have plunged, and the brokerage firm would have had to declare insolvency. The failure of this large brokerage house could have destroyed the fragile calm in financial markets. The second test was related to the concern that the Trust Company of America and the Lincoln Trust would face bank runs the following Monday. The state banking examiner had reported on Saturday morning that banks were in a precarious situation.

Two conferences were convened at the Morgan Library on Saturday night. More than 40 trust presidents met under the directive of Morgan to pool $25m to bail out the threatened trusts. Morgan locked the doors of the library to ensure that no one would leave before a resolution was reached. At dawn the reluctant presidents agreed to pledge the amount needed to save the weak trusts and were permitted to leave. The help came, however, with the condition that the two troubled trusts were to hand two thirds of their assets to a trustee named by Morgan, and their operations would be closely supervised. Concurrently, in another room of the library, a proposal was being devised for the US Steel Corporation (owned by Morgan and two partners) to buy TC&I and thereby save Moore and Schley. The deal was sealed on Sunday afternoon. Anti-trust crusader President Roosevelt gave final approval to the acquisition minutes before the NYSE opened on Monday morning.

On Monday, November 4, 1907, the DJIA closed at 57, a 39 percent drop since the beginning of the year. November 5 was election day, and banks were closed. In the following week the Treasury pumped another $40m in gold bonds into the banking system, which permitted banks to expand banknotes and alleviate the liquidity shortage. In addition, news arrived that $12.4m worth of gold was en route from London. The financial crisis finally appeared to have been averted and confidence was restored, but economic ramifications continued to reverberate. The turbulence hurt confidence in NYC banks, and many country banks demanded conversion of their deposits in NYC banks to currency. NYC banks responded to the country banks' redemption demands by restricting convertibility of deposits, which led to limitations on cash withdrawals across the country (Friedman and Schwartz 1963). Many state governments declared emergency bank holidays as bank runs spread across the nation. Convertibility restrictions remained in place until January 1908. A wave of bankruptcies hit the real sector of the economy with the credit squeeze, and economic activity contracted for 13 months from May 1907 to June 1908. Production fell by 11 percent, and unemployment increased from 3 percent to 8 percent in 1908.

The aftermath

Augustus Heinze was sued for financial malfeasance and exonerated in 1909. He ran his few mining interests in Utah for a while longer but never recovered. Charles Morse's financial career was later interrupted by charges of embezzlement of funds, for which he served a prison sentence. Charles T. Barney still had a net worth of $2.5m but was disgraced; he put a bullet through his stomach on November 14 and died. J. P. Morgan was hailed as the savior of financial markets by many, but his outsized role was also a source of concern about plutocracy.

The alarm and apprehension felt by populist and progressive political groups over the concentration of financial power in a few Wall Street hands that exercised control over both credit extension and decision-making in the boardrooms of the industry—the *Money Trust*—were expressed in the 1912 congressional hearings, chaired by Representative Arsene Pujo. The committee reported that a small group of banks held 341 directorships in 112 corporations with a market capitalization of $22b (approximately 85 percent of the NYSE capitalization). These interlocking directorships were alleged to be a source of conflicts of interest on issues of access to financing and competition in provisioning final consumer goods. The business press and the bankers, including Morgan, who testified, took the paradoxical position of both denying the existence of a Money Trust and praising the benefits of concentration of financial-industrial power. The hearings offered the public an opportunity to understand how bankers saw themselves. The immense powers that they exercised through representation on company boards, monitoring management, gathering information, and deciding which firms would get financing by underwriting decisions, bankers argued, were means to protect the interests of those who invested in the securities of these companies. The dominance of big banks was a reflection of both the public's confidence in big banks' ability to look after investors' interests and the public's trust in the market's ability to discipline any banker who would not perform this task adequately (DeLong 1991).

Bankers were also unreceptive to the idea of openness and transparency of bank activities, including detailed disclosure of their assets and liabilities, on grounds that it would be detrimental to business. One bank president, George Baker, stated that a public disclosure would halt business for reasons he could not even divulge. If depositors were unhappy, he said, they could withdraw their funds any time they wanted. George Perkins, a lieutenant of J. P. Morgan, defended and justified Morgan's control of information on the basis that it was symptomatic of investors' confidence and trust in Morgan, built by the banker's decades of hard work that proved to be beneficial his clients. The returns investors received on securities underwritten by banks were proof of the value added by Morgan's work (DeLong 1991; Smith and Sylla 1993). In response to the public's condemnation of exorbitant fees and commissions bankers responded that it was the only way to attract and retain the talent needed to perform complex financial deals (Smith and Sylla 1993).

The establishment of the Federal Reserve System

The most important outcome of the 1907 panic was the re-emergence of the idea of the lender of last resort. Following President Jackson's revocation of the charter of the second Bank of the US, the country did not have an institution that resembled a central bank. The resolution of the 1907 crisis by the tenacity, authority, and power of J. P. Morgan, with substantial help from the government, presented a dilemma to Jeffersonite opponents of the central bank. While there was no central bank, large private banks, which were viewed with similar misgivings, dominated the system. From the Jeffersonian perspective, the fact that the function of the lender of last resort was performed in large part through the intermediation of J. P. Morgan in 1907 did not sit well. Morgan's actions bore witness to the extreme concentration of wealth, prestige, and clout in the hands of an individual and the way that this power could be used to coerce economic and, and perhaps, political actors. Entrusting the stability of banking to the plutocrats had profoundly disagreeable implications for the democratic ideals advanced by Jefferson.

Moreover, even the presence of such a powerful class or an individual such as Morgan did not ensure that meltdown would be averted in the next financial debacle. In the event of a prolonged crisis, coercing bankers to commit their scarce reserves to faltering colleagues or rivals and coordinating distribution of these funds may be beyond the capacity of any private individual or group. Thus, the last panic of the nineteenth-century US tradition persuaded all parties that a lender of last resort modeled after contemporary European central banks was necessary, and the third round of the Jefferson–Hamilton debate went to Hamilton.

In 1908 Congress established the National Monetary Commission and assigned it to investigate the currency and banking systems of Europe, determine the necessary changes in the US banking system in light of international experience, and report its findings to Congress. The commission was headed by Republican Senator Nelson W. Aldrich, who undertook a two-year study. Bankers and politicians both agreed that the stability of financial markets required an institution that would serve as the lender of last resort when a liquidity crisis was imminent. Contentious points were related to the centralization of financial power, as well as the balance of public and private interests in governance of the institution. Among populists and Democrats skepticism of large centralized financial institutions still existed. After the struggles of hard vs. soft money and distributional strife between borrowers and lenders these populists and Democrats did not wish to leave the control of the monetary system to banking interests alone. Bankers, however, wanted exclusive control of the reserve system and freedom from government interference in monetary matters.

Senator Aldrich convened a secret conference in 1910 on Jekyll Island, off the coast of Georgia, in which leading bankers participated. The conference, ostensibly a duck hunt, was so secret that, throughout the week, only the first names of the participants were used for fear of leaks to the press. The outcome of the conference, in addition to an endless number of conspiracy theories, was the Aldrich Currency Report of January 1911, which laid the foundations of the Federal Reserve System. In the Aldrich Report bankers received much of what they wanted, including 15 geographically separated "Regional Reserve Associations" under the control of banks. These associations would be authorized by the federal government to hold reserves (deposits) of commercial banks, to issue the national currency that would be the government's obligation (later called Federal Reserve Notes), and to act as lenders of last resort.

In contrast to the preceding three-tiered national banking system, the regional reserve system was expected to transfer reserves flexibly and efficiently to banks that faced liquidity issues. The decentralized reserve system was designed to address the Democrats' concerns about the centralization of monetary power. However, the Democrats and populists were still apprehensive about the disproportionate power of bankers in the proposed reserve associations and the extent to which the system could function as a government-empowered tool to serve the interests of bankers (creditors) to the detriment of farmers, workers, and small businesses (debtors). President Wilson, a Democrat, modified the Aldrich template in several ways. The most important modification was the addition of the Federal Reserve Board (FRB), appointed by the president and headquartered in Washington, DC, to oversee the reserve system. The objective of the addition of the FRB was to ensure that the government had a say in the governance of the reserve system so that bank and non-bank public interests were better balanced. Although bankers publicly criticized the addition of the FRB as an intrusion of political power into private enterprise and a threat to the market system, privately, they found the compromise acceptable. Congress passed the Federal Reserve Act, and President Wilson signed it into law on December 23, 1913.

The Federal Reserve Act reduced the number of regional reserve banks to 12, with the Federal Reserve Bank of New York the first among equals. National banks were required to become members of the system. State banks were encouraged to do so, although most did not. Regional reserve banks were "owned" nominally by the member banks, which pledged 6 percent of their assets for the capital of the reserve bank. Member banks were required to keep, at a minimum, a fraction of their deposits as reserves, some of which were to be deposited at a regional reserve bank in the form of gold, Treasury gold certificates, or money convertible to gold. In return they could take loans from the "discount window" of the reserve bank at will, either in the form of additional reserves or as Federal Reserve notes. Interest on these loans was called the rediscount rate (now more commonly called the *discount rate*).

The regional reserve banks were non-profit institutions and did not engage in banking business with the public. Their boards of directors were selected largely by the member banks but were expected to reflect the interests of banks as well as the non-bank public. Governors and the chair of the FRB were selected by the president and confirmed by the Senate. The balance of power within the system initially favored the regional reserve banks vis-à-vis the FRB, but this was to change in the 1930s when the FRB acquired the ability and authority to conduct national monetary policy and regulate the banking sector, powers that went far beyond the intentions of its founders. After the 1930s the regional reserve banks were represented in the FRB's policy-making committee but functioned in an advisory capacity.

The Federal Reserve System evolved with the changing economic and political environment, but its hybrid, private–public nature remained a constant source of tension. According to the Federal Reserve legislation, it had the task of aligning private and public interests in the control of monetary conditions, but how this objective would be achieved was not detailed. Instructions such as maintaining "sound" (non-inflationary) credit conditions while accommodating the credit needs of industry, agriculture, and commerce in setting the rediscount rate provided little explicit guidance to the directors of the Federal Reserve System (Greider 1987). Thus, the boards had wide latitude in determining the credit needs of the economy and balancing the interests of bankers, farmers, small and big businesses, and merchants as they saw fit. Not surprisingly, the Federal Reserve became an incessant target of criticism from certain groups. The left of the political spectrum viewed it as an institution that ultimately defended the interests of big banks and creditors against debtors by keeping money tight. From the right it was viewed as a promoter of cheap money and a corrupting intrusion into the market system that had a tendency to create artificially low interest rates and artificial prosperity. Most of the time, however, Federal Reserve officers projected the image of an institution above the fray of social and political conflict, and the public and politicians were largely willing to leave what they viewed as technical and obscure questions of money and credit to the central bank's experts and technocrats.

Timeline

	1873 Crisis
1862	Issue of greenbacks; brokers and traders who are not allowed to join New York Stock Exchange (NYSE) start Public Stock Board; Gold Room founded.
1863–5	Banking Acts create national banking system.
1864	Open Board of Stock Brokers and Gold Exchange founded.
1865	Vanderbilt and Tobin corner Harlem Railroad.
1869	Gould attempts to corner gold market; Cooke and Company underwrite $100m worth of Northern Pacific Railroad bonds.
February 1873	President Grant signs Coinage Act.
August 1873	Cooke and Company in trouble over unsold Northern Pacific bonds; newspapers report two other railroad companies in trouble.
September 8, 1873	Several banks with loans to railroads become insolvent.
September 15, 1873	Several railroad companies and more banks and insurance companies with loans to railroads go bankrupt.
September 18, 1873	Black Thursday; Cooke and Company closes down; panic spreads.
September 20, 1873	NYSE closes; panic spreads to other centers; stocks tumble.
September 30, 1873	NYSE opens; panic ends.
October 1873–March 1879	Long Depression of the US.

	1893 Crisis
1874	Congress limits greenback circulation.
1875	Congress passes Resumption Act to make greenbacks convertible to gold by 1879.
1890	Congress passes Sherman and McKinley Tariff Acts; Bank of England rescues Baring Brothers.
1891	Recession in Europe and continuing gold outflow from US.
1892	US returns de facto to bimetallic standard.
February 1893	Philadelphia and Reading Railway Company goes bankrupt.
April 1893	Treasury's gold reserves below legal minimum limit.
May 1893	Failure of National Cordage Company; NYC banks suspend converting silver dollars and Western bank notes.
August 1893	Congress repeals Sherman Act; Treasury stops buying silver.
January 1893– June 1897	US economy in depression.
	Panic of 1907
January 1906	Dow Jones Industrial Average (DJIA) index at historic peak.
April 1906	San Francisco earthquake and fire.
July 1906	Maximum railroad rates set; railroad stocks decline.
Fall 1906	Bank of England raises its discount rate twice.
March 1907	DJIA declines by 16 percent.
Spring– Summer 1907	US reserves drain to Britain and France; bank failures in Japan; NYC has difficulty selling municipal bonds; copper market collapses; courts fine Standard Oil for anti-trust violation; stock prices slide.
October 14–15, 1907	Otto Heinze attempts to corner copper market and fails.
October 22, 1907	Knickerbocker Trust suspends operations after massive bank run.
October 23, 1907	Bank run on American Trust; Morgan organizes $8.25m loan package; instability spreads in NYC and to other parts of country.
October 24, 1907	Treasury deposits $25m in banks; stock prices plummet; NYSE asks for help; Morgan arranges $23.6m loan to NYSE.

October 25, 1907	Panic continues in NYSE; Morgan arranges $9.6m loan and averts crisis.
October 27, 1907	NYC informs Morgan it will go bankrupt unless $20m raised by November 1.
October 29, 1907	Morgan arranges New York Clearing House underwriting of $30m NYC bond issue.
November 2, 1907	Moore and Schley brokerage house near collapse; state banking examiner reports two large trust companies in precarious situation. Morgan convenes conferences to save trusts and Moore and Schley.
November 3, 1907	Plans to save trusts and for US Steel to take over TC&I finalized.
November 4, 1907	President Roosevelt approves sale of TC&I.
	The Aftermath
1908	Congress establishes National Monetary Commission.
1910	Jekyll Island conference convenes.
1911	Aldrich Report on Federal Reserve System issued.
1912	US Representative Arsene Pujo holds congressional hearings on Money Trust.
1913	Congress passes and President Wilson signs Federal Reserve Act.

Key terms and concepts

Blind pool
Call loan
Call rate
Corner
Federal Reserve System
Greenback
Gresham's Law
Industrial trust
Margin account
Margin call
Money Trust
National banking system
Pool
Trust company (financial)

Endnotes

1 Much of the historical narrative of this chapter comes from Chancellor (2000), Geisst (1997), Sobel (1988), and Stedman (1905). Friedman and Schwartz (1963) is the classic academic source for post-1867 US monetary history.
2 The margin of safety varies with factors such as the size of the loan and the volatility of the stock and the market.
3 See Steeples and Whitten (1998) for a detailed account of the 1893 crisis and depression.
4 Silver miners who expected silver coinage to raise the demand for the metal were also a part of this coalition.
5 For an hour-by-hour account of the 1907 panic see Bruner and Carr (2007).

References

Bruner, Robert F. and Sean D. Carr. 2007. *The Panic of 1907: Lessons Learned from the Market's Perfect Storm*. Hoboken, NJ: John Wiley and Sons.

Calomiris, Charles W. and Gary Gorton. 1991. The Origins of Banking Panics: Models, Facts, and Bank Regulation. Pp. 109–73 in *Financial Markets and Financial Crises*, edited by R. Glenn Hubbard. Chicago: University of Chicago Press.

Carter, Susan B., Scott Sigmund Gartner, Michael R. Haines, Alan L. Olmstead, Richard Sutch, and Gavin Wright, Eds. 2006. *The Historical Statistics of the United States* (Millennial ed.). Cambridge, New York: Cambridge University Press. Online: hsus.cambridge.org/HSUSWeb/HSUSEntryServlet.

Chancellor, Edward. 2000. *Devil Take the Hindmost: A History of Financial Speculation*. New York: Plume.

DeLong, J. Bradford. 1991. "J. P. Morgan and his Money Trust." *Wilson Quarterly* 16 (4): 16–30.

Diamond, Douglas W. and Philip H. Dybvig. 1983. "Bank Runs, Deposit Insurance, and Liquidity." *Journal of Political Economy* 91 (3): 401–19.

Friedman, Milton and Anna J. Schwartz. 1963. *A Monetary History of the United States, 1867–1960*. Princeton, NJ: Princeton University Press.

Geisst, Charles R. 1997. *Wall Street: A History from its Beginnings to the Fall of Enron*. Oxford, UK: Oxford University Press.

Gorton, Gary B. 2012. *Misunderstanding Financial Crises: Why We Don't See Them Coming*. New York: Oxford University Press.

Greider, William. 1987. *Secrets of the Temple: How the Federal Reserve Runs the Country*. New York: Touchstone.

Kindleberger, Charles P. and Robert Z. Aliber. 2011. *Manias, Panics, and Crashes: A History of Financial Crises*, 6th ed. New York: Palgrave Macmillan.

National Bureau of Economic Research. 2014. *NBER Macrohistory Database*. Online: www.nber.org/databases/macrohistory/rectdata/11/m11005.dat.

Smith, George David and Richard Sylla. 1993. "The Transformation of Capitalism: An Essay on the History of American Capital Markets." *Financial Markets, Institutions and Instruments* 2 (2): 1–62.

Sobel, Robert. 1988. *Panic on Wall Street: Classic History of America's Financial Disasters with a New Exploration of the Crash of 1987*. New York: Truman Talley Books/Dutton.

Stedman, Edmund Clarence. 1905. *The New York Stock Exchange: Its History, its Contribution to National Prosperity, and its Relation to American Finance at the Outset of the Twentieth Century*, vol. I. New York: Stock Exchange Historical Company.

Steeples, Douglas and David O. Whitten. 1998. *Democracy in Desperation: The Depression of 1893*. Westport, CT: Greenwood Press.

Wimmer, Larry T. 1975. "The Gold Crisis of 1869: Stabilizing or Destabilizing Speculation under Floating Exchange Rates." *Explorations in Economic History* 12: 105–22.

10 The crash of 1929

Memories of most financial calamities eventually fade away. To new generations they seem like dated, largely puffed-up anecdotes. Even scholars and experts often think of past crises as mere subjects of curiosity that are no longer pertinent to modern times, and consign them to the proverbial dustbin of history. If there is one exception, however, to the tendency to forget or discount the past, it is the Wall Street crash of October 1929.

In the summer of 1929 record-high stock prices were considered to signal the prosperous, productive, new-era US economy. Between early September and the end of October, however, prices fell by 40 percent. By fall 1932 the stock-price index was down 80 percent from its 1929 peak. In the aftermath of the crash about 40 percent of banks went bankrupt, the US economic engine came to a stop, industrial production contracted by more than 50 percent, and the rate of unemployment increased alarmingly. This momentous event was seared into the public conscience for decades to come and has become the standard to which every new financial crisis is compared.

The 1929 crash and the subsequent Great Depression was also a turning point in economic policy and theory. In the realm of policy widespread legislative changes restructured financial markets. New federal agencies and the reconstituted Federal Reserve System (Fed) imposed and enforced rules and regulations on private financial institutions to ensure the stable functioning of the banking system and exchanges. In the intellectual arena the crisis shook faith and confidence in the laissez-faire doctrine that predicted that self-adjusting and self-disciplining powers of markets were sufficient to maintain stability in both the financial and real sectors of the economy. A more cautious attitude, which both expressed the conviction that the market system is superior to all other modes of economic organization and professed the acceptance that markets also are prone to chronic instability and, therefore, need external assistance to not self-destruct, became dominant.

The economic landscape[1]

The decade of the 1920s started with a slump. Industrial production dropped by 27 percent during the 12 months after July 1920 and did not

Figure 10.1 US industrial-production index, 1920–32 (monthly).

Note: Seasonally adjusted series.

Source: FRED, Federal Reserve Bank of St. Louis.

recover until October 1922 (Figure 10.1). Industrial production also stagnated in 1924 and 1927. Despite these setbacks, the cumulative growth rate was impressive. Between 1920 and the summer of 1929, when it peaked, the industrial-production index increased by 41 percent, averaging almost 5 percent per year. The Roaring Twenties is often described as a time of unbounded optimism and wealth accumulation.

The primary source of the brisk growth on the supply side was the increase in productivity in response to improvements in technology, business organization, and management methods. Research and development created new production techniques, and corporate mergers exploited economies of scale and increased overall efficiency. Fordism reduced unit costs through assembly-line work organization, specialization, mass production, and product standardization, and used wage incentives to raise the labor effort. Scientific management and the time-motion methods of Taylorism were implemented across industries to streamline the corporate organization and production process.

The availability of mass-produced goods and the expansion of the electric-utility network revolutionized consumption and spending patterns on the demand side. The Ford Model T, introduced in 1908, was the forerunner of affordable durables that catered to the emerging consumer society. Technological innovations introduced new commodities, such as the radio, telephone, motion pictures, and airplanes, and higher incomes and the discovery of consumer credit stimulated consumption spending. Whereas households could borrow only at usurious rates earlier, small-loan companies that extended consumer credit at reasonable interest rates multiplied during the first decades of the century. Installment-finance companies made loans toward the purchase of large consumer durables, primarily automobiles. Consumer spending rose steadily and accounted for two thirds of total national expenditure toward the end of the 1920s. The expanding use of automobiles and trucks required paved, all-weather roads, and the construction industry boomed with rising urbanization, the growth of cities, and the spread of suburbs. The extension of home loans by thrift institutions contributed to the building of new subdivisions.

While output, productivity, and employment were high and rising, the benefits of the boom were not shared evenly across society, and income inequality sharpened. The top 10 percent's share of household income increased from 38 percent to 46 percent between 1920 and 1928, and the top 1 percent received 20 percent of total household income in 1928 (Piketty and Saez 2003). Wealth distribution was even more unequal. The net worth of the richest 1 percent of households accounted for 47 percent of total personal household wealth (Wolff 2002)—and their share of financial wealth was even greater. The labor movement was docile, and the progressive upheavals of the late nineteenth century were a distant memory. The unionization drives of craft and mine workers had failed after unsuccessful strikes, and the 1921 recession further weakened the labor movement. The rate of unionization declined from 18 percent to 10 percent during the first half of the 1920s and stayed there for the remainder of the decade.

The overall stance of the government was pro-business, made clear by President Calvin Coolidge (1925; he was in office from August 1923 to March 1929) with his famous words, "The chief business of the American people is business." Tax rates were low, the government was small, and regulations were minimal. The Fed had started to exercise its power to control credit in the economy, and the boom-bust banking cycles and liquidity crises were believed to be a thing of the past. Within the system there was tension between the Federal Reserve Board (FRB) in Washington and the Federal Reserve Bank of New York (FRBNY), the leader of the regional reserves. Under the leadership of Governor Benjamin Strong, once a lieutenant of J. P. Morgan, the FRBNY monitored the monetary conditions in the financial capital of the country by buying and selling short-term government securities in the open market (known as *open market operations*) and by changing the discount rate at which it made loans to the member banks. While the gold standard still governed international monetary transactions, domestically, these tools effectively dissociated credit conditions from the supply of gold and improved the stability of overall economic activity.

Speculative disturbances occured, but they were localized. The most infamous of these was the Florida real-estate bubble of 1925. Early in the decade Florida had been promoted as a tropical leisure paradise by real-estate developers who marketed plots of land, mostly to the urban middle classes. Heavy advertising and easy credit helped to generate enthusiasm and raise land prices. Soon there was rampant speculation. It was common to sell the right to buy land for a fraction of the price, which allowed buyers to leverage their purchases and drove prices upward. Buyers often purchased plots from brokers and dealers without ever laying their eyes on the land.

Speculation spread from land to commodities. The scale of construction was such that the hauling of supplies created gridlock in the Florida railroads. The FRB started to question whether monetary policy was too lax and interest rates too low. However, the FRB's concern was inconsequential because, by law, the regional reserve bank had the power to conduct operations to raise the discount rate and limit credit. The speculative fever started unraveling in 1925 as real-estate-price appreciation slowed down. As capital gains disappeared speculators began to liquidate their inventory, prices dropped, and foreclosures occurred with more frequency. Two hurricanes in 1926 were the final pins that popped the bubble, which left behind many abandoned subdivisions at various stages of development and became a major setback for Florida's development over the next two decades. For the economy as a whole, however, it was a peripheral matter. The overall feeling of prosperity and optimism, together with the anticipation of high returns and capital gains in the midst of rising productivity and corporate earnings, were too robust to be dissipated by a real-estate blunder that was happening a thousand miles away from Wall Street.

The banking system

The resources of US banks grew throughout the 1920s. First, deposits increased with higher national income. Second, New York City replaced London as the finance capital of the world after World War I, and money from across the world started flowing into the US. Third, the FRBNY cut the rediscount rate in 1925 and again in 1927, permitting banks to borrow funds cheaply from the FRBNY to lend in the lucrative financial markets.

Because the 1929 crash is at times blamed on foreigners and the Fed it is worth discussing the motivations of this FRBNY policy. The second cut in the rediscount rate was instigated at the request of western European governments. The gold standard, which set the values of national currencies in terms of gold,[2] was suspended during World War I. In 1925 the UK returned to the gold standard but set the value of the pound sterling vis-à-vis gold, and, therefore, the dollar, at the pre-war parity. This rate was unrealistically high because sterling had lost value due to inflation in the preceding years. The overvaluation of sterling made UK commodities uncompetitive in international markets, and investors across the globe switched from the overvalued pound to the US dollar. International trade and capital flows brought gold to the US and threatened the UK financial system as early as 1925. To sustain financial stability in western Europe the central-bank presidents of the UK, France, and Germany asked the Fed to lower the rediscount rate to slow down and then reverse the money flow into the US.[3] Financial instability in Europe could have had negative consequences for the US in the event that problems stopped the war-debt payments it received from Europe. The FRBNY then lowered the rediscount rate in August 1927 from 4 percent to 3.5 percent to avoid a crisis in Europe.

In comparison with previous decades, corporations relied more on earnings and securities issues to finance fixed-capital investments, and became less dependent on long-term bank loans. Through their affiliates commercial banks underwrote corporate securities and marketed securities to the public at both the wholesale and retail levels (Friedman and Schwartz 1963: 244). Thus, the banks' role as intermediaries between securities investors and issuers became more prominent relative to that between depositors and commercial borrowers. In addition, bank loans made against the collateral of securities and the trading of securities on their own accounts became more widespread.

The stock market

During the 1920s stock issues grew rapidly. Manufacturers of new products, such as radios and airplanes, floated stocks to finance fixed-capital investment. Established public companies issued new stocks to finance expansion. The horizontal mergers of the 1920s brought together geographically separated enterprises that operated in the same line of business, e.g. utilities, department stores, and movie theaters, under unified management to improve organizational efficiency and open new outlets. These centralized holding companies issued securities to finance purchases of other operations and property, or to build new establishments. While most of these corporations were highly leveraged, equity financing also was attractive, especially when stock prices were rising. Finally, investment trusts issued stocks based on their portfolios of common stocks of other companies (more on investment trusts later).

The demand for stocks increased far faster than supply. The accumulation of wealth in combination with its concentration in the hands of the rich kept interest in the stock market high and stock prices buoyant. The urban upper-middle classes also participated in the stock market in increasing numbers. The higher incomes of the middle class permitted higher levels of savings. Stock returns had exceeded bond returns, particularly during the inflationary first decades of the century, and made common shares a more attractive store of savings. The public's perception that corporate management was becoming more responsive to shareholder interest, coupled with improved methods of portfolio allocation and diversification, increased confidence in equity investment.

Stock ownership was promoted by prominent members of academia, business, and finance, many of whom spoke on the radio and wrote in newspapers and magazines in glowing terms about the future of the US economy and profit prospects. There were also numerous self-styled "experts" who were purported to have intimate knowledge of the market, especially of little-known, specific stocks. They dispensed free advice and tips to investors in the media. These experts were typically highly optimistic and enthusiastic about stocks. The upper-middle classes increasingly channeled savings to stocks, which they saw as lucrative, long-term investment vehicles. In addition to wealthy and middle-class investors, speculators who anticipated capital gains also bought stocks. They usually leveraged their purchases by margin loans. Speculative trades accounted for most of the action during the tumultuous months of the stock market in 1928 and 1929.

The impression that the whole country was heavily involved in trading stocks during the 1920s has become part of American lore, but it is hardly accurate. Hard numbers are not available on the number and types of stock buyers, but Sobel (1988: 355–6) puts the number of stockholders at around three million, out of a population of 120 million, mostly urban, upper-middle-class people. Most of these were probably long-term investors who sought dividends, but distinguishing between investors and speculators is difficult. The number of margin accounts, the best indicator of the extent of speculation, was around 600,000. Galbraith (2009 [1954]: 78) puts the number of active speculators at less than a million. While the number of people involved directly in the market was small relative to the population, the social impact of stock-market activity was disproportionately large. The stock market became the center of attention in the media. Interpreting past performance of stocks and predicting their future was an intrinsic part of the culture and the subject of constant discussion. Bernard Baruch, a prominent financier and speculator of the day, was reportedly shocked to hear stock tips from a panhandler. While relatively few participated directly, a much larger number apparently passed the time talking about the stock market.

While the days of the robber barons were gone and professionals were in charge of corporate finance, efforts were still being made to influence stock prices. Investment trusts and banks that traded on their own accounts acted strategically to boost share prices before unloading their holdings. It was common for traders to pool their resources to push the price of a stock higher. A successful pool, with some assistance from radio and newspaper commentaries and tip sheets, created public interest in the stock. Pool participants then sold the stock at the higher price and shared in the proceeds. The public was aware that price manipulation occurred, but there was no backlash. As long as prices kept on rising and gains appeared to continue without limit, there were no complaints (Galbraith 2009 [1954]: 79; Sobel 1988: 363).

Call loans

Call loans and margin accounts, introduced in the last chapter, played a major role in fueling the demand for stocks during the 1920s. To recap, banks extended call loans to brokers, who, in turn, used these funds to finance the margin accounts of their customers. Investors and speculators were able to purchase stocks from brokers on credit against cash, usually 10 percent to 20 percent of the loan, and the collateral of the stock they purchased. In the event that stock prices, and hence collateral values, declined, brokers requested that their customers make up the difference in cash or additional securities. Margin buying at 10 percent meant that a buyer with $100 cash could purchase $1,000 worth of stocks. With a 5 percent rate of return, a 10:1 leverage ratio would boost total earnings to $50, or the return on capital to 50 percent. The downside, of course, is that a 5 percent loss symmetrically wiped out 50 percent of the capital.[4]

Banks were fond of extending call loans. They were payable on demand and highly liquid as a result. The wide spread between call rates and the FRBNY discount rate was a rich source of revenue. Rising stock prices probably also created the perception of very low default risk. Many brokers were bank subsidiaries. Call loans were contracted at the money desk of the NYSE, where stockbrokers and lenders' brokers negotiated the call rate and transferred funds and collateral (Rappoport and White 1993). Soon other actors entered the market as suppliers to take advantage of high call rates. Corporations flush with cash—compliments of high sales and Coolidge's tax cuts—and, later, international lenders also offered funds to the call-loan money market (Sobel 1988: 362).

Financial markets viewed margin accounts favorably and promoted them because they were believed to attract people with limited means to the stock market. Rising numbers of investors were expected to expand the stock market, but margin trading was used primarily by speculators to leverage their assets. Call-loan volume is often taken as a measure of the prevalence of speculation (Galbraith 2009 [1954]; Sobel 1988), and in the early 1920s it was $1.0b to $1.5b. By the end of 1927 it had jumped to $3.5b, indicating that credit extended to speculators rose more than three-fold in seven years.

Leveraging by retail stock customers was practiced with unprecedented fervor in the 1920s to amplify dividends and capital gains. It was also practiced at the institutional level by *investment trusts*.

Investment trusts

The *investment trust* was created in the 1920s to offer primarily middle-class investors access to an expertly supervised, diversified portfolio of stocks. An investment trust built a stock portfolio by purchasing the common stocks of various corporations. It then issued its own shares of common stock backed by this stock portfolio. Hence, shareholders of the investment trust indirectly owned the trust's portfolio of common stocks; the stock of the trust itself was a derivative financial instrument, the value of which was derived from the underlying stock portfolio. When the underlying portfolio yielded dividends or paid capital gains these benefits, after subtracting the trust's management fees, accrued to the trust's shareholders. Trust issues constituted one third of all new stocks in 1929 (Galbraith 2009 [1954]), increasing the country's volume of common shares without a corresponding expansion in the country's physical capital. Hundreds of investment trusts were organized by investment banks, brokers, securities dealers of assorted reputations, and investment trusts themselves.

Experts, including Wall Street authorities, prominent bankers, and academics, served on trust management teams and offered advice on portfolio allocation (Galbraith 2009 [1954]: 55). Trusts often did not divulge information on their stock portfolio and justified this practice on the grounds that to do so would reveal their trade secrets. Hence, their capital consisted of unveiled brain power and veiled financial assets. The lures of diversification and first-rate expert management nevertheless drew many middle-class investors who were willing to pay a premium for the trust stocks to take advantage of the expertise of leading authorities. Investment-trust stocks were sold at prices substantially higher than the value of the stocks that backed them.

The popularity of trusts among investors yielded large revenues to the sponsors in the form of fees and premiums. The sponsors soon discovered other means to enhance their profits. First, they borrowed against the trust's assets to expand the size of the portfolio and magnify the returns. Second, they created a new trust using the unsold stock of a parent trust as capital. The new trust, in turn, leveraged this capital and issued more stocks. Galbraith (2009 [1954]: 60–5) tells the story of one such leveraged chain trust. Investment bank Goldman, Sachs and Company established the investment trust Goldman, Sachs Trading Corporation in December 1928 with a market capitalization of $100m. In July 1929 the Trading Corporation founded the Shenandoah Corporation; a month later Shenandoah formed the Blue Ridge Corporation, and the Trading Corporation acquired Pacific American Associates. In eight months the Goldman, Sachs chain operation issued $425m worth of stock.

The proliferation of trusts through chains further expanded the volume of stock issues. It also created the illusions of greater choice for the common investor and more diversification across investment trusts. For the executives the chain trusts yielded more fees, but these were not their only gains. During the establishment of chain trusts they often set aside shares of the new trust for themselves with an eye on the capital gains to be made as soon as the new trust's share price appreciated; they then traded in their own shares to manipulate the price.

Stock prices before 1928

Stock prices are expected to vary directly with corporate earnings. Figure 10.2 illustrates the relationship between the real (inflation-adjusted) Standard & Poor's (S&P) Composite Index and earnings per share. Earnings figures are the ten-year moving average of mean corporate earnings.[5] Overall, earnings per share grew by 35 percent, cumulatively, from 1920 to the end of 1927, and the stock-market index during the same period rose by 120 percent. However, there was a significant decline in corporate earnings per share during the 1921 recession and smaller dips in 1924 and 1927, in line with the contraction in industrial production. The stock index declined during the recession of 1921, but the 1924 and 1927 episodes did not have a perceptible effect on the stock-price index.

During the 1924–6 period the stock index increased at the impressive rate of about 50 percent. Stock prices and earnings per share largely

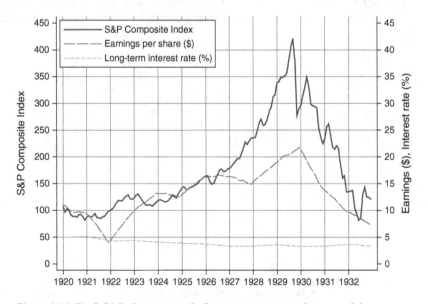

Figure 10.2 Real S&P Composite Index, earnings per share, and long-term interest rate, 1920–32 (monthly).

Source: Shiller (2005).

trended together until 1927, although stock prices rose at a swifter pace. The real discrepancy between the two series came after 1927, when the index jumped by 32 percent while earnings declined. The FRB was concerned that the stock-price increase was incommensurate with earnings growth and that the FRBNY was keeping the discount rate too low. Even Governor Strong was worried, but the stock-market decline in early 1926 did not have adverse consequences for the larger economy and dissipated the fears of a bubble and crash. In fact, it reinforced confidence in the stock-price trend, reflecting expected profitability growth and the strength of the fundamentals.

Another fundamental of the stock price is the interest rate. Stock prices are expected to rise as the interest rate declines. However, during the period under study the relationship was erratic. Figure 10.2 plots the behavior of the ten-year government-bond interest rate. As shown, stock prices increased between 1920 and 1927, and the interest rate indeed declined steadily from 5 percent to 3.5 percent, the sharpest drop occurring early in 1921. But during the boom year of 1927 the interest rate was virtually constant, dropping from 3.34 to 3.33 percent.

Prelude to the crash: 1928–9

Historical accounts date 1928 as the start of the speculative fever in earnest. Figure 10.3 reports that the daily Dow Jones Industrial Average (DJIA) grew by 33 percent over the year, while earnings per share rose by 23 percent. The initial bull run that started in March raised the stock

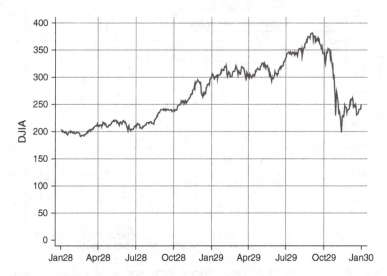

Figure 10.3 Dow Jones Industrial Average, 1928–9 (daily).

Source: S&P Dow Jones Indices.

index by 15 percent before leveling off in June and turning into a brief bear market with very heavy trading. The second bull run started in September and gained momentum in November after Hoover was elected president.

Monetary policy was not expansionary in 1928. The FRBNY tightened monetary conditions by raising the discount rate between February and July 1928 from 3.5 percent to 5 percent. The long-term bond rate climbed higher, from 3.3 percent to 3.6 percent, over the course of the year. However, higher interest rates did not slow down the expansion of call loans, and speculation continued feverishly. Call rates rose from 5 percent to as high as 10 percent over the year, and the spread between the discount rate and the call rate remained advantageous for lenders (White 1990). Call-loan volume rose from $4.4b at the end of 1927 to $4.9b in mid 1928, and was $6.4b at the end of 1928. Moreover, US corporations and foreign banks flooded the credit market with their surplus cash to take advantage of the high-yield, high-liquidity debt. Their share in call loans rose from 41 percent to 60 percent (Kindleberger 1973: 113). The fact that the debt was backed by liquid stocks and the belief that stock prices would continue their upward trajectory likely offered further comfort to lenders.

The evidence indicates that the Fed was not behind the credit expansion, and borrowing increased despite the cost of loans turning against margin borrowers. Moreover, in addition to higher call rates, margin requirements on call loans started rising after October 1928 (Smiley and Keehn 1988). The continuation of credit growth under these circumstances suggests that the driver of credit expansion was the rising demand for loans. Borrowers appear to have been highly optimistic, anticipating high returns on their stock investments. Bank and, increasingly, non-bank sources of credit were merely accommodating the demand.

There was widespread apprehension among policymakers regarding excessive speculation. Strong, the most innovative and influential central banker of the time, attempted to raise the discount rate in the summer of 1928 to 6 percent to curb speculation but was rebuffed by the FRB. The FRB was also concerned with speculation but preferred to use the qualitative measures of coercion, pressure, and persuasion to have banks reduce their call loans. The FRB did not favor a higher discount rate because it could adversely affect "productive" users of credit and economic performance.

During the first six months of 1929 stock prices were turbulent. The market gained 5 percent, while earnings per share increased by 7 percent. The uncertainty over whether the FRB and FRNBY would intervene through qualitative or quantitative measures attracted much attention. Call loans continued rising, albeit at a slower rate. On June 30 call-loan volume stood at $7.1b. Beginning in July, however, trading in the stock market intensified, and prices rose by 18 percent to their peak in September, while earnings per share rose by only 3 percent. On October 4 call loans reached $8.5b, higher by 20 percent since June 30, and by 32 percent since the beginning of the year. Almost 80 percent of the supply came from non-bank corporations and from abroad.

The real sector of the economy, however, was not faring as well. Industrial production peaked in July and then began to decline. The monthly rates of decline were substantial, at 1 percent in August and 0.6 percent in September (Figure 10.1). The source of the downturn is still a matter of debate (see below). In the summer of 1929, however, the public expressed no fear of recession. The Harvard Economic Society, which had warned of a possible recession early in the year, declared that there was no chance of a significant economic downturn (Galbraith 2009 [1954]: 71).

Higher stock prices were hailed by most as a sign of the strength and future affluence of the US economy—and there was no shortage of cheer-leaders for the stock market. Prominent businessmen, such as John Raskob and William Crapo Durant, who had made their name and built their wealth in General Motors, now hailed the bright prospects of Wall Street. Bernard Baruch expressed his confidence in the future of the market on radio and in newspapers and encouraged stock purchases. The public fol-lowed the statements of these successful businessmen and speculators, and the atmosphere of confidence produced many would-be imitators of the moguls.

Academia added more fuel to the speculative fire. Professor Charles Dice of Ohio State University praised captains of industry for having the vision and wisdom to engage with the world of finance, heralding the progress of the Coolidge market (Galbraith 2009 [1954]: 14). Professor Joseph Davis of Stanford, Edmund Day of Michigan, Joseph Lawrence of Princeton, and Edwin Kemmerer of Yale were among Wall Street's enthu-siasts. The judgment of many of these academics reflected the laissez-faire ideology of the time and the public's confidence in the stability and effi-ciency of markets. Several commentators, such as Galbraith, however, question whether the source of their enthusiasm was purely intellectual and scholarly conviction. Many market enthusiasts, including Davis and Day, had a vested interest in high-performing markets because they served as advisors to investment trusts and banks and had lent their pres-tige to these businesses. The most prominent academic to lead the cheers for the stock market was Irving Fisher, a professor of economics at Yale University and one of leading economists of the century. Fisher was ear-nest in his faith that stock prices reflected the strength of the economy and followed his own advice; he invested heavily in the stock market, although he reportedly did not diversify.

Not everyone followed this state of affairs with enthusiasm. Alexander Dana Noyes, the financial editor of *The New York Times*, warned as early as January 1, 1929, that historical experience demonstrates that easy credit and intense speculation ultimately lead to collapse and financial strin-gency (Sobel 1988: 354). Paul Warburg, an investment banker, one of the architects of the Fed, and an eyewitness to the 1907 panic, pointed out that unrestrained speculative price increases, fed by a mounting debt burden, would eventually lead to the collapse of the stock market and the entire economy. The Standard Statistics Company, a credit-rating agency, viewed the situation as unsustainable. Finally, Roger Babson, business analyst and entrepreneur, notified the public on September 5 that a crash was imminent.

These forewarnings were met with derision and dismissed summarily by bankers, academics, and the business media, including *The Wall Street Journal* and *Barron's*. Each passing day without a crash was taken as validation of the speciousness of prophesies of doom. Skeptics were viewed as outdated naysayers, who failed to appreciate the new economic frontiers that promised continuous expansion of productivity and profitability. Listening to their advice would have meant speculators foregoing capital gains, bankers missing out on interest charged on loans to brokers, investment trusts giving up generous fees, and long-term stock investors missing opportunities for future dividends. Cheerleaders easily outnumbered pessimists.

Other experts in positions of power viewed stock prices with caution but chose not to speak out or take any action. E. H. H. Simmons, President of the NYSE, for instance, believed that excessive speculation could be harmful but was ambivalent about whether that was the case in 1929. Ultimately, he viewed the function of the exchange as ensuring free and fair markets and did not make judgment calls about whether speculation had become excessive.

Perhaps the most interesting debate took place inside the Fed. After the death of Governor Strong in October 1928 the disagreement between the FRB and the FRBNY surfaced once again. Only the regional reserve banks could influence credit conditions directly, by open market operations and discount-rate changes, although these changes needed to be approved by the FRB to take effect; otherwise, the FRB functioned primarily in a supervisory capacity. Both the FRBNY and the FRB were concerned about speculation and the stock-market boom and agreed on the need to reduce credit flow for stock purchases. However, they again disagreed on the means to achieve this. The FRB viewed the prevailing discount rate as too low for speculation but too high for producers and merchants. It opposed the FRBNY's plans to raise the discount rate because, while raising the rate may have slowed credit extension to speculators, it would have harmed other customers of credit who needed it for production and commerce, adversely affecting the level of economic activity. Instead, the FRB asked the FRBNY to exercise its moral suasion with the member banks to reduce call loans and to impose restrictions on banks' usage of loans from the FRNBY. The FRBNY, however, argued that such measures were unfeasible because it did not have the power to control how banks used its loans. This conflict paralyzed the monetary authority in early 1929.

The question of what the monetary authority should or could do in the face of a speculative boom has been encountered repeatedly during the past two centuries and is still a topic of discussion today. Central bankers were engaged in similar disputes in 1929. They first questioned how Fed officers would know whether a stock-price pattern was driven by the fundamentals or whether it was a bubble. The common objection to intervention is that the monetary authority's information is no better than that of private agents, and, therefore, it is no more capable of judging whether a stock-price increase is justified by the fundamentals. If there is no bubble interventions, such as limiting credit and raising the interest rate, may contract production and commerce unnecessarily.

The second argument against intervention is that deflating a bubble is a delicate process. If the Fed's actions pop the bubble too quickly panic and financial instability may ensue. The potential collateral damage to the overall economy makes the policy authority apprehensive about intervening. Squeezed between doubt over whether any action is necessary and the possibly hazardous consequences of action, the central banker's easiest course may be to do nothing.

The third problem that the Fed faces is whether it has the appropriate tools to bring stock prices down. The problem was particularly severe in 1929. One option, of course, was to raise the discount rate and shrink loans to the banks. However, the discount rate was substantially lower than the call rate, and credit originated largely from sources outside the influence of the FRBNY. Thus, a higher discount rate probably would not have affected the extension of call loans. Moreover, a very large increase, which might have been necessary to force banks to reduce call loans, would have had severe consequences for the real sector. The effectiveness of the other instrument—advice, admonition, moral suasion, and jawboning to persuade the banks to act in a prudent fashion—was dubious as the Fed was not as powerful a regulator in the 1920s as it has been in modern times.

According to most accounts, the FRB adopted a passive stance in early 1929 in the face of criticism from financial circles, politicians, and academics, and in fear of creating turbulence in markets. According to Galbraith (2009 [1954]: 35), the FRB's cautionary announcements on speculation were motivated not by the desire to limit reckless behavior but to absolve itself of any responsibility regarding speculative excesses. The market decline in March 1929 increased the FRB's timidity. National City Bank President and FRBNY director Charles Mitchell, with the approval of the FRBNY Governor, George L. Harrison, pledged $25m of call loans to traders in the event the FRB followed up the idea of supervising banks' lending activities (Friedman and Schwartz 1963: 260). The FRB's passivity continued until August 9, when they approved the FRBNY's decision to increase its discount rate from 5 percent to 6 percent. The change was inconsequential. The margin between the call loan and the discount rates was approximately 3 percent, still making it very profitable for banks to continue borrowing from the FRBNY and making call loans.

President Coolidge had been enthusiastic about the stock market's growth and ignored the Fed's expressions of concern, but Hoover, the new president, did not agree with him. Both Hoover and Secretary of the Treasury Mellon followed prices in late 1928 and 1929 with apprehension and worried about excessive speculation; their views paralleled those of the FRB.

The fall

The Great Bull Market, which began in 1924, ended on September 3, 1929. A gradual decline in the stock-price index started on September 5, and by the end of the month the DJIA had dropped by 10 percent. In early October 1929 share prices continued to fall, but the market was expected to recover. The sentiment on the street was of enduring confidence in the fundamentals of the US economy, combined with faith in big operators and investment trusts to sustain the market through bargain purchases or rescue operations in the event the situation got worse. On October 15 economist Fisher proclaimed that the stock market reached a "permanently high plateau" and attributed the price decline to the actions of a few marginal traders who had financed stock purchases with loans and faced difficulties in paying their debts—a necessary cleansing. The index fell by another 5 percent between October 1 and 22, and banks increased their margin calls throughout this period. October 23 was a particularly bad day, when the stock-price index dropped by 6.3 percent. The panic started the next day.

Black Thursday, October 24, was the lead-up to the disaster. The panic started in the morning when brokers, believing that their customers would be unable to respond to margin calls, started placing *stop-loss orders*, i.e. orders to sell a security when the price reaches a certain level. Prices collapsed, and the NYSE ticker fell behind, which added to the uncertainty and fueled panic. The panic spread to the rest of the country, and several exchanges, such as Chicago, were forced to suspend operations for the day. Wall Street bankers met to pool funds and buy shares to support the market. Organized support emerged in the afternoon. Bankers boldly asserted and displayed their power and authority on the floor of the NYSE by buying shares of the largest companies to allay the fears of traders, and some degree of stability was achieved. At the end of the day the DJIA had declined by only 2.1 percent with trading close to a record 13 million shares.

During the following two days the captains of industry and finance reassured the public that the worst was over. The market had merely undergone a correction and come out stronger after a few reckless speculators were purged. The fundamentals were sound. The press expressed its admiration for the bankers who had seemingly brought the panic to an end. President Hoover joined the chorus that praised the foundations of the US economy.

The disaster hit after the weekend. On October 28, Black Monday, the DJIA fell by 13.5 percent, and close to ten million shares were traded. Bankers met once again in the afternoon, but this time the concern was self-preservation, or figuring out ways to liquidate the loans they had extended and limit the losses from the forthcoming wave of defaults. They released a statement expressing their objective to let prices fall, albeit in an orderly and proper manner, which meant the loss of all hope for speculators and margin buyers.

On the following day, October 29, or Black Tuesday, there was a deluge of sell orders as speculators disposed of their stocks to meet margin requirements; the DJIA fell by another 11.7 percent. Investment trusts were hurt most. Shares of the investment trust Goldman Sachs Trading Corporation, which were traded at $104 per share a few months earlier, fell to $1.75. At the end of the day there were rumors of banks selling stocks, and once esteemed bankers quickly became objects of scorn. Executives of the NYSE considered suspending trading for a few days, but decided against it in view of the risk of such a move causing further deterioration of confidence. At the end of the day a record volume of 16.4 million shares had been traded. Between September 3 and October 2, the DJIA dropped by 40 percent, wiping out all the gains of the previous 12 months. The sharpest declines occurred during the last two days.

On October 30 things started looking up, with reassuring words from industrialists, including J. D. Rockefeller. On that day the DJIA rose by 19 percent, and the public's mood improved somewhat. The NYSE offices closed from Thursday afternoon until Monday, and the FRBNY cut the discount rate to 5 percent.

Although prices appeared to recover between January and April 1930, this was only temporary. In the summer of 1932 the stock market reached its nadir, 81 percent lower than its September 1929 peak in inflation-adjusted terms. This was the lowest the stock market had been since the nineteenth century.

What happened? Interpretations

Was the stock market of the 1920s a bubble? As pointed out above, there were contradictory answers back then, and, unsurprisingly, the debate has not abated to this day.

Was the stock market overvalued?

Fisher (1933), the leading US economic theorist of the time, was a sincere believer in the fundamentals-driven market and asserted that there was no bubble in US stocks in 1929. He claimed that technological innovations, new commodities, research and development, patents, and new methods of business organization had brought about a new age of high productivity and profitability, which validated the high stock prices. The maturing of the exchanges had eliminated the previous century's stock volatility. Professionally managed modern markets were no longer subject to insider manipulations. The emergent investor class was better educated and more informed, used scientific methods of investing, such as present-value calculation, and managed risk through portfolio diversification. These developments all brought more stability to the market. Even after the crash Fisher revised his assessment of the stock market's performance only marginally and claimed that up to three quarters of the price boom between 1926 and 1929 was justified by technological and organizational improvements in the production process.

Some modern commentators offer evidence in support of Fisher's contention that the economic indicators were strong. Sirkin (1975) and Bierman (1991, 1998) review the price-earnings (P/E) ratios of individual stocks and assess whether they were "reasonable" under plausible projections of future earnings-growth rates and discount rates. Sirkin focuses on the Dow Jones Industrials and argues that P/E ratios at the peak of the market in 1929, with few exceptions, were justifiable under the scenario that earnings per share would grow at around the median rates observed over the 1926–9 period for another five to ten years. Similarly, Bierman rejects the idea that stock prices were overvalued in 1929 because P/E ratios in 1929 were in line with historical norms and, except for utilities stocks, were sensible, given the "reasonable" expectations for earnings growth over "reasonable" time periods. Along different lines, McGrattan and Prescott (2004) argue that Fisher was correct in claiming that stocks were not overvalued because, once the corporate intangibles, such as technological know-how, are taken into consideration in addition to the tangible assets, the total value of the corporations justified their high share prices and market capitalizations.

Other economists disagree. White (1990) notes that the time periods and earnings-growth rates used in calculations that supposedly justify the P/E ratios of 1929 were far in excess of the historical norms of the business-cycle experience and, therefore, can hardly be considered reasonable. Shiller's (2005) cyclically adjusted P/E (CAPE) ratio is reported in Figure 10.4 in a historical perspective. The CAPE ratio reached 33 in 1929, a record that stayed intact until 2000.[6] By this metric the stock market was overvalued dramatically.

De Long and Schleifer (1991) use a different method to address the question of overvaluation. They focus on the share prices of investment trusts, whose fundamental value should equal the value of their stock portfolio after adjusting for taxes, liquidity premiums, and management fees. Buyers of trust stocks were presumably less sophisticated investors.

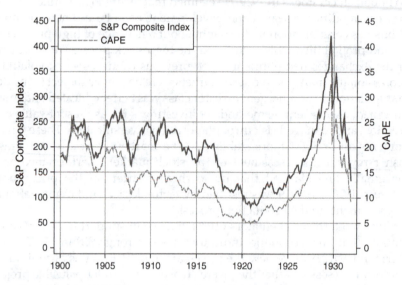

Figure 10.4 Real S&P Composite Index and CAPE, 1900–32 (monthly).

Source: Shiller (2005).

If these buyers responded to noise, and trust-stock prices rose substantially above their fundamental value, then the standard theory predicts that the smart money would have shorted trust stocks and brought prices back in line with the fundamental value. Based on a sample of trust stocks, DeLong and Schleifer note that there was no evidence of stabilizing speculation. The premium on investment-trust stocks rose throughout 1929 and averaged as high as 47 percent by the third quarter. DeLong and Schleifer note that the premium of chain-trust-stock prices, i.e. trusts that hold only the stocks of other trusts, cannot be justified with management skills. The authors use the premium on trust shares as a measure of over-optimistic investor behavior. Projecting this premium to the S&P stock index, they estimate that average stock prices were overvalued by 30 percent above the fundamentals.

In a similar vein, Rappoport and White (1993) compare call rates with interest rates on short-term paper and try to tease out information about lenders' perceptions regarding the likelihood of a stock-market bubble. While interest rates generally increased after 1928 with the more restrictive monetary policy, the increase in call rates was much higher than the short-term commercial-loan rate and far more volatile. Between spring 1928 and spring 1929 the commercial-paper call-rate spread increased by eight percentage points, a substantial amount, considering the commercial-paper rate was around 6 percent. Moreover, the pattern of higher call rates and spreads was established even before the market grew apprehensive about the Fed's actions regarding the loan market in February 1929. Rappoport and White conclude that the premium on call loans reflects lenders' increasing anxiety regarding the stock-market bubble, the rising likelihood of a crash, and the collapse in collateral values.

Explaining the bubble and the crash

If the stock market in 1929 reflected future profit prospects in a prospering and expanding economy, and there was no overpricing, why did the market crash in 1929? According to the standard asset-pricing theory, all available information about the present value of earnings is embodied in the current price of the stock, and, therefore, only an unexpected piece of information can cause the price to change. Commentators draw attention to several bits of news as possible culprits for stock-price changes.

For instance, the Smoot–Hawley Bill passed the House in May 1929, and moved through the Senate.[7] The bill proposed raising tariffs on thousands of agricultural and industrial goods and provoked retaliation from other countries and the disruption of international trade. Then, on September 20, the business and finance empire of Clarence Hatry, who had issued unauthorized stock, failed in London. Further, on October 11, the Massachusetts Department of Public Utilities did not allow Boston Edison to split its stock, arguing that it would encourage speculation, and instigated an inquiry into the company's rates.

While commentators attach varying degrees of importance to these news reports, most economists discount the likelihood that these events by themselves created a generalized decline in profit expectations. Shiller (2005: 95, 97) surveys newspaper articles of the time and reports that they were devoid of any significant news on the fundamentals. The most prominent items prior to and during the crash were news on price declines, the competing assurances of Wall Street and Washington that the economy was sound and the worst was over, and commentary on the pessimistic mood of the markets. Galbraith (2009 [1954]) and White (1990) point out that the effects of the events mentioned above were limited in scope, and could not have spread across the entire market. Others argue that they could be significant in combination with anti-speculation rhetoric.

Bierman (1998) holds President Hoover, UK Chancellor of the Exchequer Lord Snowden, and the media culpable for creating fear among the public, and even in the Fed, by their constant, often sanctimonious talk about the "orgy of speculation." In this atmosphere, suggests Bierman, an event such as the Boston Edison incident or the FRBNY's raising discount rates could collapse stock prices. Thus, he states, there was no overpricing to start with; unfounded fears of a bubble among political leaders alarmed markets and depressed prices. Note that this explanation is strays from that of optimizing agents simply revising stock valuations in light of the arrival of new information; it relies on investor decisions based on non-fundamental, extraneous factors and market psychology to describe a negative bubble. Cecchetti (1992) also emphasizes political factors. Citing President Hoover's memoirs penned in 1952 as evidence, Cecchetti puts the onus on the president's "anti-market" stance during the boom and his hostile rhetoric. He claims that Hoover's public statements cautioning the public about speculation contributed to the triggering of the crash.

An exogenous shock that may have triggered the crash is the Fed's policy and the ensuing recession. Friedman and Schwartz (1963) attribute the onset of recession in June 1929 (Figure 10.1) to the tightening of monetary policy by the FRBNY after the fall of 1928 (later joined by the FRB) to restrict speculation and discourage call loans. Contractionary monetary policy and the consequent downward pressure on the price level induce people to hold more money and reduce spending, thereby lowering the level of economic activity. If profit expectations decline with the level of economic performance they pull down stock prices. Galbraith (2009 [1954]: 90) discounts the recession explanation by pointing out that the summer recession was a modest decline and that similar declines had happened before without the disastrous consequences of 1929.

A very different interpretation of the relationship between monetary policy and the crash argues that there was a bubble economy during the 1920s that was created by inflationary policies pursued by the FRBNY. According to Austrian-school economist Rothbard (1963), the FRBNY had kept discount rates low with the complicity of the legislative and executive branches of the government. Politicians sought to ensure the supply of easy credit to the powerful constituencies of businesses and the farmers. In addition, FRBNY Governor Strong reduced the discount rate in 1927 to help the UK as well as J. P. Morgan (Rothbard 1979). The prospect of easy money created the classical Austrian malinvestment boom. The combination of low discount rates and President Coolidge and Secretary of the Treasury Mellon cheering the advances of stock prices and the new era of the US economy fueled stock speculation. The flow of funds to speculators through call loans permitted stock prices to rise far above justifiable values. The hazard of this policy, i.e. an unsustainable speculative boom, was recognized in February 1929, but by the time the FRBNY raised its discount rate it was too late. This reading of the history puts the blame on politicians who catered to their constituencies, the foreign central banks, and the Fed for instigating monetary ease.

White (1990) explains the 1920s experience as a case of an intrinsic bubble. The momentous transformations of the 1920s, including changes in technology and industrial structure, new products, and the rise of a consumer society, heralded higher earnings and dividends and, thus, higher stock prices. During this period of rapid transformation the fundamentals became more difficult to judge. Some of the new product firms, such as RCA, had never paid dividends; some of the old firms were experiencing displacements, e.g. Ford's replacing its Model T with the Model A; and

General Motors was emerging as the leading auto company. The composition of investors was also changing, and included a rising number of women and first-time investors from the upper-middle classes. Efforts to cater financial-market services to these classes were on the rise. It was a period of a high intrinsic uncertainty, coupled with high expectations, which was conducive to the emergence of a bubble. The era came to an end, according to White (1990), when industrial production started lagging due to the restrictive monetary policy pursued by the Fed. Investors revised earnings and dividend expectations in light of the new information that began to arrive in the summer of 1929. With the recession, expectations were adjusted in a downward direction, and demand for stocks, and stock prices, declined.

Shiller (2005: 67, 113) emphasizes that the 1920s was a period of increased awareness and interest in the stock market, as measured by the quadrupling of articles on the market in periodicals, and the domination of a new era of economic thinking that created perceptions of lower risk, expectations of a permanently better future, and excessive optimism among investors. Moreover, economics professors and experts continually promoted, in best-selling books and newspaper articles, stock investment and its advantages over buying bonds (Shiller 2005: 113, 196). Positive prices, income, wealth, and cultural feedback loops led to a higher demand for stocks and amplified stock-price increases. Thus, the larger volume of credit was not a cause of overvaluation but a symptom. It was overoptimism fed by rising stock prices that induced greater demand for and supply of credit. Regarding the point of the crash, Shiller (2005: 97–8) believes that pieces of adverse news were not individually important but that their accumulation created an *attention cascade* whereby people reinterpreted the previous bits of information and their impact on the stock market under an increasingly pessimistic light.

Kindleberger and Aliber (2011) note that the period prior to the crash exhibited displacement, expansion, euphoria, and distress in succession. They identify technological innovations, such as the expansion of automobile production, highways, electrification, movie theaters, and consumer usage of radios and telephones as the displacements that raised profit opportunities in the US. Surging fixed-capital investments in these sectors brought about a rapid expansion of economic output and credit. Burgeoning call loans signaled euphoric conditions and speculation in the stock market. The increase in their volume was so impressive that Kindleberger and Aliber (2011: 80) suggest that declining industrial production after July 1929 was attributable to the allocation of credit from production and consumption to the call-loan market. This emphasis on the call-loan market is challenged by Cecchetti (1992), who discounts the importance of call loans in the summer of 1929 because their volume constituted merely 4.4 percent of the total market value of the NYSE. As most stock trading was taking place via the call-loan market, however, call loans probably had a disproportionately large effect on the stock prices.

Kindleberger and Aliber (2011: 98) observe signs of distress from June to the last week of October 1929 as banks slowed down credit extension to the real sector of the economy. Loans to the stock market, however, continued rising until early October. Signs of financial distress probably surfaced fully in mid October when loans by US banks and foreigners started to decline (Kindleberger 1973: 118). Finally, despite prominent New York financiers' efforts to support stock prices, panic set in the week before October 28.

Again, the BMK and Austrian accounts concur on the importance of credit conditions in creating the stock-market bubble but differ on the causal relationship between loans and prices. Was it the ease of loans that fueled speculation, or were lenders accommodating the demand for loans to make speculative investments? The evidence shows that the demand for call money continued unabated and increased in volume after the FRBNY increased the discount rate in 1928. The fact that the call rate rose as high as 15 percent in 1929 suggests that speculation and demand for credit were driving the increase in lending. With ample resources at their disposal, banks as well as non-bank institutions facilitated speculation by accommodating credit demand.

The banking panic

Banking failures in the years after the crash have attracted substantial scholarly attention. The number of banks in the US had increased rapidly after 1887 and peaked at 31,000 in 1921. In the 1920s the banking industry was overbuilt, and competition had reduced profitability (Walter 2005). Many of these banks were established in rural areas and were small and badly capitalized. During the 1920s bank failures were common, especially among smaller banks in the rural Midwest that were vulnerable to regional agricultural problems. They also had difficulty competing with the branches of national banks. An average of 635 banks failed annually between 1921 and 1929, a number far larger than the failures of the previous decade, but these failures did not pose a threat to the stability of the banking system.

The real structural break came after 1929. Thirteen hundred and fifty banks failed in 1930, 2,293 in 1931, 1,453 in 1932, and an estimated 4,000 in 1933. Approximately 40 percent of the banks that were in operation in January 1929 had been wiped out by March 1933. In the first round of failures in November 1930 rural banks were hit hard, but some larger state banks also found themselves in trouble. The downfall of the Bank of the United States in December 1930, which was a member of the Fed, was the largest commercial bank failure in the US to date. New waves of banking crises struck the economy between brief respites. In March 1931 bank runs affected Chicago especially hard. In the third wave of early 1933, which caused two large banks in Detroit to shut down, governors in many states, including Michigan and Washington, declared bank holidays and closed the banks. Richardson (2007) underscores that the experiences of banks varied widely. Many banks suspended their operations, although not all of them faced heavy deposit withdrawals. Some banks were able to reopen without outside assistance. Some exhausted their borrowing capacity and shut their doors permanently. Others did not suspend operations but ended up running out of cash or merging with other institutions.

Economists and historians pinpoint March 1933 as the turning point in the 1930s banking crises. On March 4, 1933, Franklin D. Roosevelt became president. He declared a nationwide bank holiday from March 6 to 9, later extending it to the March 13. On March 9 Congress passed the Emergency Banking Act, which gave extraordinary powers to the administration to deal with banking crises and allowed the Fed to supply loans to banks in liberal amounts. The Banking Act of June 1933, popularly known as the *Glass–Steagall Act*, addressed the problem on a more permanent basis.

There are two debates related to bank failures in the aftermath of the 1929 crash. The first concerns the reasons for the large scale of failures. The second is the contribution of the 1929 crash to the bank failures and the Great Depression. The remainder of this section deals with the first question. I will consider the second question in the next section in the discussion of the causal relationship between the stock-market crash and the Great Depression.

As mentioned earlier, the source of the banking failures could be either illiquidity or insolvency. The debate between these competing hypotheses in the context of the 1930s bank failures has been lively. Friedman and Schwartz (1963) take the position that the problem was one of liquidity. While some rural banks had made poor loans throughout the 1920s and encountered problems, these were local problems of minor significance. Most banks did not make excessive loans, and their overall quality of credit was good at the end of the 1920s. In November 1930, March 1931, and January 1933, however, the combination of Midwestern banks' troubles due to crop failures, the failure of the Bank of the United States, and the failures of European banks indebted to US banks created a loss of confidence in commercial banks. Many banks that were forced to liquidate their assets to build reserves, often at highly discounted prices, went under. The Fed could have provided liquidity to the system and bought time for the cash-constrained institutions, but it failed to do so, which led to exacerbation of the crisis. Nor did policymakers resort to imposing restrictions on the conversion of deposits to currency, or bank holidays. In the absence of countermeasures waves of liquidity shortages wreaked havoc on the system.

The challenge to the liquidity hypothesis came from Temin (1976: 106), who argues that the problem was one of insolvency due to poor-quality bank loans. According to this argument, bond values started declining as early as 1928, which suggests that bank assets were losing value before the crash. Second, worsening economic conditions, e.g. crop failures and declining private spending, further damaged bank's balance sheets across the board in 1929. White's (1984) statistical comparison of the characteristics of failing and non-failing banks in 1930 offers evidence in support of Temin's argument. White finds that weak asset portfolios underlie the failures in 1930: lower agricultural incomes and defaults hurt banks in the South and the Midwest, and declining bond values hurt larger banks and trusts. These factors made the banking system more susceptible to the monetary contraction that was underway.

Richardson (2007) argues that both illiquidity and insolvency played roles in the banking crises as periods of panic and "ordinary" business alternated between 1930 and 1933. The relative importance of the two sources of trouble varied with the acute and chronic types of banking distress. During periods of panic or acute distress, most notably in November 1930, illiquidity was the primary source of bank suspensions. During periods of chronic distress, or non-panic periods, banks closed down due to insolvency and impending bankruptcy.

The crash of 1929 and the Great Depression

Because the Great Depression immediately followed the stock-market crash of 1929 these two events are merged in the minds of many. Economists' opinions on the causal relationship between the 1929 crash and the Great Depression, however, vary. According to Friedman and Schwartz (1963: 306), there is little relationship between the two events. The crash was an outcome of the Fed policies that contracted the economy in the summer of 1929. The crash itself did not create a loss of confidence in the banking system or trigger the depression. Instead, it was the misguided policies of the Fed that transformed what would have been an ordinary recession into a deep and long-lasting slump. The succession of banking failures led to the destruction of one third of deposit money. While the money stock of the nation shrank drastically, the Fed did not increase reserve notes to offset monetary contraction or assist the failing banks. The shortage of money reduced spending, raised default rates, and pushed the economy into a tailspin.

Friedman and Schwartz (1963) do not convince many economists. Temin (1976), for instance, points out that spending and economic activity declined prior to monetary contraction, and, therefore, the latter cannot be the cause of the depression. Both Temin (1976) and Bernanke (1983) find Friedman and Schwartz's hypothesis implausible in light of the limited extent of monetary contraction relative to the depth of the depression.

Several economists find a causal relation that runs from the crash to the depression. Mishkin (1978) identifies the *wealth effect* as the link between the two events. The explanation lies in declining household net worth. In 1929 and 1930, in inflation-adjusted terms, the value of household financial assets fell. To make things worse, the ensuing deflation increased the value of financial liabilities. Middle-class households experienced a financial squeeze as deflation reduced the value of their primary asset, i.e. their homes, and increased the value of primary liabilities, i.e. mortgage and consumer debt, in real terms. Declining overall wealth and redistribution of wealth away from middle-class households prompted consumers to cut down on their spending and build liquid balances. Lower aggregate demand plunged the economy into a depression.

Bernanke (1983) offers an alternative explanation that relies on banks' inability to perform intermediation services between borrowers and lenders during a state of disorder in the financial system. Bernanke takes exception to the idea of perfect markets and grounds his argument in imperfections or inefficiencies in the banking system. After the crash it was more difficult for banks to distinguish between good and bad borrowers. Costs incurred by banks in screening and monitoring borrowers and assessing the default risk, or *credit intermediation costs*, increased. In the absence of perfect or complete markets, where they could have traded these loans to hedge their risks, banks chose to limit their potential losses by contracting loans and ended up inhibiting the regular flow of credit. The subsequent credit rationing transformed the downturn into a depression.

Galbraith's (2009 [1954]: 186) account focuses on the structural fragilities of the real sector of the economy. He believes that the economy had certain attributes that were highly brittle and vulnerable to the shock created by the crash. Aggregate demand was sensitive to declining asset values because income distribution was highly unequal, and the small securities-owning class carried out a disproportionate share of spending. Highly leveraged holding companies and investment-trust chains were exposed to huge losses if and when leveraging worked in reverse. Large numbers of highly interconnected financial institutions raised the likelihood of bank failures turning into an epidemic. Policymakers and experts were oblivious to the state of the economy and incapable of adopting appropriate measures in times of trouble. The collapse of corporate structures destroyed the ability to borrow and the willingness to lend. In this context the momentous decline of stock prices spread across the economy with little resistance.

Kindleberger and Aliber (2011: 80–1) note that during the euphoric 1920s the positive feedback loop between higher stock prices and the flow of credit to the stock market came at the expense of loans to producers and consumers. The economy began to turn downward in the summer of 1929, not because the Fed reduced the money supply but because there was a shortage of credit in the real sector of the economy. When the crash hit, the subsequent liquidity freeze pushed the economy into a depression.

The legislative response to the crash

The crash of 1929 and the subsequent banking failures raised questions about the stability of markets and the need to impose rules and regulations on banks and exchanges to avoid financial crises. Congress passed, and the president signed, a series of acts after 1933, including the Glass–Steagall Act of 1933, the Securities Act of 1933, and the Securities and Exchange Act of 1934, and instituted a series of new rules and regulations to prevent a recurrence of the financial extravagance of 1928 and 1929. Among these the Glass–Steagall Act was the most prominent. The act separated commercial and investment banks. It defined the primary role of commercial banks and their affiliates as being an intermediary between depositors and retail borrowers, i.e. firms and households who need funds to purchase homes, durables, machinery, and equipment. No depository institution was permitted to buy, sell, underwrite, and distribute securities (with a few exceptions concerning government and investment-grade bonds) or to issue bonds against their assets. The objective of this provision was to prevent commercial banks from engaging in high-risk activities with depositors' money. The act also extended federal supervision of commercial banks. Regional Fed banks were assigned to oversee the books of the member banks to ensure that they did not engage in speculative activities. Thus, commercial banks ended up controlling huge amounts of deposits but were prevented from taking high risks with depositors' money. The banking laws of the 1930s made the commercial banking system very dull indeed.

In return for parting with lucrative activities commercial banks received some rewards. The newly established Federal Deposit Insurance Corporation (FDIC) insured deposits in commercial banks up to $10,000 (reduced to $5,000 in 1935). This new federal agency sustained depositor confidence in the banking system, which had been badly injured in previous years. The FDIC was funded by insurance premiums paid by commercial banks. The FDIC turned out to be controversial because many lawmakers initially questioned the wisdom of the federal government getting involved in the insurance "business" and the possibility that this innovation would induce banks to engage in high-risk activities. Concerns regarding moral hazard or the perverse incentives that *deposit insurance* might have created were addressed by policymakers, who imposed restrictions on risky behavior. In addition to the limitations on securities trading mentioned above, Regulation Q of the US Code of Federal Regulations prohibited banks from paying interest on demand deposits and limited competition for deposits by imposing interest rate caps on savings and time deposits.

The 1933 and 1935 acts also redefined the Fed and altered the balance between the FRB and the regional reserve banks. Under the guidance of Fed Chairman Marriner Eccles, and against the protests of private bankers and the regional reserve banks, the FRB was reconstituted and renamed the Board of Governors of the Federal Reserve. The regional reserve banks' power diminished as they took on an advisory role. The revamped Board of Governors seized the authority to set reserve requirements and the discount rate, to run monetary policy through the Federal Open Market Committee, and, as a measure against speculation, to set margin requirements on call loans, as high as 100 percent if necessary.

The Securities Act of 1933 required initial-public-offering issuers to register their securities with the federal regulator and provide complete and accurate information to prospective investors. The Securities and Exchange Act of 1934 created the Securities and Exchange Commission (SEC) to enforce the 1933 act. The 1934 act, however, was more encompassing, and regulated securities trading in the secondary markets. Nationwide securities exchanges and the activities of investment banks, brokers, and dealers fell under the purview of the SEC. To achieve greater transparency in markets and provide timely, reliable information to securities buyers and sellers, the SEC required securities-issuing companies to file periodic reports. The SEC's duties also included supervision of the system to ensure that corporate abuse, such as insider trading, price-fixing, stock-market-pool operations, accounting fraud, and activities intended to misinform and mislead investors, did not take place. In 1938, again to improve market stability and stop downward price momentum, the SEC adopted the *uptick rule*, which restricted short selling.[8]

Under the new regulations the main role of investment banks was to help firms raise funds. Their primary activities were underwriting IPOs, marketing securities, and providing advice and management expertise on mergers and acquisitions, services for which they received substantial fees. Parallel to these activities, but separate due to a potential conflict of interest, they also provided investment advice to clients in return for fees. Finally, they served as market makers by buying and selling securities on their own account. Thus, in comparison with commercial banks, there was greater opportunity for investment banks to engage in high-risk activities, but as non-depository institutions they could do so with either their own or borrowed money.

Timeline

1921	US economy undergoes deep recession.
1924	Recession.
1925	Florida real-estate bubble; FRBNY lowers discount rate.
1927	FRBNY lowers discount rate.
January 1928	FRNBY raises discount rate from 3.5 percent to 5 percent.

March 1929	Hoover becomes president; stock market declines; FRB and FRBNY debate how to respond to speculative call loans.
May 1929	Smoot–Hawley Tariff Bill passes the House.
July 1929	Industrial production peaks.
August 9, 1929	FRBNY raises discount rate to 6 percent.
September 3, 1929	US stock market peaks.
September 20, 1929	Clarence Hatry's empire fails; London Stock Exchange crashes.
October 11, 1929	Massachusetts Department of Public Utilities instigates inquiry into Boston Edison's rates and refuses to permit company's request to split stock.
October 24, 1929	Black Thursday panic; contained by bankers purchasing shares.
October 28, 1929	Black Monday panic; stock market declines 13 percent.
October 29, 1929	Black Tuesday panic; stock market declines 12 percent.
November 1930	First round of banking failures.
March 1931	Second round of banking failures.
July 1932	Stock market reaches lowest level, 90 percent below 1929 peak.
January 1933	Third round of banking failures.
March 6, 1933	Nationwide bank holiday declared; Congress passes Emergency Banking Act.
June 1933	Congress passes Banking Act of 1933 (Glass–Steagall Act).

Key terms and concepts

Attention cascade
Credit intermediation cost
Deposit insurance
Glass-Steagall Act
Investment trust
Open market operations
Stop-loss order
Uptick rule
Wealth effect

Endnotes

1 This chapter's historical narrative draws on Chancellor (2000), Friedman and Schwartz (1963), Galbraith (2009 [1954]), Geisst (2004), Kindleberger (1973), and Sobel (1988).

2 Gold parities, in turn, set currency exchange rates.
3 For a historical account of inter-war monetary relations between the US, UK, France and Germany see Ahamed (2009).
4 For the sake of simplicity, interest payments on loans are ignored in these calculations.
5 Both series come from data compiled by Shiller (2005). When tracing stock-price changes over long time periods I use the Shiller data because they are inflation-adjusted. The stock-price data are the S&P Composite Index, which in 1957 was renamed the S&P 500 Index. Whenever I use the Shiller series I follow his nomenclature. The ten-year moving average of earnings is the mean value of the earnings reported in the previous ten years. The moving average of earnings smooths out short-term fluctuations and reflects the longer-term trends in earnings.
6 The CAPE is a long-term average P/E ratio calculated for the S&P Composite Index. It uses the ten-year moving average of monthly earnings in the denominator. The presumption here is that the average of past earnings over a long period is a predictor of future earnings.
7 The bill was enacted into law in June 1930.
8 The uptick rule permits a short sale only at a price higher than the price at which the security was traded most recently.

References

Ahamed, Liaquat. 2009. *Lords of Finance: The Bankers Who Broke the World*. London: Penguin Books.
Bernanke, Ben S. 1983 June. "Nonmonetary Effects of the Financial Crisis in the Propagation of Inflation." *American Economic Review* 73 (3): 237–76.
Bierman, Harold. 1991. *The Great Myths of 1929 and the Lessons to be Learned*. New York: Greenwood Press.
Bierman, Harold. 1998. *The Causes of the 1929 Stock Market Crash: A Speculative Orgy or a New Era?* Westport, CT: Greenwood Press.
Cecchetti, Stephen G. 1992. "Stock Market Crash of 1929." Pp. 573–7 in *The New Palgrave Dictionary of Money and Finance*, edited by P. Newman, M. Milgate, and J. Eatwell. London: Macmillan.
Chancellor, Edward. 2000. *Devil Take the Hindmost: A History of Financial Speculation*. New York: Plume.
Coolidge, Calvin. 1925. Address to the American Society of Newspaper Editors, Washington D.C., January 17. Online: www.presidency.ucsb.edu/ws/?pid=24180.
Delong, J. Bradford and Andrei Schleifer. 1991. "The Stock Market Bubble of 1929: Evidence from Closed-End Mutual Funds." *Journal of Economic History* 51 (3): 675–700.
Fisher, Irving. 1933. "The Debt-Deflation Theory of Great Depressions." *Econometrica* 1 (4): 337–57.
Friedman, Milton and Anna J. Schwartz. 1963. *A Monetary History of the United States, 1867–1960*. Princeton, NJ: Princeton University Press.
Galbraith, John Kenneth. 2009 [1954]. *The Great Crash 1929*. Boston: Mariner Books.
Geisst, Charles R. 2004. *Wall Street: A History from its Beginnings to the Fall of Enron*. Oxford, UK: Oxford University Press.
Kindleberger, Charles. P. 1973. *The World in Depression, 1929–1939*. Berkeley: University of California Press.

Kindleberger, Charles P. and Robert Z. Aliber. 2011. *Manias, Panics, and Crashes: A History of Financial Crises*, 6th ed. New York: Palgrave Macmillan.

McGrattan, Ellen R. and Edward C. Prescott. 2004. "The 1929 Stock Market: Irving Fisher Was Right." *International Economic Review* 45 (4): 991–1009.

Mishkin, Frederic. 1978. "The Household Balance Sheet and the Great Depression." *Journal of Economic History* 38 (4): 918–37.

Piketty, Thomas and Emmanuel Saez. (2003). "Income Inequality in the United States, 1913–1998." *Quarterly Journal of Economics* 118 (1): 1–39.

Rappoport, Peter and Eugene N. White. 1993. "Was There a Bubble in the 1929 Stock Market?" *Journal of Economic History* 53 (3): 549–74.

Richardson, Gary. 2007. "Categories and Causes of Bank Distress during the Great Depression 1929–1933: The Illiquidity versus Insolvency Debate Revisited." *Explorations in Economic History* 44: 588–607.

Rothbard, Murray N. 1963. *America's Great Depression*. Princeton, NJ: Van Nostrand.

Rothbard, Murray N. 1979. "Reliving the Crash of 1979." *Inquiry* 15–19.

Shiller, Robert J. 2005. *Irrational Exuberance*, 2nd ed. New York: Currency Doubleday. Online: www.econ.yale.edu/~shiller/data/ie_data.xls.

Sirkin, Gerald. 1975. "The Stock Market of 1929 Revisited: A Note." *Business History Review*, 49 (2): 233–41.

Smiley, Gene, and Richard H. Keehn. 1988. "Margin Purchases, Brokers' Loans and the Bull Market of the Twenties." *Business and Economic History* 17: 129–42.

Sobel, Robert. 1988. *Panic on Wall Street: Classic History of America's Financial Disasters with a New Exploration of the Crash Of 1987*. New York: Truman Talley Books/Dutton.

Temin, Peter. 1976. *Did Monetary Forces Cause the Great Depression?* New York: W. W. Norton.

Walter, John R. 2005. "Depression-Era Bank Failures: The Great Contagion or the Great Shakeout?" *Federal Reserve Bank of Richmond Economic Quarterly* 91 (1): 39–54.

White, Eugene Nelson. 1984. "A Reinterpretation of the Banking Crisis of 1930." *Journal of Economic History* 44 (1): 119–38.

White, Eugene Nelson. 1990. "The Stock Market Boom and Crash of 1929 Revisited." *Journal of Economic Perspectives* 4 (2): 67–84.

Wolff, Edward N. 2002. *Top Heavy: The Increasing Inequality of Wealth in America and What Can Be Done About It*. New York: The New Press.

11 Mighty magic of the market

The discussion of asset-price bubbles revolves around the notion of the fundamental price and the relationship between the fundamental and market prices. Why does the equality of the two prices matter? The answer to this question is related to one of the central issues in economic theory and policy—whether market exchanges produce socially beneficial outcomes. This chapter presents two competing sides in this debate, both of which are well within the confines of mainstream economic theory. According to the first camp, the free, mutually beneficial transactions of individual economic agents in the marketplace not only maximize individual utility and profit but lead to socially optimal outcomes by "getting the prices right"; that is, the prices fully reflect the costs and benefits of goods and services. If this view is correct then, from the public-policy perspective, the performance of the market in allocating scarce resources cannot be improved upon. Consequently, external interference with the market process may create distortions that force prices to deviate from the true costs and lead to production of too much of some goods and too few of others, and thus lower social welfare. The second camp, however, draws attention to persistent social, ecological, and financial problems, such as income inequality, pollution, and recurring bubbles and banking crises, as signs of market failure. In this view, various peculiarities of markets mean that individual optimization does not necessarily lead to socially optimal outcomes; therefore, government interventions through regulation and other means are necessary to correct failures of the market system.

In the intellectual arena this debate is traced back to Scottish moral philosopher Adam Smith's metaphor of the *invisible hand*, or the anonymous, self-regulating power of the market. Smith's best known work, *The Wealth of Nations*, is a wide-ranging treatise that presents the nature, structure, and dynamics of the capitalist system. It is a critical, foundational economics text, as the two primary competing traditions of the discipline draw from Smith's observations on the forces of conflict and harmony in society. The first is classical political economy, which emphasizes economic classes, identified in terms of their position with regard to the means of production, as analytical categories and studies the evolution of the capitalist system in terms of the contradictions between wage-earners and profit-recipients (among other classes) in the processes of production and distribution. David Ricardo and Karl Marx were the foremost early representatives of this tradition.

The second tradition eschews class distinctions and focuses on the consequences of market exchange among individuals and how the pricing of commodities and factors of production allocates resources among competing ends. This line of thinking has matured into the currently dominant paradigm of *neoclassical economics*, which views exchange as the primary economic activity and treats production and distribution as instances of market transactions. Given the dominance of the neoclassical tradition in academia today, it is not surprising that modern textbooks identify Smith's examination of the benefits of mutual exchange and the power, or "magic," of the invisible hand as his essential contribution to intellectual history.

The primary objective of this chapter is to summarize the two sides of the debate in mainstream neoclassical economics about whether markets yield "efficient" outcomes. Efficiency is defined in the narrow neoclassical sense of the allocative, productive, and informational outcomes of market exchange.[1] The next chapter extends the discussion to financial markets. Given the centrality of the doctrine of the invisible hand in the discipline, however, I start with a brief digression on moral philosophy and the evolution of the idea of the invisible hand from Smith to neoclassical economics.

Moral philosophers

The core questions of moral philosophy are the origins of morality, the judgment of right and wrong, or how we live or ought to live our lives, and the basis of civil society. How is it possible for individuals with varying and often conflicting interests, concerns, opinions, and attitudes to live with some degree of harmony alongside each other? How does a society composed of essentially selfish individuals sustain itself and survive? How are the rights and responsibilities of members of a society balanced? As social and economic systems evolved over millennia responses to these questions also changed and served as the intellectual and ideological foundations to defend or challenge the status quo.

Until the sixteenth century the dominant philosophy was scholasticism, which answered these questions by appealing to a combination of Biblical authority and Aristotelian natural philosophy. St. Thomas Aquinas' integration of the Catholic faith and Aristotelian reason in the thirteenth century served as the foundation to infer moral/right and immoral/wrong. The Church promulgated and enforced the doctrine, and faith in the doctrine formed the foundation of the social consensus. The condemnation of charging interest on money loans is an example of the canonical law's integration of immoral/sinful and unnatural. Usury was sinful because it amounted to charging for time, which is owned by God and not by the lender. It was unnatural because the natural end use of money was as a means of exchange, not to create more money.

After the sixteenth-century Renaissance, the influence of the Catholic Church in public matters began to diminish. The answer to the question of how individuals cohere to create a society was sought in the authority of the absolutist state in which the monarch had unlimited political power. Niccolo Machiavelli (1469–1527) saw individuals as wicked and deceitful, and advised the prince on the means (including the use of violence) to establish and to maintain political and social order over his subjects. According to Thomas Hobbes (1588–1679), who wrote in the midst of civil wars that wreaked havoc in England, the intrinsic egotism of individuals, if not kept in check, made social life and civilization impossible. In his book *Leviathan* Hobbes called life in its natural state "solitary, poor, nasty, brutish, and short." The prerequisite for civilized, social life, then, was the centralized, absolutist nation state that laid down the rules and laws and coerced individuals to abide by these strictures. The state's paternalistic power monopoly that was ready to resort to violence to obtain its subjects' obedience was the foundation of civil society. The centripetal force of compulsory conformity counteracted the centrifugal force of individual selfishness that would otherwise lead to civil discord and social disintegration.

This perspective also constituted the justification for the absolutist state's interventions in the economic realm during the sixteenth and seventeenth centuries. *Mercantilism*, the dominant economic doctrine of the time, measured the wealth of a nation in terms of its bullion reserves. With the aim of accumulating gold within the country, the state granted exclusive privileges to selected companies (recall the Mississippi and South Sea companies) to carry out overseas trade, and provided military protection to merchants to ensure export surpluses and the inflow of specie from abroad.

However, momentous changes in the eighteenth century rendered mercantilism and the notion of the interventionist state untenable. In England the enclosure movement turned rural commons into private property, forced poor villagers from their land, and turned them into wage laborers. The putting-out system combined production and commercial activities. The budding capitalist class's control over the production process increased, and wage labor supplanted the medieval guild system. Merchants and capitalists who were handicapped by a lack of access to state-bestowed monopoly grants demanded what they considered to be their individual natural rights: the removal of mercantilist restrictions and all other state-instituted barriers to competition so that they could expand their operations and enter new markets.

By the end of the seventeenth century these emerging political and economic forces were already gaining the upper hand against the absolutist state. The Glorious Revolution of 1688 and the Declaration of Rights in 1689 circumscribed the authority of the monarch in England and instituted a system in which the king and Parliament shared political power. These developments brought about a transformation of economic and political philosophy that identified the individual and individual rights as ingredients of the natural order. In the natural sciences, revolutionary changes had already culminated in Newtonian physics. It was more commonly accepted that the natural order and the laws of the physical universe could be discovered by means of empirical observation and abstract thought. Newton's Law of Gravitation, for instance, explained the movement of bodies in terms of a self-regulating natural order. Outside intervention was unnecessary.

These ideas eventually spilled over to social and political thought. If there was a natural order in social life, as in the physical world, then the notion of intrinsic chaos that can be alleviated only by the canonical dictates of right and wrong or the coercion of the absolutist state was no longer acceptable. The task was to find out the *natural laws* through which social balance was achieved. In the seventeenth and eighteenth centuries moral philosophers such as John Locke sought to uncover the natural laws that regulate social relations and that are revealed in the free expression of human activity. This search and discovery of the natural order in society was imperative to ensure that the human-made "positive" laws and conventions, which were the foundations of the state, were drawn in conformity with the natural law.

By the beginning of the eighteenth century the subject matter of the emerging discipline of political economy was the discovery of the natural laws that govern the creation of wealth and the organization of production and commerce. Political economists who wrote in the tradition of natural law also targeted the status quo by demonstrating how state-induced restrictions on trade and manufacturing were against the natural law and, therefore, anathema to the public good. Smith was a product of this era of enlightenment.

Adam Smith

Smith (1723–90) is universally recognized as the father of the economics discipline. He was educated at Oxford University and later became Professor of Moral Philosophy at the University of Glasgow. He lived during the era of pre-industrial capitalism, when the factory system was just emerging in Britain.[2]

Smith initially gave several tentative answers to the question of how self-interested individuals can cohere and sustain societies in *The Theory of Moral Sentiments*, which was published in 1759 and turned out to be a widely debated, successful book. His first idea was that, while people are selfish, they are by nature also capable of empathy. The ability to understand the actions and reactions of others by putting oneself in their shoes makes it possible for self-interest not to damage society. Smith's second idea was that people's admiration of wealth, and willingness to serve the wealthy, held society together. Third, people have a conscience, a higher form of love, which overrides their selfishness. By this intrinsic quality people form moral judgments and codes of conduct that supersede selfishness. Smith's final thought was that people seek wealth in vanity, in magnitudes beyond their capacity to consume it. As they accumulate more wealth they enrich society because many more benefit from this enrichment by working in the service of the wealthy.[3]

Smith addressed the question of the foundation of social life again in his magnum opus *The Wealth of Nations*, published in 1776. Smith pointed out that, contrary to the mercantilist doctrine, the source of a nation's wealth is not its bullion stock but its division of labor. Using the famous example of the pin factory, he illustrated how specialization in specific tasks improves skills, dexterity, judgment, and overall productivity and facilitates more efficient use of time and induces technological innovation. What necessitates this division of labor, in turn, is the intrinsic human propensity to exchange one thing for another to improve one's own well-being. The motivation to engage in exchange is self-interest: people offer commodities they produce to others not out of benevolence but in return for other commodities so that they can provide themselves with the necessities of life.

While each person, then, has a stake in the survival of the civil society in which they interact, the existence and daily maintenance of the society does not need conscious, deliberative human effort or action (except in a few areas noted below). Although individuals make uncoordinated, independent production and consumption decisions in pursuit of their own self-interest without any regard for the needs of others, the natural order of the market, or the anonymous forces of competition, spontaneously achieves social coherence and harmony of individual interests.

The magic of markets ensures first that profit-seeking sellers offer a composition of goods and services that aligns with the needs and wants of the buyers *and* their ability to pay. Competitive forces will drive out of the market producers who do not offer what customers want and can afford. Second, the price at which each good is offered is equal to the unit cost of production of the commodity (including the wages of the producer) so that buyers pay the lowest price possible. Producers who offer a product at a price higher than the unit cost of production will be undercut by their competitors. Collusion between producers of the same or similar commodities to inflate prices above the cost of production cannot be sustained because their high profits attract new competitors to the industry who eventually drive the price down—provided, of course, that there are no human-made laws that violate the natural law by prohibiting enterprise. In the natural order the price of a commodity cannot deviate from its unit cost of production. Finally, competition constantly pushes producers to increase productivity and lower production costs through technological innovations, specialization, and the reorganization of the production process.

The only role for deliberative coordinated human action in this context is to establish the positive legal framework and institutions that accord with the natural order, to ensure protection of private property and free participation in exchange, and to remove obstacles that stand in the way of competition.

Smith's importance as a moral philosopher lies in his explanation of how the natural law operates to govern and regulate the society that, on the surface, is an amalgam of self-interested behavior, atomistic decentralized actions, complexity, and confusion. As an economist he articulated systematically for the first time how competition shapes and leads the evolution and growth of the economic system and accumulation of wealth via the division of labor and specialization. It is important to note, however, that Smith was not necessarily a market purist who was opposed to any kind of state intervention in markets. He was opposed primarily to monopolies, and he was critical of state policies that restricted competition.

Unlike some modern champions of "free markets," however, he acknowledged that the state still had important roles to play in the economy. For instance, he was willing to allow the state to shelter infant industries from competition so that they could develop and eventually become competitive in the global market. He further recognized that the state had a role in provisioning certain goods that are beneficial to the society, such as roads and education, because they would not be sufficiently lucrative to attract profit-seeking producers and, therefore, tend to be underproduced when left to the whims of the market.

From Adam Smith to neoclassical economic theory

En route to neoclassical economics, Smith's conception of human behavior, i.e. self-interested but capable of empathy, was replaced by utilitarian philosophy's "calculus of pleasure and pain." According to Jeremy Bentham (1748–1832), the father of the utilitarian philosophy, the objectives of pleasure maximization and pain minimization govern all human behavior, including economic decision-making. The individual is considered the sole judge of his or her pleasure, and, therefore, the experience of satisfaction is subjective. Moreover, Bentham argued that pleasure and pain are quantifiable in various dimensions, including intensity, duration, and extent. Later, the idea of quantifiable pleasure and pain, combined with mathematical tools of optimization imported from physics, was instrumental in constructing an economic theory upon the foundation of utility (and profit) maximization.

In the early 1870s Englishman William Stanley Jevons, Leon Walras of Switzerland, and Austrian Carl Menger independently published books that demonstrated that the economic-optimization problem, i.e. maximizing utility and minimizing pain, can be solved by weighing the marginal benefits and marginal costs of economic choices. An optimizing consumer improves her welfare by purchasing another loaf of bread instead of a pint of beer as long as the benefit (pleasure) produced by the last dollar spent on bread is higher the cost (pain or sacrifice) of not spending that last dollar on beer. At the optimal point, or the point at which the consumption basket cannot be improved upon, the last dollar spent on each good must deliver the same amount of marginal benefit. This insight from the works of the three marginalist revolutionaries constitutes the foundation of neoclassical economic theory, which is the dominant paradigm in the economics discipline today.

Neoclassical economic theory is built upon the optimizing behavior of two primary agents: households (consumers) and firms (producers). A household receives income from the sale of factors of production it owns, and uses this income to buy final goods and services for consumption purposes. Thus, it makes dual decisions related, first, to the demand for goods and services in the product markets and, second, to the supply of factors of production in the factor markets. The objective of the household in making these decisions is to maximize satisfaction or utility from consuming goods and minimizing the "pain" of work and the postponement of consumption (saving). The firm demands factors of production in the factor markets and employs these factors of production to produce and supply goods and services in the product market. The objective of the firm is to maximize profits. The preferences of households, factor endowments, and technology (the fundamentals) are treated as exogenous factors.

The central economic problem follows from two premises. First, human needs and wants are practically unlimited; the higher the level of consumption, the higher the level of satisfaction and well-being. Second, resources, or factor endowments, are limited. There are, for instance, only 24 hours in a day, which sets the upper limit to how much labor can be supplied and thereby sets an upper limit on the quantity of goods that can be produced. The core economic question then is how to allocate scarce resources among competing goods. Textbooks offer allocation by command, central planning, and markets as the three alternative solutions to the problem.

Smith used the term *invisible hand* in only a few peripheral settings, but in the hands of neoclassical economics it became the central metaphor in illustrating the magic of resource allocation via markets. In the neoclassical explication of the notion of the invisible hand economic agents are placed in an environment of perfect competition. The neoclassical concept of perfect competition is different from Smith's notion of competition. On the one hand, Smith (and the political-economy tradition in general) describes competition as a continuous rivalry between two or more producers with varying degrees of market power to expand their profits and protect and expand their market shares. This is a dynamic process that shapes the long-term evolution of the economy. The neoclassical concept of perfect competition, on the other hand, is a static state in which individual buyers and sellers lack market power and, therefore, are unable to influence the price of the commodity.[4] Prices are determined by anonymous forces of market supply and demand that aggregate the utility- and profit-maximizing plans of individual agents.

With these pieces in place the allocation process through anonymous market forces, i.e. the price system, can be described. To illustrate the self-regulating forces of the market consider a two-commodity world in which only bread and beer are produced and consumed. Suppose the initial state of the economy is one in which the compositions of the output and consumption baskets match and all resources are fully employed (so there is no waste). To simplify exposition assume that income and technology do not change. Now, consider a change in preferences, e.g. bread is discovered to have antitoxins that lengthen life. Households increase the quantity of bread in their consumption baskets at the expense of beer. Bread becomes relatively scarce, and beer becomes less so, raising the price of bread and lowering the price of beer. The higher relative price of bread causes resources to move from the breweries to the bakeries as producers revise their output plans in accordance with the price signals they receive.

Utility- and profit-maximization motives dictate the pattern of market adjustment in response to the new information on the health benefits of bread. A somewhat simplified story of the adjustment runs as follows. As a result of the higher demand for bread the benefit from the last loaf of bread purchased (*marginal benefit*) and, therefore, the willingness to pay for it, now exceeds the initial price of a loaf of bread. Because each dollar spent on bread now yields more satisfaction utility maximization dictates more bread (and fewer beer) purchases. However, two factors contribute to the closing of the gap between the marginal benefit and the price of bread as purchases rise. First, on the supply side excess demand for bread motivates bakers to raise production by hiring brewery workers, whose services are no longer needed in beer production. These workers are likely to be less skilled in baking than in brewing and, therefore, less productive than those who are already working in the bakeries. Therefore, employment of the former brewery workers in the bakeries drives the cost of each additional loaf (*marginal cost*) higher. Increasing marginal costs imply that bakers would be willing to offer more bread, but at a price high enough to cover their expenses.[5] Second, on the demand side, each additional loaf of bread consumed adds less utility than the previous loaf due to diminishing marginal utility. As the marginal benefit declines so does the willingness to pay.

This adjustment of rising output will continue as long as the marginal benefit of another loaf of bread is higher than its marginal cost or price so that excess demand persists. It ends eventually when the marginal benefit is equal to the marginal cost or price. Beyond this point there is no incentive for consumers to buy more bread because the utility obtained from the next loaf will be below its cost. The price stabilizes once the benefit obtained from the last unit of bread consumed is identical to the cost of that loaf of bread's production. At this price the quantity of bread demanded is equal to the quantity supplied, and there is nor shortage or surplus.

The story in the beer market is symmetrical. Diminished demand for beer creates a situation where marginal cost exceeds marginal benefit, which leads to a declining price and quantity. The invisible hand of the price mechanism shifts resources from breweries to bakeries in accordance with changing preferences.

Note that there are substantial differences between Smith's vision of the self-regulating market model and the neoclassical version. Smith was concerned about the effectiveness of the market system in achieving long-term wealth accumulation through specialization. He viewed competition as an evolutionary process that describes the dynamics and long-term trajectory of the economy. Neoclassical economic theory, however, starts from a given distribution of scarce resources, preferences, and technology and then focuses on how mutually beneficial, exchange-determined prices allocate resources among the multitudes of commodities.

In defense of the market system: allocative and productive efficiency

The competitive market outcome described above is alleged to have certain socially desirable properties. The first is known as *allocative efficiency*. Bread and beer in the example are produced in just the right quantities in the sense that the final composition of the production basket coincides with the desired composition of the consumption basket. There are no frustrated customers in bakeries that ran out of bread, or brewery owners burdened with bottles of unsold beer. The market outcome is aligned with how much consumers intend to buy and producers intend to sell at the current price. To appreciate the social-welfare implications of this allocation note that at the point of efficient allocation described above consumers pay for a loaf of bread a price that is lower than or equal to the *highest* price they are willing to pay; and producers receive a payment for each loaf that is higher than or equal to the *lowest* price they are willing to accept. This outcome yields the maximum social benefit, as any other combination of prices paid and received would be inferior. Thus, there is no room for improvement.

Second, the market outcome exhibits *productive efficiency*: both bakers and brewers use the most efficient methods in production because, otherwise, they would be undercut by competitors who use technologically superior, lower-cost methods. Thus, consumers buy each commodity at the lowest possible price, given the technology and factor endowments.

Propositions of allocative and productive efficiency constitute an influential defense of the market allocation of resources against command and central-planning solutions, as well as a denunciation of proposals to impose regulations on industries. The rewards and discipline of the market ensure that resources are utilized in accordance with the preferences of final consumers and that there is no waste in the production process.[6]

In defense of the market system: informational efficiency

Markets' ability to achieve outcomes that are efficient in both the allocative and productive senses was a powerful argument in the hands of those who favored laissez-faire capitalism, or the non-interventionist state. After 1917, however, socialists in the Soviet Union had started to build an alternative economic system, based on state ownership as opposed to private ownership of the means of production. Resource-allocation decisions under socialism were made not by market interaction between consumers and private producers, i.e. capitalists, but by the central-planning organization that determined what and how much would be produced in accordance with the perceived needs of the society; it would then produce and distribute goods through state-owned production units and stores.

How the central planner determined this allocation was a theoretical and practical challenge for the socialists. Ironically, one solution to the problem was suggested by the neoclassical version of the invisible hand. Socialist economic theorists pointed out that it was doubtful that the market system could allocate resources optimally through the self-regulating process described by the invisible hand in real time. Their claim seemed especially plausible during the 1930s, when the capitalist system was in the throes of the Great Depression. Instead, socialist theorists suggested, the market-allocation model could be simulated by computer to determine the market-clearing quantities of each commodity, and then production could be coordinated via central planning.

This simulation would work as follows. Efficient allocation of resources occurs at prices that equate quantity supplied with quantity demanded in each market. Socialist economic theorists suggested that central planners could collect information on preferences, resource endowments, and the technology—or the fundamentals—and extract supply and demand relationships from these data. Once these supply and demand relationships were fed into a computer, the computer could find the equilibrium prices and quantities far more effectively than the markets themselves. In practice, the central planner would replicate the market by setting prices through a trial-and-error process, responding to surpluses and shortages. Once the set of prices at which all markets clear was determined the planner would also know how much of each commodity to produce. Socialists argued that the central-planning system was better equipped to attain the ideal state of efficient resource allocation than the seemingly self-regulating, private-ownership-based market system.

The leading opponents of the socialists in this *economic calculation debate* were Austrian-school economists Ludwig von Mises and Friedrich Hayek. They pointed out that it is a formidable task to collect information on preferences, resources, and endowments in multitudes of markets across millions of agents. Moreover, these pieces of information are in continuous flux because preferences, endowments, and technology change constantly. Thus, it is practically impossible for any agency to collect useful information on individual economic actors' intentions, and it is futile to attempt to extract the right set of prices for the optimal allocation of resources.

The more influential part, however, of the Austrian-school response was this: the function that no agency can perform is, in fact, carried out continuously and efficiently by anonymous market forces. Hayek (1937) argued that the true ingenuity of the market system lies in the fact that it collects, processes, and aggregates disparate knowledge that is scattered across millions of buyers and sellers, and then summarizes and delivers it to all economic agents in the form of price signals. Information about each household's preference for bread or each baker's hiring decision is practically inaccessible. However, rising preferences for bread are revealed to bakers in the form of the higher prices consumers pay for bread. The subsequent change in bakers' hiring decisions is transmitted in the form of higher wages for bakery workers. All the information on the changes in the fundamentals is embodied in price signals and optimizing agents need pay attention only to the latter. This property of the markets is called *informational efficiency*. The better that market prices reflect the multitude of information on individual supply and demand intentions, the more informationally efficient markets are.

This perspective distinguishes the Austrians from other neoclassicals. While Menger, the founder of the Austrian school, shared the *methodological individualism* of Jevons and Walras and made utility maximization the cornerstone of economic thinking, he did not agree with the static-equilibrium framework. Instead, he viewed the economy in dynamic terms, wherein agents continually responded to price signals to exploit profit opportunities. Later, Hayek defended the market system not in terms of the optimality properties of the static-resource-allocation problem; rather, he stated, the market system is superior to all alternatives because only markets transmit information on changing fundamentals and emerging profit opportunities, and thereby induce entrepreneurial activity, innovations, and economic growth.

Market failures

The debate among mainstream economists today is not whether to replace the capitalist system with an alternative, but how well markets perform various functions, including allocating resources, producing at the lowest unit cost, and gathering and disseminating information. Skeptics point out instances where the alleged efficiencies in competitive markets fail to materialize because of spillover effects. Market failures may also be the outcome of market imperfections or frictions, i.e. the assumptions of perfect competition upon which the efficiency arguments are built do not hold. Market failures come in many variants and a full discussion is beyond our scope. A few examples, however, are sufficient to illustrate their significance and set the stage for the next chapter, which focuses on financial markets.

One type of market failure is the spillover effect of a transaction between two parties on a third party. It is called an *externality*. Filling the tank of a car for $40, for example, may be viewed as a simple exchange between the owner of the gas station and the driver. The $40 pays for the manufacturing, transportation, and storage of the fuel, as well as the services provided by the station owner. This voluntary exchange by definition improves the welfare of both parties, and as long as no one else is adversely affected by this exchange social welfare improves as well.

However, this bilateral transaction affects others who are not directly involved. There are hidden costs in the use of gas that are not covered by the price paid, such as emissions from the exhaust pipe that harm the quality of the air and cause health problems. Such costs are instead paid by society in the form of extra visits to the doctor and a haze that lowers visibility. The price paid for a tank of gas reflects only the private production costs; it does not include the true social cost. Put differently, in the competitive market the gas is underpriced due to the externalized pollution cost, and, therefore, it will be consumed and produced in a quantity higher than is socially optimal. If the pollution cost is internalized to the buyer and seller of gas by, say, the imposition of a tax that would pay for the pollution costs the private cost and price would be higher, buyers would purchase less of the product, and production levels would be lower.

Externalities also may be positive. For instance, vaccinations not only protect the individual but reduce the likelihood of contagion, benefiting the community. As the social benefit is higher than the private benefit, however, left to the market system private purchases would fall behind the socially desirable quantity, and vaccinations would be produced at a level lower than is socially optimal.

The second category of market failures relates to the failure of the assumptions of perfect competition. One example is agents not being price takers. Natural monopolies, e.g. railways in Britain in the nineteenth century, or consolidated businesses, such as US Steel and Standard Oil in the

1890s, were instances in which the sellers had sufficient market power to influence price. Manufacturers often create market power by distinguishing their products from the competition by branding, packaging, or advertising. Both allocative and productive efficiencies fail when a single seller or a few sellers limit competition and attain higher profits by restricting output and selling the product in more limited quantities at a price above the marginal cost.

Another source of deviation from assumptions of perfect competition that has attracted much attention in recent decades is the asymmetric distribution of information across buyers and sellers. Asymmetric information specifically refers to the situation in which one party in a transaction has more information than the other. In this situation market exchange gives rise to two types of problems that preclude optimal outcomes. The first is the *adverse selection* problem. One famous illustration of the problem is Akerlof's (1970) market for "lemons" and "cherries." Suppose two individuals, one who leads a high-risk (the lemon) and the other who leads a low-risk lifestyle (the cherry), are buying life insurance. If the company had perfect information it would charge a higher premium to the first customer and a lower premium to the second. However, it usually does not have perfect information and faces the problem when calculating premiums of how to discern the risks of each policy. It may try to alleviate the problem by screening applicants to better assess risk factors (e.g. by finding out about smoking habits, driving records). The company may also try to draw up insurance contracts that cover every possible contingency, or purchase insurance for the insurance contract sold to the policyholders. However, there are costs to these undertakings, which may be high, or even prohibitive.

In these circumstances the best course of action for the company is to charge an "average" premium to each customer. The outcome is hardly optimal for the firm because it will win the undercharged, high-risk customer, who won't miss a good deal, and lose the overcharged, low-risk customer, who is likely to withdraw from the market. This market is clearly inefficient because of adverse selection, or the lemons driving out the cherries.

Similar examples may be taken from the used-car, mortgage, and other markets where informational asymmetry is prevalent. However, the consequences of the problem may go deeper. Because the insurance company knows that customers have more information, and that high-risk customers drive out low-risk customers, it has no incentive to trade at all. Thus, adverse selection may cause the market to disappear altogether and eliminate the possibility of mutually beneficial exchange. *Missing markets* in the face of uncertainty over the heterogeneous quality of customers preclude the efficient allocation of resources through exchange.

The second type of problem asymmetric information creates is *moral hazard*. A customer who buys a health-insurance policy may visit the physician more frequently than she otherwise would. Or, after buying a life insurance policy, the customer, who now enjoys the comfort of knowing that his children are provided for if anything goes wrong, may be more lax about putting on his seat belt. Moral hazard refers to the perverse incentives that induce agents to engage in wasteful or higher-risk activities when costs are incurred by another party. Again, the insurance company's incomplete knowledge about customers' proclivities and its recognition of the moral-hazard problem may cause it to withdraw from market exchange.

From the public-policy perspective the possibility that markets may fail to allocate resources efficiently poses two interrelated questions: how significant are these market failures? And what is the appropriate policy response to a market failure? Again, there are two opposing viewpoints.

The first group discounts the importance of the spillover effects and market imperfections, and expresses confidence in market incentives and profit-seeking behavior to correct market failures whenever they surface. Market imperfections signal profit opportunities waiting to be exploited, and entrepreneurs tend to take advantage of them by offering new products that meet the needs of economic agents. For instance, reinsurance companies offer policies to insurance companies who wish to manage risk and protect themselves from adverse contingencies. Used-car buyers can access information through a variety of products that offer information, such as consumer reports and the repair history of individual cars. Markets also design proper incentives in view of moral hazard. For example, requiring health-insurance customers to pay co-insurance reduces excessive visits to the doctor.

In the case of spillover effects the source of the problem is viewed as the absence of property rights and a market to price the externality. A solution to air pollution, for instance, is to create a market for carbon emissions so that air becomes a commodity and is priced appropriately by supply and demand. If individuals were assigned property rights to air they could negotiate with the polluters the price that would compensate for the negative effect of low-quality air on their lives. A higher price would induce polluters to reduce emissions. One well publicized carbon-trading scheme is cap-and-trade. The idea is to assign carbon emitters property rights in terms of how much carbon they can emit in a year and permit them to trade these quotas in the "air pollution" market. The maximum emission would be limited by the overall cap. Profit-maximizing firms would then have the incentive to adopt techniques to lower emissions and sell their permits to others. Firms that do not or cannot reduce emissions would be forced to purchase permits from others at a cost, which, in turn, would give them incentives to lower their output.

The second group believes that externalities and market imperfections are ubiquitous and persistent, and they are skeptical that markets can always generate appropriate incentive structures and solutions to remedy failures. They note that markets are often missing or incomplete in the first place due to the impediments and costs to create them. When negative effects of externalities are distributed across a large number of disparate people, for instance, victims face significant logistical costs of organization and coordination to negotiate with, say, polluters. Thus, individually, each victim has the incentive to hold back and become a free-rider.

As a general rule, the efficient functioning of markets requires the existence of complete markets, in which economic agents can make hedge trades to protect themselves against all contingencies. The oil-futures market is an example, but these markets are far from complete. The creation of a full array of contingency markets may be prohibitively expensive due to information costs, the costs of bargaining in the assignment of property rights, and the costs of overseeing and enforcement, which are jointly referred to as *transaction costs*.

In the presence of coordination problems and high transaction costs markets may fail to generate solutions to resource misallocation that arises from externalities and imperfections. In these cases the imposition and enforcement of rules, regulations, taxes, and subsidies is called for in order to align social and private costs (and benefits), to police monopolies, and to alleviate informational deficiencies so that resources can be better allocated. Internalizing negative externalities by requiring polluters to clean up or reduce pollution, or promoting certain types of behavior by introducing higher taxes on gas, subsidizing cars with higher gas mileage, subsidizing vaccinations, or requiring seat-belt usage are typical interventions when market failures are prevalent. Other examples of rules and regulations include making transactions more transparent by requiring participants to reveal explicit and comprehensive information, and the imposition of a liability system that forces participants to be more forthcoming in markets to avoid lawsuits.

From a market-solution perspective, however, government interventions to address market failures are not only unnecessary but can also be harmful. The harmful effects are attributed to two main sources. First, regulations can be self-defeating because they may create moral hazard and perverse incentives by changing the behavior of economic agents. Seat-belt or motorcycle-helmet requirements may not mitigate the risks faced by the life-insurance company because drivers who are forced to wear seat belts or helmets may drive faster, believing that their odds of getting seriously hurt are now lower. Second, widening the scope of government intervention may create large bureaucracies, self-interested regulators, political scheming, and the co-optation of regulatory agencies by the industry. Instead of correcting prices these factors may introduce new distortions. Regulations create waste because they motivate companies to devote resources, which could have been used productively elsewhere, to influence regulators and policymakers and exploit loopholes in the regulations. In addition to perverse incentives, these factors also create disincentives that stifle innovation and entrepreneurship. The inefficiencies government intervention creates in resource allocation are collectively called *government failure*.

Key terms and concepts

Adverse selection
Allocative efficiency
Economic calculation debate
Externality
Government failure
Informational efficiency
Invisible hand
Marginal benefit
Marginal cost
Market failure
Mercantilism
Methodological individualism
Missing market
Moral hazard
Moral philosophy
Natural law
Productive efficiency
Transaction cost

Endnotes

1 There exists a larger debate over whether neoclassical concepts of efficiency that ignore income-distribution questions (because it takes endowments as a given) and power relations are meaningful in regard to social welfare (see Samuels (1972)). The net cast in this chapter is indeed very narrow.
2 On moral philosophers and Adam Smith see Heilbroner (1999) and Screpanti and Zamagni (2005: 77–82). See also Heilbroner (1997) for annotated extracts from Smith's works.
3 The term "invisible hand" makes its first appearance in this context, in which affluence trickles down to the poor, who labor in the service of the wealthy.
4 To recap from Chapter 4, the necessary conditions for perfect competition are the presence of many buyers and sellers; generic homogeneous products that rule out non-price competition; free entry into and exit from markets; and uniform distribution of information so that no one has informational advantages they can exploit.
5 Put differently, for consumers, the opportunity cost or relative price of each additional loaf of bread, measured in the number of bottles of beers foregone, increases.
6 Note, however, that these notions of efficiency take the initial endowments as a given. Thus, this justification of the virtues of the market system is silent about the existing income distribution and does not raise the question of whether

redistribution would improve economic outcomes (unless there is a willingness to impose a normative judgment that redistribution of endowments would lead to more desirable outcomes).

References

Akerlof, George A. 1970. "The Market for Lemons: Quality Uncertainty and the Market Mechanism." *Quarterly Journal of Economics* 84 (3): 488–500.

Hayek, Friedrich. 1937. "Economics and Knowledge." *Economica* New Series 4 (13): 33–54.

Heilbroner, Robert L. 1997. *Teachings from the Worldly Philosophy*. New York: W. W. Norton and Company.

Heilbroner, Robert. 1999. *The Worldly Philosophers: The Lives, Times, and Ideas of the Great Economic Thinkers*, 7th ed. New York: Touchstone.

Samuels, Warren J. 1972. "Welfare Economics, Power and Property." Pp. 61–148 in Gene Wunderlich and W. L. Gibson, Jr. (eds.) *Perspectives on Property*. University Park, PA: Institute for Research on Land and Water Resources, Pennsylvania State University.

Screpanti, Ernesto, and Stefano Zamagni. 2005. *An Outline of the History of Economic Thought*. Oxford: Oxford University Press.

12 The conjurations of financial markets

The historical accounts presented so far have offered examples of how financial products contributed to the accumulation of productive capacity, the growth of new industries, and the improvement of welfare. The emergence of joint-stock companies, insurance services, and options contracts facilitated the development of long-distance trade and the growth of unprecedented wealth in the seventeenth century. Large-scale, fixed investments, such as canals and railways—the veins of the industrial revolution—could be built only by combining the wealth of many individuals through selling equity and various types of debt instruments. In the twentieth century consumer credit enabled middle-class households to purchase homes, cars, and durable consumer goods. On the other side of the ledger, the availability of different types of financial assets allowed wealth holders to enjoy returns on their savings and build diversified portfolios that balanced return and risk in accordance with their preferences.

However, such favorable assessments of the world of finance are hardly universal. The same historical episodes also attest that financial markets can become a speculative rollercoaster, and financial assets can turn into instruments that generate immense wealth for a few without creating significant social benefit. There is an abundance of news stories about misbehaving financial institutions and professionals who receive big rewards without creating commensurate value.[1] When rewards come at someone else's expense they do not enhance social welfare. Worse, when financial products become a source of instability and vulnerability for the entire economy the masses pay the cost in terms of lost jobs, savings, and homes.

These alternative perspectives on the industry pose the question of whether financial-services providers contribute to people's well-being by creating products that meet their wants and needs—similar to those offered by bakers and brewers—or whether they are opportunistic entities that live off the productive sectors of the economy and, even worse, pose a threat to the stable functioning of the economy.

In this chapter I will discuss the debates over the efficiency of financial markets and how they succeed or fail in producing social good.

These issues are intimately linked with the pricing of financial assets and whether these prices reflect true costs and returns. I first extend the allocative-efficiency discussion of the previous chapter to financial markets and discuss two possible, and critical, market failures. The bulk of the chapter, however, is devoted to the question of informational efficiency, which has attracted a great deal of attention in academic circles since the 1970s, and became a topic of public conversation after the crash of 2007–8. The question of whether asset prices reflect all of the relevant information about the fundamentals is related to the topic of asset-price determination, presented in Chapter 5. This discussion will also prepare the groundwork for the theoretical and historical material covered in subsequent chapters.

The invisible hand in financial markets

The basic role of financial markets is to bring together surplus and deficit units so that liquid funds are channeled to build fixed capital. The efficiency of financial markets can be illustrated by an example of a generic loan market. The interest rate on the loan is the rate of return from the perspective of the lender and the cost of borrowing from the perspective of the borrower. It varies with the relative supply of and demand for loanable funds. The greater the demand for funds by the deficit units relative to the supply of savings, the higher the interest rate (or the lower the price of loans).[2] If, for instance, firms want to invest in a brand new technology that promises to yield higher profits then competition for funds will raise the rate of interest and induce lenders who want to take advantage of the higher rate of return to offer more funds to borrowers. On the demand side the rising cost of borrowing is likely to put some restraint on borrowers' enthusiasm for funds. This adjustment process eventually eliminates the excess demand, at which point the interest-rate rise comes to a stop. The market outcome is a higher volume of funds channeled to deficit units so that they can carry on with new fixed-investment projects, and a higher interest rate, so that lenders can receive a share of the revenues produced by the new projects. At the end of this exchange there are no disappointed surplus/deficit units who cannot lend/borrow as much as they want at the market interest rate. The market outcome is allocatively efficient because the interest rate settles at a level at which lenders receive a rate of return that is higher than or equal to the lowest return they are willing to accept; and borrowers pay a cost that is lower than or equal to the highest rate they are willing to pay. Neither lenders nor borrowers can improve on this outcome.

In order to appreciate the efficiency of financial markets more fully one has to remember that lenders vary widely in terms of their time horizons and willingness to take risks. In comparison with the older people, for instance, the young who save for retirement are more likely to make long-term plans and have higher risk tolerance simply because they have more time. Businesses are also diverse in terms of their time horizons and the riskiness of their projects. Some borrow short-term funds to cover working-capital expenses, e.g. wages, utilities, and inventories, to bridge the gap between production and sale of goods, while others need long-term loans to finance investments in machinery and buildings that will pay for themselves over a long period of time. In addition, some businesses may be undertaking high-risk projects with new technologies and new commodities in unproven markets, whereas other businesses in established markets may be virtually free from the risk of default. Financial markets offer a plethora of instruments that meet the needs of these agents. Borrowers and lenders with various time and risk preferences and attributes meet in many markets in which instruments of various maturities and risks are traded, and these instruments determine the price of time and risk for each instrument through the interactions of supply and demand, matching lenders and borrowers. Funds are allocated among different projects in accordance with the time horizons and risk tolerance of agents. The availability of many types of financial instruments also enables a larger number of lenders and borrowers to participate in financial transactions, find counterparties, and carry out investment plans.

Diversification, risk sharing, and hedging illustrate the efficiency-enhancing effects of a multitude of assets, e.g. types of loans, bonds, stocks, and derivatives. Wealth holders hedge or manage risk through portfolio diversification, reducing the adverse effect of the collapse of a particular firm or sector on their portfolio by holding financial assets from different sectors of the economy. The more diversified the portfolio and the less correlated the returns of the individual assets, the more the value of the portfolio is insulated from the adverse effects of poorly performing assets. Diversification also allows for high-risk-high-return projects to be realized through *risk sharing*. A pharmaceutical company may be unwilling to devote the bulk of its internal funds to find a cure for Alzheimer's disease if the probability of success is very small, even when the expected returns, both private and social, would be enormous if the research were fruitful. However, the project is given a fighting chance when it is financed by selling securities to the public, which permits distribution of the risk among many investors. Thus, diversification both lowers the portfolio risk and facilitates the realization of high-risk-high-return projects.

This last point extends the benefits of financial markets from direct stakeholders to the larger society. Economic growth is realized through innovative technologies, new commodities, and expansion of productive capacity. If firms cannot carry out fixed-investment plans due to a lack of financing they are forced to delay or cancel new projects and new production lines. When the latter are inhibited economic growth and well-being suffer.

Financial derivatives add means to manage risk. Derivatives, like forward and option contracts, are financial instruments that derive their value from underlying assets. Asset holders can protect the value of their portfolio against possible adverse shocks by selling their assets in the forward markets or buying the right to sell them at a specific price by a certain date. Proliferation of the variety and volume of derivatives offers investors more opportunities to "insure" their portfolio and more incentives to participate in financial markets, which increases the availability of funds for deficit units.

However, not all economists are as enthusiastic about the effectiveness of financial markets in performing these functions efficiently. Impediments to the efficiency of markets, including the externalities and market imperfections discussed in the last chapter, apply to financial markets as well.

Market failures

Previous chapters presented and illustrated how asset-price bubbles and banking panic may emerge in the presence of various types of externality and market imperfections. Bubbles and bank runs are examples of market failure that lead to the inefficient allocation of resources and waste. This section focuses on two sources of inefficient outcomes in the financial markets, systemic risk and asymmetric information, which have attracted the most attention in recent theory and policy debates. It discusses in greater detail how they lead to financial-market failures, as well as the debate over how to alleviate them. Systemic risk and asymmetric information are also featured extensively in the experience and policy discussions of the post-1980 period.

Systemic risk

Similar to the purchase of gas, a financial contract can have externalities or spillover effects that influence third parties. These spillover effects are prevalent in financial markets due to the interdependence among various entities created by inter-institution loans, depositor behavior or the possibility of bank runs, and the real economy's dependence on loans. A default, for instance, does not pose a risk only to the lender bank. To the extent that the default raises questions about the bank's ability to repay its own debt to other financial institutions, or causes a loss of confidence in the banking system and triggers a bank run, the individual contract creates risks for the entire system. *Systemic risk* refers to the possibility that the failure of a financial institution will adversely affect other institutions and expose the whole system to the risk of collapse. It is a negative externality because the social risks of the contract are higher than the private risks. The larger and more connected the failing firm, the higher the likelihood of catastrophic consequences. Moreover, systemic risk is generated by the system endogenously. During periods of upswing more contracts are signed, more debt is created, and systemic risk rises.

Systemic risk poses a quandary to policymakers because in the presence of a negative externality the social cost of a firm's failure is significantly higher than the private cost paid by the failing firm's creditors and shareholders. In order to avert these social costs and prevent the spread of failures public authorities are often compelled to assist large financial institutions that are in trouble. Since such assistance often comes at the cost of moral hazard as well as political discontent among taxpayers who ultimately pay for the bail out, it is important to find ways to mitigate systemic risk.

One common proposal to avoid systemic risk is the imposition of regulations to ensure that agents do not take excessive risks. Thus, the first line of defense against systemic risk is to reduce risk exposure by closely supervising lenders and borrowers and avoiding excessive debt. Typical examples of countermeasures against excessive debt include imposing capital requirements on lenders and income or asset requirements on borrowers. The design of these regulations should pay attention to the fact that systemic risk is generated internally and that these measures should be sensitive to economic trends, i.e. be more strict during periods of upswing when systemic risk rises.

After the subprime crisis of 2007–8, when new types of unregulated lending institution and derivatives proliferated, heightening systemic risk, there were proposals calling for restrictions on the size of financial institutions as well. These will be discussed in more detail in Chapter 17.

Skeptics of government intervention question the expansion of regulatory power. First, they doubt that government has the wherewithal to effectively regulate markets in the constantly changing world of financial institutions, innovative instruments, and globalization. It lacks the necessary resources, flexibility, and expertise to adapt regulations to this environment. Regulations that rapidly become anachronistic may hurt the economy by making financial institutions uncompetitive and impeding the growth and development of financial markets, to the detriment of households and businesses in their search for funds to finance homes and fixed-investment projects. Second, skeptics point out, regulations are ineffective because firms avoid regulations by relocating outside the jurisdictions of government agencies (*jurisdictional arbitrage*) or by creating new instruments that are not covered by existing regulations (*regulatory arbitrage*), always staying a step ahead of the agencies. Third, regulations are wasteful because firms will devote resources that could have been used in productive activities to lobby regulatory agencies and, thereby, distort markets by influencing regulations in their favor (*regulatory capture*).

Finally, government taking on responsibility for stabilization in the financial markets produces the belief, among the public and financial institutions that regulators will be less likely to stand aside and permit large, highly interconnected firms to fail in times of turbulence. This belief will create perverse incentives in the private sector. When banks are confident that government will act as a savior they are more likely to take greater risks to attain higher returns because there is no downside to their reckless behavior.

Proponents of laissez-faire, instead, focus on whether markets are capable of generating institutions and instruments to self-discipline and manage risk. As early as 1850 bankers created clearing houses to spread individual risk across the member banks and make it easier for them to absorb shocks. More recently, new securities and commodity exchanges, like the Chicago Mercantile Exchange (CME), mitigate default risk by spreading it across members, acting as counterparty in all transactions, and imposing collateral, minimum-capital and disclosure requirements on members. Most economists are not convinced, however, that such arrangements provide sufficient incentives for firms to behave in a prudent fashion and alleviate the systemic risk.

Asymmetric information

Asymmetric information and the consequent adverse-selection and moral-hazard problems are especially pertinent to financial markets because financial decisions are intrinsically forward looking, and not everyone is equally informed about what the future may hold. Various historical episodes covered in the earlier chapters illustrate how asymmetric information between banks and their depositors can create liquidity crises in the banking system.

The adverse-selection problem is endemic to the entire financial system. For example, both the surplus and deficit units are aware of the fact that issuers of assets are better informed than buyers about the quality of their projects, expected profitability, and the likelihood of default. Suppose lenders are offered two alternative securities of differing quality. If they have complete information about the quality they will pay in accordance with it. Without complete information, however, they will offer the "average" price for each security (similar to the insurance company of the last chapter which charges an average premium to each customer). The seller of the high-value security is, of course, unlikely to sell it at a price lower than its true value, whereas the issuer of the low-value security will be happy to sell it at the average price. The security of the less-worthy borrower ends up overvalued while the more worthy borrower faces an inordinately high financing cost, and the latter will move out of the market. Moreover, the lender who is aware of the asymmetric-information problem and that the lower price signals low quality may drop out of the market altogether, knowing that only undeserving counterparties will be willing to engage in exchange. Adverse selection leads to suboptimal outcomes at both the individual and social levels.

Asymmetric information also results in a moral-hazard problem. In comparison with shareholders and debt holders, executives and managers have better information about how funds are utilized and how their companies are run on a day-to-day basis. George Hudson, Daniel Drew, and Jay Gould routinely exploited their positions to enrich themselves at the expense of shareholders through the unauthorized issuance of stocks. During the 1920s investment trusts manipulated their own stock prices to reap higher returns. The misalignment of the interests may also take the form of managers trying to improve the company's short-term performance to maximize bonuses at the expense of the long-term growth that would benefit investors. The *principal–agent problem* in economics refers to the divergence of interests of the principals (e.g. shareholders, lenders) and their agents (e.g. executives, managers) who are expected to look after principals' interests. Principals do not have first-hand knowledge of how managers are running the company and, therefore, run the risk of being harmed by the self-interested actions of their agents. The existence of moral hazard may again induce wealth holders to limit their participation in financial markets and slow the flow of funds from savers to users.

Solutions to asymmetric-information problems are sought both in markets and in externally imposed regulations. The market solution includes financial institutions that specialize in collecting information about the credibility of borrowers and monitoring their performance on behalf of lenders. Commercial banks, for instance, serve as intermediaries between depositors and the retail borrowers. They act on behalf of depositors by screening borrowers through an examination of their past and expected future incomes and assets, an evaluation of the creditworthiness of the project for which financing is sought, and monitoring the conduct of the borrower to ensure that the loan is used for the purpose stated on the loan application. Thus, they alleviate the problems of adverse selection and moral hazard.

Some users, especially large corporations, obtain financing directly by issuing bonds and equities instead of borrowing from commercial banks. In this event investment banks provide information to investors on the quality of the security by underwriting initial public offerings. The underwriting process consists of a syndicated or individual investment bank taking over the task of distributing securities to the public. In effect, the investment bank buys the securities from the issuer, sells them to the public, and profits from the fees and the spread between the buy and sell prices.

Underwriting is a highly profitable enterprise but, as the fortunes of Jay Cooke illustrate, it also involves risk. It is in the underwriter's interest to do a diligent job in gathering in-depth information to assess future prospects and the expected profitability of the issuer of the security. From the perspective of the public the willingness of an investment bank to underwrite a security can be taken as evidence of the high quality of the issuer and the reliability of its management. During the Pujo Hearings this was precisely the function that bankers emphasized to justify their practices. Bankers, personified by J. P. Morgan, asserted that they were protecting the interests of investors by demanding corporations provide periodic financial statements to the underwriting banks and taking seats on corporate boards so that they could monitor and oversee borrowers' operations.

Ratings agencies, such as Standard & Poor's and Moody's, are also expected to increase the system's transparency and mitigate information asymmetry. These agencies assess the riskiness of a debt instrument and report a summary evaluation of its creditworthiness as a letter grade. Potential investors can easily obtain rankings of debt instruments, ranging from prime investment grades all the way down to "in default," and make their decisions accordingly.

One problem with these market solutions is that they replace one asymmetric-information problem with another: who is watching the watchers? At the height of the subprime boom of the 2000s investment bank Goldman Sachs assembled portfolios of very low-quality securities and marketed them to investors whose portfolios it managed at the same time as it made bets against these bonds, while its traders infamously boasted about "ripping the face off" their clients. Shady, corrupt, or fraudulent banking practices that take advantage of the ignorance of depositors and securities holders (admittedly, sometimes with their own connivance) were widespread before the 1930s and after the 1980s. Rating agencies can be a source of misinformation when their services are paid for by securities issuers because they have an incentive to overrate the bonds.

The alternative approach to alleviating the effects of asymmetric information is to require borrowers as well as intermediary institutions to follow rules and regulations in the disclosure of information and attain greater transparency concerning their activities. This route requires the creation of public agencies to oversee the system and to enforce regulations. In the wake of the crash of 1929 Congress passed legislation that established new institutions, e.g. the Securities and Exchange Commission and Federal Deposit Insurance Corporation, and expanded the powers of others, e.g. the Federal Reserve System, to supervise and monitor the activities of commercial banks, investment banks, and securities exchanges. At the simplest level, financial institutions can be required to file periodic reports on their activities and balance sheets with a regulator, who makes these reports public. These reports allow investors to make more-informed decisions. Financial institutions may also be required to go through periodic auditing by independent agencies.

The efficient-market hypothesis

From Hayek's (1937) perspective, the primary function of the market system is to gather, aggregate, and disseminate information about the fundamentals. The *efficient-market hypothesis* (EMH) states that the market price of an asset incorporates and reflects all of the currently available information on expected earnings, safe interest rates, and risk and liquidity premiums that are relevant to the determination of the value of the asset, thereby ruling out systematic mispricing and bubbles. In this section I first lay out in some detail the foundations and implications of the EMH. This discussion revisits many themes introduced in Chapter 5 and illustrates how the fundamental price is established in an environment characterized by randomness.[3]

The foundations of the EMH can be traced back to Louis Bachelier's research on the statistical properties of security-price movements (Bachelier *et al.* 2006). Bachelier, a French mathematics doctoral student, defended his dissertation *Theory of Speculation* in 1900. Among other things, the dissertation demonstrated that bond-price movements can be modeled as a succession of random steps drawn from a probability distribution. To appreciate the contribution of Bachelier's statistical modeling, a quick review of probability distribution is in order.

Probability distributions and the normal distribution

A probability distribution describes the probabilities of possible outcomes of a random event. Consider Jack and Jill, who are playing a coin-toss game. If the outcome is tails (T) Jack pays Jill $1; if heads (H) Jill pays Jack $1. Suppose they play this game four times, using a fair coin. The *random variable* is the winnings of Jill (or Jack). We cannot know in advance Jill's winnings with certainty, but we know the possible outcomes and corresponding probabilities. The probability distribution that summarizes this information is reported in Table 12.1 and the histogram in Figure 12.1.

If the coin tosses yield four heads Jill will lose $4, and the probability of this outcome is 1/16; she would lose $2 in the event that there are three heads and one tail, and the probability of this outcome is 4/16 (and so

Table 12.1 Probability distribution of pay-offs to Jill in the coin-toss game

Outcome	Probability	Pay-off to Jill
Four heads	1/16	$4 loss
Three heads and one tail	4/16	$2 loss
Two heads and two tails	6/16	$0
One head and three tails	4/16	$2 gain
Four tails	1/16	$4 gain

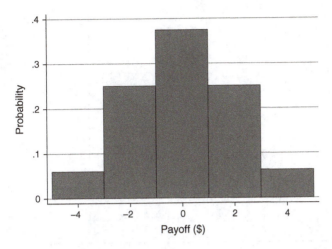

Figure 12.1 Probability distribution of pay-offs to Jill in the coin-toss game.

forth). The sum of the probabilities, or the area under the histogram, is equal to 1 because the distribution describes all the game's possible outcomes. The expected value of Jill's gains is the mean value of the distribution, or the average of pay-offs weighted by the associated probabilities. In this game the mean value is equal to zero: $-\$4(1/16) - \$2(4/16) + \$0(6/16) + \$2(4/16) + \$4(1/16) = 0$.

As there are only five possible outcomes, the probability distribution of this game is discrete. If the coin-toss game were to be played 10,000 times, however, there would be far more numerous possible outcomes that would have approximated a smooth continuous distribution (which now would range from a $10,000 loss to a $10,000 gain, but the expected gain/loss would still be $0). Moreover, this continuous distribution would approximate a bell curve, also known as the *normal distribution*, illustrated in Figure 12.2. The normal distribution is not an empirical distribution derived from experimentation, such as coin tosses, but a mathematically derived theoretical distribution that is very commonly used in statistical modeling.

The normal distribution is summarized by two parameters. First, the mean, coinciding with the median and the mode, is the exact center of the bell curve that divides it into two symmetrical halves. The mean determines the location of the distribution, or where it is centered. The symmetry of the distribution indicates that the deviations from the mean are, on average, offsetting. The shape of the distribution, thick in the middle and tapering toward the tails, implies that small changes (in the area of the mean) are more likely to occur than large changes (located in the tails

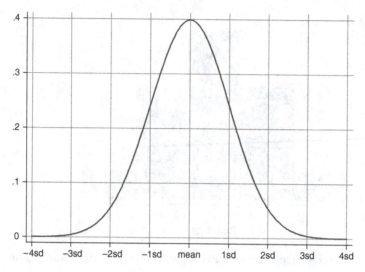

Figure 12.2 The normal distribution.

of the distribution). The second parameter of the distribution is the standard deviation (sd), which measures the dispersion of the distribution. Graphically, one standard deviation is the horizontal distance on the base line between the mean value and the points of inflection (on either side) along the curve. These are marked as ±1sd in Figure 12.2. The less concentrated the possible outcomes around the mean value, the higher the standard deviation and the wider the spread of the normal distribution. As the area under the curve is equal to 1, a wider spread means a lower peak value of the curve.

   One important property of the normal distribution is that the area under the curve bounded by ±1sd is equal to 0.682, which means that the realized value of the random outcome will be within one standard deviation of the mean with the probability of 68.2 percent. Further, the outcome will be within two standard deviations with the probability of 95.4 percent, and within three standard deviations with the probability of 99.6 percent. Thus, the probability of possible values that lie farther from the mean drops precipitously, getting very close to zero. In other words, outlier events of more than three of four standard deviations from the mean are extremely unlikely to happen. This property is often described as the normal distribution having *thin tails*.

   The normal distribution, also known as the Gaussian distribution after mathematician Carl Gauss who discovered it in 1809, is very popular among researchers. Its popularity derives in part from its accuracy in describing randomness in certain physical and social phenomena in life.

Many random variables, such as people's height, weight, IQ scores, blood pressure, measurement errors, and the weights of cereal boxes, roughly follow the normal distribution (or a log-normal distribution, which describes the distribution of the logarithm of the random variable).

Another reason for the popularity of normal distribution is that the mean of a randomly generated independent variable, e.g. coin tosses, converge in the limit to normal distribution, a result known in statistics as the central limit theorem. Thus, many other types of distributions tend to be close to normal distribution. Finally, analytical tractability of the normal distribution that permits explicit solutions to problems makes it a favorite among researchers. It is mathematically extremely convenient to use in modeling exercises because just two well defined parameters, the mean and the standard deviation, summarize the entire distribution. Bachelier also chose to model security-price movements as random events drawn from a normal distribution.

The random-walk hypothesis

Consider the path of a drunkard who lets go of the lamppost he is holding and begins to take steps in an empty, level parking lot. In his inebriated state, he may move in any one of four directions with equal probability. Also suppose that he immediately forgets the direction of his last step. For an observer who wants to predict the direction and length of the drunkard's next step this lack of memory implies that the previous step does not carry any information. The best prediction of the drunkards's next location, then, is the average of four possible directions, or his current location. Although we may be sure that he will take a step, it is impossible to predict the direction. The path of the drunkard is called a *random walk*.

The pattern is also known as Brownian motion, named after the botanist Robert Brown, who observed in 1827 under the microscope that a pollen particle submerged in liquid moved randomly. The pollen's random movement is explained by the fact that the liquid is full of invisible molecules that move independently at different velocities and strike the pollen at different angles. The movement of the pollen is the net effect of its collisions with molecules.[4] Bachelier's contribution to the theory of finance was to show that the price of securities over time could be mathematically modeled as the path of the drunkard or the movement of the pollen. In his model the price constantly changes in response to independent, random shocks. The direction and force of these shocks are drawn from a normal distribution. The independence of the shocks over time implies that asset-price movements have no memory, and, thus, the future price cannot be predicted from past prices.

Bachelier's random-walk model has some interesting properties in addition to the unpredictability of the next step of the drunkard (or the price change). The drunkard's path is going to deviate from the lamppost as a greater number of steps are taken, but there is no reason to expect that he will return to the lamppost. The independence of each new step from the previous step implies that there is no history or any gravitational force (or bungee cord) that will pull him back to the lamppost.[5] The assumption of normally distributed steps also implies that the size of each step is likely to be small and land him a short distance away from the last location. Three- or four-standard-deviation long steps, as if the drunkard takes a ballet leap, are virtually impossible. Finally, it is presumed that the standard deviation of the probability distribution of the movements is constant. The distribution of the size of the next step (or the price change) does not vary with the distance from the lamppost (or the initial price level).

Figure 12.3 illustrates these points. At Period 1, the price of the asset is $100. The normal distribution drawn on Period 2 indicates that the price

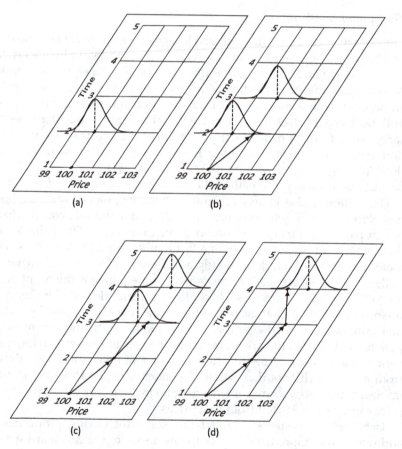

Figure 12.3 An illustration of a random walk.

that will prevail in this period is the current price plus the value of the random shock. As the expected or average value of the random shock is zero, the best prediction of the price of Period 2, or the mean of the probability distribution of the price, is the current price of $100 (Figure 12.3(a)). Suppose that a positive shock occurs in Period 2, and the price level turns out to be $101 (Figure 12.3(b)). Now the best prediction of the Period 3 price is $101. In Figure 12.3(c) the Period 3 price turns out to be $101.50. The expected price of Period 4 is $101.50. Note that the series of actual price changes, $1.00 in Period 1, $0.50 in Period 2, are both independent shocks drawn from normally distributed price changes. Except for its mean value the distribution of price is unchanged from one period to the other, or its standard deviation is constant.

To visualize the random walk in the stock market over a long period of time consider Figure 12.4. The dark line in Figure 12.4 is the inflation-adjusted monthly S&P Composite Index from 1900 to 1990. The thin lines are two random-walk series created by a random-number generator from the same normal distribution. Each random-walk series starts from the value of the index on January 1, 1900. The only factor that distinguishes the two series is that they draw different random shocks in each period.

Figure 12.4 is interesting in several ways. First, the thin lines illustrate how mere randomness can cumulatively create widely different price patterns over a 90-year period. Second, neither of the random-walk series has a trend, or a center of gravity, to which price eventually reverts. To

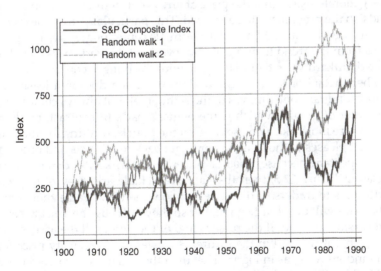

Figure 12.4 Real S&P Composite Index and two random walks (monthly).

Source: Random walks generated by the author. Real S&P Composite Index is from Shiller (2005).

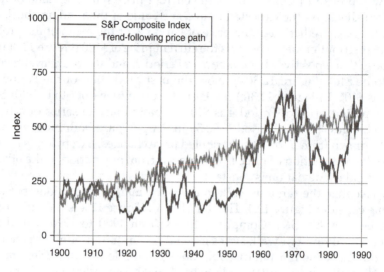

Figure 12.5 Real S&P Composite Index and a trend-following price path (monthly).

Source: Price path generated by the author. Real S&P Composite Index is from Shiller (2005).

appreciate this point better consider another hypothetical stock price represented by the thin line in Figure 12.5. In this case the hypothetical stock price is generated such that the price at any point in time has memory or depends on the previous value observed. This particular price series is not a random walk because it has a deterministic center of gravity. The price deviates from the trend temporarily but eventually reverts back to it. It is as if the drunkard were tied to the pole with the bungee cord.[6]

Another metaphor for the non-random walk is a dog on a leash that constantly and randomly moves to the right or left but always comes back to the center of gravity, which is the owner's path. In contrast, random-walk lines are more like a dog set free on the prairie, running in whatever direction it pleases without an owner to get back to. This second observation is important because, if asset prices behave like the deterministic series, as in Figure 12.5, then they are predictable and they offer profit opportunities to traders. If the price is below the trend value they know that the price will eventually go higher so they will buy the asset to sell it after reversion to trend. If the price is higher they will sell the asset short, knowing that it will fall in the future. However, if the security price follows a random walk, as in Figure 12.4, then there is no way to predict the future and beat the market.

The third observation that follows from Figure 12.4 is the resemblance between the actual stock-price series and the random walks. By comparison, the price series generated in Figure 12.5 appears to be too "regular" and is not a good rendering of the actual series. However, one should not be too hasty to conclude from these observations that random walk is an adequate description of the actual S&P Composite Index and that stock prices are indeed unpredictable. Validation or rejection of the random-walk hypothesis cannot be conducted merely by visual inspection; it calls for rigorous statistical tests. Moreover, there may be modeling alternatives to the random walk.

The final point to draw from the comparison of random walks and the actual stock series in Figure 12.4 is that the actual stock prices exhibit a larger number of sharp, one-period changes than the random-walk series. It is as if the drunkard, against Bachelier's expectations, leaps every once in a while and lands at a distant location. These discontinuities raise doubts about whether the normal distribution, according to which outliers are very unlikely, is a proper description of the distribution of price changes.

Figure 12.6, which reports the daily percentage of the Dow Jones Industrial Average (DJIA) changes from 1900 to 2010, provides a more stark illustration of this observation. The mean and standard deviation (sd) of the daily price changes are 0.03 percent and 1.15 percent respectively. The question is whether the normal distribution offers an adequate approximation of the price changes experienced over this period. If daily price changes are distributed normally then a ±10 percent or larger change from the mean is at least a 9sd event. The normal distribution table tells us

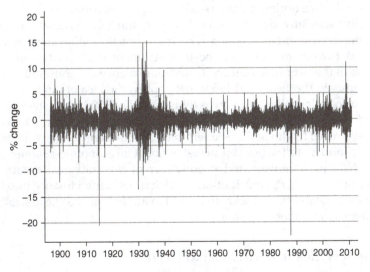

Figure 12.6 Dow Jones Industrial Average daily volatility, 1896–2010.

Source: Author's calculations based on S&P Dow Jones Indices.

that the probability of a 9sd event is one in 7.1×10^{18} days, which is one in 7.1 quintillion days. The age of the universe is 13.8 billion years, or 3.8×10^{12} (3.8 trillion) days. Even the life of the universe is too short for a 9sd event to occur, but, over the time span of 115 years, we have already had 15 such events. There are too many outlier events or large changes for which the normal distribution cannot account. Fat or *thick-tailed distributions* that recognize a higher probability of outlier events are more appropriate than thin-tailed distributions in modeling. Indeed, Fama (1965) underscores that normal distribution is only one of several possibilities for modeling random walk, and shows that random-walk models based on thick-tailed distributions provide better descriptions of the actual data.

This finding is significant for risk-management techniques that rely on probability distributions in assessing the likelihood of adverse events. It appears that using the normal distribution to calculate risk is seriously flawed because it underestimates the likelihood of extreme changes in price and overlooks the associated risks. This can be very damaging for portfolio risk management. Unfortunately, normal distribution has became the distribution of choice in mathematical financial models that became popular on Wall Street after the 1980s.

What does the high frequency of outlier events tell us about the behavior of prices? If price changes merely reflect independent shocks, many of which are offsetting, then their magnitudes are expected to be relatively small, as suggested by the normal distribution. The presence of large deviations, in turn, may be attributable to interdependent shocks, e.g. several negative shocks that arrive in sequence, or, more importantly, to economic agents' interdependent responses to shocks, as if they are prone to bouts of collective optimism and pessimism, or herd behavior.

Bachelier was awarded a doctoral degree, but his dissertation went unnoticed for a number of years. The theory of Brownian motion was developed further by some of the most eminent mathematicians and physicists of the twentieth century. In addition, there were scattered works in economics in the 1940s and 1950s that applied the idea of random walk to stock prices. Bachelier's work was revived in the 1950s when statistician Leonard Savage discovered the dissertation and passed it on to Paul Samuelson of MIT, who had made seminal contributions to many fields in economics and had a particular interest in financial economics. Samuelson quickly became a convert and proselytizer of the statistical theory of finance, and Bachelier's contributions, which transformed finance into the calculus of probabilities, quickly took hold in academia, and the discipline of mathematical finance was born.

From random walk to efficient-market theory

The notion that financial markets are efficient in the sense that openly traded security prices reflect the "best intelligence concerning them" was presented in a book on stock markets written by George Gibson in 1889 (Shiller 2005: 178). However, the EMH wasn't fully developed until the 1960s, when Paul Samuelson of MIT and Eugene Fama of the University of Chicago extended Bachelier's insights to argue that, in financial markets dominated by optimizing investors, informational efficiency implies the unpredictability of future stock prices. Their formulation, in due course, became part of the economic canon as well as an intense subject of dispute. As optimization implies that all currently available relevant information is factored into the asset price; only new information can change the value of the security. New information is intrinsically random or unpredictable because, had it been predictable, it would have been part of the current information, and optimizing agents would have incorporated it into their decision-making. Hence the seemingly paradoxical result that the more informationally efficient the market, the more difficult it is to predict what the price will be in the next period.

To visualize the problem at hand consider an investment in a publicly owned pharmaceutical company that announces the discovery of a blockbuster drug. The intrinsic price of the company's stock will rise in expectation of higher profits, but not everyone will agree immediately on the new value. After all, there is a great deal of uncertainty regarding the effectiveness of the new drug, what competitors have in store, and so forth. It is also possible that some investors may be closer to the source of information, or that they may vary in terms of their proficiency in processing the new information. Individual investors may also have different assessments of the fundamentals, or their information sets may include private information about the industry or the company in addition to the publicly available information. Consequently, it is possible that investor A will expect the intrinsic price to rise by 5 percent, while Investor B anticipates 15 percent. Such differentials will trigger trades. If the market price happens to rise by, say, 10 percent at some point, Investor A will sell and Investor B will buy. These trades constitute a process of *price discovery*. During this process investors with better information and better judgment about the new intrinsic value can make systematic profits at the expense of their counterparties. Such gains and losses, however, are temporary. Once the dust settles and new information is fully processed by all market participants the new market price will emerge as the best estimate of the fundamental price, at which point systematic profit opportunities will disappear.

Thus, the EMH does not imply that there will be no turbulence in asset prices. Rather, asset prices change with the turbulence in the fundamentals. In addition, there will be volatility during the price-discovery process while the newly arrived information disseminates among agents. Institutions and technological innovations that enhance the collection, processing, and distribution of information, that expedite decision-making, and that increase market transparency will accelerate the price-discovery process and reduce both the amplitude and duration of price volatility observed during the adjustment period.

Neither does the EMH imply that economic agents do not make mistakes. In fact, there are two types of error made by economic agents, and it is important to distinguish between them. First, the information set of each agent includes publicly available information, which puts all agents on the same level playing field. It does not necessarily follow, however, that individual predictions of the fundamental price based on public information will coincide. It is plausible, due to the peculiarities of agents, that there are idiosyncratic differences between the individual information sets or their utilization. An investor may overestimate the new intrinsic price, while another may underestimate it. Optimizing behavior entails that such errors are non-systematic, or uncorrelated, and they are randomly distributed across agents. Correlated errors contradict the optimization assumption because they imply that the agent is systematically overlooking a relevant factor and, therefore, not making full use of the information set. Uncorrelated errors across investors cancel each other out and do not affect the market price.

The second type of error is systematic but transitory. Information sets may include agents' private knowledge about the fundamentals. Each agent knows that other agents may have private information concerning the potential success of the new drug, and tries to discern this information from other investors' bids. Sophisticated variants of fundamentals-based analysis and the EMH recognize that these attempts to obtain information about the fundamentals from other investors' actions may cause deviations from the intrinsic price (similar to those discussed in the section on intrinsic bubbles). In the event that agents erroneously interpret an increase in price as a signal of other investors' private knowledge of the fundamentals, thereby discounting their own assessment of the fundamentals, deviation from the intrinsic price will increase. This situation will eventually be followed by a correction when the error is reckoned and the price moves back to the fundamental value. This temporary deviation is not taken as an invalidation of the EMH because the decision is still based on each investor's best perception of the fundamentals.

Independence of sequential price movements may be attributed to the random arrival of news or the independent actions of decision makers, but proponents of the EMH recognize that these are restrictive assumptions. Positive (or negative) news often comes in succession and is non-random, and unsophisticated naïve investors, who trade on noise instead of the fundamentals, are easily swayed by rumors, and buy and sell en masse. These observations raise the possibility of a correlation of price changes over time or non-random price movements. As mentioned in Chapter 5, in the context of market rationality, Fama (1965) maintains that the EMH will hold even in the presence of these factors. These occurrences will not cause systematic deviations from the intrinsic price as long as there are sophisticated investors who have access to sufficient funds to take advantage of mispricing.

First, these smart investors will learn the patterns of dependency in the news and adjust their expectations accordingly. If positive news is expected to be followed by further rounds of the same then the smart money's current bids will reflect the second-round effects as well. As the following rounds of price changes are immediately incorporated into the current price, price movements will again be independent. Second, the unwarranted optimism of naïve investors cannot cause a sustained rise of the market price above the intrinsic price because the smart money will take advantage of the profit opportunity by dumping the overvalued security on naïve investors. The actions of astute investors will correct the deviation.

The visceral sensations of investors in efficient markets are probably similar to those of riders on Disneyland's Space Mountain rollercoaster. This ride simulates an erratic spaceship that travels in pitch darkness. The riders cannot see the track, and, although they know that the carriage will twist, turn, climb, and plunge, it is impossible to anticipate the direction and magnitude of the next movement. The thrill of the ride is facing the unexpected. The efficient securities market is comparable. Investors are similar to the rollercoaster riders in that they are hurtling forward in total darkness toward an unpredictable future. While there is no pre-constructed track, investors know that the evolution of the fundamentals lays down the rails of the market continuously, but only an instant ahead of the speeding carriage.

Three versions of the efficient-market hypothesis

The very act of optimizing investors exploiting every piece of available informational advantage in pursuit of profit transmits the information into the price of the security and thereby eradicates the profit opportunities. Fama (1970) proposed three versions of the argument. The *weak form of the EMH* is closely associated with the random walk and states that an asset price cannot be predicted from its past values. It is impossible to profit systematically by trading on information on historical price patterns because they do not carry any information about the future. The *semi-strong form* states that investors cannot profit systematically by trading on any publicly available information because relevant news will disseminate quickly among profit-seeking investors and become incorporated into their assessment of the asset price. As the new price will reflect fully all publicly available information there will be no systematic profit opportunities. Finally, the *strong form of the EMH* states that even investors who trade on inside information cannot profit systematically because the actual price will eventually reflect both private and public information. While traders with privileged information may initially beat the market, their success will soon be news and other investors will either seek the same information or emulate their investment strategies, thereby smothering the informational advantage.

If no one can systematically earn higher than the average market return or beat the market then stock-picking expertise is a myth. There should be no systematic difference between the returns of portfolios put together by mutual-funds managers and those compiled randomly. Perhaps the smartest investment strategy, therefore, is to invest in index funds that mimic the composition of a market index (such as the S&P 500). The latter minimizes effort, offers diversification, and costs the least in fees. This is not to say that one cannot receive systematically higher returns than the market average. These higher returns, however, are attributable to investing in riskier assets, not to smarter stock picking, and they are merely compensation for the higher risks taken by investors.

Value analysis and technical analysis

The provocative implications of the EMH regarding investment strategy are better appreciated in comparison with two traditional alternatives: *value analysis* (also known as fundamental analysis) and *technical analysis*. Both approaches presume that future stock prices are predictable to some extent, and, therefore, that there are opportunities for profit making through stock picking.

According to value analysis, economic fundamentals drive the value of the stock in line with the standard asset-valuation formula, but the market price does not always reflect intrinsic value correctly. It is possible for the price to hover above or below the intrinsic price for extended periods of time, although such deviations cannot last indefinitely. Eventually, the fundamentals assert themselves, and the price moves to the fundamental value. The objective of value analysts is to discover undervalued companies through an in-depth study of their markets, balance sheets, and earnings potential. If value analysis determines that a company is undervalued the smart strategy is to purchase and hold the stock until the price rises to reflect the company's true profitability. The investment will pay off both in dividends and capital gains. Warren Buffett, whose strategy is to make leveraged purchases of undervalued stocks that he can afford to hold on to for a long time, is reputed to be the master of this type of investing.

Technical analysis attempts to predict a future security price by identifying regularities in past price movements and relying on the conviction that these patterns will repeat in the future. Technical analysts are also known as *chartists* because they infer the future behavior of prices from historical patterns illustrated in price charts. Due to improvements in technology sophisticated statistical techniques have largely replaced charts, but the thrust of the chartist effort remains the same. Implicit in the approach is that investor psychology is the primary mover of the market, and the future behavior of market participants can be discerned from their past behavior as revealed in historical price patterns. Unlike value analysts, technical analysts do not heed the fundamentals, and they may have only a vague or even no notion of the intrinsic value of a security.

If chartists can successfully identify repeating historical patterns they can profit by predicting future movements of prices. Among the alleged patterns, "zig-zag trending" spots significant peaks and lows and posits that investors follow the trend between these resistance and support points. The "resistance level" pattern identifies the ostensible psychological upper resistance level (e.g. the DJIA 15,000), which agents do not believe it is possible to supersede. Therefore, the chartists sell every time the index approaches the threshold, and push the index lower. The "head and shoulders" formation, i.e. three bumps in the stock price with the middle one (head) higher than the other two (shoulders), is an indication that price will plummet (after the second shoulder). The chartist investment strategy, then, is to get ahead of the curve by recognizing patterns ("When will the trend reversal happen? What is the resistance level? Is it a shoulder?") before everyone else, selling assets that are expected to decline in value and buying assets whose prices are expected to increase.

Technical analysis is inconsistent with the weak version of the EMH. The EMH predicts that chartists' profits cannot be persistent because once optimizing investors discover a pattern of, say, a steady price increase followed by a steady decline, they will take advantage of it by shorting the asset whenever they observe prices climbing. As the forward supply of the asset rises and pushes the future price down the pattern will disappear. In a world of optimizing agents charting is self-defeating because optimization does not allow history to repeat itself.

The semi-strong version of the EMH predicts that value analysis cannot yield persistent profits either. Advantages enjoyed by value investors will be short-lived because other investors, motivated by profit opportunities, will eventually catch up with these more astute investors. As investors pursue the same strategy in greater numbers the discrepancy between the actual and the intrinsic price and, thus, profit opportunities, vanish.

How do the EMH's proponents explain the inordinately long string of successes of value investors such as Lawrence Tisch and Warren Buffett, who seem to beat the market quite consistently? Their answer is luck. If millions of people are tossing coins a few are likely to get an inordinate number of heads in sequence, no matter how low the probability. The same is true for investors who may have had lucky streaks. However, inferring future success from past achievements is an inductive fallacy.

Keynes on market efficiency

The EMH was formulated rigorously in the 1960s. Leaving aside, however, the theoretical and technical embellishments and sophisticated statistical testing, the basic idea of the coincidence of the market and intrinsic prices was hardly novel. In fact, John Maynard Keynes (1936) laid the ground-work for an alternative description of the securities markets in Chapter 12 of his *General Theory*, which challenged the pre-1930s as well as the post-1960s orthodoxy. In his view, investors do not behave as expected utility maximizers, their actions are highly interdependent, and the smart money may fail to correct deviations from the intrinsic price. Thus, prices reflect the market sentiment on the value of the assets rather than investors' deci-sions based on discounted expected returns. According to Keynes, there are three keys to understanding investor behavior: state of confidence, convention, and animal spirits.

The state of confidence, convention, and animal spirits

Keynes (1936) points out that standard economic theory omits the critical fact that the investor's decision depends not only on long-term forecasts of future yields but also on the *state of confidence* in these forecasts. Suppose that, according to the best prediction, the stock-market-price index will double within a year. This will still not tempt an investor to buy stocks if she believes that there is a high likelihood it will not be realized. When forecasts are based on flimsy knowledge about possible outcomes and their probabilities the state of confidence in them will be weak. The higher the intrinsic uncertainty about what the future holds, the lower the inves-tor's confidence in her best forecast of the fundamental values of assets.

In circumstances of precarious knowledge and a lack of confidence in forecasts the investor falls back on simple interrelated principles or rules of thumb, which Keynes (1936) summarizes by the term *convention*. First, the investor acts as though the current state of affairs will be sustained in the future (unless she knows that something will actually happen). Investors do not believe that the future is going to be the same, but they have no choice but to ignore prospects of change when they do not have sufficient knowledge about that change. Second, investors view the cur-rent state of general opinion about markets as an adequate assessment of future prospects, and they abide by these opinions, unless, again, some-thing actually changes. Third, they fall back on the judgment of the aver-age and conform to the rest of the market. The presence of organized securities exchanges offers the convention-following investor peace of mind because she knows that there are outlets to liquidate her investment in the event of bad news.[7]

The willingness of investors to follow convention and stand by the judgment of the average or the majority creates inertia in the marketplace and an appearance of stability. Paradoxically, this is also a fragile state. Due to investors' weak knowledge base and limitations on their ability to discriminate between news in terms of importance and relevance investor behavior and asset prices are susceptible to sharp changes in response to news that may not even be germane to the determination of the intrinsic price. The interconnectedness of investors' actions can generate sudden waves of optimism or pessimism and new benchmarks of conventional judgment emerge.

The third component of Keynes's vision concerns this question: if expected utility maximization does not apply then what motivates investors, mired in intrinsic uncertainty, to act and invest in the first place and put their capital at risk? His answer is *animal spirits*, or the psychological urge to act:

> There is the instability due to the characteristic of human nature that a large proportion of our positive activities depend on spontaneous optimism rather than mathematical expectations, whether moral or hedonistic or economic. Most, probably, of our decisions to do something positive, the full consequences of which will be drawn out over many days to come, can only be taken as the result of animal spirits— a spontaneous urge to action rather than inaction, and not as the outcome of a weighted average of quantitative benefits multiplied by quantitative probabilities.
>
> (Keynes 1936: 161)

It is misleading to interpret this passage in the narrow rational-irrational dichotomy of standard economics. According to Keynes, agents obviously do not behave "rationally," in the sense of optimization, when it is not feasible. Their actions, however, are "rational" in the sense that they are reasonable under the circumstances, as underscored in the following passage:

> It is our innate urge to activity which makes the wheels go round, our rational selves choosing between the alternatives as best as we are able, calculating where we can, but often falling back for our motive on whim or sentiment or chance.
>
> (Keynes 1936: 163)

Animal spirits do not indicate arbitrariness or capriciousness, nor do they defy analysis. They vary with the state of confidence and the sense of trust in the firm and sector, as well as in the level of overall economic activity.

Interdependence of investors' actions

In portraying how the interdependence of investors' actions and market psychology may detach the market price from the intrinsic value, Keynes (1936: 156) likens financial decision-making to voting in a then popular beauty contest. A newspaper posted pictures of several women and asked people to vote for the "prettiest." Once all the votes were in and the queen was crowned the paper gave a prize to one person selected by lottery from among those who voted for the winner. One route readers may take is to vote for whomever they think is the prettiest and hope that most voters agree. However, if the objective is to win the prize, regardless of who is crowned, the superior strategy is to guess who the majority thinks is the prettiest contestant and vote for that person. Thus, the voter's choice is determined by her perception of other voters' preferences.

Keynes (1936) argues that investors, like the beauty-contest voters, base their decisions not on their own estimates of the fundamentals that determine the value of an asset but on the perception of other investors' assessment of the asset.[8] Difficulties in assessing the fundamentals far into the future and the costs and risks of arbitrage and shorting incentivize traders to adopt a short time horizon and chase short-term capital appreciation rather than invest in long-term growth, innovation, and profit. Smart investors are in the business of determining the average market opinion of the value of the asset, not the intrinsic value of the asset.

In the Keynesian vision of the financial markets, then, cumulative price distortions and market failures are ordinary events. In this environment private profits do not necessarily translate into social benefits. When security prices do not reflect their true value some worthy projects fail to raise financing and go unrealized, while some less worthy projects attract inordinate amounts of funds. Thus, financial markets may generate immense wealth for market professionals without creating commensurate social value.

Keynes has been judicious on the question of whether financial markets have social value. He distinguishes between two types of activities. Enterprise, on the one hand, is the long-term investment activity, which pays attention to the true worth of assets based on the fundamentals and targets benefitting from long-term profitability. Speculation, on the other hand, tries to make short-term gains by predicting the psychology of the market. Keynes argues that short-term speculative behavior is harmless, provided it is marginal to the enterprise. However, once the situation is reversed and speculation becomes the central activity of the market, pushing enterprise to the periphery, financial markets no longer serve to allocate resources in accordance with long-term profitability and fail to contribute to the growth and well-being of society.

Keynes was pessimistic in 1936 about which side would win in twentieth-century capitalism. He believed that the separation of ownership and management, which compounds the precarious knowledge base about future prospects, and the expansion of securities markets, which allows continuous revisions of security values, make it more likely for speculation to dictate the future course of markets, unless countermeasures are taken. He suggests as possible countermeasures a transfer tax on financial assets to deter frequent trading and encourage long-term commitment, and the state taking on a greater role in organizing long-term, socially advantageous investment (Keynes 1936: 160, 164).

Evidence for the efficient-market hypothesis

The EMH fits comfortably in the core of orthodox economics, which puts a premium on axiomatic structure, mathematical elegance, statistical applications, and market efficiency. The mathematical-finance methods it has created also influenced, albeit with a lag, trading practices in financial markets. However, acceptance of the EMH is not universal, and its critics often argue in line with Keynes's objections. The behavioralists, for instance, argue that the EMH does not hold when investors rely on heuristics and arbitrary anchors. Elsewhere in this book I point out that the hypothesis may not hold in the presence of market imperfections. Grossman and Stiglitz (1980) note the logical flaw that perfect efficiency implies zero profit opportunities and, therefore, a total lack of incentive to collect information or trade. Thus, without inefficiency, there would be no trading and no markets.

These competing theoretical positions have also stimulated an immense amount of empirical research on whether financial markets are efficient. Tests of the weak form of efficiency focus on the statistical properties of stock prices to detect whether there is a systematic relationship between the current and lagged prices. The absence of such a relationship would imply that the future price of the stock cannot be predicted from previous prices. One way to test the semi-strong version is to conduct event studies that examine whether there are above-normal returns following an event such as an announcement of earnings, mergers, or a stock split. If such public information is efficiently reflected in the price then the price should change immediately and there should be no profit opportunities following the announcement.

Another method is to check whether portfolios of professional money managers earn systematically higher than average market returns. Proponents of the EMH often point out, in line with the theory's predictions, that this is not the case. One can also question whether there are frequent incidents that contradict the EMH. The persistence of what the chartists call the January effect (stock prices are higher between December and January), for instance, is a challenge from the EMH perspective. Obvious cases of mispricing, such as a subsidiary having higher capitalization than its parent company, are difficult to explain on the basis of the fundamentals. An alternative testing strategy is to determine whether there is a relationship between valuation metrics, such as initial P/E ratios and future returns. A negative correlation contradicts the EMH because it suggests that it is smarter to purchase stocks when the P/E ratio is smaller.

One influential line of testing offered by Shiller (2005: 191) is reproduced in Figure 12.7. If stock prices fully reflect discounted earnings then the two should move in tandem. Shiller calculated three alternative dividend present-value series under different assumptions of discounting and compared these with the stock-price index. Figure 12.7 sheds doubt

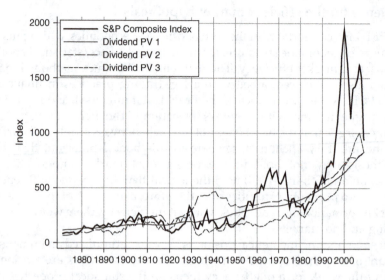

Figure 12.7 Real S&P Composite Index and dividend present values, 1871–2009 (annual).

Source: Shiller (2005).

on the EMH by demonstrating that over the 1871–2009 period stock prices were far more volatile than dividends. Moreover, excess volatility has increased in the recent era of more "mature" financial markets.

A discussion of the technicalities and interpretations of empirical tests of the EMH is beyond our scope, but it is worth noting that reviewers of the literature have concluded that empirical work falls short of resolving the debate. The evidence that has emerged has often been conflicting. Results are questioned and criticized because of divergent views on the appropriateness of the empirical models' specifications, statistical significance, and alternative interpretations of the findings. Anomalies were dismissed as insubstantial when they contradicted prior beliefs; inconclusive tests did not change minds.[9] At any rate, statistical tests of questions of whether security prices are predictable or markets are beatable are probably of little import now. However valuable they may be in other contexts, the subtleties of statistical testing as criteria to judge the efficiency of financial markets fell by the wayside when the brutal swipe of the market crash and financial crisis caused the economy to collapse in 2007–8.

Key terms and concepts

Animal spirits
Chartist
Convention

Efficient-market hypothesis
Jurisdictional arbitrage
Normal distribution
Price discovery
Principal–agent problem
Random variable
Random walk
Regulatory arbitrage
Regulatory capture
Risk sharing
Semi-strong form of EMH
State of confidence
Strong form of EMH
Systemic risk
Technical analysis
Thick-tailed (fat, heavy) distribution
Thin-tailed distribution
Value analysis
Weak form of EMH

Endnotes

1 According to Michael Lewis' (1989) chronicles, the earnings of bond traders in the 1980s were vastly out of proportion with their contribution to the social good. Indeed, in popular culture finance professionals are often portrayed as people who push money around and collect ample commissions and fees.
2 Bear in mind that borrowers supply debt instruments, e.g. bonds, in return for loans. A higher demand for loans means a higher supply of bonds and, therefore, lower bond prices.
3 Financial journalists John Cassidy (2009) and Justin Fox (2009) offer very engaging and detailed accounts of the intellectual history of the EMH against the background of the evolution of financial markets.
4 The applet http://galileo.phys.virginia.edu/classes/109N/more_stuff/Applets/brownian/brownian.html illustrates the random-walk path of pollen in liquid.
5 Bachelier also demonstrated that the drunkard's expected distance from the lamppost is proportional to the square root of the time elapsed. Albert Einstein derived the same result a few years later, although he had not read Bachelier's work. Another Frenchman, Jules Regnault, had applied random walk to stock market price movements, discovered the square-root rule, and published his findings in 1863.
6 The random-walk paths are generated by assuming that the price in period t is equal to the price in period $t-1$, a drift term that adds a constant amount to the series (equal to 0.8) and a normally distributed random error term ε (with mean equal to zero and standard deviation equal to 12): $p(t) = p(t-1) + 0.8 + \varepsilon$. The starting January 1900 value of the stock index is 175 (Shiller, 2005). The random error is generated by the NORMINV function of Excel. The simulated series in Figure 12.5 is an autoregressive process whereby the price is drawn back to the underlying deterministic trend value by a fraction of the magnitude of deviation. The equation is $p(t) = 30 + 0.08t + 0.8p(t-1) + \varepsilon$, where ε is again the

normally distributed random error with mean equal to zero and standard deviation equal to 12.

7 Keynes also notes that, while an investment is liquid individually, there is no liquidity in the aggregate. If investors can sell their holdings without a perceptible influence on price then they have the safety of liquidity. When there is a generalized rush to sell assets, however, buyers may not be easy to find, and the hope of liquidity crashes along with the security price.

8 Of course interdependence among investors goes deeper. Since each investor recognizes that other investors will follow the same strategy they have to consider the average market opinion of the average market opinion of the value of the asset.

9 For reviews of statistical tests of the EMH from supporting and skeptical perspectives see Lo (2008) and Malkiel (2012) respectively.

References

Bachelier, Louis, Mark Davis and Alison Etheridge. 2006. *Louis Bachelier's Theory of Speculation: The Origins of Modern Finance*. Princeton and Oxford: Princeton University Press.

Cassidy, John. 2009. *How Markets Fail: The Logic of Economic Calamities*. New York: Farrar, Straus and Giroux.

Fama, Eugene F. 1965. "The Behavior of Stock-Market Prices." *The Journal of Business* 38 (1): 34–105.

Fama, Eugene F. 1970. "Capital Markets: A Review of Theory and Empirical Work." *The Journal of Finance* 25(2): 383–417.

Fox, Justin. 2009. *The Myth of the Rational Market: A History of Risk, Reward, and Delusion on Wall Street*. New York: Harper Business.

Grossman, Sanford J. and Joseph E. Stiglitz. 1980. "On the Impossibility of Informationally Efficient Markets." *American Economic Review* 70 (3): 393–408.

Hayek, Friedrich. 1937. "Economics and Knowledge." *Economica* New Series, 4 (13): 33–54.

Keynes, John Maynard. 1936. *The General Theory of Employment, Interest, and Money*. London: Macmillan.

Lewis, Michael. 1989. *Liar's Poker*. New York: Penguin Books.

Lo, Andrew S. 2008. "Efficient Markets Hypothesis." In *The New Palgrave Dictionary of Economics*, 2nd ed., edited by Steven N. Durlauf and Lawrence E. Blume. Online edition: Palgrave Macmillan. Online: www.dictionaryofeconomics.com/article?id=pde2008_E000050. doi:10.1057/9780230226203.0454.

Malkiel, Burton G. 2012. "The Efficient Market Hypothesis and the Financial Crisis." Pp. 75–98 in *Rethinking the Financial Crisis*, edited by Alan S. Blinder, Andrew W. Lo, and Robert M. Solow. New York: Russell Sage Foundation.

Shiller, Robert J. 2005. *Irrational Exuberance*, 2nd ed. New York: Currency Doubleday. Online: www.econ.yale.edu/~shiller/data/ie_data.xls.

13 The 1980s

Financial capitalism unchained

The period from 1945 to 1970 witnessed rising productivity, rapid economic growth, and improved living standards throughout industrialized countries. It was free from deep and long recessions that marked the earlier era of capitalism. The Great Depression was still fresh in people's minds, but it was widely accepted that judicious use of monetary and fiscal tools prevented excessive turbulence of the business cycle. The labor–capital discord had faded away under corporatist welfare states. Relative to the bank-run and crash-ridden experiences of the earlier era, the financial system was tranquil under the rules and regulations put in place in the 1930s.

This era came to an end in the 1970s with the breakdown of the postwar international monetary system and the apparent failure of standard monetary and fiscal measures in mitigating concurrent inflation and recession. Academics and policymakers grew more skeptical of the efficacy of government policies to tame the business cycle. Proponents of laissez-faire policies questioned the effectiveness and the necessity of regulations in specific industries. Celebrations of unregulated markets and private wealth, as well as a denunciation of discretionary policymaking and regulatory measures, dominated public discourse.

During the 1980s the financial landscape was transforming. Non-depository institutions, like mutual money-market funds, became a major force that competed with commercial banks for savings. Commercial banks took steps toward investment-banking activities as banking regulations eased. Investment banks expanded their securities brokerages and trading operations. New financial instruments proliferated. The *financialization* of the US economy, i.e. the domination of the larger economy and governance by financial markets, institutions, and interests, commenced. Over the course of the decade these developments also brought about a more turbulent financial market marked by the failure of the thrift institutions, defaults, and the largest one-day stock-market crash ever witnessed in the US. Nonetheless, these events did not slow down the momentum of change and by the end of the 1980s financialization was advancing rapidly.

The rise and fall of the golden age of capitalism

International monetary relations[1]

Until World War I international monetary relations were governed by the gold standard, whereby each country set the value of its currency against a fixed amount of gold. Gold parities, in turn, determined exchange rates among currencies. After the war the gold-standard system could not be fully re-established, and monetary relations were in a state of flux. During the Great Depression countries competitively devalued their currencies to lower the price of their products, expand export markets, and protect domestic producers from foreign competition. However, no country's goods can be cheaper when all countries devalue their currencies. The outcome of the currency warfare was the imposition of prohibitive import taxes, which led to the implosion of international trade in the 1930s.

In 1944 representatives of the Allied countries created a post-World War II international monetary system that would ensure currency stability and shun trade warfare. Known as the *Bretton Woods system*, it replaced the gold standard with the *gold exchange standard*. Under the new system the US dollar became the reserve currency. Its value was linked to gold at the rate of $35 per ounce, and the US agreed to convert US dollars to gold at the request of foreign governments and central banks. Other countries, in turn, pegged the value of their currencies in terms of the US dollar. To avoid competitive devaluations individual countries were not permitted to change the value of their currencies unilaterally, and the International Monetary Fund (IMF) was established to monitor the system.

In the event that any country experienced temporary trade deficits and required foreign currency to pay for imports the IMF provided loans until the problem was resolved. When deficits were chronic, however, the country was permitted to devalue its currency to make its products competitive, but only in consultation with the IMF and on condition it would implement IMF-recommended economic reforms. The system also imposed restrictions on the international mobility of financial assets because these flows, often associated with speculation, were perceived to be a detriment to the stability of global monetary relations and nation states' conduct of monetary and fiscal policy. The international monetary system was generally free from currency crises, at least until 1970, and international trade flourished in this stable environment. International fixed-direct investment grew as multinational companies organized manufacturing on a global scale. Exchange rates exhibited little volatility, and national currencies were not objects of speculation.

By the end of the 1960s the Bretton Woods system was cracking. Because the US dollar was used as the international medium of exchange and the reserve currency central banks across the globe had accumulated it in large stocks. After 1958 the US government had partially relaxed capital controls under pressure from Wall Street, and the outflow of dollars that escaped domestic banking regulations further added to the accumulation of dollars abroad, particularly in Europe. As long as foreigners were willing to hold it, the dollar was as good as gold, and the system was sustainable. However, the fact that dollar holdings across the globe grew at a much faster rate than US gold reserves eventually cast doubt on the ability of the US to support the $35-per-ounce conversion rate. European governments began to ship their dollar holdings to the US for conversion to gold. In the face of global speculation against the dollar and the depletion of gold reserves President Nixon first suspended the convertibility of dollars to gold and then closed the gold window permanently in 1971.

The vanishing of the international currency anchor spelled the end of the Bretton Woods system. By 1973 industrialized countries had abandoned the pegged exchange rates and allowed the values of their currencies to be determined in the global currency market. Concurrently, they began to remove limitations on the global trading of financial assets. Unlike pegged exchange rates, under this flexible exchange-rate system the value of a currency varied with fluctuations in the supply of and demand for the currency by importers, exporters, multinational corporations, portfolio investors, and currency speculators. Higher exchange-rate volatility also led to the growth of currency futures markets, which offered protection to global traders who needed hedges against unfavorable movements in exchange rates. For example, the Chicago Mercantile Exchange (CME) established the International Money Market for trading foreign-exchange futures contracts in 1972. Currency speculators participated in this market to make bets on future movements of currencies.

The Keynesian consensus

During the decades following World War II economists and policymakers had widely accepted the Keynesian diagnosis that the source of fluctuations of economic activity was the volatility of private consumption and investment demand. Overall economic activity stagnated during periods of lackluster household and business spending. The Great Depression had demonstrated that market forces could not be relied on to correct economic contraction by themselves. The solution to recessions was to stimulate private demand in the economy through expansionary fiscal policies, such as higher government spending and transfers, lower taxes, and/or monetary policies, e.g. lower interest rates. The cost of expansionary policies could be inflation, but, with memories of unemployment during the Great Depression still fresh, that was considered a reasonable price to pay. Provided that the terms of the trade-off between inflation and unemployment were at a socially acceptable level, both economists and policymakers were in favor of demand-management policies.

Not everyone agreed with the Keynesian diagnosis or therapy. The intellectual leader of the critics, Milton Friedman of the University of

Chicago, fervently opposed Keynesian theory and practice on the grounds that the sources of economic instability were the government and the monetary authority, and warned that demand-management policies would be destabilizing (Friedman 1962, 1968). His calls to limit the scope of government intervention in the economy were largely ignored until the early 1970s. However, opinions changed after 1970, when inflation and unemployment rates increased simultaneously. *Stagflation* challenged the notion of a stable trade-off between the two macroeconomic evils as well as trust in the effectiveness of countercyclical demand-management policies. Whereas the Keynesians attributed the stagflation largely to the extraordinary shocks that tripled the price of oil twice in the 1970s and the consequent rise in energy costs, Friedman blamed it on the social-engineering attempts of woolly minded academics and government policymakers.

Friedman warned of the harm of demand-management policies and found a sympathetic audience in a discipline already predisposed to relying on unregulated markets to solve economic problems. By the end of the 1970s the pendulum had swung back as more and more economists supported the idea that markets ensure full employment of resources, and laissez-faire policy once again became dominant. Keynes was announced "dead." In the political arena these views formed the intellectual foundations of the Reagan and Thatcher counter-revolutions of the following decade. The doctrine of *neoliberalism*, which called for privatization, deregulation, dismantling of welfare programs, curbing of union power, and unimpeded flow of commodities and capital across national boundaries, became dominant at the global level. As Ronald Reagan articulated in his inaugural address in 1981: "In this present crisis, government is not the solution to our problems; government *is* the problem."

At the microeconomic level the ascendancy of "free" market ideas started the movement for the removal of the rules and regulations implemented in previous decades. Regulations were dismantled first in the airline and trucking industries during the presidency of Jimmy Carter. In the banking sector commercial banks sought ways to free themselves from the restrictions imposed by the Glass–Steagall Act.

The financial sector

Before the 1970s the primary activities of commercial banks were to collect deposits and extend commercial and consumer loans from the deposit base. They controlled vast amounts of deposits, but banking laws prevented them from undertaking high-risk-high-return investments with depositors' money. Their primary source of revenue was the interest-rate differential between the loan and deposit rates. Investment banks primarily assisted firms in raising financing via initial public offerings (IPOs) and offered advice on *mergers and acquisitions* (M&A). A plethora of agencies supervised financial markets to prevent imprudent practices, market manipulation, and insider trading. The scope for speculation was limited under these conditions. Post-Great Depression laws and regulations had made the domestic financial sector rather dull, which is not to say that the banking system was free from trouble. The credit crunch in 1966, the bankruptcy of Penn Central Railroad in 1970, and the failure of Franklin National in 1974 sent shock waves throughout the system, but regulators insulated each incident successfully.

The 1970s witnessed revolutionary changes in the infrastructure of financial markets. Innovations in information and communications technologies created much faster, round-the-clock trading opportunities in comparison with any previous market. Due to these developments not only was information compiled and disseminated more swiftly across the globe, but traders were also able to access and respond to new information more quickly. The expansion of international financial transactions, as a result of the removal of the Bretton Woods-era restrictions on capital flows, and growing technological interconnectedness, made geographically separated financial markets more integrated and interdependent. Business executives, Wall Street, most academic economists, and the media celebrated the information revolution for opening up new opportunities to investors and improving the efficiency of markets. While some skeptics cautioned that the rapid propagation of information could lead to impulse buying, herd behavior, innovative ways of manipulating the marketplace, and momentum investment, their voices were muffled in the festive mood.

Within the changing financial environment various institutions became more prominent, including money-market funds, which grew significantly. Interest-rate ceilings on bank deposits and the high inflation rates of the 1970s made depository institutions less attractive places to hold money, and people increasingly shifted their savings to mutual money-market funds that offered better returns. Declining deposits hurt commercial-bank profits and further motivated these institutions to challenge the existing regulatory structure. They fought against rules that barred them from participating in lucrative securities- and derivatives-related activities. In the securities markets large institutional investors (e.g. pension funds, mutual funds) that traded very large blocks of securities became more prominent. Their actions, especially when correlated, had a substantial effect on the stock market and added to the volatility of prices. The number of *hedge funds*, private investment partnerships that served limited numbers of very large investors, also multiplied. Unlike mutual funds, hedge funds were not subject to Securities and Exchange Commission (SEC) regulations. Hedge-fund managers invested funds for a limited number of very wealthy clients who were supposedly sophisticated enough to look after themselves. Their label notwithstanding, hedge funds were highly leveraged and typically took high-risk positions.

Among investment banks the competition for fees on securities under-writing and M&A assistance increased as new domestic and foreign banking houses entered the market. In response many investment banks shifted their focus from these traditional sources of revenue to finan-cial research, investment management, and dealer-broker services. The research activity evaluated individual stocks, bonds, derivatives, and cur-rencies in terms of price, risk, and volatility. Bankers used this informa-tion to offer buy-and-sell advice to their customers. They actively managed institutional and individual investor portfolios through in-house hedge funds, private equity, or mutual funds in accordance with their clients' return and risk objectives. Both research and investment management became sources of lucrative fees for investment firms.

Dealer and broker services traded financial instruments either on behalf of the clients or on their own account. As a trader of securities, the firm acted as a market maker by selling and buying financial assets, and prof-ited from the spread between the bid and ask prices. By trading on their own account, known as *proprietary trading*, investment banks also placed bets on expected market movements. Market making and proprietary trading unlocked a vast source of profits but also exposed investment banks to more risk because they held an inventory of assets in their own portfolio. As investment houses did not have access to deposits to finance these activities, they raised the necessary funds through short-term bor-rowing in the money markets.

Carrying out underwriting, consulting, portfolio-management, broker-age, and proprietary-trading activities simultaneously amounted to a con-flict of interest. A bank, for instance, has an incentive to promote an IPO that it has underwritten to its clients, or take positions on its own account, depending on what its customers are trading. Such conflicts of interest require the bank to build firewalls to inhibit inter-desk flows of informa-tion, and regulators to keep an ever vigilant eye on investment banks' operations.

Another emergent profit source for investment banks was the fast-growing derivatives market. Derivatives, such as futures contracts and options, have been commonplace since the seventeenth century, but the 1970s was a turning point in the ascent of derivatives. New exchanges were established to trade standardized derivatives, and the seeds of new derivatives, such as swap contracts and securitization of previously illiq-uid bank loans, were sown.

Leveraged buyouts and junk bonds[2]

The 1980s started with the deepest recession the US had experienced since the 1930s. The contraction was the outcome of draconian measures taken by the Federal Reserve System (Fed), including raising interest rates to over 20 percent, to lower double-digit inflation. Not surprisingly, the stock

Figure 13.1 Real S&P Composite Index, 1980–90 (monthly).
Source: Shiller (2005).

market stalled until mid 1982 (Figure 13.1), but the recovery was swift, gaining momentum after 1984. Between August 1982 and August 1987 the S&P 500 increased in inflation-corrected terms by 256 percent. The driving force of the securities markets appeared to be the innovations of financial markets, including a wave of corporate takeovers fueled by junk bonds.

The takeover wave

A merger refers to two or more companies that combine their assets and operations and continue their activities as a new, single entity. An acquisition, or takeover, refers to one company buying another company fully and becoming the new owner of its assets and liabilities with or without the consent of the shareholders and managers of the acquired company. While a merger connotes more of a symmetrical relationship between the two entities than an acquisition, in practice the distinction is often blurry, and in many mergers the more powerful company swallows the weaker. In the present context the distinction is not important, and I will use the terms merger, acquisition, and takeover interchangeably.

The 1980s witnessed the fourth largest M&A wave in the twentieth century in the US. The basic takeover story of the 1980s ran as follows. An investor, a consortium of investors, or a private equity firm identified a public corporation as the takeover target. The target could be a corporation perceived as undervalued in the stock market or with substantial assets but relatively low profits. The buyer would purchase shares of the target corporation and, once its ownership reached 5 percent of the shares, it filed with the SEC, in accordance with regulations, to indicate its intention to take over the target. The two companies then started to negotiate the price to be paid to the shareholders of the target company, how the payment would be made, i.e. in cash or stock of the acquirer, and the future of the target company's executives, managers and, perhaps, customers and workers. If these negotiations were finalized to the satisfaction of both parties then a friendly acquisition proceeded.

If, however, the target company did not agree with the terms of acquisition, either the buyer gave up or a takeover war started. The executives and boards of the target companies often viewed takeover attempts as hostile and adopted defensive strategies of giving in to "greenmail," i.e. paying off the attacker by purchasing its stock at a premium price, seeking a "white knight," i.e. a more desirable buyer, or taking the "poison pill," i.e. diluting shares to weaken the grip of the unwelcome buyer. Occasionally, the buyers offered executives of the target company "golden parachutes"—large payments and compensation—to break down their resistance and to persuade them to leave.

In addition to the prevalence of hostile takeovers, the acquisition wave of the 1980s was also distinctive in the methods used to finance purchases, summarized by the term *leveraged buyout* (LBO). Buyers took on vast amounts of debt to finance purchases, often higher than 90 percent of the purchase price, against the collateral of the cash flow and assets of the target firm. The strategy was to buy the company with maximum debt and then use the company cash flow and assets to service the debt. Often buyers took the firm private after the takeover. After managerial and operational changes, which at times meant dismantling the company, buyers put the company up for sale, either in full or in pieces, in expectation of capital gains. The prominent actors of the takeover boom of the 1980s were corporate raiders and junk-bond financiers.

The raiders

The term *corporate raider* is attributable to the pervasiveness of aggression and hostility in the 1980s takeover wave, the eagerness of buyers to split up the acquisition for sale, and the proceeds they realized in the form of fees and capital gains.[3] The LBOs boom began with the acquisition of Gibson Greeting Cards in 1982 by the Wesray Corporation, led by former Treasury Secretary William E. Simon, for $80m: $1m cash, $53m debt, and the remainder from the sale of Gibson's physical assets. Gibson Greetings was taken public in 1983 by issuing stock valued at $330m. The one-year pay-off to Simon was $66m, or a two-hundredfold increase in his initial investment. Many other buyout attempts followed. Among the significant ones, Gulf Oil escaped a takeover attempt by T. Boone Pickens in 1984 by selling out to white knight Chevron for $13.4b. Carl Icahn took over TWA in 1985, but his bid to buy US Steel failed. Ronald Perelman purchased the Revlon Corporation for $2.7b in 1985. The purchase of RJR Nabisco by KKR, led by Henry Kravis, in 1989 for $31.1b ($29.9b in debt, $1.2b in equity) was the most publicized LBO of the decade. The story was turned into the book and movie *Barbarians at the Gate*.

Anticipating the next target of the raiders also created profit opportunities. *Risk arbitrageurs* specialized in seeking out vulnerable companies. Once they identified companies they profited by buying the stock of the target company and selling short the stock of the acquiring company because usually with the takeover the former rose and the latter fell. The most famous—and later notorious—of these actors was Ivan Boesky who, among his many exploits, earned $65m from Chevron's acquisition of Gulf in 1984 and $50m from Philip Morris' purchase of General Foods in 1985. Boesky stated to a receptive audience, "Greed is all right. . . greed is healthy," in his 1986 commencement speech at the University of California–Berkeley Business School, lines later engraved in popular culture. Taking positions in stocks of the target and acquiring companies exposed risk arbitrageurs to potentially heavy losses in the event the takeover was not completed. Access to reliable and, if possible, inside information was key to high-risk arbitrage profits. Inside trading was, of course, beyond the SEC-drawn boundaries of legitimate information allowed in trading.

The mainstream economic theory of the time largely supported the corporate-takeover movement and claimed that the raiders' aggressive actions would improve the efficiency of corporations and benefit shareholders directly (Jensen 1988). The thrust of the argument is that many large companies had grown careless with heavy bureaucracy, complacent management, and inefficient operations. The executives and managers of the company were not serving the best interests of the owners or shareholders. This is an example of the principal–agent problem mentioned in Chapter 12. In modern public companies ownership and management are separated. The agents, i.e. executives, managers, and the board, are employees of the principals, i.e. shareholders; they are hired to serve the interests of the latter by doing their best to enhance the performance of the company and maximize profits. When the owners cannot monitor the day-to-day operations of the company, however, the managers may put their own interests ahead of the interests of the owners and prioritize their own job security, salaries, and bonuses at the expense of long-term profits. As a result returns to the owners suffer. Its supporters saw corporate takeovers as a remedy for this malady. The threat or act of corporate takeover would improve the efficiency of public corporations and returns to shareholders by forcing changes in traditional management practices, replacing the outdated governance structure, executives, and managers, eliminating underperforming divisions, and dismissing underachieving personnel.

This particular solution to align the interests of shareholders with the performance of management has come to be known as maximizing *shareholder value*. During the 1980s, when the efficient-market hypothesis was ascendant, there was a ready metric to judge how well executives were serving the interests of owners. If the share price aggregates all of the information regarding the discounted future profitability of the company then the objective of the executives is to maximize the share price, or the shareholder value. Jack Welch of General Electric achieved this objective in the early 1980s by cutting costs, i.e. laying off much of the management, closing low-performing divisions and factories, and cutting the payroll, all with an eye on raising the share price. Welch implemented his plans from inside the company; the raiders came from the outside as defenders of shareholder rights.

From the public-interest perspective the important question is whether LBOs improved social welfare. Raiders were hailed as social benefactors by theorists and practitioners because the removal of inefficiencies and the improvement of company performance were thought to advance overall welfare through cheaper and better products for customers.

The financiers

Debt-financed, or leveraged, buyouts of public companies had been carried out since the 1950s but rose to prominence in the 1980s. The following example illustrates the idea of leveraging. Suppose an investor is considering purchasing a company at a price of $100. The company normally makes an annual profit of $20. If the investor buys the company with his own money the profit rate would be 20 percent on the equity. However, suppose that the investor borrows $90 at 10 percent interest against the collateral of the target company, and completes the purchase with $10 equity and $90 in loans. Out of the $20 profit $9 will go to the interest payment on the loan, and the remaining $11 is the profit—that is 110 percent profit on the $10 equity, which is higher than the non-leveraged purchase by a factor of 5.5. Further, tax deductions on interest payments and accelerated depreciation (due to the Economic Recovery Act of 1981) lowered the tax burden and made LBOs even more attractive.

However, the more important financial innovation of the time was a new and more lucrative source of borrowing. Raiders faced limitations when they borrowed from the banks against the collateral of company shares because margin requirements limited leverage. They also were personally liable for the bank loans. Raising funds by selling bonds backed by the target firm's assets or future revenues was a way to avoid these restrictions. There were no regulatory limitations on how much money could be raised by selling bonds. Moreover, bond financing passed the risk of failure on to bond investors. Raiders needed investment banks to underwrite the bond issue, and during the surge of takeovers a new class of financiers assisted raiders by underwriting their debt.

The so-called bulge-bracket firms, such as Goldman Sachs, Morgan Stanley, First Boston, and Lehman Brothers, which served governments and the largest institutional and private investors, dominated investment banking in the 1970s. During the increasingly competitive 1980s smaller banks, such as Salomon Brothers and Merrill Lynch, took advantage of special niches to expand and match the "old guard" in size. Drexler Burnham Lambert distinguished itself in this context by promoting an extremely aggressive strategy of underwriting high-yield bonds, or *junk* bonds. At one point Drexler was listed among the five largest US investment banks.

Credit-rating firms grade bonds in terms of their default risk. The term junk bond is reserved for medium-grade bonds that rank below the low-risk *investment-grade bonds*, but above the high-risk *speculative bonds* (on Standard and Poor's bond-rating scale junk bonds are rated BBB). Medium quality means that the issuing firms have adequate ability to service their debt but are highly susceptible to adverse circumstances. Thus, these firms had to offer higher interest rates than the blue-chip corporations (or offer cheaper bonds) to attract lenders. Junk bonds made up only a small percentage of the bond market before the 1980s, which indicated that these firms' primary recourse to credit was the banking system.

The radical idea of Michael Milken, who headed the high-yield-bond desk at Drexler, was that these companies were "fallen angels." They were unfairly shut off from the investment-grade-bond market because the ratings of their bonds overestimated the default risk. Milken argued that the historical default rates of these companies were lower than their credit ratings suggested, and, therefore, their bonds were actually excellent investment opportunities. Moreover, Milken championed these companies as candidates to become future captains of industry; in view of their excellent prospects their backward-looking, high-risk reputations were misleading. Thus, Drexler's high-yield division began to work with these companies to issue large volumes of junk bonds. Drexler dominated both the primary and secondary trading in this rapidly expanding segment of the market.

Junk bonds underwritten by investment banks quickly became the primary borrowing tool in LBOs as well. Drexel was the undisputed master of the field, although others, such as Salomon Brothers and Morgan Stanley, had joined the junk-bond market. Milken was able to attract investors by advertising that the perceived default rates of the bonds he marketed were lower than the norm. He also cultivated the customer base by matching issuers of and investors in junk bonds (and collected commissions and fees from both sides). His annual convention, known as the Predators' Ball, brought together potential investors, raiders, and company executives, as well as the political and academic figures that helped raise the profile of the junk-bond business. The primary buyers of junk bonds were institutional investors, such as insurance companies and mutual funds. Savings and loan institutions also invested in junk bonds after the loosening of banking regulations in the early 1980s.

The LBO wave offered a lucrative source of profits for investment banks. In comparison with standard investment-banking charges, fees were much higher for underwriting junk bonds, arranging temporary loans for raiders, and providing them with advice. Milken raised hundreds of millions of dollars of funds from investors in blind pools, which essentially meant that the investors knew that the money would be used for acquisitions but did not know much else. Among others, Drexler financed Pickens' bids for Gulf Oil and Unocal, Icahn's bid for Philips 66, Ted Turner's purchase of MGM/UA, Perelman's purchase of Revlon, and KKR's purchase of RJR Nabisco. For a while Milken was the highest-paid financial executive in 1987, with an annual income of $550m. It came to light, however, that, throughout this period unsavory practices, such as insider trading and kickbacks between the agents of junk-bond buyers and Drexel/Milken, were widespread.

In the public discourse junk bonds were said to "democratize capital" by facilitating the access of smaller, temporarily wobbly companies to long-term capital so that they could strengthen, grow, create jobs, and contribute to the productive capacity of the country. They were also hailed for assisting the takeover of fossilized companies, resulting in streamlined management and improved productivity and competitiveness (Yago 1990). Not all, however, shared the enthusiasm for junk bonds. Some commentators suggest that the success of the Milken operation was largely illusory. Milken created hundreds of partnerships with associates from within and outside of Drexler. He used these partnerships to manipulate the market, embezzle the incentives that issuers offered to the buyers, and defer defaults by parking troubled bonds with friendly mutual funds and savings and loans institutions (Akerlof and Romer 1993; Black 2005: 255).

Critics of leveraged buyouts

When private equity became a controversial subject more than two decades later, in the midst of the presidential primaries, columnist George Will (2011) responded to the critical comments of several Republican candidates:

> Firms such as Bain [private equity firm founded by Mitt Romney, then running for the republican nomination for president] are indispensable for wealth creation, which often involves taking over badly run companies, shedding dead weight and thereby liberating remaining elements that add value. The process, like surgery, can be lifesaving. And like surgery, society would rather benefit from it than watch it.
>
> (Will 2011)

Will's opinions concur with shareholder-value theory, but not everyone agreed that LBOs were socially beneficial. According to critics, takeovers were predatory exploits that benefitted raiders at the expense of the target company's employees and bondholders. The primary means to raise profits and to service the debt was cost savings, one form of which was laying off workers. Cost savings were also realized through cutting wages, benefits, and other operating expenses, looting pension funds, and reducing ongoing or planned investments. It was common practice for raiders to split the company and sell its physical assets in a piecemeal fashion. One point of contention in discussions over LBOs is whether downsizing improved short-term profits at the expense of long-term profitability, weakening a corporation's competitive position. However, little systematic information is accessible, as much of the pertinent data regarding the performance of the LBO firms of the 1980s are proprietary. The available empirical evidence shows that, on average, employment in LBO firms increased but at a slower rate than that observed in similar firms that did not experience LBOs. Wages were also lower in the LBO firms (Kaplan and Stromberg 2008).

Regardless of the ultimate success or failure of the LBO firms, the raiders themselves turned a profit because there was a profound asymmetry in terms of sharing the benefits and costs. The takeover entrepreneurs put little equity of their own into the projects and, therefore, had little at stake. They were, however, rewarded handsomely with their bonuses and advising and management fees, regardless of the eventual outcome of the takeover. If the project turned out to be profitable they made capital gains as well. The risk of failure, on the other hand, was borne by the bondholders, who received pennies on the dollar in the event the acquired company defaulted on its debt. Many companies that were burdened by excessive debt indeed went bankrupt.

The savings and loan debacle[4]

Savings and loan (S&L) institutions, or thrifts, were created to extend home loans to middle-class families. Under legislation put in place in the 1930s they were regulated by the Federal Savings and Home Loan Banking Board (Bank Board), and their deposits were insured by the Federal Savings and Loan Insurance Corporation (FSLIC), which was funded by the S&L industry and backed by the government.

The 1970s were challenging times for S&Ls. They lost depositors to money-market funds, which offered higher interest rates and, therefore, better protection from inflation. The Fed's disinflationary policies between 1979 and 1981 raised money-market interest rates further and added to the flow of depositors moving away from S&Ls. Mortgage loans, however, had stalled in the slowing economy. At the beginning of the 1980s many S&Ls were on the verge of insolvency, and the FSLIC itself was shaky due to undercapitalization. The solution to S&L issues, sanctioned by the administration and Congress, was to "grow out of their problems" and evolve into viable institutions by expanding deposits, making higher-return investments, and improving their revenue stream. The turning points for the fortunes of S&Ls were the passing of the Depository Institutions Acts of 1980 and 1982 and the Tax Act of 1981, which altered how thrifts conducted business on both sides of the balance sheet, reduced capital requirements from 5 percent to 3 percent, and created a seemingly more favorable environment.

On the asset side of the balance sheet growth required significant changes in the size and composition of thrifts' investment portfolios. It involved, first, making more fixed-rate loans at the high interest rates of the early 1980s. Provided that short-term interest rates declined quickly and the loan-deposit interest-rate differential widened, the strategy would have improved earnings. Second, an expanding share of adjustable-rate mortgages (ARMs) permitted thrifts to offer mortgage rates that varied with overall credit conditions. Third, S&Ls expanded their lending authority beyond residential mortgages to property deals and commercial real estate.

The new banking legislation also permitted the federally chartered S&Ls to invest in corporate bonds. S&Ls took advantage of this change by investing heavily in junk bonds, which offered higher yields. In response to the federal legislation California, Texas, and Florida passed legislation that removed state-level restrictions, which allowed state-chartered S&Ls to expand the scope of their investments. Changes in federal tax laws encouraged investment in real estate, contributed to the coming building boom, and thereby expanded the thrift loan market.

On the liability side of the balance sheet legislative changes helped to attract more depositors by removing Regulation Q, which had capped the deposit-interest rate, and by raising the insurance limit on individual deposits to $100,000, albeit without a corresponding increase in deposit-insurance premiums. Thrifts also grew less dependent on local customers. They increasingly borrowed funds wholesale from Wall Street deposit brokers, who gathered funds from corporations and rich customers, divided them into appropriately smaller sizes, and channeled them to thrifts to take advantage of higher rates of interest and deposit insurance.

Changes in laws and regulations amounted to the government adopting the strategy of *forbearance* vis-à-vis thrifts. The government authorized lenient accounting rules that allowed companies to inflate profits and hide losses. Thrifts were permitted to report anticipated earnings on real-estate investments on balance sheets as though they were already realized. They were also able to defer reporting losses from sales of bad loans.

The government offered additional incentives to the larger S&Ls to acquire insolvent institutions in anticipation of freeing the FSLIC from making deposit-insurance payments. For instance, suppose that a failing thrift has deposits of $5b that are not backed by reserves or other assets. After the merger this liability would be passed on to the acquirer and reduce its net worth by the same amount. To assist the merger regulators "handed" $5b of paper assets—called *supervisory goodwill*—to the acquiring institution. Supervisory goodwill was counted as an asset, amortized over as long as 40 years. The net worth of the acquiring firm was now unchanged, but it was in a position to expand loans and profits from a larger deposit base. Supervisory goodwill created the impression that the balance sheet of the S&L industry was more robust than it had actually been.

Due to these incentives more thrifts entered the market and larger S&Ls were created, albeit with precarious capital bases and often with minimal management experience. Thrifts invested substantial amounts of their new funds in high-risk-high-return development projects, both as loans and direct equity. Bad loans were often sold without the company showing losses, and the proceeds were invested in seemingly profitable projects. Making loans to and taking equity positions in the same real-estate-development projects limited diversification and exposed thrifts to magnified risk. In the meantime incompetence and corruption were widespread, and some S&L executives appropriated company funds for their own use.

While deregulation of thrifts proceeded, underfunding and understaffing weakened the powers of its regulator, the Bank Board. The number of inspectors and supervisors was reduced, and examination of thrifts' activities became less frequent. Edwin Gray, previously an anti-regulation advocate, became the chair of the Bank Board in 1983. Once in office he was alarmed by the aggressive lending practices of S&Ls and, after 1985, attempted to re-regulate the industry by limiting non-mortgage loans and direct-equity investment, increasing capital requirements, and recapitalizing the deposit-insurance fund. He also proposed a thorough examination of thrift loans (Black 2005). His efforts were met with strong opposition in both the executive and legislative branches of government. The policymakers concurred with the private experts they consulted, including Alan Greenspan, then a private consultant, who preached that markets were capable of regulating themselves through competition and did not need outsiders to set and enforce rules. Directors of the largest thrifts were well connected in Washington, and politicians often intervened against regulation on their behalf rather than looking after the public interest.

Akerlof and Romer (1993) attribute the S&L debacle to "looting." The environment of lax regulation, lenient accounting, low penalties, and government-guaranteed deposit insurance created perverse incentives for executives to extract as much value as possible for themselves and then to default on their obligations. According to Black (2005), most S&Ls were insolvent but stayed afloat by running Ponzi schemes, thanks to the funds from deposit brokers and an acquiescent government. By the mid 1980s there was turmoil in the financial landscape. Empire Savings of Mesquite,

Texas, failed in March 1984. After Home State Savings Bank of Cincinnati failed in March 1985 the governor of Ohio, facing the depletion of the state deposit-insurance fund, closed state-chartered Ohio S&Ls. Maryland followed in May 1985. The ultimate implosion occurred a few years later.

Options pricing and portfolio insurance

The efficient-market hypothesis (EMH) made inroads on Wall Street in the early 1970s. The leading promoter of the theory was Princeton University economics professor and investment advisor Burton G. Malkiel, whose book *A Random Walk Down Wall Street* was first published in 1973 and is now in its tenth edition, having sold more than a million copies. The book promoted the EMH among professionals and investors, criticized value analysis and chartist investment strategies, and offered investment advice to the masses.

Wall Street professionals were fond of two implications of the theory. First, the EMH made a strong case that the proliferation of financial instruments and the growth in the volume of transactions improve the market's informational efficiency, validating what was to become the largest source of fees for investment banks, brokers, and dealers. Second, the EMH effectively stated that government regulation is unnecessary. If the market ensures that the fundamental asset price will prevail then an external regulator was a needless cost and burden. Worse, external regulations were harmful because they distorted markets and hurt innovations. Beyond these points of agreement, most traditional Wall Street professionals looked down upon the EMH as ivory-tower theorizing with little relevance to how markets really worked, rejected the implication that stock picking is a futile exercise, and viewed academics as poor investors. However, academics were prepared to make their mark on the practical side of finance. They started in the 1980s with options pricing and portfolio insurance.

The Black–Scholes–Merton model of options pricing

Options as instruments to protect portfolio value from unfavorable future price movements have existed for decades. To review, an option is a financial derivative through which an investor buys the right to buy (*call option*) or sell (*put option*) an asset at a predetermined price (*strike price*) before or at the option's expiration date. Options are important in financial markets because they offer a means to investors to insure the value of their assets against unfavorable fluctuations in price. A portfolio holder who is concerned about a possible drop in the value of a stock she holds, for instance, can buy protection in the form of a put option. In the event the price drops below the strike price she would exercise the option by selling the stock and limiting her losses. If the market price remains above the strike price then she would not exercise the option. Her only loss would be the price paid for the option. The put option locks in a cash position and transfers the risk of a decline in the value of an asset to the counterparty. For much of their history option transactions were over-the-counter (OTC), bilateral exchanges designed to the specifications of the counterparties. The trading of standardized (and, therefore, less costly and more liquid) options was instituted in the Chicago Board of Options Exchange in 1973. After 2003 the New York-based electronic International Securities Exchange became the largest market where standardized options could be traded at any point before the expiration date.

A practical formula that expresses the "fair" value of an option as a function of a set of observable variables had long been the holy grail of financial economics. The problem was that while the list of factors that influences the option price was common knowledge the values of some of the variables were unobservable, and, therefore, an operational theory of option-price determination could not be formulated. The discovery of the formula was not just an academic exercise. Knowing the true worth of an option would enhance portfolio holders' ability to manage risk, use option instruments more confidently, and, therefore, expand investing in securities (and other derivatives). Bachelier himself attempted to answer the question of fair option value in his dissertation. Edward Thorp, a University of California–Irvine mathematics professor (who, among other things, developed and published a winning strategy in blackjack), had discovered heuristic option-pricing rules in the 1960s and made a substantial fortune by putting them into practice in the hedge fund he managed. However, he did not publicize his methods, and heuristic rules would likely not have satisfied the academic economist's criteria of theoretical rigor.

The solution that satisfied the penchant of academic financial economists for foundational axiomatic postulates and mathematical elegance arrived in 1973 with the publication of Fisher Black and Myron Scholes' groundbreaking article on options pricing, and Robert Merton's refinement and extension of their work in another article (Black and Scholes 1973; Merton 1973). These two articles set the stage for the quantitative finance revolution that took hold of Wall Street in the coming decades. The Black–Scholes–Merton (BSM) option-pricing model came to be considered, in company with the Pythagorean theorem and Einstein's theory of special relativity, as one of the ten equations that changed the world. The mathematics of the model is complex, but for the present purposes an elementary understanding of the BSM solution and an appreciation of its implications will suffice.

To simplify the exposition suppose that an option can be exercised only on the expiration date,[5] the underlying stock does not pay any dividends before the expiration date, and the safe interest rate is zero. Two observations can be made. First, the call (put) option will not be exercised if the stock price turns out to be lower (higher) than the strike price. Thus, the value of the option is related to where the market price is expected to be relative to the strike price at the time of expiration. The greater the likelihood that the market price of the underlying stock at the time of expiration will be above (below) the strike price, the higher the price of the call (put) option. If the expected price of the underlying stock at the expiration date is less (more) than the strike price then the value of the call (put) option is zero.

The key variable, then, in determining the price that an option buyer would be willing to pay is the expected spot price on the date of expiration. However, the fact that this variable is not observable is an obstacle for researchers. The BSM model shows that this problem can be circumvented by neutralizing the risk associated with the uncertainty of the future spot price. The first step is to identify the observable variables that influence the future spot value of the stock and, thus, the option price.

Under the simplifying assumptions made above these variables and their effects on the call-option price are as follows. First, if the current value of the underlying stock rises, ceteris paribus, it becomes more likely that the market price on the expiration date will be above the strike price, and, therefore, the value of the option increases. Second, the lower the strike price, the higher the value of the call option because of the higher probability of the stock price being above the strike price on the expiration date. Third, the longer the time that remains until the expiration date, the higher the value of the option because the chances of a favorable (rising) price movement are higher. These three variables are readily observable. The fourth variable, however, is not. It is the expected volatility of the underlying stock price over the life of the option. The higher the volatility of the underlying asset, the greater the chance that the asset price will be higher than the strike price and, therefore, the more valuable the option will be. Typically, researchers measure volatility as the standard deviation of historical stock prices and assume that this value will remain unchanged in the future.[6]

For the next step the BSM model uses arbitrage principles to derive an equation whereby the theoretical fair price of an option is determined as a function of only the four observed, or proxied, variables listed above (plus other observable variables in more complex versions of the model). The intuition behind the formula is as follows. If the market price of the stock is higher than the strike price at the expiration date the pay-off for holding a call option is the difference between the two prices; otherwise, it is zero. Given the first four variables listed above, BSM shows that it is possible to create a hypothetical portfolio in the underlying stock, partially funded by borrowing, which replicates the option's pay-off.[7] The important point is that, in a frictionless market with unrestricted arbitrage, the two pay-offs should be identical.

The no-arbitrage condition then implies that the fair price of the option should be equal to the cost of creating the hypothetical replicating portfolio. To understand why consider the following exercise. Suppose that the market price of the call option happens to be higher than the cost of the replicating portfolio. Investors will then make riskless arbitrage profits by selling call options and buying shares in the underlying stock of the hypothetical portfolio, which will lower the market price of the option. Conversely, if the market price is less than the fair price then arbitrage dictates that investors should buy call options and sell short shares of the underlying stock. The fair option price is settled when arbitrage profits vanish or the call-option price is the same as the cost of the replicating portfolio. The BSM model was an impressive feat because it demonstrated that expected changes in the underlying asset price, which had baffled earlier researchers for decades, had no relation to the fair option price.

To appreciate the insights of the BSM model next note that, during the option's lifetime, the price of the underlying stock changes constantly. Therefore, the price of the option should change continuously as well. The BSM formula's fair option price mirrors the adjustments in the replicating portfolio as the latter responds to changing market conditions. BSM referred to these adjustments as *dynamic hedging*; investors can eliminate their exposure to risk on a continuous basis by trading in options at their fair value.

It is worth pointing out that the BSM formula was derived under restrictive assumptions, some of which have serious consequences if violated. First, the volatility of the stock price, estimated as the standard deviation of past price behavior, is assumed to be constant and known with certainty. Second, it is assumed that (the logarithm of) the stock price over the remaining life of the option follows a normally distributed random walk, so there will be no extreme changes in the value of the stock. These assumptions are common features of standard financial models. As mentioned in the last chapter, however, historical evidence suggests that there are reasons to question the validity of these assumptions.

From a theoretical perspective the BSM formula was influential because its basic principles, such as replicating portfolios, were applicable in various other contexts. On the practical side the importance of the BSM formula was that it determined the fair price at which investors could virtually eliminate risk by hedging their positions via derivatives contracts. The trader or investor could now compute the fair price of an option simply by plugging the values of the relevant variables into a financial calculator. This innovation promised to bring in multitudes of new investors who had previously been concerned about risk, and to deepen financial markets. It also helped the flourishing of multitudes of new types of derivatives, such as options of futures (or derivatives on derivatives), that could be used in managing risk.

The adoption of the BSM model by practitioners at the exchanges and the proliferation of its applications as a risk-management tool signaled the surge of quantitative finance on Wall Street. More than anyone else, mathematicians, physicists, and software programmers were endowed with the mathematical, statistical, and technical skills necessary to carry out the tasks of constructing and replicating portfolios and writing the computer algorithms. A new breed of trader, quantitative analysts, or *quants*, who based investment decisions on mathematical and statistical models, and a new branch of engineering, financial engineering, emerged. In the meantime new exchanges, communication networks, data processing power, and software development facilitated the application of theory in daily practice. For the old-timers mathematical models of finance were too elegant, precise, sanitized, and oblivious to the "feel of the market," which they believed was the more important factor in ascertaining the direction that prices were moving. Nonetheless, mathematical finance came to dominate both the theory and the practice as derivatives flourished in the 1980s.

Portfolio insurance

The purchase of a put option on an asset functions as "insurance" by locking in a cash position in the event that the price of the asset falls below the strike price and, thereby, limits the owner's loss. For institutional investors with complex and diverse portfolios, however, the purchase of put options for each item in the portfolio is an unwieldy task. The need for *portfolio insurance* arose from the lack of adequate put options for diversified portfolios. In 1976 Hayne E. Leland and Mark Rubinstein, professors of finance at the University of California–Berkeley, found a solution to this problem. The BSM model used the arbitrage argument to price existing options; Leland and Rubinstein turned the arbitrage argument around to create option substitutes where options did not exist. Their solution consisted of replicating the put option by creating a synthetic portfolio composed of stocks and riskless assets. If the portfolio manager of a pension fund is concerned about the declining stock market she can limit future losses by readjusting (dynamically hedging) the composition of the synthetic portfolio in line with changing market conditions, or, basically, selling the synthetic portfolio short (Leland and Rubinstein 1988).

In 1981 Leland O'Brien Rubinstein Associates (LOR) began to sell portfolio insurance to institutional investors. In practice the creation of such portfolios required financial engineers' mathematical, statistical, and programming expertise. LOR not only innovated and developed the expertise but also, by their own account, shared knowledge with their competitors. Portfolio insurance was simplified after exchanges started to trade stock-index-futures contracts after 1982 and index options after 1983. Pension funds could now hedge their positions by trading index-futures contracts or index-option equivalents of its portfolio. As the microprocessor and communications technology advanced, portfolio adjustment was increasingly left to *program trading*, whereby computers made buy and sell decisions automatically in response to new incoming data. By 1987 the size of the portfolio-insurance industry exceeded $90b.

What LOR and others were selling was not insurance but a portfolio-management strategy that was simple in principle, i.e. if the value of the portfolio is going down get out of the market to minimize losses, but highly sophisticated and, allegedly, precise in execution. This strategy implied that the higher the amplitude of stock-price fluctuations, the more stock-index futures or options are traded. One concern regarding portfolio insurance was the relationship between market volatility and dynamic hedging. As in the BSM model, portfolio insurance assumed that volatility is constant and known with certainty. This assumption amounted to stating that portfolio-insurance transactions do not influence market volatility. If the size of these investors and the volume of their transactions are small relative to the size of the market then the assumption would be plausible; there would always be sufficient liquidity in the market, and portfolio insurance would work. However, when the volume is large relative to the size of the market, due to the large size of institutional portfolio-insurance investors or the interdependence of their actions, then portfolio insurance adds to the momentum of price fluctuations and exacerbates price collapses. When simultaneous sales precipitate sharp price falls buyers and liquidity may disappear. Warren Buffet, a prominent critic of this feature of portfolio insurance, stated the following in his annual letter to Berkshire Hathaway, Inc. shareholders after the October 1987 crash:

> Portfolio insurance [is] a money-management strategy that many leading investment advisors embraced in 1986–1987. This strategy—which is simply an exotically-labeled version of the small speculator's stop-loss order—dictates that ever increasing portions of a stock portfolio, or their index-future equivalents, be sold as prices decline. . . . The less these companies are being valued at, says this approach, the more vigorously they should be sold. As a "logical" corollary, the approach commands the institutions to repurchase these companies—*I'm not making this up*—once their prices have rebounded significantly. Considering that huge sums are controlled by managers following such Alice-in-Wonderland practices, is it any surprise that markets sometimes behave in aberrational fashion?
>
> (Buffett 1987)

Index arbitrage

Another type of program trading that became common in the 1980s, due to the emergence of index futures markets, was *index arbitrage*. The CME began to trade S&P 500 index-futures contracts in 1982 and Major Market

Index-futures contracts in 1984. Theoretically, the futures price of an index is expected to reflect the current information on the fundamentals and, therefore, be equal to the current price (adjusted for time and transaction costs). Any difference between the current and futures price indices offers arbitrage opportunities. If the observed futures price of the index is higher than the current price, for instance, arbitrageurs can profit by simultaneously buying the stocks in the index in the current market and selling stock-index futures. This activity, of course, is expected to align the current and futures stock-price indices and stabilize the system.

Computer technology enabled automatic execution of index arbitrage. Investors' computers were programmed to take offsetting positions on stocks and index futures whenever a discrepancy arose between the prices of a stock index and its futures index. Their computers, in turn, were linked to traders' computers. As soon as a market signal arrived at investors' computers the trade was executed automatically.

The futures exchanges took place in the CME, and the current exchanges occurred in New York. Prices were expected to line up in the two centers through the actions of arbitrageurs. If large sales in the CME pushed futures prices below current prices, for instance, index arbitrageurs would buy futures-index contracts in Chicago and sell stocks in New York, which would correct the discrepancy. At least, that was what the academics believed. The seasoned professionals were more circumspect.

The crash of 1987

On October 19, 1987, the US stock market experienced the largest one-day drop in its history. On Black Monday the S&P 500 dropped by 20.5 percent, the DJIA dropped by 22.6 percent, and the number of shares traded exceeded the typical volume by an order of more than three. On October 19 and 20 stock markets in Western Europe and the Far East declined by sharp margins as well. It was a bewildering incident and its magnitude caught many by surprise.[8]

What happened?

Figure 13.2 presents the daily nominal S&P 500 closing prices in 1987. The daily index exhibited an impressive 32 percent rise from the beginning of the year until late August and then stalled. The price index was basically flat throughout September, with alternating drops and rallies. Perhaps the most important news during this period was the Fed's announcement of higher interest rates on September 4 under its new helmsman, Alan Greenspan, who had replaced Paul Volcker in August. While the Fed's concern regarding inflation and higher interest rates might have signaled a future slowdown of the economy, there was no perceptible adverse effect on the stock market in September.

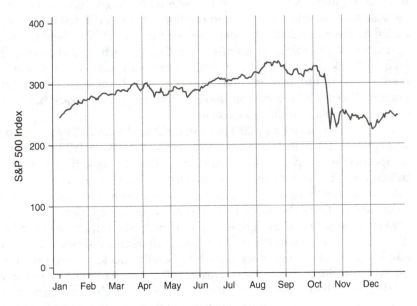

Figure 13.2 Nominal S&P 500, 1987 (daily).

Source: S&P Dow Jones indices.

The slide started during the first week of October. European countries had increased interest rates, and there was conversation regarding the possibility of the Fed doing the same. Some US banks had, indeed, increased their prime rates. On Wednesday, October 14, the Department of Commerce announced that the August trade deficit was higher than previously expected, although still lower than that of the previous month. On the same day a bill to discontinue tax breaks for LBOs was introduced to the House Ways and Means Committee. An incident that might have increased political uncertainty and anxiety was an Iranian missile attack on a US-owned tanker in the Persian Gulf on Friday, October 16, but the US did not respond because the tanker was not in international waters and did not carry the US flag. Between Monday, October 5, and Friday, October 9, 1987, the S&P 500 declined by 5.2 percent; by the end of the following week it had declined by another 8.6 percent.

On Monday, October 19, stock prices were lower in the Far East and European stock markets. The New York Stock Exchange (NYSE) also started the day with low prices and few bids. When the CME opened there was very heavy selling of futures contracts, which caused futures-index prices to drop. One might have expected that index arbitrage would have slowed the drop in futures prices, as arbitrageurs would purchase futures in Chicago and sell current stocks in NYSE, but the situation was too volatile, and both futures and spot stock prices continued to slide. Moreover, the futures index and the stock markets increasingly fell out of synch because the execution of trades on the floor of the NYSE fell behind and added to the confusion. Disorder prevailed in the NYSE, where the floor specialists were unable to find buyers for the avalanche of sell orders. The lagging stock ticker failed to provide timely information on where the market stood, and brokers and dealers stopped answering their telephones. The exit of the market makers from the system exacerbated illiquidity and added to the price collapse.[9]

The S&P 500 plunged by 20.5 percent on Black Monday. The magnitude was approximately the same as that of the October 28–29, 1929, drop—and comparison of the two incidents was inevitable. The question of whether this could be the start of another Great Depression was foremost on everyone's mind, but there were, surprisingly, no notable adverse repercussions in the real sector of the economy in the subsequent weeks and months.

Many things could have gone wrong in the credit market afterward but did not. On the demand side of the credit market the shock could have amplified effects if investors who had bought stocks on margin were forced to produce cash to meet margin calls, if market makers and stock mutual funds had needed credit to meet their clients' demands, and if risk arbitrageurs who had purchased stocks with debt had had to meet their obligations. The supply side also would have been in crisis if lenders who faced higher uncertainty and declining collateral values had stopped extending credit and called in loans to boost their reserves. In the absence of liquidity borrowers would have been forced to sell their assets and deepen the market collapse. But none of these events occurred. It was auspicious that the crash did not take place during a period of distress or of heightened caution among lenders.

Moreover, the Fed alleviated the anxiety in credit markets by promptly increasing the supply of money and lowering interest rates. Alan Greenspan had great confidence in self-stabilizing markets, but, by his own account, he was a student of the history of financial crises. He knew how investors' declining confidence could easily transform into a self-feeding panic and credit freeze. The Fed publicly announced to banks that they would have access to as much liquidity as they needed to avoid a panic and a halting of interbank lending, and to speed up the return to normalcy. The Fed also privately advised some bankers that by continuing their regular business of lending and making payments they would serve both the public and their individual interests (Greenspan 2008: 106–8).

Another reason for the lack of repercussions could be the limited effect of the crash on aggregate demand for goods and services. A stock-market crash and the destruction of wealth may affect the real sector through its impact on household-consumption expenditures, and a large drop in spending may lead to the contraction of production and lay-offs. However, while the magnitude of the loss of net worth (approximately $750b–$1,000b) was substantial, its effect on consumption was relatively small, estimated at around \$30b–\$70b, or about 1 percent to 2 percent of consumption spending (Feldstein *et al.* 1988).

Unlike the October 1929 crash, stock prices did not continue to decline in the following months. Many corporations bought their own shares in large quantities, which suggests that they considered their stocks to be underpriced. Stock prices remained low and turbulent but the downward trend did not continue. Real output grew at an increased pace throughout 1988, and, soon, the crash of 1987 was deemed a nonevent—though it was still a mystery that required an explanation.

Why did the market crash?

The 1987 crash baffled professionals, politicians, and academics because none of the news of the preceding weeks was novel or substantial enough to alter expectations of earnings flows, cause a two-week slide in stock prices, and initiate a dramatic sell-off (Schwert 1992). Shiller (2005) surveyed approximately 900 institutional and private investors immediately after the crash and asked them to identify the news that preoccupied them prior to the crash. The responses indicate that there was no single piece of news that made the investors excessively anxious about earnings flows or created expectations of market collapse.

The Reagan administration assigned to the Brady Commission the task of determining the underlying cause of Black Monday. The commission report recounted the news mentioned above as the triggers of the crash and singled out computerized trading mechanisms, specifically, portfolio insurance, as the primary source that propagated and amplified the price shock. Program trading remained a popular explanation of the crash in the media, and the exchanges later adopted the Brady Commission's recommendation of creating *circuit breakers* to prevent panic selling. The circuit breaker, also known as collar and price limit, is designed to suspend trading temporarily when the price index drops by a certain amount during a certain period to allow for disorder and confusion to subside, to give participants a chance to assess the state of the market calmly, and, hopefully, to restore stability.[10]

Economists concurred that computerized trading mechanisms may have added to the confusion and volatility but did not consider their role as central. Roll (1988) points out that the collapse was worldwide, while program trading was characteristic of US markets. Shiller (2005) views program trading as merely another feedback mechanism that magnified the price collapse, but not as the primary culprit.

From an economist's perspective the primary question regarding why the crash occurred is whether stocks were overpriced before October 1987. Most economists believe that stocks were overpriced from 1986 onward but disagree on the magnitude. Assessments vary with the version of the

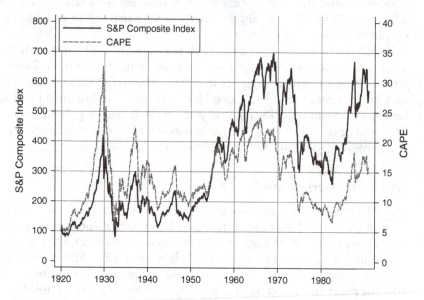

Figure 13.3 Real S&P Composite Index and CAPE, 1920–90 (monthly).
Source: Shiller (2005).

P/E ratio used. According to Schwert (1992), it was approximately 37, the highest value observed since 1926. The Campbell–Shiller cyclically adjusted P/E (CAPE) from 1920 to 1990, shown in Figure 13.3, indicates that the value was around 18, only moderately higher than the long-term norm of 15. Higher figures had been observed in the 1960s without subsequent crashes.

Perhaps the more interesting question is investors' perception of stock prices prior to the crash, or whether there were reasons for them to anticipate a crash. Bates (1991) compares the put- and call-option prices over 1985–7 and finds that, during much of this period, put options were more highly valued than call options, which suggests that stocks were considered overpriced. However, this relationship held only until August 1987 and not after. This evidence does not strongly suggest that the market was expecting a downturn. In response to Shiller's (2005) questionnaire most investors said they believed that the market was overpriced, but Shiller discounts the response as an ex-post statement that exhibits hindsight bias.

Among the fervent supporters of the EMH, French (1988) argues that the fundamentals of earnings expectations and discount rates cannot explain the 1987 crash. He states that stocks were overpriced and that a correction was in order. While French's explanation for mispricing may be categorized as an intrinsic bubble, like most others who favor fundamentals-based approaches he prefers to call it a pricing mistake rather than a bubble. He believes that the market was overpriced due to investors' misperceptions. Each investor's information set consisted of two components: information on prices and trade volumes observed publicly by everyone, and each investor's private information about share values. French claims that, in estimating the value of stocks during the boom months leading to October 1987, investors put too much weight on the optimistic first component of the information set and too little weight on the more cautious second component, or their own assessments. The correction occurred when investors revised their market evaluation in view of the seemingly small adverse news of October that validated the private information and shifted the weights. Moreover, the price declines of the previous days also revealed to each investor that other investors were re-evaluating the fundamentals downward. The outcome was the sharp drop in the stock market.

Another version of the EMH-mispricing argument comes from Black (1988). His explanation has two salient features. First, a higher market and increasing financial wealth increase investors' penchant for risk. Second, the market price fluctuates around the fundamental value and is "mean-reverting": that is, if it rises above the fundamental value it falls back down. However, it is difficult to judge how far the price needs to drop to reach the fundamental value because the latter is unobservable. According to Black, during the months of stock-market boom before October 1987 investors took on more risk and price volatility increased. Jointly, these factors require investors to increase the magnitude of their expected mean reversion. However, until October, investors underestimated the actual mean reversion that would return stock prices to the fundamental equilibrium. Put differently, investors overestimated the market returns, and the market price deviated upward from its proper level. The time of reckoning came when the stock market started sliding in early October in response to the disruptive news widely publicized in the press. The triggering event was the very large blocks of stocks put up for sale by portfolio insurers on October 19 following the news of the previous week. Investors who received this new piece of information, in addition to the turbulence of the previous two weeks, reasoned that the fundamental price was overestimated. When they began to sell the collapse occurred.

Feldstein *et al.* (1988) also attribute the crash to a market correction warranted by the changing fundamentals, such as the trade surplus, the Fed's interest-rate hike, and so forth. The common theme is that investors made mistakes of some combination of overestimating the earnings growth and underestimating inflation-corrected interest rates, which led to the overvaluation of assets. Further, there was market nervousness due to questions regarding the unfamiliar consequences of portfolio insurance during a market shakedown. When adverse news on the fundamentals finally arrived these mistakes were recognized, and a market correction followed. From this perspective—the mainstream perspective—the October crash offered supporting evidence to the argument that stock prices are driven by the fundamentals, albeit with possible temporary deviations.

Shiller's (2005) explanation stems from the behavioralist end of the spectrum and views the incident as a negative bubble. Judging by the CAPE ratio, stocks were not significantly overvalued, but the magnitude of the collapse was enormous. The results of the questionnaires indicate that the utmost concern of the investors on the morning of October 19 was not any specific news that would affect the stock prices but the perception of market anxiety over declining prices. Shiller attributes the pessimism in the market in part to the pre-crash stories in the business press that drew parallels between October 1929 and October 1987. Shiller's interpretation of the cause of the 1987 crash is that it was the outcome of a negative psychological price-to-price feedback loop. Investors sold stocks due to their perceptions of other investors' nervousness; price declines induced even more investors to sell stocks. Program trading in this context played an important role by changing the nature of the feedback loop, enabling investors to pursue more aggressive, faster-response trading strategies. The key to what happened was the investors who contemplated the rising likelihood of a crash.

Another take on portfolio insurance and index arbitrage emphasizes not the mechanics of these trades but their effects in terms of transforming the time horizons of market participants. Decades earlier Keynes had warned about investors in modern markets being more occupied with short-term profit opportunities than long-term investment, income, and capital accumulation. Technological innovations facilitated faster and larger volume trades to exploit profit opportunities originating in price differentials. These actions not only raised markets' short-term bias but made them more unstable. Warren Buffett wrote on the 1987 crash:

> We have "professional" investors, those who manage many billions, to thank for most of this turmoil. Instead of focusing on what businesses will do in the years ahead, many prestigious money managers now focus on what they expect other money managers to do in the days ahead. For them, stocks are merely tokens in a game, like the thimble and flatiron in Monopoly.
>
> (Buffett 1987)

The end of the decade

The year 1987 was the decade's turning point. Not only did the stock market collapse but the takeover movement that was fed by junk bonds came to an end, S&Ls imploded, and their depositors were saved by a massive government bailout.

Unraveling of junk bonds and leveraged buyouts

Junk bonds gained notoriety when prominent people associated with their issuance and distribution were tarnished by scandals. In May 1986 the SEC brought insider-trading charges against a Drexler employee, Dennis Levine. Levine implicated Ivan Boesky among others, and the probe, led by the US Attorney's Office, widened. Boesky, in turn, cooperated with the investigation and implicated Michael Milken. The SEC charged Drexler with securities violations in 1988, and the US Attorney's Office started to investigate Drexler under the Racketeer Influenced and Corrupt Organizations (RICO) Act, which until then was used to prosecute organized crime. In the meantime Drexler's situation became more precarious when its internal investigation of Milken's high-yield activities discovered kickbacks, bribes, and failures in fulfilling fiduciary responsibilities to customers. Drexler settled the criminal and SEC charges in 1989, and agreed to pay $650m in fines. A grand jury indicted Milken for fraud and racketeering in March 1989. In April 1990 Milken pleaded guilty to securities and tax violations and was sentenced to ten years in prison (later reduced to two) and paid fines totaling $600m. Boesky was sentenced to three and a half years in prison and a $100m fine.

The LBO activity financed by junk bonds continued for a while longer. In the midst of all its legal troubles Drexler supported the RJR Nabisco takeover by selling $5b worth of junk bonds. The insider-trading and corruption scandals that put Boesky, Milken, and others in prison harmed the reputation of the junk-bond industry, but the successful run of junk bonds was coming to an end for other reasons. Investors recognized that in terms of risk these bonds were like stocks. Stock prices vary with earnings and are, therefore, more volatile than bond prices. Junk-bond prices were similarly highly variable because adverse earnings promptly raised the possibility of default and borrowing costs for firms that rested on unsteady financial foundations. Investors reasoned that junk bonds were riskier than advertised and that their risk-adjusted returns did not outperform investment-grade bonds. The demand declined and the heyday of junk bonds came to an end. Drexler filed for bankruptcy in 1990.

Legal problems, S&L troubles, the mounting debt burden of the many acquired companies, and the Fed's raising of the interest rate after 1989 added to the decline of the LBO movement. As earnings dropped and interest rates increased, the LBO companies faced greater challenges in meeting debt obligations and raising finance. Some fought against the tide by issuing zero-coupon bonds and in-kind payments. Moreover, the quality of takeovers was decreasing, and some late LBOs were blatantly nonsensical. The most publicized example is the purchase of Allied Stores and Federated Department Stores (which owned, among others,

Bloomingdales) in 1986 by Robert Campeau, a Canadian real-estate developer with no experience in retail business, for a total of $10.1b in what was called the "biggest, looniest deal ever," all financed by junk bonds (Fortune 1990). The combination of high debt and slowdown in the retail business forced this once profitable group of companies to file for bankruptcy protection in January 1990.

The S&L implosion

After 1986 the S&L problems grew in size, and the losses of insolvent thrifts became more difficult to hide. In January 1987 the FSLIC was almost $4b in the red. The unsustainable situation finally collapsed when the price of crude oil fell 50 percent, which sent the Texas commercial-real-estate market into a tailspin. As property values and rental income declined and vacancy rates increased, the quality of loans that thrifts extended to developers, as well as the quality of equity they held in real estate, deteriorated. More than half of the nationwide S&L losses in 1987 occurred in Texas.

Throughout 1988 the Bank Board attempted to avert the spread of the crisis by consolidating and putting the insolvent S&Ls up for sale; they were able to sell approximately 200 S&Ls institutions. Finally, the Bush administration and Congress passed the Financial Institutions Reform, Recovery, and Enforcement Act of 1989, which established the Resolution Trust Corporation to liquidate insolvent thrifts and provide funds to pay depositors. The total cost of the federal bailouts to the taxpayers was $124b by the end of 1999, after assets of the failed banks were fully disposed. According to one estimate, looting and fraud in thrifts at least doubled the cost of the bailout (Akerlof and Romer 1993). The Department of Justice convicted many S&L executives, and some served prison sentences.

The legacy of the 1980s

The 1980s was a turbulent decade, but it did not end with a cautionary note about the excesses of financial markets. Quite the opposite. The forces that were unleashed gained momentum and led the way to an even more extravagant 25 years as the relative size of the financial sector continued to grow. The junk-bond wave ended, but other types of fixed-income investments rose to prominence. The most important was securitization, or issuance of bonds, backed by the cash flow of mortgage, automobile, student, and credit-card loans. Securitization permitted the widespread trading of previously illiquid loans and thereby expanded the supply of debt instruments. While these bonds initially did not attract as much attention as junk bonds, they later turned into collateralized debt obligations (CDOs) and played a central role in the subprime-mortgage crisis of

2007–8. Portfolio insurance was discredited, but financial engineering had dug its roots deep. Exotic, engineered derivatives that allegedly increased liquidity and helped risk management proliferated. Most experts hailed these financial instruments for widening and deepening the markets and contributing to the expansion of productive capacity and welfare.

After the 1980s the promise of riches and widespread use of quantitative techniques attracted many of the best brains with the requisite statistical, mathematical, and programming expertise to Wall Street. The quants rose to prominence here because the skill set needed to create derivatives was not the old-style, first-hand market experience but the knowledge of stochastic properties of prices and the technical knowledge to create synthetic portfolios, swaps, and such. There were skeptics who noted that these derivatives were more likely to play a destabilizing role as instruments of speculation. In the midst of the celebration of wealth creation, however, they were dismissed in policymaking circles, media, and academia.

The 1980s was a transformative decade that set the cultural tone of the following period. Music videos, television soaps, and magazine programs were saturated with fascination with wealth. The signature phrase of one show, "champagne wishes and caviar dreams," summed up the spirit of the times. There was also critical social commentary on the financial markets. The lives and times of the 1980s bond traders, i.e. the "masters of the universe" and "big swinging dicks," were chronicled derisively in Oliver Stone's feature film *Wall Street,* Tom Wolfe's (1987) *The Bonfire of the Vanities,* and Michael Lewis' (1989) autobiographical *Liar's Poker.* If these works were intended as morality tales about the excesses of the financial market they failed; these unflattering portraits did not turn away potential recruits from Wall Street. Lewis (2009: xv) was surprised to discover that college seniors read his account of the daily routine of arrogant, unscrupulous, and infantile traders as a "how-to manual" to secure careers on Wall Street.

Nor did the financial misadventures of the 1980s raise questions about the adverse consequences of deregulation. Not only were financial firms increasingly permitted to engage in activities that were banned as late as the 1970s, but the scope of these activities widened throughout the 1990s. Politicians, when they were not dismantling regulations outright, directed regulatory agencies to be more lenient in their enforcement and cut their budgets and supervisory powers to ensure that these directives were followed. Thus, the turbulence of the 1980s did not plant any doubt in the minds of experts and policymakers regarding the efficiency and self-regulating capacity of markets. The fact that the real economy escaped serious problems following the financial crisis was taken as a sign of the resilience of the economy (Greenspan 2008: 110).

It is also interesting that the discovery of insider trading, price manipulation, and fraud did not result in mistrust of the self-disciplining powers of the market. There were three alternative views on the corruption and fraud scandals: the protagonists, some of whom ended up in prison, were either victims of overzealous regulators or attorneys, rotten apples in an otherwise well functioning financial system, or products of a reckless financial system in which money was the measure of everything. The first view blames the government and the regulators for gratuitously intruding into the S&L industry and junk bonds, vindictively targeting institutions and individuals and turning them into scapegoats. Charles Keating Jr., imprisoned chief executive of the Lincoln Savings and Loan, which cost taxpayers between $2b and $3.4b, sued the government for destroying his corporation and personal fortune. The second perspective does not whitewash the illicit practices but treats corruption and fraud as individual failures. These illegal activities may have been abetted by looser regulations and lax enforcement but blame rests on the corrupt and fraudulent individuals, and their actions are not manifestations of structural flaws of the financial industry. The third approach views the preponderance of illegal and unethical behavior as symptomatic of the changing nature of the financial system. Governance at the national and corporate levels sets the rules of competition as well as the means of its implementation, i.e. laws, social sanctions, and customs. These rules state, for instance, that an investment bank has a fiduciary responsibility to look after the interests of its clients and not to push them to buy bonds for which it is receiving a kickback from the issuer; or that a business should not hide the weaknesses on its balance sheet in an effort to mislead or deceive investors. The job of regulators, in part, is to supervise financial institutions and ensure transparency to protect the integrity of the system.

In the 1980s the scope of competition among financial institutions expanded with the relaxation of legal and regulatory regimes and the introduction of new financial instruments. The new environment relied more on market forces and less on external regulation to arrange mutual rights, responsibilities, and penalties. Executives and managers were rewarded exclusively on the amount of profit they generated, with little attention paid to the means they employed. Given the greater autonomy of financial institutions, individual incentives to pursue any avenue to generate profits, and the lack of oversight at the corporate level, fraud, deception, and corruption evolved into tolerable practices. Paradoxically, investors, who often got hurt by such practices, were complicit in this process. As long as asset prices kept rising and their paper wealth increased investors accepted the superiority of unregulated markets and did not ask questions.

By the end of the decade financialization had switched into a higher gear. Wall Street and its counterparts across the globe transformed into a dominant force that shaped the economy and politics, and the idea of market omnipotence and beneficence raced into the 1990s.

Key terms and concepts

Bretton Woods system
Call (buy) option
Circuit breaker
Corporate raider
Dynamic hedging
Financialization
Forbearance
Gold exchange standard
Hedge fund
Index arbitrage
Investment-grade bond
Junk bond
Leveraged buyout
Mergers and acquisitions (M&A)
Neoliberalism
Portfolio insurance
Program trading
Proprietary trading
Put (sell) option
Quant
Risk arbitrage
Shareholder value
Speculative bond
Stagflation
Strike price
Supervisory goodwill

Endnotes

1 For the establishment and downfall of the Bretton Woods system see Helleiner (1996).
2 For journalistic accounts of takeovers and junk bonds in the 1980s see Bruck (1989) and Burrough and Helyar (1990). A scholarly, mostly sympathetic, view of takeovers can be found in a symposium published in the *Journal of Economic Perspectives* in 1988.
3 When corporate raiders transformed into private equity firms in the 1990s they rebranded themselves as "activist shareholders" and dropped the unflattering "raider" label.
4 For a firsthand account of the extent of political intrigue and fraud in the S&L crisis from a regulator's perspective, see Black (2005). For economic theorists' view of the episode, see Akerlof and Romer (1993).
5 This kind of option is called the European option. The American option can be exercised at any time before the expiration date. The names are unrelated to geography.
6 The put-option price varies inversely with the current value of the stock and directly with the strike price. As in the case of the call option, the value of the

put option decreases as the expiration date gets closer and is lower if volatility is lower.

7　Creating the replicating portfolio is a task for financial engineers and does not concern us here.

8　Lewis (2009: Part 1) offers a handy compilation of contemporary expert commentaries on the crash from newspapers and magazines.

9　The sheer size of the crash, which is also observed clearly in Figure 12.6, was a warning to the mathematical finance models that were based on the assumption of normally distributed price changes. The point that the number of outliers in price changes is far in excess of what the normal distribution can accommodate was made in the last chapter. To underscore the same point, the 22.6 percent drop in the DJIA is a 20-standard-deviation event, and its odds are one in 7.0×10^{86}, or, roughly speaking, once in billions and billions of big bangs.

10　For instance, currently the NYSE stops trading for one hour if the DJIA drops before 2 pm by more than 10 percent of its average closing value of the previous month.

References

Akerlof, George A. and Paul M. Romer. 1993. "Looting: The Economic Underworld of Bankruptcy for Profit." *Brookings Papers on Economic Activity* (2): 1–73.

Bates, David S. 1991. "The Crash of '87: Was It Expected? Evidence from Options Markets." *The Journal of Finance* 46 (3): 1008–44.

Black, Fischer. 1988. "An Equilibrium Model of the Crash." *NBER Macroeconomics Annual* 3: 269–75.

Black, Fischer and Myron Scholes. 1973. "The Pricing of Options and Corporate Liabilities." *Journal of Political Economy* 81 (3): 637–54.

Black, William K. 2005. *The Best Way to Rob a Bank is to Own One: How Corporate Executives and Politicians Looted the S&L Industry.* Austin: University of Texas Press.

Bruck, Connie. 1989. *The Predators' Ball: The Inside History of Drexler Burnham and the Rise of the Junk Bond Raiders.* New York: Penguin Books.

Buffett, Warren E. 1987. *Chairman's Letter to the Shareholders of Berkshire Hathaway.* Online: www.berkshirehathaway.com/letters/1987.html.

Burrough, Bryan and John Helyar. 1990. *Barbarians at the Gate: The Fall of RJR Nabisco.* New York: Harper and Row.

Feldstein, Martin, Franco Modigliani, Allen Sinai and Robert Solow. 1988. "Black Monday in Retrospect and Prospect: A Roundtable." *Eastern Economic Journal* 14 (4): 339–42.

Fortune. 1990. "The Biggest Looniest Deal Ever." 121 (14): 48–63.

French, Kenneth R. 1988. "Crash-Testing the Efficient Market Hypothesis." *NBER Macroeconomics Annual* 3: 277–85.

Friedman, Milton. 1962. *Capitalism and Freedom.* Chicago: University of Chicago Press.

Friedman, Milton. 1968. "The Role of Monetary Policy." *American Economic Review* 58 (1): 1–17.

Greenspan, Alan. 2008. *The Age of Turbulence: Adventures in a New World.* New York: Penguin Books.

Helleiner, Eric. 1996. *States and the Reemergence of Global Finance: From Bretton Woods to the 1990s.* Ithaca, NY: Cornell University Press.

Jensen, Michael. 1988. "Takeovers: Their Causes and Consequences." *Journal of Economic Perspectives* 2 (1): 1–48.

Kaplan, Steven N. and Per Stromberg. 2008. "Leveraged Buyouts and Private Equity." *Journal of Economic Perspectives* 23 (1): 121–46.

Leland, Hayne E. and Mark Rubinstein. 1988. "The Evolution of Portfolio Insurance." Pp. 3–10 in *Dynamic Hedging: A Guide to Portfolio Insurance*, edited by Donald L. Luskin. New York: John Wiley and Sons.

Lewis, Michael. 1989. *Liar's Poker*. New York: Penguin Books.

Lewis, Michael, ed. 2009. *Panic: The Story of Modern Financial Insanity*. New York: W. W. Norton and Company.

Malkiel, Burton G. 2012 [1973]. *A Random Walk Down Wall Street: The Time-Tested Strategy for Successful Investing*. New York: W. W. Norton and Company.

Merton, Robert. 1973. "Theory of Rational Option Pricing." *Bell Journal of Economics and Management Science* 4 (1): 141–83.

Roll, Richard. 1988. "The International Crash of October 1987." *Financial Analysts Journal* 44 (5): 9–35.

Schwert, G. William. 1992. "Stock Market Crash of October 1987." Pp. 577–82 in *The New Palgrave Dictionary of Money and Finance*, vol. 3, edited by P. Newman, M. Milgate, and John Eatwell. New York: Stockton Press.

Shiller, Robert J. 2005. *Irrational Exuberance*, 2nd ed. New York: Currency Doubleday. Online: www.econ.yale.edu/~shiller/data/ie_data.xls.

Will, George F. 2011. "Newt Gingrich Commits a Capital Crime." *Washington Post*, 13/12/2011.

Wolfe, Tom. 1987. *The Bonfire of the Vanities*. New York: Farrar Straus Giroux.

Yago, Glenn. 1990. *Junk Bonds: How High Yield Securities Restructured Corporate America*. New York: Oxford University Press.

14 The 1990s

The triumph of financial capitalism

Between July 1990 and March 1991 the US economy underwent a recession, which economists attributed variously to the savings and loan (S&L) implosion and the burst of the real-estate bubble, the high-interest policy from 1986 to 1989, and the Kuwait War oil-price increase in 1990. Real gross domestic product (GDP) declined by 1.4 percent over the contraction, the rate of unemployment peaked at 7.8 percent in June 1992, and the inflation-averse Federal Reserve (Fed) belatedly lowered interest rates to stimulate the economy. Bill Clinton won the presidency by making unemployment and jobs the main issue of the 1992 election.

The economy recovered swiftly after 1992. Between 1992 and 2000 it grew at an average rate of 3.6 percent per annum, the longest recession-free period in US history. Public debt declined, and the stock market rose more than fourfold in real terms, dwarfing the previous booms and creating financial wealth of unprecedented magnitude. Productivity gains accrued primarily to the wealthiest as income and wealth distribution became more unequal (Piketty and Saez 2003; Wolff 2002), but such matters attracted relatively little attention. Proponents of unregulated markets attributed economic growth to deregulation, downsizing (laying off workers), lower international trade barriers, and lower deficits. Technology enthusiasts attributed growth to the digital revolution. Some said it was just luck.[1]

This is not to say that financial markets were free from turbulence. First, there were problems that originated from abroad. The Mexican tequila crisis of 1994, the Far East financial crisis of 1997, and the Russian default of 1998 called for coordinated emergency solutions led by the International Monetary Fund (IMF) and the US Treasury to provide liquidity to emerging markets and to stabilize global markets. The Fed assisted these efforts in an advisory role. External financial assistance to countries always arrived with draconian conditions that contracted domestic economies and gave priority to payment of Western investors' debt. Most countries complied; only Russia refused. Second, two major domestic disturbances, the fall of the hedge fund Long-Term Capital Management (LTCM) in 1998 and the burst of the dot-com bubble (1998–2001), shook US financial markets. There were also a series of corporate malfeasance and fraud cases that ruined some very large publicly owned companies, at huge costs to their shareholders. The complicity of several large banks and independent auditing agencies in these incidents raised red flags regarding the degree of oversight in the financial markets.

The transformation of the contours of financial markets was far more consequential than these individual failures. First, financial institutions put the skills of quants to use creating more complex financial instruments, and derivatives proliferated. These instruments were too complicated for most traditional finance professionals to understand, were not traded on open exchanges, and, therefore, increased the opacity of the financial system. Nonetheless, they were purported to stabilize and deepen the markets via better quantification and management of risk.

Second, at the urging of commercial banks Congress and the Fed continued to dilute the Glass–Steagall Act and finally repealed it altogether in 1999. Wall Street complained that regulations hindered financial innovation and threatened the status of New York City as the global financial center; consequently, the legislative and executive branches of government as well as the Fed did their best to eliminate financial regulations or weaken their enforcement. Industry leaders, academics, and policymakers asserted that external supervision to prevent reckless risk-taking was no longer necessary due to the maturity of markets and improved risk-management tools, as well as modern financial institutions that were capable of self-discipline.

The third important change was the emergence of the *shadow banking system*. Shadow banking institutions, which included commercial banks, borrowed funds in the short-term money markets to make loans. While their activities replicated traditional bank lending, they operated outside banking regulations. In addition to raising leverage, shadow banking offered financial institutions ways to remove assets from their balance sheets to evade capital requirements and hide their risk exposure.

The academics preached, Wall Street echoed, politicians agreed, and the media broadcast the belief that securitization and derivatives improved efficiency and stability of financial markets, and that the industry had the power and ability to police itself and avoid reckless behavior. The few attempts to bring more transparency to derivatives were thwarted by the vigorous efforts of the finance industry and the complicity of the government. While the public applauded, Wall Street and Washington joined hands in cheering and celebrating the triumph of the financialization of capitalism.

The banking system

Throughout the 1980s commercial banks pressured the Fed, Congress, and the administration to loosen the rules of the Glass–Steagall Act so that they could expand their activities into the securities business. They argued that the restrictions were a relic of the 1930s, redundant in a world of sophisticated investors, a mature financial market with credit ratings agencies and an effective SEC, and a detriment to the global competitiveness of US banks. The Fed began to relax the act's restrictions in 1986 by permitting banks to raise limited revenue from securities operations. Later it allowed banks to enter the underwriting business, including commercial paper and mortgage-backed securities, over the objections of Fed Chair Paul Volcker.

The trend gained momentum in the 1990s as the Fed further relaxed constraints on the securities operations of commercial banks. In 1998 bank holding company Citicorp attempted a merger with the Travelers Group, an insurance-services company that owned investment house Salomon Smith Barney. Although it was in violation of the Bank Holding Company Act, the merger took place under a two-year-review loophole that granted a temporary waiver and created Citigroup, a financial supermarket that combined banking, insurance, and securities broker-dealer services. What ensued was immense lobbying of the Fed, Congress, and the administration that targeted the removal of all the legal obstacles that commercial banks faced in entering investment-banking activities. Shepherded by Robert Rubin, previously co-chair of Goldman Sachs, and Secretary of the Treasury under President Clinton, and at the time serving as a Citigroup board member, these efforts were successful. Congress repealed the Glass–Steagall Act with the passage on November 4, 1999, of the Financial Services Modernization Act, also known as the Gramm–Leach–Bliley Act. On the same day Rubin became CEO of Citigroup. President Clinton signed the act into law and congratulated its architects:

> So I think you should all be exceedingly proud of yourselves . . . today what we are doing is modernizing the financial services industry, tearing down these antiquated laws and granting banks significant new authority. This will, first of all, save consumers billions of dollars a year through enhanced competition. It will also protect the rights of consumers.
>
> (US Department of the Treasury 1999)

On the investment bank-side of the sector trends that had emerged in the 1970s, e.g. the shift from traditional securities underwriting and mergers-and-acquisitions (M&A) consulting to securities dealing on organizations' own accounts and portfolio management, became more prominent. The fee-based business model led banks to expand their more profitable securities- and derivatives-related activities. They became major players in securitizing loans and marketing these to their customers. In addition, the corporate structure of investment banking changed. Traditionally, investment banks were organized as partnerships that were owned and run by a limited number of people. This structure was gradually replaced by public ownership. Although many executives owned shares of their companies, with the disappearance of the partnership structure they were, first and foremost, employees of the shareholders, and their job was to manage and run the corporation in return for compensation. In comparison with the partnership system, they now had a lesser stake in the long-term performance of the firm. As their salaries and bonuses were linked to the short-run performance of the firm they were more likely to maximize short-term profitability at the expense of long-term goals, and to engage in ventures that yielded higher returns in the short-run at the expense of rising medium- to long-run risk. Rewards for short-term success were generous and penalties were relatively slight (golden parachutes were offered to those who were dismissed).

In the midst of diminishing regulatory oversight, however, banks' concurrent securities underwriting and marketing raised the risk of conflicts of interest. The highly publicized Chinese wall between securities analysis and the trading desk was increasingly breached. The practices of financial institutions intentionally giving bad advice to their clients, inflating stock prices, and offering special deals to CEOs and other prominent business customers became commonplace.[2]

Yet the most important new institution was the shadow banking system, which, as mentioned, refers to the set of non-depository financial intermediaries that were not subject to banking regulations or safety nets, but performed borrowing and credit-extension services similar to depository institutions. In the banking-balance-sheet example given in Chapter 3 it was assumed that the bank uses deposits to extend loans. In fact there is another source of funds: the bank can also borrow from money markets to leverage its long-term lending capacity. In this case short-term borrowing is added to the liabilities, and long-term lending is added to the asset side of the balance sheet. Shadow banking institutions issued short-term (usually three-month) commercial paper to borrow from pension funds, money markets, and regular banks, and channeled the bulk of the funds to purchase securitized-debt instruments, mortgages, and other types of long-term loans. They posted these long-term assets as collateral for the commercial paper they sold. At the simplest level the shadow bank benefited from the interest-rate spread between the long- and short-term interest rates (although, as discussed later, this was not their sole revenue and they also served other purposes). Shadow banking entities include, in varying degrees and at different capacities, commercial and investment banks, non-bank mortgage originators, hedge funds, private equity funds, and mutual funds.

Commercial banks were an integral component of the shadow banking system. While the scope of commercial banks' securities operations had widened, the system was not free from government regulation. Both the Fed and the 1988 Basel Accord (Basel I)[3] set the minimum amount of capital that banks needed to hold as a percentage of their risk-adjusted loans to ensure that they could sustain operations even in the face of losses. The Fed's capital requirement was 5 percent of the loans, and the Basel I guideline was 8 percent. From the perspective of the banks the capital requirement was costly because these funds did not earn interest. Many large commercial-banking institutions attempted to evade capital requirements by creating independent shadow banking entities that were not subject to regulations.

One potential issue related to the short-term-financing model was that the maturity mismatch between borrowing and lending by the shadow banking institutions required them to roll over their debt continuously, effectively paying it and borrowing again, usually from the same lender. Moreover, they were subject to margin calls by lenders in the event that the value of the collateral they posted declined. The dependence of shadow banking institutions on short-term funding and high leverage made them vulnerable to turbulence in financial markets. They faced rollover risk, which is money-market creditors refusing to refinance debt. In addition, they did not have the privilege of access to the lender of last resort in the event that their short-term lenders called back loans, creating the equivalent of a bank run.

The alphabet soup of financial complexity

Securitization and exotic derivatives multiplied during the 1990s with the growth of mortgage- and asset-backed securities and swaps. These complex financial arrangements, offering borrowers and lenders a plethora of instruments to serve unique financial needs and transfer and diversify risk, have to come to be known as *structured finance*. Their proliferation had sweeping consequences.

Securitization

The US residential-mortgage market is one of the largest markets in the world, measured in trillions of dollars. Prior to the 1980s a mortgage was an exclusive contract between a bank or thrift and a homebuyer; the lender extended the loan and held it until the interest and principal were paid in full. There was no secondary market in which the mortgage originator could sell the loan to another party to pass on the risk or to generate new funds to make more loans. Given the illiquidity of the mortgage loan, the lender had the incentive to screen and monitor the borrower very carefully to avoid the risk of default.

The only exception to this practice was the government-sponsored enterprise (GSE). US governments have historically promoted home ownership and in 1938 established the Federal National Mortgage Association (Fannie Mae), which bought Federal Housing Administration (FHA)-insured mortgage loans from the banks and the S&Ls so that more funds were made available to lenders to issue further mortgages. Fannie Mae financed its purchases of mortgages by selling bonds to the public. These bonds were popular among investors because federal insurance of mortgage loans meant zero default risk.

In 1968 the government spun off the Government National Mortgage Association (Ginnie Mae) from Fannie Mae and converted Fannie Mae into a private corporation that was fully owned by shareholders. Ginnie Mae was owned by the government. In 1970 the government also created the Federal Home Loan Mortgage Corporation (Freddie Mac) as a private entity to compete with Fannie Mae; Freddie Mac was turned into a publicly owned corporation in 1989. Ginnie Mae limited its purchases to mortgages that were insured by government agencies, such as the FHA and Veterans Administration. Fannie Mae and Freddie Mac, however, were permitted to expand the scope of their purchases to mortgages that did not carry government-agency insurance. These mortgages, nevertheless, were required to be *conforming loans* that met specific criteria concerning loan-income-ratio limits, size, and documentation regarding the borrower's income and wealth. As not all mortgages purchased by Fannie Mae and Freddie Mac carried government-agency insurance it was possible for these GSEs to default on their bonds in the event of widespread mortgage defaults. However, in addition to whatever comfort conforming-loan requirements and government oversight may have given to the Fannie Mae and Freddie Mac bond buyers, these investors interpreted government sponsorship as an implicit guarantee. The public perception of low risk permitted both corporations to raise funds cheaply by selling bonds.

The first generation of mortgage securitization arrived in 1968, when Ginnie Mae created pools of mortgages and issued *pass-through securities*, certificates backed by the cash flow of the pools. Investors in the certificates effectively became lenders to homebuyers and, in return, were entitled to a share of the interest and principal cash flow into the mortgage pool on a pro-rata basis.[4] Freddie Mac in 1971 and Fannie Mae in 1981 followed suit by introducing their own certificates.

GSE-issued securities are generically called *agency-label* securities. The foray of banks into this field occurred in 1977 when the Bank of America issued and Salomon Brothers (an investment bank specializing in fixed-income securities) underwrote the first *private-label* pass-through. One of the leaders of the effort, Lewis Ranieri of Salomon Brothers, at this time coined the word *securitization* to describe the creation of securities backed by mortgage cash flows (Ranieri 1996). These private-label securities, however, initially did not attract a great deal of interest due to the state-level restrictions on their marketing and tax laws.

However, even the agency-label pass-through certificates were not highly attractive to investors, for three reasons. First, certain investors did not want to tie up their funds for as long as 20 or 30 years, which was the maturity of most mortgages. Second, the mortgage-payment scheme was a source of discontent. A standard bond entitles the owner to periodic fixed coupon payments over the lifetime of the bond and the fixed principal upon maturity. In contrast, the mortgage lender receives a fixed monthly payment that is composed of the interest and principal payments. One problem that pass-through certificate holders faced was the *prepayment* risk, as the mortgage loan could be paid off fully before the maturity date. When interest rates decline mortgage buyers rush to re-finance. They pay off their debt in full and obtain another mortgage at a lower rate. Thus, owners of the pass-through certificate may not receive their expected interest payments, and they can re-lend the amount paid early only at a lower interest rate. The third problem with pass-through certificates was that they did not offer many options to diversify loan portfolios. They did not appeal to investors who were risk intolerant due to the prepayment option. Nor did they lure investors who sought high yields in return for taking high risks.

The search for a solution to these problems led to the second generation of securitization. Two investment banks that worked with Freddie Mac—Salomon Brothers and First Boston—created the *collateralized mortgage obligation* (CMO) in 1983. The CMO was a *structured debt instrument*, whereby a family of bonds with different risk and return characteristics was created against the cash stream of a mortgage pool's collateral. A simple example of a CMO is one that addresses the differences in time preferences of investors. Over time the interest share of the fixed monthly mortgage payment shrinks while the principal component increases. One may create a CMO that consists of two types of bonds that are backed separately by the principal and the interest cash flows. Investors in interest-only (IO) securities are paid out of the interest payments and receive declining payments over time. Lower interest rates and accelerating prepayments reduce the value of IO securities. Payments on the principal accrue to the investors in principal-only (PO) securities; if interest rates decline and prepayments increase the price of the PO bonds rises. IO and PO securities offered choices to investors with different time horizons.

The more common type of CMO divided a mortgage pool into tranches that offered investors debt instruments with varying risks and returns. The earliest and simplest CMO divided the mortgage pool into three tranches and offered a different bond for each tranche: senior, mezzanine, and junior (equity). The senior tranche had the lowest risk and return, while the junior had the highest. Tranches are often viewed as a waterfall of cash flow that fills layered basins, starting with the senior tranche and then overflowing sequentially to the others. The alternative description from the default side had the first 8 percent of the pool's defaults absorbed by the junior-tranche bondholders and the next 2 percent by the mezzanine bondholders. The senior bonds were affected only if defaults exceeded 10 percent. By historical standards, the occurrence of defaults that exceeded 10 percent of mortgages was extremely unlikely, and, therefore, the senior-tranche bonds were considered very safe, usually receiving the highest credit ratings.

The rising popularity of CMOs had a profound effect on the mortgage market. Mortgage originators increasingly sold their mortgage loans to securitizers or became securitizers themselves. The overwhelming share of these securities was issued by the GSEs. Private institutions participated in securitization in rising numbers after the tax laws of 1986 removed the obstacles faced by private-label funds. Over the course of the 1990s the annual volume of *mortgage-backed securities* (MBSs)[5] increased from \$260b to \$833b (Inside Mortgage Finance 2012). Private-label securities hovered around 15 percent of the volume but increased to approximately 20 percent by the end of the decade. The next chapter examines the trends in MBS issuance in more detail.

The most important customers of the CMOs were the institutional investors, including pension funds, mutual funds, insurance companies, and local governments. Some hedge funds also invested heavily in CMOs with borrowed money. In addition, many investment and commercial banks held CMOs as assets, either to diversify their asset portfolio or as inventories of the higher-risk equity tranches of their own products.

One incident in 1994 signaled that the CMO market was not very stable and that interest changes could have great ramifications. Investment bank Kidder Peabody was one of the three largest private-label CMO producers of the time (in addition to Bear Stearns and Lehman Brothers). Askin Capital Management was a customer and satellite of Kidder, and three of the hedge funds it controlled had highly leveraged investments in private-label CMOs. When interest rates increased in February 1994 Askin Capital suffered losses on its PO bonds and experienced difficulties in financing its CMO holding. Askin's liquidity troubles spilled over to Kidder, and both firms were wiped out. As shockwaves spread, private-label CMO buyers disappeared and prices declined. Both investors and securitizers suffered losses, and the private-label market came to a standstill for two years.

Soon the scope of securitization expanded as securities collateralized by auto, student, credit-card and other types of consumer loan, often generically referred to as *asset-backed securities* (ABSs), joined the fray. The next step was the creation of *collateralized debt obligations* (CDOs), structured debt instruments backed by pools of other synthetic debt instruments (e.g. CMOs, ABSs) and even corporate bonds, royalties, leases, and derivatives such as credit default swaps (CDSs). Drexler, Burnham and Lambert created the first CDO in 1987. CDOs were promoted as being backed by a wider asset base and therefore offering a more diversified investment vehicle than CMOs.

If tranches of a CMO were different-grade sausages made of mixed beef products, tranches of a CDO were varieties of sausages manufactured from sausages of beef, chicken, pork, and vegetables, in total freedom from Food and Drug Administration regulations. By construction, CMOs and, even more so, CDOs were opaque instruments, and their lack of transparency about their content complicated pricing via markets. The secondary markets in CMOs and CDOs were very thin. They were not structured to be traded on exchanges, and only the issuer could have served as the market maker. Therefore, traditional supply and demand did not play a role in their pricing. The returns on CMOs and CDOs, and their pricing, were determined by financial engineers' mathematical architecture and computer programs that distributed the cash flow among the various bonds collateralized by a pool of securitized assets.

Swaps

The swap is a type of financial derivative that emerged in the 1980s and rose to prominence in the 1990s. Swaps came in a multitude of types and forms. An earlier type was the *interest-rate swap*. Suppose that Corporation A holds debt with a floating interest rate, determined by a fixed rate plus a reference rate, such as LIBOR.[6] Continuous changes in the LIBOR expose Corporation A to interest-rate risk. One way it can protect itself from a future interest-rate increase and rising debt burden is to find a counterparty that holds a fixed-rate debt, Corporation B, and swap the interest cash flows. In effect, Corporation B would make fixed interest payments to Corporation A, and Corporation A would make floating interest payments to Corporation B, based again on the reference interest rate plus a margin. A *currency swap*, in turn, is a contract whereby counterparties swap their assets, liabilities, or interest payments that are denominated in different currencies to protect themselves from exchange-rate fluctuations. While they have been around since the 1970s, Salomon Brothers arranged the first modern currency swap in 1981 between the World Bank and IBM, whereby the parties exchanged interest-payment flows denominated in Swiss francs and German marks.

Another type of swap was invented in 1994 by traders in the banking house JP Morgan and soon caught the attention of the world of finance.[7] The *credit default swap* (CDS) is an "insurance" contract that a debt holder buys from a counterparty against default or downgrade of the debt. The objective of the CDS is to protect the lender from default risk. Suppose Party A holds a ten-year bond with a face value of $1m. If Party A is concerned about the default risk of the bond he can hedge by signing a CDS with Counterparty B. A simple CDS contract would stipulate that, over the lifetime of the contract, Party A pays Counterparty B an annual premium (known as the swap spread), determined as a percentage of the notional value of the debt. Counterparty B, in return, pledges that in the event the issuer of the bond defaults she will compensate Party A for the loss. Compensation takes the form of either a *physical* or *cash settlement*. In the case of a physical settlement the seller of the CDS pays the bondholder the face value of the bond and, in return, receives the bond from Party A. In a cash settlement the seller pays the CDS buyer the difference between the face value and the market value of the bond for which the CDS has been purchased. The primary difference between these methods, of course, is that in the event of a physical settlement the buyer must be in possession of the bond, whereas for a cash settlement that is not necessary. Cash settlements became more common as "naked" purchases, i.e. purchases of CDSs without possessing the debt obligation, became prevalent.

Swaps were over-the-counter (OTC) contracts, structured to the specifications of the two parties. They proved to be a lucrative business for investment banks that served as intermediaries between counterparties with mutual needs. Salomon Brothers' fee for the World Bank–IBM swap was $210m. There were no regulations that barred commercial banks from taking part in the swap market, and they soon joined in.

In the last chapter I mentioned how futures contracts and put options can be used as insurance policies against a decline in the value of an asset. Along the same lines, interest-rate, currency, and credit default swaps are often viewed as insurance policies for protecting oneself against interest, exchange-rate, and default risks respectively, or as a means to transfer risks to counterparties. But in finance insurance refers merely to hedging one's risks by taking offsetting portfolio positions via derivatives, a very different game from traditional insurance. Unlike in traditional insurance, swap contracts may be purchased by people who do not own the asset. Swap sellers are not subject to regulations such as capital requirements. Nor do they manage risk by pooling premiums and using actuarial tables to calculate the probabilities of adverse events. The most important implication of these features of swap derivatives is that they also serve as means of speculation. The next two chapters will explore this role in more detail.

As swaps are not traded in exchanges or clearing houses their volume can be estimated only on the basis of surveys. The market size is measured in terms of the notional amount over which swap contracts are drawn. According to the International Swaps and Derivatives Association, an industry group that reports total notional swap contracts based on surveys, over the 1990s the sum of notional amounts of outstanding interest-rate and currency swaps rose twenty-threefold, from $2.5t to $58.3t (ISDA 2013). The CDS, by contrast, was a newcomer, and its global market was estimated at $300b in March 1998, with US firms accounting for half of the notional principal (Tett 2009: 58). Originally, CDSs were drawn on corporate bonds, and until 2005 there were no credit swaps on MBSs. The next chapter explains why.

Value-at-risk

After the crash of October 1987 financial companies searched for an easily quantifiable measure of risk exposure to assess their vulnerability to

market slides. Statistical techniques that had gained a foothold in financial markets by that time offered an answer: the *value-at-risk* (VaR), or the
worst-case scenario a firm may encounter. The VaR measures the worst
losses a portfolio can expect at a threshold probability over a time period
under normal market conditions and no trade. For instance, a one-day
99 percent VaR of $50,000 means that there is a 99 percent chance that the
portfolio will lose a maximum value of $50,000 in a one-day period; or the
firm expects to lose more than $50,000 once in 100 days. One method to
calculate the daily VaR is to create a frequency diagram of the historical
daily price fluctuations from the lowest to the highest value. If there are
1,000 daily observations the worst 1 percent losses are the ten observations located at the extreme left tail of the frequency diagram. Let's assume
that these ten observations have price drops of 5 percent or higher. If the
value of the portfolio is $1m then the one-day 99 percent VaR is $50,000.

The second method of calculating the VaR assumes that price changes
are distributed normally and approximates the historical data with the
normal distribution curve. Under the normal distribution assumption it is
easy to calculate the VaR. From the standard normal distribution table, the
99 percent left-tail cut-off point is –2.58 (or 2.58 standard deviations below
the mean).[8] The VaR is the product of the value of the portfolio, standard
deviation of the distribution, and the value of the cut-off point. If the standard deviation of the price variation is 2 percent then the 99 percent VaR
of the portfolio described above is $51,600 [$1m·0.02·(–2.58)]. In summary,
all that is needed to calculate the VaR is the standard deviation of the distribution of the price changes and the standard normal distribution table.

The VaR can be used to assess what is at stake under alternative combinations of confidence level and time horizon. A more substantive use of
the metric is to determine how much capital should be set aside to ride out
a period of turbulence. In this context judicious use of the VaR requires
selecting a high confidence level to ensure that the likelihood of exceeding
the VaR is very low. The time horizon should also be long enough to permit raising funds to replenish capital funds or to liquidate assets to lower
the riskiness of the portfolio (Jorion 2000).

Given its mathematical convenience, the VaR's calculation under the
assumption of normally distributed price changes has become common
practice. Financial institutions routinely report their VaR in financial
statements to inform their shareholders of the company's risk positions.
The catch is that, if returns are not normally distributed, the VaR yields an
understatement of firms' risk exposure and a false sense of confidence.
Figure 12.6 illustrates the inadequacy of the normal-distribution-based
VaR to capture extreme events. Over the 1896–2010 period almost 20 percent of the daily rate of change of the DJIA exceeded three standard deviations. However, according to the normal distribution, only 0.3 percent of
the observations should exceed three standard deviations, and, therefore,
it is hardly an adequate approximation of the true empirical distribution

of the actual risk faced by the firm. Such miscalculation contributed to the collapse of LTCM, the largest hedge fund of the 1990s.

The rise and fall of Long-Term Capital Management

Long-Term Capital Management (LTCM) was a very high-profile hedge-fund company founded by John Meriwether, formerly a star trader and vice-chairman at Salomon Brothers. Meriwether resigned from Salomon in 1991, following a government bond-trading scandal that involved one of his subordinates. In 1994 he brought together his old Salomon team of high-powered traders, all quantitative-finance PhDs, as partners under the roof of LTCM. The partners also included a former vice-president of the Fed Board, David W. Mullins. Two academic superstars, Myron Scholes and Robert Merton of BSM-model fame, added prestige to the operation and, in the case of Scholes, effective salesmanship. The minimum amount required to invest in the fund was $10m, and withdrawals were not permitted during the first three years. Clients were required not to question the specifics of trades. The fund was to receive a 2 percent charge on assets annually and 25 percent of the profits (in comparison with standard hedge-fund charges at the time of 1 percent and 20 percent respectively). Before long Meriwether had collected $1.25b from 80 investors, including banks, sovereign funds, and pension funds, as well as the luminaries of Wall Street and Hollywood, and launched LTCM.[9]

The rise

LTCM's selling point was that it combined the best brains available with the brawn of the most comprehensive global databases, most advanced software, and fastest computers in search of the highest returns. The mystique surrounding LTCM notwithstanding, its investment strategy was simple in principle. It was based on convergence arbitrage or relative-value trades. The technique in *convergence arbitrage trading* is to identify deviations from the "normal" state of the market and then to make bets on the market eventually returning to the normal state.

Suppose two very similar assets have different returns at a point in time. The standard example is US Treasuries with a slight difference in maturity dates. Consider two 15-year Treasury bonds that are issued one quarter apart. The newer, "on-the-run" issue is typically traded at a premium because it is more liquid and more of it is traded in the market. The older, "off-the-run" issue is likely to have been "shelved" by investors; it is traded less frequently and at a lower price. Given that they have the same issuer and lifespan, and that their maturity dates are very close, the older and newer Treasuries are virtually identical in terms of returns and risks. Therefore, their prices should be practically the same; the initial price difference should eventually disappear.

The objective of the convergence trader is to profit from this initial price differential. A numerical example will illustrate how. Suppose that the old and young issues trade at $100 and $103 respectively, and the arbitrageur has $100 of capital. He can make money by going short on the younger and long on the older security, borrowing and selling the younger security in the spot market at $103 and simultaneously buying and holding the older security at $100. Once prices converge, hopefully before the date on which the younger security is to be returned to the lender, the arbitrageur can sell the older security and buy the younger security, both at the same price, and deliver the latter to the lender. The initial price difference of $3 is the profit (ignoring transactions costs), or the rate of return on equity of $100 is 3 percent. Note that the convergence trade is *market neutral*; it does not matter whether the final price rises or falls. The arbitrageur makes $3 profit, provided the prices of the young and old bonds converge, regardless of whether that price turns out to be $110 or $90.

One drawback to this plan is that the difference between the old and new security prices is likely to be far smaller than 3 percent, most probably a fraction of a percentage point, and, therefore, the convergence profits will be very small. Still, significant profits can be made if the arbitrageur leverages the operation. Consider the following extension of the numerical example. Suppose the arbitrageur borrows $900 additional cash at 1 percent interest and increases the scale of its operation tenfold. After convergence the profit will be $21 (3 percent on $100 of equity plus 2 percent (3 percent – 1 percent) on $900 of borrowed funds), or the rate of return is raised from 3 percent to 21 percent on equity. As always, leveraging magnifies the risk alongside the profit opportunities. If the 3 percent price differential remains unchanged the unleveraged arbitrageur will lose 3 percent on equity; the leveraged arbitrageur will lose 39 percent (3 percent on $100 and 4 percent (3 percent + 1 percent) on $900 is $39). The finance PhDs running the LTCM trades believed that markets are informationally efficient and that prices will ultimately converge to the fundamentals. They searched for windows of opportunity where the price had not yet fully adjusted to the fundamental value and took advantage of these phases of transitory inefficiency. Merton Scholes often described LTCM as a gigantic vacuum that sucked up the nickels everyone else overlooked.

LTCM built a very successful business model based on the apparently simple convergence trading strategy that was, in principle, the same as that employed a few years earlier at Salomon Brothers. Its success had three ingredients. First, LTCM (the fund) started with a sizeable capital base, which became even larger over time, and then borrowed very huge sums to leverage its investments. By 1997 its capital was $7b. During much of its operation it leveraged this capital base by an average factor of 20 by borrowing from banks. One standard method to borrow short-term funds is the *repurchase* or *repo agreement*: the borrower sells assets to the lender with the understanding that it will purchase them back later at a fixed price. Banks usually charge a "haircut" to the borrower in repo purchases as protection from the possible decline in the value of the asset. LTCM used repo agreements extensively, with the notable difference that it negotiated very favorable, no-haircut terms with lenders despite the fact that banks had little information about LTCM's operations. The combination of the large capital base and ability to borrow cheaply made a very large vacuum that could suck up lots of change.

Second, the LTCM partners had been utilizing mathematical finance and statistical models intensively and for a long period of time as a closely knit group, and they took full advantage of their experience to get the best deals (Lowenstein 2001). They searched for and identified arbitrage opportunities across the globe, especially in emerging markets, using very large databases and software better and faster than anyone, and exploited opportunities before others jumped in. LTCM also concealed its operations from the outside world, often dealing with different banks for different legs of a trade to ensure that outsiders did not discover their trade secrets. Whereas lenders usually grow nervous of a dearth of information, LTCM's reputation was sufficient to keep them, as well as investors, from asking questions, at least during the first years of operation—and the more they were kept in the dark, the more LTCM's mystique grew.

The third component of the corporate strategy was risk management. There is always the risk that the convergence may not take place within the anticipated time frame. To reduce this risk LTCM hedged its bets via securities and derivatives and maintained a purportedly highly diversified portfolio. Provided that returns to individual assets were uncorrelated, it was unlikely that the whole portfolio would be adversely affected by market disruptions. LTCM assessed its risk position on the basis of the VaR calculation. The acceptable maximum level of risk was selected as the historical volatility of the US stock market, measured as the standard deviation of the S&P 500. The portfolio was managed to maximize the expected returns subject to the constraint that the overall risk level of the portfolio was no higher than that faced by an investor in the S&P 500 Index fund. As was usual in these calculations, the risk model assumed that stock-market volatility is constant and price fluctuations follow a normal probability distribution so that there are no large price jumps (Jorion 2000).

In its first two years LTCM was extremely successful due to trades in Treasury bonds, IO mortgage-backed securities, and Italian government bonds. It posted rates of return for investors that exceeded 40 percent both in 1995 and 1996 (after fees). LTCM soon expanded its arbitrage trading to new areas, e.g. it bet on the fall of spreads between European and Japanese bonds. In the stock market it engaged in *pairs trades*. Daily fluctuations in the stock prices of competing firms in specific sectors exhibit some correlation because they are affected by events that affect the whole industry. Pairs trades take advantage of instances when the correlation temporarily breaks down. When prices of two similar firms diverge the trader makes a bet by buying the cheaper stock and selling short the expensive stock. Again, these trades are market neutral. LTCM also made bets on risk arbitrage (simultaneously buying and selling the stocks of merging companies).

In comparison with Treasuries, these types of convergence trades were riskier. However, the partners' confidence in the efficiency of markets, their own expertise, and mathematical models was so supreme that they usually responded to any widening spread by doubling up their positions. Their performance until 1998 reinforced the self-assurance of the partners as well as the sense of awe among its lenders and investors. Spreads eventually diminished, prices converged, and bets paid off handsomely.

As it ran out of arbitrage opportunities, the firm also pursued other types of investment, such as emerging-market sovereign bonds, equity options, interest-rate swaps, and CDSs. Perhaps the most inventive trading strategy was the *volatility trade*. As discussed in the previous chapter, the option price rises with the volatility of the stock price. The BSM model calculates the option price based on historical volatility, i.e. the standard deviation of the stock price, and assumes that the volatility is constant and price changes are normally distributed. Volatility trading reads this relationship in reverse: instead of calculating the option price from the observed volatility, it estimates the implied volatility of the stock price from the current option price.

Volatility trading compares the implied volatility from the BSM equation (based on the observed option price) with the "true" expert estimate of volatility. If the two are different then there may be profit opportunities. During the 1997 East Asian financial crisis, for instance, stock-market fluctuations raised market volatility and, therefore, the prices of both put and call options. However, the expert opinion in LTCM was that the true volatility was lower, and, therefore, observed volatility was expected to decline. What this meant for options prices was that they were overvalued and expected to decline to their true values. Thus, LTCM started to sell both call and put options. If the volatility and option prices indeed declined options would not be exercised, and the fund would turn profits from the option fees.

Scholes and Merton received the Nobel Prize in Economic Sciences in 1997 for their work on the options-pricing theory (Black had passed away two years earlier). Notwithstanding the accolades the prize bestowed to the power of mathematical finance in managing risk, and the brainpower behind LTCM, the fund's spectacular run had slowed down in 1997. While its rate of return to investors was still a respectable 17 percent after fees, it was far behind the US stock market, which had gained 33 percent in that year. The equity of the fund was $7b. At the end of the year LTCM returned $2.7b of capital to the investors, despite disgruntlement from the latter, because investment opportunities were shrinking. However, the partners themselves increased their own equity to $1.9b. In early 1998 the fund's total assets on its balance sheet were valued at $130b, approximately $5b in equity and $125b borrowed from banks; the leverage ratio exceeded 25:1. The notional principal of LTCM's derivatives position was a staggering $1.25t. Only six banks had derivatives positions on notional principal that exceeded $1t at the time (Jorion 2000). The daily VaR of the fund was calculated at $45m, and the partners were in search of more exotic trades, sometimes with rising levels of recklessness (Lowenstein 2001: 128–9).

The fall

The first significant negative shock came in 1998 when Salomon Brothers began to dismantle its bond-arbitrage desk and sell off its mortgage-related securities positions. LTCM, which held similar assets, suffered losses because it underestimated the negative impact of the sell-off on the price of these assets. In May and June of 1998 LTCM lost 16 percent of its equity, and its leverage rose to 30. The fund responded by liquidating some of its portfolio and reducing the daily VaR to $34m. Although this action increased the cash position and lowered leverage, the fund chose to sell more liquid assets and thereby made its overall portfolio less liquid.

On August 17, 1998, Russia devalued the ruble, defaulted on $13.5b worth of debt, and declared a moratorium on payments to foreign creditors. At that time LTCM held Russian bonds and had hedged its position by selling rubles in the futures market. The calculation was that in the event Russia defaulted the ruble also would fall, and LTCM's profits in the foreign-exchange market would offset the loss on bonds. Unfortunately for the fund, the hedge failed because the Russian government also halted trading of the ruble. However, the real shock was the contagion that the Russian crisis created. Investors across the globe, already alarmed by the previous year's crash in the Far East, switched to risk-free assets, namely, US Treasuries and cash. The flight to safe assets was devastating for LTCM. At the time the fund's portfolio was long various financial instruments, e.g. junk bonds, sovereign debt, interest swaps, and short Treasuries, because the partners had calculated that values of these assets were undervalued relative to Treasuries and anticipated diminishing spreads. The much touted diversified portfolio was in fact composed largely of illiquid assets whose values collapsed all at once during the panic and run to the safety of US Treasuries and cash. Treasury prices peaked as other asset prices collapsed. Widening spreads squeezed the fund as convergence trades failed en masse. As leveraging worked in reverse the fund hemorrhaged. On August 21 LTCM lost $550m, higher than its daily VaR by a factor of 16. By the end of August capital was down by 50 percent, and the leverage ratio climbed to 55:1.

Another big source of losses was the volatility trades. After the East Asian crisis in fall 1997 the implied volatility of the stock indices stood at 20 percent. However, LTCM had calculated that the true volatility based on historical experience was approximately 15 percent and, consequently, believed that options were overvalued. Confident that the volatility would decline to its conventional level and options would not be exercised, LTCM sold large volumes of options. In early September, however, implied volatility on stock indices across the globe climbed above 30 percent, and options prices increased. Option counterparties began to make margin calls on LTCM that further hurt the fund's bottom line. Throughout September daily losses regularly exceeded $100m. As the volume of loans had scarcely changed, declining equity in the company meant that the leverage ratio rose, as high as 100:1 by mid September. On September 21 the fund lost another $550m. Volatility trades alone cost the firm a total of $1.3b.

Starting in late August, and throughout September, LTCM took corrective action to reduce its risk exposure. First, Meriwether tried to raise as much as $1.5b of new capital by attracting new investors with offers of special terms on fees, but he was unsuccessful, both because tempestuous global markets made investors more cautious and Meriwether's attempt in itself raised doubts about the state of LTCM. The fund had lost its luster and was now forced to share its previously heavily guarded operations with prospective investors. The more that potential investors, who included the banks that made loans to the fund, discovered about the position of the once secretive LTCM, the more they declined to offer their assistance and, at least according to some fund partners, instead positioned themselves to exploit the portfolio of the fallen fund.

The second line of action was to liquidate assets to lower the leverage ratio and build LTCM's cash position. Declining markets and the drying up of liquidity made this route even more difficult to pursue. First, the fund had already sold its more liquid assets, and much of its remaining portfolio was composed of higher-risk illiquid assets that were difficult to dispose of. Second, in the midst of a rush to liquidity it might have been feasible for a small, nimble hedge fund to unravel its positions, but LTCM was the quintessential 800-pound gorilla. Its positions were so large that a sale attempt would have caused prices to collapse and buyers to disappear. Third, the fund tried to buy back its shorts and return them to the lenders. The potential sellers of these assets, knowing that LTCM was now cornered, offered them at very high premiums and further squeezed the fund. Fourth, banks, which now had access to the fund's books, had, perhaps opportunistically, started to unwind their similar positions ahead of LTCM, which further tightened the fund's liquidity constraint.

LTCM's descent was followed with concern on Wall Street. Banks had been complicit in creating the outsized LTCM by offering loans with no haircuts. Lenders are expected to be vigilant about how their loans are used, but in the case of LTCM they were content with ignorance, or temporarily blinded by their faith in the genius of the fund's partners. The unraveling of the fund and the potential default would hurt lenders, though the greater concern was the possible system-wide consequences. The bankruptcy of LTCM meant defaults on derivatives trades that exceeded a trillion dollars in notional principal. If counterparties who had purchased options from LTCM suddenly found out that their "insurance" had evaporated they could dump their assets in the market.

The effect of the ruble crisis on the stock market had been a 10 percent decline between mid August and mid September; bank stocks had dropped in much larger magnitudes, reaching 40 to 50 percent. The failure of LTCM could have triggered a catastrophic systemic shock. By mid September Meriwether was looking for more than $2b of new equity, signaling the deterioration of the fund's circumstances. Reminiscent of 1907, the largest banks attempted to coordinate fundraising to inject equity into the fund, but these attempts failed because banks could not reach an agreement amid market turbulence and their own precarious situation.

The equity of the fund had dropped from $4,700m to $400m between the beginning of the year and September 23, 1998, the date when the curtain fell for good. The final resolution required the intervention of the Federal Reserve Bank of New York. In a Fed-brokered agreement the 14 largest banks contributed a total of $3.625b to purchase a 90 percent share in the fund. Bear Stearns was the only bank that refused to participate in the consortium, an action not forgotten by its peers or the Fed. LTCM partners held on to the remaining 10 percent equity. The total losses of LTCM are estimated at $4.6b, distributed across numerous investors. Among others, UBS wrote off $700m of loans; Dresdner Bank, $145m; and Credit Suisse, $55m. The consortium bought enough time for LTCM to dissolve in an orderly fashion. The fund was liquidated fully in 2000, and the consortium banks were paid back. The rescue mission was not a government bailout, and no taxpayer money was used. Nonetheless, there was a populist backlash that accused the Fed of protecting billionaires and aggravating moral hazard and too-big-to-fail problems. Sarcasm was not spared on the seemingly sophisticated lenders and billionaire investors who were supposed to be able to look after themselves. Yet public indignation did not translate into calls for the expansion of regulation or oversight of the financial institutions or of derivatives.

Interpretation

The task of explaining what went wrong from the insider's viewpoint fell on Scholes (2000). Scholes found fault with risk-management practices, criticized the VaR methodology, and called for financial firms to conduct stress tests on their portfolios to gauge potential losses in times of extreme turbulence in markets. However, as the primary cause of the collapse he singled out the fundamentals, specifically the risk premium. What brought LTCM down, according to Scholes, was the generalized run of market participants dumping their assets, initiated by an external shock. Investors had come to believe that the IMF would assist emerging countries in times of trouble and would not let them default on their debt. When the IMF stood on the sidelines as Russia defaulted this belief was shattered. Consequently, investors' risk premium and liquidity preference skyrocketed. When everyone sells and no one buys liquidity evaporates. It will be recalled that orthodox economists have been applying the same line of reasoning, i.e. exogenous shocks create liquidity crises, to explain financial crises since the South Sea Bubble.

This diagnosis treats illiquidity as the outcome of an exogenous shock and overlooks the issues of overleveraging and excessive confidence in the economic models that underlie the trading strategy. The alternative way of looking at the LTCM debacle is to view the lack of liquidity as the symptom of the problem, not the source. The fund had understated its risk exposure drastically in view of rising volatility in the market and ended up overleveraged. Its hedging strategy also failed because massive shorting of Treasuries had correlated positions on its balance sheet, all of them highly vulnerable to a single risk factor: liquidity. With the crisis and panic in the rush to liquidity, the relative price of short positions increased and spreads widened instead of narrowing. LTCM was caught because it was overleveraged, and the mathematical models dismissed the possibility of a shock of such proportions.

The quant partners were in a state of disbelief because financial models dictated that, in a world of optimizers, the spreads should have converged. The Russian default should not have affected, say, the positions on Brazilian debt or UK interest swaps as long as the fundamentals of the latter were unrelated to the former. The theory ignored the possibility that through the interdependent actions of economic agents panic and contagion could wreak havoc in markets and push prices cumulatively away from their fundamental values. The oversight seems surprising because such massive runs to liquidity have been observed repeatedly throughout history. The October 1987 meltdown occurred only 11 years previously, but the LTCM models simply ignored the possibility. It is true that returns would align and spreads would shrink, but that eventuality could follow a very bumpy course, and the dictum (often attributed to Keynes) that "The market can remain irrational longer than you can remain solvent" applies.

The dot-com bubble, 1998–2001

In the summer of 1995 Netscape Communications Corporation, an internet-browser company, offered shares to the market for the first time. Its business plan was to give the browser away free to users and raise revenue from the sale of server software and service contracts to users setting up and operating their websites. Netscape's market share was reportedly 75 percent, although there were competitors in the wings, including Microsoft's Spyglass (later Explorer) that was to come free with the Windows 95 operating system. Investment bank Morgan Stanley, the primary underwriter of the initial public offering (IPO), had initially planned to sell 3.5 million shares at $12 to $24 per share. By August 8 the bank raised the public offering to 5 million shares and the price to $28. When the Netscape IPO took place on August 9 the share price rose as high as $74.75. At the close the price stood at $58.25, and the market capitalization of Netscape was $2.2b (New York Times 1995). It was an exceptionally successful opening day for a stock on Wall Street. The success came despite the fact that Netscape had never made any profit. It had lost more than $4m in the first six months of 1995, and analysts did not expect profits for another two years. The Netscape IPO heralded the arrival of a new phase of the information-technology revolution.[10]

The information-technology revolution

Throughout the 1980s many experts and policymakers raised concerns about the US's loss of its manufacturing base and economic power to the Far East and Europe. However, these concerns were soon replaced by a celebration of the rise of the new economy in Silicon Valley, which featured technological superiority and entrepreneurial culture. The old economy was pronounced passé. Information technology, like the factory system, railways, and assembly lines of earlier eras, was viewed as a revolutionary transformation that would change the nature of production, distribution, exchange, and global patterns of specialization. By the mid 1990s technology firms, exemplified by Intel, Sun Systems, Hewlett–Packard, Microsoft, and Oracle, were already well established corporations and recognized as the leaders in transforming the core of economic activity from traditional manufacturing to collection, processing, storage, and dissemination of information.

These firms manufactured faster and more powerful central processing units, desktop computers, and servers, and created sophisticated software that ran on advanced hardware. Such innovations made it possible for more enterprises to avail themselves of the benefits of the new technology. In businesses of all sizes, digital technology improved productivity by streamlining production, distribution, inventory management, account keeping, and communications. It also reduced costs by replacing administrative and clerical staff as well as certain types of crafts workers. As home computers became more user-friendly and less expensive, consumers also participated in the technology revolution. There is widespread agreement among observers that the advance in information technology was one of the primary factors that explained the uninterrupted economic growth and stock-market boom from 1992 to 2001.

By the mid 1990s there was yet again a new revolution: the internet and the web. The government, military, and universities participated in the creation of the first communication and data-sharing computer networks in the 1960s. In the 1970s and 1980s common network protocols facilitated the merging of many networks. By the end of the 1980s the global civilian network, commonly referred to as the internet, encompassed North America and Europe and had made inroads into Asia. Governmental agencies and universities used it for communications, research, and education. The European Organization for Nuclear Research (CERN) created the World Wide Web, a system of interlinked hypertext documents that resided in computers across the globe and that could be accessed via the internet. CERN made the web freely available to all users in April 1993. Internet browsers enabled users to search for and access information on the web. One of the revolutionary browsers with a graphical interface, Mosaic, was developed in 1993 at the University of Illinois at Urbana–Champaign with funding provided by the US government. Later it was commercialized under the name Netscape Navigator.

Two sets of firms took advantage of the commercial opportunities of the internet and the web. The first set of companies created the hardware and software for the communication infrastructure. Large communications companies, such as WorldCom, built the "communications super-highway" of fiber-optic-cable networks that enabled the flow of huge volumes of information quickly and efficiently. In the heyday of the boom internet traffic was said to be growing at 1,000 percent annually, and the communication companies were borrowing billions of dollars to construct wider-bandwidth fiber-optic networks to meet the anticipated demand for high-speed internet access. Others, such as Cisco Systems, manufactured the routing-hardware infrastructure. Firms such as Netscape, AOL, and Yahoo! offered internet access, web portals, and browsing services.

The second set of companies used the internet and the web to access business and retail customers and offer cheaper and more efficient means of shopping and delivery of goods and services. Virtual commerce competed with traditional brick-and-mortar stores by offering a larger variety of goods and services at lower prices and for home delivery. Amazon and eBay are successful examples of such companies.

The commercial potential of web-based projects depend on *economies of scale*, whereby the larger size of an operation reduces the unit cost of production, and *network economies*, which occur when the value of a good or service rises with the number of users. Examples of network economies include the telephone and social networks—even a Friday night party. The higher the number of people who sign up, the more people who can be reached, and the more attractive and valuable the commodity becomes for other users. The expansion in the number of businesses and people who used the internet to access information raised the prospects for entrepreneurs to reach and offer services to potential customers. After 1994 commercial websites proliferated.

The business model

The business model of web companies was to "get big fast" and to exploit the "first-mover advantage" (Goldfarb *et al.* 2007). The strategy required the creation of a large customer base to deliver a wide variety of products and services at lower prices and greater convenience via the web. Time was of the essence because the key to the success of these types of firms was to generate traffic to its website, and build a brand name and consumer awareness of the company and the product. Earlier access to customers and market share was expected to become self-sustaining due to network effects; in turn, this would reduce competition. A company that consolidates its market share and collects information about its customers earlier than its competitors can reinforce its position by tailoring its products to individual tastes and imposing technical and marketing standards on the industry.

To capture the hearts, minds, and wallets of customers and ward off competitors start-ups needed to be loss-leaders while stimulating their sales and building network economies. Thus, a start-up firm needs to identify a novel product or service that appeals to customers and then access large amounts of funds so they can meet their expenses during the early business-building and growth stages. One success story is the online bookstore Amazon.com. Amazon was established in 1995 and went public in 1997. It spent its first years investing heavily in expanding its customer base and did not target profit-making for a period of four to five years. In fact, it reported an extremely modest profit at the end of 2001 (0.05 percent of revenues). Under such a business plan a company faces a negative cash flow for an extended period of time, during which it can sustain itself only by using its capital to meet its overheads. Its survival requires venture capitalists or shareholders with deep pockets who are willing to give a fledgling enterprise a fighting chance.

Enterprising internet-commerce companies offered products that ranged from social-networking and auction services to virtual stores that sold books, groceries, toys, and pet supplies. Many companies offered similar or identical products and chased the same customer base. Competition was intense, and most of the companies had no chance of survival because it is logically impossible for all companies to have large markets shares. By definition, network effects benefit only a few.

Nevertheless, internet companies attracted huge volumes of capital. The emerging "new era" thinking promised unprecedented productivity gains through new means of communication, marketing, productivity, inventory control, and supply chains. Although not many investors fully comprehended the potential of the new technology, they were confident that the future held ever larger profit prospects. Using the "e-" prefix or ".com" suffix was sufficient to make any company seem to outsiders like a visionary enterprise on the verge of a breakthrough (Shiller 2005: 77, 107).

There were four sets of players in the dot-com game. The first set consisted of the entrepreneurs, or the ideas people, a fluid group who acted as company founders, executives, and employees. Entrepreneurs identified a new market, invented a new method of marketing, or wrote software that expanded the capabilities of the digital network. They were usually technology-savvy young people who worked for stock options and stood to realize huge profits from their equity holdings if the dot-com firm took off and had a successful IPO.

The second set of players was comprised of individuals and private-equity-partnership firms with a large amount of capital who offered financing to start-ups in return for stock options. The success of the entrepeneurs' ideas required seed and sustenance money, which could be substantial because internet firms typically operated at a loss during their early years. The primary source of funds during the establishment and growth stage of dot-com firms was *venture capitalists*, who sought to identify star companies of the future and lay claim to potential fortunes. The third set of agents was investment banks that arranged the internet firms' IPOs when they were ready to take off. Finally, the fourth set included investors who staked a claim on the sector through two channels at two different stages. First, wealthy individuals and institutional investors became limited partners or investors in venture-capital firms. Venture-capital firms managed the money of these investors in return for fees and a share of the profits. Thus, investors owned equity indirectly in technology firms via venture capital. Second, investors participated in the game directly by buying stocks after the company went public.

The traditional objective of an IPO is to generate funds for the firm to be used for fixed-investment plans, but the objective of a technology-firm IPO was quite different. Investment banks designed the offer price and quantity of shares to maximize capital gains on the first day of the IPO. They were aided in this effort by the fact that these IPOs were highly publicized in the media. In addition, the quantity of shares offered was usually kept small, and restrictions were imposed on the transaction of shares. The combination of a highly advertised IPO and a small number of circulating shares caused prices to increase by several orders of magnitude on the first day. Investors who purchased shares at or near the IPO offer price benefitted from immediate capital gains.

The magnitude of these gains attracted more investors, who fueled the stock-price increases. On the other side, entrepreneurs, venture capitalists, and early-round investors, who held the bulk of the stock options, reaped huge capital gains, at least on paper, in a single day. As the media touted the new industry, share values of the public dot-com companies reached new heights. Widely reported stories of unprecedented gains, in turn, created a positive-feedback mechanism that attracted more entrepreneurs, venture capitalists, and early investors to the technology sector (Kindleberger and Aliber 2011: 182). Finally, in return for their role in generating this wealth, investment banks were rewarded handsomely in underwriting fees.

Many of the companies that secured significant capitalization were yet to sell a single item or realize any profits, and the founders of many of these companies often had little or no business or managerial expertise. The capital they attracted was buying into an "idea" that might or might not pay off in the midst of intense competition. However, the novelty of the product, incessant media promotion, and intense advertising were influential. The capital flow continued, and the dot-com bubble was well on its way in 1998. The geographic center of the new technology was Silicon Valley, near San Francisco, but many state and local governments in the US heavily invested in their own technology corridors, unimaginatively labeling them Silicon Alley, Prairie, Park, Coast, Hill, and so forth, with advanced-technology office spaces to create synergy and attract young technology entrepreneurs and start-ups.

The boom and the bust

The stock market boomed in line with the new technologies, products, and firms, and the new merger movement they initiated. The increase in stock-market indices took place against the background of the Fed easing monetary policy and lowering short-term interest rates, especially after the turbulence caused by LTCM. Financial crises in Asia, Latin America, and Russia also compelled many investors to direct their funds to safer assets, adding to the volume of financial wealth in the US. The exceptional performance of the stock market is illustrated in Figure 14.1. Over the decade the S&P 500 index rose by 116 percent in inflation-corrected terms, but the surge occurred in the second half of the decade. The price index rose by merely 14 percent over the first five years of the decade, at an annual rate of approximately 2.7 percent.

The rest of the decade was an entirely different story. The index jumped 32 percent in 1995, 17 percent in 1996, 24 percent in 1997, 22 percent in 1998, and 16 percent in 1999. It was a phenomenal streak by any measure. Reminiscent of 1928 and 1929, it was hailed as a permanently high stock market, the triumph of innovative technology and the potential of individualistic, entrepreneurial, low-regulation, US-style capitalism. James Glassman and Kevin Hassett, then fellows at the American Enterprise Institute, argued in their 1999 book, *Dow 36,000*, that US stocks were, in fact, undervalued and that the DJIA would more than triple to 36,000 in a few years. They encouraged people to jump in while stocks were still cheap. As Figure 14.2 illustrates, the only comparable market performance occurred in the second half of the 1920s. Not everyone was in agreement with the optimistic assessments, however. If the P/E ratio is

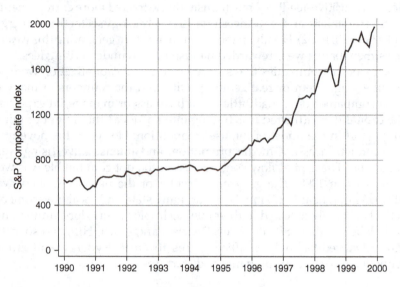

Figure 14.1 Real S&P Composite Index, 1990–2000 (monthly).
Source: Shiller (2005).

any indicator stocks were overpriced by historical standards. As seen in Figure 14.2, cyclically adjusted P/E (CAPE) ratio rose steadily throughout the period and reached nearly 45, a historical record.

Figures 14.1 and 14.2 give, if anything, a subdued notion of what was really going on in the technology sector. As technology stocks are traded predominantly on the NASDAQ exchange, the NASDAQ Composite Index gives a more accurate picture of developments in this frontier segment of the securities market and of the impact of the digital revolution. Figure 14.3 reports the NASDAQ Composite between 1998 and 2002. For comparison purposes, the S&P 500 is reported in the same chart, and both indices are normalized to 100 on January 1, 1998. The NASDAQ Composite peaked on March 10, 2000, rising 220 percent in the span of 37 months. Over the same period the S&P 500 rose by 25 percent. Yet even the NASDAQ Composite may be considered too broad an index to capture the internet effect because it includes all high-tech companies, some of which were already a part of the "old" economy. Ofek and Richardson (2002, 2003) identify 400 "pure" internet companies, excluding technology companies with internet-related business, e.g. Cisco, Microsoft, MCI, that were not exclusively internet companies. The authors report that the "pure" internet-company-stock index grew by about 500 percent over the same period.

Alan Greenspan initially followed the stock-market boom with some trepidation. Greenspan, a disciple of Ayn Rand, economic consultant, chair of the Council of Economic Advisors of President Gerald Ford, and

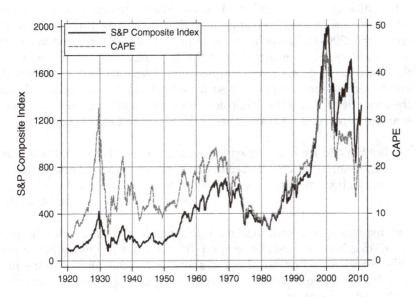

Figure 14.2 Real S&P Composite Index and CAPE, 1920–2010 (monthly).

Source: Shiller (2005).

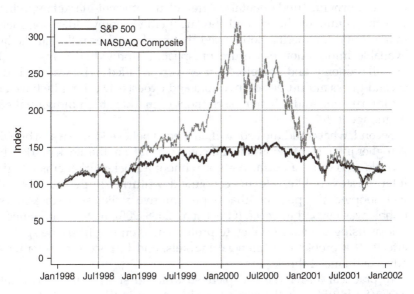

Figure 14.3 The dot-com bubble, 1998–2001 (daily).

Source: Calculated by the author from S&P Dow Jones Indices and NASDAQ Indices.

a firm libertarian who believed in the efficiency and self-disciplining power of markets, had been appointed chairman of the Fed in 1987. By the end of the 1990s he had achieved revered status in Washington as a result of the satisfactory performance of the macroeconomy under his watch (high economic growth was coupled with low inflation) as well as the Fed's swift and firm response to serious shocks to the economy, including the crash of 1987 and the implosion of LTCM, to avert economic dislocation and bank runs. On December 5, 1996, he asked at a speech:

> But how do we know when *irrational exuberance* has unduly escalated asset values, which then become subject to unexpected and prolonged contractions as they have in Japan over the past decade?
>
> (Greenspan 2008: 177) [italics added]

Greenspan's speech sent markets tumbling the next day, from Tokyo to New York. Nevertheless, Greenspan did not follow up his question with either words or action but chose to show renewed deference to the markets. Within a week markets recovered and continued their upward trend with even more rigor.

The dilemma that faced central bankers in 1996 was similar to that faced in 1929 in the US, and in 1834 and 1847 in Britain. First, how does one know there is an asset-price bubble and that rising prices do not merely reflect improving fundamentals? After all, the efficient-market hypothesis was the dominant theory, and the "new era economy" idea dominated markets and the media. Both stated that market prices reflected the best available information on future prospects of individual firms and the overall economy, and, therefore, prices were justified. Who was the Fed to second-guess multitudes of investors and experts? Did it really have better information and a better assessment of markets than individual economic agents?

Second, what could the Fed do if, indeed, it believed there was a bubble? A higher interest rate would let off some steam from the stock market, but it could also cause a crash. With or without a stock-market crash, higher interest rates could create an economic downturn.[11] In the late 1990s the Fed adopted the position that a pre-emptive strike at a stock-market bubble was beyond its reach (Greenspan 2008: 208). Instead, it defined its role as using monetary policy to protect the economy from the spillover effects of a problem in financial markets, and to restore order after an adverse financial shock.

In practical terms, the Fed pledged to lower short-term interest rates and offer liquidity to the market in abundance in the event that markets declined by large enough magnitudes to endanger stability. The pledge is known as the *Greenspan Put*—as though investors had bought put options to sell their portfolios: should a calamity arise the Fed steps in and provides sufficient liquidity to markets until the problem is resolved. As anticipated, there were those who expressed doubts about the moral-hazard implications of the Greenspan Put. In fact, moral hazard was amplified because the Greenspan Put came on top of deregulation and a false sense of security regarding the derivative "insurance policies" that promoted excessive risk-taking behavior. The full consequences of the Fed's stance surfaced a decade later.

The turning point in the stock market came in March 2000. As mentioned, the NASDAQ Composite peaked on March 10, 2000, and then started its precipitous decline (Figure 14.3). Investors dumped their holdings en masse. By the end of 2000 the NASDAQ index had collapsed by 50 percent, and by the end of 2001 it had declined by another 20 percent. The losses were spread across the industry, affecting established technology firms as well as start-ups. The media extensively publicized the failures of dot-com companies that had burned through their capital and were forced into liquidation. Selective reporting of eccentric internet projects provided fodder for humor, parody, and satire. While anecdotes gave the impression that most dot-com companies had folded, many, in fact, survived the turmoil (Goldfarb *et al.* 2007), although the earlier optimism was muted, and a great deal of paper wealth was destroyed. Various companies, such as Amazon and eBay, weathered the storm and came out of it stronger, with better-established market positions and fewer competitors.

Perhaps the largest negative economic impact at this time was on the debt-ridden communication-infrastructure sector. During the boom demand for high-speed internet access increased significantly, but it was far short of the expectations of the communication companies that invested in the construction of the fiber-optic network. Lewis (2009a) puts the actual annual traffic growth at approximately 70 percent to 150 percent, far below expectations, which reached, at the time, as high as 1,000 percent. Thus, an immense excess of fiber-optic capacity was created. This infrastructure sat idle for years without generating profits, and dwindling profits meant that companies did not have the revenue to meet their debt obligations. Excess capacity, lagging profits, and the debt burden, sometimes in combination with mismanagement and fraudulent accounting, caused the stocks of telecommunication companies, such as Global Crossing, Nortel, and WorldCom, to crash, and these huge companies filed for bankruptcy.

Banks were not involved in the creation of the bubble, and the burst did not affect their balance sheets, nor was there a credit freeze. The loss of wealth, estimated as high as $5t, however, had a negative effect on consumption spending, which contributed to the eight-month recession from March to November 2001, during which GDP declined by 0.3 percent.

Interpretation

In the immediate aftermath of the crash many commentators searched for an explanation of its causes. They identified a number of proximate factors that might have contributed to the collapse. In preparation for the Year 2000 (Y2K) switch most companies had invested billions in new hardware and software to replace their old computer systems and programs. Therefore, there was a drop in technology purchases in the first months of the new millennium. In addition, the findings of the United States v. Microsoft anti-trust case were scheduled to be released on April 3. The prevailing expectation that the ruling would go against Microsoft created anxiety among technology investors. Yet another piece of news that may have scared technology investors was the large sell-off of prominent high-tech stocks, e.g. Dell, Cisco, IBM. According to Shiller (2005), however, none of the news was significant enough to explain the break on March 10.

From an economist's perspective the first interesting question regarding the bursting of the bubble is whether technology stocks were overpriced. Many observers draw attention to market anomalies as evidence of mispricing (Ofek and Richardson 2002; Shiller 2005: 181–2). One example is the frequently observed jumps in stock prices following a superficial name change, e.g. the addition of .com or .net, which did not add any new information regarding expected cash flow and, therefore, should not have created a price change. Another example is the unrealistic market capitalization of subsidiary companies that, on occasion, climbed above that of the parent company. One extreme case was the valuations of 3Com and its subsidiary Palm Inc. At its IPO Palm's market capitalization was $53.4b. The value of 3Com, which owned 94 percent of Palm, was $28.5b, which meant that the rest of the assets of 3Com were worth –$21.7b!

Another way to assess mispricing is through the P/E ratio. Figure 14.2 plots CAPE. This metric reached its record value in March 2000, suggesting overvaluation of the overall market by historical standards. It could be argued, however, that the high P/E ratio reflected a transformative change in profitability and, therefore, was not indicative of overvaluation. Ofek and Richardson (2002) use their sample of pure internet companies to gauge whether the latter claim is plausible. They conclude that the entire internet industry would have had to grow two to three times as fast as the fastest-growing firms in the overall economy for ten years to justify the observed internet-company share prices, which they deem improbable.

Again, the fundamentals-based approach disputes this conclusion. Pastor and Veronesi (2006) challenge Ofek and Richardson's (2002) claim that high share prices (as well as the volatility of technology stocks) were associated with a high degree of uncertainty about the profitability and future growth rates of the revolutionary-tech sector, which induced investors to discount historical experience. They argue that the magnitude of uncertainty was large enough to increase the value of the firms and ex ante to justify stock prices.

If the fundamentals-based approach is correct and firms were not overvalued ex ante then what explains the boom and the bust? As usual, the

Fed's policies came under scrutiny. After a period of easy monetary policy the Fed raised the federal funds rate six times, a total of 1.75 percentage points between June 30, 1999, and May 16, 2000, from 4.25 percent to 6 percent, explaining that the objective of these rate hikes was to draw back the liquidity supplied to markets in the aftermath of the Russian default and the LTCM affair, and to prevent the economy from overheating. Nevertheless, expectations of an economic slowdown may have lowered profit expectations and stock sales. The Christmas season of 1999, in fact, hinted at economic weakening.

Pastor and Veronesi (2006) claim it was the arrival of news that corrected the over-optimistic expectations formed amid high uncertainty. The technology-sector stock prices rose until 2000 and eventually fell in 2000–1 with reports of lower than anticipated profitability. Another fundamentals-based answer to the question relies on adjustments to technological changes. The technological-revolution argument offered by Pastor and Veronesi (2009) is summarized in the context of nineteenth-century US railroads (see Chapter 8). The nature of risk faced by owners of technology stocks changed over the course of the technology revolution from idiosyncratic to systematic risk. In the early stages of the revolution technology firms and the sector were small, and the portfolio-risk exposure to these stocks could be reduced through diversification. As the technology matured and integrated with the old economy, the riskiness of the technology stocks became more closely correlated with general market fluctuations and, thus, became systematic and less diversifiable. In the beginning, then, low risk and productivity growth jointly drove the stock price higher, but later the risk premium rose and put downward pressure on prices; it eventually took over the positive productivity effect, and the stock price started to decline. By this account, the rise and fall of technology stocks reflected the life cycle of the internet revolution.

In contrast, Goldfarb *et al.* (2007) accept that stocks were overvalued and offer an explanation based on optimizing behavior under the conditions of asymmetric information. The investment decisions of individual venture capitalists are conditioned by their information sets. Some of this information was public, or shared by everyone. Some of it was private, or available specifically to an individual or group. Each venture capitalist knows that others have their own private information but does not know what it is—hence asymmetric information. The venture capitalist can only try to infer what others privately know from their buy and sell decisions, or the movement of the market.

In the late 1990s, according to Goldfarb *et al.* (2007), venture capitalists observed rising stock prices in the technology market that contradicted their private information on what prices should be. These rising prices created a belief cascade whereby individual venture capitalists discounted whatever private reservations they might have had about the prospects of internet companies and put more weight on the investment pattern that had emerged in the market. Growing confidence among venture capitalists on the viability of the "get big fast" strategy and "first-mover advantage" replaced traditional evaluation criteria and disconnected the price from the fundamentals. As information on the true profitability of internet companies arrived with a lag, this belief cascade temporarily dominated markets, and share prices escalated sharply. However, this cascade was also fragile in the sense that it collapsed quickly once information arrived regarding the true prospects of internet firms and the weaknesses in their business models.

The suddenness of the dot-com crash was a symptom of another level of informational asymmetry in the market, one that existed between venture capitalists and investors. Investors in venture-capital firms and information-technology stocks were more removed and less informed about markets than venture capitalists—something they were well aware of. Once investors received the bad news, *after* the venture capitalists, they were even hastier than the venture capitalists in decreasing the flow of funds to the industry to cut their losses, both directly through reducing stock purchases and indirectly through reducing investing in venture-capital firms. The abruptness of their actions precluded a more orderly adjustment, and the outcome was a crash rather than a milder correction.

Another explanation based on market imperfections is offered by Ofek and Richardson (2002, 2003). Their explanation has two elements. First, internet-firm shareholders were heterogeneous, retail (not institutional) investors, many of whom were under-informed and inexperienced regarding technology stocks. Ofek and Richardson claim that the overvaluation of stocks suggests excessive optimism on the part of these noise investors. Their actions led to overtrading, high prices, and volatility that were unrelated to the fundamentals. Theoretically, the smart money should have shorted the stocks and driven prices back to intrinsic levels. The second component of the Ofek–Richardson explanation is that short selling of internet stocks did not occur because there were limitations on shorting, as evidenced, among other things, by higher borrowing costs, few lenders, and high volatility. Often, technology stocks were simply not available for borrowing due to temporary restrictions imposed by the underwriters. The explanation for the crash follows from the same logic. In the spring of 2000 a large number of internet firms removed restrictions preventing investors from selling their shares. The outcome was not only an increased supply of shares but also the removal of shorting constraints, which precipitated the price collapse.

Shiller (2005: 129–30) emphasizes the role of feedback and psychological factors and argues that the internet-stock boom was a fad. He notes that the far more important factor in explaining the crash was the public recognition, reiterated strongly in the business press, that many internet companies were losing money fast and that their P/E ratios were improbable. These publications served as a feedback mechanism that amplified declining confidence in internet stocks, which eventually spilled over to the rest of the market and ultimately brought about the recession of 2001.

Key terms and concepts

Agency-label security
Asset-backed security
Cash settlement
Collateralized debt obligation
Conforming loan
Convergence trade
Credit default swap
Currency swap
Economies of scale
Greenspan Put
Interest swap
Mortgage-backed security
Network economy
Pairs trade
Pass-through security
Physical settlement
Prepayment risk
Private-label security
Repurchase (repo) agreement
Securitization
Shadow banking system
Structured debt instrument
Structured finance
Value-at-risk (VaR)
Venture capital
Volatility trade

Endnotes

1 For insider evaluations of economic conditions and policymaking in the 1990s from very different perspectives see Stiglitz (2003) and Greenspan (2008: Chapters 7–9).
2 New York State Attorney General Eliot Spitzer prosecuted prominent US banks for these fraudulent and unethical activities. The outcome was the Global Settlement in 2002, whereby ten large banks (including Credit Suisse First Boston, Merrill Lynch, Goldman Sachs, and JPMorgan Chase) agreed to pay $1.4b in fines and to separate their analysis departments from their investment-banking businesses. See US Securities and Exchange Commission (2003) for details. A further investigation in 2003 resulted in several mutual funds being fined $1b for permitting their privileged customers to engage in illegal "after-hours trading" at the previous day's prices and high-frequency "market timing" trading.

3 Basel I was a set of guidelines on credit extension agreed upon by central bankers and regulators of advanced industrial countries for banks to implement. These guidelines were superseded by Basel II in 2004 and Basel III in 2010.
4 In practice, banks or thrifts that had made mortgage loans issued the pass-through security and Ginnie Mae approved and guaranteed the certificates.
5 I will use the generic term mortgage-backed security to refer to all mortgage-related securities including the CMOs.
6 LIBOR (London interbank offered rate) is the average interest rate at which the largest banks in London borrow from other banks. It is an internationally recognized reference for a short-term interbank loan rate.
7 See Tett (2009) on how CDSs were created and gained a foothold in the industry.
8 The standard normal distribution table reports probabilities that a random variable, distributed normally with a mean of zero and a standard deviation of one, will be less than or equal to a specific value. It is available in appendices of statistics textbooks.
9 Lowenstein (2001) offers a detailed account of the fortunes of LTCM.
10 On the story of the rise and fall of the internet companies see Cassidy (2002). Lewis (2009b) provides a compendium of contemporary commentary on the dot-com bubble.
11 Stiglitz (2003: 64) notes that there were, of course, other measures that the Fed could have considered to calm markets, such as raising margin requirements or speaking against the capital-gains tax cut in 1997, but it did not entertain these alternatives.

References

Cassidy, John. 2002. *Dot.con: The Greatest Story Ever Sold*. New York: Harper Collins.

Goldfarb, Brent, David Kirsch and David A. Miller. 2007. "Was There Too Little Entry During the Dot Com Era?" *Journal of Financial Economics* 86: 100–44.

Greenspan, Alan. 2008. *The Age of Turbulence: Adventures in a New World*. New York: Penguin Books.

Inside Mortgage Finance. 2012. *The 2012 Mortgage Market Statistical Annual*, vol. II. Bethesda, MD: Inside Mortgage Finance.

ISDA (International Swaps and Derivatives Association). 2013. "Market Surveys Data, 1987–2010." Online: www2.isda.org/functional-areas/research/surveys/market-surveys/.

Jorion, Philippe. 2000. "Risk Management Lessons from Long-Term Capital Management." *European Financial Management* 6 (3): 277–300.

Kindleberger, Charles P. and Robert Z. Aliber. 2011. *Manias, Panics, and Crashes: A History of Financial Crises*, 6th ed. New York: Palgrave Macmillan.

Lewis, Michael. 2009a. "In Defense of the Boom." Pp. 239–58 in *Panic: The Story of Modern Financial Insanity*, edited by Michael Lewis. New York London: W. W. Norton and Company.

Lewis, Michael, ed. 2009b. *Panic: The Story of Modern Financial Insanity*. New York: W.W. Norton and Company.

Lowenstein, Roger. 2001. *When Genius Failed: The Rise and Fall of Long-Term Capital Management*. New York: Random House.

New York Times. 1995. "Underwriters Raise Offer Price for Netscape Communication." August 9.

Ofek, Eli and Matthew Richardson. 2002. "The Valuation and Market Rationality of Internet Stock Prices." *Oxford Review of Economic Policy* 18 (3): 265–87.

Ofek, Eli and Matthew Richardson. 2003. "Dotcom Mania: The Rise and Fall of Internet Stock Prices." *Journal of Finance* 58 (3): 1113–37.

Pastor, Lubos and Pietro Veronesi. 2006. "Was There a Nasdaq Bubble In The Late 1990s?" *Journal of Financial Economics* 81: 61–100.

Pastor, Lubos and Pietro Veronesi. 2009. "Technological Revolutions and Stock Prices." *American Economic Review* 99 (4): 1451–83.

Piketty, Thomas and Emmanuel Saez. 2003. "Income Inequality in the United States, 1913–1998." *Quarterly Journal of Economics* 118 (1): 1–39.

Ranieri, Lewis S. 1996. "The Origins of Securitization, Sources of its Growth, and its Future Potential." Pp. 31–43 in *A Primer on Securitization*, edited by Leon T. Kendall and Michael J. Fishman. Cambridge, MA: The MIT Press.

Scholes, Myron S. 2000. "Crisis and Risk Management." *American Economic Review* 90 (2): 17–21.

Shiller, Robert J. 2005. *Irrational Exuberance*, 2nd ed. New York: Currency Doubleday. Online: www.econ.yale.edu/~shiller/data/ie_data.xls.

Stiglitz, Joseph E. 2003. *The Roaring 1990s: A New History of the World's Most Prosperous Decade*. New York: W. W. Norton and Company.

Tett, Gillian. 2009. *Fool's Gold: How the Bold Dream of a Small Tribe at J. P. Morgan was Corrupted by Wall Street Greed and Unleashed a Catastrophe*. New York: Free Press.

US Department of the Treasury. 1999. *Statement by President Bill Clinton at the Signing of the Financial Modernization Bill*. November 12. Online: www.treasury. gov/press-center/press-releases/Pages/ls241.aspx.

US Securities and Exchange Commission. 2003. *Ten of Nation's Top Investment Firms Settle Enforcement Actions Involving Conflicts of Interest Between Research and Investment Banking*. 2003-54 Joint Press Release April 28, 2003, Washington D.C. and New York. Online: www.sec.gov/news/press/2003-54.htm.

Wolff, Edward N. 2002. *Top Heavy: The Increasing Inequality of Wealth in America and What Can be Done About It*. New York: The New Press.

15 The latest act

Subprime mortgages and derivatives

On Thursday, September 18, 2008, Treasury Secretary Henry Paulson issued a warning that the credit arteries of the economy were clogged and that a cardiac arrest was imminent. Ben Bernanke, chair of the Federal Reserve System (Fed), announced to congressional leaders that, unless Congress acted boldly, the US was only days away from a financial meltdown and a predicament worse than the Great Depression (Wessel 2009: 203–4): "If we don't do this, we may not have an economy on Monday," he warned. A few days later, when his own party stood in the way of opening up the blocked channels of finance, President George W. Bush stated, "If money isn't loosened up, this sucker could go down." Policymakers were facing the endgame of the accelerating downward slide of the financial sector that had started two years earlier.

In 2006 mortgage defaults and foreclosures had increased, and a number of large mortgage-originator companies, including some of the largest, filed for bankruptcy. Unsurprisingly, the cost of mortgage insurance increased in 2007. Then in March 2008 the government prevented the bankruptcy of the fifth-largest US investment bank, Bear Stearns, by brokering its sale to another bank, JPMorgan Chase. On September 6 the government took over the mortgage giants, Fannie Mae and Freddie Mac. The last domino to fall was the fourth-largest US investment bank, Lehman Brothers, which went bankrupt on September 15. In the following two days chaos ensued.

A run on money-market funds began; interbank lending came to a halt; credit flow to the real sector of the economy froze; the insurance giant American International Group (AIG) teetered on the edge of bankruptcy, compelling the Fed to authorize an $85b line of credit; the Securities and Exchange Commission (SEC) announced a temporary emergency ban on short selling financial stocks; and the Dow Jones Industrial Average (DJIA) fell by 3 percent. When Paulson and Bernanke assembled with congressional leaders on September 18 they anticipated that Congress would authorize the executive branch to intervene to thaw the liquidity freeze so that banks, hopefully, would start lending to each other, as well as to nonbank businesses, and restore the financial sector of the economy.

In describing the 2007–8 subprime crash, commentators frequently mention the metaphor "the perfect storm." The term has become familiar after Sebastian Junger, in his 1997 book of the same name, described the rare convergence of distinct weather disturbances over the northeastern US that created the 1991 Halloween Nor'easter storm. One should be cautious, however, in using this metaphor in reference to the 2007–8 financial crisis. A perfect storm refers to independent catastrophic events that coincide with, and thereby magnify the effects of, each other. This perspective relegates what happened in the financial markets to an abnormal event, reduces it to happenstance and, notwithstanding its destructive power, ultimately trivializes the incident. Nonetheless, it is a common viewpoint as demonstrated by many commentators' proclamations that "nobody expected this crisis" or that it was a "once in a lifetime crisis."

Perhaps an alternative interpretation of the weather metaphor is more appropriate for the conditions of the financial markets of the 2000s. If the separate weather systems that ultimately converge and wreak havoc are the consequences of underlying climate forces, such as global warming, then a perfect storm is not a mere fluke or an exceptional situation: it is the symptom of a set of identifiable factors. Even if it is difficult to forecast when and where perfect storms would occur, we know that changing atmospheric conditions increase their likelihood, and we should anticipate encountering more of them in the future. Treating the emergence and convergence of distinct destructive weather systems as an anomaly would then not only be erroneous but also reckless and irresponsible. The right course of action would be to identify and track, with greater precision, the systematic factors that make perfect storms more likely, take measures to weaken or eliminate these factors, and devise means to protect people from their damage.

Similarly, the transformation of the financial markets since 1980 created forces and tensions that aggravated systemic fragility and made calamities more probable. During the 2000s these forces and tensions surfaced in the forms of unsustainable and unprecedented increases in home prices and household indebtedness, extreme leveraging in unregulated shadow banking institutions, and the explosive growth of bilateral swap derivatives as instruments of speculation.

Several experts cautioned about the vulnerability of the financial system. The business press in the early 2000s reported that there was a housing bubble, but most scholars and policymakers did not give much credence to the idea. Dean Baker (2002) was a noteworthy exception, expressing concern about unsustainable increases in home prices. Claudio Borio and William White (2003) of the Bank of International Settlements cautioned central bankers that the thriving economy, against the background of a liberalized financial system, was generating excessive debt, instability and risk. Robert Shiller (2005) offered historical data on home prices and argued that the increase in home prices was disconnected from the fundamentals. Raghuram Rajan (2005) and Nouriel Roubini (2006) issued dire warnings to central bankers about the growing fragility of the financial markets at the most prominent levels of policymaking and academia, but they too were summarily dismissed as misguided and then ignored by their peers.

However late and few these warnings might have been, they still demonstrate that the systematic problems that endangered the financial system were visible at least in part. Beneath the surface of a healthy economy these forces were driving the economy into a perfect storm. The complacency engendered by the seemingly endless generation of fees, returns, profits, and bonuses related to mortgages, securitization, and derivatives, as well as the intellectual dominance of the vision that financial markets were performing their magic to the benefit of lenders, borrowers, and intermediaries, perhaps explains why the majority of the experts paid no attention to these perils or ruled them out when they were mentioned.

The complacent majority probably also took comfort in the fact that although what many commentators were calling "once in a lifetime" crises had been occurring with regularity since 1980—so far they had been dealt with quite effectively, without substantial collateral damage. Unfortunately, the crisis of 2007–8 turned out to be vastly different from the turbulence experienced in the previous two decades. While the actions of the Fed and the government were able to contain the previous crises, this time their traditional tools of crisis management proved ineffectual. The Great Recession, which followed the 2008 crash, was the US's deepest and longest contraction since the 1930s. Even after June 2009, the official end of the recession, the rate of unemployment remained stubbornly high, and the economy continued to operate below its potential level. This chapter and those following describe the mortgage-securitization process, shadow banking, and CDSs that constituted the fragile foundations of the financial structure; they chronicle the crisis and the policy responses over 2007 and 2008; and they summarize the contending explanations of why the crisis occurred.[1]

The housing market

Home ownership is an elemental ingredient of the American dream; private homes are popularly accepted as the appropriate environment in which to raise families and build neighborhoods. US governments since the 1930s have deemed home ownership a desirable goal to enhance social stability, and they designed and implemented public-policy measures to advance it. Beyond its worth in sentimental and social values, home ownership is a financial decision. A home is the principal item of wealth of most US households. Unlike rent, mortgage payments build equity, and homebuyers can take advantage of tax deductions on interest and property-tax payments. If home prices increase in line with the rate of inflation, home ownership protects the value of wealth. Homeowners may also stand to make capital gains if they can sell their homes.[2]

Whether home ownership is a good investment requires over-time comparisons of home prices. However, the housing stock is extremely heterogeneous, with great variations in location, size, shape, vintage, construction materials, and so forth. Therefore, the construction of a home-price index is far more complex than calculating, say, a stock-price index. A well known attempt to create a home-price index for the US was undertaken by professors Karl E. Case and Robert J. Shiller. The thick line in Figure 15.1 is the annual Case–Shiller index for home prices relative to the value of other goods from 1890 to 2012 (based on repeat sales of homes). Four distinct periods are observed in this diagram.

The first period was from 1890 to the mid 1910s, when the index oscillated around 100. The volatility of the early years is likely attributable to the paucity of systematic data. During the second period, from 1920 to the early 1940s, the average real home value was depressed. In the mid 1940s the home-price index jumped and then remained relatively flat for a long stretch of time, albeit with significant fluctuations, particularly during the inflationary late 1970s and the late 1980s. Stability of real home prices from the 1940s to the mid 1990s suggests that home ownership was a safe bet against inflation but not necessarily a reliable source of capital gains

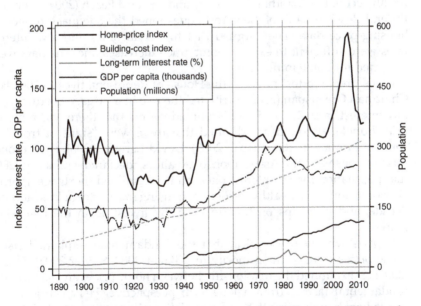

Figure 15.1 Case–Shiller home-price index and home-price fundamentals, 1890–2011 (annual).

Sources: GDP per capita calculated from FRED, Federal Reserve Bank of St. Louis; Shiller (2005).

(although this nationwide average obviously masks the performance of local housing markets where price booms may have been more substantial and longer-lasting). The real-home-price index in the mid 1990s stood at roughly the same level it did a century earlier. The most conspicuous change in the average home price, however, took place after 1997. Between 1997 and 2006 it jumped by 79 percent, from 109 to 195, an annual average increase of 6 percent. This was a nationwide phenomenon, although the price increases on the coasts and in the South were more accentuated. As Figure 15.1 makes clear, the price boom was an unparalleled event in the US housing market.

One question regarding the housing boom is whether this was a bubble or something that can be explained by the fundamentals. It is straightforward to identify the fundamentals that govern the demand and supply of homes: on the demand side a higher population and per capita income, along with a lower cost of borrowing, will raise the demand for housing. On the supply side home prices are expected to rise with the prices of construction and land.

During the boom years most policymakers, academics, and industry experts believed that the increase in average home prices was connected to the fundamentals, and did not express concern about excessive price escalations. Ben Bernanke, the head of President Bush's Council of Economic Advisors in 2005, attributed rising housing prices largely to the healthy economy. Jonathan McCarthy and Richard Peach (2004), from the Federal Reserve Bank of New York, questioned the adequacy of federal housing-price data. They argued that higher incomes and low interest rates were sufficient to explain home-price increases once the data were corrected for home improvements.

In his prepared testimony to the House of Representatives in 2002 Fed Chairman Greenspan (2002) attributed the rise in mortgage borrowing to low interest rates. In 2005 he discounted claims that there was a home-price bubble, although he admitted that there were "signs of froth" in some local markets (Greenspan 2005). David Lereah (2006), chief economist of the National Association of Realtors, declared as late as 2006 that population forces, interest rates, and streamlined mortgage approvals would support a healthy residential housing market for at least another decade, and gave tips on how to profit by investing in the real-estate market.

Experts who were skeptical that the fundamentals explained rising home prices were in the minority (e.g. Baker 2002; Shiller 2005). Shiller (2005: 13) examined the relationship between home prices and some of the fundamental factors from a long-term perspective. His historical data (reproduced in Figure 15.1) on population, interest rates, and home-construction costs do not indicate changes in these variables after 1997 that are commensurate with observed home-price increases. The population increased at a secular rate, without sharp variations. Long-term interest rates (a ten-year rate that is highly correlated with mortgage rates) had trended downward since 1983, but they were not extremely low by historical standards. Construction costs had begun to decline during the late 1970s and were flat throughout the 1990s. Per capita income did not exhibit a break in the 1990s. Finally, there is no severe shortage of land in the US. While real estate may be very expensive in certain areas, such as New York City and San Francisco, the US is abundantly endowed with land, and people as well as businesses have options to relocate when costs become prohibitive. This availability of substitutes should have helped to keep prices in check.

There were other signs that indicated home prices were out of the ordinary. One metric that mortgage lenders commonly use as an indicator of a home's affordability is the ratio of the home price to the annual income (net of debt obligations) of the prospective buyer. Too low a ratio means that the borrower may not be buying as good a home as she can afford; a high ratio signals a greater likelihood of difficulty in making mortgage payments. Over the 1975–2000 period the ratio averaged 2.4, fluctuating between 2.3 and 2.5 (Joint Center for Housing Studies (JCHS) 2008: 33). It jumped to 2.7 in 2001 and reached 3.6 in 2006.[3] Many homebuyers were borrowing beyond their means, which suggests that they somehow anticipated access to extra funds in the future. It is unlikely that homebuyers anticipated labor income to be a source of higher future income that would make mortgage payments affordable. Wages and salaries (the primary income source of most Americans) since the 1970s had been basically flat.

Another metric to judge whether homes are mispriced is the *price-rent ratio*, which is similar to the P/E ratio. The fundamental price of a house, like that of a stock, should reflect the discounted present value of the earnings it is expected to generate. The latter is the imputed rent stream. Similar to the P/E ratio, systematic deviations from the customary value of the price-rent ratio may be taken as an indicator of mispricing in the housing market. Krainer and Wei (2004) estimate that the ratio rose steadily after 1997 and, by 2002 (the last year of their study), stood 18 percent above the historical norm.

The third indicator of home overpricing is the vacancy rates in rental and ownership units. If home prices are higher due to the fundamentals causing a relative shortage of homes then households are expected to substitute relatively low-cost rental units for home purchases. Therefore, vacancies in rental units are expected to decline as home prices rise. Yet rental-vacancy rates increased between 2000 and 2004, from 8 percent to 10 percent (JCHS 2008). Vacancy rates in ownership units also rose between 2005 and 2007 and stood 50 percent higher than the historical norm. As Baker (2008: 80) points out, neither of these observations supports the opinion that a shortage of homes was the driving force behind home-price increases.

In retrospect, the viewpoint articulated by Greenspan, Bernanke, and Lereah in the mid 2000s about home-price appreciation certainly missed the mark. However, two questions remain to be answered. First, what factors account for the sharp increase in home prices after 1997? Second, why did the turndown in the housing market, an essentially local market and a relatively small sector of the overall economy, shake the foundations of the US and global economy so deeply that attempts to contain it by the government, the Fed, and regulators were generally unsuccessful? Answers to these questions relate to the securitization of mortgages and other types of debt, the leveraging of households and financial institutions, and the opaqueness of the financial sector due to deregulation and over-the-counter (OTC) derivatives trades.

The mortgage market and securitization

Chapter 14 presented the history of securitization. Here I will give a more detailed account of the mechanics of securitization, the forces it unleashed, and its links to the housing bubble. As a point of reference, consider the pre-securitization originate-and-hold mortgage contract (Figure 15.2) with two actors: the borrower (the homebuyer) and the lender (a bank or thrift institution). When the prospective borrower applied for a loan the lender checked her credibility in terms of net wealth, income, credit score, and the *loan-to-value (LTV) ratio,* i.e. the ratio of the loan to the value of the house.[4] The lender hired an appraiser to get an independent valuation of the property, as the property was the collateral for the loan. Once the mortgage contract was signed the bank extended the loan and held on to the contract, which meant that the borrower made monthly principal and

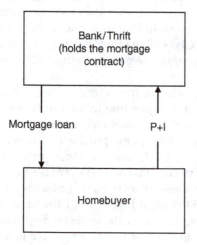

Figure 15.2 Traditional originate-and-hold mortgage loan.

interest payments (P+I) to the lender until the mortgage was fully paid. Until the 1980s, other than the government-sponsored enterprises (GSEs) that purchased conforming loans, there was no secondary market in which the lender could sell the mortgage.

The mortgage-securitization chain

This originate-and-hold structure transformed into originate-and-sell, as mortgage securitization gained a foothold after the 1970s, first by the GSEs and then by the banks. The new mortgage market was a complex, multistage affair with many stakeholders. The following summary of the securitization process, seen in stages A through E in the accompanying Figure 15.3, is adopted from Ashcraft and Schuermann (2008). It should be noted that some actors and flows are omitted from the diagram for the sake of brevity.

Stage A: The borrower received the loan from an originator, which was a bank/thrift institution or a non-bank mortgage originator. The primary difference between the two types of originators is that non-bank lenders were non-depository institutions that specialized in making mortgage loans. These monoline originators did not have access to deposits to finance loans, and, thus, they relied exclusively on lines of short-term credit extended by the "warehouse lenders" in the money market against the collateral of the mortgages. Mortgage brokers often served as intermediaries between homebuyers and originators in return for fees. The originator did not hold on to the loan but sold mortgages to a securitizer (or securitized the debt itself) in due course. The monoline lenders paid their warehouse debt with the proceeds of the sale of mortgages to the securitizer.

Stage B: The securitizer, also known as the issuer or arranger, pooled the mortgages it purchased or originated and issued bonds backed by the income streams of these pools. Securitizers could be GSEs, commercial or investment banks, or their subsidiaries. Non-depository securitizers relied on the money markets to fund mortgage purchases. Securitizers that were depository institutions financed mortgage purchases both out of deposits and by borrowing in the money markets. The securitization process involved packaging mortgages, creating structured assets against the collateral of interest and principal payments of these pools, underwriting the securities,[5] filing with the SEC, and arranging credit rating of securities.

Private-label securitization was usually carried out by a bank-sponsored trust or fiduciary called a *special purpose vehicle* (SPV). SPVs were bankruptcy-remote entities, or legally separate from sponsors' other obligations. The sponsoring institution assigned to the SPV the purchasing and pooling of the loans, the issuing of securities, and the managing of payments to investors from the income flow of the mortgage pool. The

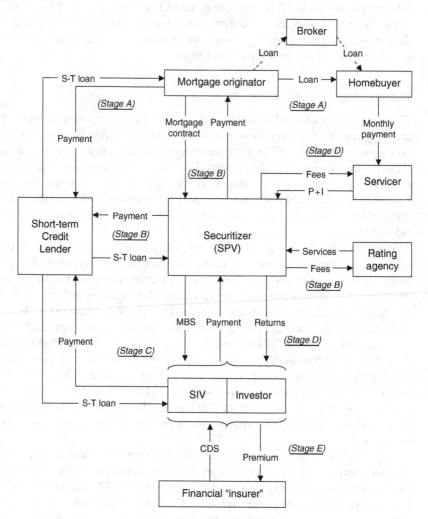

Figure 15.3 Mortgage securitization chain.

legal separation of the sponsor and its subsidiary SPV was intended to ensure that obligations to the mortgage-backed-security (MBS) investors were separated from the bank's other obligations and to safeguard investors from misfortunes that may befall the parent. As discussed in the last chapter, an MBS was initially a simple asset backed by a residential- or commercial-mortgage pool. It quickly evolved into structured debt or a collateralized mortgage obligation (CMO), which was divided into tranches with varying risk and return characteristics to serve investors' differing levels of risk tolerance. Securitization gradually expanded to more complex and less transparent synthetic collateralized debt obligations (CDOs) that were backed by various other types of structured debt, such as pooled mortgage, credit-card, student-loan, and auto-loan securities. Soon CDOs were issued that were based on pools of CDOs (called CDO^2) and pools of CDO^2s (called CDO^3). As there was no secondary market for these securities MBSs and CDOs were priced via mathematical-statistical modeling.

The assessment of the default risk of MBSs and CDOs was performed by the credit-rating agencies, such as Standard and Poor's, Moody's, and Fitch. The grades that these agencies assigned to bonds were a primary source of information for investors. While, historically, the rating agencies had sold this information to bond buyers, this practice had disappeared in the 1970s. By the 1990s issuers of the securities were paying the rating agencies for their services, and ratings were freely available to all.

Stage C: Investors purchased MBSs and CDOs from the securitizer. These investors included private investors, GSEs, pension funds, insurance companies, and sovereign funds, as well as banks themselves. Two features of this link in the chain are worth emphasizing. First, asset managers, such as hedge funds, mutual funds, or investment banks, were located between the SPVs and most of the final investors. As agents of the investors, asset managers handled the portfolios of the final investors; consequently, the securities were often marketed directly to asset managers. Second, banks created yet another layer of complexity in the system through *structured investment vehicles* (SIVs). Similar to SPVs, SIVs (and a similar entity called conduits) were sponsored by banks, but they were legally independent and, therefore, off the balance sheets of the sponsors. The primary task of SIVs was to borrow from the money markets by selling short-term commercial paper to invest in MBSs and CDOs that had longer-term maturities.[6]

SIVs served several purposes. First, they added to the profits of the sponsor bank from the spread between the long- and short-term interest rates and amplified the magnitude of the profit by high leveraging. Second, they served as repositories for the securitizer banks' unsold MBSs and CDOs. SIVs often turned into storehouses for the unsold lowest-grade debt, later called toxic waste. Thus, the bank (or its SPV) unloaded its loans to this separate entity and cleared dubious-quality products on the asset side of its balance sheet. Third, SIVs offered banks a means to circumvent capital requirements. Once the loans were removed from the balance sheet and capital was freed up banks could extend more credit. Thus, while SIVs raised the profitability of banks, they also hid the weaknesses in banks' capital structure and made markets less transparent. Due to their reliance on short-term borrowing SIVs were also heavily exposed to turbulence in the money market.

Stage D: Because the original lender was now out of the picture the home-buyer made monthly interest and principal payments to a servicer, which also was in charge of holding escrow accounts for taxes and insurance and managing delinquent loans and foreclosures. After deducting its fees the servicer transferred these payments to the SPV. The SPV made the periodic payments to the investors of the MBSs and CDOs from these funds.

Stage E: Some MBS and CDO investors hedged their portfolios by purchasing CDSs from the "financial insurer." This last link of the chain will be discussed later.

While the large number of actors that offer specialized services gives the impression that multi-stage securitization process was a very crowded field, in fact, perhaps two dozen institutions (GSEs, commercial and investment banks, thrifts, monoline lenders), either directly or via their subsidiaries, dominated the chain, and many performed several tasks simultaneously. The same prominent financial institutions were, all at the same time, the primary securitizers, originators, servicers, underwriters, short-term creditors, and investors (Inside Mortgage Finance 2012b). The fact that many banks were in both the securitization and asset-management businesses naturally raised the question of conflict of interest.

Everyone is a winner!

Figures 15.4 and 15.5 give an idea of the scope and scale of securitization. Figure 15.4 reports annual securitization rates as measured by the ratio of the value of MBSs to the value of mortgage loans over the 2001–11 period. Between 2001 and 2007 the securitization rate increased from 61 percent to

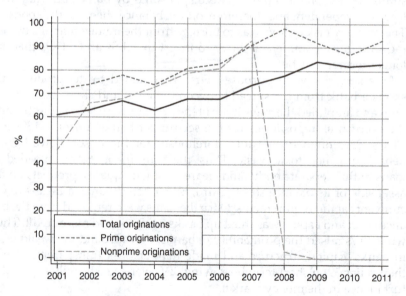

Figure 15.4 Securitization rates, 2001–11 (annual).

Source: Inside Mortgage Finance (2012b: 2).

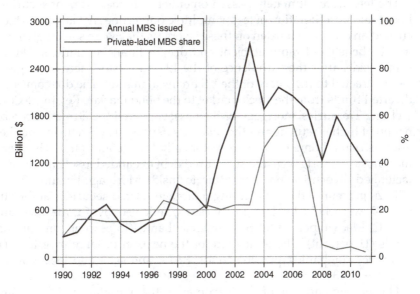

Figure 15.5 MBS origination and distribution by originator, 1990–2011 (annual).

Source: Inside Mortgage Finance (2012b: 6).

74 percent. Figure 15.5 shows that new MBS issues more than quadrupled between 2000 and 2003 and then hovered around $2t annually from 2004 to 2007. Private-label or non-agency MBSs accounted for roughly 20 percent of MBSs until 2003. The more interesting feature of Figure 15.5, however, is the reversal at the peak of the boom. Between 2004 and 2007, non-agency MBS shares abruptly increased, and in 2005 and 2006 sometimes even exceeded the agency share.

Mortgage securitization was celebrated and promoted across the board by its many stakeholders. Mortgage originators profited from the fees paid by homebuyers (closing costs and points) and the premium that the securitizer may have paid over the par value of the mortgage. Depository institutions that originated mortgages removed loans from the asset side of the balance sheet and freed cash for further rounds of credit extension. The securitizer was willing to pay a premium for mortgages as long as the sale of MBSs yielded sufficiently high profits. The securitizers' profit came from the fees that they collected from the securities investors and the premium that investors may have paid over the par value of the securities. Money-market-fund lenders collected interest payments for the loans they made to the originators, the securitizers, and the SIVs. Handsome fees were generated for mortgage brokers, servicers, underwriters, rating agencies, and portfolio managers.

The fees were ultimately passed on either to homebuyers or securities investors. A proliferation of fees at multiple points does not appear to have created an excessive burden on these actors, as they were seemingly reaping the benefits of more efficient and deeper financial markets. On the supply side, after the turbulence of the 1990s investors across the globe were attracted to the safety of the US financial market. The dot-com crash diverted funds from the stock market to the bond market. Relative to low-yielding Treasuries, mortgage-backed assets offered the attractive combination of higher returns and the relative safety of the US housing market, with its rising home prices and historically low default rates. The metamorphosis of mortgages into structured debt expanded asset choices, and facilitated diversification. According to Inside Mortgage Finance (2102b: 271), 20 percent of the outstanding mortgage-related securities at the end of 2007 were held by foreign investors, followed by Fannie Mae and Freddie Mac (16 percent), US commercial banks (15 percent), and mutual funds (11 percent). The total share of the next set of large investors, i.e. insurance companies, pension funds, S&Ls, and state and local governments, was 23 percent.

On the demand side of the loan market the abundance of funds and new types of mortgage instruments helped more people to become homeowners. Between 2000 and 2006 the percentage of homeowners in the population rose from 66 to 69 percent, a historical record. In 2005 President Bush was pleased to note that more Americans than ever had become homeowners, an important step toward his goal of an "ownership society." Some existing owners used home-equity loans to maintain their standard of living, pay for education, or purchase consumer durables. Others refinanced, traded up to larger, better homes with better prospects of market appreciation, or bought second homes.

The viability of the mortgage-securitization chain relied critically on homebuyers continuing to make payments on mortgages. The ultimate source of income for everyone in the chain was the monthly payments of the homebuyers, and for the system to function it was imperative to avoid widespread defaults and foreclosures. A loss of confidence in the ability of homebuyers to meet their obligations would have led to the downgrading of the MBSs, a decline in collateral values, and money-market lenders halting short-term financing to the originators, securitizers, and SIVs.

Flies in the ointment

There were two immediate flaws in the mortgage-securitization chain. First, it was afflicted with perverse incentives at every stage that aggravated the risk in the system. The profits of the originators and securitizers depended on the volume of mortgages and securities issued. Both were also able to pass the risk to the next agent in the chain. Originators targeted making as many loans as possible regardless of the default risk because the sale of mortgages transferred the risk to the securitizer. The securitizer also aimed at pooling as many mortgages as possible without much attention to their riskiness because once MBSs and CDOs were sold the risk would be transferred to the investors. Investors appeared not to be disconcerted by the fact that they were at the tail end of the chain. They discounted the default risk because these securities, especially the senior tranche MBSs and CDOs, were graded highly by the rating agencies. They believed, too, that rising real-estate prices "ensured" that homes were solid collateral for the securities in the event of a default.

In fact, a closer look at the market reveals that this risk avoidance was not foolproof. At any point in time originators had inventories of mortgages yet to be sold to securitizers, and securitizers had inventories of mortgages yet to be pooled and securitized, as well as securities yet to be sold to investors. Thus, they were exposed to the risk of a downturn in housing prices. In addition, securitizers were often under obligation to replace or repurchase loans from their investors in the event of breaches of representations and warranties (although the mere determination of a breach would entail a prolonged legal process). In short, originators and securitizers did not fully remove the exposure to default risk. This attribute of the mortgage process might have been an advantage from an overall market perspective. The "failure" to transfer risk to others in full would have been considered beneficial had agents exercised more caution and diligence in view of the residual risk exposure.

However, perverse incentives easily dominated the mortgage chain. Executives and managers were generously rewarded with salaries and bonuses for the profits they generated. The fee and premium-on-par business model motivated them to maximize short-term profits via excessive leveraging and risk-taking without much consideration for the longer-term consequences of their actions. Perverse incentives contributed to the declining quality of mortgage loans, predatory lending and borrowing, grade inflation of MBSs and CDOs, deceptive investment practices, and amplified systemic risk.[7]

The second problem was that the process was reliant on short-term borrowing at the stages of mortgage origination, the purchase of mortgages by the securitizers, and SIV operations. Hedge funds also borrowed in money markets to leverage their positions. The collateral used in these loans was homes, mortgage loans, or the MBSs and CDOs. Excessive reliance on short-term loans at all stages of the chain was the key vulnerability of mortgage securitization. The collateral was subject to *mark-to-market* accounting, which means that if the value of the collateral declined the lender would make margin calls to the borrower to make up the difference. Thus, a market downturn would put additional pressure on borrowers to come up with more cash. Moreover, any credit incident that shook the confidence of short-term lenders would slow down credit extension and affect the mortgage chain at all levels. Short-term financing meant that borrowers had to go back to the money market periodically, usually every three months. If lenders refused to roll over the loans, then origina- tors, securitizers, or investors/SIVs would be forced to liquidate their assets, perhaps at a loss, to meet their obligations.[8] A generalized deterio- ration of asset values and declining net worth could then easily lead to insolvencies throughout the chain.

A smorgasbord of mortgage loans

The climbing global demand for mortgage-backed assets prompted origi- nators to generate more mortgage loans to be securitized. There were sev- eral types of borrowers in the housing market. The highest-quality borrowers were those with excellent credit scores, steady incomes, an abil- ity to make down payments, and good collateral. These prime borrowers, who had the lowest default risk, received the *prime loans*, or conforming loans. Once this segment of the market was saturated, however, lenders searched for other types of borrower, and they were quite creative and successful in finding new customers and designing new types of loans for them. A step below the prime borrowers were the near-prime borrowers, who had decent credit scores but incomplete documentation and higher home-price-to-income and LTV ratios. *Alternative-A*, or *Alt-A*, mortgages served this group of borrowers. These mortgages were extended primar- ily by a handful of firms, including thrift giants IndyMac, Countrywide, and Washington Mutual (WaMu), independent mortgage lenders, and investment-bank subsidiaries. In comparison with the prime loans, lend- ers charged higher interest rates on the Alt-A loans.

Lowest in the hierarchy were the subprime borrowers, those with little or no credit history, low credit ratings, and the highest risk of default. Typically, these people would have been turned down by lenders, but, in the midst of rising demand for structured debt instruments, they consti- tuted the final opportunity to feed the demand for MBSs. Given these borrowers' higher risk, interest rates on *subprime loans* were higher than those on Alt-A loans.[9]

Figure 15.6 presents total mortgage originations over the 1990–2011 period and the shares of prime, Alt-A, and subprime mortgages. Annual mortgage loans were on the rise from 1990 to 2000, with local peaks in 1993 and 1997. The big change came after 2000. Between 2000 and 2003 the volume of loans quadrupled, from $1t to $4t, and then declined to $3t by 2006.

Jointly, Figures 15.5 and 15.6 reveal, first, that the annual issuance of new mortgages and MBSs moved in tandem. The second important find- ing is that the sharp increase in the non-agency share of securitization in Figure 15.5 coincided with the rising share of subprime loans, shown in Figure 15.6. Until 2003 the number of Alt-A and subprime loans made up

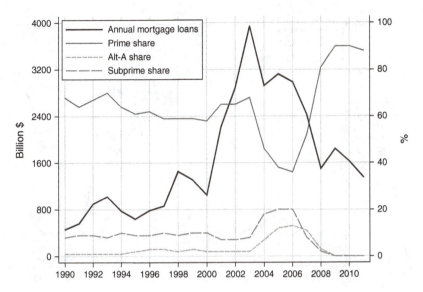

Figure 15.6 Distribution of mortgage originations by type, 1990–2011 (annual).
Source: Inside Mortgage Finance (2012b: 17).

approximately 2 percent and 10 percent of the total respectively. After 2003 both types of non-prime mortgage increased their shares. Between 2004 and 2006 they jointly accounted for close to 35 percent of all new mortgage loans extended, and nearly matched the share of prime loans.[10] Securitization of Alt-A and subprime loans was primarily a private-sector affair because the GSEs, at least initially, did not purchase non-conforming loans. The pattern observed in Figure 15.4 complements these observations. Securitization rates of the total and prime mortgages followed roughly parallel trends. The securitization rate of non-prime (Alt-A and subprime) mortgages, however, increased at a much faster rate and doubled between 2001 and 2007, and matched the securitization rate of prime mortgages between 2004 and 2007.

Figure 15.7 also presents another important piece of information. Private-label MBSs increased after 2000 and peaked in 2005–6, and this growth was driven mainly by the securitization of Alt-A and subprime mortgages. In addition, three quarters of the private-label MBSs were backed by non-prime mortgages. In summary, between 2004 and 2006 the share of non-prime mortgage contracts, the share of non-agency MBSs, and the share of non-agency securitization backed by non-prime loans all peaked concurrently. Non-prime securitization and the growth of the non-prime mortgage market appear to have been driven primarily by the actions of non-agency institutions.

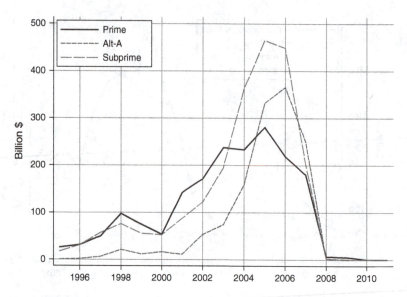

Figure 15.7 Distribution of private-label MBSs by mortgage type, 1995–2011 (annual).

Source: Inside Mortgage Finance (2012b: 28).

In addition to locating new types of customers, the mortgage industry also promoted new types of loans that offered more flexible and seemingly more favorable payment options to borrowers. *Adjustable-rate mortgages* (ARMs) had been available for some time as an alternative to fixed-rate mortgages. The buyer of a conventional, fixed-rate mortgage knows the amount of the monthly payment and its interest and principal components over the lifetime of the loan because the interest rate does not change. The interest rate on an ARM, however, is variable. Typically, ARMs were hybrid loans that started with low fixed (at times "teaser") interest rates for an initial period of time (two to three years), and then the interest rate was adjusted in line with a reference-index rate, such as the London interbank offered rate (LIBOR) or a one-year Treasury rate, or a rate at the lender's discretion. If interest rates declined the mortgage buyer benefitted from this arrangement, but higher interest rates would spell trouble for her. Even then, the ARM offer was attractive, particularly to customers who planned to live in the home for a short while and then sell it, hopefully realizing a capital gain. Figure 15.8 shows the share of ARMs in total mortgages (the balance is fixed-rate mortgages) from 1992 to 2007. The share of ARMs in mortgage loans fluctuated sharply in the 1990s, reaching as high as 50 percent in 2004.

There were other types of non-conventional mortgage contracts. *Interest-only loans* were fixed- or adjustable-rate mortgages that required the

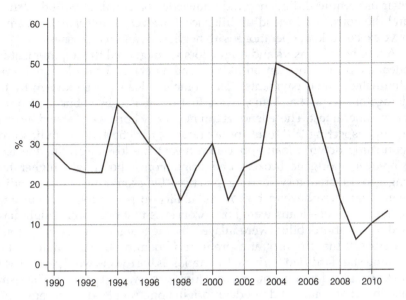

Figure 15.8 Share of adjustable-rate mortgages, 1990–2011 (annual).

Source: Inside Mortgage Finance (2012a: 17).

borrower to make only the interest payments initially (usually the first five years) and postpone principal payments. In the case of the *option ARM*, the borrower was permitted for a while to pay even less than the interest due, with the balance added to the principal of the loan. Normally, the borrower amortizes the loan over time and builds equity. In the case of option ARMs, however, negative amortization occurred, or the outstanding debt increased. As long as home prices were rising the debt was sustainable because the borrower could refinance or sell her home at a value higher than the amount she owed.

If the home value dropped, however, it would be nearly impossible to refinance or pay the debt fully by selling the house. The best recourse then would be to walk away from the home. Note that when the borrower takes the latter course of action the lender is also at a disadvantage because it now owns a physical asset that is declining in value. Jarsulic (2010: 103) reports that 50 percent of WaMu's option ARM borrowers (69 percent of the thrift's loans) were in negative amortization at the end of 2007. IndyMac was in a similar situation, with 34 percent of its option ARMs in excess of original mortgage values. Both thrifts failed.

These novel mortgage products had been available in one form or another for a long time, but their utilization in the 1990s posed brand new challenges and heightened risk exposure for the economy. Non-conventional loans were far more complicated and risky than fixed-interest loans, and, therefore, their use required diligence and knowledge on behalf of both the lender and the borrower. Instead of diligence, however, counterparties seem to have executed loan operations with negligence and recklessness.

A number of brokers and originators soon ignored the requirement for adequate documentation on income and assets, and they lowered, even eliminated, down payments. "Stated-income loans," also known by the derogatory term "liar loans," were first originated by subprime-lending giant Ameriquest. These lenders did not verify borrowers' stated income, e.g. by inspecting W-2 forms or tax returns, nor check their credit scores, as turning down a loan application meant the loss of origination fees. Moreover, mortgage brokers and originators who sought higher fees engaged in predatory lending practices by promoting and extending loans that were beyond borrowers' ability to pay. NINJA—no-income, no-job, no-asset—loans were born. Concerns that borrowers might have had about affordability were allayed by the suggestion that they could always sell the property at a profit in a booming housing market. Lax lending standards led to rising LTV ratios as borrowers were permitted to make smaller down payments, sometimes as low as 0 percent. The rising likelihood of default did not deter originators from lending because they expected to sell the loans immediately, to be securitized down the chain.

During this time academics and policymakers viewed innovations in the mortgage market in a positive light, as these developments seemingly enhanced access to the mortgage market of people who had previously been excluded (such as the young, people with low net worth, and households who had missed a few payments on their credit cards due to an illness, unemployment, or divorce), created a more-inclusive market, and helped more people achieve their objective of home ownership. However, the combination of declining loan quality and the matching of the most complex loans with the highest-risk, non-prime borrowers created a highly combustible mixture. These dangerous practices were largely hidden from the outside world and came to light later when examiners inspected the books of some of the largest failed lenders. Jarsulic (2010: 101–7) recounts how IndyMac, WaMu, and New Century generated and purchased Alt-A and subprime loans without proper review and knowingly extended loans with negative amortization that would fail as soon as house prices stopped rising. When the market started to decline, and they had trouble meeting their debt obligations, these thrifts shifted the burden to taxpayers by raising funds through the sale of federally insured certificates of deposits, and doubled down to create even more loans to stay afloat in the hope that they could survive until home prices started to rise again.

Credit default (and other) swaps

As discussed in the last chapter, CDSs on corporate bonds had been available since the late 1980s, but they were not common for MBSs and CDOs until the 2000s. The reason for the absence of CDSs for MBSs and CDOs is the one important difference between corporate bonds and mortgage- and asset-backed securities. An MBS is based on thousands of pooled mortgages. A mortgage pool defaults one mortgage at a time, affecting the value of the MBS drop by drop. The default (or downgrading) of an MBS is a slow, protracted process, unlike that of the corporate bond, which comes in one swift blow. Given the ambiguity of the definition of default of an MBS, it is far more complicated to write a CDS contract on an MBS than on a corporate bond.

The solution to the problem of how to draw CDSs for MBSs or CDOs was found in 2005. Because these securities default incrementally a CDS contract was created that would oblige the CDS seller to make payments to the buyer incrementally as well. The contract linked the "default payments" to fluctuations in the MBS price, or, in principle, marked them to market. When the MBS price declined (as it would when there are more defaults) the CDS buyer would issue a margin call on the seller to post more collateral. Conversely, when the market value of the MBS increased the seller would ask the buyer to post collateral. One impact of mark-to-market CDS contracts was that cash settlements varied with the market value of debt, and, thus, the balance sheets of the buyers and sellers became more volatile.[11]

Interestingly, the first customers of the CDSs on MBSs were not investors who were seeking to buy "insurance" against default but, instead, hedge-fund speculators who wished to place bets against the residential real-estate market. The first CDS contracts were drawn between these hedge funds on one side and Goldman Sachs and Deutsche Bank on the other.[12] However, neither of these banks was the ultimate supplier of the CDSs. These institutions hedged their positions by buying offsetting CDSs from the large insurance and reinsurance companies. Many operators soon sought to turn a quick profit by selling CDSs and then turning the contract over to yet another seller of protection. Most of the CDSs on MBSs and CDOs ended up being "one-way" contracts offered by large insurance and reinsurance companies, such as AIG, Swiss Reinsurance, and AON, written without the protection of hedge CDSs. In addition to hedge-fund speculators, financial institutions also bought CDSs on the mortgage-related securities they held to reduce their default-risk exposure and to free up regulatory capital (capital requirements were lower for hedged loans). Before long retail investors and asset managers were also in the market to purchase CDSs, with the primary purpose of hedging (as illustrated by the lowest cell in Figure 15.3).

The notional outstanding value of the CDSs rose sixty-eightfold, from $900b in 2001 to $62t in 2007 (ISDA 2013). For some perspective on the magnitude of these numbers, note that the total value of final goods and services annually produced across the globe was approximately $60t. Global financial net household wealth, i.e. shares and other equity, bonds, deposits, and insurance and pension funds, in the mid 2000s was approximately

$120t (Shorrocks *et al.* 2012), and the value of the total MBSs outstanding was $5.3t in 2002 and $9.4t in 2007 (SIFMA 2014). The sheer magnitude of the size and rate of growth of the notional value of the CDSs suggest that they were not merely instruments of hedging but a means of betting on future defaults. The scale of the operation also gives an idea of how lucrative a business it was for the financial institutions that arranged these swap contracts.[13] Finally, as they were primarily OTC contracts between two parties, their sizes and terms unknown to other parties, the figures signal how little transparency there was in a huge segment of the market.

CDSs often are called means for hedging or insurance. As noted in the previous chapter, there are critical differences between CDSs and traditional insurance policies. First, as the CDS buyer does not need to hold the asset the CDS could be, and was, easily used instead as an instrument to place bets on company defaults. Second, the swap seller was not regulated like an insurance company, which was required to abide by capital requirements and to demonstrate its ability to pay clients in the event of a disaster. Any counterparty could sell CDS contracts, and there was no oversight on whether sellers of CDSs would be able to meet their obligations. Third, an insurance company calculates the expected loss by using actuarial tables that report the probabilities of accidents, fire, death, and so forth, based on data over large populations. Provided the company has a large customer base so that the law of large numbers applies, the company can determine the profit-making premium. This risk-management strategy did not apply to CDSs. There was nothing comparable in the financial sector to actuarial tables on accidents, deaths, or fires. The only way a CDS seller could manage risk was to write a "hedge CDS," that is, enter into another swap agreement as a buyer.

Opinions on the benefits and costs of derivatives were sharply divided. The banking industry was obviously enthusiastic because derivatives were a significant source of profit. Most economists also favored them because they allegedly aided in risk management, and thereby brought more confidence to the market, motivated more lending and borrowing, and improved financial markets' allocative efficiency. Some economists applauded derivatives contracts, as widespread speculation and the higher volume of traffic facilitated the price-discovery process. A larger number of participants and significant volume in the market could only enhance market efficiency. Speculation, following Milton Friedman's (1953) dictum, was deemed to be stabilizing. The rising complexity of derivatives was taken as a sign of the maturity of financial markets.

Greenspan (2002) articulated the pro-derivatives majority view in his testimony to legislators:

> Both deregulation and innovation in the financial sector have been
> especially important in enhancing overall economic resilience. New

financial products—including derivatives, asset-backed securities, collateralized loan obligations, and collateralized mortgage obligations, among others—have enabled risk to be dispersed more effectively to those willing to, and presumably capable of, bearing it. Shocks to the overall economic system are accordingly less likely to create cascading credit failure. Lenders have the opportunity to be considerably more diversified, and borrowers are far less dependent on specific institutions for funds. Financial derivatives, particularly, have grown at a phenomenal pace over the past fifteen years, evidently fulfilling a need to hedge risks that were not readily deflected in earlier decades. Despite the concerns that these complex instruments have induced . . . the record of their performance, especially over the past couple of stressful years, suggests that on balance they have contributed to the development of a far more flexible and efficient financial system—both domestically and internationally—than we had just twenty or thirty years ago.

Others were not as optimistic about the stabilizing powers of speculation via derivatives. Because swaps were not traded on the organized exchanges or recorded in clearing houses there was little systematic independent information on their volume or market values. The lack of information on the CDS positions of individual firms added to the lack of transparency in financial markets. The CDS market became more complex as issuers increasingly sold CDSs for complex MBSs and CDOs during the 2000s. Many CDS issuers had little knowledge or information about the content, value, and risk of these structured debt instruments. While CDSs were, in principle, subject to mark-to-market accounting, the opacity of collateralized securities and their prices' reliance on mathematical modeling made valuing the related CDSs problematic. Skeptics were concerned that in a context of myopic time horizons, short-term gains, and a lack of transparency the proliferation of speculative instruments was more likely to be a source of systemic risk rather than ballast against it.[14]

Warren Buffett (2002) articulated how derivatives contributed to the perverse incentives, opacity, and systemic risk in financial markets:

> [T]he parties to derivatives . . . have enormous incentives to cheat in accounting for them. Those who trade derivatives are usually paid . . . on "earnings" calculated by mark-to-market accounting. But often there is no real market . . . and "mark-to-model" is utilized. This substitution can bring on large-scale mischief. As a general rule, contracts involving multiple reference items and distant settlement dates increase the opportunities for counterparties to use fanciful assumptions. . . . Another problem with derivatives is that they can exacerbate trouble that a corporation has run into for completely unrelated reasons. This pile-on effect occurs because many derivatives contracts

require that a company suffering a credit downgrade immediately supply collateral to counterparties. . . . Many people argue that derivatives reduce systemic problems, in that participants who can't bear certain risks are able to transfer them to stronger hands. These people believe that derivatives act to stabilize the economy, facilitate trade, and eliminate bumps for individual participants. And, on a micro level, what they say is often true. . . . [However, the] macro picture is dangerous and getting more so. Large amounts of risk, particularly credit risk, have become concentrated in the hands of relatively few derivatives dealers, who in addition trade extensively with one other. The troubles of one could quickly infect the others. On top of that, these dealers are owed huge amounts by non-dealer counterparties. Some of these counterparties . . . are linked in ways that could cause them to contemporaneously run into a problem because of a single event . . . Linkage, when it suddenly surfaces, can trigger serious systemic problems. . . . [T]he derivatives are financial weapons of mass destruction, carrying dangers that, while now latent, are potentially lethal.

Key terms and concepts

Adjustable-rate mortgage
Alternative-A (Alt-A) loan
Interest-only loan
Loan-to-value ratio
Mark-to-market accounting
Option ARM
Price-rent ratio
Prime loan
Special purpose vehicle
Structured investment vehicle
Subprime loan

Endnotes

1 The subprime-mortgage crisis, covered in this and the next chapters, generated a deluge of books by academics and journalists for the general public. While they come from various perspectives and do not necessarily agree on the diagnosis and prescriptions, many of these books are perceptive, insightful, informative, often polemical and entertaining, and filled with revealing details about the decision-making process at the highest echelons, including the penchants of academics and the psyches of bankers and policymakers. Among the notable works are those by journalists Cassidy (2009), Lewis (2010), Lowenstein (2011), McLean and Nocera (2010), Sorkin (2009), Tett (2009), and Wessel (2009). Geithner (2014) and Paulson (2010) offer the eyewitness testimony of insiders on policy actions to contain the crisis. Academics and experts writing for the

general public include Baker (2008), Blinder (2013), The Financial Crisis Inquiry Commission (2011), Gorton (2010), Jarsulic (2010), Johnson and Kwak (2010), Rajan (2010), Roubini and Mihm (2011), Shiller (2008), and Stiglitz (2010). Lo (2012) reviews 21 books by financial journalists and scholars on the crisis. Friedman (2011), Blinder *et al.* (2012) and Wolfson and Epstein (2013) are edited collections of scholarly work on the topic. These are partial lists and certainly miss many other worthy books. The feature films *Too Big to Fail* (2011, based on Sorkin (2009)) and *Margin Call* (2011), and the documentaries *Frontline: The Warning* (2009), *Frontline: Inside the Meltdown* (2009), and *Inside Job* (2010) deserve special mention for making the subject matter accessible to the educated general public and revealing the spirit of the times; they are highly entertaining, too.

2   For discussions of the US residential real-estate market from a historical perspective see Shiller (2005: Chapter 2; 2008: Chapters 2 and 4).

3   The quality of the housing data is mixed. The later JCHS studies reported ratios based on different sources and methodologies. Nonetheless, the historical trends, including the turning points, remain unchanged.

4   A low LTV ratio implies that the borrower makes a large down payment and holds more equity in the property. Therefore, the lender is exposed to a smaller loss in the event of default.

5   In GSE securitization banks often served as underwriters.

6   Although it was a legally separate entity, an SIV's ability to raise funds in the money market relied on the reputation of the bank that stood behind it.

7   These problems are related to asymmetric information and will be discussed in more detail in the next chapter.

8   The sponsoring banks, therefore, had established credit lines to the SIVs in case of need.

9   For a detailed discussion of the attributes of prime, Alt-A, and subprime mortgages see Mayer *et al.* (2009).

10 Other types of loans not shown in the figure are jumbo loans and home-equity loans.

11 As there was no secondary market for the MBSs and CDOs, the questions of how the market price would be determined, especially in a time of turbulence, added another complication to these transactions.

12 See Lewis (2010) on the emergence of the swap market on MBSs.

13 As large as the volume of notional CDSs was, it was dwarfed by interest-rate and currency swaps. The volume of these contracts, whereby counterparties exchanged fixed- and floating-interest obligations and different currency-denominated obligations respectively, exploded in the 2000s, reflecting the prevalence of speculative forces in the economy. Between 2001 and 2007 the notional volume of the sum of interest-rate and currency swaps outstanding increased from $70t to close to $382t. Again, the figures suggest that these derivatives were used predominantly as instruments of speculation or to bet on interest-rate and currency movements.

14 Among the regulators there were several who raised an alarm. As early as 1998 Brooksley Born, chair of the Commodity Futures Trading Commission (CFTC), had argued that the lack of transparency of swaps put the financial security of many savers at risk and urged the regulation of OTC derivatives. She met with the stiff resistance of the White House, Congress, and Wall Street. At the Senate Financial Committee hearing on the subject Born faced Alan Greenspan, Treasury Secretary Robert Rubin, Deputy Treasury Secretary Larry Summers—"the Committee to Save the World" and the "Three Marketeers," according to *Time* magazine's cover of February 15, 1999—and the head of the SEC, Arthur Levitt. The power quartet warned

senators that any discussion of the CFTC concept release would create turmoil in financial markets and stifle innovation. Born was browbeaten and dismissed as being out of her depth. The senators agreed, and Congress passed legislation in the same year to limit the CFTC's power to regulate derivatives. Born resigned from the CFTC soon after.

References

Ashcraft, A. B. and Til Schuermann. 2008, March. *Understanding the Securitization of Subprime Mortgage Credit*. Staff Report No. 318. New York: Federal Reserve Bank of New York.

Baker, Dean. 2002. *The Run-Up in Home Prices: Is it Real or is it Another Bubble?* CEPR Briefing Paper. Washington, DC: CEPR.

Baker, Dean. 2008. *Plunder and Blunder: The Rise and Fall of the Bubble Economy*. Sausalito, CA: PoliPoint Press.

Blinder, Alan S. 2013. *After the Music Stopped: The Financial Crisis, the Response, and the Work Ahead*. New York: The Penguin Press.

Blinder, Alan S., Andrew W. Lo and Robert M. Solow, eds. 2012. *Rethinking the Financial Crisis*. New York: Russell Sage Foundation.

Borio, Claudio and William White. 2003. *Whither Monetary and Financial Stability? The Implications of Evolving Policy Regimes*. Bank of International Settlements. Paper prepared for the Jackson Hole Symposium on "Monetary policy and uncertainty: Adapting to a changing economy" on 28–30 August 2003.

Buffett, Warren E. 2002. *Chairman's Letter to the Shareholders of Berkshire Hathaway*. Online: www.berkshirehathaway.com/letters/2002.html.

Cassidy, John. 2009. *How Markets Fail: The Logic of Economic Calamities*. New York: Farrar, Straus and Giroux.

The Financial Crisis Inquiry Commission. 2011. *The Financial Crisis Inquiry Report: Final Report of the National Commission on the Causes of the Financial and Economic Crisis in the United States*. (Official Government Edition.) Washington, DC: US Government Printing Office.

Friedman, Jeffrey, ed. 2011. *What Caused the Financial Crisis?* Philadelphia: University of Pennsylvania Press.

Friedman, Milton. 1953. "The Case for Flexible Exchange Rates." Pp. 157–203 in his *Essays in Positive Economics*. Chicago: University of Chicago Press.

Geithner, Timothy F. 2014. *Stress Test: Reflections on Financial Crises*. New York: Crown Publishers.

Gorton, Gary. 2010. *Slapped by the Invisible Hand: The Panic of 2007*. Oxford, UK: Oxford University Press.

Greenspan, Alan. 2002. *Federal Reserve Board's Semiannual Monetary Policy Report to the Congress*. Testimony before the Committee on Financial Services, US House of Representatives. Online: www.federalreserve.gov/boarddocs/hh/2002/february/testimony.htm.

Greenspan, Alan. 2005. *Federal Reserve Board's Semiannual Monetary Policy Report to the Congress*. Testimony before the Committee on Financial Services, US House of Representatives. Online: www.federalreserve.gov/boarddocs/hh/2005/july/testimony.htm.

Inside Mortgage Finance. 2012a. *The 2012 Mortgage Market Statistical Annual*, vol. I. Bethesda, MD: Inside Mortgage Finance.

Inside Mortgage Finance. 2012b. *The 2012 Mortgage Market Statistical Annual*, vol. II. Bethesda, MD: Inside Mortgage Finance.

ISDA (International Swaps and Derivatives Association). 2013. "Market Surveys Data, 1987–2010." Online: www2.isda.org/functional-areas/research/surveys/market-surveys/.

Jarsulic, Marc. 2010. *Anatomy of a Financial Crisis: A Real Estate Bubble, Runaway Credit Markets, and Regulatory Failure*. New York: Palgrave Macmillan.

Johnson, Simon and James Kwak. 2010. *13 Bankers: The Wall Street Takeover and the Next Financial Meltdown*. New York: Pantheon Books.

Joint Center for Housing Studies of Harvard University. 2008. *The State of the Nation's Housing 2008*. Cambridge, MA: JCHS.

Krainer, John and Chishen Wei. 2004. "House Prices and Fundamental Value." *Federal Reserve Bank of San Francisco Economic Letter*. 2004–27.

Lereah, David. 2006. *Why the Real Estate Boom will not Bust - And How You Can Profit From It: How to Build Wealth in Today's Expanding Real Estate Market*. New York: Crown Business.

Lewis, Michael. 2010. *The Big Short: Inside the Doomsday Machine*. New York and London: W. W. Norton and Company.

Lo, Andrew W. 2012. "Reading about the Financial Crisis: A Twenty-One-Book Review." *Journal of Economic Literature* 50 (1): 151–78.

Lowenstein, Roger. 2011. *The End of Wall Street*. New York: The Penguin Press.

Mayer, Christopher, Karen Pence and Shane M. Sherlund. 2009. "The Rise in Mortgage Defaults." *Journal of Economic Perspectives* 23 (1): 27–50.

McCarthy, Jonathan and Richard W. Peach. 2004. "Are Home Prices the Next 'Bubble'?" *Economic Policy Review* 10 (3): 1–17.

McLean, Bethany and Joe Nocera. 2010. *All the Devils are Here: The Hidden History of Financial Crisis*. New York: Portfolio/Penguin.

Paulson, Henry M. 2010. *On the Brink: Inside the Race to Stop the Collapse of the Global Financial System*. New York: Business Plus.

Rajan, Raghuram G. 2005. "Has Financial Development Made the World Riskier?" *Proceedings of the Federal Reserve Bank of Kansas City*, 313–69. Online: www.kc.frb.org/publicat/sympos/2005/pdf/rajan2005.

Rajan, Raghuram G. 2010. *Fault Lines: How Hidden Fractures Still Threaten the World Economy*. Princeton, NJ: Princeton University Press.

Roubini, Nouriel. 2006. "The Biggest Slump in US Housing in the Last 40 Years . . . or 53 Years." Online: www.roubini.com/analysis/44763.htm.

Roubini, Nouriel and Stephen Mihm. 2011. *Crisis Economics: A Crash Course in the Future of Finance*. New York: The Penguin Press.

Shorrocks, Anthony, James B. Davies and Rodrigo Lluberas. 2012. *Credit Suisse Global Wealth Databook*. Zurich, Switzerland: Credit Suisse Group AG.

SIFMA (Securities Industry and Financial Markets Association). 2014. "US Mortgage-related Issuance and Outstanding." Updated May 1, 2014. Online: www.sifma.org/research/statistics.aspx.

Shiller, Robert J. 2005. *Irrational Exuberance*, 2nd ed. New York: Currency Doubleday. Online: www.econ.yale.edu/~shiller/data/ie_data.xls.

———. 2008. *The Subprime Solution: How Today's Global Financial Crisis Happened, and What To Do About It*. Princeton, NJ: Princeton University Press.

Sorkin, Andrew Ross. 2009. *Too Big to Fail: The Inside Story of How Wall Street and Washington Fought to Save the Financial System from Crisis—and Themselves.* New York: Viking.

Stiglitz, Joseph E. 2010. *Freefall: America, Free Markets, and the Sinking of the World Economy.* New York: W. W. Norton.

Tett, Gillian. 2009. *Fool's Gold: How the Bold Dream of a Small Tribe at J.P. Morgan Was Corrupted by Wall Street Greed and Unleashed a Catastrophe.* New York: Free Press.

Wessel, David. 2009. *In Fed We Trust: Ben Bernanke's War on the Great Panic.* New York: Crown Business.

Wolfson, Martin H. and Gerald A. Epstein, eds. 2013. *The Handbook of the Political Economy of Financial Crises.* New York: Oxford University Press.

16 The latest act

The crash of the 2000s

Mathematician, scientist, engineer, and inventor Archimedes of Syracuse reportedly said, "Give me a place to stand and with a lever I will move the whole world." Approximately two millennia later two levers lifted the world of finance to new heights. First, many households used loans to purchase unaffordable homes. Second, banks and other intermediaries reaped record profits from activities funded by short-term loans. We do not know what Archimedes believed would have happened once the world moved; after all, the question was not pertinent because he was making a hypothetical statement. However, the case of financial markets of the 2000s is out of the realm of hypotheticals. Accumulation of wealth offered a long lever, and deregulation and the shadow banking institutions provided the fulcrum to put the idea into practice. Most commentators trusted that the elevation of financial markets would carry the entire economy to a more productive and prosperous plane by strengthening the foundations of capital accumulation and risk allocation. The minority view was that the mortgage chain was a house of cards built on unsustainable debt structures, which would inevitably collapse, resulting in dire collateral damage in the real sector of the economy.

We now know that the second outcome occurred. The downfall of the financial system took two years, from 2006 to 2008. It started with declining home prices and monoline subprime-mortgage-originator bankruptcies, then spread to the government-sponsored enterprises (GSEs) and shadow banking vehicles, and, finally, threatened the large investment and commercial banks.

Leverage, leverage, everywhere

Figure 16.1 illustrates the two expectations-augmented leverage cycles that underlie the financial boom and the collapse.[1] The rightmost box in the upper portion of the figure shows that the relaxation of lending standards, expansion of non-prime mortgages, and alternative mortgage-payment schemes made credit accessible to increasing numbers of prospective homebuyers. The loosening of household credit constraints induced many

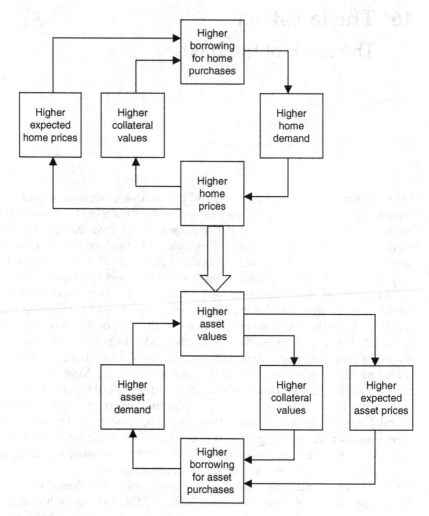

Figure 16.1 Leverage feedback loops.

renters to become homeowners, and the higher demand raised the price of residential property. Rising home prices increased homeowner wealth as well as the value of the collateral they could post for the next loan. Current homeowners were able obtain additional credit to trade up to bigger and better homes or purchase second homes. They were also able to take second mortgages and use the borrowed funds for home renovation, durables purchases, education, and to pay off of higher-interest debt. Further increases in the demand for homes elevated prices further, and the process repeated itself. Normally, higher prices are expected eventually to diminish the excess demand for homes because they will, on the one hand, stimulate homebuilders to construct new homes, and, on the other, push some potential buyers back to the rental market. The cycle then abates and home prices stabilize at a higher level. However, another mechanism prevented price stabilization.

The outer arrows on the left-hand side of the upper loop in Figure 16.1 show that higher prices also fed expectations of home-price appreciation. The expectation of higher home prices, in turn, had two effects. First, more homebuyers entered the market to speculate. Second, portfolio holders downgraded the risk of default on MBSs and purchased more of these assets. Thus, there were both more borrowers and more available credit, which augmented the volume of mortgages and demand for homes. The outcome was a self-sustaining increase in home prices, or a bubble. As evidence of the magnitude of leveraging by households, Blinder (2013: 49) points out that home-mortgage debt in the US was steady at around 60 percent of gross domestic product (GDP) from 1980 to 1996; between 1997 and 2008 it jumped to 95 percent. Shiller (2005) reports that in surveys people expressed the belief that homes would appreciate annually in double digits, a figure that was difficult to justify by the prevailing housing-price fundamentals listed in the last chapter.

When *Barron's* in 2002 and *The Economist* in 2003, among other print media, questioned whether the US housing market was experiencing a bubble and whether higher prices were sustainable most experts asserted that the housing market was local and that, while there may be problems in certain areas, a generalized price bubble and implosion were unlikely. After all, homes were not as liquid as stocks or bonds and, unlike stocks and bonds that are traded on exchanges, they could not be dumped in the market in bulk in the face of disappointing news, such as the evaporation of capital gains. Therefore, a generalized housing-market crash was deemed improbable. Clearly, this assessment overlooked the fragility of the financial infrastructure of the housing boom; that is, in the background, the housing bubble was feeding a credit bubble in the financial sector.

The shadow banking system emerged in the late 1980s and 1990s, but it hit its stride in the 2000s with the growing popularity of the mortgage-backed securities (MBS) and the collateralized debt obligations (CDO). Banks held mortgage-backed assets either directly themselves or indirectly via their shadow banking subsidiaries, e.g. structured investment vehicles (SIVs), conduits, and in-house hedge funds, and financed these holdings by selling commercial paper in the money market against the collateral of the MBSs and CDOs they held. The lower portion of Figure 16.1 illustrates the feedback loop that fed MBS and CDO prices. Rising home prices, as well as the prevailing macroeconomic and financial stability, reduced risk premiums and increased asset prices. Banks assessed the value of their holdings at current values; i.e. assets were valued using mark-to-market accounting practices. Higher MBS and CDO prices raised the value of bank assets, which could then be posted as additional collateral for further short-term borrowing. The borrowed funds were used to purchase additional mortgage-backed securities. These purchases, in turn, generated further rounds of rises in MBS and CDO prices, the value of bank assets, and short-term borrowing. The process also fueled expectations of asset-price appreciation. These expectations again entered the leverage cycle, as illustrated in Figure 16.1 by the right outer branch loop that amplified the increases in price at each round and formed a credit bubble.

The great unraveling

The upswing of these leverage cycles came to an end in the mid 2000s, first in the housing and then in the credit market, and was followed by the downward spiral. The downturn took place in three overlapping phases. In the first phase declining home prices increased mortgage defaults and pushed non-depository mortgage originators to insolvency. Second, the housing-market collapse reduced the value of MBSs and CDOs, which, in turn, pulled down the net worth of structured investment vehicles (SIVs), as well as the GSEs. Third, the crisis spread to large investment and commercial banks and thrifts as the balance sheets of these institutions deteriorated along with asset values. The entire system unraveled as households and financial institutions put their assets up for sale; massive deleveraging further depreciated values as risk premiums rose, and buyers withdrew from markets.

The situation was complicated by the fact that financial institutions' balance sheets lacked transparency due to the ambiguity of the value of the complex structured securities held as assets, the sheer scale of over-the-counter (OTC) derivatives contracts, and the toxic assets possibly concealed in subsidiary accounts. Uncertainty about the net worth of institutions heightened perceptions of default risk. Rising concerns about the solvency of the counterparties as well as the declining value of their own assets made banks less willing to extend loans to other financial institutions, industry, or commerce.[2]

The collapse of home prices and subprime lending

According to the Case–Shiller index, average home-price growth slowed in 2005, and the index peaked in January 2006 (Figure 15.1). After March 2006 it began to taper off. The outcome was due in part to the fundamentals asserting themselves. Higher home prices had created a boom in the construction sector and an excessive number of residential units. According to the Joint Center for Housing Studies (JCHS) (2008), annual single-family housing starts had trended sharply higher after 2000, growing steadily from 1.2m in 2000 to 1.7m in 2005. The vacancy rate had also increased during the same period, and the rate of growth of inflation-adjusted rents had declined and turned negative after 2004. As the supply of subdivisions and housing units caught up with speculative demand, the downward revision of expected price growth was inevitable. For homeowners, declining home values closed the door on them being able to meet their debt obligations by refinancing or selling their house. In the meantime the honeymoon period of adjustable-rate mortgages (ARMs) had passed, and many borrowers were facing steep increases in their monthly mortgage payments as interest rates were reset. Thus, many homeowners were caught between a mortgage debt that exceeded the value of their home and tighter financing constraints.

The feedback mechanism, seen in Figure 16.1, that had started the housing-price boom now created a cumulative depreciation of home values. As home prices declined so did the value of homeowner collateral. Lower collateral, in turn, lowered the household's net worth, reducing its capacity to borrow and refinance. As defaults and foreclosures spread, the excess supply of homes pushed down prices even further, causing the cycle to repeat. The effect of the negative price shock was especially severe due to the prevalence of subprime loans and risky mortgage products that pulled the value of many homes underwater. As people came to anticipate home-price declines, the contraction of both demand and prices was aggravated by self-fulfilling expectations.

After January 2007 the situation worsened. Not only had deleveraging accelerated, but the effects of lower home prices and increasing defaults spilled over to both the subprime originators and the construction industry. First, subprime lenders now owned an expanding inventory of fore-closed homes that they could not liquidate. They also held mortgage contracts that they could not sell because securitizers now viewed sub-prime mortgages as too risky. At the end of February 2007 Freddie Mac announced it would no longer be buying subprime mortgages or MBSs collateralized by subprime loans. At the same time, in response to escalating homebuyer-default risk and the depreciating market value of mortgages, warehouse creditors were making margin calls on the monoline mortgage originators and closing revolving credit lines.

Subprime originators were squeezed on all sides by the rising defaults of mortgage holders, the drying up of short-term financing, the need to come up with cash to meet margin calls, and their inability to unload their own existing mortgage inventory. As early as May 2006 subprime lender Ameriquest announced the closure of its retail branches, and thousands of employees were laid off; another lender, Merit Financial Inc., had filed for bankruptcy. In early 2007 Ownit Mortgage Solutions, American Freedom Mortgage, Mortgage Lenders Network USA, Accredited Home Lenders Holding, New Century Financial, DR Horton, and Country Financial, some of which were subprime giants, filed for bankruptcy.

Second, residential-construction activity slowed in the midst of higher vacancy rates, unsold homes, and rising defaults. New housing construction declined by 17 percent in 2006 and 29 percent in 2007 (JCHS 2008). Homeowners' ability to meet mortgage obligations deteriorated as the business cycle turned down and unemployment rose. The number of loans in foreclosure doubled to one million in 2007. The hardest hit segment was the subprime loans (JCHS 2008), and it was only a matter of time before the slowing down of overall economic activity amplified the deleveraging cycle.

Ben Bernanke and others attempted to calm markets by playing down the possible destructive ramification of defaults. The first action of the Federal Reserve System (Fed) to mitigate the economic slowdown was to signal future monetary easing. The federal funds rate and the discount rate, which had been on the rise since 2004, were kept level from mid 2006 to fall 2007. In public statements the Fed claimed that the overall economy was well insulated from subprime-market problems. In his congressional testimony on March 28 Bernanke stated:

> At this juncture, however, the impact on the broader economy and financial markets of the problems in the subprime market seems likely to be contained. In particular, mortgages to prime borrowers and fixed-rate mortgages to all classes of borrowers continue to perform well, with low rates of delinquency. We will continue to monitor this situation closely.
>
> (Bernanke 2007b)

The shadow banking system and the GSEs under stress

In 2007 the conditions of the financial-market conditions had become more severe due to the burst of the credit, or bond, bubble. Declining home prices, rising defaults, and foreclosures depreciated the value of mortgage-related securities. This development was of great concern to both the shadow banking institutions and the GSEs.

According to Jarsulic (2010: 64), the combined size of SIVs and conduits was as large as 20 percent of US banking assets in 2007. Their overleveraged investments and excessive reliance on short-term funding made these entities vulnerable to exogenous shocks. As soon as the values of their collaterals began to decline SIVs and conduits were squeezed. Short-term lenders made margin calls on existing loans and refused to roll over matured loans. Investment vehicles were forced to deleverage and sell their assets to raise cash. However, this was not an orderly process. The credit bubble burst, and mortgage- and asset-related security prices crashed.

Rising CDS spreads signaled that MBSs and CDOs were losing value, but due to the opacity of the balance sheets no one quite knew exactly by how much. The mathematical models used to price these securities were of hardly any use because they assumed any changes would be incremental and ignored the likelihood of home prices deteriorating sharply. Amid the subprime defaults there were no buyers for the junior-tranche toxic assets. As a result the net worth of the vehicles declined dramatically. The sponsor banks had no choice but to step in and take SIVs and conduits back on to their balance sheets. The transfer of these assets back to the banks was, of course, not a solution to the system-wide problem because it effectively weakened the balance sheets of the sponsoring banks. Citigroup, the largest banking conglomerate in the country, experienced perhaps the largest deterioration in value as a result of absorbing its subsidiaries.

The fact that the GSEs were originally chartered to purchase qualified mortgage loans did not insulate them from problems in the subprime market. Their assets consisted largely of mortgages and MBSs, and this undiversified portfolio was vulnerable to a downturn in the residential real-estate market. Fannie Mae's and Freddie Mac's exposure to the subprime segment of the housing market had also expanded in the lax regulatory environment. Although they were latecomers to the subprime market, the GSEs held subprime mortgages and MBSs backed by non-prime loans in their portfolio. Thus, the economic slowdown and the spillover of the crisis from the subprime to the prime sector raised anxiety about the state of the GSEs. The rapid erosion of their net worth threatened these institutions with insolvency. The bankruptcy of institutions that held trillions of dollars' worth of mortgage-related assets would have shattered the markets. In March 2007 Ben Bernanke (2007a) issued a warning that the GSEs were a source of systemic risk.

Big banks in trouble

The crisis soon reached the large banking institutions that directly or indirectly had participated in the credit bubble. The financial viability of many big banks was in doubt due to the combination of their deteriorating balance sheets and the opacity of their assets. On June 7, 2007, Bear Stearns, the fifth-largest US investment bank, suspended redemption of shares of its two in-house hedge funds that dealt in MBSs, due to a shortage of cash. Both hedge funds were subsequently closed. Investors in these hedge funds, including the UK's Barclays Bank, initiated litigation against Bear Stearns for embellishing profit reports and misleading investors.

Public confidence in the self-disciplining powers of banks was diminishing. In June 2007 Federal Deposit Insurance Corporation (FDIC) Chair Sheila Bair issued warnings to regulators on the dangers of relying on the self-policing of capital requirements by banks. In July Standard and Poor's placed more than 600 MBSs on credit watch, suggesting that their downgrade was likely. In early August retail-mortgage originator and MBS

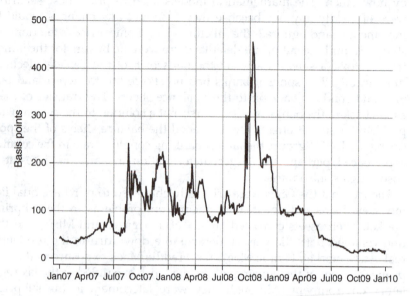

Figure 16.2 TED spread, 2007–9 (daily).

Source: Author's calculation from FRED, Federal Reserve Bank of St. Louis.

investor American Home Mortgage Investment Corporation was unable to roll over its short-term loans and filed for bankruptcy. This failure signaled that the mortgage crisis was gaining momentum and spilling over from the subprime into the prime sector.

Perhaps the best indicator of the feeling of apprehension in the market during this period is the TED spread, which is the difference between the three-month dollar London interbank offered rate (LIBOR) and the three-month Treasury-bill interest rate. These are respectively the short-term interbank loan rate and safe interest rate (on dollar-denominated assets). During times of high confidence and of the perception of low risk in the banking system the interbank lending rate is very close to the risk-free interest rate on US government paper, and the TED spread is very small. Between January 2002 and August 2007, for instance, it varied between 10 and 93 basis points and averaged 35 points.[3] From August 8 to August 20, 2007, however, the TED spread rose from 57 to 242 basis points, indicating a sudden increase in anxiety and in the perception of heightened risk among banks (Figure 16.2). Throughout the following months bad news arrived on a regular basis.

The biggest shock to date came on August 9, 2007, when French investment bank BNP Paribas announced that three of its funds that dealt in subprime debt were suspending redemptions to investors due to lack of liquidity. The Fed, the European Central Bank, and the Bank of Japan responded immediately and injected the equivalent of approximately $400b into the banking system to prevent a liquidity freeze. A week later the largest US mortgage lender, Countrywide Financial, narrowly escaped bankruptcy by exhausting its $11.5b line of bank credit, and subprime lender Ameriquest closed down at the end of August. By the fall of 2007 the largest global banks had started making frequent announcements of losses and loan write-downs. In September Citigroup, facing liquidity problems, borrowed $3.4b from the Fed; Northern Rock, a British mortgage lender and securitizer, could not raise funds in the money market and was saved by liquidity support from the government; and Swiss bank UBS announced a $690m loss. In October, Merrill Lynch announced that its third-quarter loss was $8.5b. Although the TED spread declined from its August peak, it remained above 100 basis points throughout the fall and had risen above 200 again by December, indicating that lenders knew that the financial sector was in trouble and that the level of risk was high. Rising anxiety clogged the credit channels between the largest banks.

Throughout this period the Fed led the charge to contain the turmoil and to ensure that lending did not come to a halt by providing liquidity to the financial system. It lowered the discount rate four times in 2007 by a total of 150 basis points so that commercial banks could strengthen their reserves. The target federal funds rate was reduced three times by a total of 100 points to facilitate interbank lending. In addition to these traditional interest-rate policies, the Fed also created the Term Auction Facility (TAF) in December to inject money directly into the banks. TAF lent funds to depository institutions against various types of collateral. Unlike the use of the Fed's discount window, news of loans via TAF was not publicly released so that banks could borrow while avoiding the stigma of resorting to emergency measures and maintaining their reputation. In addition, the Fed established short-term, reciprocal swap lines with the European and Swiss central banks to meet the liquidity needs of the banking system abroad.

In October the Departments of Treasury and Housing and Urban Development spearheaded the HOPE NOW initiative, an alliance of the government, mortgage lenders and servicers, MBS investors, and housing counselors to assist homeowners who were facing foreclosures. However, the initiative proved to be ineffective. Also in October Citigroup, Bank of America, and JPMorgan Chase announced an $80b "super-SIV" that would purchase high-grade MBSs from special purpose vehicles (SPVs) to stabilize asset prices, but the plan was abandoned in December.

The first months of 2008 saw more failures. Bank of America acquired troubled mortgage lender Countrywide Financial, and the UK government nationalized Northern Rock. The big shock, however, was the bank run on Bear Stearns in March. Bear Stearns had large amounts of MBS and CDO investments on its books that were financed by short-term borrowing; its leverage ratio was 35:1. The declining value of MBSs and concerns about the amount of worthless assets in Bear Stearns' portfolio raised questions regarding its solvency. Although the company insisted that it had a large pool of cash, rumors of a cash shortage caused a bank run by short-term lenders that refused to roll over the debt. Between March 10 and 13, 2008, the company's cash position dropped from $18b to $2b, and its share price plummeted.

While Bear Stearns, the least respected investment firm in the industry and never forgiven by its brethren for its refusal to participate in the resolution of the Long-Term Capital Management (LTCM) affair, was near bankruptcy, the Fed and the Treasury sought a savior. JPMorgan Chase agreed to purchase Bear Stearns' assets for $2 a share (shares were trading above $90 only a month earlier) on March 16. The purchase price was set by Secretary of the Treasury Paulson, who intended to send a message to shareholders and executives that they would feel the pain of their bad investments.[4] The Fed sweetened the deal by providing $29b to JPMorgan Chase to cover possible losses from the Bear Stearns acquisition, a necessary action, according to Bernanke (2012), to avoid a bankruptcy that would have created chaotic conditions in the financial markets.

During the summer of 2008 declining securities prices were taking their toll. Credit-rating agencies downgraded bond insurers AMBAC and MBIA in June. In July the share prices of Fannie Mae and Freddie Mac dropped by 50 percent. The Great Recession had started officially in December 2007—and by 2008, as the economy contracted and the rate of unemployment increased, many homeowners were having difficulty meeting their monthly payments and the crisis was spilling over to large thrift institutions. Although they are regulated depository institutions, thrifts had specialized in Alt-A loans and relied on short-term borrowing to finance these loans. In July 2008 IndyMac, a regulated thrift institution, failed. It was the fourth-largest bank failure in US history.

In April 2008 the IMF estimated that the total losses from the credit crisis could reach $945b. Banks and brokers had lost a total of $435b since the beginning of 2007 due to losses in the values of MBSs, CDOs, ABSs, and leveraged loans (Bloomberg 2008).

The curtain falls

The final act of the collapse began with the GSEs in September 2008. The Fed had opened lines of credit to Fannie Mae and Freddie Mac, and the Securities and Exchange Commission (SEC) attempted to limit shorting of GSE debt to salvage them. These measures proved unsuccessful, and on September 7 the Treasury put both institutions under government control.

Large banking institutions that had invested heavily in MBSs and CDOs could no longer continue funding these positions because short-term liquidity had dried up. To meet their obligations to their lenders they were forced to sell their assets at prices well below what they had paid, which not only failed to raise the needed funds but also depressed prices further in a very opaque market. One solution to the problem was to find a white knight that would buy out the troubled firm and infuse capital. The possible saviors were large depository institutions, some of which were less affected by the liquidity shortage due to access to deposits, and foreign banks. Of the four large investment banks that remained, Merrill Lynch negotiated a deal with Bank of America.

The weakest of the four, Lehman Brothers, looked for suitors, including Bank of America, Korean Investment Bank, and Barclays Bank. Lehman executives requested assistance in the form of guarantees that the Fed had offered in the Bear Stearns acquisition in March. Although the Treasury and the Fed were actively involved in finding a buyer for Lehman, they refused to consider their own even partial involvement in a bailout in view of the moral-hazard problem. In marathon negotiations reminiscent of J. P. Morgan's efforts in 1907 and the LTCM rescue in 1998 Paulson, Bernanke, and the chair of the Federal Reserve Bank of New York, Timothy Geithner, pressured the largest US banks to absorb the toxic assets of Lehman to facilitate a deal with Barclays, the only possible buyer remaining as of September 14, 2008.

At the last minute UK regulators refused to allow Barclays' acquisition of Lehman because the deal needed to be approved by shareholders, which could take as long as a month. The fact that the US government did not offer any guarantees against possible Lehman losses was likely the more serious obstacle. UK regulators were concerned about exposing the UK financial system to risk. The next day, September 15, Lehman Brothers declared bankruptcy, and the failure sent shockwaves throughout the financial world. Until then large institutions in trouble had somehow always been "saved." Now it appeared that no institution was too big to fail. On a more practical level, Lehman acted as a broker and dealer for many financial institutions across the globe under many jurisdictions, and its failure raised questions regarding how these accounts would be settled. The day after the Lehman bankruptcy the share price of the Primary Reserve Fund, a $60b money-market fund that had made large loans to Lehman, "broke the buck": that is, its income did not cover expenses and losses and its share fell below $1. This event was equivalent to bank deposits falling below par value, and it started a run on money-market funds by their investors.

Bank insolvency was not the only hazard faced by the financial system. While negotiations over Lehman continued, AIG, the insurance giant with $1t worth of assets and $96b of shareholder value, issued distress signals. Various AIG subsidiaries had invested in MBSs and CDOs, and their net worth was declining. Far worse, the Financial Products division of the company (AIGFP), which had sold CDSs on hundreds of billions of dollars of the notional value of mortgage-related debt, was running out of cash. Because MBSs and CDOs had lost value purchasers of swap contracts were making margin calls on AIG. However, unlike the traditional regulated subsidiaries of AIG, the unregulated AIGFP did not have liquid assets with which to post payments, and the liquid resources of other subsidiaries were out of reach under the regulations. In addition, AIGFP could not borrow as the loan market had dried up.

The enormous positions of this small division exposed the entire corporation to insolvency. Between September 11 and 17 AIG's share price dropped by 88 percent. AIG continued to burn through cash, and rating agencies downgraded its debt. AIG's bankruptcy would have had chaotic consequences for the balance sheets of its counterparties and intensified the downward spiral of the system. In the end the Fed was forced to reverse the "no bail-out" position it took on Lehman and authorized an $85b line of credit to AIG.

On September 17 the SEC announced a temporary ban on short selling financial stocks to halt the decline of financial stocks. During the following seven days the two remaining large investment banks, Goldman Sachs and Morgan Stanley, filed applications to become regulated bank holding companies, which would give them access to Fed funds. Many smaller investment banks followed suit shortly after. In addition, Moody's downgraded Washington Mutual's (WaMu) debt to junk status. The thrift had been in trouble due to its exposure to ARMs, and on September 25 the government finally put WaMu into receivership. Its assets were acquired by JPMorgan Chase. WaMu was the largest depository-institution failure in US history. The WaMu acquisition was followed by a bank run on Wachovia, another large bank holding company that had been having difficulty as a result of ARMs and other risky loans. On October 1 Wells Fargo announced that it would acquire Wachovia. The bank-stock-price index (KBW) declined by 25 percent between September 15 and October 9, 2008.

Markets' unease throughout this period can be observed from the TED spread. Figure 16.2 shows that between September 10 and 17 the spread tripled to 300 basis points. After October 1, while the Treasury and the Fed frantically improvised to bring a sense of normalcy to the economy, the TED spread continued its escalation and reached its peak of 458 basis points on October 10.

The TARP and QE

Throughout 2008 the Department of the Treasury and the Fed attempted to insulate the problems of individual institutions and prevent a spillover to the rest of the economy. They assisted troubled institutions by seeking buyers (Bear Stearns, Lehman, Wachovia), offering guarantees to suitors to facilitate deals (JPMorgan Chase), injecting capital and cash (GSEs, TAF program), or bailing them outright (GSEs, AIG). Paulson refused to extend guarantees for Lehman due to the moral hazard, but in the post-Lehman emergency conditions moral hazard was of little concern. Extraordinary times required extraordinary measures from the Treasury and the Fed.

On September 18 Paulson and Bernanke issued to the congressional delegation their ominous verdict that the economy was facing a meltdown and requested that Congress authorize the Department of Treasury to spend $700b to stem the tide. The Treasury drafted the legislation for the *Troubled Asset Relief Program* (TARP) on September 20, which proposed purchasing toxic assets from financial institutions. After much haggling and the initial defeat of the proposed legislation in the House of Representatives Congress passed TARP, and President Bush signed it into law on October 1.

The large-scale purchases of illiquid MBSs and CDOs were expected to stabilize the prices of these assets, slow the downslide of the net worth of financial institutions, and encourage banks to resume lending. However, plans were quickly modified because it was not feasible to carry out the toxic-assets-purchase plan in such a short time frame. On October 14 the Treasury announced that it would directly inject $250b of capital into the nine largest banks under the TARP authority in return for preferred shares. On November 10 the Treasury Department announced that it would use TARP funds to recapitalize financial companies. As of June 30, 2012, $416b of TARP funds had been spent; about 60 percent of this was used to infuse capital into banking institutions. Citigroup and Bank of America were the primary beneficiaries. Other main users were automakers and auto finance companies (19 percent), AIG (16 percent), and mortgage servicers for loan modifications (11 percent). By the same date TARP users had repaid $303b of the funds to the government (Wilson 2013).

The Fed continued to lower interest rates and enhance commercial-bank reserves in 2008. It reduced the target federal funds rate seven times, bringing it to the 0–0.25 percent bracket by the end of the year. The discount rate was reduced eight times, reaching 0.50 percent. Under normal circumstances traditional short-term interest rate tools are expected to lower long-term rates, enhance credit extension, and stimulate the economy, but their effectiveness was questionable under conditions of declining confidence and a contracting economy. Moreover, their potency evaporated rapidly as interest rates approached the zero lower bound.

In recognition of the limitations of conventional tools, the Fed continued its unorthodox policy of pumping liquidity directly into the market, known as *quantitative easing* (QE). The first round of this innovation occurred in the last quarter of 2008 and the beginning of 2009 (QE1). QE2 and QE3, the second and third rounds of quantitative easing, took place in November 2010 and September 2012 respectively. QE1 had started with the establishment of the TAF. After the Lehman bankruptcy the Fed not only expanded the TAF lines but also established various new facilities and opened direct lines of credit that authorized the extension of trillions of dollars of emergency liquidity into depository institutions, investment banks, bank holding companies, insurance companies, short-term money markets, SIVs, the GSEs, non-financial corporations, and small businesses against an ever widening array of collateral assets, including government bonds, GSE bonds, MBSs, CDOs, and commercial paper.[5] Fed policymakers anticipated that large-scale acquisitions of long-term troubled securities, such as MBSs, would lower the risk premium on these assets and raise their prices. The outflow of MBSs from and the inflow of cash into private portfolios were also expected to induce asset holders to rebalance their portfolios by substituting other assets for the incoming cash, and thereby expand asset demand and prices in general.

Between September and November of 2008 the value of the assets on the Fed's balance sheet ballooned from $900b to $2.2t. Most of these loans were non-recourse loans, meaning that in the event the value of the collateral assets dropped the Fed would absorb the losses, but an increase in value would accrue to borrowers. The discount window became available to financial institutions other than depository banks. The Fed was transformed into a lender of last resort for institutions beyond the conventional, regulated depository institutions. In addition, the Fed renewed reciprocal swap lines with the central banks of many industrialized countries to ease the global liquidity freeze.

Critiques of the Treasury and Fed responses

The primary objectives of TARP and QE1 were to stabilize the banking system and to re-establish lines of credit to revive economic activity. It was anticipated that with restoration of confidence in the financial system wealth holders would return to asset markets. However, the actions of policymakers were met with public protests from across the political spectrum. Many saw the TARP and Fed facilities as rescue missions to help executives, shareholders, and creditors of financial institutions. Little assistance was given to the mortgage holders who were victims of deceptive lending practices or who suffered job losses during the Great Recession and were now facing foreclosure. The publicly funded financial rescue that amounted to socializing the costs of reckless banking behavior (while the benefits were still private) hurt the public's sense of fairness, and planted the seeds of populist movements on the right (Tea Party) and the left (Occupy).

The majority of experts, and perhaps the public, agreed that there was no choice for government institutions but to become involved in saving the financial system. However, they did not always agree on the means and methods. One line of criticism of the Fed's interest rate policy and QE was that excessive monetary expansion would trigger runaway inflation. Taylor (2011), for instance, warned that the declining interest rates would lower the value of the US dollar vis-à-vis other currencies, raise the price of imported goods, and, hence, increase inflation. Most others discounted this concern because inflation was of little concern during the deepest and longest economic contraction since the 1930s. If anything, the problem faced by the Fed was deflation, or a declining average price level, that would have added to recessionary pressures by discouraging borrowing and spending. Indeed, the threat of inflation has not materialized. At the time of writing, six years after the first round of QE1, inflation shows no signs of surfacing.

The second line of criticism was that the transfer of funds to troubled financial institutions would warp incentives and damage the economy in the long run (e.g. Rajan 2010: 149). The bail out of the GSEs was harmful, the argument went, because such institutions do not really belong in a market economy and their presence creates inefficiencies. More importantly, TARP and QE1 placed few conditions on the assistance offered to banks; interest rates on Fed loans were practically nil. Stakeholders in banks ended up benefitting handsomely from excessive and risky lending during the upswing, but passed on the costs to the taxpayers during the downswing. Free support from government institutions was flirting with moral hazard. Anticipation of government bailouts in times of systemic trouble lowered the cost of risk and encouraged banks to engage in higher-risk and higher-return operations. Moreover, bank mergers and the rising concentration of business in the financial sector in 2008 compounded the problem of moral hazard. Their growing size gave financial institutions even more reason to anticipate that the government had no option but to bail them out during times of turbulence.

The third line of criticism focused on the ineffectiveness of TARP and QE1 in stimulating the real sector of the economy and helping mortgage holders who were underwater. The Treasury and the Fed assisted banks in the expectation that they would weather the storm and resume lending to Main Street, but they built no mechanism into the measures to enforce credit extension to the real sector. Indeed, banks largely did not use these funds in places where they would have alleviated the economic contraction or given some breathing room to people who were facing foreclosure. Instead, banks channeled the government funds back to US government securities to make guaranteed profits from the interest-rate differential. Substantial amounts also found their way to high-return stock markets across the globe. The public was further outraged when the media reported that bank executives, against the instructions of the Treasury, had paid themselves bonuses from the TARP funds, and that the main beneficiaries of the AIG bailout were investment banks that had purchased CDSs against toxic securities—some of which the banks themselves had created and marketed.[6]

In retrospect, capital injections and relief from troubled assets strengthened banks' balance sheets. TARP and QE1 appear to have stabilized the financial sector by 2009. However, they were not as successful in alleviating economic contraction. While the Great Recession ended officially in

2009 and the US economy started to grow again, the economy operated below capacity for years to come. In 2013 the rate of unemployment was around 7 percent, indicating that the US economy was still performing below historic levels of full employment.

Some economists who were appalled by the munificence of the Treasury and the Fed to the banks at the expense of taxpayers argued that the better option to ensure the flow of credit to the real sector and to distribute the costs of crisis resolution fairly would have been the temporary nationalization of the banking system. They indicated that the banking system was suffering from an insolvency crisis and that some banks were practically bankrupt. Temporary nationalization of the banks would involve the government infusing capital into insolvent banks by taking common equity and controlling-interest positions. Banks' shareholders and creditors, beneficiaries of the system in good times, would now bear the burden of losses in bad times and pay the price for their failures.

Nationalization would inflict pain on shareholders because dilution of shares reduces dividends and their claims on future profits. Bank debt would be renegotiated with creditors, who would get a "haircut" or accept a loss on the value of the debt. As the largest shareholder, the government would also have the power to change a bank's senior management team, put a stop to rewarding undeserving executives, improve balance-sheet transparency, eliminate the bank's toxic assets, and, most importantly, manage the bank to ensure that the flow of credit to businesses and households would continue uninterrupted. After the banking system was placed once again on a solid foundation the government would return its shares to private investors by selling them in the open market.

Sweden had adopted this approach during its financial crisis in the early 1990s. The FDIC had nationalized Continental Illinois in 1984 (and sold it a decade later) and IndyMac in 2008 (again, to sell it a few months later). The logistics of how nationalization would be carried out and whether the Swedish and FDIC experiences were relevant to the 2008 crisis were a subject of lively discussion among economists. While, for political reasons, nationalization was not an option at this time, many prominent economists, including Joseph Stiglitz, Paul Krugman, and Simon Johnson, argued that temporary nationalization would have been fairer and less costly than propping up shareholders, creditors, and executives of banks with taxpayer handouts.

Why did it happen?

Before the collapse a majority of experts shared the opinion that the financial system was on a solid foundation. After the collapse they identified an astoundingly large number of weaknesses in the system. The Financial Crisis Inquiry Commission (2011), for instance, attributed the subprime crisis to risky subprime mortgages and their securitization, the failure to supervise the financial market and enforce regulations, the breakdown of corporate governance and risk management in major banks, excessive leveraging, lack of transparency, government institutions' inadequate grasp of developments in the financial markets and their deficient preparation for a crisis, a systemic breakdown of ethics and accountability at all levels from mortgage brokers' quarters to executive suites, government measures to promote home ownership, and the lax monetary policy of the Fed.

The five-way theoretical taxonomy offered and applied in previous chapters helps to organize competing explanations of the crisis. One set of hypotheses searches for the answer in the fundamentals of the level of economic performance, risk assessment, and global savings. The second approach places the blame squarely on the misguided public-policy choices of the government and the monetary policy pursued by the Fed. While there may be differences in the theoretical positions of these two approaches, it will be observed that they are largely in agreement. They both emphasize perverse incentives created by government institutions, even if they may disagree on the appropriateness of the use of the term "bubble." The third line of argument brings the effects of financial-market imperfections under scrutiny, revealing that problems of asymmetric information and other imperfections were compounded by deregulation, lack of transparency, and the shadow banking system. The fourth approach stresses behavioral factors. The final approach focuses on endogenously created systemic fragility as the primary cause of the crisis.

The fundamentals: recession and risk reassessment

Economists at the fundamentals-based end of the spectrum dismiss the idea of a bubble. Eugene Fama, for instance, describes the events of the 2000s as outcomes of optimizing responses of economic agents to the perceived fundamentals (Cassidy 2010). Higher asset prices were mere reflections of the market's best estimates of rising home values at a time of low interest rates and the promotion of home ownership. According to Fama, the onset of the recession in 2007 that led to mortgage defaults was the cause of disorder in the market. Due to lax lending practices and other attributes of the mortgage market these defaults turned out to be substantially higher than the historical norms. The rising defaults, in turn, led homebuyers and investors to reassess home- and mortgage-related security values, and revise them downward. The peculiarities of the non-prime-mortgage market accentuated the downturn, but the driving force of the decline was the overall economic contraction created by some exogenous macroeconomic factor.

The other component of the fundamentals that compounded the problem was risk perceptions. Cochrane (2009–10) argues that the subprime defaults and even the Lehman bankruptcy were small events that could have been absorbed with relative ease by the US economy. What transformed these relatively small shocks into a major meltdown was the reversal of public expectations that the government would routinely bail out the faltering large financial institutions. The government's prior actions on the GSEs, Bear Stearns, and elsewhere had the systemic effect of creating the expectation that troubled too big to fail institutions would not be allowed to go under. When the government surprisingly reversed course in the Lehman case, and the public's expectations were not fulfilled, the perceived risk premium shot up, lending came to a halt, and the run for liquidity started. From this perspective, the panic was simply the outcome of agents raising risk and liquidity premiums in response to arbitrary government actions.

The fundamentals: the global savings glut

Another fundamentals-related explanation is that the global *savings glut*, or excessive global savings, pushed long-term interest rates lower and raised asset prices (Rajan 2010). The expansion of export-oriented production in China and elsewhere built imbalances into the world economy, where some countries ran chronic trade deficits while others ran surpluses. Trade-surplus economies, by definition, spent less than they produced and, consequently, accumulated savings that turned into a glut. The US was a chronic-deficit country, which spent more than its income and made up the difference through the inflow of savings from the surplus countries. Foreign savings flowed into the US as foreigners purchased US securities. MBSs and CDOs were attractive assets for foreigners due to higher returns (in comparison with Treasury bonds), historically low default rates in the US housing market, and climbing home prices.

The policymakers are the culprits

Many economists believe that the Fed's interest-rate policy had a role in bringing about the crisis, but opinions about its significance vary widely. With the country coming out of the dot-com crash, the Fed began to cut short-term interest rates in January 2001 to alleviate recessionary pressures. Over the course of 2001 the federal funds rate was lowered from 6 percent to 1.75 percent, and by September 2003 it was down to 1 percent. Only in June 2004 did the Fed start raising the interest rate gradually; it was up to 5.25 percent by June 2006. Lower interest rates were often justified as a means to avoid deflation and to mitigate the stubbornly high unemployment rates, even while the economy recovered. According to Rajan (2010), the lack of an adequate safety net for the jobless forced policymakers to rely on a discretionary policy of low interest rates to stimulate the economy and lower the unemployment rate. Several experts, such as Taylor (2011) and Posner (2011), place the responsibility for the unsustainable boom in housing primarily on these low short-term interest rates.

While the housing boom had started before federal funds rate cuts, the low interest rates sustained and exacerbated the flow of funds to the real-estate sector and fed the mortgage and refinancing boom. Taylor claims that if the Fed had begun raising interest rates as early as 2001 instead of keeping them low until 2004 the housing boom would have been moderated.

While short-term interest rates were low, some economists point out that, by historical standards, this was not the case for long-term interest rates and therefore greater housing demand cannot be explained by lower mortgage costs (Jarsulic 2010; Shiller 2005). On the securities-market side low interest rates had some effect on the demand for mortgage-backed assets. Blinder (2013: 45–6) concurs that Fed policies led to low interest rates on safe Treasury bonds, and investors who sought higher returns reached for higher-yielding and riskier bonds, including MBSs. Blinder maintains, however, that low interest rates fall short of explaining how and why MBS and CDO investors vastly underestimated the riskiness of these assets and ended up channeling so much money into these bonds. The majority of economists believe that monetary policy bore some degree of culpability, but relatively few are willing to reduce the cause of the bubble to the single factor of low short-term interest rates, or even to recognize it as the primary factor.

The second line of argument that blames the Fed is that it fueled moral hazard and aggravated the magnitude of the crash. The Greenspan Put encouraged investors to take on more risk in pursuit of higher profits by effectively privatizing profits and socializing losses. Investors in high-risk securities, which included banks, were confident that, if their bets did not pay off and financial markets plunged, they would not suffer inordinate losses because the Fed would come to the rescue by providing liquidity.[7] The rising level of risk made the financial sector more vulnerable to adverse external shocks.

Some commentators shift the focus from the Fed to the legislative and executive branches of government that promoted home ownership among the middle- and lower-income classes. First, Fannie Mae and Freddie Mac pumped trillions of dollars into the housing market by purchasing mortgages from banks and securitizing these mortgages. Second, the GSEs heedlessly invested in enormous amounts of toxic MBSs and flooded the real-estate market with even more money (Rajan 2010: 36–8; Wallison 2011). Third, the GSEs, in addition to engaging in fraudulent accounting practices, had a hand in the relaxation of loan-underwriting standards that plagued the industry. The GSEs adopted this aggressive stance, the argument goes, in part because they were profit-maximizing institutions that wanted to take advantage of higher-yielding mortgage-related assets, but mainly because they were pushed by the Clinton and Bush administrations, and Congress, to make home ownership more accessible, either in response to worsening income distribution or to enhance the ideology of an "ownership society." The result was the unsustainable boom in the housing market and related securities. The GSEs also played a critical role in the crash. Because their balance sheets were burdened with toxic MBSs and CDOs the downturn in the real-estate market and declining mortgage-related asset values reduced their net worth precipitously and brought the GSEs to the edge of bankruptcy.

According to other experts, the GSEs were more victims than culprits of the crisis (Blinder 2013: 117; Jarsulic 2010: 148–50; Johnson and Kwak 2010: 145). They were victims because their enormous, undiversified portfolios created a huge exposure to the misfortunes of the residential real-estate market. They were not the primary perpetrators because the GSEs' mortgage purchases, at least initially, were more tightly controlled and confined to prime loans. The GSEs were latecomers to the subprime market and played a supporting role to the banks in the issuance of subprime MBSs (Figures 15.5 and 15.7). The evidence for the GSEs being the main buyers of MBSs is not strong either. At the end of December 2006 Fannie Mae and Freddie Mac held 18 percent of outstanding mortgage-related securities; their shares were 16 percent in 2007 and 2008 (Inside Mortgage Finance 2012: 271).

Experts who hold the Fed, the government, and the GSEs culpable for the subprime-mortgage boom and bust do not necessarily overlook the responsibility of banks. Rajan (2010: 134), for instance, mentions that bankers' reckless risk-management practices turned what could have been an emergency into a meltdown. However, Rajan considers the bankers' role as secondary because they were merely responding to incentives to do what comes naturally to them: taking advantage of opportunities to realize greater profits. It was not surprising that greed got the better of them in an environment where money was the sole measure of worth. However, the root cause of the problem remains government and Fed actions, i.e. lax monetary policy, the Greenspan Put, excessive promotion of home ownership, a warped incentive structure, and moral hazard that had weakened market discipline. While the excesses of financial executives may be inexcusable, the real fault lies with the government institutions.

Market imperfections: price manipulation

The explanations presented so far—the recession, global savings glut, and the policy choices of the Fed and the government—are exogenous shocks to the financial system. An alternative approach sees that faults lie in markets themselves—or, more precisely, in the misbehavior of markets. Prices deviated from their intrinsic values and inefficiencies resulted because of market imperfections.

The first type of market imperfection is price manipulation. Under perfect competition individual buyers and sellers do not have the power to influence prices so no one can take advantage of other agents by exercising influence over price. Prices disseminate information on risk and return attributes and reflect the true value of assets. The large number of competitors and advanced information technology in financial markets may have given the impression that they were efficient in the sense that borrowers accessed funds at the lowest possible risk-adjusted costs and lenders earned the highest risk-adjusted returns at prevailing market prices. However, it was discovered in 2008 that price manipulation and misrepresentation of value by large financial institutions was, in fact, ubiquitous.

After 2008 many financial institutions were taken to court by their investors and lenders, and investigated by agencies including the Department of Justice, the SEC, the Fed, the Department of Housing and Urban Development, as well as the states, for the fraudulent sale of securities and market manipulation, misleading investors on the quality and riskiness of mortgage-related assets, and selling flawed mortgage products. Some of these lawsuits are still in progress but as of August 2014 six largest banks had settled many of these cases by agreeing to pay $126.5b (Bank of America: $74.58b; JPMorgan Chase: 27.09b; Citigroup: $12.14b; Wells Fargo: $9.90b; Morgan Stanley: $1.91b; Goldman Sachs: $0.88b) (*The Wall Street Journal*, August 22, 2014, C1). In addition, Fannie Mae paid $0.40b in fines for inflating earnings. These figures underscore the prevalence of product misrepresentation by some of the largest financial institutions. The combination of the complexity of the securities and the laxity of regulators and ranking agencies facilitated the masking of the fundamentals and their disconnection from market prices.

Another price-manipulation scandal concerned the determination of LIBOR, the average London interbank borrowing cost reported by 18 large global private banks. It is the most common benchmark rate for all other interest rates, e.g. for mortgages, credit cards, student loans, as well as interest-rate swaps. Given the enormous amounts of notional values of interest rates and currency swaps, banks that hold swap derivatives can realize huge gains or losses from changes in the LIBOR. It was reported in May 2008 that banks had manipulated LIBOR frequently to profit from their derivatives positions. In 2013 Fannie Mae sued nine banks for $900m of losses due to LIBOR manipulation. However, the significance of the practice for the 2007–8 crisis was elsewhere. Many banks under-reported their borrowing costs during the crisis to avoid publicizing the difficulty they were having accessing loans (*The Economist* 2012). Misrepresentation of their true status meant that borrowing rates were not accurate reflections of the fundamentals, or prices did not perform their information-signaling function. By December 2013 European authorities had fined ten banks, including two from the US, $3.3b for LIBOR manipulation. Further investigations in Europe and the US were still ongoing in 2014.

Market imperfections: asymmetric information

The second source of market imperfection was related to the structure and distribution of information. The mortgage-securitization chain was composed of many agents who interacted as buyers or sellers under conditions of asymmetric information. This complex structure added its own twists to the adverse-selection and moral-hazard problems (Ashcraft and Schuermann 2008). In a well functioning market participants are expected to exercise due diligence in their transactions to protect their reputation and preserve their customer base. Money managers are expected to act on behalf of investors by watching over the quality of bundles of debt-backed bonds put together by the securitizers; otherwise, portfolios will suffer and managers will not be able to hold on to their clients. Constant scrutiny by money managers, in turn, will motivate securitizers to pay proper attention to the return and risk attributes of the mortgages they purchase. Finally, securitizers' due diligence in mortgage purchases will compel originators to exercise the same type of assiduousness in selecting borrowers. This is how market discipline is expected to work to mitigate problems of moral hazard between money manager and investor, of adverse selection between securitizer and originator, and between the originator and the mortgage borrower, each of whom has an incentive to protect his reputation vis-à-vis customers or clients.

However, such market discipline did not prevail in the mortgage chain. Instead, as mentioned in Chapter 15, incentives to maximize the volume of mortgages and related securities and, thereby, the fees eclipsed reputation considerations. To post returns comparable to those of their competitors asset managers shifted portfolios from corporate bonds to MBSs because the latter had the same credit rating but higher returns. For managers, questioning the quality of MBSs and not investing in them based on perceived risk amounted to missing a chance to amass hefty fees during the upswing, as well as to risk upsetting clients who felt that they were failing to take advantage of profit opportunities. Thus, managers ended up taking high-risk positions with their clients' wealth.

Financial myopia and perverse incentives were contagious. Securitizers, not being watched closely by the asset manager, were, in turn, freed from conducting due diligence in purchasing and packaging good-quality mortgages. They maximized short-term profit by securitizing as much debt as possible without due attention to risk. Farther up the chain securitizers' behavior removed the disciplining forces on originators, whose duty it was to screen mortgage borrowers. Originators also maximized mortgage volume by creating more complex and risky mortgage instruments to expand the market and selling them without any consideration of the creditworthiness of the borrower. Not only did slipshod lending standards inevitably follow, but the most complicated mortgage products were matched with the highest-risk subprime borrowers. Moral hazard ran amok.

As discussed in previous chapters, markets may internally generate specialized institutions and instruments to mitigate problems posed by asymmetric information. If they had had reliable information about the true value of the assets investors could have exercised some power over securitizers and thereby originators by not purchasing high-risk MBSs and CDOs and by forcing them to be diligent in selecting mortgages and borrowers. In modern markets one source of information on the quality of the debt is the rating agencies, which are expected to make independent assessments of securities' default risk. However, rating agencies were not a solution in the 2000s. Where the rating agency was paid by the securitizer it had the perverse incentive not to show due diligence in providing reliable information. Instead, rating agencies had incentives to engage in grade inflation to avoid losing securitizer's business in the future.

The alternative market solution to the investors' problem is the CDS. The CDS market, ideally, protects investors from lemon securities by offering a venue to buy insurance against possible defaults. In a well functioning market one would expect that the CDS seller would make a complete assessment of the security and charge a higher premium for a higher-risk asset. The premium, in turn, signals to the investor the risk level of the asset and permits her to make a better-informed investment decision. But CDSs failed to perform this function adequately. First, as discussed in the next section, CDSs on mortgage-backed assets were a very recent innovation that emerged in 2005. More importantly, it was not proper insurance. The readiness of suppliers to sell CDSs for mortgage-related securities, despite their unfamiliarity with these opaque products and insufficient funds to meet their obligations in the event of widespread defaults, probably gave investors the impression that security prices were justified by the fundamentals. CDSs contributed to the bubble by giving investors a false sense of security.

Market imperfections: costs of arbitrage

The third type of market imperfection discussed in previous chapters is the costs and risks of arbitrage and shorting that may prevent market prices from reverting to their fundamental values. Indeed, there is evidence that much of the smart money, mostly hedge-fund managers, believed that home-price and related asset-price increases were unsustainable and that bubbles were underway. Why didn't they keep prices in the housing market in check by arbitrage?

One way arbitrage may work in the housing market is substitution between occupancy and rental units. Home (and mortgage-related-security) prices should not rise persistently above their fundamental value else potential buyers will choose renting over buying. Second, housing prices should not fall below the fundamental value else renters will enter the market as buyers and push prices higher. However, this is not a highly efficient channel for arbitrage. Glaeser and Gyourko (2007) argue that differences between the characteristics of homebuyers and renters, differences between owned homes and rental units, hidden costs of ownership (such as maintenance), and the high volatility of housing prices make physical arbitrage in homes unwieldy.

The second way to pursue arbitrage in the housing market is to short mortgage-related securities when their prices rise above the fundamental value. If successful the sale of securities in the forward market will halt the expectation of continuing security-price appreciation, slow the flow of funds to the housing market and thereby the demand for homes. Again, though, there were obstacles. The fact that secondary markets in MBSs and CDOs were virtually non-existent, and that these securities could not be borrowed, made it impractical to short them.

The third method of arbitrage was to make bets against mortgage-related securities, especially the higher-risk mezzanine and equity tranches that were more likely to default, by purchasing naked CDSs. Arbitrage might have worked if the smart money's actions had generated a sufficient volume of funds betting on MBS defaults (or on MBS price depreciation). Indeed, a few hedge-fund managers who believed MBSs and CDOs were overpriced made their first bets in 2005, one year before the housing market (and two years before the securities market) went into a tailspin.[8] Once again there were constraints. The standard fundamental, noise trader, and synchronization risks applied to bets that securities would default. To hold on to these bets short sellers were forced to post additional collateral when MBS and CDO prices continued to rise and convergence with the fundamental value was delayed.

Holding on to CDS bets over a long period of time required very deep pockets or continuous access to borrowing, facilities that shorters did not necessarily have. They frequently faced rising borrowing costs. They also encountered dissatisfied investors who did not like or agree with bets against the still rising markets and threatened to withdraw their money. Although, near the end, large banks, such as Goldman Sachs, had joined the shorters (after all, securitizers knew better than anyone the quality of the MBS packages they had created), overall, bets against the MBSs and CDOs via CDSs came late and had little deflating effect on the asset bubble. In fact, there is evidence that the smart money found it more advantageous and less risky to ride the bubble instead of betting against it. The bubble-riding behavior was summarized by Citigroup's Chairman and CEO Charles O. Prince in the *Financial Times* on July 9, 2007: "When the music stops, in terms of liquidity, things will be complicated. But as long as the music is playing, you've got to get up and dance. We're still dancing." Prince, however, did recognize that the situation was unsustainable. He added: "At some point, the disruptive event will be so significant that instead of liquidity filling in, the liquidity will go the other way. I don't think we're at that point."

Ironically, limits to arbitrage were blamed after the collapse as well, this time for prolonging the depression of mortgage-related-security prices. These items were now undervalued, and the smart money should have borrowed funds to purchase them. However, lenders were alarmed by the crisis and credit froze. The continuing decline in the price of securities increased the risks of arbitrage, and arbitrageurs were again unable to perform their corrective function (Allen and Carletti 2010).

Market imperfections: systemic risk

The fourth form of market imperfection was externalities, or systemic risk. Financial institutions were interconnected through various channels, including investment in securities issued by other institutions, inter-bank lending, OTC-derivatives positions, reliance on money-market financing, and dealer activities. Many of these institutions were excessively leveraged and needed to roll over their short-term loans regularly to continue operating. Interdependence, exposure to common risk factors, and high leverage made the entire system vulnerable to an adverse event. Once home prices and the values of some mortgage-related assets plunged, the damage was not limited to specific originators who faced defaults or investors who held a specific security.

The impact spilled over to the entire system because short-term lenders, not knowing which originators, securitizers, or SIVs were in more trouble, not only limited credit to faltering institutions but tightened it across the board. Banks that faced balance-sheet deterioration and a shortage of credit broadened the price decline to other long-term assets as they attempted to build up cash through deleveraging. In the inter-bank loan market potential lenders were unable to assess the value of collateral reliably due to the ambiguity of many long-term assets' market values. Insolvency risk was hard to evaluate because of counterparties' opaque balance sheets, an outcome of the complexity of structured debt, OTC derivatives, and the probable existence of low-quality assets hidden in SIVs. Lenders became extremely cautious. Efforts by individual institutions to save themselves created a credit freeze that put the system as a whole in greater danger.

Regulatory failure

The escalation of market imperfections and systemic risk was closely associated with the changing regulatory environment. Appropriate regulation may mitigate problems of asymmetric information by forcing financial institutions to be more transparent, but the dominant worldview, shared by the large majority of businesses, politicians, academics, and the public since the 1980s, was that the financial market can mitigate market imperfections, discipline itself, and manage risk through prudent decision-making as well as the availability of hedge instruments. In this environment many financial-market regulations were dismantled, enforcement was relaxed, and regulatory agencies were weakened by defunding and personnel cuts.

Thus, policymakers and regulatory agencies bear heavy responsibility for the crisis. Again, the mortgage chain of Figure 15.1 offers a roadmap to trace regulatory failures. The Fed had the authority to supervise mortgage originations and to impose and enforce loan standards, but it ignored the deterioration of loan standards and exhibited an unwillingness to restrain the growth of the non-prime market. The decline and eventual repeal of the Glass–Steagall Act allowed commercial banks to engage in securities operations. Banks not only issued MBSs and CDOs in massive volumes but also held them as assets, and there was no oversight of the quality of these products, the opaqueness of which only increased over time. Further, the Fed and the Office of the Comptroller of the Currency (OCC) ignored banks avoiding capital requirements by means of off-balance-sheet entities such as SIVs, and disregarded increasing leverage. The Office of Thrift Supervision was negligent in its supervision of thrift institutions that generated and accumulated non-prime loans and assets backed by these loans, which ultimately led to the collapse of giants like Countrywide, IndyMac and WaMu.

Investment banks were outside the purview of the Fed. While these banks were accumulating large amounts of MBSs and CDOs, in 2004 the SEC attempted to bring them under its supervision to audit their operations and risk-management practices, and to implement the Basel capital requirements. Investment banks agreed to do so, but their participation was "voluntary" and the SEC effort was ineffectual. Finally, Congress had legislated that OTC derivatives be free from regulation even after the Commodity Futures Trading Commission (CFTC) suggested that they were a source of risk.

Johnson and Kwak (2010) argue that deregulation was the outcome of Wall Street interests dominating the legislative and executive branches of government in the post-1980 era. The power of Wall Street derived from generous donations to political campaigns, intense lobbying, the revolving door between Wall Street firms and government executive offices and, perhaps most importantly, the commonly shared belief by politicians, businesses, academics, and the public that what is good for Wall Street is good for the economy at large. Thus, the government institutions merely did Wall Street's bidding when they followed policies that degraded standards in the mortgage- and the mortgage-related-securities market, masked the riskiness of these assets, increased leveraging, promoted speculative bets via derivatives, and offered the largest financial institutions free reign to pursue profits.

The behavioralist account

Shiller (2008) does not dispute the importance of factors such as declining lending standards, the spread of non-conventional mortgage instruments such as ARMs, low interest rates, securitization, leveraged investments in MBSs and CDOs, flawed credit ratings, and inattentive regulators but claims that these were symptoms of the bubble rather than causes. The real source of the housing bubble was the "social contagion of boom thinking" (Shiller 2008: 41) fed by new-era stories in the media. Agents came to anticipate that home prices would continue to rise indefinitely and at a very rapid pace. Observed increases in prices, favorable news reports, and "getting rich by real estate" schemes that saturated the airwaves all confirmed these expectations and created amplifying feedback loops. Rising prices fed new rounds of price increases through loops of leveraging, asset appreciation, and economic expansion.

Peer effects were important in drawing homebuyers and investors into this mindset. Whether it was herd behavior or agents believing that other homebuyers and investors had better information about the fundamentals, interdependent actions led to the cascade of over-optimistic (and over-pessimistic, after the crash) evaluations of the future of the market. Home buying turned into a social contagion. What distinguished the housing bubble of the 2000s from past real-estate booms was that it became a countrywide phenomenon as investors reasoned that now, after the dot-com crash, this was the way to make money. From this perspective, argues Shiller (2008), factors that seemingly contributed to the subprime boom were, in fact, outcomes or symptoms of the infectious boom mentality.

For example, the Fed pursued easy monetary policy because it believed that either the housing boom was not a bubble or that any troubles it might have created could be contained. Mortgage lending became more lax because borrowers, lenders, securitizers, and investors believed that home prices would continue to rise. Credit-rating agencies did not consider themselves overgenerous because they believed that price rises would persist and that risks were low. Along the same lines, regulators did not consider themselves negligent because a housing crisis of the proportions seen later was considered inconceivable. Even if some individuals had qualms about the continuation of price increases they were hesitant or constrained by the market to take a contrarian action in the midst of the euphoric boom.

Shefrin and Statman (2012) delve deeper into the *aspirations gap* to explain the behavior of homebuyers. The aspirations gap refers to the desired standard of living of households and their current standard of living; i.e. if the living standards to which households aspire run ahead of those they enjoy currently then there is an aspirations gap. The real incomes of the middle and lower classes had changed little since the 1980s, as returns to higher productivity were collected by the higher-income classes. While the overall economy was growing, the aspirations of the middle classes concerning home ownership, education, and consumption levels rose as well, albeit without a commensurate increase in income. Home ownership for most Americans, more than an investment decision, is the realization of the American dream and, therefore, has a significant cultural component. When households' dreams run ahead of their incomes they are prone, even predisposed, to take greater risks. Borrowing at seemingly convenient terms became the means to reach the levels of spending to which they aspired. Indebtedness swelled as a result of the combination of homebuyers' tendency to focus more on the short-term benefits of non-standard loans than on their long-term costs, their belief in their ability to meet mortgage payments, their excessive optimism about the housing market, and predatory lending practices.

Middle- and lower-income classes with stagnant incomes were not the only agents to experience an aspirations gap. According to Shefrin and Statman (2012), bankers were also subject to an aspirations gap in their pursuit of even greater wealth, more and bigger bonuses than their peers, and higher status, which made them prone to engage in higher-risk activities as the means to higher returns.

Systemic financial fragility

All commentators agree that in the 2000s the financial system became increasingly fragile. Opinions on the source of the fragility vary, however. While Cochrane (2009–10) attributes it to the government-fed moral-hazard trap, Bernanke (2012) draws attention to the shadow banking system, its over-leveraged investments, and excessive reliance on short-term funding. Others point to rampant moral hazard in the mortgage chain or lax regulation.

In contrast to these approaches, the Bagehot–Minsky–Kindleberger (BMK) approach offers a wider perspective and context that views fragility not as the result of a particular series of unfortunate events and circumstances but as a condition bred endogenously by competitive forces in the financial system. The BMK approach does not dispute that market imperfections and frictions or negligent regulators played important roles in heightening exposure to systemic risk, nor does it question the role of the psychological predispositions of individuals. However, it does not view these factors as "causal" in the sense that the crisis is reducible to them. They played roles in precipitating the crisis, but they were incidental. Instead, the evolution of the system itself over the credit cycle made it more fragile and vulnerable to adverse shocks.[9]

According to the proponents of the BMK approach, or the tradition that emphasizes the structural-institutional features and internal dynamics of the capitalist system, the subprime crisis was the culmination of a process that had started with the Reagan–Thatcher neoliberal policies that favored unregulated markets, privatization, and the abandonment of policies that target full employment. The big displacements that put their stamp on the next three decades were less regulated markets and technological innovations. Many were impressed by the performance of the economy, at least most of the time, during this period. The volatility of the business cycle diminished after the mid 1980s, suggesting a more stable economy. What has come to be known as the *Great Moderation* is attributed variably to deepening capital markets, technical innovations that improved inventory management, and the Fed's skillful use of monetary policy (Bernanke 2004). The new-era notion that the rise of entrepreneurial spirit and enhanced productivity had pushed the economy to a higher plateau dominated business, politics, academia, and the public. This mode of thinking intensified efforts of businesses and policymakers to remove the remaining regulations in the financial sector or relax their enforcement, and not to impose regulations on new financial instruments. The savings and loan crisis, LTCM, and the dot-com bubble were only temporary setbacks; they did not diminish confidence in the system or change its trajectory. If anything, the fact that these episodes did not scar the economy too deeply fortified faith in the system's stability.

Underneath the apparently healthy economy, however, structural imbalances were growing. The most prominent of these imbalances was the polarization of income inequality. Economists who concur with the Minskyan outlook argue that the primary sources of inequality were institutional.[10] They view rising income and wealth inequality as outcomes of the neoliberal regime, including the abandonment of full-employment and labor-market-protection policies, the attack on labor unions and minimum wages, the promotion of tax cuts for the wealthy, and the relocation of manufacturing abroad. The real wages of an overwhelming majority of Americans remained stagnant as productivity gains accrued to the wealthy. Middle- and lower-income families relied on multiple workers, multiple jobs, and eventually on debt to maintain their standard of living. The longevity of the seemingly prosperous neoliberal period is explained in part by the rising but unsustainable consumer debt that kept consumption spending buoyant (Palley 2009).

During this era the credit-expansion mechanism transformed (Erturk and Gokcer 2009), and the consequent liquidity expansion fed the growth of the economy. Depository institutions, which were the traditional intermediaries, faced rising competition from a multitude of other types of financial entities that collected funds in the money markets and channeled them to users by making loans. Rising reliance on short-term funds made banks' intermediation function between depositors and borrowers increasingly marginal. To compete with the shadow banking institutions traditional banks created their own shadow banking institutions and resorted to the money market to raise financing. The consequences of this transformation for Minskyan endogenous credit expansion were remarkable.

Banks used money-market funds and off-balance-sheet entities to circumvent capital requirements and thereby increase their capacity to make loans, but this was only part of the story. There was also a very close link between security prices and the capacity to create credit. Banks posted long-term securities as collateral when they issued short-term liabilities to borrow from money markets. As illustrated in the lower half of Figure 16.1, higher asset prices enabled banks to post more collateral and expand their short-term borrowing. They then used these funds to acquire long-term assets, raising asset prices even further. Expectations of mortgage-related asset-price appreciation boosted prices and the spiral of credit growth still further. Price appreciation also gave the appearance of strong balance sheets and created the impression that banks and their subsidiaries were operating in a low-risk environment. Euphoria set in.

Thus, the credit-market dynamics of the neoliberal era generated the forces that led to the rising demand for credit, higher capacity to create debt, and underestimation of risk. The period of growth and steady gains bred fragility in the financial system because, as leverage ratios increased, Alt-A and subprime loans, higher-risk mortgage products, and opaque mortgage-related securities proliferated, and the quality of credit deteriorated. This unsustainable state of affairs inevitably came to an end once mortgage payments exceeded households' ability to pay, and the house of cards tumbled down.

Timeline[11]

	2007
January–April	Subprime lenders, including industry giants Ownit Mortgage Solutions, American Freedom Mortgage, Mortgage Lenders Network USA, Accredited Home Lenders Holding, New Century Financial, DR Horton, and Country Financial, file for bankruptcy.
February 26–27	Greenspan warns US economy nearing recession; DJIA falls 3.3 percent; Freddie Mac announces it will no longer buy subprime mortgages and MBSs.
March 6	Bernanke warns GSEs are source of systemic risk.
June 7	Two CDO hedge funds of Bear Stearns suspend redemptions to investors.
June 25	FDIC Chair Bair warns regulators should not leave capital-requirement decisions to banks.
July 11	Standard and Poor's places 612 subprime MBSs on credit watch.
July 19	DJIA at record high above 14,000; Bernanke announces subprime crises may cost the US economy $100b.

August 1	Bear Stearns liquidates its two problem hedge funds and halts redemptions in a third.
August 6	American Home Mortgage Investment Corporation files for bankruptcy.
August 9	PNB Paribas suspends redemptions on three funds that invested in subprime debt; European Central Bank injects €95b into European market.
August 10	Fed, European Central Bank, and Bank of Japan inject $266b into market.
August 16	Fitch downgrades Countrywide, the largest US mortgage lender; Countrywide exhausts $11.5b credit lines with banks.
August 17	Fed warns of heightened recession risk and lowers discount rate.
August 31	Subprime lender Ameriquest closes down, and Citigroup acquires its assets; President Bush announces plans to assist mortgage borrowers in trouble.
September 12	Citibank borrows $3.375b from Fed.
September 13	UK government announces liquidity support for Northern Rock.
September 18	Fed lowers federal funds and discount rates.
October 15–17	Consortium of US banks, supported by US government, announces "super-SIVs" to purchase MBSs.
October 31	Fed lowers federal funds and discount rates.
November 1–20	Liquidity in interbank market diminishes; Fed injects $41b into money supply.
December 4	President Bush announces temporary freeze on several ARM.
December 11	Fed lowers federal funds and discount rates.
December 12	Fed announces TAF.
December 24	Banks abandon super-SIV plan.
2008	
January 11	Bank of America acquires Countrywide.
January 21	Stock markets around world decline.
January 22	Fed lowers federal funds and discount rates.
January 30	Fed lowers federal funds and discount rates.
February 17	UK Treasury nationalizes Northern Rock.
March 11	Fed establishes TSLF to make loans against various federal and private debt, including MBSs.
March 14	Run on Bear Stearns; share price plummets.
March 16	JPMorgan Chase acquires Bear Stearns, with Fed providing up to $30b to cover possible losses; Fed establishes PDCF and lowers discount rate.

March 18	Fed lowers federal funds and discount rates.
April 8	IMF reports total losses from credit crisis could be as high as $945b.
April 30	Fed lowers federal funds and discount rates.
May 2	Central banks inject $82b into banking system.
June 5	Monoline bond insurers AMBAC and MBIA downgraded.
July 10	Fannie Mae and Freddie Mac share prices drop 50 percent.
July 11	Regulated thrift IndyMac fails.
July 13	Fed opens lines of credit to Fannie Mae and Freddie Mac; Treasury allowed to purchase GSE shares.
July 17	MBS-related losses of major financial institutions at $435b.
September 7	US government places Fannie Mae and Freddie Mac under conservatorship.
September 14	Bank of America acquires Merrill Lynch.
September 15	Lehman Brothers files for bankruptcy.
September 16	Rating agencies downgrade AIG's credit; Primary Reserve Fund (money-market fund) "breaks the buck"; run on money markets funds.
September 17	Fed authorizes $85b line of credit to AIG; the SEC announces temporary emergency ban on short selling financial stocks.
September 18	Paulson asks Congress for $700b to be used in purchase of toxic assets.
September 19	Fed announces establishment of AMLF.
September 20	Paulson submits draft legislation for TARP.
September 21	Fed approves Goldman Sachs and Morgan Stanley's applications to become bank holding companies.
September 25	WaMu placed in receivership; JPMorgan Chase acquires WaMu's bank assets.
September 29	House defeats TARP bill; stocks collapse; Treasury announces temporary guarantee program for money-market-fund shareholders.
October 1	Congress passes TARP and President Bush signs Emergency Economic Stabilization Act; Wells Fargo announces it will acquire Wachovia.
October 6	Fed announces $900b short-term loans to banks.
October 7	Fed announces $1.3t loan against commercial paper; Internal Revenue Service (IRS) relaxes rules on repatriating corporate money held abroad; FDIC raises deposit insurance coverage to $250,000.

October 8	Fed and central banks of England, Japan, Europe, Switzerland, China, and Canada cut emergency lending rates to banks by half a percentage point.
October 11	DJIA loses 22.1 percent, S&P 500 loses 18.2 percent over previous week; G7 countries agree to conduct coordinated actions to unfreeze credit markets.
October 14	Treasury announces it will inject $250b into nine largest banks by buying preferred stock under TARP authority.
October 21	Fed announces plans to purchase $540b of short-term debt from money-market mutual funds.
October 28	Treasury buys $125b of preferred stock in nine banks in first round of Capital Purchase Program.
October 29	Fed lowers federal funds and discount rates.
November 4	Fed loans $133b.
November 12	Treasury abandons plan to purchase toxic assets and decides to use $410b of TARP money to recapitalize financial companies.
November 17	Treasury gives $33.6b to banks under TARP authority; three large insurance companies and auto companies request access to TARP funds.
November 20	Fannie Mae and Freddie Mac temporarily suspend mortgage foreclosures.
November 24	Citigroup share price drops 60 percent in a week; Treasury, Fed, and FDIC agree to rescue $20b from TARP and provide more liquidity access, guarantees, and capital in return for preferred shares.
November 25	Fed pledges $800b more to help financial system, much of which used in GSE-issued or guaranteed MBSs.
December 16	Fed lowers federal funds rate to 0–0.25 percent, and discount rate to 0.50 percent.
December 19	Treasury authorizes up to $17.4b of loans to automakers.

Key terms and concepts

Aspirations gap
Great Moderation
Quantitative easing
Savings glut
Troubled Asset Relief Program

Endnotes

1 The leverage diagram is adapted with several modifications from Carlin and Soskice (2014).
2 For detailed accounts of the events that led to the final collapse see Brunnermeier (2009) and Jarsulic (2010). For a more detailed chronicle of the events, see The Financial Crisis Inquiry Commission (2011).
3 One hundred basis points are equal to one percentage point.
4 The final share price was raised in May to $10 after Bear Stearns' shareholders threatened to litigate. Policymakers wanted to avoid a protracted bankruptcy process in the hope that a clean closure would add stability and confidence to the market.
5 These facilities included the Term Securities Lending Facility (TSLF), Primary Dealer Credit Facility (PDCF), Asset-backed Commercial Paper Money-market Mutual Liquidity Facility (AMLF), Commercial Paper Funding Facility (CPFF), Money Market Investor Funding Facility (MMIFF), and Term Asset-backed Securities Loan Facility (TALF). For a list of the borrowers from TSLF, PDCF, and CPFF, and the number and size of their borrowings, see Jarsulic (2010: 167–9).
6 For the breaks given by the government to various banks see Johnson and Kwak (2010: 168–70).
7 There is a separate line of criticism of the Fed that focuses on its negligence in the enforcement of regulations. I will consider this argument later.
8 Lewis (2010) has a fascinating account of the trials and tribulations of several hedge-fund managers who made bets against the housing market.
9 For Minskyan interpretations of the subprime crisis, see Crotty (2013), Erturk and Ozgur (2009), Palley (2009), and Wray (2008).
10 Other economists agree that income inequality worsened throughout this period and had an impact on the subprime crisis but emphasize different reasons and channels. Rajan (2010), for instance, attributes rising inequality to unequal access to education and the relatively higher demand for highly skilled workers. To alleviate the negative social and economic effects of rising inequality, he continues, government resorted to subsidizing home ownership, which precipitated the accumulation of unsustainable debt.
11 For a more detailed international timeline see The Statesman's Yearbook (2011).

References

Allen, Franklin and Elena Carletti. 2010. "An Overview of Crisis: Causes, Consequences and Solutions." *International Review of Finance* 10 (1): 1–26.
Ashcraft, A. B. and Til Schuermann. 2008. *Understanding the Securitization of Subprime Mortgage Credit.* Staff Report No. 318. New York: Federal Reserve Bank of New York.
Bernanke, Ben S. 2004. *The Great Moderation.* Remarks at the Meetings of the Eastern Economic Association, Washington, D.C. February 20. Online: www.federalreserve.gov/BOARDDOCS/SPEECHES/2004/20040220/default.htm.
Bernanke, Ben S. 2007a. "GSE Portfolios, Systemic Risk, and Affordable Housing." Speech before the Independent Community Bankers of America's Annual Convention and Techworld, Honolulu, Hawaii. March 6. Online: www.federalreserve.gov/newsevents/speech/bernanke20070306a.htm.

Bernanke, Ben S. 2007b. *Economic Outlook*. Testimony before the Joint Economic Committee, US Congress. Federal Reserve Board. March 28. Online: www.federalreserve.gov/newsevents/testimony/bernanke20070328a.htm.

Bernanke, Ben S. 2012. "Some Reflections on the Crisis and the Policy Response." Pp. 3–13 in *Rethinking the Financial Crisis*, edited by Alan S. Blinder, Andrew W. Lo and Robert M. Solow. New York: Russell Sage Foundation.

Blinder, Alan S. 2013. *After the Music Stopped: The Financial Crisis, the Response, and the Work Ahead*. New York: The Penguin Press.

Bloomberg. 2008. "Merrill Lynch Posts Fourth Straight Quarterly Loss (Update 2)." July 17. Online: www.bloomberg.com/apps/news?pid=newsarchive&sid=atGti_UmcPnM&refer=home.

Brunnermeier, Markus K. 2009. "Deciphering the Liquidity and Credit Crunch 2007–2008." *Journal of Economic Perspectives* 23 (1): 77–100.

Carlin, Wendy and David Soskice. 2014. *Macroeconomics and the Financial System: Stability, Growth and the Role of Policy*. New York: Oxford University Press.

Cassidy, John. 2010. "Interview with Fama." *New Yorker*, January 13. Online: www.newyorker.com/online/blogs/johncassidy/2010/01/interview-with-eugene-fama.html.

Cochrane, John H. 2009–10. "Lessons from the Financial Crisis." *Regulation* 32 (4): 34–7.

Crotty, James. 2013. "The Realism of Assumptions Matter: Why Keynes-Minsky Theory Must Replace Efficient Market Theory as the Guide to Financial Regulation Policy." Pp. 133–58 in *The Handbook of the Political Economy of Financial Crises*, edited by Martin H. Wolfson and Gerald A. Epstein. New York: Oxford University Press.

The Economist. 2012. "The Libor Scandal: Rotten Heart of Finance." July 7. Online: www.economist.com/node/21558281.

Erturk, Korkut and Gokcer Ozgur. 2009. "What is Minsky All About, Anyway?" *Real-World Economics* (50): 3–15. Online: www.paecon.net/PAEReview/issue50/ErturkOzgur50.pdf.

The Financial Crisis Inquiry Commission. 2011. *The Financial Crisis Inquiry Report: Final Report of the National Commission on the Causes of the Financial and Economic Crisis in the United States*. (Official Government Edition.) Washington, D.C.: US Government Printing Office.

Financial Times. 2007. "Citigroup Chief Stays Bullish on Buy-outs." July 9. Online: www.ft.com/intl/cms/s/0/80e2987a-2e50-11dc-821c-0000779fd2ac.html#axzz32cP1S6il.

Glaeser, Edward L. and Joseph Gyourko. 2007. *Arbitrage in Housing Markets*. NBER Working Paper No. 13704. Cambridge, MA: National Bureau of Economic Research.

Inside Mortgage Finance. 2012. *The 2012 Mortgage Market Statistical Annual*, vol. II. Bethesda, MD: Inside Mortgage Finance.

Jarsulic, Marc. 2010. *Anatomy of a Financial Crisis: A Real Estate Bubble, Runaway Credit Markets, and Regulatory Failure*. New York: Palgrave Macmillan.

Johnson, Simon and James Kwak. 2010. *13 Bankers: The Wall Street Takeover and the Next Financial Meltdown*. New York: Pantheon Books.

Joint Center for Housing Studies of Harvard University. 2008. *The State of the Nation's Housing 2008*. Cambridge, MA: JCHS.

Lewis, Michael. 2010. *The Big Short: Inside the Doomsday Machine*. New York: W.W. Norton.

Palley, Thomas. 2009. "The Limits of Minsky's Financial Instability Hypothesis as an Explanation of the Crisis." *Monthly Review* 61 (11): 28–43.

Posner, Richard A. 2011. "Afterword: The Causes of the Financial Crisis." Pp. 279–94 in *What Caused the Financial Crisis*, edited by Jeffrey Friedman. Philadelphia: University of Pennsylvania Press.

Rajan, Raghuram G. 2010. *Fault lines: How Hidden Fractures Still Threaten the World Economy*. Princeton, NJ: Princeton University Press.

Shefrin, Hersh and Meir Statman. 2012. "Behavioral Finance in the Financial Crisis: Market Efficiency, Minsky, and Keynes." Pp. 99–135 in *Rethinking the Financial Crisis*, edited by Alan S. Blinder, Andrew W. Lo, and Robert M. Solow. New York: Russell Sage Foundation.

Shiller, Robert J. 2005. *Irrational Exuberance*, 2nd ed. New York: Currency Doubleday. Online: www.econ.yale.edu/~shiller/data/ie_data.xls.

Shiller, Robert J. 2008 *The Subprime Solution: How Today's Global Financial Crisis Happened, and What to Do About It*. Princeton, NJ: Princeton University Press.

The Statesman's Yearbook. 2011. "Credit Crunch Chronology: April 2007–September 2009." In *The New Palgrave Dictionary of Economics*, edited by Steven N. Durlauf and Lawrence E. Blume. Online edition: Palgrave Macmillan. Online: www.dictionaryofeconomics.com/article?id=pde2011_C000621. doi:10.1057/9780230226203.3843.

Taylor, John. 2011. "Monetary Policy, Economic Policy, and the Financial Crisis: An Empirical Analysis of What Went Wrong." Pp. 150–71 in *What Caused the Financial Crisis*, edited by Jeffrey Friedman. Philadelphia: University of Pennsylvania Press.

Wallison, Peter J. 2011. "Housing Initiatives and Other Policy Factors." Pp. 172–82 in *What Caused the Financial Crisis*, edited by Jeffrey Friedman. Philadelphia: University of Pennsylvania Press.

Wilson, Linus. 2013. "Troubled Asset Relief Program (TARP)." In *The New Palgrave Dictionary of Economics*, edited by Steven N. Durlauf and Lawrence E. Blume. Online edition: Palgrave Macmillan. Online: www.dictionaryofeconomics.com/article?id=pde2013_T000257. doi:10.1057/9780230226203.3891.

Wray, L. Randall. 2008, April. *Financial Markets Meltdown: What Can We Learn from Minsky?* Public Policy Brief No. 94. Annandale-on-Hudson, NY: Levy Economics Institute of Bard College.

17 Two legacies of the subprime sinkhole

According to a General Accountability Office study, the cumulative economic toll of the subprime crisis on the US economy in terms of lost output was as much as $13t (United States Government Accountability Office (GAO) 2013). Total household wealth of $9t was wiped out. The combination of fiscal stimulation measures implemented to alleviate contractionary forces and the shrinking tax base quadrupled the government deficit (as a percentage of gross domestic product (GDP)) between 2007 and 2009. The Great Recession was not, by any measure, an ordinary slowdown of economic activity, but the deepest and longest economic contraction in US history since the Great Depression.

Deep economic crises can be turning points in both theory and policy. The experience of the 1929 crash and the Great Depression contradicted the belief in self-correcting and self-disciplining markets and forced the modification of the dominant economic theory. The emergent theory acknowledged the market system's shortcomings, the need for discretionary monetary and fiscal policies to tame the business cycle, and a wider scope of regulations to stabilize the financial system. Then the pendulum swung back in the 1970s when the simultaneous increase in the rates of inflation and unemployment cast doubts on the government's ability to stabilize the economy. The vision that sees markets as inherently stable and attributes the primary source of instability to government policy errors once again became prevalent in academia, policy circles, and the media.

The fact that economists failed to anticipate the 2007–8 crisis and misjudged its destructive force, and that markets failed to avert destabilizing pressures, made it seem as though the history of the 1930s was repeating itself. The twin crises in theory and policy once again loomed large: were the ways in which economists asked questions, set up models, and looked for verification of those models seriously flawed? What is the appropriate way to organize financial markets to reduce the likelihood of another costly meltdown? These questions have generated lively and contentious discussions in both learned journals and the media. This last chapter summarizes where we stand in these debates as of mid 2014.

The subprime crisis and the economics discipline

The fact that most economists did not foresee the subprime meltdown, ignored or dismissed the few who blasted trumpets of alarm, and then underestimated the depth and duration of the subsequent economic contraction was a source of embarrassment for the profession. Not surprisingly, the crisis instigated soul-searching in the scholarly community. Economists build knowledge through constructing models that represent selected features of the economy; they use these models to formulate hypotheses on how variables of interest interact and evolve, and search for evidence that support or contradict the hypotheses. Is it possible that the mainstream of the profession constructed models that were dissociated from real life, passed over the key questions, evaded the evidence that contradicted the canon, and put people's livelihoods in jeopardy by systematically ignoring the hazardous consequences of these models' real-life applications?

Some eminent economists, including Nobel Prize winners Paul Krugman (2009) and Joseph Stiglitz (2010: Chapter 9) levy harsh criticisms against mainstream economists for producing theories based on unrealistic assumptions and irrelevant to the real world, for being fixated on the elegance of formalization, for ignoring questions that do not lend themselves easily to mathematical modeling (such as crises), and for neglecting the lessons of history. In the field of finance the target of these criticisms was the efficient-market hypothesis (EMH).

The basic EMH rests on the assumption that independent expected utility-maximizing agents operate in perfectly competitive markets and form rational expectations of future outcomes. Under this assumption markets are efficient: all the relevant information on the fundamentals is fully embodied in the observed price of the asset. Price changes are traced to profit expectations, the safe interest rate, and risk and liquidity premiums. Changes in the fundamentals may be subtle, and first impressions of these variables may fall short of explaining the observed price changes. The researcher's task is then to look deeper into them and discover the hidden fundamental forces. In the case of the subprime crisis the growth in home- and mortgage-related-asset prices is attributed by the fundamentals-based and the Austrian-school approaches to excessive monetary expansion by the Federal Reserve System (Fed), the government's promotion of home ownership via cheap credit, and the perverse incentives that these policies created for the private sector. This vision essentially absolves the markets from wrongdoing; that is, a crash is merely a market correction due either to an exogenous shock that causes revision of profit, risk, or liquidity perceptions, or the inevitable product of unsustainable government action.

Two alternative visions to these "market knows best" perspectives are the market-failure and the behavioralist approaches that challenge the essential assumptions of the EMH and propose different views on how markets are structured and individuals make decisions. Economists who emphasize market imperfections abide by the utility-maximization axiom but draw attention to the consequences of market flaws and pathologies, such as moral hazard, adverse selection, systemic risk, missing markets, and imperfect capital markets. These considerations doubt the proposition that markets can always correct price deviations automatically, i.e. prices may fail to carry out their allocation and information-dissemination functions efficiently and eventually cause asset-price bubbles and banking crises.

The behavioralist vision emphasizes the limitations of the optimization hypothesis and the psychological and evolutionary foundations of human behavior. Behavioralist economists conclude that investment decisions are not based on cost-benefit analysis but on heuristics or rules of thumb. The latter may not only be disconnected from the fundamentals but also generate interdependent actions among decision makers. Consequently, cumulative deviations from the fundamental price are possible.

Both the market-failure and the behavioralist approaches enhance our understanding of how the economy functions and advance our knowledge, but are they harbingers of new conceptual frameworks for economic analysis? The answer is "no" because neither of these alternatives moves too far away from the gravitational force of the core economic orthodoxy, or even attempts to break from it. Rather than replacing the neoclassical core, their proponents are expanding it in order to solve the stubborn puzzles and anomalies that it cannot explain. Perhaps the primary reason for the strength of the gravitational pull is that both models, similar to orthodox economic theory, start from individual agents in their attempt to understand social phenomena. This mind-set is more dominant in the market-imperfection approach, which employs the axiomatic core of expected utility maximization but places agents in environments that feature market imperfections and frictions. Mainstream economics has already successfully assimilated imperfectly competitive market models in many sub-fields, such as international trade, industrial organization, and labor economics. Various financial-market frictions could be built into the standard finance models with relative ease as well. This would change the complexion of the discipline in the sense that the emphasis would be more on the question of how market efficiency varies with market characteristics, but the basic method of creating knowledge about the financial system would be unchanged.

The primary unit of analysis of the behavioralist approach is, again, the individual. However, it draws attention to feedback mechanisms between the economic, social, and cultural environment and human behavior, as well as the interdependence of human actions. Thus, the approach is innovative in the sense that it treats human behavior, to some extent, as an outcome of the environment, and, hence, is potentially a more significant deviation from the neoclassical core. However, most practitioners of the behavioralist approach are not willing to give up standard economics and, in fact, declare that their objective is to extend the axiomatic basis of the neoclassical approach to incorporate psychological factors rather than to challenge or replace its core principles. Not surprisingly, their policy proposals are quite modest and focus on how to design incentives to ensure that people make more-informed and more-optimal long-term decisions.

The economic crisis forced many economists to assess and modify the standard model by incorporating the insights of the market-imperfection and behavioralist approaches. Already, proponents of the EMH appear to have softened their positions. Rather than insisting that markets are efficient, they now pose the question of how efficient markets are and how to make them more efficient (Malkiel 2012). How much this re-examination will change the contours of the discipline, however, is yet to be seen. The possibility that the theoretical complacency of the pre-crisis period will make a comeback is always there. After all, a meltdown comparable to 1929 did not happen, and economists are well trained in discounting history.

In comparison with the market-imperfection and behavioralist approaches, the Bagehot–Minsky–Kindleberger (BMK) tradition is a more fundamental challenge to standard economic theory. This approach rejects the ahistorical notions of expected utility maximization as the sole foundation of economic analysis and of markets as locations of stabilizing, mutually beneficial exchange. It posits that the behavior of individual agents can be understood only in the context of the historically contingent environment within which they are situated. Markets generate instability internally and can lead to socially undesirable outcomes. The BMK approach gives priority to the institutions, structure, and evolutionary dynamics of the capitalist system in building economic knowledge. From this perspective financial crises are not merely symptoms of specific pathologies or flaws in markets but the outcome of the normal functioning and internal contradictions of the credit system. It is important to explain the role of psychological biases and market frictions to understand the mechanisms of the crisis. However, they are incidental in the wider span of the BMK account.

Since the subprime crisis some mainstream economists have mentioned Bagehot, Minsky, and Kindleberger more frequently than usual and at times even expressed appreciation for the BMK account of financial crises.[1] However, it is highly unlikely that this appreciation will translate into a deeper reconsideration of the foundations of standard economic analysis and methodological individualism. As is often the case with the most vigorous dissenters, the BMK tradition is likely to be cast to the periphery of the discipline by the practitioners of the dominant theory.

The subprime crisis and financial-market regulation

The foremost policy debate in the aftermath of the subprime-mortgage crisis was how the financial system should be restructured to prevent excessive leveraging and systemic risk in the future. There were calls to bring back the Glass–Steagall Act, to establish new regulatory agencies, and to dismantle big banks. Cautionary statements about the unintended consequences of government interventions accompanied these proposals. One outcome of these debates was the Dodd–Frank Wall Street Reform and Consumer Protection Act, which was signed into law in 2010. The rules and regulations of the act are still being created, and how they will be enforced is even now a subject of discussion in Congress and elsewhere.[2]

Opinions on the proper scope of the government's role in the marketplace largely reflect the competing visions on how the economy is structured and how it works. The salient issues are the significance of market failures, the ability of the market system to provide solutions to failures, the propensity of individuals to vacillate between excessive optimism and pessimism, the endemic instability of the financial markets, and the advantages and pitfalls of government regulation.

Skeptics of extra-market fixes

The EMH side of the debate discounts the need for outside interventions to correct the imperfections that are not already mitigated by traders, for the following six reasons. First, its proponents have confidence in unregulated markets to generate their own solutions in the event of market failures. Information asymmetry, incomplete markets, or externalities will signal profit opportunities, and profit-seeking actions will eliminate the imperfection. Specialized firms that collect and distribute information, spread risk among participants, and provide incentives for transparency, innovative products that offer hedging and risk management, and incentives to protect reputations alleviate market frictions.

Second, extra-market means are counter-productive because they introduce even worse frictions and distortions into the market that will create moral hazard, hinder the generation and efficient allocation of savings, and inhibit financial innovation and competitiveness. Third, regulations create incentives for a select number of economic interests to exert political influence and manipulate regulatory agencies in their favor. Co-optation by a few will lead to political corruption.

The fourth argument is that the government's efforts to tame financial markets are futile. Financial firms will create new types of instruments that are not covered by existing regulations and escape the oversight of regulatory agencies. Companies will gravitate toward the most lenient regulator. Different regulations in different geographical areas will also motivate businesses to move from more- to less-regulated corners of the market.

Fifth, the regulatory solution is inappropriate when the real problem lies elsewhere, such as government policies to promote home ownership or the stagnant incomes of the lower- and middle-income classes. The lesson to be drawn from this diagnosis is that the US economy needs to make structural changes that will eliminate the need for policy actions that may have unintended consequences. The final objection relates to moral hazard. Expanding the role of the regulatory agencies and, thereby, their accountability during times of trouble, will make it more likely that government will assist businesses in times of trouble. If businesses believe this is the case they will have an incentive to take greater risks and magnify systemic risk.

In sum, according to opponents of regulation, rules and regulations are unnecessary, inefficient, pernicious, unworkable, diversionary, and self-defeating. The validity and implications of these objections, however, are subject to debate. The experience of the recent past sheds doubt on the claim that specialized institutions and the motivations of self-discipline and reputation protection are sufficient to alleviate market imperfections. The costs of the alleged distortions created by government intervention should be assessed in comparison with the costs of instability created by unregulated financial markets. In fact, the search for better rules and regulations could be more rewarding than the blanket condemnation of extra-market interventions as "too costly."

Further, the finance industry has ruthlessly co-opted regulatory agencies and political power since 1980, but, again, the solution to the problem does not necessarily lie in dismantling the regulatory structure.[3] The answer to the problem may lie in part in building more-robust institutions that are independent of pressure applied by small but disproportionately powerful interest groups. Increasing the transparency of regulatory agencies and their interactions with the executive and legislative branches of the government, limiting the influence of big money in elections, and ensuring the broader participation of the population in the political process are also necessary measures to avoid regulatory capture.

The prevalence of regulatory and jurisdictional arbitrage in the recent past is also evident. The alternative to dispensing with regulations, however, is to design better regulations. Regulatory arbitrage requires comprehensive, general rules that apply across the board, without exceptions. In this age of multinational financial institutions, a worldwide financial market, and global financial crises, regulatory measures need to be coordinated across countries to be effective. Finally, economists agree that the difficulties experienced during the 2007–8 crisis were merely a warning of deeper structural problems. There exists, however, a wide diversity of opinion on the sources of these fractures and how they should be addressed. Nevertheless, acknowledging the existence of these problems does not preclude debate over the inherent flaws of the financial sector and the need for restructuring.

A behavioralist's counsel

Another interesting proposal to solve financial turbulence through reliance on market forces comes from Robert Shiller (2008: Chapter 6; 2012). While Shiller has been a long-time, prominent critic of the EMH, he prescribes the following method to avoid turbulence and bubbles in the future: let financial markets flourish, but on the foundations of a new institutional framework that involves wider and deeper participation of a better-informed and educated general public. Shiller sees both positives and negatives in the current state of financial markets. On the one hand, financial flows facilitate the creation of value in the forms of new physical capital, homes, consumer durables, access to education, and comfortable retirement. Financial innovations offer people the means to hedge risks. However, certain activities, such as making bets against the future direction of prices, may circulate money without improving allocative efficiency or producing new value, and add to the fragility of the system. Shiller believes, however, that it is possible to harness the power of finance to generate proper incentives and produce social good. To this end, he calls for the "democratization of finance."

The democratization of finance involves the implementation of a series of market-based reforms that take advantage of the innovations in communications, information, and finance technologies. Shiller's proposals are informed by the insights of behavioral economics, psychology, and interdisciplinary research into human behavior. In line with the behavioralist emphasis on the role of social contagion and information cascades, i.e. periods of over-optimism and over-pessimism, one crucial reform is the reinforcement of the information infrastructure. An enhanced information and communication infrastructure is necessary to enable the financial-sector consumers to make educated and informed decisions, obtain protection against turbulence, and, thereby, mitigate against the emergence of positive and negative bubbles. The components of such an infrastructure include: (a) improved financial education and comprehensive professional advice so that people can avoid unnecessary risk, (b) corporate information disclosure to assist risk assessment, (c) integrated data systems to evaluate financial status and manage risk at the individual level, and (d) contracts that offer prudent default options (that would, for instance, encourage savings).

Next, there should be new markets, institutions, and derivative instruments for better-prepared individuals to manage risks. These innovations include mortgages, the terms of which can be adjusted continuously, insurance against home-price decline or job loss, occupational-income-futures markets (and other hedge derivatives), and markets to short real estate. Government has an important role in the creation of this market infrastructure. It should subsidize the general public's access to financial education and to professional financial advice, create a financial-product safety commission to protect small investors, credit-card users, home-buyers, and other users of financial services,[4] and impose regulations to ensure the dissemination of comprehensive, effective financial information in clear language. Shiller (2008) suggests that as people become better users of financial information they will find ways to control their gambling urges, tame the biases in their decision-making, and be less subject to sharp vacillations between excessive optimism and pessimism.

Keynes (1936) argued that myopic behavior and the domination of speculation over enterprise in financial markets were outcomes of the existential issues of intrinsic uncertainty and the nature of the public corporation. Interdisciplinary research into decision-making, in the tradition of Herbert Simon, emphasized the cognitive and informational limitations of human beings as the source people using rules of thumb, along with the various psychological biases that impinge on these rules. The extent to which the advance and improved utilization of technology and more complete financial markets would alleviate these concerns remains an open question.

Keeping an eye on externalities, moral hazard, and fragility

The most visible debate in the years following the crisis was over the need for a regulatory system that would alleviate systemic risk and moral hazard. The major points of the discussion have been what to do about financial institutions that are *too big to fail* (TBTF) or *too systemic to fail* (TSTF) and the regulation of over-the-counter (OTC) derivatives.

The source of the TBTF problem is the combination of the size and interconnectedness of certain financial institutions.[5] The Lehman Brothers experience demonstrated the hazards of the bankruptcy of a bank that operates simultaneously as a highly leveraged investor, securitizer, dealer, and broker with in-house private equity and hedge funds in addition to its global links with other banks, dealers, brokers, hedge funds, and investors. Its failure sent shock waves throughout the financial system, undermined confidence, froze credit markets, and created worldwide contagion.

An orderly bankruptcy proceeding is immensely difficult when the failure of a single firm can produce such magnified tremors. Such firms expose the entire economy to systemic risk. As the collateral damage of a financial meltdown and a credit freeze are borne by Main Street, which may have had little to do with the reckless actions of Wall Street, the political authority cannot simply stand aside and wait for the system to purge itself of the high-risk players who made bad bets. In the financial crisis of 2007–8 the government did not have much choice but to assist the troubled TBTF firms (except Lehman Brothers), either by intermediating their purchase by another bank or by bailing them out. Knowing that they would be rescued, however, the banks would see no downside to engaging in high-risk activities because all losses belonged to the government and, by extension, the taxpayer. TBTF firms effectively hold the entire economy to ransom.

The widespread public anger and revulsion over the government's assistance, at taxpayer expense, to large financial institutions that had taken excessive risks once again brought up the question of what to do with the TBTF firms. On moral, political, and economic grounds, there was consensus across the ideological spectrum that it was imperative to take measures to prevent another bailout. Ironically, at the same time, bank mergers throughout 2008 created a far more concentrated banking industry, and exacerbated the TBTF problem.

Economists favoring less regulation discount the systemic risk and view TBTF as a government-created moral-hazard problem (Cochrane 2009–10). From a social perspective, agents act imprudently because government creates perverse incentives by giving the impression that some firms are TBTF. If the government could avoid creating this impression private agents would adjust their behavior by appropriately assessing risk and refraining from socially destructive reckless actions. Restoring market discipline is the solution to the problem.

Economists and experts who believe that market forces themselves bear primary responsibility for the emergence of systemic risk assign an active role to regulators in controlling destabilizing forces. They offer varieties of solutions and frequently disagree among themselves about the effectiveness and feasibility of specific measures. Some of these suggestions include new regulatory adjustments and fixes to alleviate systemic risk; other economists and experts propose more drastic reforms in the structure of financial intermediation and the banking industry.

The regulatory adjustments include imposing higher capital ratios on banks, increasing the oversight of banks by regulators, and creating a government *resolution authority* to design and implement a smooth termination of teetering large banks. The imposition of higher capital requirements reduces the risks associated with excessive leveraging and provides banks with a buffer to ease the effects of adverse shocks to the system.[6] While bankers may agree that lower leverage would benefit the system overall, they still oppose stringent capital requirements because lower leverage ratios imply lower profits. Imposition of higher capital requirements was considered during the deliberations of the Dodd–Frank Act but was ultimately rejected. Instead, the act authorized the newly created federal Financial Stability Oversight Council (FSOC) to impose, through the Fed, a higher capital requirement on an individual bank when it is deemed necessary.[7]

One variation of the higher-capital-requirement idea is to require banks to raise debt by issuing long-term bonds that would be treated as "convertible contingent capital." In the event that the declining stock price of a wobbly bank reaches a trigger point, the contingent capital would convert into equity capital and provide a cushion to the troubled firm by erasing some of its liabilities. Such a conversion comes at the expense of the holders of the convertible bonds who end up as shareholders, as well as those shareholders whose claims on profits would be diluted. Thus, the costs of failure are borne by the creditors and the shareholders rather than by the taxpayer.

Another regulatory proposal is to create a resolution authority, possibly designed after the Federal Deposit Insurance Corporation (FDIC). The FDIC routinely designs and implements orderly terminations of smaller insolvent banks without the involvement of the bankruptcy courts. Similarly, the resolution authority would take over a failing, albeit large, institution such as Lehman, replace the management, and run daily operations while allotting the cost of failure among shareholders and the creditors. After stabilizing the institution it would liquidate it by dismantling it or by selling it to another bank or the public at an opportune time. The design of convertible bonds and the resolution authority, of course, presents a number of logistical problems, such as the determination of the trigger point and the jurisdiction of the authority.

One idea incorporated into the Dodd–Frank Act requires banks with assets of more than $50b and non-bank financial companies specified by the FSOC to prepare and file "living wills" with the Fed and the FDIC. These plans outline the allocation of losses among the management, creditors, and shareholders, as well as the dismantling of the company in an orderly manner should bankruptcy be imminent.

These regulatory fixes may address particular pathologies and provide some semblance of stability, but they may turn out to be palliative measures. In light of the lessons from the subprime-mortgage crisis, there is skepticism over whether these solutions will be sufficient to prevent future collapses, as financial agents eventually find ways to evade them through regulatory and jurisdictional arbitrage or regulatory and political capture. The alternative and more drastic route to supervision is to restrict the playing field and power of these firms. Some economists and experts advocate sweeping structural changes in the landscape, often summarized as "breaking up the TBTF banks."

Johnson and Kwak (2010), among others suggest mitigating the TBTF problem by imposing an upper limit on the size of banks, measured in terms of some metric, such as volume of assets. One solution that was proposed and defeated during the Dodd–Frank deliberations was capping a bank's assets to a percentage of GDP.[8] Another proposal was to return to some version of the Glass–Steagall Act by confining within certain boundaries the activities of banks that are potential recipients of taxpayer support. Perhaps the best known example of such restrictions is the *Volcker Rule*, named after Paul Volcker, former chair of the Fed, advisor to President Obama, and a vocal skeptic of the social benefits of financial innovations. In view of the large role of the banks in mortgage-backed-security (MBS), collateralized-debt-obligation (CDO), and credit-default-swap (CDS) trades in the 2007–8 crisis, Volcker proposed banning banks from using deposits in high-risk speculative activities, such as proprietary trading. A diluted version of the Volcker Rule was incorporated into the Dodd–Frank Act and implemented at the end of December 2013.

Some economists favor far more stringent conditions that would ulti-mately force banks to return to their primary intermediation functions. Volcker himself preferred that banks that have access to public funds abandon all high-risk activities, such as owning or running hedge funds and private equity funds (which the Dodd–Frank Act did not ban). A number of economists and experts argue in favor of *utility banking*. The public-utility model of banking restricts bank activities to specific services related to deposits, loans, and payments, and prohibits others. Banks are public utilities in the sense that they offer certain basic services that are needed by everyone in society, and their status as utility providers justi-fies the government subsidies they enjoy, including deposit insurance, access to low-interest loans and to the lender of last resort. In return for these benefits they should be required to supply financial services at a reasonable cost and not to misuse their access to government resources. Speculative, high-risk activities by a company that enjoys public privi-leges and a government backstop are abusive practices because the risks are effectively passed on to the taxpayers.

Another suggestion to diminish the power of the TBTF banks is to increase competition by creating alternative suppliers of banking services. Postal banks, wherein wages and salaries are directly deposited and checks can be written, offer an alternative public-payment system. The private–public partnership of local-development community banks can provide savings and checking accounts, business and consumer loans, retirement accounts, and financial advice to customers.

Breaking up the big banks would, of course, have an adverse effect on bank profits. Not surprisingly, these proposals generated vehement objec-tions from the bankers. The standard argument against the "breaking up" idea is that size has its own advantages, such as fueling financial innova-tions, remaining competitive in the global markets, keeping costs low, and meeting the needs of larger customers. There are academics and experts on both sides of the debate. While critics of radical measures argue that the costs of breakup would exceed the benefits, proponents of dismantling the TBTF firms point out that there is little empirical evidence on the alleged benefits of size but undeniable documentation of the vast abuse of economic and political power by the TBTF institutions.[9]

A parallel debate is taking place regarding OTC derivatives. Again, all sides agree that derivatives have a useful role as hedge instruments. Critics of derivatives, however, point out that the widespread utilization of naked options and swaps exacerbated the fragility of the economy without producing much social good. Rather than reducing individual risk, they raised the opacity of financial markets and intensified systemic risk. In the aftermath of the crisis critics called for all derivatives trading be moved from OTC to regulated clearing houses or organized exchanges. Such a move would ensure full transparency of counterparty positions so each side can better assess risk. Organized exchanges or clearing houses would ensure that counterparties have enough capital to cover their obligations and meet their margin requirements. The counterparty risk also would be mitigated by a well capitalized clearing house that takes over the contract in the event one party fails to meet its obligation. This is not a foolproof system because clearing houses may fall short of performing these functions in cases of widespread meltdowns. More radical proposals to avoid the risks generated by the derivatives market include banning naked contracts altogether.

If such restrictions were imposed they would put a dent in the very lucrative OTC businesses of large banks. As expected, banks insisted that exchanges and clearing houses may work for simpler derivatives contracts but do not meet their clients' needs for more complex arrangements. The Dodd–Frank Act took limited steps in the direction of more regulation by moving some derivatives to exchanges, improving transparency, and imposing higher margins, but it left more complex derivatives in the OTC market and did not ban naked contracts.

* * *

The crisis of 2007–8 had disastrous consequences as people lost their homes, pensions, and jobs. New entrants to the workforce were forced in large numbers to settle for lower earnings and transitory employment. As a result of their bumpy career starts their lifetime earnings are likely to be adversely affected. What is the likelihood that a future generation will be spared from a similar experience?

The shape, durability, and success of a new financial architecture designed to provide stability to the economic and financial system are historically contingent. The crash of 1929 and the Great Depression were momentous events. They shook the economic and social systems to their foundations, and produced a sharp break from past practices. Government and regulators assumed a more active role and imposed a set of rules and regulations to ensure that the reckless behavior of private agents in financial markets was avoided. Economics provided the theory that explained why these interventions are necessary and desirable. During the post-1980 neoliberal era the evolution of financial markets, the resistance of large financial institutions to restrictions on their activities, their growing economic and political power, and "free-market" ideology led to the dismantling of this system in favor of less regulated markets.

By comparison, the 2007–8 financial crisis and the Great Recession have not been as violent as the experience of the 1930s. Due to massive government intervention the Great Recession did not, fortunately, turn into another Great Depression. Perhaps for the same reason, neither did it realign economic and political powers, significantly rehaul financial institutions, or implement a new financial structure to curb speculative behavior. The debate over the design of the new financial system is not yet entirely settled; however, unless the economic and political balance of powers and the modes of economic thinking, which so far have remained largely intact, are altered soon, the hindsight of four centuries of experience on recurring financial crises gives ample reason to expect the repeat of financial boom-and-bust cycles in a not too distant future.

Key terms and concepts

Resolution authority
Too big to fail
Too systemic to fail
Utility banking
Volcker Rule

Endnotes

1 See DeLong (2012), Blinder (2013), Shefrin and Statman (2012), and Malkiel (2012) on the relevance of Minsky's work to the subprime crisis.
2 See Blinder (2013: Chapter 11) for a summary of the evolution of the Dodd–Frank Act.
3 The Fed's support for securitization, subprime loans, non-standard mortgage loans, and proliferation of OTC derivatives can be seen as examples of regulatory or political capture by the big banks. Still, an overwhelming majority of economists would not agree to the Fed's elimination simply because it is potentially subject to manipulation by big banks.
4 The Dodd–Frank Act established the Consumer Financial Protection Bureau.
5 Note that the TBTF institutions also include non-bank financial companies, such as Fannie Mae, Freddie Mac, AIG, and the Long-Term Capital Management hedge fund.
6 Capital requirements are at the core of the Basel Committee on Banking Supervision.
7 The main task of the FSOC is to oversee the financial sector, specifically, TBTF companies, to detect the systemic risks in the system and serve as a consultant as well as a facilitator of communications among the Fed, the FDIC, and other regulators. Closer cooperation and coordination among regulators is expected to design and implement stabilizing measures more effectively. The identification and monitoring of excessive risks in the financial system is also expected to provide regulators with an opportunity to take countermeasures against emerging threats to the financial system.
8 Johnson and Kwak (2010: 214–5) suggest maximum limits of 4 percent of GDP for commercial and 2 percent for investment banks. The authors point out that these limits would have affected only the six largest US banks, whose total assets were as high as 63 percent of GDP (217).

9 Among others, Johnson and Kwak (2010: 208), Roubini and Mihm (2010: 230), Stiglitz (2010: 164), and Wray (2013) make the case for reforms that would re-transform finance from "casino" back to "boring" banking. For counterarguments see Blinder (2013: 268).

References

Blinder, Alan S. 2013. *After the Music Stopped: The Financial Crisis, the Response, and the Work Ahead*, New York: The Penguin Press.

Cochrane, John H. 2009–2010. "Lessons from the Financial Crisis." *Regulation* 32 (4): 34–7.

DeLong, J. Bradford. 2012. "This Time it's *Not* Different: The Persistent Concerns of Financial Macroeconomics." Pp. 14–36 in *Rethinking the Financial Crisis*, edited by Alan S. Blinder, Andrew W. Lo, and Robert M. Solow. New York: Russell Sage Foundation.

Johnson, Simon, and James Kwak. 2010. *13 Bankers: The Wall Street Takeover and the Next Financial Meltdown*. New York: Pantheon Books.

Keynes, John Maynard. 1936. *The General Theory of Employment, Interest, and Money*. London: Macmillan.

Krugman, Paul. 2009. "How Did Economists Get It So Wrong?" *New York Times Magazine*. Online: www.nytimes.com/2009/09/06/magazine/06Economic-t.html?_r=1.

Malkiel, Burton G. 2012. "The Efficient-Market Hypothesis and the Financial Crisis." Pp. 75–98 in *Rethinking the Financial Crisis*, edited by Alan S. Blinder, Andrew S. Lo, and Robert M. Solow. New York: Russell Sage Foundation.

Roubini, Nouriel, and Stephen Mihm. 2010. *Crisis Economics: A Crash Course in the Future of Finance*. New York: The Penguin Press.

Shefrin, Hersh, and Meir Statman. 2012. "Behavioral Finance in the Financial Crisis: Market Efficiency, Minsky, and Keynes." Pp. 99–135 in *Rethinking the Financial Crisis*, edited by Alan S. Blinder, Andrew S. Lo, and Robert M. Solow. New York: Russell Sage Foundation.

Shiller, Robert J. 2008. *The Subprime Solution: How Today's Global Financial Crisis Happened, and What to Do About It*. Princeton, NJ: Princeton University Press.

Shiller, Robert J. 2012. *Finance and the Good Society*. Princeton, NJ: Princeton University Press.

Stiglitz, Joseph E. 2010. *Freefall: America, Free Markets, and the Sinking of the World Economy*. New York: W. W. Norton and Company.

United States Government Accountability Office (GAO). 2013. *Financial Regulatory Reform: Financial Crisis Losses and Potential Impacts of the Dodd- Frank Act*, GAO-13-1980. Washington, DC: GAO.

Wray, L. Randall. 2013. "A Minskyan Road to Financial Reform." Pp. 696–710 in *The Handbook of the Political Economy of Financial Crises*, edited by Martin H. Wolfson and Gerald A. Epstein. New York: Oxford University Press.

Glossary

Adjustable rate mortgage: Mortgage with a variable interest rate that changes with credit-market conditions.

Adverse selection: Outcome of asymmetric information in which too many low-quality and too few high-quality market goods, assets, or factors are traded.

Agency-label security: Mortgage-backed securities issued by GSEs.

Allais paradox: Paradox that shows the inconsistency of observed individual choices with predictions of expected utility theory.

Allocative efficiency: Allocation of resources in which the quantities of commodities produced are in accordance with demand. It is achieved when the benefit obtained from the last unit is equal to the cost of producing the last unit.

Alternate-A (Alt-A) loan: Loan that is riskier than a prime loan, due to factors such as deficient documentation and unsteady income, but less risky than a subprime loan.

Animal spirits: Human attribute that explains decisions as outcomes of spontaneous urges to act rather than probabilistic expectations (according to Keynes).

Annuity: Financial contract whereby one party makes a contribution or a loan to another party in return for receiving periodic payments over a period of time (historically, the latter have been as long as 99 years).

Arbitrage: Simultaneous purchase and sale of an asset (or equivalent assets) in order to profit from price differences across markets. (See: Law of one price)

Aspirations gap: Difference between the standard of living to which individuals or households aspire and the current standard of living.

Asymmetric information: Situation in which one side of the transaction knows more than the other.

Attention cascade: Tendency of individuals or the media to focus on a particular story for a long period of time.

Availability heuristic: Tendency in decision-making to put more weight on readily available information rather than consider alternatives.

Banknote: Paper currency issued by banks and originally backed by specie.

Bank run: Sudden demand by a large number of banknote holders, depositors, or short-term lenders to withdraw their funds from banks.

Bill of exchange: Written note whereby one party (drawer or issuer) promises to pay a specified sum of money to a counterparty (payee) at a fixed time or on demand. (See: Promissory note)

Bimetallism: System in which both gold and silver are used as monetary standards.

Bond: Debt instrument sold by the issuer (corporation, government) in order to borrow funds. The issuer is obliged to pay the bondholders (creditors) the coupon value periodically and the face value when the bond matures.

Bounded rationality: State in which a decision problem cannot be clearly delineated due to informational, computational, and cognitive limitations and people base their decisions on a bounded set of choices and accept satisfactory solutions rather than the optimal. (See: Economic rationality, Satisficing)

Bretton Woods system: Post-World War II international monetary system based on gold-exchange standard.

Call (buy) option: Contract whereby one party buys the right (but not the obligation) to buy an asset at a certain price (strike price) before or at a specific date (exercise date).

Capital gain/loss: Difference between an asset's current sale price and the initial purchase price.

Capital market: Market where equities and long-term debt instruments are traded.

Cash settlement: Settlement of a derivative (futures, options, swap) contract by cash transfer of the profit or loss amount rather than physical delivery. (See: Physical settlement)

Certainty effect: Tendency to prefer a less risky (more certain) outcome even when its (probabilistic) expected value is lower than the alternative.

Chartism: Investment strategy based on forecasting the future behavior of prices from their historical patterns. (See: Technical analysis)

Circuit breaker: Measure designed to stop trading when the market index falls below a threshold.

Clearing house: Agency for settling claims and accounts, including check payments and futures and options trades, among member financial agents.

Cognitive dissonance: People's tendency to ignore, reject, avoid, or explain away new information that contradicts their belief system.

Collateral: Assets pledged by a borrower to a lender as security for repayment of a loan that are seized by the lender if the borrower defaults.

Collateralized debt obligation: Structured security backed by the cash flow of mortgage-backed securities and other asset-backed securities.

Collateralized mortgage obligation: Structured security backed by the cash flow of mortgage-backed securities.

Commercial paper: Promissory notes issued by corporations to meet short-term working-capital needs.

Commodity money: Specific commodity, which has a use value of its own, that serves as money.

Common stock: Public-company stock that has company voting rights. Common-stock holders are not entitled to a guaranteed dividend and, in the case of bankruptcy, have a claim on capital only after creditors and preferred shareholders.

Completeness axiom: For any two alternatives—A and B—the individual either prefers A to B, or B to A, or is indifferent between A and B.

Confirmation bias: People's tendency to favor information that validates prior beliefs.

Conforming loan: Mortgage loan that conforms to GSE guidelines (on size, debt-to-income ratio, and documentation).

Convention: Rules of thumb and strategies investors adopt when uncertainty about the future cannot be reduced to probabilistic decision-making (according to Keynes).

Convergence trade: Investment strategy that exploits price differences in similar assets by buying the cheaper asset in the spot market and selling the expensive asset in the futures market in the expectation that prices will converge by the delivery date.

Corner: Gaining control of a stock in order to raise the price and squeeze short sellers.

Corporate raider: Individual or a company that attempts a usually hostile takeover of another company, and replaces management and redesigns operations in order to raise its market value.

Coupon: Fixed periodic payment on a fixed-income security.

Coupon rate: Ratio of coupon value to face value of a fixed-income security.

Credit: A contractual agreement whereby one party offers resources to another party in return for the second party's pledge to pay for these resources at a later date, usually with interest.

Credit default swap: Derivative instrument in which the buyer makes a periodic payment to the seller until a loan matures in return for the seller pledging to pay the face value of the loan to the buyer if the loan defaults.

Credit intermediation cost: Bank's costs of screening and monitoring borrowers.

Currency swap: Contract to exchange the payment stream of a loan denominated in one currency with the payment stream of a loan denominated in another currency.

Debt deflation: Declining value of collateral (e.g. a home in a mortgage contract) that may cause borrowers to end up owing more than the value of their investment (home).

Debt financing: Situation in which an agent funds expenditures by selling debt instruments to creditors.

Debt instrument: Financial obligations, such as bonds, commercial paper, certificates of deposit, issued in order to raise funds.

Default risk: Risk of borrowers not being able to meet debt obligations.

Deficit unit: Economic unit with income less than its expenditures.

Deposit insurance: Guarantee to compensate depositors for their losses if a bank fails.

Depository institution: Financial institutions that accept deposits from the general public (commercial banks, thrifts, and credit unions).

Derivative: Financial asset, the value of which is based on the performance of an underlying financial asset(s).

Discounting (commercial paper):   Purchase of commercial paper before maturity at a reduced price.

Discount rate (central bank):   Interest rate a central bank charges on short-term loans to member banks (also called the re-discount rate).

Discount rate (present value calculation):   Rate at which an expected future income stream is discounted. It is the required rate of return to make the purchase of an asset worthwhile.

Diversification: Investment strategy to reduce the risk exposure of a portfolio by combining various assets, the returns on which are not positively correlated.

Dividend: Portion of the earnings of a public company distributed to the shareholders.

Dynamic hedging: Strategy of continuously hedging a portfolio position via synthetic options in response to changing market conditions.

Economic-calculation debate: Debate over whether efficient allocation of resources through simulation of the price system by central planners is feasible, and superior to real-time market outcomes.

Economic model: Simplified verbal, mathematical, or geometric construct that describes relationships and causal links among a set of endogenous and exogenous economic variables.

Economic rationality: Postulate that an individual decision maker ranks all feasible choices and consistently selects the basket that yields the higher benefit (utility or profit) or lowest cost.

Economies of scale: Situation in which the output rises more than proportionately with the scale of production.

Efficient-market hypothesis: Argument that asset prices always incorporate all relevant information and that an investor cannot beat the market systematically.

Endogenous variable: Variable that depends on other variables in the model and explained within the model.

Equity: Asset that represents ownership interest.

Equity arbitrage: Investment strategy to purchase and sell similar (same) assets simultaneously to exploit price differences.

Equity (balance sheet):   Difference between assets and liabilities on the balance sheet.

Equity finance: Company raising funds for its expenditures by selling common or preferred stocks.

Exchange trading: Trading of assets via organized markets, like the stock market. In comparison with the OTC market, products are standardized and trading is transparent.

Exogenous variable: Variable whose value is not explained by the model but taken as given.

Expectational error: Difference between the expected value of a variable and its actual realized value.

Expected utility maximization: Hypothesis that the utility of an action under uncertainty is its mathematical expectation or the weighted average value it yields based on the possible outcomes and their probabilities.

Externality: Situation in which private costs/benefits do not match the public costs/benefits and thus products are over- or underproduced relative to the optimal amount.

Extrinsic bubble: Cumulative deviation of the asset price from its fundamental value that is attributable to investors basing their decisions on a factor unrelated to the fundamentals.

Face value: Value of a security as it is stated on the certificate. (See: Par value)

Factors of production: Primary inputs in to the production process (land, labor, and capital).

Fallacy of composition: Inference that if something is true for individual components then it is also true for the whole.

Fiat money: Paper money recognized as legal tender by government fiat but not backed by specie.

Financial intermediary: Financial institutions, like banks, that facilitate transactions between surplus and deficit units.

Financial market: Markets in which financial instruments (stocks, short- and long-term debt, derivatives, and currencies) are traded.

Financial system: System that encompasses the institutions, markets, mechanisms, and instruments through which excess funds of surplus units are allocated among deficit units to finance the latter's expenditures.

Financialization: The growth of the financial sector both in relative size and in terms of its dominance of other sectors in the economy.

Fixed-income security: Investment whose periodic returns are known in advance.

Fixed-rate mortgage: Mortgage with an interest rate that does not change over the life of the loan.

Flexible income security: Investment whose payments are not fixed but determined by an underlying measure such as earnings.

Floating debt: Short-term debt that is continuously refinanced. Examples are commercial paper and Treasury bills.

Forbearance: Postponement of the payment of loans to provide relief to the borrower for a specified period of time.

Forward contract: Agreement to buy or sell a commodity or an asset at a certain price for delivery at a specific date in the future. Forward contracts are usually traded OTC.

Forward market: Market in which forward contracts are exchanged.

Fractional-reserve system: Banking system in which only a fraction of deposits are held as reserves by banks and the rest is loaned out.

Framing effect: Cognitive bias that presents otherwise equivalent choices differently (e.g. as a gain or loss) and that causes systematically different choices.

Free banking: Banking system in place in the US between the 1840s and 1860s, when some states relaxed conditions of entry into banking.

Futures contract: Agreement to buy and sell a commodity or an asset at a certain price for delivery at a specific date in the future. Futures contracts are standardized and exchanged in regulated markets and are, therefore, more liquid than forward contracts.

Futures market (Futures exchange):   Organized, regulated market in which futures contracts are exchanged.

Fundamental risk: The risk that fundamentals move against arbitrageurs/ short sellers after they make bets against mispricing in the market.

Glass–Steagall Act: Post-Great Depression law that banned commercial banks from engaging is investment-banking activities (among other provisions).

Gold-exchange standard: Post-World War II international monetary system in which the value of the US dollar was set in terms of gold and the values of other currencies were pegged to the US dollar.

Gold standard: Monetary system in which gold is the standard measure of money and other forms of money are convertible to gold at fixed rates. International monetary system in which the value of each national currency is set in terms of gold and international payment imbalances are settled in gold.

Government debt: Total debt owed by the government to creditors (public debt, sovereign debt).

Government failure: Situation in which government intervention to correct market failure creates further misallocation of resources.

Great Moderation: Post-1980s period of reduced volatility of business cycles and inflation in the US.

Greenback: Paper currency issued during the US Civil War. It was legal tender but not convertible to specie.

Greenspan Put: Widespread perception after 1998 that the Fed would use monetary policy to ensure liquidation of stocks as if there is a put option.

Gresham's Law: Principle stating that if coins with the same par value have different precious-metal content then the coin with more metal content will be hoarded and disappear from circulation, or "bad money drives out good."

Hard money: Money backed by precious metal.

Hedge finance (Minsky):   Finance regime in which borrowers have sufficient revenue to make interest and principal payments on loans and are on schedule to pay off their debt.

Hedge fund: Unregulated investment vehicle that pools funds from a limited number of very wealthy individuals and seeks high returns, usually by taking leveraged, risky positions in securities and derivatives.

Hedging: Risk-management strategy of taking offsetting positions (long and short) in related securities to minimize the risk of market fluctuations.

Herd behavior: Investors' tendency to act interdependently as a large group rather than making their own decisions independently.

Idiosyncratic risk: Risk that is not correlated with market risk and can be mitigated via portfolio diversification.

Independence of irrelevant alternatives axiom: If an agent chooses basket A to basket B then the availability of basket C will not affect the ranking between A and B. (See: Rational choice theory)

Index arbitrage: Investment strategy that seeks to profit from the price discrepancy between a stock index and stock-index-futures contracts.

Industrial trust: Combination of firms for the purposes of reducing competition and controlling prices in an industry.

Information cascade: Tendency to ignore one's own information in favor of information based on other people's actions.

Informational efficiency: Degree to which prices collect, aggregate and disseminate all the information relevant to the fundamentals.

Initial public offering: First sale of a stock to the public.

Interest swap: Contract to exchange one stream of interest payments for another, usually fixed-interest payments for variable-interest payments.

Intrinsic bubble: Cumulative deviation of the asset price from the fundamentals that is attributable to investors systematically miscalculating the fundamentals.

Intrinsic uncertainty: Type of uncertainty about the future that cannot be gauged probabilistically because the odds of outcomes and even the outcomes themselves are not known with a high degree of confidence.

Investment bank: Non-depository financial institution that specializes in underwriting securities and assisting in M&As. It also provides portfolio management, investment advice, and market-making services.

Investment trust: Financial institution that issued its own stock against its portfolio of common stocks (in the 1920s).

IOU: Informal document that acknowledges a debt owed.

Irredeemable debt: Government debt that cannot be paid off without the debt holder's permission.

Joint-stock company: Business owned by shareholders.

Junk bonds: Bonds that carry a higher default risk and also higher expected returns than investment-grade bonds.

Jurisdictional arbitrage: Locating a business in a legal jurisdiction with more lenient regulations.

Laissez-faire: Economic doctrine that upholds the autonomous nature of individuals and markets in regulating economic affairs and opposes government intervention in business and commerce.

Law of one price: In a perfectly competitive market with no distortions arbitrage behavior ensures that equivalent assets (or commodities) have the same price.

Legal tender: Money that is legally recognized and enforced as payment in meeting financial obligations.

Lender of last resort: Institution that extends credit to banks when all other options of raising liquidity are exhausted. It is usually the central bank.

Leverage: Use of debt or financial derivatives to raise returns on investment. The amount of debt used in financing assets.

Leveraged buyout: Acquisition of a public company by a substantial amount of debt collateralized by the assets and income flow of the target company, usually with the aim of taking it private.

Limited liability: Limitation of an investor's financial liability to the amount invested in a company.

Liquidity: Ease of convertibility of an asset into cash.

Liquidity crisis: Situation in which there is generalized lack of buyers for the asset offered.

Liquidity freeze: Acute shortage of credit in financial markets because lenders severely reduce or stop rolling over or making new loans.

Liquidity premium: Return investors demand as compensation for the cost of tying up cash in an asset that is not easily convertible to cash.

Liquidity risk: Risk that an asset cannot be quickly sold in the market without a significant discount.

Loan-to-value (LTV) ratio: Ratio of a mortgage loan to the appraised value of the property.

Long position (or Long):   Buying and holding an asset with the expectation that its value will rise. (See: Short position)

Malinvestment: Misallocation of resources to the production of physical capital goods because of artificially low interest rates.

Margin account: Brokerage account from which investors can borrow funds at a margin to purchase securities against the collateral of a security.

Margin call: Broker demanding a margin-account holder to deposit additional cash when the value of the collateral security in the margin account drops.

Margin requirement: Fraction of the security price a margin-account holder must pay in cash (the rest is paid by a loan from the broker that is collateralized by securities).

Marginal benefit: Benefit obtained from the last unit consumed.

Marginal cost: Cost of production of the last unit of output.

Market capitalization: Total value of shares issued by a public company.

Market demand: Relationship between the price and the quantity buyers are willing to purchase at each price.

Market failure: Situation in which unregulated competitive market outcomes are inefficient in the allocative, productive or informational sense.

Market maker: Financial institution that readily buys and sells a security at publicly quoted bid and ask prices, and profits from the bid-ask spread.

Market rationality: Idea that market forces ensure that the observed price will be equal to the intrinsic price and discipline any individual agent who does not rely on market fundamentals.

Market supply: Relationship between the price and the quantity sellers are willing to offer at each price.

Maturity mismatch: Situation in which liabilities on a balance sheet are short-term and assets are long-term.

Mercantilism: Economic doctrine according to which the wealth of a nation is measured by its bullion stock.

Mergers and acquisitions: Consolidation of companies through amalgamation or acquisition of one company by another.

Methodological individualism: Approach that attempts to explain social phenomena on the basis of the behavior of individual agents.

Minsky moment: Sudden collapse in asset values during the credit cycle when liquidity-seeking speculators/investors are forced to sell their higher-quality securities.

Missing (incomplete) markets: Situation in which the unregulated competitive market system cannot produce efficient outcomes because the relevant market does not exist.

Money: Item that serves as medium of exchange, store of wealth, and measure of value.

Money market: Market where short-term financial instruments are traded.

Money trust: Control of industry, commerce, and finance by a few powerful bankers.

Moral hazard: Situation in which one party has the incentive to engage in risky behavior because it can shift the costs of potential losses to the other party.

Mortgage-backed security: Structured security that is backed by the cash flow of a pool of mortgages.

Naked short (shorting): Selling short an asset without borrowing it in the first place or ensuring that it can be borrowed before its delivery date to the buyer.

National banking system: Banking system established in 1863 and 1864 in the US, which lasted until the establishment of the Fed, characterized by hierarchically structured banks with federal charters.

Neoliberalism: Political and economic philosophy that supports deregulation, privatization, trade and capital liberalization, and minimizing the economic role of government as a means to improve efficiency and achieve growth in the economic system.

Network economies: Situation where the value of a product expands with the number of people using it.

Net worth: Difference between assets and liabilities on a balance sheet.

No-arbitrage condition: Situation where assets are priced according to their discounted expected earnings. When it prevails investors cannot make above-market returns unless they are willing to take on more risk.

Noise trader: Investor who makes buy and sell decisions with little or no regard to the fundamentals of the asset price.

Noise-trader risk: Risk that asset mispricing worsens due to the actions of noise traders.

Normal distribution: Theoretical frequency distribution of a random variable. It has a bell shape with most observations clustered around the mean and very few near the tails.

Open market operation: Central bank's buying or selling short-term government debt in an open market.

Optimization: Selecting the alternative that yields the highest utility or the lowest cost under given constraints.

Option: Financial contract whereby one party buys the right (but not the obligation) to buy or sell an asset at a certain price (strike price) during a certain period of time or at a specific date (exercise date). (See: Call option, Put option)

Over-the-counter trading: Trading of assets by bilateral contracts. In comparison with exchange trading, OTC products are not standardized and their trading is more opaque. (See: Exchange trading)

Pairs trade: (See: Convergence trading)

Par value: Value of a security as it is stated on the certificate. The dollar amounts of interest and principal payments on a bond and dividend on preferred stock are calculated as percentages of par values. Common stocks usually do not have par value. (See: Face value)

Pass-through security: Earlier and simpler form of mortgage-backed security.

Perfect competition: Market structure in which no individual buyer or seller can influence the price, and exchanges take place at the price determined by anonymous forces of market supply and demand.

Physical settlement: Settlement of a derivative (futures, options, swap) contract by physical delivery of the item. (See: Cash settlement)

Ponzi finance (Minsky):   Finance regime in which borrowers do not have sufficient revenue to make the interest and principal payments.

Ponzi scheme: Investment scam in which earlier investors are paid out of the money raised from new investors.

Portfolio insurance: Investment strategy that hedges the value of a stock portfolio against an unexpected decline in its market value by trading a synthetic replicating portfolio (e.g. short selling stock-index futures or buying stock-index put options).

Preferred stock: Public-company stock that does not have voting rights in company decisions. Preferred stocks have prior claim over common stock in receiving dividends, and on capital in the case of bankruptcy.

Prepayment risk: Risk of early payment of the principal of a mortgage contract.

Present value: Current value of an amount that is to be received in the future, taking into account the interest rate that would be earned over time, and the risk and liquidity characteristics of the contract.

Price discovery: Dynamic process of determination of the price of a security through the interactions of buyers and sellers.

Price-earnings ratio: Ratio of the market price of a common stock to its annual earnings per share.

Price-rent ratio: Ratio of the price of a house to its annual rental value.

Primary market: Markets where new issues of securities are offered for the first time. (See: secondary market, underwriting)

Prime loan: Mortgage loan extended to a borrower who has a good credit rating, documentation, and overall low default risk.

Principal-agent problem: Situation in which the interests of the principals (e.g. shareholders) and their agents (managers) diverge, and the agents pursue their own self-interest rather than the interest of the principal with which they are entrusted.

Private company: Company whose stock is held by a narrow group of owners (managers, founders, employees, venture capitalists) and not openly traded in the market. (See: Public company)

Private equity: Equity that is not traded publicly on open exchanges.

Private-label security: Mortgage-backed securities issued by non-GSE financial institutions.

Procedural rationality: Principle that agents who face cognitive, informational and computational limitations make decisions using reasonable procedures and appropriate deliberations.

Productive efficiency: Situation in which a commodity is produced at the lowest possible cost given input prices and the technology, ensuring no resources are wasted.

Program trading: Usually computerized, automatic trading of large volumes of securities in accordance with index values reaching predetermined values.

Promissory note: Written note whereby one party promises to make a specified sum of money to the counterparty at a fixed time or on demand. (See: Bill of exchange)

Proprietary trading: Bank trading securities on its own account for profit rather than for its clients in return for commissions and fees.

Public company: Limited-liability company whose stock is owned by individual or institutional investors and is traded in the open market. (See: Private company)

Put (sell) option: Contract whereby one party buys the right (but not the obligation) to sell an asset at a certain price (strike price) before or at a specific date (exercise date).

Qualitative (moral) anchor: Tendency to rely on stories and moral justifications in decision-making.

Quant: A quantitative analyst who applies advanced mathematical and statistical techniques to financial analysis, risk management and designing synthetic derivatives.

Quantitative anchor: Tendency to rely on arbitrary quantitative indicators (e.g. the most recent peak price) in decision-making.

Quantitative easing: Central bank's actions to stimulate the economy by buying financial assets of various maturities from financial firms to promote liquidity and to raise the price of these assets (instead of using the more conventional central-bank method of buying Treasury bills).

Random variable: Variable whose value is a function of a known probability distribution.

Random walk: Path of a variable that does not follow a discernible pattern and is unpredictable.

Rate of return: Gain (loss) on an investment over a period of time expressed as a percentage of the initial investment cost.

Rational bubble: Increase in an asset price based on rational expectations of future price increases.

Rational choice theory: Approach to modeling, understanding and interpreting social phenomena based on the idea that individuals behave consistently to maximize benefits and minimize costs given their subjective preferences.

Rational expectations hypothesis: Expectation-formation hypothesis according to which agents' expectation of the future value of a variable is consistent with the prediction of the relevant economic theory.

Redeemable debt: Government loans that can be paid off before the end of the contract without the debt holder's permission.

Regulatory arbitrage: Circumvention of regulations by exploiting loopholes (e.g. by creating financial instruments that are not covered by the regulations).

Repurchase (repo) agreement: Short-term contract in which one party borrows by selling securities to another party on the understanding that it will buy them back at a future date at a predetermined price.

Reserve ratio: Ratio of a bank's reserves to its deposits.

Risk arbitrage: Investment strategy that seeks to profit from the anticipated stock-price changes of the acquiring and target companies in
mergers and acquisitions.

Risk premium: Return above the safe interest rate that will compensate
an investor for holding a riskier asset.

Safe interest rate: Interest rate on a risk-free asset (e.g. Treasury bills).

Satisficing: Decision-making on a limited set of choices and the acceptance of satisfactory solutions that meet a threshold. (See: Bounded
rationality)

Savings glut: Savings generated in trade-surplus countries and loaned
to the US in the early 2000s, ostensibly leading to low long-term interest
rates.

Secondary market: Capital market in which previously issued bonds
and stocks are traded. (See: Primary market)

Securitization: Securities issuance backed by a portfolio of assets
including mortgages and other debt instruments.

Security: Certificate which shows the ownership of a stock, bond, or
other debt instrument.

Shadow banking system: Non-depository institutions that make loans
financed by borrowed funds.

Share: Certificate of ownership of one of the equal fractional parts into
which the capital stock of a publicly owned company is divided.

Shareholder value: Value of a company to the shareholder calculated on
the basis of the discounted earning flow of the company.

Short position (or Short): Selling a borrowed asset or an asset to be borrowed (usually from a broker) before its delivery date in the expectation that its value will drop. The seller anticipates buying the asset at
a lower price in the future to return to the lender (See: Long position)

Smart money: Sophisticated or experienced investors who make buy
and sell decisions on the basis of careful analysis of all the available
information on the fundamentals of the security price.

Soft money: Paper money that is not (rigidly) backed by precious metal.

Solvency: Ability of a firm to meet its long-term financial obligations.

Sovereign debt: Total debt owed by the government to the creditors
(public debt, government debt).

Special purpose vehicle: Legally separate entities set up by firms to
acquire and finance financial assets. Commonly used by banks in the
securitization process.

Specie money: Money in the form of precious metal (usually gold or
silver coin).

Speculation: Investment strategy of making bets on the future movements of asset prices.

Speculative finance (Minsky): Finance regime in which borrowers
have sufficient income to make interest payments but need to resort to
new loans to make principal payments.

Spot market:　Market in which commodities or assets are traded for immediate delivery and payment. (See: Futures market)

Stagflation:　Combination of economic stagnation and inflation.

State of confidence:　Degree of confidence investors have in their best forecasts of the future.

Stock:　Certificate of ownership of a public corporation that entitles the owner to a claim on earnings.

Stockbroker:　Agent who executes stock sales and purchases for clients in return for a fee or commission.

Stockjobber:　Agent who trades stocks on her own account with the objective of profiting from the buy-sell price spread.

Stop-loss order:　Order placed with a broker to sell or buy a security when it reaches a certain price in order to limit losses.

Structured finance:　Complex financial arrangements offering borrowers and lenders a plethora of instruments to serve unique financial needs and transfer and diversify risk.

Structured investment vehicle:　Legally separate entities set up by banks to borrow short-term debt to invest in securities.

Subprime loan:　Mortgage loan made to a borrower with a poor credit rating, documentation, and higher default risk than Alt-A borrowers. (See: Alt-A loan, Prime loan)

Subscription:　Legal commitment to purchase a financial instrument. It usually required a fraction of the price as down payment. The subscription agreement specified the terms of purchase and the schedule of payment.

Substantive rationality:　Principle of understanding economic agents' decision-making in terms of their goals of optimization.

Sunspot:　Random variable that is unrelated to the fundamentals.

Supervisory goodwill:　Federal regulator permitting the negative net worth of a failing S&L acquired by another thrift be valued as a capital asset and amortized over 20 to 30 years.

Surplus unit:　Economic unit whose income is greater than its expenditure.

Synchronization risk:　Risk that not all short sellers/arbitrageurs will bet against a mispricing simultaneously.

Systematic risk:　Risk that affects the entire market and therefore cannot be mitigated through portfolio diversification.

Systemic risk:　Risk that the failure of one or a few financial institutions will spill over to the financial system and the rest of the economy due to interconnections among financial institutions.

Technical analysis:　Investment strategy based on forecasting the future behavior of prices from historical patterns. (See: Chartism)

Too big to fail:　Situation where the government has to take measures against the failure of a business because the size of the company will create too much collateral damage.

Too systemic to fail: Situation where the government has to take measures against the failure of a business because the interconnectedness of the company will create too much collateral damage.

Toxic waste: Nonperforming MBSs and CDOs securitized by the highest-risk portions of the underlying securities.

Transaction cost: Costs incurred in market exchange, including information, search, enforcement, and negotiation costs.

Transitivity axiom: Rational choice theory requires that choices are consistent: if alternative A is preferred to B and B is preferred to C then it follows that A is preferred to C. (See: Rational choice theory)

Troubled Asset Relief Program: Treasury program introduced in October 2008 to purchase toxic bank assets and later used to inject capital into banks and other financial institutions.

Underwriting: Means by which an investment bank (or a syndicate) takes over the risks associated with new issuance of securities. In return for a fee the investment bank evaluates, guarantees a price for, and markets new issues to potential investors on behalf of the issuer.

Utility banking: Banking models in which the activities of depository institutions that receive a government backstop are limited to payments, deposits, and retail real-sector loans.

Value analysis: Investment strategy determining whether a security is mispriced based on measuring its intrinsic value and taking positions accordingly.

Value-at-risk: Statistical measure of the potential loss of a portfolio over a period of time.

Venture capital: Money invested in innovative high-risk-high-return small businesses and start-ups.

Volatility trading: Investment strategy that speculates on changes in the dispersion of asset prices.

Volcker Rule: Restrictions that prevent depository institutions from trading on their own behalf.

Wealth effect: Impact of changes in real wealth on consumption spending.

Wildcat banking: Unusual practices of some banks during the free-banking era, such as setting up banks in remote locations to escape redemption of banknotes.

Yield to maturity: Rate of return on a bond held to maturity.

Index

This is a lucid and illuminating book with much to teach both the student and instructor. It comes as close to a page turner as a book on finance and economics can be. The approach adopted of first documenting financial crises and then explaining those using alternative theoretical approaches is very effective. This method applied as a climax of the book to the 2007–2008 financial crisis successfully reinforces earlier lessons.

Shahrukh Rafi Khan, Visiting Professor of Economics,
Mount Holyoke College, USA

This book offers and employs a rich theoretical framework for examining, assessing, and understanding the multiplicity of forces generating specific crises over an especially long run – from tulip mania and the Mississippi Bubble all of the way up to what the author coins as "The Latest Act: The Crash of the 2000s." In my judgment, Bilginsoy has authored an especially comprehensive, thorough, and readable book on the subject of crisis and crises.

John Hall, Department of Economics,
Portland State University, Oregon, USA

This new volume by Cihan Bilginsoy will take its place alongside Kindleberger and Aliber's "Manias, Crashes, and Panics" and Reinhart and Rogoff's "This Time It's Different" as a valuable introduction to the financial booms and crashes which continue to shape our world. While "Manias, Crashes, and Panics" focuses attention on market and international dynamics, and "This Time It's Different" on sovereign debt, Bilginsoy goes beyond these texts in his recounting of the historical background and institutional mechanics of a wide range of boom–crash episodes, and in his comprehensive discussion of economists' debates about why they happened. Indeed, a great strength of this book is its author's even-handed approach to different economic points of view: readers can think along with established experts about the deeper logic of these events. Consequently, this book – written to be accessible to non-economics university students – will be equally valuable for professional economists and investors.

Gary A. Dymski, Professor of Applied Economics,
Leeds University Business School, University of Leeds, UK